LEARN ITALIAN

Learn Italian for Beginners in Your Car like Crazy.
Lessons for Travel & Everyday. How to Speak Italian
with Grammar, Common Phrases, Vocabulary,
Conversations and Short Stories

Table of Contents

ITALIAN GRAMMAR

Learn Italian for Beginners in Your Car Like Crazy.

Language Learning Lessons for travel and Everyday.

How to speak Italian with Vocabulary and Conversations.

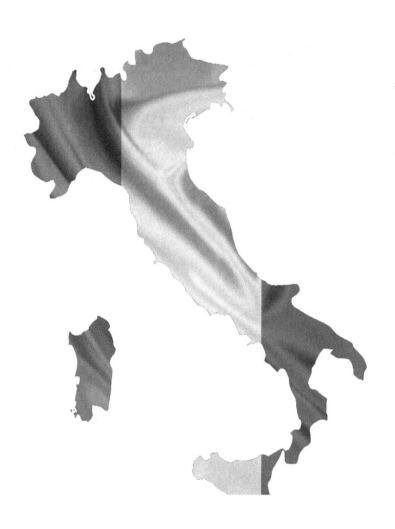

13

INTRODUCTION

Italy has a rich cultural history. Its lifestyle, art, food, wine, fashion, sporting events, architecture and scenic beauty attract some 40 million tourists each year. The influence of Italy is seen everywhere in Europe today. Today there are alot of large Italian speaking community all over europe and australia and there are plenty of restaurants, shops and industries offering authentic Italian products. Students of Italian have many opportunities to use the language in everyday life. There is an abundance of Italian restaurants, businesses and social groups where Italian is spoken. Knowledge of the Italian language can open doors to a wide range of employment opportunities in the commercial, educational, scientific, chemical, automotive and hospitality fields. It also provides access to a rich culture known throughout the world for its contribution to art, architecture, music, ballet, literature, film, fashion and of course, food! through the centuries, Italian inventors such as Marconi and Galileo, composers like Vivaldi and Verdi, poets such as Dante Alighieri, film directors such as Fellini and Rossellini, artists like Michelangelo and Leonardo da Vinci, as well as other great artists, philosophers, musicians and designers have had a profound influence on the world. Today, Italy continues to set trends and is synonymous with fashion and style. Designers such as Valentino and Armani are well known all over the world, as are sporting personalities such as Valentino Rossi and Francesco Totti. Musician/ song writers like Eros Ramazzotti, Laura Pausini and Andrea Bocelli, as well as actors Roberto Begnini and Monica Bellucci have captured the hearts of young and old all over the world.

Italian is a relatively easy language to learn because of its similarity to English. Both English and Italian are derived from Latin so they share a similar sentence structure. Italian is written in Roman script as is English, but the Italian alphabet only has a twenty-one letters. Studying Italian also provides the background for further studies of other Romance languages, such as French, Spanish and Portuguese.

MANY ITALIAN WORDS HAVE BEEN ADOPTED BY THE ENGLISH LANGUAGE. HOW MANY OF THESE WORDS DO YOU KNOW?

Pasta - risotto

Presto - pizza

Minestrone - soprano

Gelato - focaccia

Opera - antipasto

Chiaroscuro - vendetta

Bruschetta - tempo

Ciao - mozzarella

Adagio - gondola

Lasagne - allegro

CHAPTER 1: THE ALPHABET AND THE BASIC SOUNDS

The modern Italian alphabet has less letters than the English one: J, K, W, X and Y do not occur in native terms. Nevertheless, these letters do appear in dictionaries, for archaic spellings, and for a few foreign and international terms officially adopted in Italian, as well.

The following table includes these letters too, though showing them in deep green, to stress their less common use. Each entry shows the pronounciation of the letter in Italian, trying to make the closest match with English sounds. An important thing to remember is that all the Italian vowels are clipped, i.e. their duration, or sound length, is very short, compared to the average English vowels. The last column on the right shows the "name" of each letter, i.e. what they are called in Italian.

LETTER	PRONOUNCIATION	NAME
A	Always as an English a in cat, fact, or as an o in how, cloud, mouse.	*a*
B	Always as an English b.	*bi*
C	As an English k, except when the following vowel is e or i: in this case it sounds as the English cluster ch in chest, chip, chisel. The letter c also forms some special clusters, discussed in the following page.	*ci*
D	Always as an English d.	*di*

E	Depending on the word, it may have two slightly different sounds: either as an English a in hay, layer, may (this is popularly called a narrow "e" or closed "e"), or as an English e in send, tent, hen (this one is popularly called a wide "e" or open "e"). To mark this difference, two different accents are placed above the vowel: an acute accent, slanted rightwards (é), gives the "closed" sound , while the grave accent, slanted leftwards (è), gives the "open" sound. Unlike in French, in Italian accented vowels such as é and è are used very sparingly: most words are spelled with an ordinary e. Obviously, for the spoken language, the correct sound must be remembered. But the student should not worry about this too much: in most cases, a word pronounced with an incorrect sound (for example a wide "e" in place of a narrow "e") would be understood all the same.	*e* (narrow sound)
F	Always as an English f in fame, knife, flute, but never like of.	*effe*
G	As an English g in gravel, goblet, except in three cases: when followed by vowels e and i, it sounds as English j in jelly, jigsaw; when followed by n, forming cluster gn (discussed in the following page); when followed by l, forming cluster gl (discussed in the following page).	*gi*
H	It is completely soundless: never as in house, hope, hammer, but as in heir, honest. Its use will be explained further on. It also takes part to special clusters, discussed in the following page. But h	*acca*
I	It always sounds as an English y in yellow, troyan. A similar sound is that of English ee in fleet, seem, but the length of the Italian sound is shorter.	*i*
J	A few names have a letter j, always pronounced as an English y in yell, lawyer.	*i lunga*
K	In foreign or international words, it always sounds as an English k.	*kappa*
L	Always as English l.	*elle*

M	Always as an English m.	*emme*
N	Always as an English n.	*enne*
O	Always as an English o, in some cases with a "narrow" or "closed" sound as in blow, soul, row, or sometimes with a "wide" or "open" sound as in cloth, spot, dog. These sounds are spelled with the acute accent (ó) for the closed sound, and with the grave accent (ò) for the open sound. However, the use of ó and ò is very limited, and the correct sound must be known. Also in this case, a word pronounced with the wrong accent is usually understood all the same.	*o (wide sound)*
P	Always as an English p.	*pi*
Q	Always as an English q, it is always followed by vowel u.	*qu*
R	This sound is always "rolled", like a Scottish r in Edinburgh, or a Spanish r in señor. It is obtained by making the tip of the tongue vibrate almost against the hard palate, next to the back of the upper teeth. It never sounds as an English r, nor as a French r.	*erre*
S	As an English s, sometimes strong as in strip, fuss, spare, and sometimes weak as in easy, abuse, lies. The letter s also belongs to some special clusters, discussed in the following page.	*esse (strong sound)*
T	Always as English t	*ti*
U	The sound is similar to an English w in win, rowing, but u is a vowel, while w is a consonant.	*u*
V	Always as an English v.	*vu or vi*
W	In foreign or international words, it may either sound as a German w in würstel, watt (i.e. like an Italian v), or as an English w in window (i.e. as the Italian vowel u). When Italians are in doubt, they usually pronounce the letter w in the German way, as suggested by the name given to this letter, which means double v.	*doppia vu*
X	In foreign or international words, it always sounds as an English x.	*ics*

Y	In foreign or international words, it always sounds as an English y, i.e. exactly as the Italian vowel i.	*i greca or ipsilon*
Z	According to the word, it sounds either as an English ds in godzilla, or as ts in cats.	*zeta (with the ds sound)*

NOTES

LETTER J - in some Italian words, such as gioiello (= jewel), maiale (= pig), and a few others, the vowel i is followed by a further vowel that belongs to the same syllable. This i will therefore have a rather "swift" sound, i.e. a short duration, more or less as the letter y would be pronounced in English in yellow, coyote, yolk: no more than 100 years ago, this i would have been often spelled j (i.e. giojello, majale), to show this particular sound due to the following vowel. The Italian name for j means long i.

Nowadays, this spelling has become totally obsolete, and j only occurs in a few first names and surnames. However, it is always pronounced as an Italian i.

LETTER Y - it is a reminiscence of the Greek alphabet, as suggested by the name Greek i given to this consonant. But while this letter in Greek sounds like German ü, in Italian it sounds exactly like vowel i, and since it was redundant, it was gradually dropped.

SPECIAL CLUSTERS

The pronounciation of some consonants changes when they come together and form one syllable (monosyllabic clusters).

CLUSTER	PRONOUNCIATION
CE, CI CIA, CIE, CIO, CIU	While ca, co and cu are pronounced as in English, ce and ci have a soft sound (palatal pronounciation), like in English che and chi. When the cluster ci is followed by a further vowel, the i loses its sound, and becomes merely graphic (only to show that c has to be pronounced as English "ch"). Therefore, cia sounds like cha (not chya), cie is pronounced che, cio as cho, and ciu as chu.

25

CHE, CHI	The letter h between c and e, or between c and i, gives the cluster a hard sound (guttural pronounciation): che sounds like an English ke, while chi sounds like an English ki.
GE, GI **GIA, GIE, GIO, GIU**	The clusters ga, go and gu are pronounced like in English, but ge and gi have a "soft" sound (palatal pronounciation), like English je and jy (or jih). Also in this case, when cluster gi is followed by a further vowel, i becomes mute, and the English "j" sound is followed by the second vowel, thus gia sounds like ja (not jya), gie is pronounced je, gio as jo, and giu as ju.
GHE, GHI	An h inserted between g and vowel e or i gives the cluster a hard sound (guttural pronounciation): ghe sounds like an English gue in guest , while ghi sounds like an English gui in guild.
GLI **GLIA, GLIE, GLIO, GLIU**	When gl is followed by vowel i, it has the same sound as ll in Spanish words like caballo, lluvia, etc. This exact sound does not exist in English, although a rather similar one is obtained pronouncing the sentence "I will call you", in which a double l is followed by y + another vowel. The Italian sound is obtained by pressing the point of the tongue against the back of the teeth and flattening it against the hard palate. When gli is followed by vowels a, e, o and u, the sound of i is lost; glia sounds like Spanish lla (close enough to English llya, but y should not be heard much), glie as Spanish lle, glio as Spanish llo, and gliu as Spanish llu. Instead, when gl (without an i) is followed by vowels a, e, o and u, it is simply pronounced as in English, in words like glass, glove, glue.

GN	It is pronounced exactly as a Spanish ñ, in señor, mañana. The gn cluster is always followed by a vowel.
SCE, SCI	The cluster sc only has a special sound when followed by vowels e and i, in which case it sounds like an English sh in sharp, shelf, shop. In any other case (sca, sco, scu) the pronounciation is like the English one in scar scorpion, scuba.
SCIA, SCIE, SCIO, SCIU	When the cluster sci is followed by a vowel (scia, scie, scio, sciu), the sound of i is lost; thus scia sounds like English sha, scie is pronounced she, scio as sho, and sciu as shu.

ENGLISH SPELLING OF ITALIAN SOUNDS

The pronounciation of the Italian consonants should not be difficult for English-speakers, but most vowels have a different sound. There are two important points to keep well in mind at all times:

! In Italian, the pronounciation of the vowels does not change according to the word (only e and o have "wide" and "narrow" sounds, yet not very different), whereas for instance an English "e" is pronounced in different ways (leave, hen, break). As a general rule, the sound of Italian vowels is not affected by other letters. There is only one exception, already discussed in the previous paragraph 1.2: when i belongs to particular clusters, its sound is not heard.

! The Italian vowels are always pronounced clipped, i.e. with a very short duration (sound length), whereas in English they are often held, so to obtain a "long" sound, particularly when they occur at the end of a word. For example, the English undergo is pronounced as if the word was spelled undergoe, although the word ends with o alone. In Italian, this sound would be shorter, as if the word was spelled undergoh, (without pronouncing the h), and the great majority of Italian words ends in a similar way, i.e. with a vowel.

Vowels are the greatest obstacle in attempting to mimic the Italian sound by using syllables pronounced in the English way; there is no other way to obtain clipped vowels than to add an "h" after each of them (ah, eh, oh, etc.) This phonetic spelling looks a little awkward, for instance libreria (for bookshop) looks like "lyhbrehryhah"; but this will no longer be necessary once the student has fully learned the basic pronounciation rules. Practice hard your vowels, so to get rid of these funny spellings very soon!

In these first chapters, a phonetic spelling (i.e. the English spelling of the word's sound), between quotation marks and in italics style, has been added to each Italian word, as a further help for the beginner; at more advanced stages, it will be abandoned, assuming that the student has gradually become confident with the

27

PRONOUNCIATION RULES.

The introduction paragraph shows a few examples, and explains why I preferred to use this method rather than the international phonetic system. Further notes about the phonetic spelling are the following ones:

! The sound of the Italian vowel a is obtained by spelling it "..ah..", always sounding as in bath, but obviously clipped, i.e. much shorter than in English.

! The Italian e is spelled "..eh..": it may sound as letter e in bet, or as letter a in may not pronouncing the y.

! The Italian i is obtained by "..yh.." or "..y..", always sounding as the letter y in gym;

! The Italian o is spelled "..oh..", sometimes sounding as letter o in box, and sometimes as in coal, though with a shorter sound than in English.

! The Italian u is spelled "..w..", always sounding as letter w in want.

! The Italian c is spelled "..k.." when its sound is "strong" (guttural), as in card, come. The "soft" (palatal) sound, like the English cluster ch in church or cheese, is spelled "..ch.." (remember not to omit the sound of h in this case!).

! In a similar way, the Italian g is spelled "..g..", when its sound is "strong" (guttural), as in goal, guide; its "soft" (palatal) sound, like an English j, is spelled "..j..", sounding like jam or jungle.

! The Italian cluster sc, when the sound matches the English cluster sh in shade or fish, is spelled "..sh.." (again, do not omit the sound of h in this case!).

! The Italian gn sound is spelled using a Spanish "..ñ..", as señor.

! For the Italian cluster gl another Spanish group has been used, "..ll.." (always with a reminder note). In the GRAMMAR AND EXERCISES section of this website, this phonetic spelling has been preferred, because it is the closest to the Italian pronounciation. Instead, in the USEFUL EXPRESSIONS sections I preferred to use its quasi-equivalent English ...lly... spelling, because the readers whose only purpose is that to use the sentences on a holiday, would find this spelling easier to understand, without having to learn the language in depth.

! The sound of the Italian r is always "rolled": there is no graphic way for showing this, so simply keep in mind the pronounciation of this letter.

ACCENT (or STRESS)

Accent will be the subject of the next paragraph, but I would like to introduce in advance that in the English sound version, the stressed syllables are shown in bold: these syllables carry the stress in pronouncing the relevant word. For example:

! animale (animal) is pronounced "ahnyhmahleh" (stress on the syllable ma)

! tavolo (table) is pronounced "tahvohloh" (stress on the first syllable ta)

! perché (why, because) is pronounced "pehrkeh" (stress on the last syllable che)

So now, according to the pronounciation table and to the above-mentioned notes, you should be able to pronounce correctly any Italian sound.

Take a test with the following words:

ITALIAN	ENGLISH SOUND	MEANING
bianco	"byahnkoh"	white
strada	"strahdah"	road
mare	"mahreh"	sea
grazie	"grahtsyeh"	thanks
luogo	"lwohgoh"	place, location
amico	"ahmykoh"	friend
facile	"fahchyleh" (English "ch")	easy
centro	"chentroh" (English "ch")	center to lift
alzare	"ahltsahreh"	Paris
Parigi	"Pahryjyh"	

DOUBLE CONSONANTS

Many Italian words have double consonants. They can be found in any part of the word, but never as first letters or as last letters.

In most cases they are followed by a vowel, as in dubbio = doubt, gatto = cat, etc.; but in some cases they may be followed by r, as in labbra = lips, attrito = friction, etc.

Instead, another consonant never occurs before a double consonant.

Also English has several words with double consonants, as supple, bottle, abbot.

In Italian, though, double consonants sound stronger than in English; this is obtainable by breaking the sound, for example as if the word cattle was spelled ca-ttle: the tt sound should therefore be heard more. Any consonant can be doubled, except letter h (never doubled, because it is always soundless), or for non- standard ones (j, k, w, x, y).

Here you can see relevant example of double consonants:

dubbio (doubt)   affare (bargain, business)

gatto (cat)   passato (past)

labbra (lips)   collare (collar)

attrito (friction)   anno (year)

SOME CLUSTERS TOO MAY BE DOUBLED:

...cci like English "...tchyh", as in stracci (rags)

29

...cce like English "...tcheh", as in accesso (access)

COMPOUNDS OF ...CCI + VOWEL OBVIOUSLY FOLLOW THE SAME PRONOUNCIATION, DROPPING THE I SOUND:

...ccia (sounds like "...tchah"), as in faccia (face)

...ccio (sounds like "...tchoh"), as in riccio (curl; porcupine)

...cciu sounds like "...tchuh" as in acciuga (anchovy)

Similar clusters with g (...ggia, ...ggio, etc.), follow the same phonetical rules as above, sounding as

"...djah", "...djoh", etc.

Rarely, the cluster ...ccie or ...ggie (with an i) may also occur, but they sound exactly as the clusters ...cce and ...gge mentioned above; in these cases i (merely phonetic) is also redundant, so modern spellings tend to drop it.

DOUBLE VOWELS ARE QUITE RARE IN ITALIAN, THOUGH POSSIBLE IN A FEW CASES.

They always sound as the normal individual vowels, but in these cases a longer sound should be heard:

cooperare (to cooperate)

zii (uncles)

veemenza (vehemence)

ACCENT (OR STRESS)

Although there is no strict rule, in most Italian words the accent or stress falls on the penultimate syllable. Although the stress is carried by the whole syllable, it is much easier to remember which vowel carries it: for instance, in the word possibile (possible) the stress is carried by the second syllable (-si-) (unlike in English), but it is easier to remember that the first vowel, i.e. i, is stressed. In the following examples accented vowels are used for the Italian spelling, to show which is the vowel that carries the stress. However, keep in mind that it is very unusual for Italian words to be spelled with accented letters, with very few exceptions discussed further in this page.

To help the reader, the stressed syllables have also been marked in the "English spelling" version by using

bold letters, as explained at the end of the previous paragraph.

A few examples:

lampadìna	*"lahmpahdyhnah"*	*light bulb*
carbòne	*"karbohneh"*	*coal*
supermercàto	*"swpehrmehrkahtoh"*	*supermarket*
senatòre	*"sehnahtohreh"*	*senator*
aereoplàno	*"ahehrehohplahnoh"*	*airoplane*
arcobaléno	*"ahrkohbahlehnoh"*	*rainbow*
riconoscènte	*"ryhkohnohshenteh"* (English *"sh"* !)	*thankful*

30

But in some other words the stress is carried by an earlier syllable:

		movable (as an adjective)
ràpido	*"**rah**pyhdoh"*	*fast, quick*
telèfono	*"teh**leh**fohnoh"*	*telephone*
lìbero	*"**lyh**behroh"*	*free (from duty or restraint)*
pòvero	*"**poh**vehroh"*	*poor*

THE USE OF ACCENTED VOWELS IN COMMON SPELLING

Accented vowels have been used in the previous examples for the sake of an easier understanding. In ordinary spelling they are allowed, but very seldom used. Only in two cases accented vowels are commonly used:

WORDS WHOSE LAST SYLLABLE CARRIES THE ACCENT

There are many words of this kind in Italian (nouns, verb inflections, adverbs, etc.), and some are frequently used. An accent is compulsory in this case, otherwise the stress would not be heard.

Furthermore, in some cases the same word spelled without an accent even has a different meaning (see further down). A few words with a similar spelling, but whose last syllable is not stressed, are shown on the right.

Perché	"pehrkeh"	why, because
sarà	"sahrah"	it will be Sara
"sahrah"	Sarah (a name)	
perciò	"pehrchoh"	therefore
papà	"pahpah"	dad papa
"pahpah"	pope	
però	"pehroh"	but, however pero
"pehroh"	pear-tree	
più	"pyw"	more, plus

Some of these words have an accent on the last syllable because they dropped the last part of the original word they derive from (usually Latin), or because they are of French origin (most French words have an accent on the last syllable). Also several compounds of che (pronounced "ke", meaning which, that) are spelled with an accent:

perché (why, because)

poiché (because)

benché (despite) giacché (since) sicché (so, therefore) etc.

WORDS THAT HAVE A DIFFERENT MEANING DEPENDING ON THE POSITION OF THE ACCENT

31

A few words have a different meaning when different syllables carry the accent:

àncora "ahnkohrah" anchor (noun)

ancòra "ahnkohrah" again, more (adverb)

règia "rehjah" royal (adjective)

regìa "rehjyhah" direction of a movie or a play (noun)

capitàno "kahpytahnoh" captain (noun)

càpitano "kahpytahnoh" they happen, they occur (verb)

In this case, accents are not mandatory; many Italian people do not use them, because the meaning of the word, and therefore its correct accent, is clearly understood by the context of the phrase: considering the first couple of sample words, in sentences such as "strange things happen" or "he is the captain", neither of the two words (happen, captain) could be mistaken with the other.

Focus your attention on the second couple of words shown above: in the first noun (règia), the gia cluster forms one syllable, because the syllables of the word are re - gia; therefore, the pronounciation of the cluster "-jah" follows the standard rules, as has already been said earlier.

In the second word (regìa), instead, the same cluster belongs to two separate syllables: re - gì - a, so the sound too splits into "re-jyh-ah". Only the second syllable gi carries the accent, not the final a.

TYPES OF ACCENTED VOWELS USED IN ITALIAN SPELLING

This part of the paragraph is not really fundamental for a beginner, although some readers might have noticed that most of the accented vowels used so far bear a grave accent, i.e. slanted leftwards (perciò, sarà), while a few others are slanted in the opposite direction (perché).

modern italian uses the following set of accented vowels:

"grave" accents, slanted leftwards ("wide" sound pronounciation)   à è ì ò ù

"acute" accent, slanted rightwards

("narrow" sound pronounciation)   é

From the table above, you can see how only e has both forms, while all the others take only the grave (leftwards) accent.

Very seldom, an ó (with acute accent) is also found in printed texts, but its use is not mandatory, and most people prefer to spell it as a normal o.

It has already been said in this page that when the accent is carried by the last syllable, an accented vowel has to be used. Since most vowels only take the grave accent, this is the only one that can be used:

andrà	"ahndrah"	he / she will go
là	"lah"	there
lunedì	"lwnehdyh"	monday
finì	"fyhnyh"	it finished

32

falò	"fahloh"	great fire, pire
però	"pehroh"	but
laggiù	"lahjjw"	down there, over there
più	"pyw"	more - plus

But e can take two different accents; according to the word, either one or the other should be used. These are examples of words whose final e bears a grave accent ("wide" sound):

è	"eh"	he / she / it is
caffè	"kah'ffeh"	coffee or coffee-bar
frappè	"frah'ppeh"	milk shake

In other words, instead, the final e bears the acute accent ("narrow" sound):

perché	"pehrkeh"	why, because
né	"neh"	not, nor, neither
sé	"seh"	self, one's self

In very few cases, an accented e can be used within the word, to indicate which is the correct sound of the vowel:

pèsca ("wide" e) = peach pésca ("narrow" e) = fishing

This is not mandatory; actually, many people would spell both words pesca (with a normal e), because the context of the sentence is enough to understand which of the two makes more sense.

HOW TO TYPE ACCENTED VOWELS

Most people who do not use an Italian keyboard may wonder how to type accented vowels in a text, because a standard international keyboard does not have these letters among the keys. Since they belong to the ASCII set of characters, it is possible to enter them by typing their code numbers in the keyboard's number pad, while pressing the Alt key: try them out yourself, in the box below.

à = Alt+133 | è = Alt+138 | ì = Alt+141 | ò = Alt+149 | ù = Alt+151 | é = Alt+130 To type an o with an acute accent use Alt+162, but remember that ó is only found in dictionaries, as a reading aid.

Instead not all fonts have capital (uppercase) accented letters.

Times New Roman and Arial, among the most commonly used, have the following codes: try them out. À = Alt+0192 | È = Alt+0200 | Ì = Alt+0204 | Ò = Alt+0210 | Ù = Alt+0217 | É = Alt+0201

Again, to type Ó use Alt+0211, for the same limited use as above.

If your computer or the standard font you are using does not have such vowels, you can still use normal ones followed by an apostrophe:

a' | e' | i' | o' | u'

A' | E' | I' | O' | U'

Some Italian people too use apostrophes in place of accented vowels, but since this is not very correct, and the two different e's cannot be told, the use of accented vowels should be preferred, where available.

CHAPTER 2: STRUCTURES

THE NOUN GROUP

The main function of nouns in any language is to denote an entity (person, object, etc.) or concept (situation, abstract idea, etc.). Nouns are generally used together with articles (the, a) and/or adjectives (describing physical or other characteristics), which provide information about the entity or concept. Together they form a group of words called the noun group; two examples are shown below:

| una (article) | grande (adjective) | casa (noun) | a big house |
| la (article) | ragazza (noun) | inglese (adjective) | the English girl |

Although the noun group may contain other elements (e.g. adverbs, prepositional phrases, etc.), in this chapter we will only deal with the three basic elements of noun/ article/adjective, analysing them one by one. In Italian the three components of the noun group can be considered not only separately but also as a 'whole', in which the various components have to 'agree', so we will also look at how they are used together.

THE NOUN

The noun is the focus of the noun group, and in fact the article and adjectives always agree with the noun in gender (masculine or feminine) and number (singular or plural). The two grammatical features of gender and number determine the form of noun, article and adjective.

GENDER

All Italian nouns have either a masculine or a feminine gender. Gender is a purely grammatical term. Nouns referring to human beings or animals sometimes have the same grammatical gender as their natural gender, but not always (see below). Italian native speakers rarely find this a problem. However speakers of other languages often find it difficult to remember the gender of nouns and this creates a problem when it comes to making the other components of the noun group 'agree' with the noun. With non-animate objects, there is not always an obvious explanation for their gender. Why, for example, should sera 'evening' be feminine, while giorno 'day' is masculine? Non-Italian speakers either have to learn and memorise the genders of words or consult a dictionary. Italian dictionaries usually indicate the gender of nouns with abbreviations such as s.m. (sostantivo maschile) and s.f. (sostantivo femminile).

Grammatically speaking, Italian does not always have a male and a female of each animal species, for example:

! una giraffa 'giraffe' is always feminine

! un ippopotamo 'hippopotamus' is always masculine

In order to provide the missing half, we have to say:

una giraffa maschio	a male giraffe
un ippopotamo femmina	a female hippopotamus

Some animals – as in English – have two distinct names for the male and the female of the species:

un cane dog una cagna	bitch
un gallo cock una gallina	hen

Some, but not all, professional and other titles may have a distinct form for the feminine. Nouns whose masculine form ends in -e have a feminine form ending either in -a or in -essa:

cameriere cameriera	waiter/waitress
infermiere infermiera	nurse
padrone padrona	master/mistress
studente studentessa	student
presidente presidentessa	president
principe principessa	prince/princess
conte contessa	count/countess
barone baronessa	baron/baroness

Most nouns with masculine form ending in -tore have a feminine form ending in

-trice:

ambasciatore ambasciatrice ambassador

attore attrice	actor/actress
autore autrice	author
direttore direttrice	director, manager
imperatore imperatrice	emperor/empress
pittore pittrice	painter
scultore scultrice	sculptor
scrittore scrittrice	writer
senatore senatrice	senator

But note the following masculine nouns with feminine equivalent in -essa:

dottore dottoressa doctor

professore professoressa teacher

The use of the masculine/feminine forms of professional titles is fully illustrated in in the subsequent paragraph.

NUMBER

Unlike gender, the grammatical concept of singular or plural ('number') causes no problem for speakers of English. Occasionally (as in English) a singular noun is used to refer to a collective entity that one might expect to be grammatically plural, e.g. la gente 'people'. On the other hand, some objects that are singular in English may be plural in Italian, e.g. le lasagne 'lasagne' or i capelli 'hair'.

COMMON NOUN PATTERNS

The gender and number determine the ending of the noun. These patterns of endings are called inflexions. Italian nouns can be divided into several different groups, according to their patterns of inflexion.

The three most common patterns (also followed by most adjectives, see below) are:

		Singular	Plural
!	Masculine	-o	-i
!	Feminine	-a	-e
!	Masculine or feminine	-e	-i

Note: Nouns in the third group (-e) have the same ending whatever the gender.

Examples

		Singular	Plural	
1.	Masculine	tavolo	table	
		tavoli	tables	
		albero	tree	
		alberi	trees	
		sbaglio	mistake	
		sbagli	mistakes	
		ragazzo	boy	r
		agazzi	boys	
2.	Feminine	donna	woman	

37

donne	women
parola	word
parole	words
scuola	school
scuole	schools
ragazza	girl
ragazze	girls

3. Masculine

padre	father
padri	fathers
studente	student
studenti	students
bicchiere	glass
bicchieri	glasses

3. Feminine

madre	mother
madri	mothers
occasione	occasion
occasioni	occasions
chiave	key
chiavi	keys

Note: In the plural, nouns ending in -co, -go; -ca, -ga; -cia, -gia present variations in their endings, as shown below.

Nouns ending in -co, -go

Masculine nouns ending in -co or -go in the singular normally form the plural as follows:

in -chi and -ghi, with the hard c, g sound, if the stress falls on the penulti- mate syllable:

fuoco	fuochi	fire
ago	aghi	needle
buco	buchi	hole
albèrgo	albèrghi	hotel
sacco	sacchi	sack
sugo	sughi	sauce

and also in catàlogo catàloghi 'catalogue', diàlogo diàloghi 'dialogue' and a few more nouns.

in -ci and -gi, with the soft c, g sound, if the stress – indicated here by an accent for the purpose of clarity – falls on the third last syllable:

mèdico   mèdici   doctor

aspàrago aspàragi asparagus

mònaco   mònaci   monk

biòlogo   biòlogi   biologist

and also in amìco amìci 'friend', nemìco nemìci 'enemy', greco greci 'Greek', porco porci 'pig'.

NOUNS ENDING IN -CA, -GA

Feminine nouns ending in -ca, -ga form their plural in -che, -ghe, with the hard

c, g sound:

amica   amiche   friend

lega   leghe   league

Nouns ending in -ca, -ga, which refer to either men or women, normally form their plural in -chi, -ghi for male and -che, -ghe for female (and see below):

collega   colleague colleghi (m.)   colleghe (f.)

But note:

belga   Belgian   belgi (m.)   belghe (f.)

NOUNS ENDING IN -CIA, -GIA

Feminine nouns ending in -cia, -gia form their plural as follows:

in -cie, -gie when the stress falls on the i (as indicated in the examples below), and when the last syllable is preceded by a vowel:

farmacìa farmacìe pharmacy

bugìa   bugìe   lie

camìcia   camìcie   shirt

ciliègia   ciliègie cherry

acàcia	acàcie	acacia
valìgia	valìgie	suitcase

in -ce, -ge when the ending is preceded by a consonant:

arància	arànce	orange
spiàggia	spiàgge	beach
provincial	provìnce	province
frangia	frange	fringe
faccia	facce	face
pioggia	piogge	rain

Notice that the pronunciation of -cia is similar to the 'ch' in English 'charm', that   of -gia is like the 'j' in 'jacket', -cie like the 'che' in 'chest', -gie like the 'je' in 'jet'. There is no difference in pronunciation between the -cie of camicie and the -ce of arance. The i is pronounced and given its full value as a syllable only when stressed as in farmacìe and bugìe.

Note: In the plural, nouns ending in -io sometimes double the final i, sometimes not, according to whether the 'i' is stressed or unstressed:

studio	study	studi
zio	uncle	zii

OTHER NOUN PATTERNS

A large number of Italian nouns do not follow the patterns shown above. Here are some other noun patterns.

Masculine or feminine nouns with singular ending in -a

Singular -a (m./f.)		Plural -i (m.)	Plural -e (f.)
atleta	athlete	atleti	atlete
autista	driver	autisti	autiste
artista	artist	artisti	artiste
giornalista	journalist	giornalisti	giornaliste

The nouns in the above group refer to categories of people. The singular ending

-a is used whether they are male or female, but the plural form is different according to the 'natural' gender. A large number of these nouns end in -ista (English '-ist') indicating an ideology (socialista, marxista), profession (chitarrista, dentista) or sport (ciclista, tennista).

Masculine nouns with singular ending in -a

Singular -a (m.)		Plural -i (m.)
problema	problem	problemi

programma	programme	programmi
sistema	system	sistemi
Papa	Pope	Papi
poeta	poet	poeti
monarca	monarch	monarchi

This pattern is similar to that of masculine and feminine nouns ending in -a shown above, but in the plural has only masculine forms. See also masculine nouns ending in -ca, -ga above.

Feminine nouns with singular ending in -o, plural in -i

The two nouns shown below are both feminine in the singular, but differ in the plural: mani is feminine, while echi is masculine:

Singular		Plural
mano (f.)	hand	mani (f.)
eco (f.)	echo	echi (m.)

See below for other examples of feminine nouns ending in -o.

Masculine nouns with singular in -o, feminine plural in -a

A number of masculine nouns become feminine in the plural, with an irregular ending in -a:

Singular (m.)		Plural (f.)
uovo	egg	uova
miglio	mile	miglia
paio	pair	paia

Masculine nouns with singular in -o, masculine plural in -i/feminine plural in -a

Some masculine nouns have a regular masculine plural in -i as well as an irregular feminine plural in -a:

Singular (m.)		Plural in -i (m.)	Plural in -a (f.)
dito	finger	diti	dita
braccio	arm	bracci	braccia
ginocchio	knee	ginocchi	ginocchia
labbro	lip	labbri	labbra
osso	bone	ossi	ossa
gesto	gesture	gesti	gesta

lenzuolo	sheet	lenzuoli	lenzuola
muro	wall	muri	mura
urlo	shout	urli	urla

There are differences in the meaning of the two different plurals: the -a plural generally emphasises the collective nature of the plural, while the -i ending tends   to denote either a more figurative sense or the plural as a collection of separate/ individual elements. For example, le dita are the fingers of your hand, when talked about 'collectively' (ho le dita gelate 'my fingers are frozen') while i diti are the fingers considered 'individually or separately' (ho due diti rotti 'I have two broken fingers'). Le mura are the collective walls of a city (Lucca è una città circondata da mura romane 'Lucca is a city surrounded by Roman walls'), while i muri refer to all other kinds of walls. Le ossa is the plural form normally used when talking about the skeletal system (mi fanno male le ossa 'my bones ache') while the masculine plural   gli ossi is used when talking about separate bones, e.g. broken bones or dog bones (ho dato due ossi al cane 'I gave the dog two bones').

INVARIABLE NOUNS

Invariable nouns have the same form in the plural as in the singular. These include the following.

Nouns with stress falling on last syllable.

These are mainly feminine in gender, coming from an older form, of Latin origin, ending in -tate (civitate, qualitate) now abbreviated and ending in -à:

		Singular	Plural
1.	Feminine	città	town
		università	university
		libertà	freedom
2.	Masculine	caffè	coffee

FEMININE NOUNS ENDING IN -I

Singular		Plural
crisi	crisis	crisi
ipotesi	hypothesis	ipotesi
analisi	analysis	analisi

FEMININE NOUNS ENDING IN -IE

Singular		Plural
serie	series	serie
specie	species	specie

But note:

moglie	wife	mogli

FEMININE NOUNS WITH ABBREVIATED SINGULAR

These end mainly in -o and are usually abbreviations, often derived from compound words (automobile > auto, fotografia > foto):

Singular		Plural
auto	car	auto
moto	motorbike	moto
radio	radio	radio
foto	photo	foto
bici	bike	bici

NOUNS OF ONE SYLLABLE

		Singular		Plural
1.	Masculine	re	king	re
		sci	ski	sci
2.	Feminine gru	crane	gru	

WORDS BORROWED FROM ANOTHER LANGUAGE

	Singular		Plural
Masculine	bar	bar, café	bar
	sport	sport	sport
	film	film	film

	computer		computer	computer
Feminine	reclame	advert	reclame	
	gaffe	gaffe	gaffe	
	brioche	brioche	brioche	

NOTE

Remember not to add -s in the plural, however tempting (il film – i film).

Nouns with extremely irregular plurals

Here are a few nouns whose plural forms are extremely irregular:

	Singular		Plural	
Masculine	uomo	man	uomini	men
	dio	god	dei	gods
	bue	ox	buoi	oxen
Feminine ala	wing	ali	wings	
	arma	arm	armi	arms

THE ARTICLE

WHAT IS AN ARTICLE?

There are two main types of article in Italian, as there are in English: the indefinite article (articolo indeterminativo) and the definite article (articolo determinativo). They distinguish the generic from the specific, the known from the unknown

In giardino c'è un cane.

There is a dog in the garden. (unknown dog)

In giardino c'è il cane.

There is the dog in the garden. (our dog or a dog we know about)

In Italian the form of the article has to agree with the gender and number of the noun it is attached to, but also according to the initial letter of the word immedi- ately following it, whether noun or adjective. This applies also a third type of article, the partitive article.

INDEFINITE ARTICLE UN, UNO, UNA, UN'

Masculine	un	+ vowel or consonant
	Uno	+ s + consonant, gn, pn, ps, x, z, semivowel i (j, y)

Feminine un'	+ vowel
Una	+ consonant

The form of the indefinite article for a masculine singular noun is un, becoming uno before a word starting with s + a consonant, gn, pn, ps, x, z and the semi- vowel i (j, y).

un telefono	a telephone
un espresso	an espresso
un nuovo studente	a new student
uno studente nuovo	a new student
uno spuntino	a snack
uno gnomo	a gnome
uno psichiatra	a psychiatrist
uno zoo	a zoo
uno yogurt	a yogurt
uno xenofobo	a xenophobe (someone who hates foreigners)
uno pneumatico	a tyre

With a feminine singular noun the indefinite article is una, but this changes to un'

before a word starting with a vowel (a, e, i, o, u):

una bottiglia	a bottle
una spremuta	a fresh fruit juice
un'aranciata	an orangeade
un'ampia distesa di neve	a wide expanse of snow

PARTITIVE ARTICLE DEI, DEGLI, DELLE

Masculine:	dei + consonant
Masculine:	degli + vowel, s + consonant, gn, pn, ps, x, z, semivowel
	i (j, y)
Feminine:	delle + any letter

With plural nouns the function of the indefinite article is taken by the partitive article, translated by English 'some':

Masculine:	dei libri	some books

	degli studenti	some students
	degli amici	some (male) friends
Feminine:	delle amiche	some (female) friends
	delle camere	some rooms

The partitive article indicates some part (an unspecified number) of a group or cate- gory of things/people; it is formed by the preposition di combined with the definite article, and following a similar pattern, changes according to gender, number and the word that follows (see examples above).

A partitive article can also be used in the singular, indicating a quantity of uncount- able things, people or abstract concepts:

Vorrei del pane.	I'd like some bread.
Ho visto della gente che correva.	I saw some people running.
C'è ancora della speranza.	There is still some hope. .

DEFINITE ARTICLE

The form of the definite article varies according to the number and gender of the noun it accompanies, but also on whether the noun begins with a vowel, a conso- nant or certain letters or groups of letters, as seen in the table below:

	SINGULAR	PLURAL
Masculine	il + consonant	i + consonant
	l' + vowel	gli + vowel or with gn, pn, ps, s + consonant, x, z, semivowel i (j, y)
	lo + gn, pn, ps	gli + vowel or with gn, pn, ps, s + s + consonant, x, z consonant, x, z, semivowel i (j, y) and semivowel i (j, y)
Feminine	la + consonant	le + any letter
	l' + vowel	le + any letter

MASCULINE NOUNS

In the singular, masculine nouns normally take the article il but they take lo before a word starting with s + a consonant, gn, pn, ps, x, z, semivowel i (j, y) and l' before words starting with a vowel. In the plural, masculine nouns take the article i but they take gli before a word beginning with s + a consonant, gn, pn, ps, x, z and semivowel i (j, y).

il famoso cantante	the famous singer
lo strano inglese	the strange Englishman

46

lo Ionio	the Ionian (sea)
lo yogurt	the yogurt
l'inglese pazzo	the mad Englishman
i ragazzi italiani	the Italian boys
gli studenti italiani	the Italian students
gli stranieri	the foreigners
gli zii americani	the American uncles
gli yacht	the yachts

FEMININE NOUNS

In the singular, feminine nouns take the article la, but take l' before a word begin- ning with vowel. In the plural, they take the article le, which is never abbreviated.

la cioccolata calda	the hot chocolate
la spremuta	the fresh fruit juice
l'aranciata	the orangeade
le automobili bianche	the white cars
le studentesse	the students (female)

USE OF DEFINITE OR INDEFINITE ARTICLES

The use of the definite or indefinite article depends on whether the person or object   is known or unknown, or whether an individual or class/species is being referred   to, as in the examples below.

A particular, clearly identified thing or things, known or visible to the speaker and to the person(s) addressed:

Dammi gli stuzzicadenti.

Give me the toothpicks.

Referring to any toothpicks, without reference to a particular or known set:

Dammi degli stuzzicadenti.

Give me some toothpicks.

Known or unknown, specified or unspecified

(a) The definite article is used to specify known people or things

Flavia vuole portare l'amico alla festa. Flavia wants to take her friend to the party. (particular friend or boyfriend)

47

Vorrei la camera che abbiamo avuto l'anno scorso.

I would like the room we had last year. (specific room)

(b) The indefinite article is used, as in English, for an unknown or unspecified indi- vidual or thing:

Flavia vuole portare un amico alla festa.

Flavia wants to take a friend to the party. (an unspecified friend)

Vorrei una camera per stasera, per favore.

I would like a room for tonight. (any old room, unspecified)

INDIVIDUAL OR CLASS/SPECIES

(a) The definite article is used when we want to identify a whole class or species of things or creatures, distinct from other species or categories, for example an animal species or a category of films:

Il delfino è un mammifero.

The dolphin is a mammal. (= dolphins are mammals)

Mi piacciono i film americani.

I like American films.

NOTE:

How English only uses the definite article 'the' in the singular ('the dolphin').

(b) The indefinite article is used to talk about an individual dolphin or film (unless   it is a particular dolphin or film known to us):

Guarda! C'è un delfino!

Look! There is a dolphin!

Ho visto un bel film americano alla televisione.

I've seen a nice American film on television.

These are only general guidelines. In many cases the use or omission of the articles depends on different linguistic habits. Some particular uses of the definite article

In Italian we always use the definite article with the proper names of geographical features such as mountains, rivers, etc.:

le Alpi, gli Alburni   the Alps, the Alburni

il Tamigi, la Senna   the Thames, the Seine

but not with the names of cities:

48

Firenze	Londra
Florence	London

except when qualified in some way:

la Firenze del Settecento

eighteenth-century Florence

We use the definite article with the names of countries or nations:

Amo l'Italia.

I love Italy.

Il Brasile è campione del mondo.

Brazil is world champion.

We don't normally use it with the preposition in if talking about feminine countries:

Vivo in Italia. I live in Italy.

Andiamo in Spagna. We go to Spain. unless the country is qualified in some way:

Si vive meglio nell'Italia meridionale.

One lives better in southern Italy.

But we do sometimes use it to refer to masculine or plural countries:

Vivo negli Stati Uniti. I live in the USA.

 When speaking of somebody's profession we use the article with fare: Faccio l'ingegnere. I am an engineer.

but omit it with essere (note how English usage differs):

Sono ingegnere. I am an engineer.

See also 8.3.3 and 8.3.4 for further examples of these points. We can summarise these patterns in the following way:

THE ADJECTIVE

WHAT IS AN ADJECTIVE?

An adjective is a word that qualifies the meaning of a noun by adding some spec- ification or description to it. There are many different categories of adjective including demonstrative (questo, quello), interrogative (quale), possessive (mio, tuo), indefinite (alcuni, qualche) and negative (nessun). But in this chapter we only cover the use of aggettivi qual- ificativi: descriptive adjectives that describe qualities (physical or otherwise) of person or thing, and classifying adjectives, such as nationality, that describe the category or classification that the person or thing belongs to (see also Chapter 10). The other types of adjectives will be shown in Chapter 3, together with the corresponding pronouns.

Common adjective patterns

Almost all descriptive adjectives follow the same basic patterns as the nouns with their endings depending on gender and number. There are two 'classes' or groups of adjectives:

	Class 1	Class 2
Masculine	-o	-i
Masculine/feminine	-e	-i
Feminine	-a	-e

In the first group, there are four different endings for feminine/masculine/singular/ plural. In the second group, the ending is the same for both masculine and feminine:

	Class 1		Class 2	
	Singular	Plural	Singular	Plural
Masculine	piccolo	piccoli	grande	grandi (m./f.)
Feminine	piccola	piccole	grande	grandi (m./f.)

Exceptions to this pattern

Only a few descriptive adjectives have a different pattern from those shown above. Adjectives with singular -a (for both masculine and feminine) have masculine plural in -i and feminine plural in -e. Many of these have endings such as -ista, -asta,

-ita, -ida, -ota (for nouns with similar endings, see below)

Singular	Plural	
Masculine/feminine	Masculine	Feminine
socialista	socialisti	socialiste
entusiasta	entusiasti	entusiaste
ipocrita	ipocriti	ipocrite
suicida	suicidi	suicide
idiota	idioti	idiote

Il partito socialista   I paesi socialisti   Le idee socialiste

La bandiera socialista

Invariable adjectives

Invariable adjectives have the same ending, whatever their gender and number, and retain the same form whatever noun they are referring to. The most common invari- able adjectives are:

SOME COLOURS: BLU, ROSA, VIOLA, LILLA, BEIGE.

un pantalone	blu navy trousers
una gonna blu	a navy skirt
i sandali blu	navy sandals
le scarpe blu	navy shoes

COLOURS INDICATED BY TWO WORDS: VERDE BOTTIGLIA, GIALLO CANARINO, BIANCO LATTE.

camicia verde bottiglia	bottle green shirt
pantaloni giallo canarino	canary yellow trousers
lampadine bianco latte	milk white light bulbs

PARI 'EVEN, EQUAL', DISPARI 'ODD' AND IMPARI 'UNEVEN, UNEQUAL':

numero pari	even number
carte dispari	odd-numbered playing cards
pari condizioni	equal conditions
una lotta impari	an unequal struggle

ARROSTO (ROAST):

pollo arrosto	roast chicken
patate arrosto	roast potatoes
carne arrosto	roast meat

POSITION OF ADJECTIVES

Unlike English, and many other languages, the most common position for the adjec- tive in the Italian noun group is after the noun. This is the usual non-emphatic position occupied by the adjective, when it expresses a basic, intrinsic characteristic of the noun:

Ho visto un film interessante

I saw an interesting film

Abbiamo visitato una città storica

We visited an historic city

Adjectives of shape, colour and nationality almost always come after the noun. Note that adjectives of nationality never have a capital letter in Italian:

una tavola rotonda	a round table
una maglia Bianca	a white sweater
uno studente francese	a French student

Adjectives qualified, for example, by an adverb or a prepositional phrase, also come after:

una persona enormemente simpatica

a really nice person

un viaggio pieno di problemi

a journey full of problems

As do participles used as adjectives:

le mele cotte	cooked apples

However in Italian, unlike in English, where adjectives almost always come before the noun ('an interesting film'), the order of the noun group is flexible, and the position of the adjectives can change the emphasis of the sentence. Although Italian descriptive adjectives, particularly the most common (e.g. nuovo, vecchio, giovane, piccolo, bello, brutto) are placed after the noun when used to specify it or distinguish it from similar objects, they can be placed before when there is a need to describe the noun with some emphasis or imagination:

Dammi il cacciavite piccolo.

Give me the small screwdriver.

(not the big one)

Sul tavolo c'era un piccolo cacciavite.

There was a small screwdriver on the table. (description of screwdriver)

Sandra è una ragazza bella.

Sandra is a beautiful girl. (not merely nice)

Sandra è una bella ragazza.

Sandra is a really beautiful girl.

Ho comprato una macchina nuova.

I bought a new car. (rather than a second-hand one)

Paola si è messa un nuovo vestito.

Paola put on a new dress. (another, a different one)

Some adjectives have a completely different meaning from their common one when their position is changed, expressing their literal meaning when used after, but a quite different, often figurative, meaning when used before:

un film bello

a nice film

un bel problema

a pretty difficult problem

Preferisco avere regole certe

I prefer to have reliable rules

Non capisco certe regole

I don't understand certain (some) rules

un ufficiale alto a tall officer

un alto ufficiale a high-ranking officer

un uomo grande a big man (e.g. Pavarotti)

un grande uomo a great man (e.g. Napoleon)

Ci sono molti studenti poveri

There are many poor students

Poveri studenti! L'esame sarà duro!

Poor students! The exam will be hard!

Note that bello, when positioned before the noun (see example above, un bel prob- lema) changes its endings in the same way as the definite article il, la, lo, etc. and the adjective quel, quella, quello, etc.

The adjective buono, on the other hand, follows the pattern of the indefinite article

un, una, un', uno buon esempio, buona fortuna, buono studio, etc.

COMPARATIVE ADJECTIVES

One way of making a comparison between two different people, objects or other elements, is to use a comparative adjective.

La mia macchina è veloce come la tua.

My car is as fast as yours.

La mia macchina è più veloce della tua.

My car is faster than yours.

53

La mia macchina è meno veloce della tua.

My car is less fast than yours.

'as . . . as'

This is formed by using the words come or quanto to introduce the second element of the comparison. As a reinforcement, we can also use the words tanto, altrettanto or così before the first element:

Il mio nuovo ufficio è comodo quanto quello di prima.

My new office is as comfortable as the one I had before.

La mia collega è tanto carina quanto efficiente.

My colleague is as pretty as she is efficient.

Qui le melanzane non sono care come in Inghilterra.

Here aubergines are not as dear as in England.

'more than'/'less than'

The words più and meno are used to make a descriptive adjective into a compara- tive, while di or che introduce the second element of the comparison:

Sandro è più bravo di Angelo a bridge.

Sandro is better than Angelo at bridge.

È stato meno facile di quanto pensassi.

It was less easy than I expected.

È più facile criticare che risolvere i problemi.

It's easier to criticise than to solve problems.

Sara è più carina che intelligente.

Sara is prettier than she is intelligent.

The choice of di or che depends on what part of speech the second element of the comparison is, and on its position in the sentence:

più/meno . . . di + noun, pronoun, adverb, numeral

più/meno . . . che + adjective, verb, noun/pronoun preceded by preposition.

SPECIAL FORMS OF COMPARATIVE

Four very common adjectives have a special form of comparative:

buono	good	migliore (più buono)
cattivo/brutto	bad	peggiore (più cattivo)
grande	big	maggiore (più grande)

piccolo	small	minore (più piccolo)

The regular form of comparative (shown in brackets) is also possible. While there is little difference between più buono/migliore and più cattivo/peggiore, there is a difference of meaning between maggiore and più grande. Maggiore can mean 'bigger, older/elder' in a physical sense, but can also mean 'greater' in an abstract sense. Similarly, minore can mean 'smaller' or 'younger', but can also mean 'less, the lesser' when referring to an abstract quality:

> Ho due sorelle. La maggiore si chiama Diana.

> I have two sisters. The elder is called Diana.

> Noi abbiamo una maggiore responsabilità di voi.

> We have a greater responsibility than you.

> Il mio fratello minore frequenta la scuola elementare.

> My little (younger) brother goes to elementary school.

> Lui lavora con minore impegno da quando si è sposato.

> He works with less commitment since he got married.

RELATIVE SUPERLATIVES

To refer to something or somebody as having 'the most' of a certain quality, in rela- tion to other individuals, we use il più together with the relevant adjective. This is called the relative superlative:

> Silvia è la più brava studentessa della nostra classe.

> Silvia is the best student in our class.

> Pavarotti è il tenore italiano più famoso del mondo.

> Pavarotti is the most famous Italian tenor in the world.

> Il Po è il più lungo fiume italiano.

> The Po is the longest Italian river.

Again, a few common adjectives have a special form of relative superlative, as well as the regular one:

buono	good
il migliore (il più buono)	the best
cattivo	bad
il peggiore (il più cattivo)	the worst
grande	big
il maggiore (il più grande)	the biggest, oldest
piccolo	small
il minore (il più piccolo)	the smallest, youngest

55

As with the comparative, there can be a difference of meaning between the two forms il maggiore/il più grande and il minore/il più piccolo:

Secondo me, il problema maggiore dei giorni nostri è la droga.

In my opinion, the greatest problem in our time is that of drugs.

ABSOLUTE SUPERLATIVES

Absolute superlatives indicate the greatest possible degree of a quality, but without any comparison being made. Superlative adjectives are formed in Italian by adding the suffix -issimo to the end of the adjective:

un uomo bellissimo a very handsome man un'organizzazione efficientissima a very efficient organisation degli importantissimi clienti some very important clients However it is also possible in Italian to use the adverb molto to modify the adjec- tive, in a similar way to the English 'very':

un uomo molto bello

a very handsome man

un'organizzazione molto efficiente

a very efficient organisation

dei clienti molto importanti

some very important clients

As seen above, when modified by any adverb (molto, poco, troppo, abbastanza, piuttosto) the adjective generally follows the noun:

dei clienti piuttosto importanti some

rather important clients

Notice how when modified by the superlative suffix -issimo, the endings of the adjectives have the same pattern as adjectives in the first group, ending in -o/-a/

-i/-e , even if they belong to the second group (-e, -i). So we have:

Adjective in the first group	bello/i/a/e	bellissimo/i/a/e
Adjective in the second group	importante/i	Importantissimo/i/a/e

The common adjectives buono, cattivo, grande, piccolo, mentioned above, also have two forms of absolute superlative:

buono	good	ottimo/buonissimo	best
cattivo	bad	pessimo/cattivissimo	worst
grande	big	massimo/grandissimo	biggest, greatest
piccolo	small	minimo/piccolissimo	smallest, least

AGREEMENT OF NOUN, ARTICLE AND ADJECTIVE

Nearly all Italian descriptive adjectives have the same pattern of endings as the

nouns (the two patterns are shown above); only a few are invariable (see 1.2.3). Nouns, adjectives and articles used together in a noun group must agree in number and gender.

For example, if we use a feminine singular noun such as borsa 'bag', we have to use a feminine singular article la and adjective rossa:

> La borsa rossa   The red bag

If we use a masculine plural noun such as sandali 'sandals', we have to use a mascu- line plural article i and adjective rossi:

> I sandali rossi   The red sandals

The English articles and adjectives are identical in both examples ('the red . . .') while in Italian they have very different forms depending on the gender and number of the noun to which they are attached:

> Il vestito rosso   I sandali rossi
>
> La borsa rossa   Le scarpe rosse

NOUN AND ADJECTIVE OF SAME PATTERN

When noun and adjective belong to the same pattern of endings, the agreement will be obvious:

> Sul tavolo c'è un piatto rotondo.
>
> On the table there is a round dish.

Agreement of noun, article and adjective

> Ho conosciuto due ragazze italiane.
>
> I met two Italian girls.

NOUN AND ADJECTIVE OF DIFFERENT PATTERNS

It is more difficult to remember how to make the agreement when the noun and adjective belong to different patterns and therefore have different endings:

Sul tavolo c'è un piatto grande.

There is a large dish on the table.

Ho conosciuto due ragazze inglesi.

I met two English girls.

Il programma era noioso.

The programme was boring.

La radio era rotta

The radio was broken.

MORE THAN ONE NOUN (SAME GENDER)

If an adjective refers to more than one noun of the same gender, it will be plural   and have the same gender as the nouns:

>Ho comprato un libro e un vocabolario tedeschi.

>I bought a German book and German dictionary.

>Ho comprato una grammatica e un'agenda tedesche.

>I bought a German grammar and a German diary.

>More than one noun (different genders)

If the two nouns are of different genders then the adjective is generally masculine plural:

>Ho comprato un vocabolario e una grammatica tedeschi.

>I bought a German dictionary and a German grammar.

However if the second of the two nouns – the one nearest to the adjective – is femi- nine plural, the adjective may sometimes agree with it:

>Ho comprato un vocabolario e due grammatiche tedesche.

>I bought a German dictionary and two German grammars.

CHAPTER 3: VERB

Introduction

Actions, events and situations are expressed by the use of verbs. Italian has a complex system of different verb forms. In the first section of this chapter we shall intro- duce the general features of Italian verbs, both regular and irregular, with a brief explanation of basic grammatical terminology, which will help you to understand these features. In the second section, the different verb forms are illustrated in table form for the regular and the most common irregular verbs and also for the passive forms of the four regular verb types. Finally, in the third section, we look at the different verb moods and tenses individually with brief explanations on their use. Part B of the book illustrates usage more fully.

GRAMMATICAL SUBJECT

Usually the subject of a verb is the 'agent' or 'doer' of an action, the 'protagonist' of an event:

> Noi partiamo per l'America.

> We leave for America.

> Franco e Teresa partono per l'America.

> Franco and Teresa leave for America.

Sometimes we talk of facts rather than actions. Here the 'subject' of the verb is not 'doing' anything, but is the theme or main topic expressed by the verb:

> Giulia è bionda.

> Giulia is blonde.

> Questo film dura due ore.

> This film lasts two hours.

However the grammatical subject of the verb may be different from the real subject or agent of the action. This is the case with passive constructions.

PERSONS OF THE VERB

The different forms of the verb, determined by its grammatical subject, are called the persons (this is a purely grammatical term, not necessarily referring to human beings):

1	Singular first person (the speaker)	I
2	Singular second person (the person addressed)	you

3	Singular third person (the third party)	he, she, it
4	Plural first person (the speaker + other people)	we
5	Plural second person (the people addressed)	you
6	Plural third person (the third parties)	they

In each tense, Italian verbs have six different endings, depending on who or what is carrying out the action. The different endings immediately identify the 'person' – the subject of the action – unlike in English where only the third person singular has a distinctive ending ('I eat, you eat, he eats'). The first and second persons are usually evident in the context of communication (speaker/writer and receiver):

| Quanti anni hai? | Ho trent'anni. |
| How old are you? | I am thirty. |

Using a subject pronoun to refer to the third person is often unnecessary where the person (or thing) has already been mentioned:

| Quanti anni ha Maria? | Ha venticinque anni. |
| How old is Maria? | She is twenty-five. |

Consequently, it is not necessary to use subject pronouns (English 'I, you, he/she', etc.) in Italian, unless we need to give particular emphasis to the subject (see also 8.4).

VERB CONJUGATIONS

The fact that Italian verbs have a pattern of six distinct verb endings in each of the tenses creates a large number of different forms of the same verb (almost a hundred!) also called inflexions. Fortunately, most verbs follow common patterns of change known as conjugations. Each verb has an invariable part (the 'stem'), which carries its meaning, and an inflected part (the 'ending') which identifies the person, the tense, the mood, and other features. The regular conjugation patterns are shown in the verb tables below (2.2) for easy reference. Traditionally we distinguish three conjugations defined by the form that the verb takes in the infinitive (the infinitive is the form used in dictionary entries):

1st conjugation ending in **-are as parl-are** 'to speak'

2nd conjugation ending in **-ere as cred-ere** 'to believe'

3rd conjugation ending in **-ire as dorm-ire** 'to sleep'

The verbs of the 3rd conjugation (ending in -ire) follow two distinct patterns, the second of which, with endings in -isco, as in fin-ire/fin-isco 'to finish', is the most frequent. Both patterns, however, are considered as belonging to the same conju- gation, because of the -ire ending of the infinitive.

MOODS AND TENSES

MOODS

The different forms and uses of Italian verbs are traditionally grouped in seven moods. These convey the different characteristics of the actions or facts that the speaker or writer wants to communicate: certainty or doubt, politeness or straightforwardness, command, etc.

The seven moods are:

indicative

infinitive

conditional

participle

subjunctive

 gerund

imperative

The different verb forms for each verb mood will be listed below in the tables of regular and irregular conjugations and then described in separate paragraphs. The ways in which moods are used to express distinct communicative functions and mean- ings are illustrated in Part B.

TENSES

The word tense denotes the different verb forms that indicate the relationship between the action or event referred to and the time of speaking or writing (or other refer- ence point in time). There is a range of different tenses for each mood of verbs (except the imperative). In Italian, different tenses are sometimes used to distinguish features of verbs other than time relationships. For example, perfect and imperfect tenses can express the aspect of the action (see Chapter 13), while different subjunctive and conditional tenses can express different degrees of doubt, possibility, politeness, etc. (see Sections III and IV).

SIMPLE AND COMPOUND TENSES

Many tenses of Italian verbs are formed using the past participle of the main verb along with either avere or essere as the auxiliary verb. These are called compound tenses. One major area of difficulty for students of Italian is knowing which verbs   use avere in compound tenses and which use essere. In order to be able to do this, it is useful to understand the difference between transitive and intransitive verbs. All passive forms of verbs are compound forms, commonly formed with the auxiliary essere.

TRANSITIVE/INTRANSITIVE VERBS: USE OF AVERE OR ESSERE IN COMPOUND TENSES

The actions that we express by using verbs can be 'completed' with an object. There may be a direct object as in:

Lucia scrive una lettera.	Lucia writes a letter.
Cerchiamo una casa.	We look for a house.

Here the action of the verb can be completed by answering the question che cosa? 'what?'. The direct object of the verb is the noun that can answer this question without the use of a preposition (in this case una lettera and una casa):

> Che cosa scrive Lucia?
>
> What is Lucia writing?
>
> Lucia scrive una lettera.
>
> Lucia is writing a letter.
>
> Che cosa cerchiamo?
>
> What are we looking for?
>
> Cerchiamo una casa.
>
> We're looking for a house.

If we can ask and answer the question che cosa?, the verb is transitive, and it will use the auxiliary avere in compound tenses:

> Lucia ha scritto una lettera.
>
> Lucia wrote a letter.
>
> Abbiamo cercato una casa.
>
> We looked for a house.

But some Italian verbs cannot be completed by a direct object and the question che cosa? would not make sense; these are intransitive verbs and they normally use essere as the auxiliary:

> Andiamo in ufficio alle 9.00.
>
> We go to the office at 9.00.
>
> Il treno per Napoli parte alle 6.00.
>
> The train to Naples leaves at 6.00.
>
> Siamo andate in ufficio alle 9.00.
>
> We went to the office at 9.00.
>
> Il treno per Napoli è partito alle 6.00.
>
> The train to Naples left at 6.00.

Because it determines their different uses, especially in the compound tenses, knowing whether verbs are transitive or intransitive is very important. Check by either looking in a dictionary or seeing whether you can ask and answer the question che cosa? 'what?'. In dictionaries all verb entries carry the following indications:

v.t. or   v.tr. verbo transitivo

v.i. or   v.intr. verbo intransitivo

Speakers of English find it difficult to distinguish transitive from intransitive verbs, because English compound tenses only use the auxiliary 'to have' in the active forms and the auxiliary 'to be' in passive forms ('I have criticised my colleagues', 'I am criticised by my colleagues'). Problems arise also from the fact that many English verbs used transitively and intransitively have an Italian counterpart that can only be used intransitively. Below we show some examples of English phrases that cannot be translated directly into Italian, since the verbs camminare, volare, guidare and viaggiare are not gener- ally used transitively:

> I'm going to walk the dog.

> I'm Sharon. Fly me!

> Can you drive me home?

> Travel the world with Airmiles!

VERBS THAT CAN BE USED BOTH TRANSITIVELY AND INTRANSITIVELY

Some verbs can be used both transitively (with a direct object) and intransitively (without a direct object), for example aumentare, cambiare, cominciare, crescere, diminuire, finire and passare. In the first two examples that follow, the subjects of these actions – beginning and finishing – are people and the verbs have direct objects ('the lesson', 'the holidays').

> Il professore comincia la lezione alle 11.00.

> The teacher begins the lesson at 11.00.

> Finiamo le vacanze in agosto.

> We finish our holidays in August.

In the next two examples (below), the same verbs (this time with 'the lesson' and 'the holidays' as subject) cannot have a direct object:

> La lezione comincia alle 11.00.

> The lesson begins at 11.00.

> Le vacanze finiscono in agosto.

> The holidays finish in August.

In simple tenses, the forms of the verbs are identical, whether transitive or intran- sitive. But the compound tenses, such as the past, vary according to whether they are used transitively or intransitively:

> Il professore ha cominciato la lezione.

> The teacher began the lesson.

> La lezione è cominciata alle 11.00.

> The lesson began at 11.00.

> Abbiamo finito le vacanze in agosto.

> We finished the holidays in August.

> Le vacanze sono finite in agosto.

> The holidays finished in August.

When used transitively, verbs such as correre 'to run', saltare 'to jump', vivere to live' take avere:

Hanno corso un grosso rischio.

They ran a great risk.

Oggi ho saltato il pranzo.

Today I skipped lunch.

Ho vissuto una vita d'inferno.

I have lived a life of hell.

When used intransitively, the choice of avere/essere is more a matter of personal choice and linguistic habit:

Ho vissuto/Sono vissuto a Londra per 10 anni.

I lived in London for 10 years.

Giuliana ha corso/è corsa a casa.

Giuliana ran home.

I bambini hanno saltato/sono saltati giù dal letto.

The children jumped down from the bed.

Verbs like these are marked in dictionaries as v.tr. e intr. ('verb transitive and intran- sitive').

VERBS USING THE AUXILIARY AVERE EVEN WHEN USED INTRANSITIVELY

Generally Italian transitive verbs use the auxiliary avere, while intransitive verbs use the auxiliary essere in the compound tenses. However, there are quite a few verbs

that use the auxiliary avere even when used intransitively. Here are the most common:

camminare to walk

piangere to cry

dormire   to sleep

riposare to rest

giocare   to play

viaggiare to travel

passeggiare to walk

In more elaborate form

Ho camminato per due ore.

I walked for two hours.

Come hai dormito?

How did you sleep?

Avete giocato a carte?

Did you play cards?

VOICE: ACTIVE, PASSIVE, REFLEXIVE

Introduction

'Voice' describes the relationship of the verb action with its subject and object.

The different voices or relationships are:

(a) ACTIVE VOICE

Normally (see 2.1.2) the grammatical subject of the verb is the doer of the action or the main theme of the event, in which case the verb is active:

Gianni guarda Luisa.

Gianni watches Luisa.

Il meccanico ripara la macchina.

The mechanic repairs the car.

(b) PASSIVE VOICE

But sometimes the person or object on the receiving end of the action is the grammatical subject, and in this case the verb is passive:

Luisa è guardata da Gianni.

Luisa is watched by Gianni.

La macchina è riparata dal meccanico.

The car is repaired by the mechanic.

In the second example, the agent of the action is clearly the mechanic (the one who repairs the car), but the grammatical subject of the passive verb is the car.

(c) REFLEXIVE AND PRONOMINAL VOICE

A verb form is reflexive when its subject and object are the same:

Gianni si guarda allo specchio.

Gianni looks at himself in the mirror.

There are other verb forms that are not strictly speaking reflexive but are similar in form.

The following paragraphs look at the passive and reflexive/pronominal forms in detail.

65

THE PASSIVE FORM

The passive of Italian verbs is formed by the use of the past participle and the auxil- iary essere, using the same tense as the corresponding active form. The passive conjugation of verbs is shown in the verb tables in 2.2 below. The passive can also   be formed using venire or andare as auxiliary instead of essere (see 19.2), or by using the pronoun si and the third person of the verb (see 19.4). Only transitive verbs can have a passive form. Passive sentences (sentences based on a passive verb) are used when we want to focus on the action itself or the object of an action, rather than on the agent of an action.

THE REFLEXIVE AND PRONOMINAL FORM

REFLEXIVE VERB FORMS

Reflexive verbs are active verb forms accompanied by a reflexive pronoun (see 3.4.3). Look at these two examples:

>Il Sig. Franchi sta lavando la macchina.

>Mr Franchi is washing the car.

>Il Sig. Franchi si sta lavando.

>Mr Franchi is washing himself.

In the first example above, the direct object of the action of washing is the car. It is separate from the person who is doing it (the subject of the action). In the second example, the subject and the object of the action ·are the same person Franchi). This is the reflexive form, in which the reflexive pronoun refers to the person carrying out the action, but at the same time is also the object of it. The position of the reflexive pronoun is the same as that of all other unstressed personal pronouns (see 3.4): usually before the verb; but sometimes attached to the end of it, as with infinitives, gerunds and voi, tu imperatives:

>Prego si accomodi.

>Please, have a seat (make yourself comfortable).

>In genere i giovani italiani si vestono alla moda.

>In general young people in Italy dress fashionably.

>Sono le 9.00. Dovete prepararvi ad uscire.

>It's 9.00. You must prepare yourselves to go out.

>Preparati ad uscire!

>Get yourself ready to go out!

In the compound tenses, reflexive verbs are conjugated with the verb essere, even though the verbs are transitive (cf. lavare, alzare) and normally take avere in the compound tenses. The past participle has to agree with the subject:

>Stamattina i bambini si sono alzati alle 6.00.

>This morning the children got (themselves) up at 6.00.

>Mi sono vestita con calma.

>I got dressed slowly.

66

PRONOMINAL VERB FORMS

Pronominal verb forms are verb forms which use the reflexive pronoun. In Italian they are used much more frequently than in English because we can use them not only in a true reflexive pattern, but also in many other ways. In true reflexives (see above), the subject and object of the verb are one and the same. Although this is not the case with pronominal verb forms, they still embody the concept of 'reci- procal' or 'reflexive' action (an action relating or reflecting back to the subject). The different uses of the pronominal verb form will become clear from the examples below.

(a) INDIRECT REFLEXIVE

The reflexive always indicates an action that is related to the person carrying out the action (the subject). Note the use of the auxiliary essere in the compound tenses:

> Giulio si lava le mani.

> Giulio washes his hands.

> Mi metto la giacca.

> I put on my jacket.

> Stamattina non mi sono fatto la barba.

> This morning I didn't shave (myself).

In the examples above, the actions are not truly reflexive, since the subjects and the objects of the actions are not exactly identical: Giulio . . . le mani, io . . . la giacca, io . . . la barba. However we use the reflexive pronoun to stress the fact that the object of the action is closely related to the person who does it, and indeed is either part of his/her body (le mani, la barba) or a personal belonging (la giacca) In the last example, the participle can also agree with the object:

Stamattina non mi sono fatta la barba.

The reflexive pronoun can also be omitted in which case the construction no longer takes essere in the compound tenses:

Giulio lava le mani. Metto la giacca.

Non ho fatto la barba.

(b) RECIPROCAL REFLEXIVE (EACH OTHER)

A reciprocal action is when two people do something to one another:

> Arrivederci. Ci vediamo domani.

> Bye. See you tomorrow.

> Mario e Nicoletta si sposano domani.

> Mario and Nicoletta are getting married tomorrow.

> Dove vi siete conosciuti tu e Maria?

> Where did you and Maria meet (each other)?

> Ci siamo incontrati in Spagna.

We met (each other) in Spain.

Note how in the examples above the reflexive pronoun marks an event or action taking place within the subject; the two people are at the same time the subject and the object of a reciprocal action. The same actions can be expressed by the active form, in which case one person is the subject and the other is the object:

> Domani Mario sposa Nicoletta.

> Tomorrow Mario will marry Nicoletta.

> Dove (tu) hai conosciuto Maria?

> Where did you meet Maria?

> Ho incontrato il Dott. Rossi in Spagna.

> I met Dr Rossi in Spain.

(c) EMOTION OR INVOLVEMENT EXPRESSED WITH REFLEXIVE PRONOUNS

In Italian we can use the reflexive pronoun simply to stress the subjective side of an event, the importance of this event to the person (the self) who is involved in it and who is its (grammatical) subject:

> Stasera ci vediamo un bel film.

> Tonight we'll watch a nice film.

> Ho fame! Voglio mangiarmi una pizza!

> I'm hungry! I really want a pizza!

> Mannaggia! Mi sono dimenticata le chiavi!

> Damn! I forgot the keys!

In the examples above, the objects of the verbs are totally separate from, and not part of, the subjects. However the use of the reflexive pronoun shows the intensity felt by the people carrying out these actions. The same sentences can be expressed without using the reflexive pronouns, but then the statements will sound much less emotional, more objective:

Stasera vediamo un bel film.

Voglio mangiare una pizza.

Ho dimenticato le chiavi.

There are a few Italian verbs that are always (or almost always) used with a reflexive pronoun, because of the 'psychological' and subjective meaning they convey, for example:

accorgersi to realise,	to be aware
arrabbiarsi	to get angry
divertirsi	to have fun
innamorarsi	to fall in love
pentirsi	to regret, repent
vergognarsi	to be ashamed

Sbrigati! Non ti accorgi che è tardi?

Hurry up! Don't you realise that it's late?

Non arrabbiarti!

Don't be angry!

Vi siete divertiti a Roma?

Did you have a good time in Rome?

Giulia si è pentita di aver accettato quel lavoro.

Giulia regretted having accepted that job.

Non vergognarti di questo errore, non è colpa tua.

Don't be ashamed of this mistake. It's not your fault.

(d) SI PASSIVANTE

In some cases the reflexive pronoun si is used to give a passive meaning to the active form of the verb

Si parla Italiano.

Italian is spoken.

Nella mia famiglia si parlano tre lingue.

In my family three languages are spoken.

Dal terrazzo si vedono i tetti della città.

From the terrace the roofs of the city can be seen (one can see the roofs).

In the first example, the si passivante form appears identical to the si imper- sonale form ('one' speaks Italian) However, when there is a plural subject, as in the second two examples, the verb is plural, so it becomes clear that the construction is passive ('three languages are spoken', 'the roofs can be seen').

IMPERSONAL SI

The pronoun si is also used to express the impersonal form of verbs i.e. in cases when no subject of the verb is mentioned, or rather when the subject cannot be identified with a particular person or thing (English would use the indeter- minate subject 'one'):

Si lavora meglio con il fresco.

One works better in cool weather.

Stasera si va a ballare.

Tonight everybody is going to dance.

A tavola non si invecchia.

One doesn't get old at the dinner table.

(Popular saying, meant to discourage people from hurrying when eating)

Notice that the impersonal form is always formed with si and the third person singular of the verb.

TO BE HUNGRY, THIRSTY, HOT, COLD, SLEEPY

These expressions, which describe a condition based on physical sensations, in English require the verb to be followed by the relevant adjective (i.e. I am hungry, you were thirsty, etc.). Instead, in Italian they require the verb to have (avere), followed by the relevant noun that describes the sensation: i.e. to be hungry turns into to have hunger; to be thirsty into to have thirst, and so on:

avere fame = to be hungry (literally: to have hunger)

avere sete = to be thirsty (literally: to have thirst)

avere caldo = to be hot (literally: to have heat)

avere freddo = to be cold (literally: to have cold)

avere sonno = to be sleepy (literally: to have sleep)

In a similar way,

avere ragione = to be right (literally: to have right)

avere torto = to be wrong (literally: to have wrong)

Any tense of the verb avere can be used with these expressions, therefore:

egli avrà fame = he will be hungry (he will have hunger)

io ho avuto sonno = I felt sleepy (I have had sleep)

noi avemmo sete = we felt thirsty (we had thirst)

voi avevate ragione = you were right (you had right) and so on.

While to be right and to be wrong are always translated with the verb avere, to be hot and to be cold may also take the verb to feel (i.e. I feel hot, you felt cold, etc.). In Italian this is obtained by using the verb sentire (to feel), followed by the noun: avere caldo, sentire caldo = to be hot, to feel hot (literally: to feel heat) avere freddo, sentire freddo = to be cold, to feel cold (literally: to feel cold) The verb sentire is never used with hungry, thirsty or sleepy.

The Italian adjectives affamato (hungry), assetato (thirsty), accaldato (hot), raffreddato or infreddolito (cold), and assonnato (sleepy) may also be used, though more sparingly than in English. In Italian they almost describe a condition, more than a personal feeling. Compare the following examples:

essi mangiano un panino perché hanno fame = they eat a sandwich because they are hungry

affamati dopo il lungo viaggio, essi si fermarono per un pasto = hungry after the long journey, they stopped for a meal

io avevo sonno e andai a letto presto = I was sleepy and I went to bed early egli sembrava assonnato perché non aveva dormito = he seemed sleepy because he had not slept

io avevo caldo (or sentivo caldo) con la giacca, così l'ho tolta = I was hot / felt hot with the jacket, so I took it off io sono accaldato, e sto sudando = I am (feeling) hot, and I'm sweating In most cases both forms would be correct: essi mangiano perché hanno fame = they eat a sandwich because they are hungry essi mangiano perché sono affamati = (same as above) essi dormono perché hanno sonno = they are sleeping because because they are sleepy essi dormono perché sono assonnati = (same as above) However, especially in common speech, the first of the two forms is the one used more often.

There is also a difference in meaning when using raffreddato or infreddolito: raffreddato = cooled, cooled up questo è un motore raffreddato ad acqua = this is a water-cooled engine

raffreddato = running a cold noi eravamo raffreddati e starnutivamo = we were running a cold and we sneezed

infreddolito = feeling cold ella era infreddolita, e indossò un cappotto = she was feeling cold, and she put on a coat Although in the previous examples raffreddato has been used as an adjective, it is the past participle of the verb raffreddare, to cool, cool up. Its reflexive form raffreddarsi, when referred to living creatures has a common meaning of to catch a cold (although the proper way of saying this is prendere un raffreddore). Since they are very common verbs, it is useful to focus well their different use (and meaning): io raffreddo quest'aqua per ottenere ghiaccio = I cool this water to obtain ice

aprendo la finestra l'aria si raffredda = by opening the window the air cools up

vieni dentro, o ti raffredderai (colloquial) = come inside, or you will catch a cold (= you will turn cold) vieni dentro, o prenderai un raffreddore (proper form) = (same as above)

There is also a similar verb, freddarsi, whose official meaning is to become (too) cold, sometime used in common speech to replace the aforesaid raffreddarsi. Its positive (non-reflexive) form too exists, freddare, always referred to living creatures, with an idiomatic meaning of to shoot someone dead (a rather modern use of this verb):

il caffè si è freddato, non berlo = the coffee has turned cold, don't drink it

quando ho fatto la doccia l'acqua si era freddata = when I took a shower the water had become cold

vieni a mangiare o la minestra si fredderà = come to eat, or the soup will grow cold

egli / ella mirò bene, e freddò il nemico al primo colpo = he/she aimed well, and killed the enemy with the first shot As a general rule, freddarsi is preferred to raffreddarsi when a somewhat negative shade of meaning is required, e.g. to become excessively cold, or to become cold (while it shouldn't have), such as speaking of food, hot drinks, water for a shower or a bath, the air in a heated room, etc.

VERB TABLES

REGULAR VERBS: ACTIVE CONJUGATIONS

Here are the complete conjugations of four very common Italian verbs. We call these patterns regular because the stems of these verbs remain constantly the same (or invari- able) throughout the whole system of moods and tenses. Understanding the way the endings (the variable part of the verb) change, will allow us to learn all the possible forms of most Italian verbs. Notice the two patterns of the 3rd conjugation, and remember that the pattern in -isco is the most frequent.

| 1st conjugation | 2nd conjugation | 3rd conjugation |

Infinitive (Infinito)

Present (Presente)

| parl-are | cred-ere | dorm-ire |
| | | fin-ire |

71

Past (Passato)

avere parlato   avere creduto   avere dormito

                                           avere finito

INDICATIVE (INDICATIVO)

Present (Presente)

1st sing.	parl-o	cred-o	dorm-o	fin-isco
2nd sing.	parl-i	cred-i	dorm-i	fin-isci
3rd sing.	parl-a	cred-e	dorm-e	fin-isce
1st pl.	parl-iamo	cred-iamo	dorm-iamo	fin-iamo
2nd pl.	parl-ate	cred-ete	dorm-ite	fin-ite
3rd pl.	parl-ano	cred-ono	dorm-ono	fin-iscono

Imperfect (Imperfetto)

parl-avo	cred-evo	dorm-ivo	fin-ivo
parl-avi	cred-evi	dorm-ivi	fin-ivi
parl-ava	cred-eva	dorm-iva	fin-iva
parl-avamo	cred-evamo	dorm-ivamo	fin-ivamo
parl-avate	cred-evate	dorm-ivate	fin-ivate
parl-avano	cred-evano	dorm-ivano	fin-ivano

Compound perfect (Passato prossimo)

ho parlato	ho creduto	ho dormito	ho finito
hai parlato	hai creduto	hai dormito	hai finito.
ha parlato	ha creduto	ha dormito	ha finito
abbiamo parlato	abbiamo creduto	abbiamo dormito	
		abbiamo finito	
avete parlato	avete creduto	avete dormito	
		avete finito	
hanno parlato	hanno creduto	hanno dormito	
		hanno finito	

Simple perfect (Passato remoto)

parl-ai	cred-etti (cred-ei)	dorm-ii	fin-ii
parl-asti	cred-esti	dorm-isti	fin-isti
parl-ò	cred-ette (cred-é)	dorm-ì	fin-ì

72

parl-ammo   cred-emmo   dorm-immo   fin-immo

parl-aste cred-este   dorm-iste   fin-iste

parl-arono   cred-ettero   dorm-irono   fin-irono

(cred-erono)

Pluperfect (Trapassato prossimo)

avevo parlato   avevo creduto avevo dormito   avevo finito

avevi parlato   avevi creduto avevi dormito   avevi finito

aveva parlato   aveva creduto aveva dormito   aveva finito

avevamo parlato   avevamo creduto avevamo dormito
avevamo finito

avevate parlato   avevate creduto

avevate dormito   avevate finito

avevano parlato   avevano creduto   avevano dormito
avevano finito

Past anterior (Trapassato remoto)

ebbi parlato   ebbi creduto   ebbi dormito   ebbi finito   avesti parlato   avesti
creduto   avesti dormito   avesti finito   ebbe parlato   ebbe creduto   ebbe dormito
ebbe finito

1st conjugation	2nd conjugation	3rd conjugation
parl-are	cred-ere	dorm-ire
		fin-ire
avemmo parlato	avemmo creduto	avemmo dormito
		avemmo finito
aveste parlato	aveste creduto	aveste dormito
		aveste finito
ebbero parlato	ebbero creduto	ebbero dormito
		ebbero finito

Simple future (Futuro semplice)

parl-erò cred-erò dorm-irò   fin-irò

parl-erai cred-erai dorm-irai   fin-irai

73

parl-erà   cred-erà   dorm-irà   fin-irà

parl-eremo	cred-eremo	dorm-iremo	fin-iremo
parl-erete	cred-erete	dorm-irete	fin-irete
parl-eranno	cred-eranno	dorm-iranno	fin-iranno

FUTURE PERFECT (FUTURO ANTERIORE)

avrò parlao	avrò creduto	avrò dormito	avrò finito
avrai parlato	avrai creduto	avrai dormito	avrai finito
avrà parlato	avrà creduto	avrà dormito	avrà finito
avremo parlato	avremo creduto	avremo dormito	avremo finito
avrete parlato	avrete creduto	avrete dormito	avrete finito
avranno parlato	avranno creduto	avranno dormito	avranno finito

SUBJUNCTIVE (CONGIUNTIVO)

Present (Presente)

parl-i	cred-a	dorm-a	fin-isca
parl-i	cred-a	dorm-a	fin-isca
parl-i	cred-a	dorm-a	fin-isca
parl-iamo	cred-iamo	dorm-iamo	fin-iamo
parl-iate	cred-iate	dorm-iate	fin-iate
parl-ino	cred-ano	dorm-ano	fin-iscano

Imperfect (Imperfetto)

parl-assi	cred-essi	dorm-issi	fin-issi
parl-assi	cred-essi	dorm-issi	fin-issi
parl-assi	cred-essi	dorm-issi	fin-issi
parl-assimo	cred-essimo	dorm-issimo	fin-issimo
parl-aste	cred-este	dorm-iste	fin-iste
parl-assero	cred-essero	dorm-issero	fin-issero

PAST (PASSATO)

abbia parlato	abbia creduto	abbia dormito	abbia finito
abbia parlato	abbia creduto	abbia dormito	abbia finito

74

abbia parlato	abbia creduto	abbia dormito abbia finito
abbiamo parlato	abbiamo creduto	abbiamo dormito abbiamo finito
abbiate parlato	abbiate creduto	abbiate dormito abbiate finito
abbiano parlato	abbiano creduto	abbiano dormito abbiano finito

Pluperfect (Trapassato)

avessi parlato	avessi creduto	avessi dormito avessi finito
avessi parlato	avessi creduto	avessi dormito avessi finito
avessi parlato	avessi creduto	avessi dormito avessi finito
avessimo parlato	avessimo creduto	avessimo dormito avessimo finito
aveste parlato	aveste creduto	aveste dormito aveste finito
avessero parlato	avessero creduto	avessero dormito avessero finito

1st conjugation	2nd conjugation	3rd conjugation	
parl-are	cred-ere	dorm-ire	fin-ire

conditional (condizionale)

Present (Presente)

parl-erei	cred-erei d	orm-irei	fin-irei
parl-eresti	cred-eresti	dorm-iresti	fin-iresti
parl-erebbe	cred-erebbe	dorm-irebbe	fin-irebbe
parl-eremmo	cred-eremmo	dorm-iremmo	fin-iremmo
parl-ereste	cred-ereste	dorm-ireste	fin-ireste
parl-erebbero	cred-erebbero	dorm-irebbero	fin-irebbero

Past (Passato)

avrei parlato	avrei creduto	avrei dormito avrei finito
avresti parlato	avresti creduto	avresti dormito avresti finito
avrebbe parlato	avrebbe creduto	avrebbe dormito avrebbe finito
avremmo parlato	avremmo creduto	avremmo dormito avremmo finito
avreste parlato	avreste creduto	avreste dormito avreste finito

avrebbero parlato avrebbero creduto avrebbero dormito   avrebbero finito

Imperative (Imperativo)

io par-lo   cred-o   dorm-o   fin-isco

tu parl-a   cred-i   dorm-i   fin-isci

lui parl-i   cred-a   dorm-a   fin-isca

noi parl-iamo cred-iamo   dorm-iamo   fin-iamo

voi parl-ate   cred-ete   dorm-ite   fin-ite

loro parl-ino cred-ano   dorm-ano   fin-iscano

Participle (Participio)

Present (Presente)

parl-ante   cred-ente   dorm-ente   fin-ente

Past (Passato)

parl-ato   cred-uto   dorm-ito   fin-ito

Gerund (Gerundio)

Present (Presente)

parl-ando   cred-endo   dorm-endo   fin-endo

Past (Passato)

avendo parlato   avendo creduto   avendo dormito finito

Regular verbs: passive conjugation

Here is a simplified table (showing only the third person singular of each tense) of the passive forms of four regular verbs. Notice how each passive tense is formed by the corresponding tense of the auxil- iary essere (see below for the full conjugation of essere) and the past participle. In this table the participle is masculine singular, but in actual use it agrees with gender and number of the subject (see below), as do all compound forms of verbs using essere. Remember that only transitive verbs can have a passive form.

guardare   credere   sentire

Infinitive

Present Past

essere guardato/a/i/e   essere creduto/a/i/e   essere sentito/a/i/e

essere stato guardato essere stato creduto essere stato sentito

Indicative

Present

| è guardato | è creduto | è sentito |

Imperfect

| era guardato | era creduto | era sentito |

Compound perfect

| è stato guardato | è stato creduto | è stato sentito |

Simple perfect

| fu guardato | fu creduto | fu sentito |

Pluperfect

| era stato guardato | era stato creduto | era stato sentito |

Trapassato remoto

| fu stato guardato | fu stato creduto | fu stato sentito |

Simple future

| sarà guardato | sarà creduto | sarà sentito |

Future perfect

| sarà stato guardato | sarà stato creduto | sarà stato sentito |

Subjunctive

Present

| sia guardato | sia creduto | sia sentito |

Imperfect

| fosse guardato | fosse creduto | fosse sentito |

Past

| sia stato guardato | sia stato creduto | sia stato sentito |

Pluperfect

fosse stato guardato fosse stato creduto   fosse stato sentito

Conditional

Present

sarebbe guardato   sarebbe creduto   sarebbe sentito

Past

sarebbe stato guardato sarebbe stato creduto sarebbe stato sentito

Imperative

Present

sia guardato   sia creduto   sia sentito

Gerund

Present

essendo guardato   essendo creduto   essendo sentito

Past

essendo stato guardato   essendo stato creduto

essendo stato sentito

Irregular verb conjugations: introduction

Irregular verbs are those that not only change the endings, but also change the stem in some of the tenses. Italian has a large number of irregular verbs, most of them   in the 2nd conjugation, including many verbs frequently used in everyday language. Sometimes the irregular changes of the stem are unique to one verb (as in the case   of avere and essere). Sometimes several verbs may be grouped under a common pattern of irregularity, and this can help to memorise the many (but not always unpredictable) deviations from the 'norm'. The complete conjugations of five irregular verbs are shown below (2.2.4) in table form. These verbs have been chosen not only because of their frequency of use, but also because in some cases their patterns are followed by several other irregular verbs.

Irregular verbs avere, essere, dovere, potere, volere

These five verbs are among the most frequently used in Italian, and also among the most irregular. They share a common feature: they are often used in combination with another verb. The verbs avere 'to have' and essere 'to be' are used as auxiliary verbs, combining with the past participles of other verbs to form all compound tenses, while dovere 'must' potere 'can' and volere 'will' are very often used in combination with another verb in the infinitive form, to complement its meaning When used in this way, they are called verbi servili 'modal verbs'.

Ieri ho dovuto chiudere io l'ufficio.

78

I had to lock the office, yesterday.

Quando potremo incontrare il Dott. Salvi?

When can we meet Dr Salvi?

Voglio tornare a casa presto stasera.

I want to go home early tonight.

CHAPTER 4: PRESENT TENSE

Introduction

Situations, actions and events are expressed by the use of verbs (see Chapter 3). Here we look at how to describe situations, actions and events taking place at the present time (i.e. in the same period of time when we are speaking or writing). The verb tense most commonly used for this is the present indicative, as shown in our examples. The examples here are mainly in the affirmative; interrogative and negative statements are covered more fully in Chapters 15 and 16 respectively.

DESCRIBING PRESENT SITUATIONS, ACTIONS AND EVENTS

The present tense is used to describe a situation, action or event that is in effect or taking place at the present time, although not necessarily at the exact moment when we speak or write. Here are some examples:

FACTS, SITUATIONS OR DESCRIPTIONS

> L'Avv. Bianchi lavora alla FIAT.
>
> Mr Bianchi the lawyer works at FIAT.
>
> Questo film dura due ore.
>
> This film lasts two hours.
>
> Molti Italiani amano il calcio.
>
> Many Italians love football.
>
> Mi piace molto passeggiare.
>
> I like walking a lot.
>
> Mia madre è malata. Ha una malattia cardiaca.
>
> My mother is ill. She has a heart disease.
>
> Le autostrade sono invase da turisti stranieri che vengono in vacanza in Italia.
>
> The motorways are invaded by foreign tourists who come on holiday to Italy.
>
> Il turismo in Calabria è poco sviluppato.
>
> Tourism in Calabria is not very developed.
>
> Il tempo è brutto.
>
> The weather is bad.

ACTIONS OR EVENTS

Single actions and events

Perché non telefoni all'Ufficio Vendite?

Why don't you phone the Sales Department?

Oggi cucina Walter.

Today Walter is cooking.

In Italian, we use the same present tense of the verb to describe actions or events which are happening at the time we speak or write ('The Boat Show is taking place this week', 'Isabella is teaching this morning'), and those that may not be happening right now, but are a habit or regular occurrence ('The Boat Show takes place every year', 'Isabella teaches every Tuesday').

Isabella insegna stamattina./Isabella insegna ogni martedì.

Isabella is teaching this morning./Isabella teaches every Tuesday.

L'infermiera non viene oggi./L'infermiera non viene il giovedì.

The nurse isn't coming today./The nurse doesn't come on Thursdays.

Il Salone Nautico si svolge questa settimana a Genova.

The Boat Show is taking place this week in Genova.

Il Salone Nautico si svolge ogni anno ad aprile.

The Boat Show takes place every year in April.

REGULAR ACTIONS

Often, in fact, the only feature that distinguishes habitual actions from single actions is the use of adverbs or phrases used to convey the notion of habit or regular occur- rence such as:

di solito usually

generalmente generally

normalmente normally

ogni every

tutti i, tutte le every

Ogni mese, andiamo a trovare i parenti in campagna.

Every month, we go to see our relatives in the country.

Ogni giovedì mattina, c'è il mercato a Postiglione.

Every Thursday morning there's the market at Postiglione.

Tutte le settimane facciamo la spesa al Centro Commerciale "Globus".

Every week we do the shopping at the 'Globus' shopping centre.

Normalmente mio marito torna a casa prima di me.

Normally my husband comes home before me.

WORDS AND PHRASES INDICATING PRESENT TIME

With days of the week, use of the article il, la also conveys the idea of a regular weekly action:

Il venerdì mangiamo il pesce.

Every Friday we eat fish.

La domenica mia madre va a messa.

On Sundays my mother goes to Mass.

For other phrases of frequency and repetition,

EXPRESSING ONGOING ACTIONS

If you need to express something more immediate, or an action that is still going   on at the present time and is not yet completed, you can use the progressive form of the present tense. The progressive present, similar to the English 'to be doing something', is formed by using the present tense of the verb stare together with

the gerund of the verb expressing the action (lavorando, leggendo,

partendo):

I ragazzi stanno leggendo.

The boys are reading.

Il signor Rossi sta partendo.

Mr Rossi is just leaving.

Stiamo lavorando.

We are working.

Note that stare and the gerund cannot be used to translate the English 'to be doing' construction when it refers to the future, even if it's the very near future. For this   you use the regular present indicative or the future:

Il Dott. Cuomo arriva fra mezz'ora.

Dr Cuomo is arriving in half an hour.

Dove andrete domani?

Where are you going tomorrow?

Words and phrases indicating present time

The present time is also indicated by using adverbs or phrases specifying time. (For more complex time contexts, see 30.4 and Chapter 36). Here are some examples:

ora, adesso now

È tardi. Ora andiamo a casa.

It's late. Let's go home now.

Scusami, adesso non voglio parlare.

Excuse me, I don't wish to talk now.

Ho cambiato ufficio. Adesso lavoro al terzo piano.

I changed my office. I'm working on the third floor now.

subito immediatamente right now/immediately

Vieni subito qua!

Come here right now!

Attenda un attimo, per favore. Le passo immediatamente il direttore.

Hold on a second, please. I'll put you through to the manager immediately.

oggi today

Oggi mi sento felice!

I feel happy today!

Oggi è sabato.

Today is Saturday.

ancora still

È ancora presto per partire.

It's still early to be leaving.

Ho ancora fame!

I am still hungry!

questo

Quest'anno le vendite vanno bene.

This year the sales are going well.

Questa settimana lavoro fino a tardi.

This week I'm working till late.

Questo pomeriggio fa freddo.

It's cold this afternoon.

Note the shortened forms stamattina 'this morning', stanotte 'this/last night', stasera 'this evening':

Stasera Monica è nervosa.

Tonight Monica is edgy.

Stanotte non sono riuscita a dormire.

I couldn't sleep last night.

DIALOGO

In this dialogue the different forms of the present are highlighted.

Incontro di lavoro

Mario Adinolfi è impiegato alla Camera di Commercio di Bari, ma in questi giorni sta lavorando a Roma per organizzare la partecipazione di alcune industrie romane alla Fiera del Levante di Bari. La Ditta Cosmetici 2000 Spa vuole presentare alla Fiera un nuovo prodotto per la cura dei capelli e il Sig. Luca Violli, direttore delle vendite, incontra il Sig. Adinolfi per chiedere informazioni sui servizi della Fiera. Ecco un brano della loro conversazione:

DIALOGO

Violli Quanto costa l'affitto di un ufficio per il periodo della Fiera? Adinolfi Quest'anno abbiamo uffici attrezzati con servizi di segreteria,

che costano €1.500 per 5 giorni. Violli Quando posso visitare gli uffici?

Adinolfi Gli uffici si possono visitare dopo il 10 settembre. Ora stiamo ancora completando i lavori, ma Lei può fare una prenotazione adesso. Deve solo riempire questo modulo.

Violli Va bene. Chi deve firmare il modulo?

Adinolfi Può firmare Lei, o un altro responsabile della Ditta, come preferisce.

Business meeting

Mario Adinolfi is an employee at the Chamber of Commerce in Bari, but   at present he is working in Rome making arrangements for several Roman companies in the 'Fiera del Levante' Trade Fair in Bari. The company 'Cosmetics 2000' Ltd wants to present its new hair care product and Mr Luca Violli, director of sales, meets Mr Adinolfi to ask for information on the services offered by the Fair. Here is a snatch of their conversation.

Violli How much does it cost to rent an office for the duration of the Fair?

Adinolfi This year we have ready-equipped offices with secretarial services, which cost 1,500 euros for 5 days.

Violli When can I visit the offices?

Adinolfi After the 10th September. We are just finishing the work, but you can book now. You only need to fill in this form.

Violli All right. Who needs to sign the form?

Adinolfi You can sign it, or else some other representative of the company, as you prefer.

CHAPTER 5: PAST TENSE

Introduction

When speaking or writing about the past in Italian we generally use two different verb forms: a perfect form and an imperfect form. These two forms are two different aspects of Italian verbs in the past – two different points of view – and it is essential to distin- guish between them. The perfect aspect is used when we talk about the past from the point of view of the present. The imperfect aspect looks at the past from the point of view of the past; it is used to talk and write about past events as if viewing it from 'inside'.

To describe what we or someone else did, we can use any of the following:

The perfect form

Ieri ho lavorato fino alle 5.00 e poi sono andata al bar.

Yesterday I worked until 5.00 and then I went to the bar.

The imperfect form

Gli impiegati lavoravano tutta la mattina e poi andavano al bar.

The employees worked all morning and then they went to the bar.

A combination of both

Quando lavoravo lì, sono andata molte volte nell'ufficio del direttore.

When I worked there, I went several times to the director's office.

In the next few pages, we look first at the perfect aspect in its two different forms (compound and simple) then at the imperfect aspect, and finally at the two aspects used together.

The perfect aspect

When talking about events in the past that are regarded as complete, Italian uses the perfect tense. There are two forms of perfect tense: the simple perfect or passato remoto and the compound perfect or passato prossimo. The passato prossimo is a compound tense (see 2.1.5) formed of an auxiliary and participle, while the passato remoto is not a compound form, so can be defined as the simple perfect. The passato remoto is also known in English as the past historic, which has led to misunderstandings over its use.

The perfect tense most frequently used is the compound form, the passato prossimo:

Sono arrivato la settimana scorsa.

I arrived last week.

Ieri ho comprato una camicia rossa.

Yesterday I bought a red shirt.

Ti è piaciuto il film?

Did you like the film?

Avete conosciuto il direttore?

Have you met the director?

The simple perfect form (passato remoto) can also be used. Here are the same exam- ples as above, this time using the passato remoto:

Arrivai la settimana scorsa.

I arrived last week.

Ieri comprai una camicia rossa.

Yesterday I bought a red shirt.

Ti piacque il film?

Did you like the film?

Conosceste il direttore?

Have you met the director?

It is clear that the difference between the two sets of examples is not one of time,   as suggested by traditional Italian grammar terminology, which makes a distinction between passato remoto or 'far-off' past, and passato prossimo or 'near' past. This is the reason why these two tenses are best defined in English as simple and compound perfect (in Italian passato semplice, passato composto), in order not to stress any difference in 'time setting'. The sentences in the second set above, although perfectly correct, are unlikely to be used in everyday conversation, at least in northern and much of central Italy. The different functions and uses of the two past tenses are best explained by example. The passato remoto is much less frequently used than the passato prossimo. Its main function is to represent events in the past that have no connection with the present, i.e. with the time when the sentence is spoken or written. So,   when talking about the date someone was born, we can use the passato remoto if that person is no longer alive:

Dante nacque nel 1265. Visse per molti anni a Firenze.

Dante was born in 1265. He lived for many years in Florence.

Pier Paolo Pasolini nacque nel 1922. Fu uno dei più famosi scrittori del Neorealismo.

Pier Paolo Pasolini was born in 1922. He was one of the most famous Neorealist writers.

However, if we want to stress the relationship of those personalities with the present, in other words their influence on today's readers, we use the passato prossimo

Dante è nato nel 1265, e oggi si festeggia l'anniversario della nascita.

Dante was born in 1265, and today we celebrate the anniversary of his birth.

86

Pier Paolo Pasolini è nato nel 1922, e i suoi film più famosi sono ancora molto popolari.

Pier Paolo Pasolini was born in 1922, and his best-known films are still very popular today.

The passato prossimo is always used if the person is still alive at the present time:

Mio figlio è nato nel 1983.

My son was born in 1983.

Using the passato prossimo

This form is very similar to the English present perfect ('I have eaten', etc.); however they do not always correspond exactly in their use, as shown below:

Gli ho parlato apertamente.

I have spoken openly to him.

Siamo partiti alle 5.00.

We left at 5.00.

Here is an example of a passage in which you will recognise many verbs used in   the compound form of the perfect. Some of the participles shown do not follow a regular pattern;

Sono uscito alle 9.00 per andare a far spese e ho incontrato un vecchio amico che non vedevo da molto tempo. Abbiamo deciso di fare le spese insieme e siamo andati prima alla Rinascente e poi da UPIM. Alle 11.00 abbiamo bevuto un aperitivo al bar e quindi abbiamo comprato verdura e carne per preparare il pranzo. Siamo arrivati a casa a mezzogiorno e abbiamo cucinato e mangiato con appetito. Alle 2.00 il mio amico è tornato a casa sua, perchè aveva un appuntamento.

ENGLISH FORM

I went out at 9.00 to go shopping and I met an old friend whom I hadn't seen for a long time. We decided to go shopping together and we went first to 'Rinascente' and then to UPIM. At 11.00, we drank an aperitif at the café and then we bought vegetables and meat to make lunch. We arrived home   at midday and we cooked and ate hungrily. At 2.00 my friend went back home, because he had an appointment.

USING THE PASSATO REMOTO

Although the passato remoto is much less frequently used than the passato prossimo there are certain contexts in which it is used to describe events or actions.

In a historical context

The passato remoto is used frequently in historical narration, as can be seen from this example taken from a history textbook for primary schools (Strumenti, a cura   di Alfio Zoi, Editrice La Scuola, 1991, pp.188–9):

Quando nel 1152, Federico I detto Barbarossa divenne re di Germania, decise di sottomettere i Comuni ribelli. Compì cinque discese in Italia: nella prima (1154) soffocò la ribellione di Roma e si fece incoronare imperatore; nella seconda conquistò Milano e riaffermò solennemente i diritti dell'Imperatore sui Comuni (1158); nella terza assediò e distrusse Milano (1163); nella quarta occupò Roma (1168) e nella quinta fu sconfitto a Legnano dalla Lega Lombarda (Alleanza tra i Comuni, decisa a Pontida nel 1167, e appoggiata dal Papa Alessandro III). Per questo dovette riconoscere la libertà dei Comuni con il trattato di pace di Costanza (1183).

When, in 1152, Frederick I, known as Redbeard, became King of Germany,   he decided to suppress the rebellious City States. He carried out five raids in Italy; in the first (1154) he suppressed the rebellion in Rome, and had himself crowned emperor; in the second he conquered Milan and with due ceremony reaffirmed the rights of the emperor (1158); in the third he besieged and destroyed Milan (1163); in the fourth he occupied Rome (1168) and in the fifth he was defeated at Legnano by the Lombard League (an alliance between the City States, set up in Pontida in 1167, and supported by Pope Alexander III). For this reason he was forced to recognise the freedom of the City States, with the peace treaty of Constance (1183).

Note however that when historical events are seen in their relevance to the present time, again the passato prossimo is more likely to be used, even if the events happened a long time ago. Here is another example, again from the same textbook Strumenti (p. 248):

La storia moderna di Roma è iniziata nel 1870 quando la città è diventata capitale del giovane Regno d'Italia. Allora Roma contava appena 200.000 abitanti ed anche il suo aspetto urbanistico non era molto diverso da quello dei secoli precedenti . . .

Anche nel nostro secolo, e in particolare negli ultimi decenni, Roma ha continuato a espandersi per l'afflusso di lavoratori provenienti da tutto il Lazio e dalle regioni centro-meridionali.

The modern history of Rome began in 1870 when the city became the capital of the young Kingdom of Italy. At that time Rome counted scarcely 200,000 inhabitants, and as a town it did not appear very different from previous centuries . . .

In our own century, and particularly in the last few decades, Rome has continued to grow, because of the influx of workers coming from all over Lazio, and the central and southern regions.

Here the events described, some of which happened more than a hundred years ago, are relevant to today's situation (Rome is still the capital of Italy and its population is still expanding because of the influx of immigrants).

IN A NARRATIVE

The passato remoto is in general the 'perfect' form most often used in the narra- tive register and is therefore more frequently found in written than in spoken language. Here is another example of the use of the passato remoto, this time not in a histor- ical context but in a narrative literary passage (from the novel Requiem by Antonio Tabucchi, Feltrinelli, 1992, p. 7.57):

E allora vieni avanti, disse la voce di Tadeus, ormai la casa la conosci. Chiusi la porta alle mie spalle e avanzai per il corridoio. Il corridoio era buio, e inciampai in un mucchio di cose che caddero per terra. Mi fermai a raccogliere quel che avevo sparso sul pavimento: libri, un giocattolo di legno, un gallo di Barcelos, la statuetta di un santo . . .

So, come on through, said Tadeus' voice, you know the house by now. I shut the door behind me, and started off along the corridor. The corridor was dark and I stumbled into a pile of things which fell on the ground. I stopped to pick up what I had spread over the floor: books, a wooden toy, a Barcelos cock, the statuette of a saint . . .

In spoken Italian

The passato remoto used as a historical or narrative tense is most frequently found in written texts. The use of this tense in spoken conversational Italian is rare and restricted to the southern regions of Italy. So the examples of spoken Italian using the passato remoto, seen in 13.2 above, are very unlikely to be heard in northern Italy or most of central Italy, but are quite acceptable, for example, in the southern regions including Sicily.

EXPRESSING THE IMPERFECT ASPECT

The imperfect aspect of actions or events in the past is conveyed by the imperfetto in Italian. This paragraph looks at the use of the imperfect aspect by itself, while 13.6 considers its use together with the perfect. The general function of the imperfect aspect is to represent past events and actions as if seen from within the past itself. The following two sentences illustrate how the same fact, happening at the same time, can be seen from two different points of view, in other words from two aspects:

Ieri faceva molto caldo a Napoli.

Yesterday it was very hot in Naples.

Ieri ha fatto molto caldo a Napoli.

Yesterday it was very hot in Naples.

The first example (the imperfect aspect) talks about the hot weather as the condi- tion experienced by people during that particular span of time; it could be said, for Expressing the imperfect aspect instance, by someone who was actually in Naples yesterday and wants to talk about his/her own experience of the weather.

The second example (the perfect aspect) sees yesterday's weather from outside; it could be said, for example, by someone who was not in Naples (e.g. a weather forecaster) and who wants to tell someone else about the weather with a certain detachment.

The main uses of the imperfetto or imperfect aspect are listed below.

Parallel events or actions

Two past actions or events can be viewed in a symmetrical relationship, taking place within the same time span:

Mentre lavorava, Anna pensava alle vacanze in Sardegna.

While she was working, Anna was thinking about the holidays in Sardinia.

Il direttore parlava e gli invitati ascoltavano annoiati.

The director was talking and the guests were listening, bored.

These are parallel actions that take place at the same time and are part of the same situation, described as if seen from within the situation itself, rather than a set of events viewed in relation to the present time (the time when we are speaking or writing).

HABITUAL OR REPEATED ACTIONS

In the following examples, the actions are not separate actions taking place at the same time; because of their repetition, they are seen not as individual actions but   as the general state or situation of the person carrying out the actions, at the period   of time when the actions took place. In English, this situation can be expressed with the form 'used to . . .'.

A Roma andavo tutti i giorni a mangiare in trattoria.

In Rome I went to eat in a trattoria every day.

Da ragazzo facevo molto sport.

When I was a boy, I used to play lots of sport.

DESCRIBING PAST EVENTS OR SITUATIONS

All'Università c'era una gran confusione. Gli studenti, che volevano iscriversi, cercavano di capire che cosa fare mentre gli impiegati della Segreteria non riuscivano a farsi sentire nel gran chiasso. Faceva molto caldo e molti si riparavano all'ombra degli alberi nel cortile. At the University, there was a great deal of confusion. The students, who wanted to enrol, were trying to find out what to do, while the staff in the Administrative Office couldn't make themselves heard in the racket. It was very hot, and many people took refuge in the shade of the trees in the courtyard. Here we have a 'picture' of a situation where the verbs are the elements inside the picture, rather than the whole of an event or an action.

Ieri sono andato all'Università e ho trovato una gran confusione. Ho chiesto informazioni in Segreteria e mi hanno detto di aspettare. Faceva molto caldo e mi sono riparato sotto gli alberi nel cortile.

Yesterday I went to the University and I found a great deal of confusion. I asked for information in the Administrative Office and they told me to wait. It was very hot, and I took refuge under the trees in the courtyard.

Each of these actions had to be carried out before the following one could take place:

| ho chiesto | hanno detto | mi sono riparato |

NARRATIVE USING IMPERFECT

Here is a passage from the novel La Delfina Bizantina by Aldo Busi (Mondadori, 1992, p. 53), which uses verbs in the imperfect almost entirely, because it is describing a scene, the background to the action. Note how the description below ends with   two verbs in the simple perfect: finì, girò:

Era entrata nella stanza adiacente dove adesso i giornali toccavano il soffitto o comunque la sovrastavano pencolanti e minacciosi. Era una vera e propria foresta di carta con scricchiolanti sottoboschi in fondo ai quali vide farsi largo la luce del giorno e lei, la vecchia striminzita imbacuccata in un mucchio di stracci maschili e di coperte. Era in piedi davanti alla finestra rotta e le presentava la schiena. Stava incollando con impasto di acqua e farina bianca un foglio di giornale sul riquadro senza vetro. E contemporaneamente lo stava bisbigliando dalla a alla zeta. Doveva certo essere così assorta da non averla sentita, non si decideva a girarsi. Brunilì finì con calma il duplice lavoro e poi si girò . . .

She had gone into the adjacent room, where the newspapers now touched the ceiling, or at least towered over her, swaying and threatening. It was a absolute forest of paper, with creaking undergrowth at the other side of which she saw the light of day penetrating and then saw her, the shabby   old woman all muffled up in a heap of tattered men's clothes and blankets. She was standing in front of the broken window with her back turned to her. She was glueing – with flour and water paste – a sheet of newspaper on the windowless frame. And at the same time she was whispering it to herself from cover to cover. She must have been so absorbed that she hadn't heard her, she didn't give any sign of turning around. Brunilì calmly finished her twofold task, and then turned around . . .

Progressive imperfect (stare + gerundio)

One very common form of the imperfect aspect is the progressive form. This is formed using the imperfect of the verb stare together with the gerund of the main verb. This form is fairly familiar to English speakers, being similar in form and use to the English 'to be -ing'.

Che cosa stavate facendo ieri sera?

What were you doing yesterday evening?

Stavo lavorando quando mi ha telefonato Andrea.

I was working when Andrea called me.

The progressive form expresses an action in progress, i.e. not completed, at a certain moment in time. It cannot be used to convey, for example, the aspects of repetition or description of past events (as in the paragraphs above), where the simple imper- fect is used instead. The progressive aspect in Italian, as in English, can be used not only in the past, but also in the present (see 12.3).

COMBINATIONS OF PERFECT AND IMPERFECT ASPECT

SCENE SETTING: INTRODUCTION

In the paragraphs above, we saw how the imperfect expresses the elements of a past situation, in contrast with the perfect tenses, which see actions or events in their entirety and 'separateness'. To understand more clearly how the two aspects interact to depict the past we can use the metaphor of a play seen at the theatre: where the scenery or stage set is the background of the play and is represented by the imperfect. The actors, their actions, and the events of the play are in the foreground and repre- sented by the perfect.

Scene setting in novels

A traditional technique of novelists is to set a scene, using the imperfect, and to let the characters act within it, using the perfect. In each of the following two passages, taken from Leonardo Sciascia's Il Giorno della Civetta (Einaudi, 1981, pp.9 and 57), it is easy to identify the two aspects, perfect and imperfect:

> (a) L'autobus stava per partire, rombava sordo con improvvisi raschi e singulti. La piazza era silenziosa nel grigio dell'alba . . . Il bigliettaio chiuse lo sportello, l'autobus si mosse con un rumore di sfasciume

> . . . Si sentirono due colpi squarciati . . . Il bigliettaio bestemmiò: la faccia gli era diventata colore di zolfo, tremava . . .

> The bus was about to leave, it was giving out a dull roar, with sudden rasping or hiccuping noises. The square was silent, in the grey dawn . . . the conductor shut the door, the bus moved off with a disintegrating noise . . . then two shots were heard to rip the air . . . the conductor swore: his face turned the colour of sulphur, he shook . . .

> (b) Il corpo di Parrinieddu era ancora sul selciato, coperto da un telo azzurrastro. I carabineri di guardia sollevarono il telo: il corpo era contratto come nel sonno prenatale, nella oscura matrice della morte.

> Parrinieddu's body was still on the asphalt, covered by a bluish sheet. The police on duty lifted the cloth: the body was drawn up as if in a prenatal slumber, in the dark womb of death.

SCENE (AN ONGOING ACTION OR EVENT) AND A NEW ACTION OR EVENT

A less obvious example of scene setting is the way in which Italian, even in everyday speech or writing, distinguishes between actions in the past, using the imperfect to describe certain actions that are seen as a background to others. Here are a few examples, where the pattern is that of an action/event happening at a certain moment, set against the background scene of something that was going on at the same moment in time (but also before and possibly after):

> Paola è arrivata [event] mentre preparavo la cena [scene].

> Paola arrived [event] while I was preparing dinner [scene].

> Gli impiegati lavoravano [scene] quando è suonato l'allarme [event].

> The staff were working [scene] when the alarm went [event].

> Passeggiavamo [scene] tranquillamente, ma all'improvviso è scoppiato

> [action] un temporale.

> We were walking along quietly [scene], when suddenly a storm broke [action].

SCENE (A SITUATION) AND NEW ACTION OR EVENT

> Erano le 5.25 quando è esplosa la bomba.

> It was 5.25 when the bomb went off.

> Sono arrivato alla stazione proprio quando il treno partiva.

> I arrived at the station just when the train left.

In both these examples, the imperfetto represents a fact that, although happening in an instant (il treno partiva), is seen as the situation, context or background against which something happened.

Cause (imperfect) and effect (perfect)

Non sono venuto a trovarti perché avevo troppo lavoro da fare.

I didn't come to see you, because I had too much work to do.

Avevamo fame e abbiamo deciso di fare due spaghetti.

We were hungry and (so) we decided to cook a bit of spaghetti.

In these sentences the role of the imperfetto is clearly that of the background to, Or cause of, an event.

Examples of different patterns

Here are examples of how the same two verbs can be used in three different patterns as described above:

Parallel actions

Mentre io riposavo Sandro telefonava a sua sorella.

While I was resting, Sandro was on the phone to his sister.

Sequence of actions

Ho riposato e poi ho telefonato a Sandro.

I rested and then I telephoned Sandro.

Situation and action/event

Mentre riposavo mi ha telefonato Sandro.

While I was resting, Sandro telephoned me.

Further examples of imperfect/perfect aspects

Here are some further examples illustrating the different functions of imperfect and perfect; see if you can link them to the explanations above:

Ho ordinato gli articoli che mi interessavano.

I ordered the items that I was interested in.

Ieri sera pensavo a quello che mi hai detto e ho capito che avevi ragione.

Yesterday evening I was thinking about what you said to me, and I realised that you were right.

Mi dispiace, non volevo offenderti quando ti ho rimproverato.

I'm sorry, I didn't want to offend you when I told you off.

Ho visitato Firenze con quell'amico che lavorava al Museo.

I visited Florence with that friend who worked in the Museum.

Abbiamo imparato l'italiano con un professore che non diceva nemmeno una parola d'inglese.

We learnt Italian with a teacher who didn't speak a word of English.

Quando abitavo a Napoli ho visitato tre volte il Museo Nazionale.

When I lived in Naples, I visited the National Museum three times.

Per quanto tempo hai vissuto in Cina?

How long did you live in China for?

Ho vissuto a Shanghai per tre anni.

I lived in Shanghai for three years.

Quando vivevo in Cina mangiavo il riso tre volte al giorno.

When I lived in China, I ate rice three times a day.

Ieri ho mangiato riso tre volte.

Yesterday I ate rice three times.

Imperfect/perfect aspect: auxiliary verbs dovere, potere, volere

With certain verbs, the choice of tense can be even more important, since it may alter the meaning. Use of the imperfect suggests that the intention or obligation was not fulfilled (the action was not completed). The past conditional may also be used in place of the imperfect

Volevo andare in banca, ma era chiusa.

I wanted to go to the bank, but it was shut. (So I couldn't go after all.)

Ho voluto andare in banca.

I wanted to go to the bank.

(The implication is that I did go there.)

Dovevano venire ieri, ma c'era sciopero dei treni.

They should have come yesterday, but there was a train strike. (They should have come but they didn't.)

Hanno dovuto introdurre un nuovo prodotto per competere con i francesi.

They had to introduce a new product to compete with the French. (They had to introduce one – and they did.)

Potevi almeno telefonare!

You could have called!

Meno male che hai potuto telefonare.

Just as well you were able to phone.

In the first of each pair of examples above, the imperfetto can be replaced by the

past conditional:

Avrei voluto andare in banca, ma era chiusa. Avrebbero dovuto venire ieri ma . . .

Avresti potuto almeno telefonare.

Non hanno potuto salvare il ragazzo.

They were not able to save the boy. (One action is implied.)

Non potevano mai uscire perché il padre non glielo permetteva. They could never go out because their father would not allow them. (A long-term state or condition is implied.)

Imperfect/perfect aspect: conoscere, sapere

The choice of tense can also alter the meaning in the case of conoscere and sapere: the way it earn it at time La nostra azienda non conosceva il mercato inglese.

Our firm was not familiar with the English market.

Ho conosciuto il direttore di marketing alla Fiera di Genova.

I met the director of marketing at the Genova Trade Fair. (Conoscere in the passato prossimo generally means 'to meet'.)

Sapevamo che lui era disposto a trattare.

We knew that he was prepared to negotiate.

Indicators of time

L'abbiamo saputo troppo tardi.

We found it out too late.

(Sapere in the passato prossimo generally means 'to learn, to find out'.)

Present tense expressing past

There are two situations in which past events are not expressed by imperfect or perfect tenses but by the present indicative tense:

When the event in question is still going on

When the event, action or situation in question is still going on, the present tense is used with da, the equivalent of the English since:

Studio l'italiano da 5 anni.

I have been studying Italian for 5 years.

(Implication: And I'm still trying!)

(lit. 'I study Italian since 5 years')

Compare this with the following example:

Ho studiato l'italiano per 5 anni.

I studied Italian for 5 years.

(Implication: But now I've given up!)

For dramatic effect, for example reporting events in newspapers

Fuori dal bar si accende un furibondo litigio. Un signore, in giro con il cane, vede i due sudamericani che si rincorrono.

Outside the bar a furious quarrel started up. A man, out walking his dog, saw the two South Americans chasing each other.

Or in historical descriptions

Nel settembre 1939 la Germania invade la Polonia e Francia e Gran Bretagna dichiarano la guerra. L'Italia rimane fuori del conflitto fino al 1940.

In September 1939, Germany invaded Poland, and France and Great Britain declared war. Italy stayed out of the conflict until 1940.

INDICATORS OF TIME

Time indicators

To say how long ago the action took place, use fa ('ago') and the appropriate length of time:

due giorni fa	two days ago
un mese fa	a month ago
poco tempo fa	a short time ago

To express 'last' meaning 'the one just past', use the adjectives scorso or passato (note that while scorso can come before or after the noun, passato can only come after):

la scorsa settimana	last week
il mese scorso	last month
l'anno passato	last year
l'estate passata	last summer

Here are some common time phrases, which can be used to refer to the past:

ieri	yesterday
l'altro ieri	day before yesterday
ieri mattina	yesterday morning
ieri sera	yesterday evening
stamattina	this morning

Here are the days of the week:

lunedì	Monday
martedì	Tuesday

96

mercoledì	Wednesday
giovedì	Thursday
venerdì	Friday
sabato	Saturday
domenica	Sunday

NEGATIVE INDICATORS OF TIME

When the double negative phrases non ... ancora; non ... mai; non più are used with the passato prossimo, non goes before the whole verb, while the second negative element will normally go after the auxiliary, but before the participle:

La consegna non è ancora arrivata.

The delivery hasn't arrived yet.

Non è più venuto.

He didn't come any more.

Non c'è mai stata la pace in quel paese.

There has never been peace in that country.

Alternatively, the second negative element can be placed after the whole verb:

La consegna non è arrivata ancora.

The delivery hasn't arrived yet.

Non è venuto più.

He didn't come any more.

Non c'è stata mai la pace in quel paese.

There has never been peace in that country.

CHAPTER 6: FUTURE TENSE

Introduction

English speakers often assume that when talking about future events, actions or situ- ations Italian always uses the future tense of verbs (see 2.3.4). This is not always   the case. As we can see in the following examples, we can use either the future tense or the present tense, to refer to the same event or facts. We can also use a different verb or verb phrase when talking about the very near future.

USING THE FUTURE TENSE

In the examples below, the future tense of the verbs is used to indicate firm intentions or plans, or a future event that is certain:

> La settimana prossima partirò per gli Stati Uniti.

> Next week I'll leave for the USA.

> Arriveremo non appena possibile.

> We'll arrive as soon as possible.

> Spero che tu non cambierai idea.

> I hope you won't change your mind.

> Fra pochi giorni saremo in Francia.

> In a few days we'll be in France.

USING THE PRESENT TENSE

The future tense is not very much used in colloquial Italian. The present tense can be used in its place in almost every situation, just as it can in English:

> Domani parto per Genova.

> Tomorrow I'm leaving for Genoa.

> A che ora arriva l'aereo?

> What time is the flight arriving?

> La settimana prossima cambiamo ufficio.

> Next week we are changing office.

> Fra poco siamo in Francia.

> Soon we'll be in France.

WITH A TIME INDICATOR

Even events in the distant future can be expressed using the present. However, when using the present, some explicit indication placing the events firmly in the future (such as la settimana prossima, l'anno prossimo, fra un mese, etc.) helps to avoid misunderstandings, as in the following examples:

> L'anno prossimo passiamo le vacanze a New York.

> Next year we are spending the holidays in New York.

> Fra un mese siamo in Italia.

> In a month we'll be in Italy.

The future tense is generally preferable when speaking or writing in a more formal context.

EXPRESSING THE IMMEDIATE OR VERY NEAR FUTURE

There are two particular ways of talking about actions that are imminent or 'about to happen':

stare per

The verb stare is used with per and the verb infinitive:

> Stiamo per partire.

> We are about to leave.

> La conferenza sta per cominciare.

> The talk will begin soon.

> La sua fattura è quasi pronta. Sto per finire di scriverla.

> Your invoice is almost ready. I'm just finishing writing it.

essere sul punto di

The expression essere sul punto di approximately corresponds to the English 'to be on the verge of':

> Il professore è sul punto di avere un esaurimento nervoso.

> The teacher is on the verge of a nervous breakdown.

> Attenzione! Il treno è sul punto di partire!

> Attention! The train is just about to depart!

EXPRESSING THE ENGLISH 'GOING TO'

The English 'going to' can sometimes be a way of expressing the future, or an inten- tion. Occasionally it means 'physically going to'. You have to know which meaning it conveys before you can translate it into Italian:

Future or intention

> When I'm on holiday, I'm going to learn Italian.
>
> Quando sarò in vacanza, imparerò l'italiano.
>
> or   Ho intenzione di imparare l'italiano.

Physically 'going'

Tomorrow I'm going shopping.

Domani vado a fare le spese.

For other examples of future planning and intention, see 14.9 below.

the 'past in the future'

Sometimes when we talk about a point in the future (3), we need to describe events/ actions that have not yet happened at the moment of speaking (1) but that will have happened at some unspecified time (2), before the point we are talking about (3).

1	2	3
NOW	UNSPECIFIED TIME	FUTURE
(moment of speaking)	(action or event)	(point referred to)

> Oggi i giornali dicono che il Governo avrà deciso il bilancio prima di agosto.
>
> Today the papers say the Government will have decided on the budget before August.
>
> Franco dice che avremo già finito il lavoro quando arriverà lo stipendio.
>
> Franco says that we will have finished the work before the salary arrives.

This reference to the past in the future – often called the future perfect in English – is expressed in Italian by a tense called futuro anteriore 'compound future'. Here are some examples:

> Domani l'ufficio chiuderà alle 12. A quell'ora avremo già finito la nostra relazione.
>
> Tomorrow the office will close at 12. By then we'll already have finished our report.
>
> È tardi. Quando arriveremo allo stadio, la partita sarà già iniziata.
>
> It's late. When we reach the stadium, the match will already have started.
>
> Soltanto dopo che avrai migliorato il tuo italiano potrai superare l'esame.
>
> Only after improving your Italian, will you be able to pass the exam.

THE FUTURE SEEN FROM THE PAST

We do not just talk of future events with reference to the actual moment when we are speaking or writing ('the present'). We may be talking now about a point in the past, when the particular events referred to were still in the future. How to express this situation in Italian depends on the sequence of events and on the probability of their happening. We can use a variety of verb tenses/ moods:

Present or simple future tense

When the future moment has not yet come, and it is still possible that Carlo will pass by:

> Carlo ha detto che passerà più tardi.

> Carlo said he will pass by later.

> Carlo ha detto che passa più tardi.

> Carlo said he will pass by later.

The condizionale al passato 'past conditional'

The past conditional indicates the future from a past point of view. It is generally used after the moment has passed, regardless of whether Carlo actually came or not:

> Carlo ha detto che sarebbe passato (ed è venuto).

> Carlo said he would pass by later (and he did).

> Carlo ha detto che sarebbe passato (e non è venuto).

> Carlo said he would pass by later (and he didn't).

The imperfetto 'imperfect'

More colloquially, it is possible to use the imperfect to replace the compound conditional:

> Carlo ha detto che passava più tardi.

> Carlo said he would pass by later.

SOME EXPRESSIONS OF TIME IN THE FUTURE

Here are a few words frequently used to indicate future time.

Prossimo 'next'

> Domenica prossima andiamo al mare.

> Next Sunday we'll go to the sea.

> Dovremo lavorare molto nei prossimi mesi.

> We'll be very busy in the next months.

> Le telefonerò il mese prossimo.

> I'll phone you next month.

Fra (tra) 'within a certain time'

Some expressions of time in the future

Ci vediamo fra una settimana.

We'll see each other in a week.

Sandro deve partire tra poco.

Sandro has to leave in a moment.

Mi scusi, sono occupata. La richiamo fra cinque minuti.

Excuse me, I'm busy at the moment. I'll call you back in five minutes.

Presto 'soon, early, quickly'

Presto cambieremo casa.

We'll soon move house.

Le manderò presto una risposta.

I'll send an answer to you soon.

Note that presto can also be used to mean 'at an early hour', as in È presto! 'It's early!', or 'at a fast pace', as in Fa' presto! 'Hurry up!'.

Poi 'then'

Prima parleremo della riunione poi passeremo all'argomento principale.

First we'll speak about the meeting, then we'll go on to the main subject.

Dopo 'after, later'

Andiamo a fare una passeggiata e dopo andiamo a casa tua.

Let's go for a walk and after we'll go to your place.

Domani 'tomorrow'

Domani porto Filippo dal pediatra.

Tomorrow I'm taking Filippo to the paediatrician.

Dopodomani 'day after tomorrow'

Dopodomani l'ufficio rimarrà chiuso.

The day after tomorrow the office will be closed.

Stasera 'this evening, tonight'

Stasera alle 19.30 si trasmetterà la prossima puntata di "Ispettore Derek".

This evening at 7.30 p.m., will be shown the next episode of 'Inspector Derek'.

Alla fine 'at the end'

Il vertice durerà cinque giorni; alla fine verrà offerto un pranzo dall'ambasciatore inglese.

The summit will last five days; at the end there will be a dinner given by the British ambassador.

Prima o poi 'sooner or later'

Prima o poi riusciranno a risolvere il problema.

Sooner or later they'll manage to solve the problem.

Verrò a trovarti, prima o poi!

I'll come to see you, sooner or later!

D'ora in poi 'from now on'

D'ora in poi non mi sentirò più sola. Ci sei tu.

From now on I won't feel lonely. You're here.

Expressing intention and future plans

As seen above, the English 'going to' can be expressed by Italian aver intenzione di:

Ho intenzione di noleggiare una macchina.

I intend hiring a car.

Other expressions of intention and planning for the future include:

aspettarsi to expect

aver in progetto di to have planned to

decidere di to decide to

decidersi a to make one's mind up to

desiderare to wish, desire

fare progetti per to make plans for

non vedere l'ora di to not be able to wait for

promettere di to promise to

sperare di to hope to

Mi sono decisa a passare le feste natalizie in famiglia.

I've made up my mind to spend the Christmas celebrations with my family.

Gli studenti stanno facendo progetti per venire a studiare in Inghilterra.

The students are planning to come and study in England.

Il professore si aspetta di ricevere i nostri compiti domani.

The lecturer expects to receive our homework tomorrow.

I bambini non vedono l'ora di andare in vacanza.

The children can't wait to go on holiday.

CHAPTER 7: VOCABULARY

Personalità / Carattere (Personality/Character)

gentile	nice, kind
scortese	rude, impolite
buono	good
cattivo	bad
simpatico	nice
antipatico	unpleasant
generoso	generous
avaro, tirchio	stingy/mean
calmo	calm
nervoso	nervous
divertente	funny
serio	serious
spiritoso	witty
imparziale	impartial
interessante	interesting
noioso	boring
normale	normal
strano	strange
virtuoso	virtuous
egocentrico	self-centered
profondo	deep
superficiale	superficial
ordinario	ordinary
appariscente	glamorous, showy
attento	careful, attentive

disattento	careless
prudente	prudent, cautious
spericolato	reckless
sposato	married
celibe/nubile	bachelor/ette
chiacchieroni	talkative
timido	shy
tranquillo	peaceful, quiet
forte, rumoroso	louds
icuro	certain, safe
permaloso	touchy, sensitive
affettuoso	affectionate
irritante	annoying
curioso	curious, inquisitive
disinteressato	disinterested
famoso	famous
sconosciuto	unknown
forte	strong
debole	weak
intelligente	intelligent
stupido	stupid
giovane	young (person)
anziano	old (person)
allegro	happy, cheerful
triste	sad

Caratteristiche Fisiche (Physical Characteristics)

grasso	fat
magro	thin
alto	tall
basso	short

bello	beautiful
brutto	ugly
atletico	athletic
sportivo	sporty
muscoloso	muscular
gracile	frail, puny

Capelli: Pettinatura, Taglio (Hair: Hairstyle, Haircut)

lunghi	long
corti	short
lisci	straight
calvo	bald
ricci	curly
mossi	wavy
brunetta	brunette (person)
castani	brown hair
scuri	dark
bionda/i	blond
barba	beard
baffi	mustache

Abbigliamento (Clothing)

pantaloni	pants
pantaloncini	shorts
vestito	dress
gonna	skirt
maglione	sweater
maglietta	t-shirt
camicia	dress shirt

camicetta	blouse
cappotto	coat
giacca	jacket
abito	suit
impermeabile	raincoat
cravatta	tie
sciarpa	scarf
cappello	hat
guanti	gloves
scarpe	shoes
stivali	boots
calzini	socks
sandali	sandals
occhiali da vista/sole	glasses / sunglasses costume da bagno bathing suit
orecchini	earrings
cintura	belt
collana	necklace
bracciale	bracelet

Lavoro/Professioni (Work/Professions)

infermiere/a	nurse
medico	doctor
dentista	dentist
dottore/ssa	doctor
attore	actor (m)
attrice	actress
ballerina	dancer
studente/ssa	student
ingegnere	engineer
avvocato	lawyer
cameriere	waiter

barista	bartender
poliziotto	policeman
architetto	architect
cuoco	cook
calciatore	(soccer) player
autista, guidatore	driver
casalinga	housewife
lavoratore	worker
capo	boss

Interno/Dentro (Internal/Inside)

soffitto	ceiling
pavimento	floor
tappeto	carpet
cassettiera	chest of drawers
lampada	lamp
ventilatore	fan
porta	door
finestra	window
mensola (per libri)	(book) shelf
tenda	curtain
sedia	chair
poltrona	armchair
divano	couch
quadro	painting
armadio	wardrobe
credenza	dresser
scrivania	desk
cattedra	big desk
televisione	television

telecomando	remote
registratore	vcr/tape recorder
orologio	clock, watch
tastiera	keyboard
cestino	trash can
lavagna	blackboard
gomma	eraser

Stanze della Casa (Rooms of the House)

stanza	room
piano	floor
camera	bedroom
camera degli ospiti	spare bedroom
cucina	kitchen
sala da pranzo	dining room
salotto	living room
soggiorno	living/family room
lo studio	study
lavanderia	laundry room
garage	garage
terrazza	terrace
bagno	bathroom
tetto	roof
al piano terra	ground floor
al piano di sopra	upstairs

Esterno/Fuori (External/Outside)

cielo	sky
stella	star
sole	sun

luna	moon
montagna	mountain
cima	summit
collina	hill
vetta	peak
pianura	plain
valle	valley
bosco	forest
l'albero	the tree
cespuglio	bush
il fiore	the flower
campo	field
prato	lawn, grass, meadow
mare	sea
costa	coast
spiaggia	beach
sabbia	sand
sponda	bank
riva	bank/shore
fiume	river
ruscello	stream
lago	lake
laghetto	pond
roccia	rock
cascata	waterfall
parco	park
giardino	garden

Geografia (Geography)

il pianeta	the planet

la Terra	the Earth
il mondo	the world
il continente	the continent
la penisola	the peninsula
l'isola	the island
l'oceano	the ocean
il paese	the country (nation)
la campagna	the country(side)
il paese	the village
città	city
i punti cardinali	the compass
nord	North
sud	South
est	East
ovest	West
orientale	eastern
occidentale	western

la Città (the City)

edificio	building
palazzo	building, palace
statua	statue
ponte	bridge
fontana	fountain
monumento	monument
marciapiede	sidewalk
centro storico	historical center
aiuola	flower bed
panchina	bench
quartiere	neighborhood

tabellone	billboard
traffico	traffic
abitanti	inhabitants
piazza	square
semaforo	traffic light
borgo	district
largo	small square
strada	street
vicolo	alley, lane
ingresso	entrance
corso	main street, avenue
uscita	exit

Luoghi (Places)

ospedale	hospital
cinema movie	theater
supermercato	supermarket
aeroporto	airport
scuola	school
discoteca	club
ufficio postale	post office
albergo	hotel
commissariato di polizia police station	
teatro	theater
ristorante	restaurant
distributore di benzina gas station	
mercatino	market
banca	bank
libreria	library
museo	museum

chiesa	church
parcheggio	parking lot
stadio	stadium
cattedrale	cathedral
municipio	city hall
negozio	store
biglietteria	ticket office
stazione ferroviaria	train station
stazione degli	autobus bus station
fermata dell'autobus bus stop	

Veicoli: Mezzi di Trasporto (Vehicles: Means of Transportation)

macchina, auto	car
motocicletta	motorcycle
motorino	moped
bicicletta	bicycle
autobus	bus
treno	train
barca	boat
traghetto	ferry
nave	ship
aereo	airplane

"Chiedere a qualcuno la strada" (to ask someone for directions)

lontano	far
vicino	near
qui	here
accanto a	next to
davanti a	in front of

dietro	behind
di fronte a	opposite
attorno	around, about
a sinistra	on the left
a destra	on the right
al centro	in the center
all'angolo	on the corner
sopra	on top of
sotto	under
dentro	inside
fiore	outside
dritto	straight
giro	turn
dappertutto	everywhere
da nessuna parte	nowhere

Animali (Animals)

cane	dog
gatto	cat
cavallo	horse
asino	donkey
agnello	lamb
pecora	sheep
mucca	cow
vitello	calf/veal
maiale	pig/pork
coniglio	rabbit
uccello	bird
anatra	duck
gallina	hen

gallo	rooster
oca	goose
tacchino	turkey
pulcino	chick
pesce	fish
mosca	fly
zanzara	mosquito
ape	bee

Utensili & Mangiare (Utensils & Eating)

forchetta	fork
cucchiaio	spoon
coltello	knife
piatto	plate
tazza	coffee cup
bicchiere	glass
scodella	bowl
tovaglia	tablecloth
tovagliolo	napkin
tovaglioli di carta	paper towels
frigorifero	refrigerator
dispensa	pantry

Cibo: carne, frutta, verdure, condimenti (Food: meat, fruit, vegetables, condiments)

prosciutto	ham
pollo	chicken
pesce	fish
bistecca	steak
maiale	pork
tacchino	turkey
salsicce	sausage

mela	apple
arancia, arance	orange, oranges
pera	pare
fragola	strawberry
mirtillo	blueberry
uva	grape
limone	lemon
fico, fichi	fig, figs
ciliegia	cherry
pomodoro	tomato
pomodorino	cherry tomato
cipolla	onion
carota	carrot
zucchine	zucchini
patata	potato
fungo, funghi	mushroom, pl.
melanzana	eggplant
peperone	pepper (vegetable)
insalata	salad
dolce	dessert
zuppa	soup
latte	milk
succo	juice
burro	butter
marmellata	jam
burro di arachidi	peanut butter
aglio	garlic
uovo, uova	egg, eggs
formaggio	cheese
olio	oil
aceto	vinegar
miele	honey

zucchero	sugar
sale	salt
pepe	pepper (black)
pane	bread
farina	flour
riso	rice
cereali	cereal
frutta	fruit
verdura	vegetable

Aggettivi (Adjectives)

moderno	modern
antico	old
nuovo	new
vecchio	old
aperto	open
chiuso	closed
acceso	on
spento	off
valido	valid
scaduto	expired
grande	big
piccolo	small
occupato	occupied
libero	free
caldo	hot
freddo	cold
ricco	rich
povero	poor
caro	expensive
economico	cheap, inexpensive

pieno	full
vuoto	empty
comodo	comfortable
scomodo	uncomfortable
largo	loose
stretto	tight
facile	easy
difficile	difficult
numeroso	numerous
pochi	few
utile	useful
inutile	useless
forte	strong
debole	weak
forte, rumoroso	loud
tranquillo	quiet
colpevole	guilty
innocente	innocent
originale	original
unico	unique
semplice	simple
elegante	elegant
necessario	necessary
indispensabile	essential
bagnato	wet
asciutto	dry
giusto	right, correct
sbagliato	wrong
vero	true
falso	false
pesante	heavy
leggero	light

in anticipo	early
in ritardo	late
in orario	on time
affollato	crowded
pulito	clean
sporco	dirty
rapido, veloce	fast
lento	slow
lungo	long
corto	short
(a) righe	striped
scacchi	checkered
(a) pois polka	dotted
in tinta unita, semplice	plain

Sport (Sports)

calcio	soccer
scherma	fencing
pallacanestro	basketball
pallavolo	volleyball
nuoto	swimming
pallanuoto	water polo
tuffi	diving
pattinaggio	skating
sci	skiing
sci di fondo	cross-country skiing
ginnastica	gymnastics
equitazione	horseback riding
corsa	track
corsa ad ostacoli	hurdling

salto in alto	high jumping
salto in lungo	long jumping
ciclismo	cycling
motociclismo	motorcycle racing
automobilismo	auto racing
vela	sailing
canottaggio	rowing
scherma	fencing
pugilato	boxing
baseball	baseball
football americano	football
tennis	tennis
golf	golf
rugby	rugby
hockey	hockey
windsurf	windsurfing
bob	bobsledding
ping pong	ping pong
squash	squash
karate	karate
judo	judo

Attrezzatura da Sport (Sports Equipment)

pattini	skates
gli sci	the skis
bicicletta	bicycle
cavallo	horse
canoa	canoe
barca	boat
vela	sail

tavola	(surf) board
fioretto	foil
spada	sword
piscina	pool
racchetta	racket
pallone	ball
pallina	little ball/marble
pesi	weights
guantoni	boxing gloves
piscina	pool

Che tempo fa? (What's the weather like?)

sole	sun
C'è sole, soleggiato	It is sunny
pioggia	rain
piove	It is raining
neve	snow
nevica	It is snowing
vento	wind
C'è il vento, Tira vento	It's windy
nuvola	cloud
nuvoloso	It's cloudy
nebbia	fog
C'è la nebbia	It's foggy
grandine	hail
Grandine	It's hailing
sereno	fine
burrascoso, tempestoso	It's stormy
Fa bello, Fa bel tempo	It's nice
Fa brutto tempo	It's bad

122

umido	humid
afoso	muggy
Fa caldo	It's hot
Fa freddo	It's cold
Fa bel tempo	It's warm
Si gela	It's freezing
C'è tuono	There is thunder
C'è fulmine	There is lightning
è luminoso	It's bright
è buio	It's dark
temporale	storm
variabile	changeable

Le Parti del Corpo (The Parts of the Body)

testa	head
faccia	face
orecchio	ear
naso	nose
bocca	mouth
occhio	eyes
braccio	arm
gamba	leg
mano	hand
piede	foot
petto	chest
stomaco	stomach
denti	teeth
dito	finger/toe

Salute: I sintomi e le condizioni (Health: symptoms & conditions)

Mi fa male...	I have a soar...
la schiena	back
il ginocchio	knee
il piede	foot
il collo	neck
la testa	head
la gola	throat
la gamba	leg
lo stomaco	stomach

Ho mal...	I have a...
di denti	toothache
d'orecchi	earache
di testa	headache
di stomaco	stomachache

Ho...	I feel... **Mi sento...**
il capogiro	dizzy
meglio	better
la nausea	nauseas
peggio	worse
i brividi	shivery
debole	weak
strano	strange

Ho...	I have ...
un raffreddore	a cold
la tosse	a cough
le febbre	a fever
un'emicrania	a migraine
l'influenza	the flu

AVERE/ESSERE: Come ti senti? (To Have/To Be: How you feel?)

Ho freddo	I am cold
Sono malato	I am sick
Ho caldo	I am hot
Sono arrabiatto	I am angry
Ho sete	I am thirsty
Sono ansioso	I am anxious
Ho fame	I am hungry
Sono depresso	I am depressed
Ho sonno	I am sleepy
Sono stanco	I am tired

Giorni della Settimana (Days of the Week)

lunedì	Monday	
di lunedì	on Monday	
martedì	Tuesday	
lunedi scorso	last Monday	
mercoledì	Wednesday	
lunedi prossimo	next Monday	
giovedì	Thursday	
ieri	yesterday	
venerdì	Friday	
oggi	today	
sabato	Saturday	
domani	Tomorrow	
domenica	Sunday	
dopodomani	the day after tomorrow	domani

125

Mesi dell'anno (Months of the Year)

gennaio	January
luglio	July
febbraio	February
agosto	August
marzo	March
settembre	September
aprile	April
ottobre	October
maggio	May
novembre	November
giugno	June
dicembre	December

Vacanze (Holidays)

Natale	Christmas
Pasqua	Easter
Avvento	Advent
Quaresima	Lent
Capodanno	New Year's (Day)
la Vigilia di	Eve (Christmas, New Year's)
Ognissanti	All Saints' Day
Ferragosto	August 15th

CHAPTER 8: TEST

Now that you have studied this dialect, naturally you want to find out how good you are. You should be able to perform the monologues and practice sentences accurately and convincingly. But can you successfully apply what you have learned to an unfamiliar text? Could you teach this dialect to someone else? Or dialect-coach a production? To help you answer those questions, here's a little test to help you find out. Print this page, and for the passage below write in the numbers of the signature sounds and additional features you have learned. You should be able to find or create examples of every signature sound and additional feature.

Complete the sentence with the appropriate adjective of nationality in the correct form, adding any other words necessary:

Example: Berlino è una città (tedesca).

Towns and cities

1   Roma è una città _____.

2   Parigi e Marsiglia sono città _____.

3   Bonn e Heidelberg sono città _____.

4   Londra e Birmingham sono città _____.

5   New York e Washington sono città _____.

6   Stoccolma e Uppsala sono città _____.

7   Berna e Zurigo sono città _____.

8   Tokyo è una città _____.

9   La 'Tipo' è un'automobile _____.

10   La 'Brava' e la 'Punto' sono automobili _____.

11   La Repubblica è un giornale _____.

12   La Stampa e Il Corriere sono giornali _____.

13   Oggi è una rivista _____.

14   Oggi e Grazia sono riviste _____.

15   Pasolini era un regista _____.

16   I fratelli Taviani sono registi _____.

17   Marcello Mastroianni era un attore _____.

18   Sofia Loren è un'attrice _____.

19   Meryl Streep è un'attrice _____.

20   Michael Douglas è un attore _____.

More descriptions

To complete the sentences below, choose an appropriate adjective from the list below and make sure it has the correct ending:

grande/piccolo; bello/brutto; alto/basso; simpatico/antipatico; costoso/economico; nuovo/vecchio; intelligente/stupido; fresco/tiepido; caldo/freddo; interessante/noioso; originale/tradizionale; vuoto/pieno; pulito/sporco; affollato/elegante

Example: La casa è . . .

La casa è piccola.

1   Il cane è _____.

2   Il portafoglio è _____.

3   L'accendino è _____.

4   Il libro è _____.

5   La casa è _____.

6   La bibita gassata è _____.

7   La strada è _____.

8   La lezione è _____.

9   Lo studente è _____.

10   La stazione è _____.

11   Il caffè è _____.

12   Il ristorante è _____.

13   La professoressa è _____.

14   il nostro insegnante è _____.

15   La sorella di Marco è _____.

16   L'automobile è _____.

17   La borsa è _____.

18   Il giornale è _____.

19   Il mio amico è _____.

20   La bottiglia è _____.

It's beautiful!

The adjective bello, bel, bella, bell', etc.

128

Your friend has just moved. You like everything about your friend's new house and garden. Insert the correct form of bello to complete these exclamations, looking up any words you don't know:

Example: Che (bell') entrata!

1	Che _____ ingresso!
2	Che _____ camera da letto!
3	Che _____ divano!
4	Che _____ panorama!
5	Che _____ specchio!
6	Che _____ giardino!
7	Che _____ albero in giardino!
8	Che _____ sedie!
9	Che _____ alberi!
10	Che _____ bicchieri!
11	Che _____ poltrone!
12	Che _____ tappeti!
13	Che _____ scaffali!
14	Che _____ armadietti!
15	Che _____ letto!
16	Che _____ moquette!
17	Che _____ cucina!
18	Che _____ sgabello!
19	Che _____ bagno!
20	Che _____ doccia!

It's delicious!

The adjective buono, buon/buona/buon', etc.

Example: Che (buon') insalata!

Your friends have just cooked a lovely meal. Express your appreciation. Insert the correct form of buono to complete the phrases below:

1	Che _____ tagliatelle!
2	Che _____ frittata!

3   Che _____ vino!

4   Che _____ spezzatino!

5   Che _____ dolci!

6   Che _____ gnocchi!

7   Che _____ fagiolini!

8   Che _____ acqua minerale!

9   Che _____ caffè!

10   Che _____ zabaglione!

The adjective buono

Italians have various ways of giving good wishes for all the different occasions.

See you if you can remember which form of buono to use:

1 _____ divertimento!

2 _____ viaggio!

3 _____ studio!

4 _____ appetito!

5 _____ feste!

6 _____ Pasqua!

7 _____ Natale!

8 _____ compleanno!

9 _____ lavoro!

10 _____ passeggiata!

TEST ON VERB

Present tense regular verbs

Nobody is listening to you, so you decide to say some really outrageous and unbelievable things to make your friends pay attention. Complete the sentences using the correct present tense form of the verbs shown in brackets:

Example: Vostro figlio (giocare) con un coltello.

Vostro figlio gioca con un coltello.

1   I miei figli (guardare) la televisione per 8 ore al giorno.

2   Gli studenti (leggere) i giornali italiani con molto entusiasmo.

3   Ragazzi, (cucinare) voi stasera! Io sono stanca.

4   I nostri vicini di casa non (pulire) mai la casa; è sporchissima e ci sono dei

        topi in giro.

5   Io (finire) le lezioni alle 2.00 di notte.

6   Il treno da Napoli a Roma (partire) solo una volta alla settimana.

7   Mio padre (bere) 4 bottiglie di whisky al giorno. È sempre ubriaco.

8   Io e il mio amico (studiare) tutte le sere – non (avere) mai tempo per

        uscire.

9   Io (andare) da Oxford a Londra tutti i giorni in bicicletta.

10   Mio marito (avere) tre mani e quattro piedi.

        Talk about yourself

Present tense regular verbs

Practise asking and answering these questions by yourself or with an Italianspeaking friend or classmate. You can use them to find out all about your

classmates or friends:

Verbs with -are

1 A che ora pranzi?

2 Dove lavori? Dove abiti?

3 Cosa mangi per prima colazione?

4 Giochi a qualche sport?

5 Che lingue parli?

6 Che materia studi?

7 Che cosa impari?

Verbs with -ere

8   Cosa leggi di solito? Un quotidiano? Una rivista?

9   A che ora prendi l'autobus o il treno per andare a casa?

10   Scrivi lettere o cartoline agli amici?

11   Conosci qualche personaggio famoso?

12   Cosa vedi alla televisione? Il telegiornale, i film?

13   Cosa bevi al pub?

Verbs with -ire

14   La sera senti la radio o la musica?

15   Preferisci il caffè o il tè? Preferisci il vino o la birra?

16   Capisci la lezione? Capisci l'italiano?

17   A che ora finisci la cena? A che ora finisci i compiti la sera?

18   Quante ore dormi ogni notte?

19   Chi pulisce a casa tua?

20   Quando parti per le vacanze?

Present tense common irregular verbs andare, venire, dovere, potere, volere

It is Sunday evening. As usual your house is in a state of chaos, as everyone in the family prepares for the week ahead. Here are some of the comments heard; complete them with the correct present tense form of the verbs shown above:

1   Mamma, non (potere) aiutarti. Domani c'è lezione d'italiano; (dovere) fare i compiti.

2   I bambini invece non (volere) fare i compiti di francese.

3   I ragazzi inglesi non (andare) a scuola il sabato; (potere) fare i compiti sabato. Beati loro!

4   Voi (dovere) anche mettere in ordine la vostra stanza, ragazzi.

5   Non c'è niente da mangiare in casa. Perchè non (andare) a mangiare la pizza?

6   Perché non (venire) anche tu stasera, Marco?

7   Marco non (volere) andare alla pizzeria in Piazza Dante.

8   Carla ha un'allergia. Non (potere) mangiare la pizza ai funghi.

9   Tanto Carla (dovere) finire i compiti prima di uscire.

Say no . . . but find an excuse

Present tense common irregular verbs venire, dovere, potere, volere

You or whoever is being asked should answer all the questions below in the negative, and provide an excuse. In your reply, use dovere, potere or volere at least once:

Example: Mi presti la tua giacca?

No, non ti presto la mia giacca – puoi mettere la tua.

No, non voglio prestarti la mia giacca – puoi mettere la tua.

1   Vieni a casa mia domani?

2   Mi presti la tua maglia verde?

3   Il tuo meccanico ripara la macchina in pochi giorni?

4   Facciamo i compiti dopo cena?

5   Bambini, volete guardare la televisione?

6   Gli studenti scrivono gli esercizi senza problemi?

7   Il Papa guida l'automobile a Roma?

8   Tua madre prepara gli spaghetti ogni sera?

9   Mangiate i calamari quando siete al mare?

10   Tu compri i giornali italiani?

The end-of-term party

Present tense regular verbs and irregular verbs

dare, dovere, essere, fare, rimanere, sapere, stare, tenere, venire

Three of your classmates, Piero, Carlo and Gianna, are organising an end-ofterm party. You overhear snatches of their conversation. Complete them using

the correct present tense form of the verbs indicated:

1   Nella classe d'italiano ci (essere) venti studenti. Li invitiamo tutti?

2   Piero, mi (dare) l'elenco dei nomi?

3   Gianna, se (tenere) la mia penna, vado a fare una telefonata.

4   Se volete, (fare) tutto io.

5   Cosa (fare) gli altri? Anche loro (dovere) aiutare.

6   Se quelle sedie (rimanere) nell'altra stanza, abbiamo più spazio.

7   Volevamo un po' di musica, ma nessuno (sapere) suonare la chitarra.

8   (Pagare) noi il vino? Poi chiediamo i soldi agli altri.

9   E chi (preparare) da mangiare?

10   Come (stare), professor Parisi? (Venire) anche Lei alla festa?

Present tense of sapere

Your hopeless friend Mara is coming out with all of you tonight. She rings you

up every five minutes with a question or problem. Complete her sentences and

133

questions with the correct present tense form of sapere:

1   Chiamami più tardi per la conferma. Tu _____ il mio numero di

     telefono, vero?

2   Noi non _____ ancora chi viene e chi no.

3   Teresa e Carlo non _____ ancora se vengono.

4   Giorgio non _____ se viene.

5   Voi _____ dove si trova il ristorante? Allora vengo prima a casa vostra,

     così possiamo andare insieme.

6   Pronto? Sono Mara! Mi sono persa! Non _____ come arrivare a casa

     vostra.

7   I ragazzi non _____ come arrivare.

8   Ho telefonato a Giorgio. Ma neanche lui _____ come arrivarci.

9   Aiuto! Io non _____ parcheggiare la macchina. La lascio qui.

10   _____ se ci sono vigili in giro?

The imperfect tense

Complete the gaps in this account of life in the 1950s with the imperfect
tense of the verb shown in brackets:

Quando io (essere) ragazza, la vita (essere) molto diversa. Non si (potere)
fare le cose che fate voi giovani oggigiorno!

Io (vivere) in un piccolo paese nel sud d'Italia. Non c'(essere) discoteche;
non c'(essere) neanche un cinema. La sera i giovani (fare) la passeggiata
lungo la via principale. Ma le ragazze (venire) sempre accompagnate da
una zia o da un'altra parente. Ma tanto io non (volere) uscire da sola.
Mio padre (fare) l'insegnante e quindi noi (conoscere) molta gente in
paese. In famiglia (essere) in cinque . . . mio padre, mia madre, i miei
fratelli ed io.

I miei fratelli (potere) uscire di sera, anche non accompagnati. Io invece
(dovere) sempre essere accompagnata da una parente.

Anche a casa la vita (essere) più semplice. Come tutte le famiglie italiane
di quel periodo, (consumare) poca roba confezionata. (Mangiare) i prodotti
sani delle nostre campagne – meno carne certamente, più frutta e verdura

– e (bere) il vino nostro fatto in casa. Non c'(essere) la televisione ma

d'inverno si (ascoltare) la radio.

The imperfect tense

Tell your friend about your first day at university, using the following verbs at

least once: aspettare, bere, capire, dovere, essere, fare, leggere, mangiare.

C' _____ tanta confusione. Tutti gli studenti _____ la coda fuori

dell'aula principale dove _____ iscriversi. Non si _____

niente. Altri avevano già finito e _____ alla mensa o _____ un

caffè al bar. Noi _____ gli ultimi quel giorno, e quindi quando

siamo arrivati in biblioteca per fare la tessera, _____ già chiusa. La mia

amica aveva portato un libro e lo _____ mentre _____ .

Past participle

You have been on holiday at the seaside with your mother. On your return

you write a letter to a friend in Milan, telling her all about it. Here are some

sentences from the letter; complete them with the correct past participle:

Example: Ho (mangiare) troppa pasta.

Ho mangiato troppa pasta.

1   Ti avevo (dire) che eravamo in un posto molto tranquillo, no?

2   Ci hanno (dare) una stanza che si affacciava sul mare.

3   Mia madre ha (leggere) tantissimi libri e tantissime riviste.

4   Ho (fare) tanti bagni. Il mare era stupendo.

5   Abbiamo (vedere) un film bellissimo.

6   Abbiamo (bere) dei cocktail.

7   Abbiamo (prendere) tanti caffè.

8   Abbiamo (avere) tanti gelati.

9   Ho (ricevere) tanti complimenti.

10   Non ho mai (scrivere) al mio ragazzo!

The compound perfect of regular and reflexive verbs

Continue your story of the holidays, but this time you have to form the whole

135

compound perfect tense, not just the participle:

Example: Mia madre (leggere) moltissimi libri in vacanza.

Mia madre ha letto moltissimi libri in vacanza.

1   Mia madre ed io non (avere) nessun problema a trovare una camera.

2   Mio padre (partire) prima di noi.

3   Mia madre ed io (fare) una vacanza lunghissima.

4   (Stare) sulla spiaggia tutti i giorni a prendere il sole.

5   (Mettersi) un costume da bagno diverso tutti i giorni.

6   Infatti (uscire) tutte le sere.

7   (Bere) tantissimi cocktail al bar Hollywood.

8   Martedì (vestirsi) eleganti per andare ad una festa alla villa dei nostri amici
         milanesi!

9   Tutti (divertirsi) da matti.

10   E tu dove (essere) quest'estate?

Avere or essere?

Transitive/intransitive verbs

There are many verbs that can use avere or essere in the compound perfect, depending on whether they are being used transitively or intransitively. Some verbs can be used transitively (with an object) or intransitively (without an object), for example aumentare, diminuire, passare. Other verbs use avere where you might expect essere, for example intransitive verbs such as correre, costare, passeggiare. For each statement below, select the options you think are correct. There might be more than one solution:

1   a Ho passato la farmacia.

         b Ho passato davanti alla farmacia.

c Sono passato davanti alla farmacia.

2   a I costi sono aumentati molto.

         b I costi hanno aumentato molto.

         c I costi sono aumentato molto.

3   a Abbiamo passeggiato lungo il fiume.

         b Siamo passeggiati lungo il fiume.

c Abbiamo passeggiati lungo il fiume.

4 a I prezzi sono saliti.

   b I prezzi hanno salito.

   c I prezzi si sono saliti.

5 a Abbiamo vissuto insieme per trenta anni.

   b Abbiamo vissuto una vita tranquilla.

   c Siamo vissuti insieme per trenta anni.

6 a Queste scarpe sono costate 120 euro.

   b Queste scarpe hanno costato 120 euro.

   c Queste scarpe sono costato 120 euro.

7 a Maria è corsa verso la fermata.

   b Maria ha corso verso la fermata.

   c Maria è corso verso la fermata.

8 a Abbiamo passeggiato per due ore.

   b Siamo passeggiati per due ore.

   c Abbiamo passeggiato 5 km.

What had taken place earlier

Pluperfect (trapassato) avevo mangiato, ero andato/a.

Give the background to an action or event by saying what had happened

earlier. Use the pluperfect (trapassato):

Example: Avevo sete (mangiare un piatto piccante al ristorante

indiano).

Avevo sete, perché avevo mangiato un piatto piccante al

ristorante indiano.

1 Ho aiutato la mia amica a fare i compiti (lei/non capire la lezione).

2 Ho aperto la finestra (Giuliana chiudere la mattina).

3 Non avevo fame (andare al bar mezz'ora prima).

4 Finalmente ho fatto i compiti (l'insegnante/assegnare la settimana scorsa).

5 Sono ingrassata 5 chili (mangiare troppi gelati e troppo cioccolato).

6 Ho dovuto chiedere un contributo a mio padre (spendere tutti i soldi al
   pub).

7 Ero stanca (studiare tutte le sere fino a tardi).

137

8   Sono uscita (gli amici/partire per le vacanze).

9   La macchina non partiva (la batteria/scaricarsi).

10   In treno mi hanno fatto la multa (dimenticare di timbrare il biglietto).

       When was Rome built?

Simple perfect (passato remoto) parlai, andai

       Example: Il Gattopardo (essere) scritto da Giuseppe di Lampedusa.

       Il Gattopardo fu scritto da Giuseppe di Lampedusa.

The simple perfect is often used in historic contexts, in novels or where there
is no strong link to the present. Complete the sentences below using the
simple perfect form of the appropriate verbs:

1   Roma (essere) costruita nel 753 A.C., secondo alcuni storici.

2   La disoccupazione (aumentare) molto dopo l'unificazione dell'Italia e molti
       italiani (emigrare) negli Stati Uniti o in Sud America.

3   Il 26 agosto del 1978 Albino Luciani divenne ufficialmente Vescovo di
       Roma. (Morire) dopo solo trentatre giorni di pontificato.

4   Dante (nascere) a Firenze nel 1265.

5   Puccini (vivere) a Torre del Lago (Toscana)

6   Dante (scrivere) la Divina Commedia tra il 1307 e il 1321.

7   Il prete (uscire) dal bar e (dirigersi) verso la chiesa. La proprietaria lo
       (seguire), lo (fermare) e gli (dare) le chiavi della chiesa.

8   Il terremoto di Messina (avvenire) il 28 dicembre 1908 e (distruggere)
       completamente la città. Il numero di morti (essere) stimato tra le 60 mila
       e le 90 mila persone, su una popolazione totale di 150 mila abitanti.

9   Molti abitanti (salvarsi) ma (rimanere) senza casa.

10   Il bambino (sporgersi) dalla finestra e poi (cadere) dal settimo piano.

I'll do it later

The future

Answer the question saying that you are doing something later:

1   Sei mai stato negli USA?

       No, ma ci (andare) l'anno prossimo con mio marito.

2   Hai mai assaggiato il tiramisu?

No, ma lo (assaggiare) domani sera a casa di Daniela.

3   Tuo marito ti ha dato dei fiori per il tuo compleanno?

No, ma me li (dare) domani, spero, per il nostro anniversario di matrimonio.

4   I tuoi genitori sono venuti a trovarti a Oxford?

No, ma (venire) a Natale.

5   Facciamo l'arrosto domenica prossima come al solito?

No, se c'è bel tempo (fare) un picnic.

6   Hai comprato un regalo per i tuoi figli?

No, (cercare) qualcosa in centro oggi pomeriggio.

7   Va bene se veniamo da voi a Ferragosto?

No, venite dopo. A Ferragosto (essere) in campagna dai miei suoceri.

8   Hai studiato tanto! Non sei stanca?

Sì, ma (riposarsi) una volta finiti gli esami.

9   Hai bevuto il latte? Ti fa bene.

No, ma lo (bere) prima di andare a letto.

10   Avete mangiato tanto panettone a Natale?

Sì, tanto, ma ne (mangiare) ancora.

I'll do it tomorrow

The future tense and object pronouns

Never do today what you can put off until tomorrow! Your mother is nagging as usual, asking you whether you have done something or other. Answer her question, saying that you will do something domani, più tardi, la settimana prossima, fra poco, oggi pomeriggio, lunedì, stasera, etc.

If you have learnt personal pronouns already, use a direct object pronoun (such as lo, la); an indirect object pronoun (such as gli, le) or a combined pronoun (such as me lo, glielo) to replace the noun object:

Example: Hai scritto il tema?

Scriverò il tema domani.

(No, lo scriverò domani.)

1   Hai telefonato a Carlo?

2   Hai scritto alla zia per ringraziarla?

3   Hai fatto i compiti di francese?

4   Hai studiato i verbi italiani?

5   Hai riparato la gomma della bici?

6   Hai lavato la macchina per tuo padre?

7   Hai pulito la tua stanza?

8   Hai preso la medicina?

9   Sei andato/a dal dentista stamattina?

10   Hai ricordato a Marco di venire sabato?

Never again!

The future tense

After a bad experience, you – or someone else – say that you will never do something (again)! Find the correct future form of the verb in brackets:

       Example: Non (vendere) mai i mobili dei miei nonni.

       Non venderò mai i mobili dei miei nonni.

1   Il bambino non (dire) mai più le bugie!

2   Susy non (guidare) mai più così velocemente.

3   Tu non (mangiare) mai più tanto cioccolato!

4   Siamo molto offesi. Non (venire) mai più a casa vostra.

5   Mi sento proprio male. Non (bere) mai più tanto whisky.

6   Voi non (cercare) mai più i funghi!

7   Mio padre non (pagare) mai più con la carta di credito.

8   I nostri amici non (ottenere) mai più il permesso di uscire la sera.

9   Io non (fare) mai più il bagno nel mare mosso.

10   I miei genitori non (essere) mai contenti della mia scelta.

The ideal holiday

present conditional

What would you do if you had a limitless supply of money to spend on a holiday and could take anyone you like with you? Complete the story of your dream holiday by transforming the verbs in brackets into the present conditional (parlerei, etc.):

       (Andare) in Italia. (Scegliere) un posto tranquillo al mare, forse in Sicilia o in Sardegna. (Venire) anche il mio ragazzo. (Rimanere) per 10 giorni o forse 15. (Avere) una bella camera con bagno tutta per noi. (Essere) gli unici ospiti nell'albergo.

(Stare) a letto fino alle 10.00. (Fare) colazione sulla terrazza dell'albergo. Di giorno il mio ragazzo (fare) tanti bagni nel mare, o (vedere) i monumenti locali, mentre io (abbronzarsi) al sole e (mangiare) tanti gelati. (Leggere) delle riviste e (scrivere) delle cartoline ai miei amici. Il cameriere (portare) dei cocktail mentre noi (stare) sempre vicino alla piscina. Di sera, (andare) in un ristorante romantico, vicino al mare. (Mangiare) il pesce fresco e (bere) tanto spumante. Dopo tanto relax, (essere) contenta di tornare al lavoro!

Finding an excuse

The present conditional

You have decided not to attempt any New Year's resolutions – you never keep them anyway. Use the present conditional to make up sentences based on the verb phrases below, adding any excuse you can think of, for not doing things:

> Example: studiare l'italiano
>
> Studierei l'italiano, ma sono troppo stanca.

1   Fare i compiti

2   Venire in chiesa con te

3   Lavorare in giardino

4   Pulire la casa

5   Giocare a tennis

6   Smettere di fumare

7   Leggere tutti i romanzi di Tolstoy

8   Scrivere un romanzo

9   Bere meno birra

10 Mangiare meno cioccolato

11   Dimagrire di 10 kg

12 Preparare la cena

13 Prendere in noleggio un DVD

14 Andare a piedi

15 tare a casa stasera

16 Rimanere in Inghilterra quest'estate

17   Fare la vacanza in Sri Lanka

18   Pagare la bolletta telefonica

19 Spiegare i verbi italiani al mio compagno di classe

20 Vestirsi meglio

What we should have done!

Use the past conditional of the verbs given to say what you – or somebody
else – could or should have done:

        Example: Carla (arrivare) alle 10.00 ma ha perso il treno.

        Carla sarebbe arrivata alle 10.00 ma ha perso il treno.

1   Giovanni è stato stupido. (Risparmiare) comprando il biglietto in internet.

2   Peccato che mi sono sposata giovane! (Potere) diventare famosa.

3   (Andare) alla festa anch'io ma non volevo andare da sola.

4   I miei amici (andare) stamattina in centro. Ma non c'è stato tempo.

5   Luisa è stata bocciata all'esame. (Dovere) studiare di più.

6   Peppino si è offeso. (Essere) meglio non dire niente.

7   I ragazzi hanno raccolto pochi soldi. (Avere) più fortuna suonando e cantando in centro.

8   Ti sei macchiata la camicia bianca! (Potere) metterti il grembiule prima di cucinare.

9   Ragazzi, avete perso l'aereo! (Fare) meglio ad arrivare un po' prima in aeroporto.

10   Abbiamo sprecato tempo e soldi. (Divertirsi) di più rimanendo a casa.

11   Non c'era un pianoforte in casa. A me (piacere) imparare a suonare.

12   Non ho fatto il dolce. Mi (servire) la panna e non ne avevo.

13   Il treno delle 9.00 (arrivare) alle 11.00 di mattina ma ha fatto un ritardo di mezz'ora.

14   Con un volo economico io (pagare) il supplemento per i bagagli perché pesavano troppo.

15   Io (dare) un CD di musica classica a mio marito ma non sapevo quale scegliere.

16   La cameriera (pulire) la camera ma i turisti dormivano ancora.

17   I bambini (fare) il bagno ma hanno dimenticato il costume.

18   Scusa, non sapevo che fosse così tardi, (prepararsi) prima.

19   Io (scegliere) la vacanza al mare non in montagna.

20   Marco canta bene. Gli (piacere) studiare la musica.

The morning rush

Reflexive verbs present tense

Now complete this story of a typical morning in someone's house with one of
the reflexive verbs given below, in the present tense (mi lavo, etc.):

alzarsi, arrabbiarsi, lavarsi, mettersi, prepararsi, svegliarsi, truccarsi, vestirsi

Di solito (io) _____ alle 6.00. _____ i denti, _____, _____ la camicetta, la maglia, e i pantaloni. Mio marito invece _____ alle 7.00. Prepara il caffè e dopo colazione _____ e _____ per andare a lavorare. I bambini _____ alle 7.00 o alle 7.15, e dopo 10 minuti _____ con grande difficoltà. La piccola è sempre di malumore la mattina e _____ con tutti.

The morning rush . . . gone wrong

Reflexive verbs compound perfect

Now complete the story of what happened the morning the alarm failed to go off, this time using the reflexive verbs given below, in the passato prossimo (mi sono lavata etc.):

alzarsi, arrabbiarsi, lavarsi, mettersi, prepararsi, svegliarsi, truccarsi, vestirsi

Stamattina (io) non _____ alle 6.00 come al solito, perché la sveglia non ha suonato. Non _____ i denti perché non c'era tempo. Non trovavo una camicia pulita e allora _____ la maglia sporca e i pantaloni di mio figlio. Mio marito dormiva ancora e _____ solo alle 8.45, furibondo perché non l'avevo svegliato. I ragazzi _____ alle 8.00 e infatti hanno perso l'autobus. La piccola _____ con suo fratello perché non trovava le scarpe. È andata a scuola con i sandali.

A letter from Giuseppina

Reflexive verbs present, future, compound perfect

Marco's friend Giuseppina has sent him a Christmas letter with all her family's news. Fill in the gaps in these extracts with the correct reflexive verb, either in present tense (mi alzo), future (mi alzerò) or the passato prossimo (mi sono alzato). Choose from these reflexive verbs: alzarsi, impegnarsi, iscriversi, laurearsi, prepararsi, preoccuparsi, sposarsi, trovarsi.

1   L'anno prossimo Mario e Carla _____ ad Assisi; è un bellissimo posto per fare i matrimoni.

2   Anche mio fratello Giulio _____, con una ragazza che ha conosciuto in vacanza l'anno scorso!

143

3   Come _____ a Londra, Marco? Stai ancora facendo il corso d'inglese?

4   Le figlie dei nostri amici _____ molto bene a Londra l'anno scorso, perchè tutti sono stati molto gentili con loro.

5   Ho trovato un lavoro part-time come commessa; comincio a lavorare alle 8.00 quindi devo _____ presto.

6   Il mese prossimo ci saranno degli esami; cominciamo a _____ veramente.

7   Teresa ha fatto un corso di lingue all'università; _____ l'anno scorso.

8   Anche Giorgio _____ all'università. Se tutto va bene, _____

      _____ fra 4 anni.

9   Quest'anno Giorgio _____ veramente; l'anno scorso non ha fatto niente.

10   E un'ultimissima notizia sulla nostra famiglia: anch'io _____

      a cambiare lavoro!

What's Marco doing?

Present tense stare + the gerund

Virtual charades! Guess from the 'props' – e.g. bottle – what Marco is doing,

answering the questions using stare in the present tense and the gerund:

      Example: Cosa fa Marco? (la bottiglia)

      Sta bevendo.

1   Cosa fa Marco? (la forchetta)

2   Cosa fa Marco? (la bibita)

3   Cosa fa Marco? (il detersivo per pavimenti)

4   Cosa fa Marco? (il dizionario italiano)

5   Cosa fa Marco? (la tazza)

6   Cosa fa Marco? (a letto)

7   Cosa fa Marco? (il CD)

8   Cosa fa Marco? (la penna)

9   Cosa fa Marco? (la pentola)

10   Cosa fa Marco? (la rivista)

What were you doing?

The gerund

Talk about what you and your friends have been doing. Replace the word in italics with a gerund either present (-ando/-endo) or past (avendo studiato, essendo partito), making any changes necessary, to express what people were doing at the time of the main action or to give the reasons behind it:

Example: Gianna (faceva) le spese in centro. Ha visto Marco.

Facendo le spese in centro, Gianna ha visto Marco.

1   Parcheggiavo la macchina in centro. Ho visto un vigile.

2   Marco andava a scuola di corsa. Ha sentito la mia voce.

3   Prendevamo un caffè al bar. Abbiamo visto i ragazzi.

4   Mio marito tornava a casa in bicicletta. È caduto e si è fatto male.

5   I ragazzi sono arrivati alla stazione alle 11.00. Hanno visto il treno per Milano già in partenza.

6   Mio fratello sciava sulle Dolomiti e si è rotto la gamba.

7   Non avevo studiato. Quindi ho preso dei brutti voti all'esame.

8   Ora mi alzo presto e riesco a fare molto di più.

9   Beveva tantissimo, poi si sentiva sempre male la mattina.

10   Fai troppe cose insieme e rischi di non concludere mai niente.

11   Abbiamo telefonato a casa. Abbiamo saputo che nostra madre stava male.

12   Bevevo un caffè. Mi sono scottata la lingua.

13   Abbiamo fatto colazione tardi. Quindi a mezzogiorno non avevamo ancora fame.

14   Eravamo stanchissimi. Ci siamo addormentati subito.

CHAPTER 9: DIALOGUE AND INTRODUCTORY COVERSATION

This chapter is filled with useful phrases, verb conjugations, and sentences for the student of Italian to read and repeat out-loud and has native speakers for both the Italian phrases and for the English translation which immediately follows. The phrases in each page start out simply, and the complete verb conjugations for the verbs to be covered in that page are given for memorization. Then, as the chapter progresses, the pharses build into more complex sentences, using the vocabulary that has already been covered. In this way, word choice and verb conjugation should become automatic. The more the phrases are repeated, the more they become a part of one's understanding of how the language is actually used, and the more natural and easy speaking in Italian becomes! The chapter provide practice which includes and then goes beyond the examples and vocabulary provided in the earlier chapter, in order to make the spoken language truly come alive. Once, or over and over again – as much or as little as needed, and follow the pace that is best for you!

Practice - 1

Basic greetings

Buon giorno.	Good day.
Buon giorno.	Use for, "Good morning."
Buon giorno.	Use when an American would say: "Good afternoon,"or"Have a good day."
Buona sera.	Good evening.
Buona notte.	Good night.

Practice - 2

Basic greetings / Idiomatic expression city of origin, "Di dove?" / Capital cities (di)

Buon giorno, Maria.	Good morning, Maria.
Di dov'è lei?	Where are you from? (polite) (lit. From where are you?)
Sono di Londra.	(I) am from London.
Buon giorno, Maria.	Good afternoon, Maria.
Di dove sei?	Where are you from? (familiar)
Sono di Madrid.	(I) am from Madrid.
Buona sera, Maria.	Good evening, Maria.
Di dove sei?	Where are you from? (familiar)
Sono di Parigi.	(I) am from Paris.
Buona notte, Francesca.	Good night, Francis.

Buona notte, Laura.	Good night, Laura.

Practice - 3

Polite expressions of agreement

Si.	Yes.
Certo.	Of course.
D'accordo.	(I) agree.
Penso di si.	(I) think so.
Per favore.	Please.
Per piacere.	Please.
Grazie.	Thank you.
Grazie molto!	Thank you very much!
Molte grazie.	Many thanks.
Grazie tante.	Thanks a lot.
Grazie mille.	A thousand thanks.
Prego.	You're welcome.
Di niente!	You're welcome! (lit. It was nothing!)
Permesso?	May I (enter)?

Practice - 5

Polite expressions / Idiomatic expression city of origin, "Di dove?" Capital cities (di)

Per favore, Maria...	Please, Maria...
Di dov'è lei?	Where are you from? (polite)
Sono di Dublino.	(I) am from Dublin.
Per piacere, Maria...	Please, Maria...
Di dove sei?	Where are you from? (familiar)
Sono di Atene.	(I) am from Athens.
Permesso?	May I?
Di dove sei?	Where are you from? (familiar)
Sono di Berlino.	(I) am from Berlin.
Grazie, Maria.	Thank you, Maria.
Prego.	You are welcome.

Singular masculine forms of bello/buono / Names of people and countries

147

Come ti chiami?	What is your name? (familiar)
Mi chiamo Maria.	My name is Maria.
Che bel nome!	What a nice name!
Come si chiama?	What is your name? (polite)
Mi chiamo Caterina.	My name is Kathy.
Che bel nome!	What a beautiful name!
Come si chiama?	What is her name?
Si chiama Rosa.	Her name is Rose.
Che bel nome!	What a good name!
Come si chiama?	What is his name?
Si chiama Michele.	His name is Michael.
È un buon nome!	(It) is a good name!
Come si chiama?	What is its name?
Si chiama Europa.	Its name is Europe.
Che bel paese!	What a nice country!
Come si chiama?	What is its name?
Si chiama America.	It is called America.
È proprio un bel paese!	(It) is really a beautiful country!
Come si chiama?	What is it's name?
Si chiama Italia.	It is called Italy.

È proprio un paese buono (cioè gli abitanti sono buoni)!

(It) is really a good country (that is, because of its wonderful people)!

Vocabulary – At the airport

Caterina, dove sei?	Kathy, where are you?
Eccomi!	Here I am!
Dov'è l'uscita? Eccola!	Where is the gate? (= exit to board the plane) Here it is!
Dov'è la scala mobile?	Where is the escalator?
Eccola!	Here it is!
Pietro, dove sei?	Peter, where are you?
Eccomi!	Here I am!

Dov'è il bagaglio a mano?	Where is the carry on luggage?
Eccolo!	Here it is!
Dov'è la cintura di sicurezza?	Where is the seat belt?
Eccola!	Here it is!
Michele, dove sei?	Michael, where are you?
Eccomi!	Here I am!
Dov'è il biglietto aereo?	Where is the plane ticket?
Eccolo!	Here it is!
Dov'è la carta d'imbarco?	Where is the boarding pass?
Eccola!	Here it is!

ITALIAN COMMON PHRASES

Learn Italian for Beginners in Your Car Like Crazy.

Language Learning Lessons for travel and Everyday.

How to speak Italian with Vocabulary and Conversations.

VOL 1

CHAPTER 8: TEST 129

CHAPTER 9: DIALOGUE AND INTRODUCTORY COVERSATION 148

ITALIAN COMMON PHRASES 154

INTRODUCTION 172

INTRODUCTION

Italian is a Romance language spoken by about 63 million people in Italy and parts of Switzerland. Modern standard Italian was adopted by the Italian government after the unification of Italy in about 1871 and has its roots in the region of Tuscany, in central Italy. There are many dialects of Italian spoken throughout the Italian peninsula. Dialects are generally not used for purposes of mass communication and are usually spoken in local, informal contexts by native speakers. Most all Italians speak a dialect (Venetian, Neapolitan, Sicilian, etc.), but they can easily switch to standard Italian

Forty million tourists visit Italy each year. Two of Italy's major cities —Florence and Rome—are among the most visited cities in the world. On any given day of the year, this equates to 110,000 foreign tourists in Italy. Many travel guides recommend that tourists make an effort to get off the beaten path; to find that small, out-of-the-way place that few tourists ever visit. It is in these areas where the "real" Italy can be experienced; it is also in these areas where very little English is spoken by the general population. This book will be very useful for the 110,000 foreign tourists who hope to have a unique, off- the-beaten-path experience in Italy. This book will be a useful tool to help integrate both the inexperienced and experienced traveler into many essential aspects of daily life. For these tourists, a very basic understanding of the language can enhance their stay in Italy. Italians treasure politeness, and everywhere in the world people can appreciate the good manners of a "thank you" or "you're welcome." Italians will respond to your efforts to communicate in their language with wholehearted appreciation. By making an effort to learn some basic phrases and expressions, you will feel safer and more assured to take the path less traveled, you will discover useful and interesting facts, you will cope with unexpected situations, and you will be greeted with much greater kindness. This book will also be a useful resource for high school and college students who wish to enhance their in-class learning experiences. It will be a handy resource to help students sharpen their speaking ability by learning useful expressions (and their correct pronunciation) that pertain to everyday life.

Useful Common Phrases For Beginners offers grammar and pronunciation sections for easier, more effective use and contains essential information for first-time and experienced travelers alike. It features more than 1,400 words and phrases, covering all subjects that people are likely to encounter in their travels— from greetings or shopping to how to buy travel ticket or changing a flight. There is also a detailed phonetic pronunciation table plus an extensive word list and grammar guide that will enable travelers to construct basic sentences.

HOW TO USE THIS BOOK

This isn't a class that you have to drag yourself to twice a week. You can use this book however you want, whether your goal is to pick up some words and phrases to help you get around when you visit Italy or you just want to be able to say "Hello, how are you?" to an Italian-speaking neighbor. Go through this book at your own pace, reading as much or as little at a time as your heart desires. You don't have to trudge through the chapters in order, either; just read the sections that interest you.

If you've never taken Italian before, you may want to read Chapters 1 and 2 before you tackle the later ones. These chapters give you the basics that you need to know about the language, such as how to pronounce the various sounds and form simple sentences.

THE BEST METHOD TO LEARNING ITALIAN

The Italian national soccer team, known as gli Azzurri because of the blue of their jerseys, has for years ranked among the top teams in the world They've won the World Cup four times, Italian-born players routinely sign multi- million-dollar contracts for European teams, and the Italian soccer leagues offer some of the most talented competition anywhere. The overriding reason for their success? Practice, practice, practice. And that's the secret to learning Italian or any other foreign language. Exercise your language muscles every day, and soon you too will be competing with the best of them. The quickest and most effective way to learn Italian is the total-immersion method. This means traveling to Italy for an extended period, studying at any of the thousands of schools throughout the country, and speaking only Ital- ian. Many programs include a home-stay component that enhances the cultural exchange. You literally eat, breathe, and dream in Italian. Unfortunately, not everyone has the opportunity to spend weeks or months in Florence, Rome, or other Ital- ian towns sipping espresso, touring ancient ruins, and tak- ing language classes. There are other ways to learn Italian without leaving your hometown, wherever that may be. You've already taken the most important step to learn- ing Italian when you picked up this book, because the most important thing is to start studying! And any method is appropriate, whether it's reading an Italian textbook, taking a language course online, at a university or local language school, completing workbook exercises, listen- ing to a podcast, tape or CD, or conversing with a native Italian speaker. Spend some time every day reading, writ- ing, speaking, and listening to Italian to become accus- tomed to the target language. Slowly but surely, your confidence will build, your vocabulary will expand, and you'll be communicating in Italian Maybe you'll even start talking with your hands!

TIPS ON THE TOP DIFFERENCES BETWEEN ITALIAN AND ENGLISH.

When it comes to learning a language, a lot of people give up before they even start largely because of a false belief that it is too difficult to learn another language. There is no such thing as a person who is unable to learn a new language. There are different degrees of ease with which a person learns a language, but anyone can be bilingual with enough effort. This is true even when learning Italian. The first step is to believe you can learn Italian, because you really can. The second step is to relax and enjoy the process. After all, Italian is the closest language to Latin, the language that virtually all other western languages are based on. You will already have a basis in the language simply by speaking English – this will make vocabulary building that much easier. As an English speaker, you will find that Italian is actually one of the easiest languages to learn. It doesn't require learning an entirely different alphabet (like any Asian, Russian, Arabic, or Greek language), and spelling is already somewhat familiar because English is based (at least in part) on it. The Italian sentence structure is also very similar to English, making it easier to start speaking in sentences once you have acquired an adequate vocabulary. Word order is nearly identical, so once you are familiar with the basics, it should be easy to start understanding what people say (even if it takes a while to start talking in Italian). The biggest differences between English and Italian lie in their sounds and grammar. Many of the sounds are also the same, though there are some unique sounds that you may not have been exposed to previously. Nor do the same letters translate to the same sounds. For English speakers, learning to pronounce some sounds in Italian can be tricky; trying to spell words correctly is less problematic. Probably the biggest complication is the use of gendered nouns. They do not follow the rules that you may expect them to, so memorization is going to be the key to getting them right. It's important for you to understand where the differences are and why they exist. It may not be easy to understand initially, but as you delve further into the language, the rules start to make it easier to understand and predict the sounds and spellings. Native-English speakers who are learning Italian may initially stumble because some of the differences between the two languages come as a surprise. This is because we tend to take our own native languages for granted, but they reflect the way we think and our cultures. To keep you from being blindsided, here are some of the biggest differences between Italian and English.

Keep in mind, the vocabulary is going to be very different, but that is something you can sit and memorize. Getting the right grammatical rhythm is far trickier and knowing the potential problems ahead of time can help you start to reprogram your thinking as you learn.

THE 10 PRIMARY DIFFERENCES BETWEEN ENGLISH AND ITALIAN

There are many differences between these two European languages, but these are the 10 that tend to cause English speakers the most trouble when learning Italian.

ITALIAN NOUNS HAVE GENDERS

English is one of the simplest European languages because all nouns have the same articles. This means that English nouns are gender neutral, except for nouns that refer specifically to a living creature that has a gender, such as "hen" and "rooster." All Italian nouns are more complex, but for now we are going to focus on the two primary genders, masculine singular and feminine singular. (Italian also uses different articles for the plural versions of nouns, but if you know the singular gender, you just need to remember to change the article when you use the plural version of the noun.) Sometimes, the gender of a noun is directly related to the gender of the thing it's referring to. More often, the gender is completely arbitrary, and it will require memorizing the words and their genders. Gender affects sentence construction, too. The article must match the gender of the noun: the English word "the" is either masculine singular or feminine. Other parts of speech, including relative pronouns and adjectives, must also match the gender of the noun. For most native English-speakers, gender is one of the most complicated new rules to grasp. Once you've gotten the gist of it, you're well on your way to mastering Italian grammar!

ADJECTIVES COME AFTER NOUNS

Something you don't notice when speaking English is that you use the adjectives first, giving the person the description of an object before they know what the object is. For example, you can talk about the large, red truck in English. In Italian, the adjectives come after the object, so you would talk about the truck large red. That means that the person listening to you will have an image of the object, and will then impose the description over it. There are a few exceptions to this rule that you might encounter because some types of adjectives work differently. One example is a quantifier, which is an adjective that describes how many of something there are. You would say "the house blue," but "the only house." At least for now, focus on learning to think of putting the adjective second. This will help you start to speak a little faster with fewer obvious mistakes.

NEGATION

In English, there are many prefixes that can be added to various words to create the opposite of that word or negate its meaning. For example, there is the difference between "efficient" and "inefficient" or "grateful" and "ungrateful." There are also negating words, like "no" and "not." There are right and wrong times to use all of these, and it can take years for children to learn the proper use of these words. This is not a problem in Italian because you can negate any verb by simply putting "no" before it. Also, Italian uses double-negatives as the default. This is why "I don't want nothing" is correct in Italian but not in English.

ITALIAN VIEWS SOME LETTERS AS FOREIGN

English and Italian have the same alphabet, but Italian treats a few of letters as outsiders. Largely, these are letters that were not used in Latin: j, k, w, x, and y. Any word that includes these words in Italian are words that were imported into the language – that means that you will not encounter these letters very often because they do not appear naturally in Italian. This will make it easier to spell because words that have these letters are often going to be imported from English, so they will be spelled similar to (if not exactly) like you see them in English.

IN ITALIAN, THERE ARE FIVE TENSES

Compared to the minimum of 12 tenses in English (even that number is up for debate, proving just how complicated our verbs are), Italian only have five: simple past, present, imperfect, future, and conditional. To achieve the same meaning as English tenses, Italian uses auxiliary words. It will definitely be tricky in the beginning, but when you get the hang of it, you may end up preferring it.

IN ITALIAN, THE VERB "TO HAVE" CAN BE USED TO EXPRESS FEELING

In English, we talk about feelings using some form of a "being" verb, like "am." In Italian, the verb for "to have" is often used instead. For example, instead of saying "I am 20 years old," a Italian-speaker would say "I have 20 years." This is similar for many other traits, such as hunger ("I have hunger"). There's a long list of words that use this construction. Keep an eye out for the Italian verb for "to have" conjugations in your studies!

ITALIAN HAS FEWER PREPOSITIONS

English relies heavily on prepositions to provide details in discussions because we focus on describing where something is oriented in time and space. For example, "The cat is sitting on top of the chair, and the dog is sleeping under it." While Italian certainly has prepositions, there are fewer of them in Italian than there are in English. This can cause some ambiguity for English speakers who are accustomed to more precise descriptions of location. A single Italian preposition can be used for several different prepositions that we use in English, and it may take a while to learn when you can use a particular preposition. Learning exactly what is meant by these prepositions can be challenging for English speakers, but having fewer words to choose from can also make it much easier to remember all of them.

PRONOUNS CAN OFTEN BE OMITTED

In English, forming a proper sentence means always providing a subject (with commands being the only exception). Italian lets you assume what is the logical subject from context. For example, to talk about your age you would say "have 20 years," and it is implied that "I" is the subject. This will definitely take a little time to get used to, but ultimately, it can make things a lot easier.

EMPHASIS IS MOVED TO THE END OF THE SENTENCE

One of the most frustrating aspects to learn as an English speaker is that Italian does not have the same kinds of rules dictating sentence structure. It is far more fluid and changeable than English, which means trying to understand a native speaker can be almost painful in the beginning. Where English relies on words for emphasis, Italian does it through restructuring the sentence. The thing that a speaker wants to emphasis goes to the end of the sentence, which means the structure changes on the point the speaker is trying to make.

SPELLING IS MUCH EASIER IN ITALIAN

Unlike English, which is filled with homonyms and irregular spelling rules, Italian spelling is very intuitive and usually phonetic. Once you know the sounds that each letter makes, you'll always be able to spell the word just by sounding it out. There are only five vowels in Italian, and they always make the same sounds. Even though vowels may have accents added for emphasis, even those are easy to master if you know how the word is pronounced. Do be aware that the sounds you are familiar with for each letter could be different.

CHAPTER ONE: READING AND PRONOUNCIATION

Italian is based on a twenty-one-letter alphabet. Though you will come across the letters J, K, W, X, and Y in your travels, you will notice that these letters only appear in words borrowed from other languages (whiskey and jolly, to name a few). English and Italian share many cognate words that are spelled similarly in the two languages. Some of these words are modern and are related to recent technology: telefono, calcolatrice, macchina. You will recognize many words related to musical terminology (alto, soprano, trombone) and to cuisine as well (al dente, biscotti, pepperoni). The Italian sound system will be familiar to most English-speakers: almost all of the sounds you'll hear exist in English. You might notice some slight differences, particularly with the vowel sounds, but there's nothing to stop you having a go and being understood. Standard Italian pronunciation is given in this book – the same form that's used in education and the media.

symbol	english equivalent	italian example
a	father	*pane*
e	red	*letto*
ee	bee	*vino*
o	pot	*molo*
oo	took	*frutta*

VOWEL SOUNDS

Vowel sounds are generally shorter than English equivalents. They also tend not to run together to form vowel sound combinations (diphthongs), though it can often sound that way to English-speakers. The following table presents four vowel sounds that roughly correspond to diphthongs in English:

symbol	english equivalent	italian example
ay	say	*vorrei*
ai	aisle	*mai*
oy	boy	*poi*
ow	cow	*ciao/au*

CONSONANT SOUNDS

symbol	english equivalent	italian example
b	big	*bello*
ch	chilli	*centro*
d	din	*denaro*
dz	lids	*mezzo/zaino*
f	fun	*fare*
g	go	*gomma*
j	jam	*cugino*
k	kick	*cambio/quanto*
l	loud	*linea*
ly	million	*figlia*
m	man	*madre*
n	no	*numero*
ny	canyon	*bagno*
p	pig	*pronto*
r	run (but stronger and rolled)	*ristorante*
s	so	*sera*
sh	show	*shopping*
t	tin	*teatro*
ts	hits	*grazie/sicurezza*
v	van	*viaggio*
w	win	*uomo*
y	yes	*italiano*
z	zoo	*casa*

DOUBLE CONSONANTS

Native speakers of English often have great difficulty in mastering the pronunciation of double consonants in Italian. One rule to keep in mind in learning correct pronunciation is that every letter in an Italian word must be pronounced. With this in mind, it logically follows that double consonants are pronounced longer than single consonants:

sano (pronounced sa-no)	sanno (pronounced san-no)
lego (pronounced le-go)	leggo (pronounced leg-go)
fata (pronounced fa-ta)	fatta (pronounced fat-ta)
papa (pronounced pa-pa)	pappa (pronounced pap-pa)

The double s in Italian has a different pronunciation than the singles:

casa (here the **s** is pronounced as in the English hose)

cassa (here the **ss** is pronounced as in the English house)

ACCENT/STRESS

Many words are pronounced with the stress on the third-to-last or fourth-to-last syllable. There is no rule governing the placement of the stress in these cases. As you develop an ear for the language you will learn which pronunciation sounds better.

facile	**portabile**	**aspettano**
FAH-chee-leh	pohr-TAH-bee-leh	ah-SPEHT-tah-noh

INTRODUCTION TO NOUNS

Singular Nouns

Italian nouns almost always end in a vowel. Those that don't are usually words borrowed from other languages. Generally speaking, nouns that end in –o are masculine, and words that end in –a are feminine. Nouns ending in –e can be either masculine or feminine. The gender of these nouns must be learned.

libro (masculine)	LEE-broh
casa (feminine)	KAH-zah
madre (feminine)	MAH-dray
padre (masculine)	PAH-dray

KEYNOTE

When learning a foreign language, you will learn convenient grammatical rules to help you along. It is important to be open- minded. For every rule, there's bound to be an exception. The rules presented here are very basic—you will notice exceptions to these rules throughout the book.

PLURAL NOUNS

Masculine nouns that end in –o form the plural by changing the –o into an –i. Feminine nouns that end in –a form the plural by changing the –o into an –e. Both masculine and feminine nouns that end in –e form the plural by changing the –e into an –i. Here are some examples:

libro (LEE-broh)	changes to	libri (LEE-bree)
amico (ah-MEE-koh)	changes to	amici (ah-MEE-chee)
gatto (GAHT-toh)	changes to	gatti (GAHT-tee)
sorella (soh-REHL-lah)	changes to	sorelle (soh-REHL-leh)
casa (KAH-zah)	changes to	case (KAH-zeh)
tazza (TAHTS-sah)	changes to	tazze (TAHTS-seh)
dottore (doht-TOH-ray)	changes to	dottori (doht-TOH-ree)
stazione (stahts-see-YOH-nay)	changes to	stazioni (stahts-see- YOH-nee)
cane (KAH-neh)	changes to	cani (KAH-nee)

DEFINITE AND INDEFINITE ARTICLES

Nouns often are accompanied by a definite article (corresponds to "the" in English). There are seven definite articles in Italian: il, lo, l', la (singular); i, gli, le (plural). There are four indefinite articles (corresponding to "a" or "an" in English)—un, uno, un', and una are all used before singular nouns. Which definite or indefinite article you choose depends on the number (singular or plural), the gender (masculine or feminine), and the first letter of the word in question.

KEYNOTES

Italian articles are sometimes difficult to master, because they have to agree with the noun they modify and don't always correspond to articles in other languages. As a general rule, there is almost always an article in front of a noun in Italian, except when indicating a profession. In Italian, "I am a professor" is Sono professore.

INDEFINITE ARTICLES

The indefinite articles un and uno are used for masculine nouns, and un' and una are used for feminine nouns. We must look at the first letter of the word in order to come up with the correct form of the indefinite article.

If the first letter:

of the noun is . . .	Masculine	Feminine
. . . a consonant	un ragazzo	una casa
	oon rah-GAHTS-so	oo-nah KAH-zah
. . . a vowel	un amico	un'amica
	oon ah-MEE-koh	oon-ah-MEE-kah
. . . s + consonant	uno stadio	una studentessa
	oo-noh STAH-dee-yoh	oo-nah stoo-dehn-TESS-ah
. . . z	uno zero	una zebra
	oo-noh DSEH-roh	oo-nah DSAY-brah

DEFINITE ARTICLES

There are seven forms of the definite article in Italian—il, l', lo, i, gli (masculine), and la, l', le (feminine).

If the word is feminine, and the first

letter of the word is . . .	Singular	Plural
. . . a consonant	la ragazza	le ragazze
	lah rah-GAHTS-sah	leh rah-GAHTS-seh
. . . a vowel	l'amica	le amiche
	Lah-MEE-kah	leh ah-MEE-keh
. . . a consonant	il libro	i libri
	eel LEE-broh	ee LEE-bree
. . . a vowel	l'amico	gli amici
	lah-MEE-koh	lyee ah-MEE-chee
. . . z	lo zero	gli zeri
	loh DSEH-roh	lyee DSEH-ree
. . . an s + a	lo studente	gli studenti

loh stoo-DEHN-teh   lyee stoo-DEHN-tee

COGNATES

Learning Italian can be made easier by developing an ability to recognize cognates—words that look like English words and have a meaning similar to those words. There are some patterns to recognize and follow in order to sharpen your ability to recognize and use cognates.

Nouns that end in –ia in Italian usually end in –y in English.

spelling equivalents

Italian word		English equivalent
psicologia	psee-koh-loh-JEE-yah	psychology
autonomia	ou-toh-noh-MEE-yah	autonomy

Nouns that end in –ica in Italian usually end in –ic(s) in English.

Spelling Equivalents

Italian word		English equivalent
fisica	FEE-zee-kah	physics
musica	MOO-zee-kah	music

Nouns that end in –tà in Italian usually end in –ty in English.

Spelling Equivalents

Italian word		English equivalent
Università	oo-nee-vehr-see-TAH	university
Autorità	ahw-toh-ree-TAH	authority

Nouns that end in –ista in Italian usually end in –ist in English.

Spelling Equivalents

Italian word		English equivalent
dentista	dehn-TEES-tah	dentist
artista	ahr-TEES-tah	artist

177

Nouns that end in –ario in Italian usually end in –ary in English.

Spelling Equivalents

Italian word		English equivalent
diario	dee-AH-ree-oh	diary
dizionario	deet-see-oh-NAH-ree-yoh	dictionary

Nouns that end in –ore in Italian usually end in –or in English.

Spelling Equivalents

Italian word		English equivalent
professore	proh-fess-SOHR-ray	professor
attore	aht-TOHR-ray	actor

Nouns that end in –ione in Italian usually end in –ion in English.

Spelling Equivalents

Italian word		English equivalent
stazione	stahts-see-YOH-nay	station
religione	reh-lee-JOH-nay	religion

Nouns that end in –za in Italian usually end in –ce in English.

Spelling Equivalents

Italian word		English equivalent
importanza	vveem-pohr-TAHNZ-ah	importance
indipendenza	een-dee-pehn-DEHNZ-ah	independence

Adjectives ending in –ale in Italian usually end in –al in English.

Spelling Equivalents

Italian word		English equivalent
speciale	speh-CHAH-lay	special
locale	loh-KAH-lay	local

178

Adjectives ending in –oso usually end in –ous in English.

Spelling Equivalents

Italian word		English equivalent
religioso	reh-lee-JOH-soh	religious
amoroso	ah-mohr-OH-soh	amorous

FALSE FRIENDS

The following section will help you to avoid many common mistakes. False friends are words that look alike but have different meanings. There are numerous false friends in Italian and English!

KEYNOTE

There are thousands of cognates between Italian and English, but some of them can be false friends! Make sure you know the true meaning of a word before working it into your spoken language.

FALSE FRIENDS

Addizione ≠ addiction	addizione = sum
ahd-deets-YOH-nay	
annoiato ≠ annoyed	annoiato = bored
ahn-noy-YAH-toh	
apprendere ≠ to apprehend	apprendere = to learn
ahp-PREHN-deh-ray	
argomento ≠ argument	argomento = subject
ahr-goh-MEHN-toh	
assistere ≠ assist	ssistere = to attend
ahs-SEES-teh-ray	
asso ≠ ass	asso = ace
ahss-soh	
attendere ≠ attend	attendere = to wait
aht-TEHN-deh-ray	
attualmente ≠ actually	attualmente = currently
aht-too-ahl-MEHN-tay	
baldo ≠ bald	baldo = courageous
BAHL-doh	

Bravo ≠ brave   bravo = good/clever

BRAH-voh

Camera ≠ camera   camera = room

KAH-meh-rah

Cantina ≠ canteen   cantina = cellar

kahn-TEE-nah

caldo ≠ cold   caldo = hot

KAHL-doh

collegio ≠ college   collegio = boarding school

kohl-LEH-jee-yoh

comprensivo ≠ comprehensive   comprensivo = understanding

kohm-prehn-SEE-voh

concorrenza ≠ concurrence   concorrenza = competition

kohn-kohr-REHN-Zah

cocomero ≠ cucumber   cocomero = watermelon

koh-KOH-meh-roh

delusion ≠ delusion   delusione = disappointment

deh-looz-YOH-nay

disgrazia ≠ disgrace   disgrazia =misfortune

dees-GRAHTS-see-yah

editore = editor   editore = publisher

eh-dee-TOH-ray

educato ≠ educated   educato = polite

eh-doo-KAH-toh

eventualmente ≠ eventually   eventualmente = possibly, if necessary

eh-vehn-too-ahl-MEHN-tay

fabbrica ≠ fabric   fabbrica = factory

FAHB-bree-kah

Fattoria ≠ factory   fattoria = farm

faht-toh-REE-yah

inabitato ≠ inhabited   inabitato = uninhabited

een-ah-bee-TAH-toh

genitore ≠ janitor   genitore = parent
jeh-nee-TOH-ray

parente ≠ parent   parente = relative
pah-REHN-tay

largo ≠ large   largo = wide
LAHR-goh

Lettura ≠ lecture   lettura = reading
leht-TOO-rah

libreria ≠ library   libreria = bookstore
lee-breh-REE-yah

licenziare ≠ license   licenziare = to dismiss, to fire
lee-chenz-YAH-ray

lussuria ≠ luxury   lussuria = lust
loos-soo-REE-yah

magazzino ≠ magazine   magazzino = warehouse
mah-gahts-SEE-noh

messa ≠ mess   messa = mass
MEHSS-sah

Morbid ≠ morbid   morbido = soft
MOHR-bee-doh

Notizia ≠ notice   notizia = news
noh-TEETS-ee-yah

CHAPTER TWO: PRESENTATION AND GREETINGS

Buongiorno. Come sta? (Boo-on-JOR-no CO-meh stah):

Good morning. How are you?

In Italian there are two different ways of addressing people: formally and informally. To address someone formally, use the Lei form; to address someone informally, use the tu form. So, for example, the simple question "How are you?" has two possible translations: the formal Come sta (Lei)?, and the informal Come stai (tu)? The Lei form is required with almost every person over age sixteen, unless you are speaking to a family member or a close friend. Using Lei is a form of respect, but sometimes it may create a certain distance between speakers. On the other hand, some people may be offended when addressed in the tu form. To be on the safe side, start by addressing everyone with the Lei form until the person you are talking to says: Diamoci del tu (let's use the tu form), which gives you permission to use the familiar form. Students are required to use the Lei form with all their teachers/ professors, at all levels. After grade five, teachers start to address students in the polite form as well. When calling out names, teachers use a student's last name, not first name. Even among work colleagues, it is common to use the Lei form. Italians often say that even they have trouble with the use of tu and Lei/voi. Usually, but not always, they use tu with someone with whom they're on a first-name basis. In certain parts of Italy, and espe- cially in the south, the Lei form is sometimes replaced by the voi form when addressing a person formally. So,

"How are you, Mr. Smith?" can be translated as

Come state (voi), Signor Smith?

The voi form has a degree of formality that is even greater than Lei.The question of for- mality is actually easier if you're not Italian, because you can just use Lei with everyone over sixteen until you're told to say tu.

Come sta, signor Carli?

How are you, Mr. Carli?

CO-meh stah seen-YOR CAHR-lee

Come stai, amico mio?

How are you, my friend?

CO-meh STAH-ee ah-MEE-coh MEE-oh

DOTTOR RISI, BUONGIORNO. (DOT-TOR REE-ZEE BOO-ON- JOR-NO):

DR. RISI, GOOD MORNING.

Italians love to be addressed by their titles. Although in America we rarely use titles before last names (preferring instead to use the simple Mr./Mrs./Miss), Italians always use the title of their profession before their last name. Some of the most common titles are: avvocato, inge- gnere, dottore, professore, ragioniere, etc. So, to address Mr. Smith who is a lawyer, one would say: Buongiorno, avvocato (Smith). Remember that in Italy, a university degree entitles the holder to be called dot- tore. Furthermore, certain high school diplomas (ragioniere, geometra, perito agrario) will be enough to guarantee someone a title.

Most titles also have equivalent female forms; for example, a female doctor is a dottoressa and a female professor is a professoressa. However, for professions which were once male dominated, like avvo- cato, ingegnere, ministro, presidente, etc., the tendency today is to use the male title for women as well. For example, if Mrs. Rossi is a lawyer or a doctor, one could say: Buongiorno, avvocato Rossi! or Buongiorno, dottor Rossi!, omitting the use of the feminine form of the title. For titles that end in an e, the final e is dropped before the last name: l'ingegner Bianchi, whether male or female.

Arrivederla, Professoressa Binni.

Good-bye, Professor Binni.

Ar-ree-veh-DAIR-lah pro-fes-

so-RES-sah BEEN-nee

Ecco l'avvocato Maria Lima.

Here is the lawyer Maria Lima.

EC-co lahv-vo-CAH-toh Mah-REE-ah

LI-mah

BUONGIORNO, SIGNORA! (BOO-ON-JOR-NO SEEN-YO-RAH):

GOOD MORNING, MA'AM!

Buongiorno, or buon giorno, is one of the most common forms of salu- tation in Italy. It can be used both formally and informally with strang- ers or with friends, while entering a coffee shop, in a doctor's office, or while walking in the streets. For example, Italian shopkeepers expect shoppers to say Buongiorno upon entering their shop. As with 'morn- ing in English, the salutation can sometimes be shortened to simply 'giorno or 'ngiorno, followed by a nod. Other times, it is necessary to add a title to the salutation: Buongiorno, professore (Good morning, Professor), Buongiorno, dottore (Good morning, Doctor), Buongiorno, signora (Good morning, Ma'am). You seldom hear Buongiorno, signore

(Good morning, Sir) or Buongiorno, signorina (Good morning, Miss). To avoid embarrassment, when greeting a woman it is better to just say Buongiorno! and not Buongiorno, signora/signorina (Good morning, Ma'am/Miss). It is normal to greet people on the street or on the bus with Buon- giorno! However, when greeting a group of people it is not necessary to say buongiorno to each individual separately. One can just say Buongiorno a tutti (Good morning to all).

Buongiorno, Signor Rossi!

Good morning, Mr. Rossi!

Boo-on-JOR-no seen-YOR ROH-SEE

Buongiorno a tutti!

Good morning to all!

Boo-on-JOR-no ah TOOT-tee

Buona giornata!

Have a nice day!

Boo-OH-nah jor-NAH-tah

BUONA NOTTE! (BOO-OH-NAH NOT-TEH):

GOOD NIGHT!

When to switch from buongiorno to buon pomeriggio (good after- noon), then to buonasera (good evening) and to buonanotte (good night) is a question to which each Italian will give his/her own rule, as the use depends on a personal feeling of time, on the season, etc. Buongiorno is used for most of the day, as even in the afternoon it is preferred to buon pomeriggio. Even though some native Italians would use buongiorno as late as 6:00 P.M., it is probably best to not use this greeting after 5:00 P.M., when stores often reopen for their evening hours. Buonasera is used for both hello and good-bye in the evening, but it's different from buona serata, which is used when someone is leav- ing for the evening, perhaps to go to a movie.

Buona notte is the expression used when leaving people with whom you have spent the evening or when you know explicitly that a person is going to bed or back home for good.

Buona sera, avvocato.

Good evening, (lawyer).

Boo-OH-nah SEH-rah Ahv-vo-

CAH-toh

Buona serata!

Have a nice evening!

Boo-OH-nah seh-RAH-tah

Buona notte, Carlo!

Good night, Carlo!

Boo-OH-nah NOT-teh CAR-loh

Ciao a tutti! (CHAH-oh ah TOOT-tee):

Hello, everybody!

There is also a difference in formality in the use of the proper greeting. As discussed above, buongiorno can be used as a formal or informal way of greeting someone. Italians also use ciao or salve for informal greetings. When greeting friends, they may shake hands or give each other a kiss on each cheek. This is very common between men as well as women. Ciao, from the old Venetian dialect meaning "your slave"/"at your service," is a very common form of salutation, but it can be used only informally. It is usually reserved for greeting family members and close friends—for people one knows well. Ciao should absolutely not be used with people whom you do not know well, or with older people to whom you want to show respect; the use of ciao might offend them.

184

However, it is acceptable to use it in greeting an older family member: Ciao, nonno (Hello, grandpa), Ciao, zia (Hi, aunt). An interesting use of ciao is the title of the movie Ciao, professore (the cor- rect form is Buongiorno, professore). The title is meant to suggest that the younger generation is much more informal. Ciao is also used as a way to say good-bye: Ciao, ragazzi! (Good- bye, guys!) Salve is another informal way of greeting people, although less common than ciao. It can be used to express hi or hello but not good-bye. Some native speakers use this salutation when addressing someone with whom they are unsure whether to use the tu or the Lei form. In actuality, salve should be used with people whom you know quite well and with whom you should use the tu form: Salve, come stai? (Hi, how are you?) At times, however, you may hear: Salve, come sta? In such instances, if not sure whether to be formal or informal in your response, always use the more polite expression Buongiorno, come sta?

Ciao, ragazzi.

Hi/Bye, guys.

CHAH-oh rah-GAHT-tsee

Ciao, Maria!

Hi/Bye, Maria!

CHAH-oh Mah-REE-ah

Ciao, ragazze!

Hi/Bye, girls!

CHAH-oh rah-GAHT-tseh

Salve, Mario.

Hello, Mario.

SAHL-veh MAH-ree-oh

ARRIVEDERCI! (AHR-REE-VEH-DAIR-CHEE):

GOOD-BYE!

The word arrivederci (literally, 'Til we see each other again") has the meaning of good-bye. Similar to ciao, arrivederci is colloquially taking the place of the formal arrivederLa, especially when saying good-bye to a group of people. While on the phone, Italians may also use Arrisentirci! (Literally, 'Til we hear each other again! / Until next time! / Goodbye for now!) As a form of salutation, in movies or written documents, Italians may use the word addio, which is meant as a more permanent or final good-bye. In spoken language, addio is considered archaic.

Arrivederci a tutti!

Good-bye to all!

Ahr-ree-veh-DAIR-chee ah TOOT-tee

ArrivederLa, ingegnere.

Good-bye, (engineer).

Ahr-ree-veh-DAIR-lah

in-jeh-NYEH-reh

185

Bye-bye.

Good-bye.

Bye-bye

Addio per sempre!

Good-bye forever!

Ahd-DEE-oh pair SEHM-preh

A PRESTO! (AH PREH-STO):

SEE YOU SOON!

Other forms of salutation meaning "good-bye" are: A domani!, Ci vediamo!, A presto! These expressions are not very formal and are nor- mally used with people one knows well. A domani! and Ci vediamo! are usually used if you already know you are going to meet the person somewhere very soon or if you usually meet him/her somewhere. A presto! is, instead, very vague in regard to the time frame. Note that A presto! is often used to end a letter or an e-mail message. In addition, it is quite common to use the informal closing expressions arrisentirci or ci sentiamo domani/più tardi ('til later/tomorrow). The latter expres- sion could also be used in Internet chat rooms, when the exchanges occur frequently and regularly.

Other forms of good-bye salutation are:

A dopo!

See you later!

Ah DOH-po

Ci vediamo tra poco!

See you in a while!

Chee veh-dee-AH-mo trah PO-co

Stammi bene!

Keep well!

STAHM-mee BEH-neh

Ciao ciao!

Good-bye!

CHAH-oo CHAH-oo

Alla prossima!

'Til the next time!

AHL-lah PROS-see-mah

COME VA, CARLO? (CO-MEH VAH CAHR-LO):

HOW'S IT GOING, CARLO?

As we have seen previously, to ask someone the question "How are you?" use Come sta? in a polite setting and Come stai? in an informal setting. The expression Come va?, even though very colloquial, could be used in both formal and informal settings: Come va, Carlo? or Come va, professore? In a very informal and colloquial setting, Italians will often use the impersonal pronoun si before va: Come si va, Carlo? or Come si va, professore?

Come sta, signora Lavezzi?

How are you, Mrs. Lavezzi?

CO-meh stah seen-YO-rah

Lah-VETS-see

Come vanno le cose?

How are things going?

CO-meh VAHN-no leh CO-seh

Come si va, ragazzi?

How's it going, guys?

CO-meh see vah rah-GAHTS-tsee

LE PRESENTO IL DOTTOR CARLI. (LEH PREH-ZEN-TOH EEL DOT-TOR CAHR-LEE):

THIS IS DR. CARLI.

When introducing people, depending on the situation, one needs to be careful in using the Lei or tu form. Therefore, use Le presento il dottor Carli for formal introductions and Ti presento Mario for infor- mal introductions. When introducing a person to more than one individual, Vi presento is used in both formal and informal situations: Vi presento il professor Lavia or Vi presento Mario. In any situation, it is also acceptable to introduce someone without using a form of the verb presentare at all; just use Il professor Dini, or Carlo. The entire action is accompanied by a handshake (a firm handshake), and it is followed by the formal/informal Piacere (Nice to meet you.), which could be replaced by a more wordy formal response: Piacere di fare la Sua conoscenza!/Piacere della conoscenza!/Molto lieto! (masc.) / Molto lieta! (fem.) In formal situations, at the end of a conversation (when people are about to go their separate ways), one would reiterate, accompanied with the handshake: Piacere!/Piacere della conoscenza!/Piacere di aver fatto la Sua conoscenza! A response to the sayings above is Il piacere è mio! (The pleasure is mine!) These expressions, however, are becom- ing more unusual. At times, among young people in very informal situations today, the word piacere may not even be used with introductions. In cases when you may need to make your own introduction, depending on the context, you would use: Mi chiamo Luigi/Luigi Rossi/ Rossi. If it is the other person who is presenting himself/herself first, just follow his/her presentation style.

Marco Calvi. Piacere. Marco Calvi.

Nice to meet you.

MAHR-co CAL-vee peeah-CHEH-reh

Mamma e papà, vi presento il

Mom and Dad, I would like to

mio amico Luigi.

introduce to you my friend Luigi.

MAHM-mah eh pah-PAH vee

preh-ZEN-toh eel MEE-oh

ah-MEE-co Loo-EE-gee

Franco, Carlo. Carlo, Franco.

Franco, this is Carlo. Carlo, this is

FRAHN-co CAHR-lo CAHR-lo

Franco.

FRAHN-co

Dottore, Le presento i miei

Doctor, I would like to introduce you

genitori.

to my parents.

Dot-TOH-reh Leh preh-ZEN-toh

ee mee-AY jeh-nee-TOH-ree

Benvenuto! (Behn-veh-NOO-toh):

Welcome!

Italians are well known for making you feel welcome and part of their home. If someone is meeting you at the airport in Italy, you will be welcomed with Benvenuto!/Benvenuta in Italia. If you are a guest in someone's home, you will be welcomed with Benvenuto/Benvenuta nella nostra casa! (Welcome to our home!)

CHAPTER THREE: KNOWING PEOPLE AND NATIONALITY

BASICS

Enlish	Italian Equivalent
Yes.	Sì.

No	No.	
Please.	Per favore.	per fa·vo·re
Thank you (very much).	Grazie (mille).	gra·tsye (mee·le)
You're welcome.	Prego.	
pre·go		
Sorry.	Mi dispiace.	mee dees·pya·che
Excuse me. (for attention or apology) Mi scusi.		mee skoo·zee
Scusami.	skoo·za·mee	
Excuse me. (when squeezing past someone) Permesso.		per·me·so

GREETINGS

Although ciao is a common greeting, it's best not to use it when addressing strangers. Also note that in Italy the word buonasera (good evening) may be heard any time from early afternoon onwards.

English	Italian Equivalent	pronounciation
Hello	Buongiorno / Salve	bwon·jor·no / sal·ve
Hi	Ciao	chow
Good day	Buongiorno	bwon·jor·no
Good morning	Buongiorno	bwon·jor·no
Good afternoon	Buongiorno	bwon·jor·no
Good evening	Buonasera	bwo·na·se·ra
Good night	Buonanotte	bwo·na·no·te
See you	Ci vediamo	chee ve·dya·mo
See you late	A più tardi	a pyoo tar·dee
Goodbye	Arrivederci	a·ree·ve·der·chee
Bye	Ciao	inf chow
How are you?	Come sta?	ko·me sta
Good, thanks	Bene, grazie	be·ne gra·tsye
And you?	E Lei / tu?	e lay / too
What's your name?	Come si chiama?	pol ko·me see kya·ma
My name is...	Mi chiamo ...	mee kya·mo ...
I'd like to introduce you to...	Le/Ti presento ...	le/tee pre·zen·to ...

189

I'm pleased to meet you	Piacere	pya·che·re

GETTING FRIENDLY

Italian has two forms for the singular 'you'. With family, friends, children or peers use the informal form tu. When addressing strangers, older people, or people whom you've just met, use the polite form Lei. When your newly-made friends feel it's time to swap to the more informal forms they might suggest:

Let's use the tu form.

Diamoci del tu.

TITLES & ADDRESSING PEOPLE

i titoli & le maniere di presentarsi Italians will greatly appreciate your efforts to try to speak their language and you'll leave an even better impression if you use the correct titles and forms of address. So when in Rome ...

Mr/Sir	Signore	see·nyo·re
Mrs/Madam	Signora	see·nyo·ra
Miss/Ms	Signorina	see·nyo·ree·na
Doctor	Dottore	do·to·re
Professor	Professore	pro·fe·so·re
Director	Direttore	dee·re·to·re

MAKING CONVERSATION

Nice weather, isn't it?

Fa bel tempo, no?

fa bel tem·po no

How did (Juventus) go?

Cos'ha fatto (la Juve)?

ko·za fa·to (la yoo·ve)

Do you live here?

Lei è di qui?

lay e dee kwee

Where are you going?

Dove va/vai?

do·ve va/vai

What are you doing?

Che fa/fai?

ke fa/fai

Are you waiting (for a bus)?

Aspetta/Aspetti (un autobus)?

as·pe·ta/as·pe·tee

What's this called?

Come si chiama questo?

ko·me see kya·ma kwe·sto

That's (beautiful), isn't it!

È (bello/a), no?

m/f e (be·lo/a) no

This is my son.

Le/Ti presento mio figlio

le/tee pre·zen·to mee·o fee·lyo

This is my daughter

Le/Ti presento mia figlia.

le/tee pre·zen·to mee·a fee·lya

This is my friend.

Le/Ti presento il mio amico

le/tee pre·zen·to eel mee·o a·mee·ko

191

LOCAL TALK

English	Italian Equivalent	Pronounciation
Hey!	Uei!	
What's up?	Cosa mi racconta?	ko·za mee ra·kon·ta
What's the matter?	Cosa c'è?	ko·za che
Everything OK?	Tutto a posto?	too·ta pos·to
It's/I'm OK.	Va/Sto bene	va/sto be·ne
Great!	Fantastico!	fan·tas·tee·ko
No problem	Non c'è problema	non che pro·ble·ma
Sure.	Certo.	cher·to
Maybe.	Forse.	for·se
No way!	Assolutamente no!	a·so·loo·ta·men·te no
I'm here ...	Sono qui ...	so·no kwee ...
for a holiday	in vacanza	een va·kan·tsa
on business	per affari	per a·fa·ree
to study	per motivi di studio	per mo·tee·vee dee stoo·dyo
with my family	con la mia famiglia	kon la mee·a fa·mee·lya
with my partner	con il mio compagno	kon eel mee·o kom·pa·nyo

don't mention the war

Italians are great communicators so you shouldn't have too much trouble striking up a conversation. Talking about the Mafia, Mussolini or the Vatican, however, could see the conversation come to a premature halt. Try topics such as Italian architecture, films, food and soccer.

NATIONALITIES

English	Italian Equivalent	Pronounciation
Where are you from?	Da dove viene/vieni?	da do·ve vye·ne/vye·nee
I'm from Singapore	Vengo da Singapore	ven·go da seen·ga·po·re
I'm from ...	Vengo ...	ven·go ...
From England	dall'Inghilterra	da·leen·geel·te·ra

192

New Zealand	dalla Nuova Zelanda	da·la nwo·va ze·lan·da
Switzerland	dalla Svizzera	da·la zvee·tse·ra
from US	dagli Stati Uniti	da·lyee sta·tee oo·nee·tee

AGE

How old ...?	Quanti anni ...?	kwan·tee a·nee ...
is your son	ha Suo/tuo figlio	a soo·o/too·o fee·lyo
is your daughter	ha Sua/tua figlia	a soo·a/too·a fee·lya
How old are you?	Quanti anni ha/hai?	kwan·tee a·nee a/ai
I'm (25) years old.	Ho (venticinque) anni	o(ven·tee·cheen·kwe) a·nee
He's/She's ... years old	Ha ... anni	a ... a·nee

OCCUPATIONS & STUDIES

What's your occupation?	Che lavoro fa/fai?	ke la·vo·ro fa/fai
I'm a/an ...	Sono ...	so·no ...
manual worker	manovale	ma·no·va·le
office worker	impiegato/a	eem·pye·ga·to/a
tradesperson	operaio/a	o·pe·ra·yo/a
I work in ...	Lavoro nel campo ...	la·vo·ro nel kam·po ...

FAMILY

Do you have (children)?
Ha/Hai (bambini)?
a/ai (bam·bee·nee)

I have (a partner)
Ho (un/una compagno/a)
o (oon/oo·na kom·pa·nyo/a)

This is (my mother)

Le/Ti presento (mia madre)

le/tee pre·zen·to (mee·a ma·dre)

in the mouth of the wolf

An Italian will typically wish you good luck with the expression In bocca al lupo!, meaning 'In the mouth of the wolf!'. Make sure your answer is Crepi! (Die!) to ward off bad luck.

Break a leg!   In bocca al lupo!   een bo·ka·loo·po

Are you married?   È sposato?   e spo·za·to

Do you live with (your family)?

Abita con (la Sua famiglia)?

a·bee·ta kon (la soo·a fa·mee·lya)

Abiti con (la tua famiglia)?

inf a·bee·tee kon (la too·a fa·mee·lya)

I live with (my parents).

Abito con (i miei genitori)

a·bee·to kon (ee myay je·nee·to·ree)

I live with someone.

Convivo.

kon·vee·vo

I'm separated.

Sono separato/a.

so·no se·pa·ra·to/a

I'm married.

Sono sposato.

so·no spo·za·to

I'm married.

Sono sposata.

so·no spo·za·ta

I'm single.

Sono single.

so·no sin·gle

body language Italians are emotionally demonstrative so expect to see lots of cheek kissing among acquaintances, embraces between men who are good friends and lingering handshakes. Italian men may walk along arm-in-arm too, as may Italian women. Pushing and shoving in busy places is not considered rude, so don't be offended by it. Try to hold your ground amidst the scrimmage. If you don't want to tread on any toes, be aware that respectful behaviour is expected in churches. Women should ideally cover their heads and avoid exposing too much flesh – wearing shorts or skimpy tops is considered disrespectful.

FAREWELLS

Tomorrow is my last day here.

Domani è il mio ultimo giorno qui.

do·ma·nee e eel mee·o ool·tee·mo jor·no kwee

What's your address?

Qual'è il tuo indirizzo?

kwa·le eel too·o een·dee·ree·tso

What's your email address?

Qual'è il tuo indirizzo di email?

kwa·le eel too·o een·dee·ree·tso dee e·mayl

Here's my address.

Ecco il mio indirizzo.

e·ko eel mee·o een·dee·ree·tso

Here's my email address.

 Ecco il mio indirizzo di email.

e·ko eel mee·o een·dee·ree·tso dee e·mayl

195

Here's my ...

Ecco il mio ...

e·ko eel mee·o ...

What's your ...?

Qual'è il tuo ...?

kwa·le eel too·o ...

fax number

numero di fax

noo·me·ro dee faks

mobile number

numero di cellulare

noo·me·ro dee che·loo·la·re

work number

numero di lavoro

noo·me·ro dee la·vo·ro

If you ever visit

Caso mai venissi

ka·zo mai ve·nee·see een

(Scotland) ...

in (Scozia)....

(sko·tsya) ...

come and visit us

vieni a trovarci

vye·ne a tro·var·chee

you can stay with me

puoi stare da me

pwoy sta·re da me

It's been great meeting you.

È stato veramente un

e sta·to ve·ra·men·te oon

piacere conoscerti.

pya·che·re ko·no·sher·tee

Keep in touch!

Teniamoci in contatto!

te·nya·mo·chee een kon·ta·to

CHAPTER FOUR: ITALIAN FOR BUSINESS

Though you will find that many Italians are proficient in English, you will certainly gain the respect of your Italian colleagues by demonstrating a proficiency of your hosts' language. If you're traveling to Italy for business, this chapter will help you make a good impression on your Italian colleagues!

Jobs and Professions Whatever your profession, a knowledge of a wide variety of professions and jobs can only enhance your business interactions.

Accountant	il contabile	eel kohn-TAH-bee-leh
Apprentice	l'apprendista	lahp-prehn-DEES-tah
Banker	il banchiere	eel ban-KYEH-reh
Bank Teller	il cassiere	eel kahs-SYEH-reh
Biologist	il biologo	eel bee-OH-loh-goh
Broker	il mediatore	eel meh-dee-ah-TOH-reh
Cashier	la cassiera	lah kahs-SYEH-rah
Civil Servant	un impiegato dello stato	oon eem-pyeh-GAH-toh dehl-loh stah-toh
Dentist	il dentista eel	dehn-TEES-tah
Detective	l'investigatore	leen-vehs-tee-gah-TOH-ray
Doctor	il dottore	eel doht-TOH-ray
Economist	l'economista	leh-koh-noh-MEES-tah
Employee	l'impiegato	leem-pyeh-GAH-toh
Engineer	l'ingegnere	leen-jen-YEH-ray
Judge	il giudice	eel JOO-dee-cheh
Journalist	il giornalista	eel johr-nah-LEES-tah
Lawyer	l'avvocato	lahv-voh-KAH-toh
Manager	il dirigente/il manager	eel dee-ree-JEHN-tay
Notary	il notaio	eel noh-TEYE-oh
Nurse	l'infermiera	leen-fehrm-YEH-rah
Pharmacist	il farmacista	eel fahr-mah-CHEES-tah
Pilot	il pilota	eel pee-LOH-tah
Police officer	il polizotto	eel poh-leets-OHT-toh

President	il presidente	eel preh-zee-DEHN-tay
Receptionist	la receptionist	lah receptionist
Researcher	il ricercatore	eel ree-chehr-kah-TOH-ray
Scientist	lo scienzato	loh she-ehn-TSAH-toh
Secretary	la segretaria	lah seh-greh-TAH-ree-ah
Soldier	il soldato	eel sohl-DAH-toh
Stockbroker	l'agente di cambio	lah-JEHN-tay dee kahm-byoh
Technician	il tecnico	eel TEHK-nee-koh
Writer	lo scrittore	loh skree-TOH-ray

KEYNOTE

Italian business offices are open on Mondays to Fridays from 8:30 A.M. to 1:00 P.M. and again from 3:00 P.M. to 5:00 P.M. Banks are open on Mondays to Fridays from 8:30 A.M. to 1:30 P.M. and from 3:00 P.M. to 4:00 or 5:00 P.M. Stores are open Mondays to Saturdays from 9:00 A.M. to 1:00 P.M. and from 4:30 P.M. to 7:30 P.M.

Italian at Work

Here is an introduction to vocabulary related to white collar professions:

Boss, manager	il dirigente	eel dee-ree-JEHN-tay
Business Card	la carta da visita	lah kahr-tah dah VEE-zee-tah

CEO

l'amministratore delegato

lahm-meen-ee-strah-TOH-ray deh-leh- GAH-toh

Company	l'azienda	lahts-YEHN-dah
Contract	il contratto	eel kohn-TRAHT-toh

Corporate Planning la programmazione aziendale

lah proh-grahm-ahts-YOH-nay ahts-yehn-DAH-lay

Interview	l'intervista	leen-tehr-VEES-tah
Job	il lavoro	eel lah-VOH-roh
Meeting	la riunione	lah ree-oon-YOH-nay

Pay envelope	la busta paga	lah boos-tah pah-gah

Raise   l'aumento di stipendio

lohw-MEHN-toh dee stee-PEHN-dee-oh

Resume   il CV/il curriculum

eel chee-vee/eel curriculum

Salary	il salario	eel sah-LAH-ree-oh
Unemployed	disoccupato	dees-oh-koo-PAH-toh

Unemployment   la disoccupazione

lah dees-ohk-oo-pahts-YOH-nay to

Hire	assumere	ahs-SOO-meh-ray
To Fire	licenziare	lee-chehnts-YAH-ray
To Work	lavorare	lah-voh-RAH-ray

KEYNOTE

Italian workers usually receive their paychecks on a monthly basis (il mensile). In December, they normally receive their end of the year bonus, called la tredicesima (the thirteenth, as in the thirteenth paycheck of the year), which is equivalent to one month's salary.

On the phone

One must use the formal way of addressing when conducting business over the phone. To start, you'll need to know that when Italians pick up the phone, they say Pronto? (pronounced "prohn-toh").

May I speak to . . . ?	Posso parlare con . . . ?
I would like to speak to . . .	Vorrei parlare con . . .
Who is calling?	Chi parla?
Please hold.	Attenda la linea, per favore.
I'll put you through now.	Glielo passo subito.

I'm sorry, she's/he's not here.

Would you like to leave a message?

Mi dispiace, ma non c'è. Vorrebbe lasciare un messaggio?

Terms for Phone Usage

Answering machine   la segreteria telefonica

lah seh-greh-teh-REE-ah teh-leh-FOH-nee-kah

Phonebook   l'elenco telefonico

leh-LEHN-koh teh-lef-FOH-nee-koh

Phone number   il numero di telefono

eel NOO-meh-roh dee teh-LEH- foh-noh

To call   chiamare, telefonare a

kyah-MAH-ray, teh-leh-foh-NAH-ray ah

To call back   richiamare

ree-kyah-MAH-ray

To dial the number   fare il numero

fah-ray eel NOO-meh-roh

To hang up   riattaccare

ree-aht-tahk-KAH-ray

To leave a message   lasciare un messaggio

lah-SHAH-ray oon mehs-SAH-joh

To ring   suonare

swoh-NAH-ray

KEYNOTE

When making a phone call in Italy, try to be as polite as possible, especially if you don't know the person who is answering the phone. You should use the terms buon giorno, per favore, and grazie when necessary.

Office Supplies and Equipment

You need to paperclip some papers together. Now if you only knew the word for paperclip! This section will help you in getting all the supplies you need.

Blotter	la cartella da scrittoio
	lah kahr-TEHL-lah dah skreet-TOY-oh
Cabinet	l'armadio
	lahr-MAHD-yoh
Clerical assistant	l'assistente
	lah-sees-TEHN-teh
Clock	l'orologio
	loh-roh-LOH-joh
Desk	la scrivania
	lah skree-vah-NEE-ah
Desk drawer	il cassetto della scrivania
	eel kahs-SEHT-toh dehl-lah skree-vah- NEE-ah
Felt-tip pen	il pennarello
	eel pehn-nah-REHL-loh
Filing cabinet	l'armadio per pratiche
	lahr-MAH-dyoh pehr PRAH-tee-keh
Keyboard	la tastiera
	lah tahs-TYEH-rah
Paperclip	il fermaglio
	eel fehr-MAHL-yoh
Partition wall	la parete divisoria
	lah pah-REH-teh dee-vee-ZOH-ree-ah
pen	la penna
	lah pehn-nah
Pencil sharpener	il temperamatite

		eel tehm-peh-rah-mah-TEE-teh
Pocket calculator	la calcolatrice	lah kahl-koh-lah-TREE-cheh
Printer	la stampante	lah stahm-PAHN-tay
Punch	il perforatore	eel pehr-foh-rah-TOH-ray
Ruler	la riga	lah ree-gah
Scanner	lo scanner	loh skanner
Stapler	la spillatrice	lah speel-lah-TREE-cheh
Suspension file	il raccoglitore delle schede	

eel rahk-kohl-yah-TOH-ray dehl-leh skeh-deh

Wall calendar	il calendario da parete	

eel kah-lehn-DAH-ree-oh dah pah-REHteh

Wastepaper basket	il cestino	eel chehs-TEE-noh

Computers and the Internet

The Internet has forever changed the way the world conducts business. A knowledge of terms related to computing and the Internet will surely be advantageous.

KEYNOTE

You will find that many English words have found their way into the Italian language. This is especially true with words related to computer technology.

Address	l'indirizzo	leen-dee-REETS-soh
Browser	il navigatore	eel nah-vee-gah-TOH-ray
To click	cliccare	kleek-KAH-ray
Computer	il computer	eel kohm-pyou-tehr
Control panel	il pannello di controllo	

eel pahn-NEHL-loh dee kohn-TROHL-loh

Dialog box	la finestra di dialogo	

lah fee-NEHS-trah dee dee-AH-loh-goh

To download	scaricare	skah-ree-KAH-ray
Folder	la cartella	lah kahr-TEHL-lah
Hyperlink	l'ipercollegamento	lee-pehr-kohl-leh-gah-MEHN-toh
Icon	l'icona	lee-KOH-nah
Inbox	la casella di posta elettronica	

203

lah kah-ZEHL-lah dee pohs-tah eh-leht- TROH-nee-kah

Internet	la rete	lah reh-teh
Keyboard	la tastiera	lah tahs-TYEH-rah
Keywords	le parole chiavi	leh pah-ROH-leh kyah-vee
Multimedia	multimediale	mool-tee-meh-dee-AH-leh
Online	in linea	een LEE-neh-ah
Operating system	il sistema operativo	eel sees-TEH-mah oh-peh-rah-TEE-voh
Page	la pagina	lah PAH-jee-nah
Password	la parola d'accesso	lah pah-ROH-lah dah-CHEHS-soh
Printer	la stampante	lah stahm-PAHN-teh

To reboot	rifare il booting	ree-FAH-ray eel boo-teeng
To restart	riavviare	ree-ahv-VYAH-ray
Search engine	il motore di ricerca	eel moh-TOH-ray dee ree-CHEHR-kah
Site	il sito	eel see-toh
System folder	la cartella sistema	lah kahr-TEHL-lah sees-TEH-mah

In School

Studying abroad in Florence? This section provides some useful words and terms related to high school and college.

KEYNOTE

The Italian university system differs greatly from its American counterpart. The course of study usually lasts five years in Italy, and many consider the Italian university degree (la laurea) to be the equivalent of an American master's degree.

School	una scuola
	oo-nah skwoh-lah
High school	un liceo
	oon lee-CHEH-oh
University	un'università
	oon oo-nee-vehr-see-TAH
Backpack	uno zaino
	oo-noh dzeye-noh
Book	un libro
	oon lee-broh

Chalk	un gesso
	oon jehs-soh
Chalkboard	una lavagna
	oo-nah lah-VAHN-yah
Classroom	un'aula
	oon ohw-lah
Course	un corso
	oon kohr-soh
Dictionary	un dizionario
	oon deets-yoh-NAH-ree-oh
Eraser	una gomma
	oo-nah gohm-mah
Homework	i compiti
	ee KOHM-pee-tee
Junior high school	una scuola media
	oo-nah skwoh-lah meh-dyah
Notebook	un quaderno
	oon kwah-DEHR-noh
Paper	la carta
	lah kahr-tah
Piece of paper	un foglio di carta
	oon fohl-yoh dee kahr-tah
Pen	una penna
	oo-nah pehn-nah
Pencil	una mattita
	oo-nah maht-TEE-tah
Test	un esame
	oon eh-ZAH-may
Diploma	un diploma
(high school)	oon dee-PLOH-mah
Diploma (university)	una laurea

oo-nah LOHW-reh-ah

Doctoral degree   un dottorato

oon doht-toh-RAH-toh

CHAPTER FIVE: HOURS/ DAYS/ MONTH/ SEASONS

Cardinal Numbers

Knowing the numbers in Italian is not that complicated, but does require a bit of memorization. The pattern is actually very similar to the numbers in English. The numbers from one through sixteen are unique, and then the rest are actually a mix and match combination of the others. You can think of it like putting together a Lego set. Numbers in Italian are always written in one word. These rules are important to know because it'll help you decipher train schedules, dates, times, etc. It'll also help you when you go shopping or any other time when you need to use currency.

As much as it may pain us to say it, our parents were correct when they told us that math was important!

1 – uno

2 – due

3 – tre

4 – quattro

5 – cinque

6 – sei

7 – sette

8 – otto

9 – nove

10 – dieci

11 – undici

12 – dodici

13 – tredici

14 – quattordici

15 – quindici

16 – sedici

The next three start following a pattern of adding the number from seven through nine to the prefix dicia, which means ten. Dicia would be pronounced as two syllables (DEE-chah). However, notice in number 18 how the final "a" is dropped. It helps with the flow of pronunciation – it sounds better because "otto" starts with a vowel and it would be choppy to have that vowel combination together.

17 – diciassette

18 – diciotto

19 – diciannove

For the numbers starting from twenty and above, all you do is add one of the first nine numbers to the prefix venti, which means twenty.

The final "i" in venti is dropped when it comes before 21 or 28, since both one (uno) and eight (otto) start with a vowel. It is for the same reason as number 18 above, it helps with the flow of pronunciation. The same rule applies going forward every time you encounter a one or an eight.

20 – venti

21 – ventuno

22 – ventidue

23 – ventitre

24 – ventiquattro

25 – venticinque

26 – ventisei

27 – ventisette

28 – ventotto

29 – ventinove

30 – trenta

31 – trentuno

32 – trentadue

33 – trentatre

34 – trentaquattro

35 – trentacinque

36 – trentasei

37 – trentasette

38 – trentotto

39 – trentanove

40 – quaranta

For the numbers fifty and above you just follow the same pattern as for the twenties, thirties, etc.

50 – cinquanta

51 – cinquantuno

52 – cinquantadue

60 – sessanta

61 – sessantuno

67 – sessantasette

68 – sessantotto

70 – settanta

75 – settantacinque

79 - settantanove

80 – ottanta

83 – ottantatre

89 – ottantanove

90 – novanta

96 – novantasei

When you get above the number 100 you simply add the appropriate number from above to the

word cento, which means 100.

100 – cento

101 – centuno

102 – centodue

122 – centoventidue

150 – centocinquanta

When you want to say 200 you simply add the number two in front of the hundred, just as you do in English.

200 – duecento

212 – duecentododici

278 – duecentosettantotto

The same thing will apply going forward:

300 – trecento

352 – trecentocinquantadue

400 – quattrocento

500 – cinquecento

600 – seicento

700 – settecento

800 – ottocento

900 – novecento

**It's important to realize that periods and commas, in regards to numbers, are reversed in Italian.

For example, one and a half kilograms of pasta would be written like this:

1,5 kg

The same thing would apply to euros and cents. Three thousand euros and 50 cents would be written like this:

3.000,50

Here are the numbers in Italian that are greater than one thousand. Please note that the plural for mille (thousand) is mila. It's an exception to the normal rule of how a noun is pluralized.

1.000 – mille

1.001 – milleuno

1.200 – milleduecento

2.000 – duemila

To say the years in the calendar, you would simply say:

1995 – millenovecentonovantacinque

2013 – duemilatredici

2014 – duemilaquattordici

2015 – duemilaquindici

10.000 – diecimila

15.000 – quindicimila

100.000 – centomila

1.000.000 – un milione

2.000.000 – due milioni

The word for billion in Italian is milliardo.

1.000.000.000 – un milliardo

2.000.000.000 – due milliardi

ORDINAL NUMBERS

When numbers are placed in an order or are describing the relative position of one item versus another, it is referred to as an ordinal number. Ordinal numbers do not have anything to do with quantity, but only rank or position.

The first ten ordinal numbers in Italian are unique. Starting from number eleven (11), all you have to do is drop off the final vowel and add the following suffix, or stem – esimo. However, the numbers three and six do not drop the final vowel.

Here is an example using the number eleven.

undici – drop the i and add esimo to become undicesimo.

Since ordinal numbers can be used as adjectives, they must agree in number and gender to the object being described. Remember the basic rule in Italian. Each ordinal number can have the following ending:

a – feminine singular

e – feminine plural

o – masculine singular

i – masculine plural

the first cat	il primo gatto
the first car	la prima macchina
the first cats	i primi gatti
the first cars	le prime macchine

Here are the ordinal numbers for describing masculine items.

first	primo
second	secondo
third	terzo
fourth	quarto
fifth	quinto
sixth	sesto
seventh	settimo
eighth	ottavo
ninth	nono
tenth	decimo
eleventh	undicesimo
twelfth	dodicesimo
thirteenth	tredicesimo
fourteenth	quattordicesimo
fifteenth	quindicesimo
sixteenth	sedicesimo

seventeenth	diciassettesimo
eighteenth	diciottesimo
nineteenth	diciannovesimo
twentieth	ventesimo
twenty-first	ventunesimo
twenty-third	ventitreesimo
hundredth	centesimo
thousandth	millesimo
two thousandth	duemillesimo
three thousandth	tremillesimo
one millionth	milionesimo

Similar to the English language, the ordinal number will be placed before the noun. The use of abbreviations is also customary and is indicated with a small ° (masculine) or ª (feminine).

il 6° piano   the sixth floor

la 2 ª macchina   the second car

TELLING TIME

Inevitably as you are traveling around Italy the ability to tell time and understand it will be very important for catching planes, trains, and automobiles. One thing to keep in mind is that Italians are not very precise and punctual when it comes to being on time. In the land where fashion is king, it's not surprising that they tend to be fashionably late.

However, transportation schedules tend to be pretty precise, especially as you work your way up north on the peninsula. Things are not as precise as you move south of Rome towards the island of Sicily when trains originate from the north. If a train from Milan (north) to Naples (south) encounters a delay in Rome, the Naples arrival will inevitably be delayed.

Being that hour is a feminine noun (la ora), time will be expressed with the feminine version of the definite article.

The verb essere (to be) is used in both the singular and plural form.

Singular Form

is – é

é l'una (this is used only for 1:00)

Plural Form

are – sono

sono le due (this is used for everything else)

When referring to minutes, they are expressed as numbers. They either come before the hour or after the hour.

and = e (after the hour)

meno = minus (before the hour)

At fifteen (15) minutes after or before the top of the hour it is typical to use quarto (a quarter) instead of quindici (fifteen minutes).

In addition, at 30 minutes after the top of the hour, it is typical to use mezza (half) instead of trenta (thirty minutes). Mezza and meno are never used together.

The masculine or feminine version of mezzo and mezza are interchanged, and it is acceptable to use either one.

Here is how you ask for the time in Italian:

Che ora é? ("What time is it?") or Che ore sono?

Here is how you ask at what time something happens:

A che ora ? ("At what time...?")

Example: A che ora torni dal mercato?

What time are you returning from the market?

It's five o'clock.

Sono le cinque.

It's a quarter past four (literally four and a quarter).

Sono le quattro ed un quarto.

It's eight thirty (eight and thirty).

Sono le otto e mezza.

It is twenty-three minutes past three.

Sono le tre e ventitre.

It is thirty-eight past eight.

È l'otto e trentotto.

Or it is more common to say:

It is twenty-two minutes to nine.

213

Sono le nove meno ventidue.

It is a quarter to twelve.

Sono le dodici meno un quarto.

To make the distinction between AM and PM you can use these verbal qualifiers:

del mattino (during the morning)

del pomeriggio (during the afternoon)

della sera (during the evening)

della notte (during the night)

Usually the context of the situation will imply whether you are referring to AM or PM.

For plane, train, and bus schedules, and other official matters, a 24-hour military clock is used.

To figure out a time past 12:00, all you need to do is add or subtract 12.

Sono le sedici e un quarto (12 + 4 = 16)

In military time, this is expressed 16:25

In Italy many times the colon (:) is replaced by the comma (,)

In Italy 16:25 can be expressed as 16,25 or even as 16.25

More Vocabulary

before	prima
after	dopo
afterwards	dopo
early	presto
late	tardi
in time	in tempo

What time does the ... close? A che ora chiude la (il) ...?

or

What time does the ... open? A che ora apre la (il)...?

...bar	...il bar
...restaurant	...il ristorante
...store	...il negozio

...campground	... il campeggio
...zoo	...lo zoo

Notice above we use lo instead of il because zoo is a word that falls into one of the special cases (begins with a z).

...ticket office	...la biglietteria
...ice cream parlor	...la gelateria

Days of the Week

The days of the week in Italian are all masculine by convention except for Sunday, which is feminine. In Italian they are not capitalized as they are in English. Notice how the word week in Italian is settimana. The first part of the word is "sett," which comes from the number seven, or sette, to indicate the number of days in the week.

Monday	lunedì
Tuesday	martedì
Wednesday	mercoledì
Thursday	giovedì
Friday	venerdì
Saturday	sabato
Sunday	domenica

It's also interesting to note that if you were to look at a physical Italian calendar, the first day of the week that appears on the far left of the row is Monday as opposed to Sunday.

I find it's easier to memorize these days of the week when you realize that each day has a particular significance or meaning associated with it.

lunedì

lun = Moon di = day (day of the Moon)

martedì

mar = Mars di = day (day of Mars)

mercoledì

mer = Mercury di = day (day of Mercury)

giovedì

giove = Jupiter di = day (day of Jupiter)

venerdì

ven = Venus di = day (day of Venus)

sabato

sab = Sabbath in Hebrew

It may be helpful to think of this day as Saturn's day, to be consistent with the others.

domenica

From the Latin word Dominus, which means the Lord. This is the day of the Lord.

Useful Vocabulary

Yesterday	ieri
today	oggi
tomorrow	domani
sometime	prima o poi
after	dopo di
before	prima di

Whenever the days of the week are preceded by the definite article, it can mean that the occurrence happens regularly.

> Il lunedì vado alla palestra.

> Every Monday I go to the gym.

Alternatively you could also use the following sentence:

> Ogni lunedì vado alla palestra.

Some other useful phrases:

> Is there a train for Rome this Tuesday?

> C'è un treno per Roma questo martedì?

> Does the boat leave for Venice on Thursday?

> Il traghetto parte per Venezia giovedì?

Months of the Year

Just as in the previous lesson regarding the days of the week, the months in Italian are not capitalized. They are all masculine and do not require the use of an article, which in this case would be "il."

January	gennaio
February	febbraio
March	marzo
April	aprile
May	maggio
June	giugno

July	luglio
August	agosto
September	settembre
October	ottobre
November	novembre
December	dicembre

A way that can help you remember them is to think of a time when the ancients used to have ten months in a year. Then the final months of the year are associated with an Italian number.

settembre – sette (7)

ottobre – otto (8)

novembre – nove (9)

dicembre – dieci (10)

When expressing a particular day of the month in Italian the cardinal numbers are used for every day EXCEPT for the first day of the month (when the ordinal number is used). And the article il is used before the corresponding number.

This becomes clearer when you see the examples below:

On May first (1) is expressed as:	il primo maggio
On May second (2) is expressed as:	il due maggio
On June third (3) is expressed as:	il tre giugno
On July fourth (4) is expressed as:	il quattro luglio

It's also important to note that Italians write dates differently than we do in English. They will start with the smallest date unit (day) and then use the month and then the year (longest date unit).

For example, in English we would use the following to express October 1, 2014:

10/1/14

In Italian, October 1, 2014, would be expressed as:

1/10/14

This is actually not just an Italian convention, but used all throughout Europe.

It actually takes some time to get used to it. You wouldn't be the first one to confuse January 10th with October 1st. But it's an important distinction for train schedules, flights, etc.

To express the word "in" with a particular month, you can use either the Italian preposition "a" or "in."

I was born in May. (A man could say)

Sono nato in maggio.

Or

Sono nato a maggio.

I was born in April. (A woman could say)

Sono nata in maggio.

Or

Sono nata a maggio.

Some more useful phrases:

I'm going to Italy this September.

Vado in Italia questo settembre.

I like to travel in October.

Mi piace viaggare in ottobre.

Can I go to the beach in Rome in May?

Posso andare a mare a Roma in maggio?

CHAPTER SIX: WEATHER

Italy is celebrated for its temperate climate, particularly in the winter months. Like other areas of the globe however, weather conditions have changed and it is now not surprising to occasionally see snow as far south as Sicily. That said, snow in Italy will probably never reach the proportions seen on the U.S. East Coast, unless of course you choose to vacation in the Italian Alps during the winter. Summer, particularly in the inland areas (with Bologna in the Val Padana often touted as the worst) can be hot and humid. Most Italians will head for the beaches or the mountains in August just to escape the excessive heat and humidity. Temperatures in Italy are measured in centigrade so you will want to consult a conversion chart (below) to correctly calculate the daily forecast.

Vocabulary	Vocabolario
Centigrade.	Centigrado. chen-TEE-grah-doh.
Cloudy.	Nuvoloso. noo-voh-LOH-zoh.
Fahrenheit.	Farenheit. FAH-rehn-ah>eet.
Fog.	Nebbia. NEHB-bee>ah.
Hail.	Grandine. GRAHN-dee-neh.
Lightning.	Lampi. LAHM-pee.
Muggy.	Afoso ah-FOH-zoh.
Rainy.	Piovoso. pee>oh-VOH-zoh.
Sleet.	Nevischio. neh-VEES-kee>oh.
Shade.	Ombra. OHM-brah.
Snow.	Neve. NEH-veh.
Storms.	Tempeste. tehm-PEHS-teh.
Sunny.	Tempo sereno. TEHM-poh seh-REH-noh.
Temperature.	La temperatura. lah tehm-peh-rah-TOO-rah.
Umbrella.	L'ombrello. lohm-BREHL-loh.
Windy.	C'è vento. cheh VEHN-toh.

Quick & to the Point Weather Forecast

Forecast.	Previsioni.	leh preh-vee-ZYOH-nee.
Minimum.	Minimo.	MEE-nee-moh.
Maximum.	Massimo.	MAHS-see-moh.

Precipitation	Precipitazioni	preh-chee-pee-tah-TSYOH-nee.
Tides.	Le maree.	leh mah-REH-eh.
Winds.	Venti.	VEHN-tee.

Gauging the Weather   Stabilire il tempo

What is the weather today? Che tempo fa oggi?
  keh TEHM-poh FAH OHJ-jee?

What is the temperature outside? Che temperatura fa fuori?
keh tehm-peh-rah-TOO-rah fah foo>OH-ree?

It is hot.	Fa caldo.	fah KAHL-doh.
It is cold today.	Fa freddo oggi.	fah FREHD-doh OHJ-jee.
It is very windy.	tira molto vento.	TEE-rah MOHL-toh VEHN-toh.
Is it raining outside?	Piove fuori?	pee>OH-veh foo>OH-ree?

Should I bring an umbrella?
Dovrei portare un ombrello?
DOHV-ray pohr-TAH-reh oon ohm-BREHL-loh?

CHAPTER SEVEN: MENU GUIDE

Italy is known for its world-class cuisine. Culinary traditions and styles vary from region to region (and from city to city as well). Knowing how to order your meal will only enhance your dining experience.

Dining Out

Here are some general phrases related to dining in a restaurant:

Meals and Courses

meal	il pasto	eel pahs-toh
breakfast	la colazione	lah koh-lahts-YOH-neh
lunch	il pranzo	eel prahn-zoh
dinner	la cena	lah cheh-nah
snack	la merendina	lah meh-rehn-DEE-nah
antipasto	gli antipasti	lyee ahn-tee-PAHS-tee
first course	il primo (piatto)	eel pree-moh
soup	la zuppa,	lah dsoop-ah,
second course	il secondo (piatto)	eel seh-KOHN- doh
vegetable course	il contorno	eel kohn-TOHR-noh
salad	l'insalata	leen-sah-LAH-tah
dessert	il dessert/il dolce.	eel deh-sehrt, eel dohl-chay

At the Restaurant

restaurant	il ristorante	eel rees-toh-RAHN-tay
(small) restaurant	la trattoria	lah trah-toh-REE-ah
public house/inn	l'osteria	lohs-teh-REE-ah
buffet-style	la tavola	lah TAH-voh-lah
restaurant	calda	kahl-dah
pizzeria	la pizzeria	lah peet-seh-REE-ah
kitchen or cuisine	la cucina	lah koo-CHEE-nah dining
room	la sala	lah sah-lah

waiter	il cameriere	eel kah-meh-RYEH-ray
waitress	la cameriera	lah kah-meh-RYEH-rah
cook	il cuoco	eel kwoh-koh
chef	lo chef	loh shehf
pizza maker	il pizzaiolo	eel peet-seye-OH-loh
bartender	il barista	eel bah-REES-tah

KEYNOTE

A full Italian meal consists of antipasto, primo (usually a pasta or rice dish), secondo (meat, poultry, or fish) with contorni (vegetables), insalata (dressed with oil, vinegar, and salt), and il dolce (dessert).

What to Order?

Ah, so many choices, and so few days to try them all. It's easy to find a restaurant in a touristy area that offers Italian-American food (spaghetti with alfredo sauce, spaghetti and meatballs, and so on). Try to find something that's off the beaten path, and certainly try to order something that you've never tried before—you'll almost always be pleasantly surprised!

Antipasto

From city to city and region to region, you will find thousands of different types of antipasti. Many restaurants will have a buffet table set up with numerous types of antipasti to choose from. The following are some of the more common items you can find throughout Italy.

Antipasto

le acciughe

anchovies

leh ah-CHOO-geh

l'affettato misto

various cold cuts

lahf-feht-TAH-toh mees-toh

l'arancino

rice ball filled with meat and cheese

lah-rahn-CHEE-noh

la bruschetta

toasted bread topped with dices tomotoes

lah broo-SKEH-tah

la bruschetta col salmone

toasted bread topped with salmon

broo-SKEH-tah kohn sahl-MOH-neh

i calamari fritti

fried squid

ee kah-lah-MAH-ree free-tee

la caponata siciliana

eggplant and tomato stew

lah kah-poh-NAH-tah see-cheel-YAH-nah

il caprese

mozzarella, tomatoes, fresh basil, and

eel kah-PRAY-zay

i carciofi

olive oil artichokes

  ee kahr-CHOH-fee

il carpaccio

raw beef very thinly sliced

eel kahr-PAH-choh

la focaccia

flat bread

lah foh-KAH-chah

frutti di mare

mixed seafood

froo-tee dee mah-ray

i funghi imbottiti

stuffed mushrooms

ee foon-gee eem-boh-TEE-tee

la giardiniera

pickled vegetables

lah jahr-deen-YEH-rah

gli involtini di prosciutto

lyee een-vohl-TEE-nee dee

rolled, stuffed prosciutto

pro-SHOO-toh

223

le lumache

snails

leh loo-MAH-keh

la peperonata

peppers sautéed with oil and capers

lah peh-peh-roh-NAH-tah

i pomodori farciti di tonno

tomatoes stuffed with rice

ee poh-moh-DOH-ree fahr-CHEE-tee dee tohn-noh

i pomodori ripieni con riso

tomatoes stuffed with rice

ee poh-moh-DOH-ree ree-PYEH-nee kohn ree-zoh

le olive condite

marinated olives

oh-LEE-veh kohn-DEE-teh

il patè di vitello

veal patè

pah-TEH dee vee-TEHL-loh

prosciutto e melone

prosciutto and melon

proh-SHOO-toh eh meh-LOH-neh

le seppioline alla griglia

grilled cuttlefish

sehp-pyoh-LEE-neh ahl-lah greel-yah

sauté di vongole

sautéed clams

sohw-teh dee VOHN-goh-leh

i gamberi

shrimp

ee GAHM-beh-ree

vongole in graticola

clams with parsley and bread crumbs

224

VOHN-goh-leh een grah-TEE-koh-lah

vongole inciocchite

steamed clams

VOHN-goh-leh een-chohk-KEE-teh

First Course Dishes: I primi piatti

The first course mainly consists of either a pasta or rice dish. There are dozens of different types of pastas, some of which are unique to certain areas in Italy. Each type of pasta is usually matched with a specific sauce based on various factors. For example, thin, delicate pastas like angel hair or thin spaghetti, are better served with light, thin sauces; thicker pasta shapes like fettuccine work well with heavier sauces, and pasta shapes with holes or ridges are perfect for chunkier sauces. You may find that some Italians will substitute a pizza for the first course.

I tipi di pasta (Types of Pasta)

agnolotti

similar to ravioli but smaller; this is

ahn-yoh-LOHT-tee

usually stuffed with meat, cheese, or vegetables

cannelloni

large, tube-shaped pasta, usually filled

kahn-nehl-LOH-nee

with meat or cheese

cappellini

very thin pasta, often called angel hair

kahp-pehl-LEE-nee

conchiglie

shells of pasta

kohn-KEE-lyeh

farfalle

shaped like a butterfly or bow tie

fahr-FAHL-leh

fettuccine

thin noodles that are somewhat wider

feht-too-CHEE-neh

225

fusilli

corkscrews

foo-ZEE-lee

gemelli

single S-shaped strands of pasta in a twisted

jeh-MEHL-lee

loose spiral

gnocchi

potato or ricotta-based pasta dumplings

nyohk-kee

lasagne

broad, flat noodles, usually baked

lah-ZAHN-yeh

with meat, cheese, and tomato sauce

linguine

flat noodles, wider than spaghetti, but

leen-GWEE-neh

narrower than fettuccine

maltagliati

flat, roughly cut triangles

mahl-tahl-YAH-tee

orecchiette

small bowl-shaped pasta

oh-rehk-KYEH-teh

pappardelle

broad, long noodles

pahp-pahr-DEHL-leh

penne

short pasta tubes

pehn-neh

ravioli

pillows of pasta, stuffed with cheese, meat, or vegetables

rah-vee-OH-lee

rigatoni

short, large tubes

ree-gah-TOH-nee

rotelle

wagon wheel-shaped pasta

roh-TEHL-leh

rotini

double-edged spiral, tightly wound

roh-TEE-nee

spaghetti

long, thin strands of pasta

spah-GEHT-tee

tagliatelle

long, flat strands of pasta

tahl-yah-TEHL-leh

tortellini

small, folded pillows of pasta, usually stuffed with

cheese, meat, or vegetables

tohr-tehl-LEE-nee

Types of Pasta Sauces

boscaiola

tomatoes, butter, cheese, lah mushrooms, olive oil, garlic

bohs-keye-OH-lah

bolognese

meat, tomatoes, cheese

boh-lohn-YEH-zeh

carbonara

olive oil, cheese, egg, bacon

kahr-boh-NAH-rah

diavolo

tomato sauce with hot spices

DYAH-voh-loh

genovese

basil, pine nuts, garlic, olive oil

jeh-noh-VEH-seh

marinara

tomatoes, olive oil, garlic,

mah-ree-NAH-rah

sometimes olives

napoletana

cheese, tomatoes, herbs

nah-poh-leh-TAH-nah

puttanesca

tomatoes, black olives, peppers,

poot-tah-NESS-kah

olive oil, garlic

quattro formaggi

literally, four cheeses

kwaht-troh fohr-MAH-jee

siciliana

provolone cheese and eggplant

see-cheel-YAH-nah

KEYNOTE

The word peperone in Italian means pepper, as in the vegetable. A pepperoni pizza in Italian is una pizza con salamino piccante.

Pizza

asparagi

tomato sauce, mozzarella,

ahs-PAH-rah-jee

asparagus

bismark

tomato sauce, mozzarella, egg

beez-mahrk

bufala

tomato sauce, buffalo mozzarella

BOO-fah-lah

Capricciosa

tomato sauce, mozzarella, prosciutto, carciofini

kahp-pree-CHOH-zah

mushrooms, egg, artichokes, sausage, olives, artichokes

tomato sauce, mozzarella,

kahr-choh-FEE-nee

diavola

anchovies, black olives, capers, spicy salami

DYAH-voh-lah

funghi

tomato sauce, mozzarella,

foon-gee

mushrooms

funghi porcini

tomato sauce, mozzarella,

foon-gee pohr-CHEE-nee

porcini mushroms

gorgonzola

tomato sauce, mozzarella,

gohr-gohn-ZOH-lah

gorgonzola

marinara

tomato sauce, garlic, oregan

mah-ree-NAH-rah

margherita

tomato sauce, mozzarella

mahr-geh-REE-tah

melanzane

tomato sauce, mozzarella,

meh-lahn-ZAH-neh

eggplant

napoli

tomato sauce, mozzarella,

NAH-poh-lee

anchovies, capers, oregano

peperoni

tomato sauce, mozzarella,

peh-peh-ROH-nee

peppers

primavera

mozzarella, sliced tomato

pree-mah-VEH-rah

prosciutto cotto

tomato sauce, mozzarella,

proh-SHOO-toh koht-toh

cured ham

pugliese

tomato sauce, mozzarella,

pool-YEH-zay

anchovies, olives, onion, oregano

quattro formaggi

tomato sauce, mozzarella,

kwaht-troh fohr-MAH-jee

fontina, gorgonzola, pecorino cheeses

quattro stagioni

tomato sauce, mozzarella,

kwaht-troh stah-JOH-nee

prosciutto, mushrooms, egg, artichokes, olives

romana

tomato sauce, mozzarella,

roh-mah-nah

anchovies, capers, oregano, olives

salame piccante

tomato sauce, mozzarella, spicy salami

sah-LAH-meh

peek-KAHN-teh

salsiccia

tomato sauce, mozzarella, sausage

sahl-SEE-chah

tonno

tomato sauce, mozzarella,

tuna tohn-noh

verdure

tomato sauce, mozzarella, with assorted vegetables

vehr-DOO-reh

Second Course Dishes: Meat, Fish, Poultry

beef	il manzo	eel man-zoh
chicken	il pollo	eel pohl-loh
ham	il prosciutto	eel proh-SHOOT-toh
hare	il lepre	eel leh-pray
lamb	l'agnello	lahn-YEHL-loh
liver	il fegato	eel FEH-gah-toh
meat	la carne	lah kahr-nay
pork	il maiale	eel meye-AH-lay
rabbit	il coniglio	eel koh-NEEL-yoh
sausage	la salsiccia	lah sahl-SEE-chah
seafood	i frutti di mare	ee froot-tee dee mah-ray
steak	la bistecca	lah bees-TEHK-kah
turkey	il tacchino	eel tahk-KEE-noh

veal	il vitello	eel vee-TEHL-loh

Meat Preparation

rare	al sangue	ahl sahn-gway
well done	ben cotto	behn-koht-toh

KEYNOTES

Italians don't really have a term for "medium" cooked meat. The default is usually medium, but if you want it rare (al sangue), or well done (ben cotto), you'll have to ask for it specifically.

Dairy (i latticini)

butter	il burro	eel boo-roh
cheese	il formaggio	eel fohr-MAHJ-joh
milk	il latte	eel laht-tay
yogurt	il yogurt	eel yoh-gurt

Fruit (le frutte)

apple	una mela	oo-nah meh-lah
apricot	un albicocca	oon ahl-bee-KOHK-kah
banana	una banana	oo-nah bah-NAH-nah
blackberry	una mora	oo-nah moh-rah
blueberry	un mirtillo	oon meer-TEEL-loh
cherry	una ciliegia	oo-nah chee-LYEH-jah
grape	un'uva	oon-oo-vah
grapefruit	un pompelmo	oon pohm-PEHL-moh
lemon	un limone	oon lee-MOH-nay
orange	un'arancia	oon-ah-RAHN-chah
peach	una pesca	oo-nah pess-kah
pear	una pera	oo-nah peh-rah
raspberry	un lampone	oon lahm-POH-nay
strawberry	una fragola	oo-nah FRAH-goh-lah

Vegetables (i legumi)

artichoke	il carcioffo	eel kahr-CHOHF-foh

asparagus	gli asparagi.	lyee ahs-PAH-rah-jee
beans	i fagioli	ee fah-JOH-lee
carrot	la carotta	la kah-ROHT-tah
cabbage	il cavolo	eel KAH-voh-loh
celery	il sedano	eel SEH-dah-noh
eggplant	la melanzana	lah meh-lahn-ZAH-nah
garlic	l'aglio	lahl-yoh
lettuce	la lettuga	lah leht-TOO-gah
onion	la cipolla	lah chee-POHL-lah
peas	i piselli	ee pee-ZEHL-lee
radish	il ravanello	eel rah-vah-NEHL-loh
spinach	gli spinaci	lyee spee-NAH-chee

Dessert (i dolci)

cake	la torta	lah tohr-tah
cookie	il biscotto	eel bees-KOHT-toh
fruit salad	la macedonia di frutta	

lah mah-cheh-DOH-nee-ah di frutta dee froot-tah

ice cream il gelato   eel jeh-LAH-toh

Beverages: Da bere

Italy is one of the world's largest wine producers. You may be overwhelmed by the selection available in some restaurants. If you're not sure what to order, ask your waiter.

Beverages

after-dinner drink	il digestivo	eel dee-jess-TEE-voh
aperitif	l'aperitivo	lah-peh-reh-TEE-voh
beer	la birra	lah bee-rah
coffee	il caffè	eel kahf-FEH
red wine	il vino rosso	eel vee-noh rohs-soh
white wine	il vino bianco	eel vee-noh byahn-koh
wine	il vino	eel vee-noh

| water | 'acqua | lahk-wah |
| | (minerale) | (mee-neh-RAH-leh) |

KEYNOTE

When taking your order, the waiter may ask you, E da bere?, which translates as "Something to drink?" To ask for a wine recommendation, you might ask, Può consigliarmi un buon vino?

Dishes and Silverware

If you need to ask for another fork or napkin, here's the vocabulary you'll need:

bowl	la ciotola	lah CHOH-toh-lah
cup	la tazza	lah taht-sah
fork	la forchetta	lah fohr-KEHT-tah
glass	il bicchiere	eel beek-KYEH-ray
knife	il coltello	eel kohl-TELL-loh
napkin	il tovagliolo	eel toh-vahl-YOH-loh
plate	il piatto	eel pyaht-toh
silverware	le posate	leh poh-ZAH-teh
spoon	il cucchiaio	eel kook-KYAH-yoh

Ordering Your Meal

Here are some useful words to help you order your meal:

to be hungry	aver fame	ah-VEHR fah-may
to be thirsty	avere sete	ah-veh-ray seh-teh
to order	ordinare	ohr-dee-NAH-ray
to drink	bere	beh-ray
to eat	mangiare	mahn-JAH-ray
check/bill	il conto	eel kohn-toh
cover charge	il coperto	eel koh-PEHR-toh
service charge	il servizio	eel sehr-VEETS-ee-oo
menu	il menu	eel meh-noo
tip	la mancia	lah mahn-chah

What would you like?

Che cosa mangia?

keh koh-zah mahn-jah?

I would like . . .   Io vorrei . . .   ee-oo vohr-ray

I am a vegetarian.

Sono vegetariano.

soh-noh veh-jeh-tah-ree-AH-noh

I am on a diet.

Sono a dieta.

soh-noh ah dee-EH-tah

I am allergic.

Sono allergico.

soh-noh ahl-LEHR-jee-koh

KEYNOTE

Some restaurants will add a cover charge—il coperto—and a service charge—il servizio—to your bill. This, by law, must be clearly marked on the menu. As a general rule, Italian waiters will not expect a tip, though adding a few euros to your payment will be appreciated.

CHAPTER EIGHT: HOME AND APARTMENT

In Italy you can arrange to rent an apartment through travel agencies or through a real estate agent. If you make a reservation, you will be asked to leave a deposit in advance. When you arrive in the tourist resort where you have reserved the villa or apartment, you will have to sign a contract. Your name, the date of the rental, the address of the apartment, the amount of your deposit, etc., will be specified in this contract. You may be asked to pay for certain "extras" not included in the original price (in particular, tourist taxes). Gas and electricity are normally included, but cleaning seldom is. It's a good idea to ask about an inventory of goods at the start, rather than be told something is missing just as you are about to leave. Sometimes you will find an inventory in the apartment (in a drawer or cabinet). Usually, you are not required to sign it. You may be asked for a deposit, in case you break something. Make sure this is specified in the contract you sign. You will get your money back when you leave.

Useful Words and Phrases

bath (tub)	la vasca da bagno	vaska da ban-yo
bathroom	il bagno	ban-yo
bedroom	la camera da letto	hamaira da let-to
blocked	intasato	eentazato
boiler	lo scaldabagno	skaldaban-yo
broken	rotto	rot-to
caretaker	il portinaio	porteeni-o
(female)	la portinaia	porteeni-a

central heating

il riscaldamento centrale

reeshaldamento

cleaner

l'uomo delle pulizie

womo del-le pulitzie

(female) la donna delle pulizie

pooleetzee-e don-na del-le pooleetzee-e

comforter

il piumino

p-yoomeeno

deposit (security)

la cauzione

kowtz-yone

(part payment)

la caparra

kapar-ra

drain	lo scarico	skareeko
electrician	l'elettricista	elet-treecheesta
electricity	l'elettricità	elet-treecheeta
faucet	il rubinetto	roobeenet-to

fusebox   la scatola dei fusibili

skatola day joozeebeelee

garbage can   il bidone della spazzatura

beedone dei-la spatzzatoora

gas	il gas	"gas"
grill	la griglia	greel-ya
heater	il calorifero	haloreefairo

iron   il ferro da stiro   jair-ro da steero

ironing board   la tavola da stiro   tavola da steero

keys	le chiavi	k-ya-vee
kitchen	la cucina	koocheena
leak (noun)	la perdita	pairdeeta
(verb)	perdere	pairdaire
loochelight	la luce	
living room	il soggiorno	soj-jorno
maid	la cameriera	kamair-yaira
pillow	il cuscino	koosheeno
pillowcase	la federa	fedaira
plumber	l'idraulico	eedrowleeko
real estate agent	l'agente immobiliare	ajente eem-mobeelyare
refrigerator	il frigorifero	jreegoreejairo
refund	il rimborso	reemborso
sheets	le lenzuola	lentzwola
shower	la doccia	docha
sink	il lavandino	lavandeeno
stop valve	il rubinetto d'arresto	roobeenet-to dar-resto
stove	il fornello	fornel-lo
swimming pool	la piscina	peesheena
toilet	il gabinetto	gabeenet-to
towel	l'asciugamano	ashoogamano
washing machine	la lavatrice	lavatreeche
water	l'acqua	akwa
water heater	lo scaldaacqua	skalda-akwa

I'd like to rent an apartment/a villa for ... days

Vorrei affittare un appartamento/una villa per . . . giorni

vor-ray_ af-jeet-tare oon ap-partamento/oona veel-la pair . . . jornee

Do I have to pay a deposit?

Devo versare una cauzione?

devo vairsare oona kowtz-yone

238

Does the price include gas and electricity?

Il gas e l'elettricità sono inclusi nel prezzo?

eel "gas" ay lelet-treecheeta sono eerMooz.ee nel pretzo

Where is this item?

Dove si trova questo oggetto?

dove see trova kwesto oj-jet-to

Please take it off the inventory

Lo tolga dall'inventario, per favore

lo tolga dal-leenventar-yo pair favore

We've broken this

Abbiamo rotto questo

abb-yamo rot- to kwesto

This was broken when we arrived

Era già rotto quando siamo arrivati

eraja rot-to kwando s-yamo ar-reevatee

This was missing when we arrived

Non c'era quando siamo arrivati

non chera kwando s-yamo ar-reevatee

Can I have my deposit back?

Potrei riavere la cauzione?

potray ree-avaire la kowtz-yone

Can we have an extra bed?

Potremmo avere un letto in più?

potrem-mo avaire oon let-to een p-yoo

Can we have more dishes/cutlery?

Potremmo avere ancora un po' di stoviglie/posate?

potrem-mo avaire ankora oon pò dee stoveel-ye/pozate

When does the maid come?

Quando viene la cameriera?

kwando v-yene la kamair-yaira

Where can I buy/find ...?

Dove posso comprare/trovare ... ?

dove posso komprare/trovare

How does the water heater work?

Come funziona lo scaldaacqua?

home joontz-yona lo skalda-akwa

Do you do ironing/baby-sitting?

Sa stirare/badare ai bambini?

sa steer are/badare i bambeenee

Do you prepare lunch/dinner?

È in grado di preparare il pranzo/la cena?

eh een grado dee preparare eel prantzo/la chena

Do we have to pay extra or is it included?

Dobbiamo pagarlo a parte o è incluso nel prezzo?

dobb-yamo pagarlo a parte o eh eenkloozo nel pret-zo

The shower doesn't work

La doccia non funziona

la docha non joontz-yona

The sink is blocked

Il lavandino è intasato

eel lavandeeno eh eentazato

The sink/toilet is leaking

Il lavandino/gabinetto perde

eel lavandeeno/gabeenet-to paxrde

There's a burst pipe

Si è rotto un tubo

see eh rot-to oon toobo

The garbage has not been collected for a week

Non portano via la spazzatura da una settimana

non portano vee-a la spatz-zatoora da oona set-teemana

There's no electricity/gas/water

Non ce elettricità/gas/acqua

non cheh elet-treecheeta/"gas"/akwa

Can you fix it today?

Può ripararlo oggi?

pwo reepararlo oj-jee

Send your bill to . .

Mandi il conto a . .

mandee eel konto a

I'm staying at . .

Sto a . .

sto a

CHAPTER NINE: SHOPPING

Shopping is what draws many people to Italy and is probably the most enjoyable activity, and second only to food. We all know about Italian leather, fashion, gold jewelry, and design. A word of advice, however, stay away from the larger tourist areas as prices will be double those found off the beaten track. Below is a list of miscellaneous shops for everyday shopping, the stores in other words that we must all go to for one thing or another. The subsequent section addresses clothes and all this entails. Finally, the great Italian pastime, bargaining. Bargaining usually takes place in outdoor markets; however the market vendors are shrewd negotiators. Trying to get the price down will require a good amount of haggling. They invariably also speak very good English, so don't take for granted that they don't understand you.

Vocabulary / Vocabolario

Shops and Beyond / negozi e oltre

> Antique shop.
>
> Un negozio di antiquariato.
>
> oon neh-GOH-tzee>oh dee ahn-tee-kwah-ree>AH-toh.

> Author.
>
> L'autore.
>
> lah>oo-TOHR-reh.

> Bakery.
>
> Un panificio / una panetteria.
>
> oon pah-nee-FEE-choh / OO-nah pah-neht-teh-REE-ah.

> Barber.
>
> Un barbiere.
>
> oon bahr-bee>EH-reh.

> Beauty salon.
>
> Un parrucchiere.
>
> oon pahr-roo-kee>EH-reh.

Book.

Un libro.

oon LEE-broh.

Bookstore.

Una libreria.

OO-nah lee-breh-REE-ah.

Used bookstore.

Una libreria di libri usati.

OO-nah lee-breh-REE-ah dee LEE-bree oo-ZAH-tee.

English bookstore.

Una libreria che vende libri in inglese.

OO-nah lee-breh-REE-ah keh VEHN-deh LEE-bree een een-GLEH-zeh.

To buy.

Comprare.

kohm-PRAH-reh.

Cake.

Una torta.

OO-nah TOHR-tah.

Camera.

La macchina fotografica.

lah MAHK-kee-nah foh-toh-GRAH-fee-kah.

Video camera.

Una videocamera.

OO-nah vee-deh>oh-KAH-meh-rah.

Camera shop.

Un negozio di foto ottica.

oon neh-GOH-tzee>oh dee FOH-toh OHT-tee-kah.

Carats.

I carati.

ee kah-RAH-tee.

Clothes.

I vestiti.

ee veh-STEE-tee.

Clothing store.

Un negozio di abbigliamento.

oon neh-GOH-tzee>oh dee ahb-bee-lyee>ah-MEHN-toh.

Color.

Il colore.

eel koh-LOH-reh.

Highlights (hair color).

I colpi di sole.

ee KOHL-pee dee SOH-leh.

Costume jewelry.

La bigiotteria.

lah bee-joht-teh-REE-ah.

Deli.

Una salumeria.

OO-nah sah-loo-meh-REE-ah.

Department store.

Un grande magazzino.

oon GRAHN-deh mah-gahtz-TZEE-noh.

Dry cleaner.

La tintoria.

lah teen-toh-REE-ah.

Electrical converter.

Un convertitore elettrico.

oon kohn-vehr-tee-TOH-reh eh-LEHT-tree-koh.

Flea market.

Il mercato delle pulci.

eel mehr-KAH-toh DEHL-leh POOL-chee.

Flowers.

I fiori.

ee fee>OH-ree.

Flower shop.

Un fioraio.

oon fee>oh-RAH-ee>oh

Grocery store (small).

Un negozio d'alimentari.

oon neh-GOH-zee>oh dah-lee-mehn-TAH-ree.

Goldsmith's shop.

Un'oreficeria.

oon oh-reh-fee-cheh-REE-ah.

Haircut.

Un taglio.

oon TAH-lyee>oh.

Hardware store.

Un ferramenta.

oon fehr-rah-MEHN-tah.

Hectogram.

Un etto.

oon EHT-toh.

Ingredients.

Gli ingredienti.

lyee een-greh-dee>EHN-tee.

Jewelry shop.

Una gioielleria.

OO-nah joy-ehl-leh-REE-ah.

Leather goods shop.

Una pelletteria.

OO-nah pehl-leht-teh-REE-ah.

Loaf.

Un filone / Una pagnotta.

oon fee-LOH-neh / OO-nah pah-nee>OHT-tah.

Mall.

Un centro commerciale.

oon CHEHN-troh koh-mehr-CHAH-leh.

Moderately priced.

A buon mercato.

ah boo>OHN mehr-KAH-toh.

Newsstand.

Un giornalaio.

oon johr-nah-LAH>ee>oh.

Open market.

Un mercato all'aperto.

oon mehr-KAH-toh ahl-lah-PEHR-toh.

Optician.

Un ottico.

oon OHT-tee-koh.

Paper.

La carta.

lah KAHR-tah.

Paper goods store.

Una cartoleria.

OO-nah kahr-toh-leh-REE-ah.

Pastry shop.

Una pasticceria.

OO-nah pahs-teech-cheh-REE-ah.

Pastries.

I pasticcini.

ee pahs-teech-CHEE-nee.

Pen.

Una penna.

OO-nah PEHN-nah.

Price.

Il prezzo.

eel PREHTS-tsoh.

Roll.

Il panino.

eel pah-NEE-noh.

Souvenir shop.

Un negozio di souvenir.

oon neh-GOH-tzee>oh dee soo-veh-NEER.

Supermarket.

Un supermercato.

oon soo-pehr-mehr-KAH-toh.

Travel agency.

Un'agenzia di viaggi.

oon-ah-jehn-TZEE>ah dee vee>AHJ-jee.

TALKING ABOUT STORES / PARLARE DI NEGOZI

Where is there an antique store?

Dov'è un negozio di antiquariato?

dov-EH oon neh-GOH-tzee>oh dee ahn tee-kwah-ree>AH-toh?

When does it open / close?

Quando apre / chiude?

KWAHN-doh AH-preh / kee>OO-deh?

Where can I buy _____?

Dove posso comprare _____?

DOH-veh POHS-soh kohm-PRAH-reh _____?

I would like a moderately priced store.

Vorrei un negozio a buon mercato.

vohr-RAY oon neh-GOH-tzee>oh ah boo>OHN mehr-KAH-toh.

I would like a haircut please.

Vorrei un taglio per favore.

vohr-RAY oon TAH-lyee>oh pehr fah-VOH-reh.

Not too short.

Non troppo corto.

nohn TROHP-poh KOHR-toh.

I would like a cut and a color.

Vorrei un taglio e il colore.

vohr-RAY oon TAH-lyee>oh eh eel koh-LOH-reh.

I would like highlights.

Vorrei dei colpi di sole.

vohr-RAY day KOHL-pee dee SOH-leh.

Do you have a book entitled _____?

Ha un libro intitolato _____? (formal)

ah oon LEE-broh een-tee-toh-LAH-toh _____?

Do you have books by this author?

Ha dei libri di questo autore? (formal)

ah day LEE-bree dee KWEHS-toh ah>oo-TOH-reh?

Can you fix my camera?

Mi può riparare la macchina fotografica? (formal)

mee poo>OH ree-pah-RAH-reh lah MAHK-kee-nah foh-toh-GRAH-fee- kah?

Can you fix my video camera?

Mi può riparare la videocamera?

mee poo>OH ree-pah-RAH-reh lah vee-deh>oh-KAH-meh-rah?

Is there a department store nearby?

C'è un grande magazzino qui vicino?

cheh oon GRAHN-deh mah-gahtz-TZEE-noh kwee vee-CHEE-noh?

I would like ¼ pound of prosciutto.

Vorrei un etto (100 grammi) di prosciutto.

vohr-RAY oon EHT-toh (CHEHN-toh GRAHM-mee) dee proh-SHOOT- toh.

Could you give me a loaf of wheat bread?

Mi potrebbe dare un filone di pane integrale? (formal)

mee-poh-TREHB-beh DAH-reh oon fee-LOH-neh dee PAH-neh een-teh- GRAH-leh?

I would like 4 rolls please.

Vorrei quattro panini per favore.

vohr-RAY KWAHT-troh pah-NEE-nee pehr fah-VOH-reh.

I would like to buy some flowers please.

Vorrei comprare dei fiori per favore.

vohr-RAY kohm-PRAH-reh day fee>OH-ree pehr fah-VOH-reh.

Do you have an electrical converter?

Ha un convertitore elettrico? (formal)

ah oon kohn-vehr-tee-TOH-reh eh-LEHT-tree-koh?

I have to convert U.S. voltage to Italian voltage.

Devo trasformare il voltaggio americano in quello italiano.

DEH-voh trahs-fohr-MAH-reh eel vohl-tahj-joh ah-meh-ree-KAH-noh een KWEHL-loh ee-tah-lee>AH-noh.

Could you please show me some costume jewelry?

Mi potrebbe far vedere della bigiotteria? (formal)

mee poh-TREHB-beh fahr veh-DEH-reh DEHL-lah bee-joht-teh-REE-ah?

How many carats does this gold contain?

Di quanti carati è quest'oro?

dee KWAHN-tee kah-RAH-tee eh kwehst-OH-roh?

I would like to see your leather coats.

Vorrei vedere i vostri cappotti di pelle.

vohr-RAY veh-DEH-reh ee VOH-stree kahp-POHT-tee dee PEHL-leh.

Do you have English newspapers?

Ha dei giornali in inglese? (formal)

ah day johr-NAH-lee een een-GLEH-zeh?

I would like to buy a pen please.

Vorrei comprare una penna per favore.

vohr-RAY kohm-PRAH-reh OO-nah PEHN-nah pehr fah-VOH-reh.

Some paper.

Della carta.

DEHL-lah KAHR-tah.

Five pastries please.

Cinque pasticcini per favore.

CHEEN-kweh pahs-teech-CHEE-nee pehr fah-VOH-reh.

What ingredients does that cake contain?

Che ingredienti contiene quella torta?

keh een-greh-dee>EHN-tee kohn-tee>EH-neh KWEHL-lah TOHR-tah?

CHAPTER TEN: TRAVEL

W hether you're visiting Italy or you just need to explain to an Italian- speaking friend how to get across town, transportation vocab really comes in handy. This chapter helps you make your way through an airport and get through customs and helps you secure transportation when you're on the ground, either by taxi, bus, car, or train. Finally, we show you how to rent a car and how to ask for directions (but we don't tell you how to make someone else ask for directions!).

Getting through the Airport

At an Italian airport, you can likely get by with English, but the person you encounter may know only Italian. Just in case, you need to know some useful words and phrases. Besides, you'll probably want to practice the language in which you'll be immersed when you step outside the airport.

Checking in

The moment you finally get rid of your luggage is called check-in—or, in Italian, accettazione (ahch-cheht-tah-tsee-oh-neh). You also pick up your carta d'imbarco (kahr-tah deem-bahr-koh) (boarding pass) at the check-in counter.

Here are some things the ticket agent might say to you:

Il Suo biglietto, per favore. (eel soo-oh bee-lyeht-toh pehr fah-voh-reh) (Your ticket, please.) Passaporto? (pahs-sah-pohr-toh) (Passport?)

Quanti bagagli ha? (koo-ahn-tee bah-gah-lyee ah) (How many suitcases do you have?)

Preferisce un posto vicino al finestrino o al corridoio? (preh-feh-ree-sheh oon poh-stoh vee-chee-noh ahl fee-neh-stree-noh oh ahl kohr-ree-doh-ee-oh) (Do you prefer a window or an aisle seat?) L'imbarco è alle nove e quindici, uscita tre. (leem-bahr-koh eh ahl-leh noh-veh eh koo-een-dee-chee oo-shee-tah treh.

Waiting to board the plane

Before boarding, you may encounter unforeseen situations, such as delays. If you do, you'll probably want to ask some questions. The following sentences represent a typical conversation about this topic:

Il volo è in orario? (eel voh-loh eh een oh-rah-ree-oh) (Is the flight on time?)

No, è in ritardo. (noh eh een ree-tahr-doh) (No, there has been a delay.)

Di quanto? (dee koo-ahn-toh) (How much?)

Circa quindici minuti. (cheer-kah koo-een-dee-chee mee-noo-tee) (About 15 minutes.)

While you're waiting, two other questions may come in handy:

Dov'è il bar? (doh-veh eel bahr) (Where is the bar?)

Dove sono i servizi? (doh-veh soh-noh ee sehr-vee-dzee) (Where are the bathrooms?)

Taking care of business after landing

After your plane lands, you have to take care of necessities, such as finding a bathroom, changing money, looking for the baggage claim area, and securing a luggage cart and a taxi. The following questions may come in handy:

Dov'è un bancomat? (doh-veh oon bahn-koh-maht) (Where is an ATM?)

C'è anche una banca? (cheh ahn-keh oo-nah bahn-kah) (Is there also a bank?)

Dove sono i carrelli? (doh-veh soh-noh ee kahr-rehl-lee) (Where are the luggage carts?)

Going through customs

You can't get into a foreign country without going through dogana (doh-gah- nah) (customs). The customs agent asks Niente da dichiarare? (nee-ehn-teh dah dee-kee-ah-rah-reh) (Anything to declare?) You respond in one of two ways:

If you have something to declare, say Ho questo/queste cose da dichiarare. (oh koo-eh-stoh/koo-eh-steh koh-zeh dah dee-kee-ah-rah-reh) (I have to declare this/these things.) If not, say No, niente. (noh nee-ehn-teh) (No, nothing.)

In some cases, the customs agent will say Per questo deve pagare il dazio. (pehr koo-eh-stoh deh-veh pah-gah-reh eel dah-dzee-oh) (You have to pay duty on this.)

Renting a Car

If you don't have a car, you may need to rent one when you go on vacation. Whether you rent a car by phone or from a rental agency, the process is the same: Just tell the rental company what kind of car you want and under what conditions you want to rent it. The following dialogue represents a typical conversation with a rental agent:

Vorrei noleggiare una macchina. (vohr-ray noh-lehj-jah-reh oo-nah mahk-kee-nah) (I would like to rent a car.)

Che tipo? (keh tee-poh) (What kind?)

Di media cilindrata col cambio automatico. (dee meh-dee-ah chee-leen-drah-tah kohl kahm-bee-oh ah-oo-toh-mah-tee-koh) (A midsize with an automatic transmission.)

Per quanto tempo? (pehr koo-ahn-toh tehm-poh) (For how long?)

Una settimana. (oo-nah seht-tee-mah-nah) (One week.)

Quanto costa a settimana? (koo-ahn-toh koh-stah ah seht- tee-mah-nah) (What does it cost for a week?)

C'è una tariffa speciale. (cheh oo-nah tah-reef-fah speh-chah-leh) (There is a special rate.)
L'assicurazione è inclusa? (lahs-see-koo-rah-dzee-oh-neh eh een-kloo-

zah) (Is insurance included?)

Sì, con la polizza casco. (see kohn lah poh- leet-tsah kah-skoh) (Yes, a comprehensive policy.)

Navigating Public Transportation

If you'd rather not drive yourself, you can get around quite comfortably by using taxis, trains, and buses. This section tells you how to do so in Italian.

Taking a taxi

The process of hailing a taxi is the same in Italy as it is in the United States. You even use the same word: taxi (tah-ksee). Here are two phrases to use when requesting help getting a cab:

Può chiamarmi un taxi? (poo-oh kee-ah-mahr-mee oon tah-ksee) (Can you call me a taxi?) Vorrei un taxi, per favore. (vohr-ray oon tah-ksee pehr fah- voh-reh) (I'd like a taxi, please.)

In case you're asked per quando? (pehr koo-ahn-doh) (when?), you need to be prepared with an answer. Here are some possibilities:

subito (soo-bee-toh) (right now) fra un'ora (frah oon-oh-rah) (in one hour)

alle due del pomeriggio (ahl-leh doo-eh dehl poh-meh-reej-joh) (at 2:00 p.m.) domani mattina (doh-mah-nee maht-tee-nah) (tomorrow morning)

After you seat yourself in a taxi, the driver will ask where you want to go. Here are some potential destinations:

Alla stazione, per favore. (ahl-lah stah-dzee-oh-neh pehr fah-voh-reh) (To the station, please.) All'areoporto. (ahl-lah-reh-oh-pohr-toh) (To the airport.) A questo indirizzo: via Leopardi, numero 3. (ah koo-eh-stoh een-dee-reet- tsoh vee-ah leh-oh-pahr-dee noo-meh-roh treh) (To this address: via Leopardi, number 3.)

Finally, you have to pay. Simply ask the driver Quant'è? (koo-ahn-teh) (How much?).

Getting around by train

You can buy a train ticket alla stazione (ahl-lah stah-dzee-oh-neh) (at the station) or at un'agenzia di viaggi (oo-nah-jehn-dzee-ah dee vee-ahj-jee) (a travel agency). If you want to take a treno rapido (treh-noh rah-pee-doh) (express train), you pay a supplemento (soop-pleh-mehn-toh) (surcharge). These faster trains in Italy are called Inter City (IC)—or Euro City (EC) if their final destination is outside Italy.

Following are some words and phrases that can help you purchase the right ticket:

treni diretti (treh-nee dee-reht-tee) (direct trains) un locale (oon loh-kah- leh) (a slow train) in prima classe (een pree-mah klahs-seh) (first class) in seconda classe (een seh-kohn-dah klahs-seh) (second class) andata e ritorno (ahn-dah-tah eh ree-tohr-noh) (round-trip) solo andata (soh-loh ahn-dah-tah) (one-way) Devo cambiare? (deh-voh kahm-bee-ah-reh) (Do I have to change [trains]?) la coincidenza (lah koh-een-chee-dehn-dzah) (the connection) A che ora parte il prossimo treno? (ah keh oh-rah pahr-teh eel prohs-see-moh treh-noh) (What time is the next train?) Un biglietto per Perugia, per favore. (oon bee-lyeht-toh pehr peh-roo-jah pehr fah-voh-reh) (One ticket to Perugia, please.) il binario (eel bee-nah-ree-oh) (the platform, track) Da che binario parte? (dah keh bee-nah-ree-oh pahr-teh) (From which track does it leave?) Dal tre. (dahl treh) (From [track number] 3.)

Going by bus or tram

To get from point A to point B without a car, you can take a bus or a tram. This section provides the appropriate Italian vocabulary for such situations.

Some Italian cities have streetcars, or trams, and most have buses. In Italian, they spell it il tram (eel trahm). The general Italian word for bus is l'autobus (lah-oo-toh-boos). Little buses are called il pullmino (eel pool-mee-noh), and big buses that take you from one city to another are called il pullman (eel pool-mahn) or la corriera (lah kohr-ree-eh-rah).

You can buy bus or tram tickets in bars, dal giornalaio (dahl johr-nah-lah- ee-oh) (at newspaper stands), or dal tabaccaio (dahl tah-bahk-kah-ee-oh) (at a tobacco shop).

Italian tobacco shops are little shops where you can purchase cigarettes, stamps, newspapers, and so on. You find them on virtually every street corner in Italy; they're recognizable by either a black-and- white sign or a blue-and-white sign with a big T on it.

Reading the schedules can be difficult for travelers because they're usually written only in Italian. You frequently find the following words on schedules:

l'orario (loh-rah-ree-oh) (the timetable) partenze (pahr-tehn-dzeh) (departures) arrivi (ahr-ree-vee) (arrivals) giorni feriali (johr-nee feh-ree- ah-lee) (weekdays) giorni festivi (johr-nee feh-stee-vee) (Sundays and holidays) il binario (eel bee-nah-ree-oh) (the track, platform)

Asking for Directions

Have you ever been lost in a foreign place? If so, you realize how helpful it is to know enough of the native language to be able to ask for directions. Knowing the language also enables you to understand the answer. In this section, we give you some conversational tips that make it easier to find your way around.

Asking for specific places

When asking for directions, it's always polite to begin with one of the following expressions:

Mi scusi. (mee skoo-zee) (Excuse me.) Scusi. (skoo-zee) (Excuse me.) Per favore. (pehr fah-voh-reh) (Please.)

Then you can continue with your question, like the following:

Dov'è il Colosseo? (doh-veh el koh-lohs-seh-oh) (Where is the Colosseum?) Questa è via Garibaldi? (koo-eh-stah eh vee-ah gah-ree-bahl-dee) (Is this Garibaldi Street?) Come si arriva alla stazione? (koh-meh see ahr-ree-vah ahl-lah stah-dzee-oh-neh) (How do I get to the station?) Può indicarmi la strada per il centro? (poo-oh een-dee-kahr-mee lah strah-dah pehr eel chehn- troh) (Can you show me the way downtown?) Dove siamo adesso? (doh-veh see-ah-moh ah-dehs-soh) (Where are we now?) Mi sono perso. Dov'è il duomo? (mee soh-noh pehr-soh doh-veh eel doo-oh-moh) (I've lost my way. Where is the cathedral?)

Here are some possible answers to these questions:

Segua la strada principale fino al centro. (seh-goo-ah lah strah-dah preen- chee-pah-leh fee-noh ahl chehn-troh) (Follow the main street to the center of the city.) Vada sempre dritto. (vah-dah sehm-preh dreet-toh) (Go straight ahead.) Dopo il semaforo giri a destra. (doh-poh eel seh-mah-foh-roh jee-ree ah deh- strah) (After the traffic light, turn right.) È in fondo a sinistra. (eh een fohn-doh ah see-nee-strah) (It's at the end, on the left side.) È vicino alla posta. (eh vee-chee-noh ahl-lah poh-stah) (It's next to the post office.) Attraversi il ponte, poi c'è una piazza e lì lo vede. (aht-trah-vehr-see eel pohn-teh poh-ee cheh oo-nah pee-aht-tsah eh lee loh veh-deh) (Cross the bridge, then there's a square and there you see it.)

Getting oriented

Four orientations are the cardinal points of the compass:

nord (nohrd) (north) est (ehst) (east) sud (sood) (south) ovest (oh- vehst) (west)

You may hear the directions used in sentences like these:

Trieste è a nord-est. (tree-eh-steh eh ah nohrd-ehst) (Trieste is in the northeast.) Napoli è a sud. (nah-poh-lee eh ah sood) (Naples is in the south.) Roma è a ovest. (roh-mah eh ah oh-vehst) (Rome is in the west.) Bari è a sud-est. (bah-ree eh ah sood-ehst) (Bari is in the southeast.)

You need to know how to orient yourself in relation to people and buildings when following or giving directions. Following are some useful terms that describe spatial relationships:

davanti a (dah-vahn-tee ah) (in front of, opposite) di fronte a (dee frohn- teh ah) (opposite, in front of) In almost all cases, these terms are interchangeable.

dietro a (dee-eh-troh ah) (behind) vicino a (vee-chee-noh ah) (beside, next to) dentro (dehn-troh) (inside) fuori (foo-oh-ree) (outside) sotto (soht- toh) (under, below) sopra (soh-prah) (above)

You also need to know relationships between dis-tance and la direzione (lah dee-reh-tsee-oh-neh) (the direction):

dritto (dreet-toh) (straight) sempre dritto (sehm-preh dreet-toh) (straight ahead) fino a (fee-noh ah) (to, up to, until) prima (pree-mah) (before) dopo (doh-poh) (after) a destra (ah deh-strah) (on the right) a sinistra (ah see-nee-strah) (on the left) dietro l'angolo (dee-eh-troh lahn-goh-loh) (around the corner) all'angolo (ahl-lahn-goh-loh) (at the corner) all'incrocio (ahl-leen-kroh-choh) (at the intersection)

Here's some more vocab for giving and receiving directions:

il marciapiede (eel mahr-chah-pee-eh-deh) (sidewalk) la piazza (lah pee- aht-tsah) (square) il ponte (eel pohn-teh) (bridge) il sottopassaggio (eel

soht-toh-pahs-sahj-joh) (underpass) la strada (lah strah-dah) (road, street) la via (lah vee-ah) (road, street) la via principale (lah vee-ah preen-chee-pah- leh) (main street) il viale (eel vee-ah-leh) (parkway, avenue) il vicolo (eel vee-koh-loh) (alley, lane)

La strada and la via are synonymous, but you always use via when the name is specified:

E' una strada molto lunga. (eh oo-nah strah-dah mohl-toh loon- gah) (It's a very long road.) Abito in via Merulana. (ah-bee-toh een vee-ah meh-roo-lah-nah) (I live on Merulana Street.)

When giving and receiving directions, you need a command of numeri ordinali (noo-meh-ree ohr-dee-nah-lee) (ordinal numbers).

What to say when you don't understand If you don't understand the directions someone gives you, you need to ask that person to repeat the directions. Here are some useful expressions: Come, scusi? (koh-meh skoo-zee) (I beg your pardon?) Mi scusi, non ho capito. (mee skoo-zee nohn oh kah- pee-toh) (I'm sorry, I didn't understand.) Può ripetere più lentamente, per favore? (poo-oh ree-peh-teh-reh pee-oo lehn-tah- mehn-teh pehr fah-voh-reh) (Can you please repeat it more slowly?) When someone does you a favor—explaining the way or giving you directions—you probably want to say thanks. That one's easy: Mille grazie! (meel-leh grah-tsee-eh) (Thanks a million!)

Asking how far something is

You may want to know how near or far you are from your destination. Here are some typical questions and responses:

Quant'è lontano? (koo-ahn-teh lohn-tah-noh) (How far is it?) Saranno cinque minuti. (sah-rahn-noh cheen-koo-eh mee-noo-tee) (About five minutes.) È molto lontano? (eh mohl-toh lohn-tah-noh) (Is it very far?) Circa un chilometro. (cheer-kah oon kee-loh-meh-troh) (About one kilometer.) No, un paio di minuti. (noh oon pah-yoh dee mee-noo-tee) (No, a couple of minutes.) Posso arrivarci a piedi? (pohs-soh ahr-ree-vahr-chee ah pee-eh-dee) (Can I walk there?) Certo, è molto vicino. (chehr-toh eh mohl-toh vee-chee-noh) (Sure, it's very close.) È un po' lontano. (eh oon poh lohn-tah-noh) (It's a bit far away.)

Verbs on the move

You need to know certain verbs when trying to understand directions. These are some of the verbs you'll find handy for finding your way:

andare (ahn-dah-reh) (to go) girare a destra/a sinistra (jee-rah-reh ah deh-strah/ah see-nee-strah) (to turn right/left) prendere (prehn-deh-reh) (to take) proseguire (proh-seh-goo-ee-reh) (to go on) seguire (seh-goo-ee-reh) (to follow) tornare/indietro (tohr-nah-reh/een-dee-eh-troh) (to go back)

Imperatives are useful verb forms to know in a variety of situations, including when you're trying to get around in unfamiliar territory. Notice that the endings of these verbs vary, apparently without a consistent pattern. These aren't typing mistakes—they're determined by the ending of the infinitive form of the verb, -are, -ere, or –ire. You can simply believe us and memorize these verbs.

No doubt the most frequently used verb in giving and receiving instructions is andare (ahn-dah-reh) (to go).

Locations you may be looking for

When you're searching for a specific place, these sentences can help you ask the right questions.

Mi sa dire dov'è la stazione? (mee sah dee-reh doh-veh lah stah-dzee-oh- neh)

(Can you tell me where the station is?)

Devo andare all'aeroporto. (deh-voh ahn-dah-reh ahl-lah-eh-roh-pohr-toh)

(I have to go to the airport.)

Sto cercando il teatro Argentina. (stoh chehr-kahn-doh eel teh-ah-troh ahr- jehn-tee-nah) (I'm looking for the Argentina theater.)

Dov'è il cinema Astoria? (doh-veh eel chee-neh-mah ah-stoh-ree-ah)

(Where is the Astoria cinema?)

Come posso arrivare al Museo Romano? (koh-meh pohs-soh ahr- ree-vah-reh ahl moo-zeh-oh roh-mah-noh) (How can I get to the Roman Museum?)

La strada migliore per il centro, per favore? (lah strah-dah mee- lyoh-reh pehr eel chehn-troh pehr fah-voh-reh)

(The best way to downtown, please?)

Che chiesa è questa? (keh kee-eh-zah eh koo-eh-stah)

(What church is this?)

Che autobus va all'ospedale? (keh ah-oo-toh-boos vah ahl-loh- speh-dah-leh)

(Which bus goes to the hospital?)

CHAPTER ELEVEN: BODY, DOCTOR AND MEDICAL EMERGNCY

The World Health Organization ranked the Italian health system as the second best in the world, after France. However, public opinion in Italy is in stark contrast with this report. The same organization places Italy in sixth place for life expectancy. In Italy every citizen is guaranteed free medical assistance. A health card gives them access to the Servizio Sanitario Nazionale (SSN) and therefore to medicines (farmaci, medicine), visits to doctors and spe- cialists (visite specialistiche), diagnostic exams, hospital admission, etc. Essential examinations and farmaci indispensabili (indispensable medicines) are free for all. All diagnostic tests, specialist visits, and farmaci non indispensabili (dispensable medicines) must be paid for, unless they fall into one of the exempted categories (children under 6, seniors over 65 with a low income, the unemployed, and people with recognized medical conditions). Unless exempted, for dispensable drugs Italians pay un ticket (a user fee) plus the cost of the medicine.

In many tourist towns there are clinics just for tourists. The cost of each visit at the ambulatorio (doctor's office) is 15 euros; a house call is 25 euros. It is wise, before leaving your country, to acquire medical insurance to cover you while traveling. If you require medical services in Italy, be sure to obtain an invoice afterward. You will need it for the insurance claim. For medical emergencies call the pronto soccorso (first aid) at 118.

Sono un turista e non ho diritto

I am a tourist and I am not covered by

al Servizio Sanitario Nazionale.

the Servizio Sanitario Nazionale.

Quanto potrà costarmi

How much could this visit cost me?

questa visita?

SO-no oon too-REE-stah eh nohn oh dee-REET-toh ahl Sair-VEE-tsee-oh Sahn-ee-TAH-ree-oh Nah-tsee- oh-NAH-leh QUAHN-toh po-TRAH co-STAHR-mee QUEH-stah VEE-zee-tah

Dov'è il pronto soccorso?

Where is the emergency room?

Do-VEH eel PRON-toh soc-COR-so

Dov'è il reparto di cardiologia?

Where is the cardiology wing?

DO-VEH eel reh-PAHR-toh dee

cahr-dee-LO-jee-ah

Come arrivo al reparto di terapia

How do I get to the intensive-care unit ?

intensiva?

CO-meh ahr-REE-vo ahl reh-PAHR-toh

dee teh-RAH-pee-ah een- tehn-SEE-vah

Vorrei fi ssare un appuntamento con il dottore. (Vor-RAY fees-SAH-reh oon ap-poon-tah-MEHN-toh kohn eel dot-TOH-reh): I would like to make an appointment with the doctor.

If you are not feeling well and need to visit a doctor, tell him/her what your symptoms (sintomi) are. If you are not sure what is making you sick, start with general sentences, stating that you are not feeling well, such as: Mi sento male; non mi sento bene; mi sento poco bene. Of course, if you are able to identify the problem, expressions starting with Mi fa male..., Ho mal di..., or simply Ho... will definitely help in expressing it:

Ho mal di gola	(I have a sore throat);
Ho mal di testa	(I have an headache);
Ho mal di denti	(I have a toothache);
Mi fa male la pancia	(I have stomach pains);
Ho la febbre	(I have a fever);
Ho il raffred- dore	(I have a cold);
Ho l'influenza	(I have the flu).

Mi sento male. Ho bisogno di

I feel sick. I need a doctor.

un medico.

Mee SEHN-toh MAH-leh Oh

bee-ZON-yo dee oon MEH-dee-co

Dov'è l'ambulatorio medico?

Where is the doctor's office?

Do-VEH lahm-boo-lah-TOH-ree-oh

MEH-dee-co

Dottore, mi può prescrivere

Doctor, can you prescribe me something?

qualcosa?

Dot-TOH-reh mee poo-OH

preh-SCREE-veh-reh quahl-CO-zah

Adesso mi sento meglio.

I feel better now.

Ah-DES-so mee SEHN-toh MEHL-yo

Dottore, potrebbe suggerirmi un buono specialista? (Dot-TOH-reh po-TREB-beh soo-jeh-REER-mee oon boo-ON speh- chee-ah-LEE-stah): Doctor, could you please suggest a good specialist?

If you should see a specialist, be prepared to pay the necessary fee. However, it is not always easy to get an immediate appointment with a specialist. In most cases, a specialist will give you an appointment only if you are referred by a doctor. Here are the titles of some special- ists: dermatologo (dermatologist), oculista (eye specialist), otorino (ear, nose, and throat specialist), pediatra (pediatrician), oncologo (oncolo- gist). Note that the Italian and English words are often very similar.

Dov'è lo studio del dentista?

Where is the dentist's office?

Do-VEH lo STOO-dee-oh del

dehn-TEE-stah

Vorrei fissare un appuntamento

I would like to get an appointment

con un cardiologo.

with a cardiologist.

Vor-RAY fees-SAH-reh oon ah-poon-

ta-MEHN-toh kohn oon

car-dee-OH-lo-go

Ho vomitato tutto il giorno. (Oh vo-mee-TAH-toh TOOT- toh eel JOR-no): I've vomited all day.

Although it is easy to express one's medical problems with gen- eral words such as those mentioned previously, it is problematic to describe the exact symptoms to a doctor or to a specialist (specialista). This is because symptoms are often vague, subjective, and intangible; furthermore, their description normally requires a specialized language and precise details. A good description can be difficult even for native speakers.

Avrà un'intossicazione alimentare.

It is probably food poisoning.

Ah-VRAH oon-in-tos-see-cah-tsee-

OH-neh ah-lee-man-TAH-reh

Ho la diarrea da due giorni.

I've had diarrhea for two days.

Oh lah dee-ar-REH-ah dah

DOO-eh JOR-nee

Sono diabetico. (SO-no dee-ah-BEH-tee-co):

I am diabetic.

If you have an existing condition, it is important to check that your medical insurance covers this condition before traveling to Italy. It is also wise to learn the basic Italian vocabulary associated with the condition. Wearing an appropriate medical alert bracelet (braccialetto di assistenza sanitaria) or carrying a note in your wallet specifying your condition is essential and could save your life. Braccialetti for diabetes (il diabete), for heart conditions (i cardiopatici), for people with Alzheimer's (l'alzheimer), or epilepsy (l'epilessia), etc., are found worldwide.

Sono allergico a...

I am allergic to . . .

SO-no ahl-LEHR-jee-co ah

Soffro di...

I suffer from . . .

SOHF-froh dee

Sono epilettico.

I am epileptic.

SO-no eh-pee-LET-tee-co

Sono cardiopatico.

I have a heart condition.

SO-no cahr-dee-oh-PAH-tee-co

Sono incinta. (SO-no in-CHEEN-tah): I am pregnant.

The first trimester of pregnancy (gravidanza) is always the most delicate for a woman, because she must adapt to the changes in her body, but also because of the risk of miscarriage. When traveling during the first few months of pregnancy, women must take extra precautions. And at the end of the pregnancy there may be some discomfort. Before undertaking a trip during pregnancy, a woman should talk with her gynecologist (ginecologo).

Ho una forte nausea.

I'm really sick to my stomach.

Oh OO-nah FOR-teh NAH-

oo-zeh-ah

Ho un forte bruciore allo

I have a strong heartburn.

stomaco.

Oh oon FOR-teh bru-chee-OH-reh

AL-lo STO-mah-co

Dov'è la farmacia? (Doh-VEH lah far-mah-CHEE-ah): Where is the pharmacy?

Pharmacies are not hard to spot in Italy as they are easily recognizable by a lit green cross. In small towns, pharmacies are normally located on the main roads or in the town square. If a pharmacy is closed, you will find a sign indicating which neighborhood pharmacy is on call (di turno). Please remember that pharmacies in Italy normally sell pharmaceutical products only and do not sell many of the items you normally find in North American drug stores.

Ecco la ricetta medica.

Here is my medical prescription.

EC-co la ree-CHEHT-tah MEH-dee-cah

Mi servono delle aspirine,

I would like some aspirin, please.

per favore.

Mee SAIR-vo-no DEL-leh ahs-pee-

REE-neh pair fah-VO-reh

Ha pastiglie per la nausea?

Do you have any antinausea pills?

Ah pah-STEEL-yeh pair lah

NAH-oo-zeh-ah

Un piccolo consiglio, per favore. (Oon PEEK-ko-lo kohn- SEEL-yo pair fah-VO-reh): A little advice, please.

If you are not sure about a product in a pharmacy, ask the pharmacist (il/la farmacista). He/she will be happy to help you. If it is unclear how to use a product, ask him/her to explain how many times you must take the medicine and the dose. It is also important to disclose any allergies you might have.

Sono allergico al lattosio.

I am allergic to lactose.

SO-no ahl-LEHR-jee-koh ahl

laht-TOH-zee-oh

Prenda questa medicina due

Take this medicine twice daily.

volte al giorno.

PREHN-dah QUEH-stah meh-dee-

CHEE-nah doo-eh VOHL-teh

ahl JOR-noh

Le suggerisco questo sciroppo

I recommend this cough syrup.

per la tosse.

Leh sood-jeh-REE-sko QUEH-stoh

shee-ROP-po pair lah TOS-she

Ci sono effetti collaterali?

Are there any side effects?

Chee SO-no ehf-FEHT-tee

cohl-lah-teh-RAH-lee

Dov'è l'erboristoria? (Do-VEH lair-bo-ree-sto-REE-ah): Where is the health food store?

People have always turned to nature to find health remedies. In an erboristeria there are all sorts of natural products and health foods such as natural remedies, herbal teas (tisane), digestives and antialler- gies, organic foods (alimenti biologici), natural hair products, etc. The old generation in Italy will always offer advice on how to cure your cold, your cough, your sore throat, etc., naturally. Homeopathy is the most common alternative medicine in Italy.

C'è una farmacia omeopatica

Is there a homeopathic pharmacy

qui vicino? close by?

Cheh OO-nah far-ma-CHEE-ah

oh-meh-oh-pah-TEE-cah

kwee vee-CHEE-no

Ha dei prodotti antirughe?

Do you have any antiwrinkle

Ah day pro-DOT-tee ahn-tee- products?

ROO-geh

Vorrei comprare delle vitamine.

I would like to buy some vitamins.

Vor-RAY cohm-PRAH-reh dehl-le

vee-tah-MEE-neh

CHAPTER TWELVE: SPORT

Chi gioca oggi? (Kee JO-cah OD-jee): Who's playing today?

Soccer is by far the most popular sport in Italy and is followed on a daily basis by the majority of Italians: men and women, children and seniors alike. Soccer players are highly regarded; their status is at the same level, if not higher, as Hollywood celebrities. When one asks Chi gioca?, by default, he/she is referring to that day's soccer game. Similarly, when one talks about la nazionale or the Azzurri, he/she is talking about the national soccer team. Italians are very proud of their favorite club team and their national team. The Azzurri national team is among the very best in the world and has won the World Cup (Coppa del Mondo) on four different occa- sions: 1934, 1938, 1982, and 2006. Only Brazil has a better record. Other very popular sports in Italy are Formula Uno, pallacanestro or basket, ciclismo, pallavolo, and boxe (boxing). Baseball and football americano (to distinguish it from soccer/football) are not popular sports in Italy.

Contro chi gioca la nazionale?

Against which team is the national

KOHN-tro kee JO-cah lah nah-tsee-

team playing?

oh-NAH-leh

Chi è stato convocato?

Which players were selected (to be

Kee eh STAH-toh kohn-vo-CAH-toh

part of the national team)?

Quando è la partita di ritorno?

When is the second-leg match?

QUAHN-doh eh lah pahr-TEE-tah

dee ree-TOR-no

In quale stadio stanno giocando?

In which stadium are they playing?

Een QUAH-leh STAH-dee-oh

STAN-no jo-CAHN-doh

Secondo te, chi vincerà lo scudetto/il campionato? (SEH- kohn-doh teh kee veen-cheh-RAH lo scoo-DET-toh/eel cahm-pee-oh- NAH-toh): In your opinion, who will win the scudetto (championship shield)/(soccer) championship?

On Saturday and Sunday, Italians religiously follow the campionato with their many different leagues. The first soccer tournament dates to 1898. The Serie A (Premiere League), the most important league, is the source of discussions, speculations, and debates, from August through the end of May. These lively discussions take place among family members, friends, and colleagues, but also in newspapers and on radio and television shows. The discussion becomes even more intense with the European Champions League games (Coppa dei Campioni [Champion's league]), usually played during midweek. Even during the summer, when the soccer championship is resting, Italians are discussing the calcio-mercato, that is, the many trades between clubs to acquire the best players.

Since 1946, Italians have been legally betting on soccer games with Totocalcio (soccer pool) and its famous schedina (betting pool), which is run by CONI, the Italian Olympic Committee, and whose profit is used to promote all sports in Italy. The idea behind the schedina is simple: One must guess the results of thirteen (now fourteen) soccer games, by using a 1 to indicate a win for the home team, a 2 for a win for the away team, and an X for a tie. For fifty years the schedina was the lottery game par excellence in Italy and it was part of a national tradition. Its symbols 1, X, 2 were part of everyday language; the number 13 became the Italian lucky number as guessing all thirteen results would make you a millionaire. In the past ten years, however, the game is somewhat in decline because of the competition of many lottery games with higher jackpots.

Hai giocato la schedina?

Did you play the schedina?

Aye jo-CAH-toh lah skeh-DEE-nah

Per quale squadra fai il tifo?

Which is your favorite team?

Pair QUAH-leh SQUAH-drah fye

eel TEE-fo

Chi sono le favorite?

Which are the favorite teams (to win

Kee SO-no leh fah-vo-REE-teh

the championship)?

Qual è il tuo pronostico per

What's your prediction for today's

la partita di oggi?   game?

Quah-LEH eel TOO-oh pro-NO-stee-co

266

pair lah pahr-TEE-tah dee OD-jee

Che partita fanno vedere in televisione? (Keh pahr-TEE- tah FAN-no veh-DEH-reh een teh-leh-vee-zee-OH-neh): Which game are they showing on television?

The cost for a ticket (un biglietto) to watch a soccer match at the stadio (stadium) varies from as low as 30 euros to over 100 euros for the best seats. You will find that online tickets are exorbitantly higher. If you are a soccer fan and cannot afford or find a ticket, there are plenty of opportunities to watch a game on television or even listen to it on the radio. On the RAIRadio1 program Tutto il calcio minuto per minuto, which has been running since 1960, you can listen to all Serie A games and enjoy the live and exciting play-by-play action by some of the best radio announcers in the world. Many television networks also dedicate a large part of their Saturday and Sunday programs to soc- cer games and to programs almost completely dedicated to soccer, showing the goals and the highlights of all games, assigning a score to each individual player, the coaches, and the referees. Very common is the so-called moviola, a frame-by-frame replay used in television programs (but not in the field) to analyze the decisions of the ref- eree (arbitro) regarding penalty kicks (i rigori), goals (le reti, i goals), whether a player was offside (fuori gioco, offside) or not, etc. If you enter a room or a sports bar where a game is being shown on television, use the questions below to get instant updates. Just make sure to ask these questions at a time when the action is not too intense!

Qual è il risultato? / Quanto

What's the score?

stanno?

Quah-LEH eel ree-zool-TAH-toh /

KWAHN-toh STAHN-no

Chi vince/sta vincendo/ha vinto?

Who is winning/is winning/won?

Kee VEEN-cheh/stah veen-

CHEHN-doh/ah VEEN-toh

Chi gioca in porta?

ùWho is playing in the goal?

Kee JO-cah een POR-tah

Chi ha segnato? Who scored?

Kee ah sehn-YAH-toh

Chi è l'arbitro? (Kee eh LAHR-bee-tro): Who is the referee?

In Italy, as the expression goes, there are 50 million coaches. Every Italian believes that he or she has the knowledge to be a soccer coach (allenatore). For this reason, before each game Italians feel entitled to propose la formazione della squadra (the team lineup) for that game; during the game they like to comment on what they watch; afterward they analyze the game. If you are an avid soccer fan and would like to comment on the game you are watching or listening to, you will have ample opportunities to do so. However, do not make your com- ments during a very critical or intense time in the game; furthermore, make sure that your comments do not upset the majority of people present.

Ma perché non fa giocare Del

But why does he (the coach) not

Piero?

let Del Piero play?

Mah pair-KEH nohn fah jo-CAH-reh

Del Pee-EH-ro

Il tackle meritava un cartellino

The tackle deserved a yellow card.

giallo.

Eel TAK-kel meh-ree-TAH-vah oon

cahr-tel-LEE-no JAL-lo

Il giocatore meritava l'espulsione;

The player deserved to be expelled

era un fallo da cartellino rosso.

from the game; the foul deserved

Eel jo-cah-TOH-reh meh-ree-TAH-vah   a red card.

leh-spool-zee-OH-neh; EH-rah

oon FAL-lo dah cahr-tel-LEE-no

ROS-so

Ma l'arbitro e i segnalinee cosa

But what are the referee and the

fanno, dormono? È rigore...

linesmen doing, sleeping? It was a

altro che punizione.

penalty kick not a free kick!

Mah LAHR-bee-tro eh ee sehn-ya-

lee-NEH-eh COH-sah FAN-no

DOR-mo-no Eh ree-GO-reh

268

AHL-tro keh poo-nee-tsee-OH-neh

Chi è prima in classifi ca? (Kee eh PREE-mah een clas-SEE- fee-cah): Who is first in the standings?

For Italians, meeting friends to discuss soccer results on Sunday eve- ning or Monday morning is a way to socialize and to get informed if someone missed the live action. If you missed a game and want an instant update, you might want to visit the local sports bar, enjoy the lively discussion, and participate in the conversation. Soccer, like many other sports, is a way to break all sorts of barriers. Sports fans will definitely answer all your questions.

Qual è stato il risultato di

What was the score for AC

Milan-Roma?   Milan-Rome?

Quah-LEH eh STAH-toh eel

ree-zool-TAH-toh dee Mee-

LAHN-RO-mah

Ha vinto la Juventus?

Did Juventus win?

Ah VEEN-toh lah Yoo-VEHN-toos

Chi è il capocannoriere?

Who is the leading scorer?

Kee eh eel cah-po-can-no-ree-EH-reh

Chi ha segnato per l'Inter?

Who scored for Inter Milan?

Kee ah sehn-YA-toh pair LEEN-tair

Chi c'é nel girone dell'Inter? (Kee cheh nel jee-RO-neh del- LEEN-tair): Who is in the round-robin together with Inter Milan?

Besides Italian championship and national team games, Italians closely follow the European Champion's League tournament, a tournament in which the best European teams, the winners of the national cham- pionship, and the second- to fourth-placed teams participate. Italian teams have the best record in this championship; Italy has won eleven times and has been runner-up fourteen times. Another very prestigious tournament (torneo) is the UEFA Cup. The participants in this tournament are the National Cup winners and the three teams that placed immediately after the Champions League team. The winner of the Champions League plays against the winner of the UEFA Cup for the Supercoppa (Europe Super Cup). Following a similar format, the winner of the Italian Championship winner plays the Copia Italia winner for an Italian Supercoppa. The most prestigious European cup is the UEFA European Cham- pionship, which Italy won only once in

269

1968. These tournaments are divided into several stages: in the turno preliminare (preliminary/qualifying round), teams are divided into gironi (round-robin groups); the winners and second-place teams advance to the quarti di finali (quarterfinals) then to the semifinali (semifinals) and the finali (finals) by playing two direct elimination

games, one at home (in casa) and one away from home (fuori casa). The finals consist of one game only. The Pallone d'oro (Golden Ball) is the most prestigious award for individual players. It is awarded annually by European journalists to the single top player in any European league.

Chi gioca in casa?

Which team is playing at home?

Kee JO-cah een CAH-zah

Siamo solo al turno preliminare!

We are only in the preliminary round!

See-AH-mo SO-lo ahl TOOR-no

preh-lee-mee-NAH-reh

Chi si è qualificato per

Which teams qualified for the semifinals?

le semifinali?

Kee see eh quah-lee-fee-CAH-toh

pair leh seh-mee-fee-NAH-lee

Quando si giocano le finali?

When are the finals played?

QUAHN-doh see JO-cah-no leh

fee-NAH-lee

Chi ha comprato il Milan? (Kee ah cohm-PRAH-toh eel Mee- LAHN): Whom (which players) did AC Milan buy?

Even during the summer, when the Italian championship is not being played, Italian fans (tifosi) still have much to discuss. In fact, it is dur- ing this period that Italian teams trade players. Fans follow the calcio- mercato news and have solid opinions about the players that are needed to improve each team. Some will suggest that their squadra (team) needs a better portiere (goalkeeper) or defense (difesa); others will prefer that their team strengthen the centrocampo (midfield) or the attack (attacco). The allenatore (coach/trainer) is often the scape-

goat for a poor season. It seems each fan can come up with a solution to better the team with his/her own possible formazione (lineup). Many fans will watch the team during their allenamento (practice) or during the partite amichevoli (friendly/preseason games).

Alla Roma serve un centrocam-

Roma needs a strong midfielder.

pista forte.

AL-lah RO-mah SAIR-veh oon

chehn-tro-cahm-PEE-stah FOR-teh

Quando va in ritiro il Napoli?

When does Naples start its training camp?

QUAHN-doh vah een ree-TEE-ro eel

NAH-po-lee

È solo una partita amichevole?

Is it only a preseason/friendly game?

Eh SO-lo OO-nah pahr-TEE-tah

ah-mee-KEH-vo-leh

Chi gioca in difesa?

Who is playing defense?

Kee JO-cah een dee-FEH-zah

Chi ha vinto la tappa? (Kee ah VEEN-toh lah TAP-pah): Who won the cycling stage?

Ciclismo (cycling) is another very popular sport in Italy, with thou- sands of riders cycling every day. The Giro d'Italia, the most popular cycling race in Italy, is 100 years old; it is divided into stages which total about 2500 kilometers covering almost all regions of Italy, and it lasts almost the entire month of May. Each stage has a winner; the overall leader wears the maglia rosa (pink jersey), but there are many colored jerseys for a variety of leaders. For example, the green jersey is assigned to the leading mountain climbers. Cyclists (ciclisti) are unofficially divided into three categories; there are sprinters, scalatori (mountain climbers), and gregari (support cyclists who work for the capitano [team captain]).

Chi ha vinto la tappa a

Who won the cronometer stage?

cronometro?

Kee ah VEEN-toh lah TAP-pah ah

cro-no-MEH-tro

Di quanti chilometri è la tappa?

How many kilometers is the stage?

Dee QUAHN-tee kee-LO-meh-tree

eh lah TAP-pah

A che ora è previsto l'arrivo?

At what time is the arrival expected?

Ah keh OH-rah eh preh-VEE-sto

lar-REE-vo

Chi è la maglia rosa?

Who is the overall leader?

Kee eh lah MAHL-yah RO-zah

Dov'è il prossimo Gran Premio? (Doh-VEH eel PROS- see-mo Grahn PREH-mee-oh): Where is the next Grand Prix?

The Ferrari, or simply La Rossa, with its fifteen Formula Uno (Formula One) titles since its beginning in 1952, is perhaps the most celebrated car in the world and is a symbol of elegance, power, and speed. For- mula Uno races are followed by sports fans of every nationality and Italian fans are no exception. Alfa Romeo and Maserati are also cars that have fared well in car racing. There are two Formula One titles: The most prestigious is for drivers (piloti); the other is for costruttori (constructors). Before each Grand Prix, there are the trials (le prove) which will decide the starting order for the actual race. The car which cleared the shortest time for a lap will be assigned the pole position. During the race (la gara), cars will stop to change the tires (le ruote) and for fuel.

Chi guida la classifica dei piloti?

Who is leading the driver standings?

Kee goo-EE-dah lah clas-SEE-fee-

cah day pee-LO-tee

Chi guida la classifica dei

Who is leading the constructor

costruttori? standings?

Kee goo-EE-dah lah clas-SEE-fee-cah

day co-stroot-TOH-ree

Chi è in pole position?

Who has pole position?

Kee eh een pole position

A che posto si trova la Ferrari?

What place is the Ferrari in?

Ah keh PO-sto see TRO-vah lah

Fer-RAH-ree

Quando incomincia il campionato del mondo di sci? (QUAHN-doh een-co-MEEN-cha eel cahm-pee-oh-NAH-toh del MOHN-doh dee she): When does the skiing world championship start?

Very popular sports in Italy also include pallacanestro or basket, ten- nis, boxe, atletica leggera (track and field), pallavolo (volleyball), pal- lanuoto (water polo), motociclismo (motorcycling), sci (ski), ginnastica (gymnastics), nuoto (swimming), and scherma (fencing). Many are the international and Olympics (Olimpiadi) successes of Italian teams and athletes in these disciplines. Less popular sports are rugby, baseball, cricket, football americano (football), pallamano (handball), and hockey.

Chi ha vinto nello stile libero?

Who won the (swimming) free-style

Kee ah VEEN-toh NEL-lo STEE-leh race?

LEE-beh-ro

Quando si disputa lo slalom

When is the giant slalom race?

gigante?

QUAHN-doh see dee-SPOO-tah lo

SLAH-lohm jee-GAHN-teh

Quanti punti ha fatto Andrea

How many points did Andrea

Bargnani nella gara contro

Bargnani score against the

i Knicks?

 Knicks?

QUAHN-tee POON-tee ah FAT-toh

Ahn-DREH-ah Bahrn-YA-nee NEL-

lah GAH-rah KOHN-tro ee Knicks

Chi ha vinto il torneo interna-

Who won the Rome Masters

ionale di tennis a Roma?

Tournament?

Kee ah VEEN-toh eel tor-NEH-oh

een-tair-nah-tsee-oh-NAH-leh

dee TEN-nees ah RO-mah

Hai comprato La Gazzetta dello Sport? (Aye kohm-PRAH- toh Lah gahts-SET-tah DEL-lo sport): Did you buy the Gazzetta dello Sport?

Italy is one of the few nations that has not one but three daily newspa- pers exclusively dedicated to sports: La Gazzetta dello Sport, Il Corriere dello Sport,and Tuttosport. All three newspapers have a long tradition: the Gazzetta dates to 1896, the Corriere to 1924, Tuttosport to 1945. All three newspapers also have a wide national circulation: the Gazzetta has a circulation of over 500,000 copies; in 1982, when Italy won the World Cup, the Gazzetta sold almost 3 million copies and the Corriere almost 2 million. There are also many weekly and monthly sports magazines, many of them specializing in a specific sport.

Please remember that Italian daily, weekly, and monthly newspa- pers, as well as magazines, are sold at specialized newspaper stands (edicola), at smoke shops (tabacchino), and at local bars. Similarly, there are many cable television and pay-TV programs dedicated exclusively to sports. These give you the opportunity to watch not only various sports events but also many sports talk shows.

Hai visto l'incontro di basket

Did you watch the basketball game

alla televisione?

on television?

Aye VEE-sto leen-KOHN-tro dee

BAHS-ket AL-lah teh-leh-vee-

zee-OH-neh

Quale trasmissione televisiva ti

Which television program do you

piace di più: 90° minuto

like best: 90° minuto or La giostra del gol?

oppure La giostra del gol?

QUAH-leh trahz-mees-see-OH-neh

teh-leh-vee-ZEE-vah tee

pee-AH-cheh dee PEW: No-

vahn-TEH-zee-mo mee-NOO-toh

op-POO-reh Lah JO-strah del gol

Pensi che Beckham rimarrà con il Milan?

Do you think that Beckham will remain with AC Milan?

PEHN-zee keh Beckham ree-mahr-

RAH kohn eel Mee-LAHN

Che voto hanno dato nella pagella

What mark did Ronaldinho get in his

a Ronaldinho? (game) report card?

Keh VO-toh AHN-no DAH-toh

NEL-lah pah-JEL-lah ah

Ro-nahl-DEEN-yoh

Andiamo a fare un po' di jogging. (Ahn-dee-AH-mo ah FAH-reh oon poh dee jogging): Let's go jogging.

As previously discussed, Italians like to read about sports and watch it on television. Their involvement in personal sports activities is, however, somewhat limited. Many go to the palestra (gym), the centri benessere (wellness centers), or the centri sportivi (sports centers), but in general Italians do not attend as avidly as North Americans. The cost of a gym membership is about 20 to 30 euros per month. Italians stay in forma (in shape) by doing a lot of walking and other natural activities; also, they use bicycles much more than North Americans. In schools, two hours a week are dedicated to gym activities. How- ever, school-related sports tournaments are not nearly as common as in North America. Outside school, the most popular sports activities for Italian children are soccer, basketball, volleyball, bicycling, dance, aqua fitness, swimming, and yoga.

Dove trovo una piscina all'aperto?

Where can I find an outdoor pool?

DO-veh TROH-vo OO-nah

pee-SHE-nah al-lah-PAIR-toh

Quanto costa un abbonamento

How much is a gym membership?

per la palestra?

QUAHN-toh CO-stah oon ab-bo-nah-

MEHN-toh pair lah pah-LEH-strah

Vi sono dei campi da tennis

Are there any tennis courts available?

disponibili?

Vee SO-no day CAHM-pee dah

TEN-nees dee-spo-NEE-bee-lee

Vorrei fare un po' di sollevamento pesi.

I would like to do some weight lifting.

Vor-RAY FAH-reh oon po dee

sol-leh-vah-MEHN-toh PEH-zee

Forza Italia! (FORT-sah Ee-TAH-lee-ah): Go, Italy, go!

Sports fans all over the world support their team by going to games. Their support is often shown by cheering their team (or booing the opposite team) during the game or by displaying large support ban- ners. Holding support banners in Italy is quite common and well coor- dinated in the stadiums; slogans used by fans are often collected in books as if it were an art form. While the Italian national soccer team is playing, the fans will encourage the players with Forza Italia! or Forza Azzurri! while proudly waving the Italian flag.

Italia! Italia! Italia!

Go, Italy, go!

Ee-TAH-lee-ah Ee-TAH-lee-ah

Ee-TAH-lee-ah

Forza Milan!

Go, Milan, go!

FORT-sah Mee-LAHN

Forza Roma! Forza lupi!

Go, Rome, go! Go, Rome, go!

(lupo wolf; the reference is to the symbol of AC Roma)

FORT-sah RO-mah FORT-sah

LOO-pee

Viva la Juve! Abbasso l'Inter!

Go, Juve, go! Down with Inter!

VEE-vah lah YOO-veh Ab-BAS-so LEEN-tair

CHAPTER THIRTEEN: WEATHER, THEATER AND ART

Whether you travel to Italy, page through a coffee-table book featuring Italian artists, or listen to opera on the radio, the plethora of Italian art is unavoidable. A wide variety of amazing artwork has been created in Italy from before the Roman Empire up to the present day, and it provides a unique way to study the language while learning more about the artistic patrimony of Italy.

The Big Names

Michelangelo, Raffaello, Leonardo, and Donatello have at least one thing in common: Most people nowa- days know these artists by their first names. Obviously, they had cognomi (last names) too:

- Michelangelo Buonarroti

- Raffaello Sanzio

- Donato di Betto Bardi (Donatello)

- Leonardo da Vinci

Along the Way, Keep in Mind When referring to a particular artistic period in a century between 1100 and 1900, Italians drop the mille (thousand). For example, they call the 1300s il Trecento, the 1400s il Quattrocento, and so on. Also, you should know that there's a price to pay for everything-even church. So be aware! Some churches in Italy now request an entrance fee to offset the cost of maintenance, claiming that the artwork found on their walls, by such artists as Filippo Brunelleschi, Masaccio, and Giotto, are equal to any found in museums. Town residents are exempt from paying though.

Art in Other Forms

Marble, wood, bronze. If it was solid and durable, chances are an artist would grab a chisel and begin to sculpt Donatello, for example, was an extremely influ- ential Florentine sculptor of the Quattrocento. He did freestanding sculptures in marble, bronze, and wood, and was also known for a new way of doing shallow relief that gave a sense of depth through using perspective rather than through the use of high relief. Michelangelo believed it was his duty to liberate the figure that was straining to be released from the marble. His slave series, several of which can be viewed in Florence's Galleria dell 'Accademia, are perhaps the best examples of how he chipped away just enough marble to liberate the figures.

At the Museum

So do you want to see these great works of art for yourself? If so, check out these top-ten not-to-be-missed Italian museums:

1. Galleria dell'Accademia, Firenze

2. Galleria Borghese, Roma

3. Galleria degli Uffizi, Firenze

4. Museo della Scuola Grande di San Rocco, Venezia

5. GettingAroundandBeingYourselt Wherever You Are!

5. Museo di Capodimonte, Napoli

6. Musei Vaticani (a group of several museums housing world-class treasures)

7. Palazzo Farnese, Roma

8. Museo del Risorgimento, Milano

9. Museo Egizio and Galleria Sabauda, Torino

10. Galleria Regionale della Sicilia, Palermo

You're standing on line at the Uffizi in Florence or the Capodimonte Museum in Naples and can't wait to see all that amazing artwork. Or you're a student in an art his- tory class studying Michelangelo, Ghirlandaio, and Cara- vaggio. Put your free time to good use and review some vocabulary words that relate to art and museums.

~Vocabulary: At the Museum

English	Italian
apprentice	l'apprendista
art	l'arte
artist	l'artista
canvas	Ia tela
caption	Ia didascalia
corridor	il corridoio
frame	Ia cornice
gallery	Ia galleria
marble	il marmo
masterpiece	il capolavoro
paint, to	dipingere
paint	Ia vernice
paintbrush	il pennello
painter	il pittore
relief	il rilievo
Renaissance	il Rinascimento
sculpt	scolpire
sculptor	sculpture
studio	la bottega

Theatre or L'Opera

There might not be another pastime in Italy that is more closely associated with the Italian language than opera. The theatrical form, combining acting, singing, and classical music, originated in Italy more than 400 years ago. Most operas were originally sung in Italian, and today there are historic opera houses throughout Italy where the divas still sing. The common operatic term bel canto (beautiful sing- ing) points out why so many people refer to Italian as a language that's "sung" by native speakers. Since Italian speakers place the vowels in a forward position (in front of the mouth) just as singers do when singing, it's easy for Italians to switch from speaking to singing. That's prob- ably why so many Italians seem to be blessed with "natu- ral" singing voices. The formation of vowels is integral not only in singing opera but in speaking Italian as well. If you want to get a head start on understanding a performance, be sure to read the libretto (literally, "little book") first. The libretto is a play-by-play of all the action onstage, and reading it will enhance your time at the the- ater. Although you might not be able to follow the songs word for word, what's more important is to get a feel for the action, the excitement, and the drama.

Here are just a few operas that are recognized as mas- terpieces and are sure to give you a thrill:

• Aida, by Giuseppi Verdi, was first produced in Cairo in 1871. The opera is set in ancient Egypt and is named after the Ethiopian princess who is its heroine.

• Il Barbiere di Siviglia (The Barber of Seville) is a comic opera composed by Gioacchino Rossini and first produced in Rome in 1816. The barber of the title is Figaro, a character who also appears in Mozart's Le Nozze di Figaro, a sequel.

• La Boheme is an opera in four acts by Giacomo Puc- cini, first produced in Turin in 1896.

• Rigoletto is an opera by Verdi produced in Venice in 1851. The title is taken from its baritone hero, a tragic court jester. "La donna e mobile" (the woman is fickle) is its most famous aria.

• La Traviata is another opera written by Verdi. The title is variously interpreted to mean "the fallen woman" or "the woman gone astray." The work, in three acts, was first performed in Venice in 1853.

If you ever have the opportunity, hearing a perfor- mance at Milano's La Scala will leave you speechless. Bravissimi! To help you find your way out there, you might need to know a few vocabulary words.

Vocabulary: At the Theatre

English	Italian
act	l'atto
backstage	il retroscena
ballet	il balletto
ballet dancer	il ballerino
cadence	la cadenza
check room	il guardaroba
comedy	Ia com
media comic opera	l'opera buffa

279

concert	il concerto
conductor	il direttore d'orchestra
costumes	i costumi
curtain	ilsipario
dance	la danza
duet	il duetto
intermission	l'intervallo
lyric	illirico
music	la musica
musical	il musicale
overture	il preludio
performance	la rappresentazione
play	l'opera drammatica
producer	il produttore
production	la messa in scena
program	il programma la scena
scenery	lo scenario
show	lo spettacolo
singer	il cantante
song	il canzone
stage	il palcoscenico
symphony	la sinfonia
Tenor	iltenore
ticket	il biglietto
voice	la voce

Golden Arches in Italy?

McDonald's might have served billions of hamburgers beneath its neon arches, but it was the Romans who put the arco in architettura, using this design element to build aqueducts, stadiums, villas, and palaces. Learning about architecture is another way to increase your Italian vocab-

ulary, whether you'd like to learn about the three primary orders of columns---corinto, dorico, or ionico--or the many different types of architectural styles-bizantino, gotico, romanico, rinascimento, manierismo, barocco. Another example? The palladium window derives from an Italian architect, Andrea Palladia, who led a revival of classical architecture in sixteenth-century

Italy and designed many major buildings, including the church of San Giorgio Maggiore in Venice, built in 1566. If you are interested in learning more about architec- ture and have some time on your hands, try the ten-volume treatise De Architectura written in the first century B.C. by Vitruvius, a Roman architect and military engineer. The work is considered the bible of classical architectural theory and also served to inspire the Italian Renaissance's architects and educated men.

The Bible's Influence on Art

If a priest wanted to teach his congregation about the Bible, and virtually all the common folk were illiterate, how else could he convey his message? With pictures! That's one reason why so many churches in Italy have paintings, frescoes, and mosaics everywhere. Commis- sioned artists created pictorial representations of Biblical stories, from the flood to the martyrdom of saints, from heaven to hell, from Christ's birth to His crucifixion and resurrection. Since very few people could read, this was one way for them to visualize the sermons offered from the pulpit. Images of sinners burning in Hell probably convinced a number of churchgoers to mind their actions. It's not surprising to see so many impressive-looking churches in a country where the seat of Roman Catholi- cism is located. Throughout Italy, there are cathedrals and basilicas in styles such as Byzantine, Gothic, Romanesque,

and Renaissance. If you're looking for some of the best examples of celestial art and architecture, you can't go wrong visiting these churches:

• Basilica di San Francesco, Assisi: Built in memorial of St Francis, this unique church, with two separate levels, has a number of important frescoes by artists such as Giotto, Cimabue, Simone Martini, and Pietro Lorenzetti.

• Cattedrale, Battistero, e Campanile, Pisa: It's not just the Leaning Tower of Pisa! The green-and-white mar- ble stonework of the adjacent buildings is every bit as stunning.

• Duomo e Battistero, Firenze: The octagonal duomo by Filippo Brunelleschi can be seen for miles around, while the ceiling of the Baptistery is covered in amaz- ing mosaics.

• Basilica di San Marco, Venezia: The curving domes of the church are encrusted with golden mosaics that are the epitome of Byzantine art

• San Miniato al Monte, Firenze: This church overlook- ing a hillside has many important frescoes.

• Sant' Ambrogio, Milano: This is an amazing Gothic church in the center of the city. Visitors can even walk on the roof for a closeup look at the spires.

• Santa Maria Novella, Firenze: Wealthy businessmen commissioned several of the city's most important Renaissance artists to create frescoes in the chapels that line this church.

Next, get to know some architectural jargon.

Vocabulary: Architecture

English	Italian
abbey	l'abbazia
altar	l'altare
arch	l'arco
balcony	la loggia

baptistery	il battistero
bell tower	il campanile
canopy	il baldacchino
chapel	Ia cappella
church	Ia chiesa
cloister	il chiostro
crucifix	il crocifisso
Last Supper	il cenacola
nave	Ia navata
palace	il palazzo
pilaster	il pilastro
refectory	il refetto rio
rose window	il rosone

Survival Phrases and in Case of an Emergency

As you get to the end of this book, you may not remember the difference between transitive and intransitive verbs, or the indirect object pronouns. However, make sure you commit to memory the following Italian phrases, essen- tial for visitors who would like to ingratiate themselves with native Italians. If you try to communicate in Italian, it's likely they'll return the thoughtfulness with goodwill and graciousness.

- A domani! (See you tomorrow.)

- A presto! (See you soon.)

- Arrivederci! (Good-bye!)

- Buon giorno! (Good morning!)

- Buon pomeriggio! (Good afternoon!)

- Buona sera! (Good evening!)

- Buonanotte! (Goodnight!)

- Come sta? (How are you?)

- Come va? (How're you doing?)

- Ci sentiamo bene. (We're feeling fine.)

- Ciao! (Hi!/Bye!)

- Come si chiama? (What is your name?)

- Di dov'e? (Where are you from?)

- Piacere di conoscerLa. (Pleased to meet you.)

- Siamo qui da una settimana. (We've been here for a week.)

Just in Case: Emergency Terms

Sometimes it happens. The rental car breaks down, you lose your wallet, or worse. If you find yourself in a situation like this, don't panic, and concentrate on try- ing to explain what happened to la polizia at la stazione dipolizia.

~Vocabulary: Police Station

English	Italian	English	Italian
an accident	incidente	judge	il giudice
arrest, to	arrestare	key	Ia chiave
attorney	l'avvocato	money	i soldi
bag	Ia borsa	necklace	Ia collana
billfold	il portafoglio	police	la polizia
briefcase	Ia cartella	prison	Ia prigione
court	il tribunale	purse	il borsellino
crime	il delitto	ring	l'anello
custody	Ia detenzione	suitcase	Ia valigia
drugs	le droghe	thief	il ladro
guilt	Ia colpa	verdict	Ia sentenza
handbag	Ia borsetta	watch	l'orologio

Italian to English Dictionary

accompagnare	to accompany
acqua	water
adagio	slowly
addome	abdomen
adesso	now
aero porto	airport
affardellare	to pack
affinch~	so that
affittare	to rent

agganciare	to fasten, to attach
aglio	garlic
agnello	lamb
ahime	alas
ala	wing
allegria	happiness
allegro	happy
allenare	to train
almeno	at least
altura	hill
ambulanza	ambulance
amore	love
anatra	duck
anche	also
ancora	still, again, yet
andare	to go
anello	ring
anno	year
antefatto	prior event
anteporre	to put before
antipasti	appetizers
anzich	rather than
appartamento	apartment
appartenere	to belong
approvare	to approve, to accept
appunto	exactly
aprire	to open
arachide	peanut
aragosta	lobster
aria	air
armadio	closet
arrivare	to arrive

ascensore	elevator
ascoltare	to listen
to assegno	check
atterrare	to land
attirare	to attract
atto	act
attore	actor
aula	classroom
autostrada	highway
autunno	autumn
azzurro	blue babbo father
badare	to kiss
bacio	kiss
bagno	bathroom, bath
baia	bay
balocco	toy
bambino	child
bambola	doll
banca	bank
banchiere	banker
banco	counter
barba	beard
barca	boat
basilico	basil
battere	to beat, to hit
benche	although
bestia	beast
bevanda	drink
bianco	white
Bibbia	Bible
biblica	drink, beverage
biblioteca	library

biglietto	ticket
binario	track, platform
birra	beer
biscotto	cookie, biscuit
bistecca	steak
bloccare	to block, to cut off
bocca	mouth
bollo	stamp
bottega	shop
bottiglia	bottle
bottone	button
braccare	to hunt
braccio	arm
bruno	brown
brutto	ugly
burro	butter
busta	envelope
cadere	to fall
calciare	to kick
calcio	soccer
caldo	heat
calendario	calendar
calmo	calm
camera da letto	bedroom
cameriere	waiter
camminare	to walk
campagna	countryside
canale	channel
cane	dog
cantina	cellar
capitare	to happen
cappello	hat

cappotto	coat
capra	goat
carcere	jail, prison
carta	paper
carta di credito	credit card
cartolina	postcard
cavallo	horse
cavern	a cave
celare	to hide, to conceal
cercare	to look for
chiacchiere	to chat
chiaro	clear
chiave	key
Chiesa	church
chirurgo	surgeon
cinghiale	wild boar
cinta	belt
cipolla	onion
circo	circus
Cittadino	citizen
classe	classroom
clima	climate
cognata	sister-in-law
cog nato	brother-in-law
colline	hill
coltello	knife
compleanno	birthday
coniglio	rabbit
conte	count
conto	bill, acount
contrarre	to contract
controllare	to check

costume da bagno	bathing suit
cotone	cotton
cravatta	tie
creanza	politeness
crema	cream
cricca	gang
crostaceo	shellfish
cucinare	to cook
cugina	cousin (female)
cugino	cousin (male)
cuoio	leather
curare	to cure
dabbasso	downstairs
dabbene	honest
danno	danger, harm

CHAPTER FOURTEEN: GROOMING

C'è un parrucchiere o un salone di bellezza in questo albergo? (CHEH oon pahr-rook-kee-EH-reh oh oon sah-LO-neh dee bel-LETS-sah een QUEH-sto ahl-BAIR-go): Is there a hairdresser or beauty salon in this hotel?

In Italian hotels you will find not only shops, restaurants, swimming pools, and saunas, but also fitness centers, dry cleaning/laundry services, beauty salons, spas, hair stylists, barbershops, and more. The use of the sauna and the swimming pool is normally free for all guests. The other services, though very convenient, are generally offered at a higher price.

L'hotel offre un servizio di

Does the hotel offer a laundry

lavanderia?

service?

Lo-TEHL OF-freh oon sair-VEE-

tsee-oh dee lah-vahn-

deh-REE-ah

L'albergo dispone di un fitness

Is there a fitness center in the hotel?

center?

Lahl-BAIR-go dee-SPO-neh dee

oon fitness center

C'è una piscina/sauna in

Is there a swimming pool/sauna in

questo albergo?

this hotel?

CHEH OO-nah pee-SHEE-nah

SAH-oo-nah een QUEH-sto

ahl-BAIR-go

C'è un centro benessere in

Is there a wellness center in this

questo hotel?

hotel?

CHEH oon CHEHN-tro beh-NES-

seh-reh een QUEH-sto oh-TEHL

Potrebbe/Potresti suggerirmi un buon parrucchiere/ barbiere? (Po-TREB-beh/Po-TRES-tee sood-jair-EER-mee oon boo-ON pahr-rook-kee-EH-reh/bahr-bee-EH-reh): Could you please suggest a good hairdresser/barber?

If you go to Italy for a wedding or other special occasion, for a formal event, or for an extended visit, at some point you may need to buy toiletries or use the services of a hairdresser, beautician, etc. You will find toiletries or hygiene products in beauty salons, supermarkets, and normally pharmacies. For the services of a hair- dresser or beautician, a recommendation is often very useful. When asking a friend or relative for a recommendation, say: Potresti sug- gerirmi un buon parrucchiere, per favore? (Could you please suggest a good hairdresser?); use the polite form of the verb (potrebbe) if asking for a recommendation from someone unfamiliar. Remember that par-

rucchiere could be used for both female and male hairdressers, even though at times the feminine form parrucchiera is used.

Dove posso trovare un buon

Where can I find a good beauty

salone di bellezza?

salon?

DO-veh POS-so tro-VAH-reh oon

boo-ON sah-LO-neh dee

bel-LETS-sah

Dove potrei comprare degli

Where could I buy some hygiene

oggetti igienici e per

products and toiletries?

la toilette?

DO-veh po-TRAY cohm-PRAH-reh

DEL-yee od-JET-tee ee-jee-EH-

nee-chee eh pair la twa-LET-te

Dov'è la farmacia più vicina?

Where is the nearest pharmacy?

Do-VEH lah fahr-mah-CHEE-ah

290

PEW vee-CHEE-nah

Vorrei fi ssare un appuntamento, per favore. (Vor-RAY fees-SAH-reh oon ahp-poon-tah-MEHN-toh pair fah-VO-reh): I would like to book an appointment, please.

The world of the beauty salon or the hairdresser in Italy is not much different than in North America. To avoid waiting for hours, it is appro- priate to make reservations well ahead of time. Prices vary depending on the service requested; for a cut (taglio), for example, prices will vary from 15 to 18 euros depending on the length of your hair; a style (piega) is about 20 euros; a perm (permanente) is about 50 euros; highlights (colpi di sole) are also about 50 euros. Just as you might expect, a salone di bellezza or a centro benessere offer many more

services such as manicure and pedicure, waxing (ceretta, depilazione), massages (massaggi), baths, facials (pulizia viso), etc.

Posso venire subito?

Can you see me right away?

POS-so veh-NEE-reh SOO-bee-toh

Quanto tempo ci vuole per... ?

How long will it take for . . . ?

QUAHN-toh TEHM-po chee

voo-OH-leh pair

Taglio, colpi di sole e piega, per favore. (TAHL-yo COL- pee dee SO-leh eh pee-EH-gah pair fah-VO-reh): Cut, highlights, and style, please.

Like fashion, hair styles change from nation to nation and over time; what's in (alla moda) today might be outdated tomorrow. And what may be fashionable in North America might be completely different from what's fashionable in Italy or in Europe, in general. Therefore, when at the hairdresser, don't be afraid to ask for his or her personal and professional advice: Che tipo di taglio è alla moda in Italia? (What haircut is fashionable in Italy?) or Vorrei cambiare il look. Cosa mi con- siglia? (I would like to change my look. What would you suggest?) or Vorrei tingermi a capelli. Quale colore mi dona di più? (I would like to dye my hair. What color suits me best?)

Vorrei tagliate le punte, per favore.

I would like a trim, please.

Vor-RAY tahl-YAH-teh leh POON-teh

pair fah-VO-reh

Potrebbe stirarmi i capelli,

Could you please straighten my hair?

per favore?

Po-TREB-beh stee-RAHR-mee ee

cah-PEL-lee pair fah-VO-reh

Potrebbe farmi la manicure,

Can you please do my nails?

per favore?

Po-TREB-beh FAHR-mee lah mah-

nee-COO-reh pair fah-VO-reh

Potrebbe aggiustarmi le

Could you do my eyebrows?

sopracciglia?

Po-TREB-beh ahd-joos-TAHR-mee

leh so-praht-CHEEL-yah

Barba e capelli, per favore. (BAHR-bah eh cah-PEL-lee pair fah-VO-reh): I would like a haircut and shave, please.

In Italian barbershops you will find a very cordial, pleasant, and infor- mal atmosphere. Barbershops are often a place to socialize. Italian men also frequent wellness centers, spas, and beauty salons, and invest in a variety of personal grooming products. In Ital- ian culture, it is very important to present oneself in a respectable, professional way (curare la propria immagine).

Vorrei tagliarmi i capelli, ma

I would like you to cut my hair, but

non troppo corti, per favore.

not too short, please.

Vor-RAY tahl-YAHR-mee ee cah-

PEL-lee mah nohn TROP-po

COR-tee pair fah-VO-reh

Vorrei dare una spuntatina

I would like a trim.

ai capelli.

Vor-RAY DAH-reh OO-nah spoon-

tah-TEE-nah aye cah-PEL-lee

Quanto costa un taglio di capelli?

How much is it for the haircut?

QUAHN-toh CO-stah oon TAHL-yo

dee cah-PEL-lee

Potrebbe dare una spuntatina

Could you trim my moustache?

ai baffi?

Po-TREB-beh DAH-reh OO-nah

spoon-tah-TEE-nah aye BAF-fee

Dove posso trovare una lavanderia self-service? (DO-veh POS-so tro-VAH-reh OO-nah lah-vahn-deh-REE-ah self-service): Where can I fi nd a laundromat?

Fare bella figura (To give a positive impression) is very important for Italians. The bella figura is also reflected in the way Italians dress. Therefore, it is good to be perfectly dressed even when going out with a friend or just going on a passeggiata (stroll) through the town. Make sure that the crease of your pants is perfect, that your suit is clean, that your shoes are well polished, that not a single hair on your head is out of place. If you need to have your suit, shirt, or dress cleaned, look for a lavanderia or lavaggio a secco. These establishments will not only clean and iron your clothes but will also make alterations. Of course, alterations can also be made by a tailor.

Potrebbe pulirmi questo vestito?

Could I have this suit cleaned?

Po-TREB-beh poo-LEER-mee

QUEH-sto veh-STEE-toh

Potrebbe lavarmi e stirare

Could you wash and iron this shirt?

questa camicia?

Po-TREB-beh lah-VAHR-mee eh

stee-RAH-reh QUEH-stah

cah-MEE-chah

Potrebbe accorciarmi questi

Could you please shorten these pants

pantaloni e restringermi

and take in this skirt for me?

questa gonna, per favore?

Po-TREB-beh ac-cor-CHAHR-mee

QUEH-stee pahn-tah-LOH-nee eh

reh-STREEN-jair-mee QUEH-stah

GOHN-nah pair fah-VO-reh

Quando sarà pronto?

293

When will it be ready?

QUAHN-doh sah-RAH PRON-toh

CHAPTER FIFTEEN: GETTING AROUND TOWN

sking directions, hailing a cab, and reading a bus schedule are all things you might want to know how to do for your upcoming trip. This chapter will help you find your way around.

Asking for Directions

Perhaps the most frequently asked questions in all tourist destinations have to do with asking for directions. Here are some useful phrases to ask for help finding your way around:

Excuse me, where is . . . ?

Mi scusi, dov'è . . . ?

mee skoo-zee doh-veh

Is it very far?

È molto lontano?

eh mohl-toh lohn-TAH-noh

How long will it take by car?

Quanto ci vorrà in macchina?

kwahn-toh chee vohr-RAH een mahk-KEE-nah

How far away is the station?

Quanto dista la stazione?

kwahn-toh dees-tah lah staht-see-OH-nay

How much further to . . . ?

Quanto manca a . . . ?

kwahn-toh mahn-kah ah

Excuse me, I'm lost.

Scusi, mi sono perso.

skoo-zee mee soh-noh pehr-soh

Where is the nearest gas station?

Dove si trova il distributore di benzina più vicino?

doh-veh see troh-vah eel dees-tree-boo-TOH-ray dee ben-TSEE- nah pyou vee- CHEE-noh

It's close by.

È a due passi.

eh ah doo-ay pahs-see

Can you tell me where it is?

Può dirmi dov'è?

poo-owe deer-mee dohv-EH

Can you give me directions to . . . ?

Può indicarmi la strada per . . . ?

poo-owe een-dee-KAHR-mee lah strah-dah pehr ?

Directions

English	Italian
Go straight.	Vai diritto.
veye dee-REET-toh	

English	Italian
Turn left.	Gira a sinistra.
jee-rah ah see-NEES-trah	
Turn right.	Gira a destra.
jee-rah a dess-trah	
to the left	alla sinistra
ahl-lah see-NEES-trah	
to the right	alla destra
ahl-lah dess-trah	
straight ahead	sempre diritto

sehm-preh dee-REET-toh

next to   accanto

a ahk-KAHN-toh ah

in front of   davanti

a dah-vahn-tee ah

in back of   dietro

dee-EH-troh

near (to)   vicino

a vee-CHEE-noh ah

far (from)   lontano da

lohn-TAH-noh dah north nord nohrd

south   sud

sood

east   est

ehst

west   ovest

oh-vehst

Some Useful Destinations

You've left your map back in the hotel room, and you know the museum you want to visit is around here somewhere. Now if you could only remember the word for museum! This section presents some useful place names found in most cities.

bank   banca

bahn-kah

bus stop   la fermata dell'autobus

lah fehr-MAH-tah dehll AHW-toh-boos cathedral cattedrale kaht-teh-DRAH-lay

church   chiesa

kee-AY-zah

coffee shop   bar

bahr

fountain	fontana
fohn-TAH-nah	
gardens	giardini
jahr-DEE-nee	
hotel	hotel/albergo
oh-tell/ahl-BEHR-goh	
monument	monumento
mohn-oo-MEHN-toh	
museum	museo
moo-ZAY-oh	
open-air market	mercato
mehr-KAH-toh	
park	parco
pahr-koh	
restaurant	ristorante
rees-toh-RAHN-tay	
supermarket	supermercato
soo-pehr-mehr-KAH-toh	
theater	teatro
tay-AH-troh	

Types of Transportation

Many Italian cities offer a full range of transportation options. Rome, Milan, Palermo, and Naples all have subway systems that are reasonably safe and reliable.

bicycle	la bicicletta
lah bee-chee-KLEH-tah	
bus	l'autobus
LAHW-toh-boos	
bus stop	la fermata dell'autobus
lah fehr-MAH-tah dehll AHW-toh-boos	
car	la macchina
lah MAH-kee-nah	
moped	il motorino

eel moh-toh-REE-noh

motorcycle	la moto
lah moh-toh	
subway	la metropolitana
lah meh-troh-poh-lee- TAH-nah	
taxi	il taxi
eel tahk-see	
taxi stand	la stazione
lah staht-see-OH-nay dei	
train	il treno
eel tray-noh	
train station	la stazione
lah staht-see-OH-nay	

KEYNOTES

Water taxis (motoscafi) and water busses (vaporetti) are available in Venice. Taxis in Venice can be expensive, but the vaporetti are very reasonable and reliable—and they're fun, too!

Renting a Car

Public transportation and taxis are readily available in all Italian cities, but you may want to rent a car to explore off the beaten path. Keep in mind that standard transmissions in cars are the norm in Italy. If you need a car with an automatic transmission, it is best to make a reservation before you leave for your trip.

I'd like to rent a car.

Vorrei noleggiare una macchina.

vohr-ray noh-lehj-JAH-ray oo-nah MAH-kee-nah

economy car

macchina piccola

MAH-kee-nah PEEK-koh-lah

midsize car

macchina media

MAH-kee-nah MEH-dee-ah

full-size car

macchina grande

299

MAH-kee-nah grahn-day

convertible

decapotabile

deh-kah-poh-TAH-bee-leh

truck

camion

KAH-mee-ohn

automatic

automatico

ahw-toh-MAH-tee-koh

KEYNOTE

Italian law requires that non–European Union citizens possess an International Driving Permit (IDP). Car rental agencies are increasingly checking for the IDP when you pick up your rental car. You will need both the IDP and your current driver's license when traveling. You can apply for an IDP at your local American Automobile Association (AAA) or American Automobile Touring Alliance.

How much will it cost?

Quanto costa?

kwahn-toh kohs-tah

I'd like to pay by credit card.

Vorrei pagare con la carta di credito.

vohr-ray pah-GAH-ray kohn lah kahr-tah dee KREH-dee-toh

Finding Your Way Around

This section presents some useful words and phrases to help you navigate the open road.

Street Smarts

accident	un incidente
oon een-chee-DEHN-tay	
all routes/directions	tutte le direzioni
toot-teh leh dee-rehts-YOH-nee	
bypass road	un tangenziale
oon tahn-jehnts-YAH-lay	

dead end	strada senza uscita
strah-dah sehn-tsah oo-SHEE-tah	
diesel	il diesel
eel dee-zehl driver l'autista lahw-TEES-tah	
gas	la benzina
lah behn-TSEE-nah	
gas station	un distributore di benzina
oon dees-tree-boo-TOH ray dee ben- TSEE-nah	
highway	un'autostrada
oon-AHW-toh-strah-dah	
lane	una corsia
oo-nah kohr-SEE-ah	
lights	i fari
ee fah-ree	
no parking	vietato parcheggiare
vee-eh-TAH-toh pahr-kehj-JAH-ray	
no stopping	vietata la sosta
vee-eh-TAH-tah lah sohs-tah	
one way	senso unico
sehn-soh OO-nee-koh	
pedestrian	il pedonale
eel peh-doh-NAH-lay	
pedestrian	le strisce pedonali
le stree-sheh peh-doh-NAH-lee	
rush hour	l' ora di punta
loh-rah dee poon-tah	
speed limit	il limite di velocità
eel LEE-mee-teh dee veh-loh-chee-TAH	
stop	stop
stohp	
traffic lights	il semaforo
eel seh-MAH-foh-roh	

Car Talk

car	una macchina/un'automobile/un'auto
	oo-nah MAH-kee-nah/oon ahw-toh-MOH-bee- leh/oon ahw-toh
car hood	il cofano
	eel KOH-fah-noh
radio	la radio
	lah RAH-dee-oh
rearview mirror	lo specchietto
	loh spehk-KYEH-toh
seatbelt	la cintura di sicurezza
	lah cheen-TOO-rah dee see-koo-REHTS-sah
steering wheel	il volante eel voh-LAHN-tay
tire	la gomma/il pneumatico
	lah gohm-mah/eel neh-oo-MAH-tee-koh
trunk	il bagagliaio
	eel bah-GAHL-yeye-oh (pronounced like the English "eye")
windshield	la parabrezza
	lah pah-rah-BREHTS-sah
windshield	i tergicristalli
wipers	ee tehr-jee-krees-TAHL-lee

Useful Driving Verbs

Here are some essential verbs related to driving:

to pass/overtake	sorpassare
sohr-pahs-SAH-ray	
to slow down	rallentare
rahl-lehn-TAH-ray	
to yield	dare la precedenza
dah-ray lah preh-cheh-DEHN-tsah	
to get a ticket	prendere una multa
PREHN-deh-ray oo-nah mool-tah	

to give a ticket   dare una multa

dah-ray oo-nah mool-tah

to pull over to the side of the road

accostare

ahk-kohs-TAH-ray

to get gas   fare la benzina

fah-ray lah ben-TSEE-nah

to fill it up   fare il pieno

fah-ray eel pyeh-noh

to hitchhike   fare l'autostop

fah-ray LAHW-toh-stohp

to park   parcheggiare

pahr-kehj-JAH-ray

to turn   girare

jee-RAH-ray

to drive   guidare

gwee-DAH-ray

to travel   viaggiare

vee-ahj-JAH-ray

to cross   attraversare

aht-trah-vehr-SAH-ray

to go   andare

ahn-DAH-ray

to buckle your seat belt

allacciare la cintura di sicurezza

ahl-lahch-CHAH-ray lah cheen-TOO-rah dee see-koo-REHTS-sah

KEYNOTES

Italy has a reputation for chaotic streets and highways. Though your initial attempt at driving in Italy may be intimidating at first, you will find Italian drivers to be aggressive but entirely competent. Italian traffic is often described as "organized chaos," which to some extent is true.

CHAPTER SIXTEEN: COMMON WARNINGS

Vietato fumare. (Vee-eh-TAH-toh foo-MAH-reh): No smoking.

When traveling, it is useful to know the laws of the country you are in and what they prohibit. In Italy, smoking is forbidden in all public places; therefore you cannot smoke in museums, restaurants, bars, train stations, airports, cinemas, and public offices. In most cases, how- ever, if you must have a sigaretta (cigarette), look for an area or zona fumatori (smoking area): You will surely find one in train stations and airports and some large restaurants have them, too. Long-distance trains have scompartimenti fumatori (smoking compartments); how- ever, smoking is absolutely forbidden on regional trains.

Dov'è l'area fumatori?

Where is the smoking area?

Do-VEH LAH-reh-ah

foo-mah-TOH-ree

Vorrei un tavolo per fumatori,

I'd like to get a table in the smoking

grazie.

area, please.

Vor-RAY oon TAH-vo-lo pair foo-

mah-TOH-ree GRAH-tsee-eh

È vietato bivaccare qui. Dovete andare via, per favore, oppure vi faccio la multa. (Eh vee-eh-TAH-toh bee-vac-CAH-reh kwee Doh-VEH-teh ahn-DAH-reh VEE-ah pair fah-VO-reh oh-POO- reh vee FAH-choh la MOOL-tah): Loitering is forbidden here. Please go away, otherwise I have to give you a ticket.

In Italy today, the city mayors have been given the power of promot- ing certain specific laws within their territory: This means that, for example, in Venice è vietato dar da mangiare ai piccioni (it is forbidden to feed the pigeons); while in some seaside towns è vietato camminare in bikini nel centro città (it is forbidden to wear your bikini downtown), and on the beach è vietato giocare a pallone (it is forbidden to play soc- cer or volleyball) as you may accidentally hurt other bagnanti (bath- ers); and in Genova è vietato bivaccare nel centro storico (it is forbidden to loiter downtown). As a tourist keep in mind that it is forbidden to buy things from venditori ambulanti or vu cumprà (non-EU street sellers who sell fake bags and other merchandise on the beach or in tourist areas; they use this broken Italian expression [literally "would you like to buy?"] when approaching potential buyers), and if a police officer catches you while making such a purchase, there may be a large fine.

Vietato l'ingresso agli animali.

No animals allowed.

vee-eh-TAH-toh leen-GREHS-soh

AHL-yee ah-nee-MAH-lee

Si prega di spegnere il cellulare.

Please turn off your cell phone.

See PREH-gah dee SPEHN-yeh-reh

eel cheh-loo-LAH-reh

Vietato mangiare e bere.

No food or drink allowed.

vee-eh-TAH-toh mahn-jee-AH-reh

eh BEH-reh

Attenzione al gradino! (At-ten-tsee-OH-neh ahl grah- DEE-no): Watch your step!

The Italian word that translates as "Be careful!" or "Pay attention!" is attenzione. The word is ubiquitous: It is easily found on signs around all sorts of public places, or heard in various public announcements.

Attenzione! Lavori in corso.

Watch for construction! Work in

At-ten-tsee-OH-neh Lah-VO-ree

progress.

een COR-so

Attenzione! Treno in arrivo/

Watch for arriving/departing/

partenza/transito.

passing train.

At-ten-tsee-OH-neh TREH-no een

306

ar-REE-vo/pahr-TEN-tsah/

TRAHN-zee-toh

Proprietà privata. Attenti al cane.

Private property. Beware of the dog.

Pro-pree-eh-TAH pree-VAH-tah

At-TEHN-tee ahl CAH-neh

Faccia attenzione ai ladri!

Beware of pickpockets!

FAT-cha at-ten-tsee-OH-neh

aye LAH-dree

Pericolo: infi ammabile. (Peh-REE-coh-loh in-fee-ahm-mah- BEE-leh): Danger: fl ammable.

In Italy, as in many parts of the world, easily recognizable international signs are used. A yellow triangular sign with an exclamation mark is the common sign for general danger (pericolo: generico); a skull with two crossbones indicates poison (pericolo: veleno); flames indicate that the item is flammable (pericolo: infiammabile); an explosion sign indicates the item could easily explode (pericolo: esplosivo); lightning means high voltage (pericolo: alta tensione); a stick figure falling means of course that there is a possibility of falling (pericolo: caduta). Here are some more danger warnings:

Pericolo: tossico.

Danger: toxic.

Peh-REE-coh-loh tohs-SEE-coh

Pericolo: nocivo.

Danger: harmful.

Peh-REE-coh-loh no-CHEE-voh

Pericolo: dannoso all'ambiente.

Danger: damaging to the

Peh-REE-coh-loh dahn-NO-so

environment.

 pehr l'ahm-bee-EHN-teh

Pericolo: alta tensione.

Danger: high voltage.

Peh-REE-coh-loh AHL-tah

ten-zee-OH-neh

Scusi, è permesso portare la macchina fotografi ca? (SCOO-zee eh pair-MES-soh por-TAH-reh lah MAK-kee-nah fo-toh- GRAH-fee-cah): Pardon me, can I take the camera inside?

As a tourist in Italy, you'll surely find yourself in museums and other places of culture. It is important in these places to dress and act appropriately. You must fare silenzio (be silent), spegnere il cellulare (turn off your mobile phone), and in most cases it is not allowed to fare fotografie (take pictures) or usare il flash (use the flash). It is likely that even entrare con la borsa (bringing your bag inside) and portare cibo e bevande (carrying food or beverages) inside is forbidden as well. Therefore, it is good to ask what is allowed at the biglietteria (ticket office) upon entrance or to take a look at the cartelli (signs) which are usually located at the entrance of each site. Like more or less every- where, è vietato calpestare l'erba (it is forbidden to walk on the grass) in certain gardens and near significant monuments. Remember, too, that if you have a dog, it is mandatory to clean up after it.

È permesso l'ingresso ai cani?

Are dogs allowed in?

EH pair-MES-soh leen-GREHS-soh

ahee KAH-nee

Mi dispiace, deve spegnere

I am sorry, but you need to turn

il cellulare.

off your cell phone.

Mee dee-spee-AH-cheh, DEH-veh

SPEHN-yeh-reh eel chehl-

loo-LAH-reh

La prego di lasciare la borsa

I kindly ask you to leave your purse at

all'ingresso!

the entrance!

Lah PREH-go dee la-shee-AH-re lah

BOR-sa ahl-leen-GREHS-so

Non è permesso entrare in chiesa

You are not allowed in church

in pantaloncini corti/

wearing shorts/a miniskirt.

minigonna.

Non EH pair-MES-so ehn-TRAH-reh

een kee-EH-sa een pahn-tah-lon-

CHEE-nee KOHR-tee/mee-nee-

GOHN-nah

CHAPTER SEVENTEEN: EMERGENCIES

Dov'è l'uffi cio della Polizia Municipale? (Doh-VEH loof- FEET-cho DEL-la Po-lee-TSEE-ah Moo-nee-chee-PAH-leh): Where is the offi ce of the municipal police?

In the majority of Italian towns, the offices of the polizia municipale are located in City Hall, as this police force is responsible to the mayor. Their main duties are the application of norms and regulations of the towns; they are generally limited to public order, traffic, hygiene, respect for the environment, and the control of commercial establish- ments to ensure, for example, that they are open or closed according to their license and local laws. The vigile urbano is part of the polizia municipale. In the fifties and sixties, the figure of the vigile urbano became somewhat famous because of Hollywood movies; a vigile was always depicted as a folkloristic and eccentric traffic policeman, wear- ing an eye-catching uniform, hat, and white gloves, who, on top of a platform, directed traffic in Rome's busiest intersections. Today, how- ever, you will see the vigile keeping an eye on the local neighborhood; controlling the traffic flow in busy areas such as schools, hospitals, and piazzas; giving tickets for traffic offenses; or patrolling the local

open-air markets to make sure that the merchants have an appropri- ate license. It is also their duty to check the hygiene and source of the merchandise. Part of the mandate of the vigili is to intervene in case of a scippo (purse snatching), borseggio (pickpocketing), or rapina (rob- bery), and then collaborate with other forze dell'ordine (police forces) such as Carabinieri, polizia, and Guardia di Finanza.

> Dov'è il Commissariato di Polizia
>
> Where is the closest police station?
>
> più vicino?
>
> Do-VEH eel com-mees-sah-ree-
>
> AH-toh dee Po-lee-TSEE-ah PEW
>
> vee-CHEE-no

Dove si trova la più vicina caserma dei pompieri? (DOH- veh see TROH-vah la PEW vee-CHEE-nah cah-ZAIR-mah day pohm- pee-EH-ree): Where is the nearest fi re station?

The various police forces previously mentioned are responsible to the Ministries of Defense (Carabinieri), of the Interior (polizia), and of Finances (Guardia di Finanza). The Carabinieri and the polizia have different duties, even though it is very difficult to identify those dif- ferences. For passport (passaporto) issues, firearms, residence permits (permesso di soggiorno), and immigration issues, the authority is the polizia. It is also the polizia (specifically the polizia stradale, road police) that handles traffic accidents and violations. Almost every town in Italy has a Comando or caserma dei Carabinieri; while you will find a questura or commissariato/stazione di polizia only in the major cities towns. Quite different and clear are the specific duties of the Guardia di Finanza (finance police), who exercise their control along the borders, and are in charge of financial inquiries, tax evasion, money launder- ing, etc.

Other vital and essential security services are those provided by the vigili del fuoco or pompieri (firemen) and the ambulanze (ambulances).

È vicino la caserma dei Carabinieri?

Is the caserma dei Carabinieri close by?

Eh vee-CHEE-no lah cah-ZAIR-mah

day Cah-rah-bee-nee-EH-ree

Qual è il numero del pronto soccorso? (Quahl eh eel noo- MEH-ro del PRON-toh soc-COR-so): What's the number for medical emergencies?

During emergencies, the faster help can be provided, the better. It is therefore important, should you find yourself in a situation where you must make an emergency call, to memorize or carry with you some essential emergency numbers. The most important emergency num- ber in Italy is 113 (police and public emergency; this is the equivalent of 911 in North America). Other essential numbers are 115 for vigili del fuoco (firefighters); 118 for pronto soccorso (ambulance and health emergency); and 112 (Carabinieri). The European Union has adopted the number 112 for S.O.S. In Italy, since March 2008, the number has been introduced gradually, into a few provinces at a time. Until the process is complete, the 112 number will operate alongside the existing national numbers previ- ously described. Anyone is able to call all emergency numbers for free from any phone. However, only call these numbers in case of real emergencies. When calling, the best way to convey the sense of urgency is to be direct and to ask that an ambulance, the police, or the firefighters be sent immediately. Otherwise, simply state that it is an emergency.

Si tratta di un'emergenza!/

It's an emergency!

È un'emergenza!

See TRAT-tah dee oon-eh-mair-

JEHNT-sah/Eh oon-eh-mair-

JEHNT-sah

Serve un'ambulanza subito,

We need an ambulance immediately,

per favore!   please!

SAIR-veh oon-ahm-boo-LAHNT-sah

SOO-bee-toh pair fah-VO-reh

Mandate i vigili del fuoco,

Send the firefighters, please.

per favore.

Mahn-DAH-teh ee VEE-jee-lee del

foo-OH-co pair fah-VO-reh

La polizia, per favore.

The police, please.

La po-lee-TSEE-ah pair fah-VO-reh

311

Telefoni al 113, per favore! (Teh-LEH-fo-nee ahl chen-toh- treh-dee-chee pair fah-VO-reh): Please call 113 (the emergency number equivalent to 911)!

If involved in an accident, stay calm, try to offer pronto soccorso (first aid) to those who need it, and call one of the emergency numbers for help. A quick response to the emergency could help save lives. Leav- ing the scene of an accident and omitting to offer first aid is consid- ered a reato (criminal offense) and as such is punishable by law. In case of an incendio (fire), call the firemen (pompieri or vigili urbani) and clearly state that there is an incendio. To warn everyone else in the building or to call for help from fellow citizens, yell: Al fuoco! Al fuoco! (Fire! Fire!) For a general emergency, shout Aiuto! Aiuto! (Help! Help!)

C'è stato un incidente e vi sono

There has been an accident and

dei feriti!

people have been injured!

Cheh STAH-toh oon een-chee-

DEHN-teh eh vee SO-no day

feh-REE-tee

C'è un incendio!

There is a fire!

Cheh oon een-CHEHN-dee-oh

Aiuto! Al fuoco! Aiuto! Al fuoco!

Help! Fire! Help! Fire!

Aye-OO-toh Ahl foo-OH-co

Aye-OO-toh Ahl foo-OH-co

Qualcuno sta male! Presto, chiamate un'ambulanza! (Quahl-COO-no stah MAH-leh PREH-sto kee-ah-MAH-teh oon-ahm- boo-LAHNT-sah): Someone is sick! Hurry, call an ambulance!

If someone is hurt, wounded, or suddenly feels very sick, the time before the arrival of a doctor or of an ambulance is critical and of the utmost importance for the patient. If you are a doctor or you know first aid (primo soccorso), your help might save a life.

So fare i primi soccorsi!

I know first aid!

Soh FAH-reh ee PREE-mee

sohc-COHR-zee

Sono un dottore.

I am a doctor.

SO-no oon doht-TOH-reh

Sto male: vi prego di portarmi

I do not feel well: please take me to

in ospedale.

the hospital.

Stoh MAH-leh vee PREH-go dee

pohr-TAR-mee in oh-speh-DAH-leh

Mi hanno rubato la macchina. (Mee AHN-no roo-BAH-toh lah MAK-kee-nah): My car was stolen.

While traveling by car, there is always the fear that your car could be stolen—even if it has the latest sistema antifurto (antitheft devices) or damaged. In such a case, you will likely be covered by the car-rental insurance. The scenario could be worse if your purse, wallet, passport, or credit cards are stolen or lost. In all cases, report these incidents to the authorities within forty-eight hours; the number to call is either 112 or 113. You will probably have to file a denuncia (report). While traveling, please remember that these types of stressful situations can be avoided by taking precautions and always being alert, especially in crowded places. Depending on the situation, even before calling the police, inform your credit card company or cell phone company, etc., of the stolen item(s).

Mi hanno danneggiato

My car was damaged!

la macchina!

Mee AHN-no dan-ned-JAH-toh

lah MAK-kee-nah

Mi hanno scippato la borsa/

My purse/wallet/cellular phone was

il portafoglio/il cellulare.

stolen. I would like to file a report!

Vorrei fare una denuncia!

Mee AHN-no sheep-PAH-toh lah

BOR-sah/eel por-tah-FOL-yo/eel

chel-loo-LAH-reh Vor-RAY

FAH-reh OO-nah deh-NOON-chah

Ho perso il passaporto/la patente/

I lost my passport/driver's license/

la carta di credito. credit card.

Oh PAIR-so eel pas-sah-POR-toh/lah

313

pah-TEHN-teh/lah CAHR-tah dee

CREH-dee-toh

C'è stata una rapina.

There has been a robbery.

Cheh STAH-tah OO-nah rah-PEE-nah

Dov'è l'uffi cio della guardia medica? (DO-VEH loof-FEE- cho DEL-lah goo-AHR-dee-ah MEH-dee-cah): Where is the after- hours medical clinic?

All Italian towns have a servizio di guardia medica or Continuità Assi- stenziale. It is a free service that guarantees medical emergency ser- vice after hours. To use the service call the office for an appointment or directly go to the clinic; a house call is also a possibility. The guar- dia medica is open when all other medical offices are closed so that people have access to medical services twenty-four hours a day.

Potrebbe fare una visita a

Could you please make a house call?

domicilio? Sono troppo malato.

I am too ill.

Po-TREB-beh FAH-reh OO-nah VEE-

zee-tah ah doh-mee-CHEE-lee-oh

SO-no TROP-po mah-LAH-toh

CHAPTER EIGHTEEN: ESSENTIAL WORDS AND PHRASES

This quick reference section will help you with the basics. Use it if you're in too much of a hurry to flip through an entire chapter.

Meeting People

yes	sì	see
no	no	noh
Thank you.	Grazie.	GRAHTS-ee-eh
You're welcome.	Prego.	pray-goh
Please . . .	Per favore . . .	pehr fah-VOH-reh
Excuse me . . .	Mi scusi . . .	mee skoo-zee
Hello.	Salve.	Sahl-vay
Goodbye.	Arrivederci.	ahr-ree-veh-DEHR-cheeh
Good morning.	Buon giorno.	bwohn johr-noh
Goodnight.	Buona notte.	bwoh-nah noht-teh
I do not understand.	Non capisco.	nohn kah-PEES-koh
Do you speak English?	Parla inglese?	pahr-lah een-GLEH-say
What is your name?	Come si chiama?	koh-meh see KYAH-mah
Nice to meet you.	Felice di conoscerLa.	

feh-LEE-cheh dee koh-NOH-shehr-lah

How are you?	Come sta?	koh-meh stah

good	bene	beh-neh
bad	male	mah-leh

Directions

map	mappa	mahp-pah
left	sinistra	see-nees-trah
right	destra	des-trah
straight ahead	diritto	dee-REET-toh
far	lontano	lohn-TAH-noh
near	vicino	vee-CHEE-noh

Transportation

Where is it?   Dove si trova?
doh-veh see troh-vah

How much is the fare?   Quanto costa il biglietto?
kwahn-toh kohs-tah eel beel-YEHT- toh

ticket	biglietto	beel-YEHT-toh

A ticket to. . . , please.
Un biglietto a . , per favore.
oon beel-YEHT-toh pehr-fah-voh-ray

Where do you live?   Dove abita?
doh-veh AH-bee-tah

train	treno	tray-noh
bus	autobus	OHW-toh-boos

316

subway station	metropolitana	meh-troh-poh-lee-TAH-nah

airport   aeroporto
ah-eh-roh-POHR-toh

train station   stazione del treno
stahts-YOH-neh dehl tray-noh

bus station   stazione degli autobus
stahts-YOH-neh dehl-yee OHW-toh-boos

subway station   stazione della metropolitana
stahts-YOH-neh dehl-lah meh-troh-poh- lee-TAH-nah

departure   partenza
pahr-TEHN-zah

arrival   arrivo
ahr-REE-voh

parking   parcheggio
pahr-KEHJ-joh

Accommodations

hotel	hotel	oh-tell
room	camera	KAH-meh-rah
reservation	prenotazione	preh-noh-tahts-YOH-neh

Do you have a room available?

Avete una camera libera?

ah-veh-teh oo-nah KAH-meh-reh LEE-beh-rah

no vacancies	niente camere libere	nyehn-teh KAH-meh-rah LEE-beh-reh
passport	passaporto	pah-sah-POHR-toh

Around Town

bank	banca	bahn-kah church chiesa kyeh-zah
hospital	ospedale	ohs-peh-DAH-lay
museum	museo	moo-zeh-oh
pharmacy	farmacia	fahr-mah-CHEE-ah
post office	ufficio postale	oof-FEE-choh pohs-TAH-lay
restaurant	ristorante	rees-toh-RAHN-teh
shop	negozio	neh-GOHTS-ee-oh
square	piazza	pyahts-sah
street	strada	strah-dah

Shopping

How much does this cost? I will buy it

Quanto costa? kwahn-toh kohs-tah. Lo compro. loh kohm-proh

I would like to buy . . .	Vorrei comprare . . .	vohr-ray kohm-PRAH-ray
Do you have . . . ?	Avete . . . ?	ah-veh-teh
open	aperto	ah-pehr-toh
closed	chiuso	kyoo-zoh
postcard	cartolina postale	kahr-toh-lee-nah pos-TAH-leh

318

stamps	francobolli	frahn-koh-BOHL-lee
little	poco	poh-koh
a lot, many, much	molto	mohl-toh
all	tutto	toot-toh

Food and Beverages

Beer	birra	bee-rah
coffee	caffè	kahf-FEH
drink	bevanda	beh-VAHN-dah
juice	succo	sook-koh
tea	tè	teh
water	acqua	ahk-wah
wine	vino	vee-noh
dessert	dolce	dohl-cheh
fish	pesce	pesh-sheh
fruit	frutta	froo-tah
meat	carne	kahr-neh
potato	patata	pah-tah-tah
salad	insalata	een-sah-LAH-tah
vegetable	legumi	leh-GOO-mee

ITALIAN COMMON PHRASES

Learn Italian for Beginners in Your Car Like Crazy.

Language Learning Lessons for Travel and Everyday.

How to speak Italian with Vocabulary and Conversations.

VOL 2

INTRODUCTION

English-speakers will find Italian a beautiful language to listen to and an easy one to start speaking. The expressive rhythm and melody of the language, which has lent itself to the epic poetry of Dante and the grand operas of Verdi, has fascinated visitors for centuries. When even a simple sentence can sound like an aria you'll find it difficult to resist striking up a conversation. Of all the Romance languages which include French, Spanish, Portuguese and Romanian. Italian claims the closest family relationship to Latin. Because English has been heavily influenced by Latin (particularly through its contact with French), there are many basic resemblances between the two languages. Today, thanks to wide-spread migration and the enormous popularity of Italian culture and cuisine, most of us are also familiar with modern Italian words like ciao, pasta, and bello. Outside Italy, Italian is spoken by minorities in Switzerland, Slovenia and France, and more recently by large communities of immigrants in Australia, Argentina and the US. Italian has official status in the Istrian peninsula of Croatia where Italian-speaking communities have existed since the Venetians began colonising parts of the Dalmatian coast during the twelfth century. Another country where Italian is spoken is the African nation of Eritrea which remained a colony of Italy from 1880 until 1941. Today most Eritreans speak Italian only as a second language. Around the world there are approximately 65 million Italian speakers, the majority of whom live in Italy. In Italy itself, most people also speak a local majority of whom live in Italy. In Italy itself, most people also speak a local dialect. Dialects are spoken all over the country and some are so different from standard Italian as to be considered distinct languages in their own right. In fact, it wasn't until the nineteenth century that the Tuscan dialect the language of Dante, Boccaccio, Petrarch and Macchiavelli was chosen to become the standard language of the nation. Standard Italian is the official language of schools, media and administration, and is the form that will take you from the top of the boot to the very toe. All the language that we have provided here is in standard Italian. This book gives you the words you need to get by, as well as all the fun, spontaneous phrases that lead to a better experience of Italy and its people. Need more encouragement? Remember, the contact you make through using Italian will make your travels unique. Local knowledge, new relationships and a sense of satisfaction are on the tip of your tongue, so don't just stand there, say something!

> ABBREVIATIONS USED IN THIS BOOK

f	feminine
inf	informal
m	masculine
sg	singular
pl	plural
pol	polite

HOW TO USE THIS BOOK TO BEST ADVANTAGE

Except for the few who are blessed with inborn linguistic superskill, no foreign tongue is truly "easy" to learn: all are as complex and internally inconsistent as we humans who invented them. Relatively speaking, however, Italian is by far the easiest of all non- native languages for an English speaker to master. Not only does it have a structural logic less replete with exceptions and self-contradictions than most, but it's full to overflowing with cognates: words that are identical or highly similar across the linguistic divide. This is the greatest advantage that any learner of Italian possesses: he or she can amass a relatively vast vocabulary the essential foundation of language acquisition with less arduous effort than is required for any other tongue! Indeed, most English speakers already know between scores and hundreds of Italian words. This book, uniquely, is an instructional tool that focuses upon that "easierness" of Italian vocabulary acquisition.

Like any tool, of course, it can either be utilized skillfully, to the learner's great advantage, or misused and / or underutilized, to his or her loss. The suggestions that follow, then, constitute an "Owner's Manual" on the best-possible usage of this potentially powerful tool.

1. The single greatest assistance the learner can give him / herself is to get the essentials of pronunciation in mind-and-mouth first. Before all else: before the easiness of cognate rich vocabulary, even, and certainly before becoming enmeshed in the complexities of grammatical formality and syntactical structure.

First, learn how the language "sounds and says." You must first train the ears and mind and mouth! It would be impossible to overstress the importance of this: go first to this book's pronunciation chapter, and carefully read and heed both its suggestions and detailed descriptions. Only then, after absorbing an essential familiarity with Italian's vocal / aural character, actively progress toward the absorption of vocabulary itself.

In most cases, a mere four hours or less of listening and practice, as specified in the pronunciation guide, will have you well on your way to really "owning" the basic character of Italian expression. And having gained that, you'll have given yourself a great additional boost toward Italian mastery, and be well ahead of those who are ignorant of pronunciation's all-important primacy. Failing to develop accurate pronunciation from the outset, conversely, would be a continual drag upon your progress, and eventually become a handicap in need of difficult unlearning and correction.

2. Then, with the matter of "sound" confidently in ear, you'll be ready to begin absorbing Italian's vocabulary. Not all of the five thousand cognates at the heart of this book will be of need or interest to you, of course. So, especially as you begin to build vocabulary, be selective!

After you're sure of all the terms in the book's initial list, Lista di termini e frasi familiari, turn with highlighter in hand to the main list, Lista di termini identici e simili, which constitutes this volume's core. From it select a dozen or two everyday nouns from across its alphabetic spectrum. For example, from ability (abilità) and academy (accademia), through discrepancy (discrepanza), and nose (naso), and recourse (ricorso), and student (studente), on to zebra (zebra) and zone (zona), and so forth. Then choose another dozen. Then another.

Then another . . . , adding a few everyday adjectives to the mix as you go along. While you can afford to ignore the "m.," "f.," and "m. & f."coding at first, at some point during your buildup of nouns and pronouns you'll need to turn to the chapter on grammar and become comfortable with the wildly irrational issue of noun / adjective "gender."You'll have no choice in that: it must be done. But don't immerse yourself in the issue of verbs and conjugations yet! That comes last and largely outside of this volumew hen you've amassed a substantial lexicon of nouns and adjectives, and are eager to begin to learn and properly use the "action" words that will make your Italian dance and sing. Yes, verbs come last. Because they must be conjugated for most effective conversational use, and because conjugation is every language's most tangled morass, verbs are by far the toughest to master. In infinitive form, they're a snap; but in conjugated form well, that's something else. But when you've got a hundred or two easy nouns and adjectives in hand, your effort toward verb mastery will seem a worthy price to pay.

3. Finally, as you begin to build and augment your core Italian vocabulary, do not forget the time-tested / experience-proven value of a "flash" system of memory-embedding, review, and self-testing! If you're computer adept, you can create such a tool within your PC with either a database or word-processing program, or by using one of the many notebook type applications widely available. (At least one, in all likelihood, is embedded within your computer's operating system itself.) Alternatively and portably! Hand lettered 2x4 cards (English on one side, Italian with pronunciation key, gender code, and perhaps even pluralization on the other) never loses its effectiveness. In either case, the very act of transposing words into such a system is, in and of itself, a valuable aid to learning and retention. And of course, the value of a ready-review tool cannot be overstated.

THE DIFFERENCES BETWEEN ENGLISH AND ITALIAN

Italian belongs to the Romance family, which in turn is part of the large Indo-European language family.

It therefore shares many features with other Romance languages such as French or Spanish. Native-Italian learners of English, a stress-timed language, face similar kinds of problems to those faced by native speakers of the other Romance languages, which are syllable-timed.

Alphabet: Italian words are made up of the same 26 letters as employed by English, although the letters j, k, w, x and y are considered foreign and are only used in import words. Italian learners may misspell dictated words containing the English letters r and e, which sound like Italian letters a and i. Some words that are capitalized in English (days, months, languages, etc) are not capitalized in Italian.

Phonology: Italian learners typically have problems with the vowel differences in minimal pairs such as sheep / sheet bet / mat cot / coat, The tendency to 'swallow' weak vowels in English causes difficulties both in listening comprehension and in the production of natural-sounding speech.

The pronunciation of consonants include the predictable difficulties with words containing the letters th: (thin, this, other, lengths, etc). Also problematic is the failure to aspirate the h in words such as house, hill, hotel (or to hyper-correct by adding an aspirated h to all words beginning with a vowel.) Most Italian words end with a vowel, which often leads Italian learners to affix a short vowel sound to in English ending with a consonant. This, together with temptation to give full value or emphasis to all syllables, results in the stereotypical Italian production of sentences that sound like: I ata soupa for luncha.

There is another factor leading to the often heavily-accented production of English by Italian learners. Namely, that in Italian the element which the speaker wishes to give most emphasis to is usually moved to the end of the clause. This contrasts with English, in which the salient element is identified by intonation changes rather than word order changes. Italians often find it difficult also to produce the right intonation patterns when asking questions or making requests.

Grammar - Verb/Tense: Italian has 5 inflected tense forms: for the present, simple past, imperfect, future and conditional. The other tenses are formed with auxiliaries. The auxiliary do, however, has no equivalent in Italian, which leads to mistakes such as: What you do? or I no like German food.

Italian does not use the perfect tenses to make a connection to the present in the same way that English does. This results in problems such as I have done my homework on the bus. A similar lack of correspondence in the use of tenses in the two languages leads to interference errors such as: What will you do when you will leave school? or I live in Germany since 1999.

Shades of meaning, which are shown in English by varying the modal verb (must/should/ought to/might want to, etc.) are typically conveyed in Italian by an inflected form of the verb dovere (must). This often results in an overuse of must when Italians speak English.

Grammar - Other: In English the meaning of a clause is largely dependent on the order of words in it (typically Subject Verb Object). Italian, being a more inflected language, allows greater variations in word order. Furthermore, adjectives in Italian usually follow the noun, not precede it as in English. These differences can result in non-standard syntax of Italian learners of English.

Italian learners frequently have problems with the correct use of articles in English. Although both the definite and the indefinite article exist in both languages, their use often does not coincide. As a result it is common to hear sentences such as: Is he teacher? or The health is the most important in the life.

The subject pronoun is not required in colloquial Italian, so learners may say sentences such as: Is impossible.

Vocabulary: Italian and English share many words that are derived from Latin. This facilitates the acquisition of vocabulary, but comes with the associated problem of false friends. Here are some common examples. The Italian false friend comes first: bravo (good/clever) / brave; editore (publisher) / editor; fame (hunger) / fame; libreria (book shop) / library.

Miscellaneous: Italian is a phonetic language. For this reason Italian learners suffer the usual problems that native speakers of such languages have with English.

Namely, that they cannot predict with confidence a. the spelling of any new word that they hear, and b. the pronunciation of any new word that they read.

ITALIAN PRONUNCIATION

Despite the astonishingly high volume of look and sound alike crossover between English and Italian, the two languages take a markedly different approach to some spelling and pronunciational fundamentals. While Italian speech contains virtually every sound present in English, it spells some of those sounds differently, and emphasizes others with greater or lesser intensity than is common in English. Additionally, Italian includes in its vocal repertoire several subtle intonations that are all but unknown in Britain and America somewhat difficult, at first, for the English-accustomed mouth to effect and that together produce a more undulant, more "musical" language than we're accustomed to hearing and speaking.

These distinctions and nuances must be understood and absorbed from the outset if real linguistic efficiency is to be attained. First, they must be recognized by the ear.

Then, because vocabulary needs to be read to be most rapidly and deeply absorbed, they must become readily recognized on the printed page. Finally, they must become comfort- ably familiar and readily reproduced within the new Italian speaker's mouth. It cannot be overemphasized that if any one of these steps is shortchanged, the learner's eventual conversational efficiency will be severely compromised by erroneous assumption, misconception, or simple incapacity. An accurate reproduction of the "sound" of Italian must be accurately perceived by both the ear and the eye, and then effectively attained by the mouth. The two-part, several-hour aural, visual, and vocal training program outlined below will do more to advance the learner toward confident mastery of the sound of Italian than any other action he or she might undertake at this stage of development. This book's users are urged in the strongest possible terms to follow its prescriptions before undertaking attainment of Italian vocabulary and understanding of the language's underlying grammatical structure.

That is, do not begin amassing words until you've learned how they actually sound and "say." To do otherwise is to virtually guarantee the much more difficult and time-costly necessity of unlearning incorrect assumptions and habits.

TRAINING YOUR EAR

From your own audio collection, or from a friend's, or from your local library, or the bookstore where you purchased this book, obtain a tape or CD that contains spoken Italian . . . and listen to it. That's all: just lis- ten. Do not at this point try to learn words or phrases, or "understand" anything at all. Just listen! Turn off the phone, dim the lights, close your eyes, lean your head back, and simply let the speaker's voice wash over you for thirty minutes at least.

Or, better yet, a full hour. Just hearing how Italian sounds.

The ideal recording for this ear-training exercise would be one that contains no English at all, but rather is exclusively the recounting, in Italian, of a story, or a news report, or a conversational interchange, or the reading of a book, and so forth. Such all Italian recordings may be difficult to find in any but the largest metropolitan centers, however.

So you'll very possibly end up with an instructional audio in which English words and phrases are spoken first, followed by their Italian translations spoken somewhat more slowly than normal. No matter: you're not now concerned with meaning at all, but rather simply with sound. Your sole objective is to become initially familiar with the essen- tial sound, shape, intonation, stress, and rise-and-fall cadence of Italian vocalization. Nothing else. At the conclusion of your listening session, take an hour's or a day's break, and then return to the recording and listen again.

This time, be a bit more attentive not merely to the general sound and flow of Italian, but also to its constituent parts particularly the "slightly odd" ones. Again, you're not listening to comprehend, but rather to simply hear and notice. Begin to notice, for example, both the "vowel breathiness" and consonantal distinctness of the speech . . . the gently rolled R's . . . the emphasized S's . . . the odd TS and "buzzy" DZ sounds . . . the often clearly doubled D, F, K, L, P, and T sounds. Then listen again. And, if possible, yet again, until you've experi- enced a total of two to four hours of "immersion" listening.

Every minute you invest in such listening will pay itself back in time saved from future uncertainty, confusion, and misunderstanding. Count yourself done with il pasto completo ("the whole repast") when the general sound of Italian has begun to become so familiar and well imbedded in your mind that its few "weird" vocalizations cease to seem odd at all, and you can begin to confidently anticipate both the sound and the pace and feel of the language as it unfolds from word to word. You're beginning to get bored? Good!

You're progressing: it's becoming "old hat!" And with that at least four half- to full hour listening sessions well embedded in your ear you're done with initial "ear training," and ready to begin "seeing and saying" Italian.

If you have access to a PBS channel that regularly airs Italian language news coverage or an Italian instructional series (usually at midnight and / or weekend hours), or to a cable system that offers extensive Italian programming, videotape and watch / listen to several such programs for several half-hour sessions at least. If you continue to do so, or repeatedly listen to your tapes / CDs during your vocabulary building period, your understanding, competence, and skill will all be steadily strengthened, and your progress accelerated and solidified.

TRAINING YOUR EYES AND MOUTH

Open this book to any two page spread in its midsection, and there, working at an unhurried pace and pointedly ignoring both the leftmost boldface English word on each line and the lightface roman Italian word that follows it, move slowly from entry to entry, focusing solely on each term's phonetic representation. That is, the parenthesized syllable by syllable rendition of each line's Italian word.

Your objective is to attempt to vocalize that representation in mimicry of the type and quality of sound you've recently heard issue from your loudspeakers. For now, pay no attention whatsoever to words, their actual spellings, or meanings. Neither should you be concerned with the "why" of any given pronunciation. Your sole concern should be with sound. That is, an attempt to match your mouth to the phonetic representation pointedly including the ALL-CAPS accentuated syllable given for each entry.

It is likely that in some instances, particularly in your first few minutes of trying, your mouth will resist some of the constructions found many TS and TSY combinations, for example. But press on: millions of people don't find these sounds arduous at all, and many thousands more successfully learn how to form them every year.

There's nothing even vaguely "impossible" here; just a seeming abundance of strangeness and modest difficulty at the start. It will soon abate! Similarly, do not waylay yourself with curiosity about such things as the overwhelming incidence of "breathy" -AH and -EH and -OH sounds . . . or the seemingly high incidence of doubled R's . . . or the apparently inconsistent wandering of S's back and forth across natural syllabic lines. Resolution of these curiosities will occur in due course; for the time being, simply accept that they're the way Italian actually works, and concentrate on trying to make your eye and mouth make sense of them.

A detailed description of the pronunciation of each Italian alphabet character follows later in this chapter, and will be important to review and absorb. For the time being, however, your attention should be focused on whole syllable sound production.

The whys and wherefores of each letter's intonational value can wait a bit longer. Remaining unhurried and unconcerned, for the moment, whether you're getting it precisely right (you're

338

almost certainly not, at least some of the time) continue your out loud pronunciational effort from top to bottom of at least two full pages, and preferably three or four. Then call it quits for a while.

Total investment thus far: between thirty and forty-five minutes. You may not realize it yet, but you've just made a huge step into Italian! As soon as practicable, return to a spread of pages within this book's Lista di termini identici e simili (for variety's sake, pick a different alphabetical section this time) and repeat your out loud enunciation of the phonetics found there. This time, however, you are going to look carefully and repeatedly at the Italian word on each line before vocalizing its phonic representation.

You still don't care about the word's meaning (although in many instances, now, that will be self-evident), but you do want to start to make a firm connection between the word's actual spelling and its phoneticized representation. Between spelling and sound, in short. Oh oh! You've begun to notice some serious spelling and pronunciational anomalies, haven't you!

Ch- combinations, for example, that are represented with a wildly un-English hard-K sound . . . and ce- and ci-constructions that move in the opposite direction, yielding an anti-intuitive CH sound! And gh- spellings that yield a hard-G sound without a hint of H-like exhalation to them . . . and all those z's that are represented as possessing odd TS or DZ intonations. Can all this be right? Yes, it is . . . and soon enough, you'll begin to recognize the patterns.

And soon, as well, understand why. Continue your reading-and-pronouncing effort for, again, two full pages at least, and preferably several more.

By now, you should be beginning to master the production of some of the more difficult sounds specified by the phonetic code.

When you're satisfied with your progress (again, a half-hour minimum is advised), take another break before returning to. . . . Give yourself an initial acceleration test.

Again selecting a random beginning point and again completely ignoring both the whole-word spelling and the term's meaning, pick a single two or three syllable word as your starting point, and rather than merely attempting to pronounce it as the phonetic guide suggests, practice doing so at a faster and faster rate, until it's emerging from your mouth as a unified whole rather than a jerky syllable-by-syllable construction.

This may seem particularly difficult at first, especially in the case of words with consonants on both sides of syllabic breaks, both of which consonants need to be expressed! And those doubled- and tripled-across-break R's are the typically gentle Italian "roll" or "trill" of that letter, which it would also be good to start trying to master.

And the seemingly misplaced S's you've so often noticed are your signal that in Italian that sound often assumes the expressively extended "almost- hiss" you earlier noted in your tape-listening. And those other all important doubled-across-break consonants are not only a reflection of letter-doubling itself, but also of the fact that Italian distinctly double-pronounces such con- structions, rather than merely emphasizing them with increased volume as we generally do in English.

Some of these will seem excruciatingly difficult to effectively enunciate "at speed," at first a set of double B's, for example, being almost a Mount Everest of oral difficulty! But keep at it, and slowly, surely, you will begin to become not only the master of virtually any construction that falls beneath your eye, but moreover a rapid-master, capa- ble of expressing whole words rather than slowly enunciated syllable-by- syllable constructs.

Keep at it, on your one chosen word, until a dozen or more increasingly rapid repetitions have forced your mouth into the required shapes and movements to get it spoken with quick confidence. Then move on to another word, and another and another, repeating in each case the same progress from slow / careful pronunciation to confident rapid-fire expression of the whole-unit term.

That is, with a smoothly ever-diminishing space between syllables. Just as your outloud reading of the words of this English paragraph would be, through years of famil- iarity and everyday practice, essentially without intraword breaks of any kind, so also do you want to attain the point where your expression of Italian terms will be similarly unified and unpaused except between the whole words themselves.

You're undoubtedly some distance from that level of expertise still but you are headed in that direction!

One word at a time. Over and over. And soon, you'll find that each new word even those really difficult five-, six-, and seven-syllable monsters with which Italian is replete becomes all the easier to attain and really, deeply master. Hard? Not really.

All it takes, like any other skill, is practice . . . prac- tice . . . practice! For thirty minutes . . . an hour . . . maybe two. And by that point you really will be becoming comfortable and expert not only beginning to hear Italian words as they're spoken in everyday conversation, but moreover noticing that these pleasing sounds are issuing from your mouth and understanding!

It's an important point to have achieved! In sum, in a half-dozen hours or so you've not only absorbed a new sound structure, but you've also begun to be comfortable with its use and you're almost ready, now, to begin building your cognate based Italian vocabulary with accuracy and confidence.

This chapter's next section will finalize and solidify your understanding of the basics of Italian pronunciation, and it will leave you fully ready to begin absorbing language.

"SAYING" THE ITALIAN ALPHABET

As you progressed through the foregoing exercises, you noticed numerous spelling and pronunciational oddities that need to be comprehended at "letter-level" to complete your overall understanding of Italian speech. In considerable detail, then, the following will resolve what mysteries remain. Italian officially possesses, now, precisely the same alphabet as does English, although five of the letters thereof are neither native to the language nor often employed, except in the representation of nonnative words. Specifically, the letters J, K, W, X, and Y are all but invisible in the Italian lexicon, although the English-equivalent sounds that we associate with those characters are richly abundant in the language. As you have begun to appreciate in the course of the foregoing exercises, those sounds are pro- duced, in Italian, by other letters and letter combinations.

The full Italian alphabet, together with each letter's phonetic name pronunciation and representative contextual pronunciation(s), is listed below. The listing sequence is from easiest-to-absorb (by an English speaker), through somewhat-trickier, to really problematic, potentially confusing, and most-difficult-to-master.

A (AH) The Italian alphabet's initial letter yields one of the easiest and least variable of all pronunciations. Simply put, it is always and everywhere throughout Italy pronounced like an English "soft a," as in English lava or mama. Italian possesses all the other sounds that we English speakers draw from our widely variable A (such as in bather and matter and water), but those sounds are never represented in Italian by the letter A. So fix this one easily and firmly in mind: "Italian A as in father."Always.

B (BEE) Another easy one. B in Italian is pronounced identically as it is in English, in all circumstances. "Italian B as in baby."

D (DEE) Still easy. D in Italian carries precisely the same value as it does in English. "Italian D as in dear."

F (EHF-feh) Easy again! The Italian F is identical in value to its English counterpart. "Italian F as in fun."

J (ee-LOONG-gah) This letter has almost disappeared from the native Italian lexicon, and is now used almost exclusively in imported to Italian nomenclature. In the rare instances where it is employed, it generally pronounces as it does in the donating tongue. Usually, it is safe to pronounce this letter as in English. Thus: "Italian J as in jazz."

K (KAHP-pah) As with the foregoing, K is a rarely seen import to the Italian alphabet. In all cases it pronounces exactly the same way as does its English equivalent. "Italian K as in king."

L (EHL-leh) Widely used in Italian, L is pronounced as in English. "Italian L as in love."

M (EHM-meh) As in English. "Italian M as in mother."

N (EHN-neh) As in English. "Italian N as in nannie."

P (PEE) Exactly as in English: lips together, and puff it out! "Italian P as in prince."

Q (KOO) As in English, the Italian Q owns an essentially "K" sound, and is always found in combination with a u plus a second vowel that follows; that is, qua, que, qui, or quo triplets.

 In practical terms, these can all be pronounced as in similar English combinations, with a "KW" sound blending into the second vowel. Some Italian dialects tend to slightly "break" qua and qui combinations into a KOO + vowel construction, thus pronouncing quarto as (koo-AHR- toh) rather than (QWAHR-toh), and so forth. Said "at speed," howev- er, this is a barely detectable subtlety. So relax with the safe general- ization: "Italian Q as in queen."

T (TEE) As in English. Exactly and always. "Italian T as in truth."

V (VOO) Exactly as it is in English. "Italian V as in victory."

W (DOHP-pyah-voo) Nonexistent in the native-Italian lexicon, this letter occurs as an import only. In those rare instances, as throughout most of Europe, it is almost invariably pronounced like an English V.

Thus a bartender will readily understand a request for whiskey, but very probably ask what kind of (VEE- skee) you want.

"Italian W as in 'I vant to show you my etchings.'"

X (EEKS) Nonnative to Italian. Rarely seen except in words derived from Greek or Latin, or, more recently, other tongues. Generally pronounces as in English. "Italian X as in extra."

Y (EEP-see-lohn) Although Y now officially "exists" in the Italian alphabet, its use is limited to the spelling of a very few imported words, and pronounced as in the donating tongue. The 2 "Tricky" Letter Sounds

E (EH) The Italian E has two sounds: an open and a close (or closed) sound. When the E is open, it's pronounced as in English words bed, met, petty. Some Italian words with an open E are letto (leht-toh), bed; bello (behl-loh) beautiful; sette (seht-teh), seven. When it's close, the E is pronounced as in the English word wait. Some Italian words with a closed E are bere (beh-reh), to drink; sete (seh-teh), thirst; neve (neh- veh), snow. As you can see, we are using the same letters (EH) to represent both sounds: one, because the difference between the two sounds is subtle and, therefore, difficult for someone who is having his / her first encounter with the language; two, because the explanation would be too complicated at this stage; three, because open and close pronunciations will start coming automatically by the positioning of the letter in the word. The two sounds are both present in the Italian word bene (beh-neh), well.

"Italian E as in bene."

I (EE) Most of the time, the Italian I is easy: on its own, when not combined with another vowel, it pronounces like an English "long e," as in lien or machine. Thus: abilità (ah-bee-lee-TAH), ability; dissimile (dees-SEE-mee-leh), dissimilar.

However, in those instances where an I serves as the lead letter of a two-vowel combination (technically, a "diphthong"), significant change occurs. Specifically . . .

• IA, in which the two letters combine and condense in a severe way their individual pronunciations (ee and ah) into a unified single-syllable yah intonation. Thus: academy—accademia (ahk-kah-DEH-myah), NOT (ahk-kah-deh-MEE-ah); and flame—fiamma (FYAHM-mah), NOT (fee-AHM-mah)

• IE follows the same pattern, yielding yeh. Thus: ambient—ambiente (ahm-BYEHN-teh), NOT (ahm-bee-EHN-teh); and convenience—convenienza (kohn-veh-NYEHN-tsah), NOT (kohn-veh-nee-EHN-tsah)

• IO, similarly, pronounces yoh. As in decision—decisione (deh-chee- SYOH-neh), NOT (dee-chee-see-OH-neh); and obsession—ossessione (ohs-sehs-SYOH-neh), NOT (ohs-sehs-see-OH-neh)

• IU, completing the established pattern, pronounces yoo. Thus: refusal—rifiuto (ree-FYOO-toh), NOT (ree-fee-OO-toh); and conjugal—coniugale (koh-nyoo-GAH-leh), NOT (koh-nee-oo-GAH-leh)

These diphthong exceptions aside, the "I = long e" pronunciation is invariably in effect. "Italian I as in bier."

O (OH) The Italian O, like the Italian E, has both an open and a close (closed) pronunciation. When it's pronounced open, it sounds like the O in the English word strong. Italian words with an open O are porta (pohr-tah), door; posta (poh-stah), mail; porto (pohr-toh), harbor. When it's pronounced closed, it sounds like the O in the English word hope or cozy. For the same reasons as in the case of the letter E, above, we are representing both sounds with the letters OH. The Italian word poco has first an open O and then a close one. Thus: "Italian O as in poco."

R (EHR-reh) The Italian R is essentially the same as in English, with the notable distinction of often being "rolled" or "trilled," except in some instances where it is immediately followed by a consonant or the vowel i.

R's in words with one or more R's in differents spots of the word rarely roll more than one or two at most.

In most cases, the Italian R-roll, while distinct and unmistakable, is softer and "less aggressive" than found in many other European languages; an angry or emphatic Italian will roll his R's with special vigor, however!

Nothing so surely and immediately denotes a nonnative speaker as his or her consistent failure to "roll." As an aid to learning this very fundamental Italian sound and practice, many R's in the phonetic guidance in this book are doubled or tripled, indicating not that they are to be double-pronounced (as are all other double-spelled consonants), but rather "rolled."

U (OO) The Italian U produces, in most instances, a sound like an English "double o," as in boot, root, or toot. However, when directly followed by another vowel, the diphthong usually coalesces into a mild English "w-flavored" intonation.

Thus the all-important buono (good) is pronounced (BWOH-noh), NOT (boo-OH-noh). Another example is the adjective inadeguato (inadequate), pronounced (ee-nah-deh-GWAH- toh), NOT (een-ah-deh-goo-AH-toh).

The learner will discover that most such constructions "form themselves" for oral convenience, and that the variation can generally be assumed to be a self-generating exception to the otherwise-reliable "double-o" rule.

The 5 "Difficult" Letter Sounds

H (AHK-kah) The Italian H is a uniquely influential letter that needs to be well understood before we progress onward to its coconspirators in complexity, C and G.

Indeed, it can be argued that without "H- understanding," a significant fraction of the language's pronunciation will remain a perplexing, paradoxical mystery. This is because, in and of itself, the widely used Italian H is not a "pronounced" letter at all(!), but rather serves only as a symbolic indicator of the manner in which a consonant that immediately precedes it is to be enunciated. Read that sentence again, and understand clearly: by itself, the Italian H is with- out pronunciational value whatsoever.

It's without sound. Instead, it is a backward-pointing "sign" or "signal" indicative of something other than its own intrinsic sound value. Which is nil. In Italian, in short, the H is always silent. Always!

Even in imported-into-Italian words such as hamburger, hobby, and hotel, the letter H is without pronunciational value, merit, or effect.

For example, the three foregoing words are pronounced by Italians as (AHM-boor-gehr),(AAH-bee), and (oh-TEL). Despite what we'd normally expect in so airy, so heavily aspirated Italian, an H does not indicate an extra measure of soft breathiness. In an Italian mouth, an H remains utterly silent. Completely inert. Wholly without "air." Without exception!

Still, for all its silence, it is not without importance. Indeed, it owns a very great significance wherever it occurs in a native Italian word. Simply put, it tells the reader or speaker how the preceding C or G (which, except in imported words, are the only two letters that ever precede an H) is to be sounded. Nothing more. And nothing less.

Repeating for emphasis: the Italian H exists solely to "say something" about another letter. Specifically, about the C or G that precedes it. Aside from bearing this "message," it might as well not exist. It has no value of its own. Do NOT express it vocally. Ever!

Alas for English speakers, what the H "tells" its reader or speak- er about that preceding letter is, for us, often anti-intuitive in the extreme. Viz: exactly the opposite of what we'd most readily expect in the generally "soft" Italian context.

That is, instead of indicating that the preceding consonant is to be softened or "aerated," the Italian H says just the reverse. "Pronounce the C or G ahead of me with solid firmness and no hint of an airy, hissing, or resounding overtone," it says. "Do not give that preceding C a soft-and-breathy C sound (as in English champion or cheese or cherry), but rather, give it a hard K-like pronunciation (as in English cap or cook or cuticle)!"

And "Do not allow that preced- ing G to get all mushy-gooey-windy, with an English J-like sound, but insure that it comes out of your mouth with a firm roof-of-the-mouth G- like intonation (as in English ghastly or ghetto or ghost)." In sum, the Italian H directs us to do precisely the opposite of what we'd most often do in English . . . or what we'd especially assume so-breathy Italian to do! It tells us (1) to ignore itself completely, and (2) to insure that the preceding consonant is "firm" rather than "soft."

Completing and compounding all the foregoing is the fact that often, when it comes to C's and G's, the absence of an Italian H very often indicates that an English-like H sound is to be inserted!!!

Thus bringing full circle the complexity alluded to at the outset of this long discussion. It is, at first, a confusingly difficult reversal-of-expectations to get on top of! But once you've got it well and firmly in mind, you can congratulate yourself on having surmounted one of Italian pronuncia-tion's highest hurdles.

The additional detail provided at C and G, below, will complete the circle. . . . C (CHEE) As previously implied, the Italian C is a troublesome letter indeed: the producer of one of Italian's most maddeningly variable sounds. And not only variable, but often quite opposite in pronunciational value from that which we assign to this letter in English speech.

343

In summary: Italian CA, CO, CU, and C-consonant combinations including CH (!), yield an English K sound. It's the inclusion of the CH combo that is most troublesome to English speakers, of course, who are accustomed to that combination's almost-always production of a soft, aspirated sound (as in chap, cheap, chip, chop, and chum).

In Italian, the CH linkup produces precisely the opposite of what we're accustomed to: a hard English K as in keep or kill.

This sound reversal, in conjunction with the other sound reversals noted directly below, makes the Italian C one of the most fundamental of all difficulties faced, and consequently one of the most critical that the learner absorb and incorporate into his consciousness from the outset.

No less "backward"feeling,the Italian CE combination yields a surprising English CH sound, as exemplified by our cello—which of course is not "our" word at all, but rather an Italian term that, amazingly, we have brought into English with its native pronunciation intact. So while anti intuitive, at least the CE combo is easy to keep in mind: "CE as in cello (CHEHL-loh)."

Continuing the anti-intuitive (for us English speakers) theme, Italian CI combinations also produce the unexpected CH sound!

Thus, while we pronounce the word cinema as (SIN-eh-mah) in English, in Italian the same word is pronounced (CHEE-neh-mah) . . . circa is our (SIR-kah) and an Italian's (CHEER-kah), . . . and our citadel (SIT-ah- dell)is their cittadella (cheet-tah-DEHL-lah).

The Italian C's final twist regards those instances in which it is doubled.

In most instances, the CC combination pronounces, as expected, with a distinct double-K sound, as in vecchio (VEHK-kyoh), meaning old. But CCE and CCI combinations give the initial C a tee sound, before adding on the CH pronunciation that would otherwise be expected per the citations above. Thus successo (soot-CHEHS-soh), English success.

Because C is so widely employed in Italian (as in English), but with a so often notably different result, the serious learner must make mastery of this letter a primary objective. It is, arguably, the least understood and most often pronunciationally botched of all Italian characters; don't be among the substantial majority of visitors who completely misunderstand its effect!

G (JEE) The Italian G, bless it's wicked soul, is similar to the C in having little reliable personality of its own, and rather being largely at the mercy of its context to "make up its mind" about what it wants to sound like. In a word, it's a problematic letter in the extreme.

Italian GA, GO, GU, and G-consonant (including GH) combina- tions pronounce like an ordinary English "firm g." That is, an expulsion formed by the midtongue's stoppage-then-release against the hard palate as in English gate, gothic, gum, glove, ghetto, or ghost.

In Italian GE-consonant and GI-consonant combinations, how- ever, the letter G assumes an English J-like sound, just as it does in many English words—gem, general, gin and giraffe, for example. In these cases, the J-like sound is followed by the succeeding vowel value and it's succeeding consonantal sound.

Thus generico (jeh-NEHR-ree- koh), English generic, or gigante (jee-GAHN-teh), English giant. The latter word, note, exemplifies both Italian G's essential sounds.

When a GI combination extends to double-vowel length, as in GIA, GIO, or GIU (i.e., G + diphthong: GIA, GIO, or GIU), however, the I value drops out of the J-sounding mix, yielding a JAH, JOH, or JOO sound precedent to the following consonant.

Thus the ubiquitous giorno (day) does NOT include pronunciation of the I, but rather comes out as (JOHR-noh).

344

This "drop out" is one of the trickiest of Italian pronunciational oddities for many learners to remember, owing to the great frequency and generally immense importance of the I in Italian spelling.

But it can't be avoided: "GI + second vowel = silent I."

And we're not done with G yet! In the not-uncommon GL + I combination (GLI), it's the G itself that disappears from pronunciation al effect, yielding only a residual LYEE sound, as exemplified by the the sound of the letters -lli- in English words million and scallion. When GLI is followed by vowel a, e, or o, we get sounds lyah, lyeh and lyoh, respectively. Thus biglietto (bee-LYHET-toh), ticket; and bagaglio (bah- GAH-lyoh), luggage. Similarly, a GN combination also results in the G's vocal disappearance, yielding an English "NY" sound, as heard in English onion. Thus campagna (kahm-PAH-nyah), campaign.

The Italian G, alas, is common enough to make early mastery of its variant complexities highly advisable.

The latter two problems are rel- atively easy, but to get the other G- complexities well in mind, eye, and mouth will require more effort. Don't delay! S (EHS-seh)

In pronunciational terms, the Italian S isn't as diffi- cult to master as the two foregoing troublemakers but it's not far behind! It produces one of two sounds, equivalent to an English "s" or "z," although in many cases real certainty regarding which pronunciation belongs where can only be determined on a word-by-word basis. Several certainties do exist.

An Italian double-S is always reliably "ess-sy" and entirely free of buzzy-z intonation. Similarly, an S + vowel at the beginning of a word always pronounces as in English safe, serene, simple, soft, or supple. And an S followed by -c, -f, -p, -q, or -t, regardless of where that construct occurs within a word, generates a standard English S sound as well.

(The learner who creates his/her own c-f-p-q-t acronym as a memory aid will profit well from the exercise; the author's mnemonic in this regard, alas, cannot be cited in polite company!)

It is also certain that whenever the Italian sibilant S is expressed, regardless of its singular or doubled status within the spelling of the word, it is done with slightly more emphasis than is accorded to any other undoubled Italian consonant except r.

Thus the "moving around" of S's in many phonetic guides, to whatever syllabic position forces the speaker's mouth toward a "natural" emphasis of this troublesome letter.

Now the difficulties begin! Usually when an Italian S immediately precedes a b, d, g, l, m, n, r, or v, or often when it's followed by a vowel, it is pronounced with a z sound, just as that letter pronounces that intonation in such English words as please, rose, and museum. And Italian nouns and adjectives ending in a -so, -sa, -se construct often pronounce with a z sound as well e.g., sposo m. (SPOH-zoh), spouse / husband; and preciso (adj.) (preh-CHEE-zoh), precise although these are notable exceptions to the more common s intonation.

There is, alas, no reliable rule that governs these variants; the early learner who forgets to substitute a z for an s sound in one or another of these troublesome instances, or makes an incorrect transposition of sounds, will hardly be held to account by a native Italian, however.

Regionalism plays a role here, and even they misspeak their language sometimes as many English speakers garble their own with regularity! We're not done with our S troubles yet, however.

For the letter assumes distinctly different (although now, reliably unbuzzed) sounds when immediately followed by a -c in combination with various other letters. Thus: SC + E or SC + I = SH sound SC + A, SC + O, or SC + U = SK sound SCH + E or SCH + I = SK sound Clear as mud? Well, at least there were those sixteen "easy" letters!

Z (DZEH-tah) Finally, the important, widely occurring Italian Z (at least fiftyfold more common than in the English lexicon) is another troublesome letter, in that it rarely pronounces with even a hint of an English "z" sound (that is, as a simple "buzzing long e"), yet doesn't follow an invariably dependable pronunciational rule of its own, either.

In many instances, an Italian Z pronounces, most unexpectedly, like an English TS construct, such as is made at the end of (English) words like forts, meats, or weights. Because this TS sound invariably occurs within the body of the Italian word (where such a sound construct never occurs in English), it may initially seem quite odd and dif- ficult to master in midword position.

A few moments of concentrated practice, however, will make the sound both easy to produce and "nat- ural" feeling in the mouth. An apt example of this anti-intuitive (to us!) pronunciation can be found within the word aberrazione (aberration), which issues from an Italian mouth as (ah-behr-rah-TSYOH-neh).

No buzz at all, but rather just a "tee-essy" sound. As decidedly un-English as it might be imag- ined. It follows, of course, that when an Italian Z is doubled—which is very often indeed—it is not an English z sound that repeats, but rather the T portion of the single-Z pronunciation.

That is, the first of the Z pair is assigned a sharply ending T enunciation, with the second Z "repeating" in the form of the full TS construct described above.

The pronunciation of this double-Z occurrence is best exemplified by the "universal" word pizza— arguably the most widely known Italian term in existence, from Rome to London to Kansas City to Hong Kong.

From an Italian's mouth, this delicious word issues as (PEET-tsah), which notably includes the millisecond break within the T sound that effectively doubles its enunciation.

Most Americans and Brits, of course, tend to elide the second T, pronouncing a slightly lazier (PEET-suh); and a few, yes, pronounce what seems to them a more "logical" (PEET-zuh).

Still, it's gratifying to hear just how often that word is pronounced fully correctly, even thousands of miles from the sunny land where that food originated—and is still and forever a sta- ple, sold out of very nearly as many shops as purvey the pie in New York City!

In other instances, an Italian Z will assume a subtle dz sound, as in the English word adz. This pronunciation is more often than not found in Italian terms that begin with Z—e.g., zebra (DZEH-brah)—but it may also occur within a word, both singly and in a doubled form—as in zanzara (dsahn-DSAH-rah), gnat; and parabrezza (pah-rah- BREHD-dzah), windshield.

"SAYING" ITALIAN WORDS

Compared to the complexities encountered immediately above, several summary generalizations about Italian words in general can be easily stated, understood, and mastered. Letters doubled in Italian spelling are always, always!! Doubled in pronunciational value.

There are no exceptions to this rule: Italian double letters really "mean" something!

While some teachers suggest that doubles must be invariably and distinctly double pronounced, the fact is that many doubles occur amidst constructions that make double pronunciation almost impossible for the nonnative mouth to produce, without slowing to a near halt.

In those instances, a lengthened emphasis, at least, must be produced to remain true to the word's actual pronunciational value.

A single example will suffice: in an English mouth, the Italian word mamma is far more often than not elided to (MAH-mah); to an Italian, that is a nonword. Rather, he / she would very distinctly intone (MAHM-mah).

346

And while consonants represent at least 90 percent of all double-letter spellings, the rare instances of doubled vowels are also subject to the same rule.

Thus zii (TSEE-ee), plural of zio m. (uncle); and veemente (adj.) (veh-eh- MEHN-teh), vehement, are definitely nonelided.

Yet again: there are no exceptions to this rule. It is absolute! While an Italian word's stressed syllable can occur at any point within its structure, by far the most common accenting occurs in the penultimate the next-to-last syllable.

The learner who fails to note which words deviate from this standard, and thus blithely pronounces all words with stress next-to-the-end, will be a much cruder speaker than need be. But at least he/she will be right more often than not.

Finally, while Italian words, like English, are composed of syllabic subunits, they are in the end organic "whole" things rather than merely a haltingly strung together assemblage of individual sounds.

The learner's objective must always be to unify every word by reducing syllabic pausing to a minimum.

With extensive "repeat and repeat" practice of every word being brought into his or her new vocabulary, as urged earlier in this chapter, the student will enjoy a steady increase in both competence, comprehension, confidence, and communicability.

CHAPTER 1: BUSINESS

Italian business culture is formal and hierarchical. First names are not used between executives and subordinates and using the right personal and professional titles may help you clinch that deal! Business is not usually discussed over a meal, but when you do dine with Italian colleagues or business partners wait for them to initiate any discussions about business. Working in an Italian office can also be daunting, especially if you haven't mastered the language. So this book has come up with some useful phrases to help you along your way, from asking your colleague out for a drink, your boss for a pay-rise or simply venting your frustration. Warning: Some may need to be used with caution! Also, as a visitor you'll be expected to be in orario (on time). Don't get touchy though about being kept waiting.

I'm attending a ...

Sono qui per ...

so·no kwee per ...

conference

una conferenza

oo·na kon·fe·ren·tsa

course

un corso

oon kor·so

meeting

una riunione

oo·na ree·oo·nyo·ne

trade fair

una fiera commerciale

oo·na fye·ra ko·mer·cha·le

I'm here with ...

Sono qui con ...

so·no kwee kon ...

my company

la mia azienda

la mee·a a·dzyen·da my colleague

il mio collega m eel mee·o ko·le·ga la mia collega f la mee·a ko·le·ga

my colleagues

i miei colleghi

ee myay ko·le·gee

(two) others

(due) altri

(doo·e) al·tree

I'm staying at (the Minerva hotel), room (309).

Alloggio al (Minerva), camera (trecentonove).

a·lo·jo (al mee·ner·va) ka·me·ra (tre·chen·to·no·ve) I'm alone.

Sono solo/a. m/f so·no so·lo/a

I'm here for (two) days/weeks.

Sono qui per (due) giorni/settimane.

so·no kwee per (doo·e) jor·nee/se·tee·ma·ne

Here's my business card.

Ecco il mio biglietto da visita.

e·ko eel mee·o bee·lye·to da vee·zee·ta

I have an appointment with (Mr Carlucci).

Ho un appuntamento con (il Signor Carlucci).

o oo·na·poon·ta·men·to kon (eel see·nyor kar·loo·chee)

That went very well.

È andato bene.

e an·da·to be·ne

Shall we go for a drink/meal?

Andiamo a bere/mangiare qualcosa?

an·dya·mo a be·re/man·ja·re kwal·ko·za

Where's the ...?

Dov'è ...?

do·ve ...

business centre

il business centre

eel beez·nees sen·ter

conference

la conferenza

la kon·fe·ren·tsa

meeting

la riunione

la ree·oo·nyo·ne

I need ...

Ho bisogno di ...

o bee·zo·nyo dee ...

a computer

un computer

oon kom·pyoo·ter

a connection to the Net

una connessione Internet

oo·na ko·ne·syo·ne een·ter·net

an interpreter

un/un'interprete m/f oo·neen·ter·pre·te

more business cards

più biglietti da visita

pyoo bee·lye·tee da vee·zee·ta

some space to set up

un posto dove sistemare

oon pos·to do·ve sees·te·ma·re

to send an email/fax

mandare un email/fax

man·da·re oon e·mayl/faks

I'm expecting a ...

Aspetto ...

a·spet·o ...

call

una telefonata

oo·na te·le·fo·na·ta

fax

un fax

oon faks

data projector

proiettore

pro·ye·to·re

flip chart

lavagna con fogli

la·va·nya kon fo·lyee

overhead projector

lavagna luminosa

la·va·nya loo·mee·no·sa

whiteboard

lavagna bianca

la·va·nya byan·ka

Greetings/morning chat:

If it's your first day in the job, remember to address your colleagues - especially those in senior positions - with the more formal

"Lei" ("you"), regardless of gender, rather than "tu". Usually, that means verbs end in 'a' rather than 'i'.

So, for example:

"Lei come si chiama?"

(What's your name?) instead of "Tu come ti chiami?"

"Buongiorno, come va?"

(Good morning, how are you?)

Italians don't tend to keep formalities up for long, so as you settle into some polite banter, you can ask your colleagues:

"Da quanto tempo lavori qui?"

("How long have you been working here?")

"Buondì/salve"

(less formal ways of saying 'hello')

"Hai passato un buon weekend/fine settimana?"

("Did you have a good weekend?")

"Sì! Domenica era bellissima! Sono andato/a al mare!"

(Yes! Sunday was beautiful! I went to the beach!")

"No! Faceva schifo!"

(No! It was rubbish!)

"Mi dispiace che sono in ritardo, c'è uno sciopero /non partiva il mio motorino"

("Sorry I'm late, there's a strike/my scooter wouldn't start")

"Ho dimenticato di timbrare, non ero in ritardo 'sta mattina"

("I forgot to clock-in this morning, I wasn't late")

"Dove hai parcheggiato?"

("Where did you park?" is a common question to ask upon arriving at work, due to the fierce competition for parking slots)

Socialising:

"Andiamo a prendere un caffè?"

("Shall we go for coffee?")

"La macchina del cioccolato ha mangiato le mie monete"

("The chocolate machine swallowed my change")

"Andiamo a prendere qualcosa al bar?"

("Shall we get something from the bar?")

"Chiamiamo il bar e li chiediamo a portare su tre caffè?"

("Shall we call the bar and ask them to bring up three coffees?")

"Vai a casa per pranzo?"

("Are you going home for lunch?" is a very common question as Italians often go home to their families for lunch)

"Andiamo fuori a pranzo?"

("Shall we go out for lunch?")

"Cosa hai mangiato a colazione/pranzo/cena?"

("What did you have for breakfast/lunch/dinner?")

Italians are always very intrigued about eating habits...and may follow it up with, "E come l'hai cucinato?"

("How did you cook that?)

"Tre ore non è molto per un pranzo d'affari"

("Three hours isn't that long for a business lunch")

"Andiamo a fare l'aperitivo?"

("Shall we go for 'aperitivo', the equivalent of afterwork drinks, but never beer and it must involve food!)

"Chi è lo stagista? E' proprio carino"

("Who's the intern? He's really cute")

Office/tech speak:

"Ha la password per la connessione wifi?"

("Do you have the password for wifi?" – a vital question on your first day!)

"Quando è la data di consegna?"

("When's the deadline?")

"Lo faccio subito"

("I'll do it straight away")

"Mi puoi inviare una email?"

("Could you send me an email?)

"Cosa vuol dire/cosa significa?"

("What does this mean?")

"Non lo so, Googl'are"

("I don't know, Google it)

"Ok, lo posso Twitt'are"

(Ok, I'll Twitter it)

"Non credo che sia fattibile finire il progetto entro oggi"

("I don't think it's feasible to finish the project by the end of today")

"No, non stavo/ero sul Facebook, hai sbagliato"

("No, I wasn't on Facebook, you made a mistake")

"E bloccato/non funziona"

("It doesn't work" - for computer problems)

"Il tuo internet funziona?"

("Is your internet working?")

"Che palle! Non funziona internet"

("Oh balls! The internet's not working")

"Il capo non è di buon umore"

("The boss isn't in a good mood")

"Questo lavoro è noioso da morire"

("This job bores me to death"). Alternatively. and far less elegant, "questo lavoro è una palla! Voglio andarmene!" ("This job is crap! I want to leave!")

"Non ne posso più di questo lavoro"

("I'm sick of this job")

"La carta igienica è finita"

("The toilet paper's run out")

Tricky conversations:

"Mi è stato offerta un´altra opportunità di lavoro. Ci ho pensato a lungo e alla fine, ho deciso di accettarla."

("I've been offered another opportunity. I've thought about it long and hard, and have decided to take it")

"Vorrei portare alla vostra gentile attenzione la questione di un piccolissimo aumento di stipendio"

("I'd like to discuss the possibility of a small pay-rise)

BANKING

Where can I ...?

Dove posso ...?

do·ve po·so ...

arrange a transfer

trasferire soldi

tras·fe·ree·re sol·dee

get a cash advance

prelevare con carta di credito

pre·le·va·re kon kar·ta dee kre·dee·to

What time does the bank open?

354

A che ora apre la banca?

a ke o·ra a·pre la ban·ka

Where's an ATM?

Dov'è un Bancomat?

do·ve oon ban·ko·mat

Where's a foreign exchange office?

Dov'è un cambio?

do·ve oon kam·byo

I'd like to cash a cheque.

Vorrei riscuotere un assegno.

vo·ray ree·skwo·te·re oo·na·se·nyo

I'd like to change a travellers cheque.

Vorrei cambiare un travellers cheque.

vo·ray kam·bya·re oon tra·ve·lers chek

I'd like to change money.

Vorrei cambiare denaro.

vo·ray kam·bya·re de·na·ro

I'd like to withdraw money.

Vorrei fare un prelievo.

vo·ray fa·re oon pre·lye·vo

The automatic teller machine took my card.

Il Bancomat ha trattenuto la mia carta di credito.

eel ban·ko·mat a tra·te·noo·to la mee·a kar·ta dee kre·dee·to

I've forgotten my PIN.

Ho dimenticato il mio codice PIN.

o dee·men·tee·ka·to eel mee·o ko·dee·che peen

Can I use my credit card to withdraw money?

Si può usare la carta di credito per fare prelievi?

see pwo oo·za·re la kar·ta dee kre·dee·to per fa·re pre·lye·vee

What's the exchange rate?

Quant'è il cambio?

kwan·te eel kam·byo

What's the commission?

Quant'è la commissione?

kwan·te la ko·mee·syo·ne

What's the charge for that?

Quanto costa?

kwan·to kos·ta

Can I have smaller notes?

Mi può dare banconote più piccole?

mee pwo da·re ban·ko·no·te pyoo pee·ko·le

Has my money arrived yet?

È arrivato il mio denaro?

e a·ree·va·to eel mee·o de·na·ro

How long will it take to arrive?

Quanto tempo ci vorrà per il trasferimento?

kwan·to tem·po chee vo·ra per eel tras·fe·ree·men·to

For other useful phrases, see money.

listen for ...

your ...

il Suo ...

eel soo·o ...

ID

documento d'identità

do·koo·men·to dee·den·tee·ta

passport

passaporto

pa·sa·por·to

In ...

Fra ...

fra ...

(four) working days

(quattro) giorni lavorativi

(kwa·tro) jor·nee la·vo·ra·tee·vee

one week

una settimana

oo·na se·tee·ma·na

Please ...

Può ..., per favore?

pwo ... per fa·vo·re

sign here

firmare qui

feer·ma·re kwee

write it down

scriverlo

skree·ver·lo

There's a problem with your account.

C'è un problema con il Suo conto.

che oon pro·ble·ma ko·neel soo·o kon·to

We can't do that.

Non possiamo farlo.

non po·sya·mo far·lo

CHAPTER 2: INTRODUCING YOURSELF

This book provides you with ready made sentences and expressions to help you navigate many different situations.

However, it is still very important to know the basics of grammar. Understanding the mechanics of the sentences and phrases presented here will make them that much more meaningful for you and can certainly help you to understand better when people are speaking to you!

Verbs and Conjugation

The following sections will help you to formulate basic sentences and questions. You've already learned about articles and nouns. Verbs form the foundation of any language.

Here you will learn the basics about the simple present tense and simple past tense.

Verbs in the Present Tense

Most all Italian verbs fall into one of three categories: first conjugation verbs, second conjugation verbs, and third conjugation verbs.

In order to determine in which category a particular verb belongs, we must look at the infinitive form of the verb.

The infinitive is the unconjugated form of the verb (to run, to eat, etc.). First conjugation verbs end in –are; second conjugation verbs end in –ere; and third conjugation verbs end in –ire.

Some examples follow: **–are verbs (first conjugation)**

affittare ahf-feet-TAHR-ray	to rent
guidare gwee-DAH-ray	to drive
parlare pahr-LAH-ray	to speak

–ere verbs (second conjugation)

vedere veh-DEH-ray	to see
ripetere ree-PEH-teh-ray	to repeat
leggere LEHJ-jeh-ray	to read

–ire verbs (third conjugation)

dormire door-MEE-ray	to sleep
partire pahr-TEE-ray	to leave
capire cah-PEE-ray	to understand

The first step in conjugating a verb is to identify the subject I, you, he, Marco, John and I, etc.

With the correct subject pronoun, you can correctly conjugate the verb.

Subject Pronouns

The subject pronouns (also referred to as personal pronouns) are used to indicate the subject of a verb.

Singular		Plural	
io	I	Noi	we
ee-oo		Noy	
tu	you(informal)	Voi	
too		Voy	
lui,lei	he,she	Loro	they
Loo-lei, lay		law-rah	
Lei	you(formal)	Loro	you(formal)
lay		law-rah	

The next step is to conjugate the verb so that it is in the same person as the subject.

—Are Verbs in the Present Tense

Almost all —are verbs are regular—that is, they follow a pattern of conjugation. Once you learn this pattern, conjugating most —are verbs is easy! To conjugate the first conjugation verbs in the present tense, remove the —are ending and replace it with a different ending for each subject:

Singular	Plural
io parlo (I speak)	noi parliamo (we speak)
ee-oh PAHR-loh	noy pahr-lee-AHM-oh
tu parli (you speak)	voi parlate (you speak)
too PAHR-lee	voy pahr-LAH-tay
lui parla (he speaks)	loro parlano (they speak)
loo-ee PAHR-lah	law-roh PAHR-lah-noh
lei parla (she speaks)	
lay PAHR-lah	
Lei parla (you [formal] speak)	Loro parlano (you [formal] speak)
lay PAHR-lah	law-roh PAHR-lah-noh

The present tense in Italian can carry different meanings in English, depending on the context:

Io parlo italiano can mean "I speak Italian," "I am speaking Italian," or "I do speak Italian."

Io non parlo italiano can mean "I don't speak Italian" or "I am not speaking Italian."

The present tense in Italian can also be used to express an action that will take place in the future:

> Stasera guardo la televisione.

> I will watch TV this evening.

–Ere and –ire Verbs in the Present Tense Second and third conjugation verbs are verbs whose infinitive forms end in –ere and –ire, respectively. You will notice from the conjugations below that – ere and –ire verbs differ from each other only in the voi forms.

scrivere SCREE-veh-ray	to write	dormire door-MEE-ray	to sleep
io scrivo ee-oh SCREE-voh	noi scriviamo noy scree-vee-AH-moh	io dormo ee-oh DOOR-moh	noi dormiamo noy door-mee-AHmoh
tu scrivi too SCREE-vee	voi scrivete voy scree-VEH-tay	tu dormi too DOOR-mee	voi dormite voy door-MEE-tay
lui scrive loo-ee SCREE-veh	loro scrivono law-roh SCREE-voh-noh	lui dome loo-ee DOOR-meh	loro dormono law-rah DOOR-moh-noh
Lei scrive	Loro scrivono	Lei dorme	Loro dormono
lay SCREE-veh	law-roh SCREE-voh-noh	lay DOOR-meh	law-roh DOOR-moh-noh
		lei scrive lay SCREE-veh	lei dorme lay DOOR-meh

The Verbs Essere and Avere

Essere (to be) and avere (to have) are two of the most common verbs, but they both require irregular conjugations.

Essere: To Be

The verb essere (to be) is one of the most commonly used verbs in Italian. It is important to learn this verb inside and out, as you will hear it in almost every conversation you have!

In the present tense, it is conjugated as follows:

Singular		Plural	
ee-oh SOH-noh ee-oh SOH-noh		noysee-YAH-moh noy see-YAH-moh	
tu sei too say	you (informal) are	voi siete voy see-YEH-teh	you(informal) are
lui e loo-ee-eh	he is	loro sono LAW-roh soh-noh	they are
lei e lay eh	she is		
lei e lay eh	you (formal) are	loro sono LAW-roh soh-Noh	you(formal)are

It is common, but not required, to omit the subject pronoun in both spoken and written Italian:

I am American.

Io sono americano.

ee-oh SOH-noh ah-meh-ree-CAH-noh

I am American.

Sono americano.

Essere can be used to indicate provenance when followed by the preposition di + a place name:

We are from Philadelphia.

Siamo di Philadelphia.

see-YAH-moh dee fill-ah-DEHL-fee-yah

To find out where someone is from, ask the question:

Di dove sei? (informal)

dee DOH-veh say?

Di dov'è? (formal)

dee doh-VEH?

Essere can be used to indicate possession when followed by the preposition di + a noun or a proper name:

It's my wife's suitcase.

È la valigia di mia moglie.

eh lah vah-LEE-jah dee mee-ah MOHL-yay

It's Paul's.

È di Paul. eh dee Paul

To find out to whom something belongs, ask the question:

Whose is it? Di chi è? dee key eh

Whose are they?

Di chi sono? dee key SOH-noh

Avere: To Have

The verb avere (to have) is a commonly used verb in Italian.

It is conjugated in the present tense as follows:

Singular		Plural	
io ho **ee-oh oh**	I have	noi abbiamo noy ahb-bee-YAH-moh	we have
tu hai **too eye**	you(informal) have	voi avete voi ah-VEH-tay	you(informal) have
lui ha **loo-ee ah**	he has	loro hanno LAW-roh AHN-noh	they have
lei ha **lay ah**	she has		
Lei ha **lay ah**	you(formal) have	Loro hanno LAW-roh AHN-noh	you(formal) have

Do you have cousins in Florida?

Hai cugini in Florida?

eye koo-JEE-nee een FLOH-ree-dah

I have two cousins in Florida.

Ho due cugini in Florida.

oh doo-ay koo-JEE-nee een FLOH-ree-dah

The Past Tense

In order to form the passato prossimo, it is important to have mastered the auxiliary verbs avere and essere. The second component of the passato prossimo conjugations is the past participle.

In Italian the past participle is formed by replacing the –are, –ere, –ire of the infinitive with –ato, –uto, –ito, respectively.

KEYNOTE

In Italian the passato prossimo is also a compound tense that is made up of two parts: an auxiliary verb (either avere or essere) and the past participle of the verb.

The passato prossimo can have a few different meanings: Io ho viaggiato in Italia could translate as "I have traveled to Italy," "I traveled to Italy," or "I did travel to Italy," depending on the context.

Infinitive	Past Participle
mangiare	mangiato
mahn-JAH-ray	mahn-JAH-toh
vedere	veduto

veh-DEH-ray	ved-DOO-toh
partire	partito
pahr-TEE-ray	pahr-TEE-toh

For most Italian verbs (including transitive verbs— those that can take a direct object), the passato prossimo is formed with the auxiliary verb avere plus the past participle of the main verb. The auxiliary verb essere is used with most intransitive verbs (verbs that cannot take a direct object). When the auxiliary verb essere is used, the last letter of the past participle must agree in number and in gender with the subject of the verb.

The Past Tense of the Verb Vedere (to see)

ho veduto	I saw; I have seen
oh veh-DOO-toh	
hai veduto	you saw; you have seen
eye veh-DOO-toh	
ha veduto	he/she saw; has seen
ah veh-DOO-toh	
abbiamo veduto	we saw; we have seen
ahb-bee-YAH-moh veh-DOO-toh	
avete veduto	you saw; you have seen
ah-VEH-tay veh-DOO-toh	
hanno veduto	they saw; they have seen
AHN-noh veh-DOO-toh	

Some examples of the past tense using essere:

The girls have left.

Le ragazze sono partite.

leh rah-GAHTS-seh SOH-noh pahr-TEE-teh

The boys arrived late.

I ragazzi sono arrivati in ritardo.

ee rah-GAHTS-see SOH-noh ahr-ree-VAH-tee een ree-TAHR-doh

The children went to the museum.

I bambini sono andati al museo.

ee bahm-BEE-nee SOH-noh ahn-DAH-tee ahl moo-ZAY-oh

Forming a Sentence

Developing your communication skills will require an understanding of basic sentence structure in Italian. Bear in mind that the following guidelines are not carved in stone; you will hear many variations in sentence structure based on context. These basic rules will help get you started.

1. Affirmative statement: Paolo mangia la pizza. (POWH-loh MAHN-jah lah PEETS-ah)

2. Negative statement: Paolo non mangia la pizza. (POWH-loh nohn MAHN-jah lah PEETS-ah)

3. Question: Paolo mangia la pizza? (POWH-loh MAHN-jah lah PEETS-ah?)

The basic structure of an affirmative statement in Italian is subject+verb+object. Making sentences negative in Italian is as easy as placing the word non in front of the conjugated verb.

Paul and Virginia are not from Boston.

 Paul e Virginia non sono di Boston.

Paul eh Virginia nohn SOH-noh dee Boston

There are some two-part negative adverbs:

non . . . ancora   not yet

nohn ahn-KOH-rah

non . . . mai   never

nohn meye

non . . . più   no longer

nohn pyou

I've never traveled by train   Non ho mai viaggiato in treno.

nohn oh meye vee-yah-JAH-toh een tray-noh

I am no longer working.

Non lavoro più. nohn lah-VOH-roh PYOU

Asking a question in Italian is as easy as raising the pitch of your voice at the end of any sentence:

Are you American? Tu sei americano? too say ah-meh-ree-KAH-noh Adjectives An adjective is a word that describes or modifies a noun (an interesting book, an American businessman).

In English, all adjectives come before the noun that they describe. This is not the case in Italian. In Italian, most adjectives follow the noun that they modify, but there is a category of commonly used adjectives that precede the nouns.

Also, remember that, as we learned in Chapter 1, nouns have a number (singular or plural) and a gender (masculine or feminine).

Italian adjectives must agree in gender and number with the nouns that they modify.

That is, if a noun is masculine plural (fratelli [brothers], for example), the adjective that modifies it must be masculine and plural as well (fratelli maggiori [older brothers]).

This means that there can be up to four forms of each adjective: masculine singular, feminine singular, masculine plural, and feminine plural.

Possessive, Demonstrative, and Interrogative Adjectives Possessive, demonstrative, and interrogative adjectives all precede the nouns they modify.

• Possessive adjectives: il mio, il tuo, il suo, etc.

• Demonstrative adjectives: questo (this) questi (these), etc.

• Interrogative adjectives: quale (which) Adjectives That Precede the Noun

Almost all adjectives follow the noun that they modify, but there are exceptions to that rule. The following is a group of commonly used adjectives that precede the noun they modify.

Italian adjective		English equivalent
altro	AHL-troh	other
bello	BEHL-loh	beautiful
bravo	BRAH-voh	good, able
brutto	BROOT-toh	ugly
buono	bwoo-OH-noh	good
caro	KAH-roh	dear; expensive
cattivo	kaht-TEE-voh	bad
giovane	JOH-vah-nay	young
grande	GRAHN-day	large; great
lungo	LOON-goh	long
nuovo	NWOH-voh	new
piccolo	PEEK-koh-loh	small, little
stesso	stehss-soh	same
vecchio	VEHK-kee-yo	old
vero	VEH-roh	true

When the adjective ends in −e, there is no difference between the masculine and feminine forms: un ragazzo intelligente, una ragazza intelligente.

KEYNOTE

In some cases, an adjective can come either before or after the noun it modifies.

In these cases the meaning of the adjective carries a subtle change in meaning.

For example, un vecchio amico = an old friend (a friend I've known for a while), but un amico vecchio = an old friend (a friend who is elderly).

ɪ

Some Useful Adjectives for Describing Yourself Almost all adjectives follow the noun that they modify. The following is a group of commonly used adjectives that follow this rule:

Italian adjective		English equivalent
biondo	BYOHN-doh	blonde
bruno	BROO-noh	dark-haired
alto	AHL-toh	tall
basso	BAHSS-soh	short
snello	SNEHL-loh	slender
grasso	GRAHSS-soh	fat
giovane	JOH-vah-nay	young
vecchio	VEHK-kee-yo	old
brutto	BROO-toh	ugly
ricco	REEK-koh	rich
povero	POH-veh-roh	poor
buono	bwoo-OH-noh	good
cattivo	kaht-TEE-voh	bad
intelligente	een-tehl-lee-JEHN-tay	intelligent
stupido	STOO-pee-doh	stupid
pigro	PEE-groh	lazy
simpatico	seem-PAH-tee-koh	kind
antipatico	ahn-tee-PAH-tee-koh	unpleasant
generoso	jehn-ehr-OHS-oh	generous
avaro	ah-VAH-roh	greedy

noioso	noy-OHS-oh	boring
felice	feh-LEE-cheh	happy
triste	TREESS-teh	sad

Adverbs

An adverb is a word that is used to modify a verb, an adjective, or an adverb. Adverbs are invariable; that is, they have only one form. Adverbs are used in a sentence to indicate manner, time, place, cause, or degree and to answer questions such as how, when, where, or how much. The placement of the adverb in Italian can be tricky, but the general rule states that when an adjective is modifying a verb, it should be placed after the verb: Mangio volentieri in quel ristorante. (I will gladly eat in that restaurant.) When the adverb modifies an adjective, it is placed in front of that adjective: Maria è molto coraggiosa. (Maria is very courageous.) Prepositions A preposition is a word that generally precedes a noun or pronoun and links it to another word in the sentence. Prepositions can have a variety of functions in a sentence:

• Direction: He's going to the store.

• Location: It's in the cabinet.

• Time: She arrived after the game ended.

• Possession: the United States America

Here are some common Italian prepositions:

di (d')	dee	of, from
a	ah	at, to, in
da	dah	from, by
in	een	in
con	kohn	with
su	soo	on
per	pehr	for
tra, fra	trah, frah	between
verso	VEHR-soh	toward
tranne	TRAHN-neh	except
senza	SEHNZ-ah	without
sotto	SOHT-toh	under
oltre	OHL-treh	beside
sopra	SOH-prah	above
dietro	dee-AY-troh	behind
prima	PREE-mah	before
davanti	dah-VAHN-tee	in front

KEYNOTE

The prespositions fra and tra both mean between or among, and they can be used interchangeably. Depending on where you are in Italy, you may hear one over the other, but they are both universally known and accepted as correct.

Articulated Prepositions

The prepositions a, da, di, in, and su, when used with a definite article, combine with the definite article to form one word. These are often referred to as prepositional articles, contractions, or articulated prepositions.

Vado a+il negozio = Vado al negozio. I am going to the store. Sono i bagagli di+gli studenti = Sono i bagagli degli studenti. They are the students' suitcases.

	il	lo	i'(m)	la	I(i.)	I	gli	le
a	al	allo	all'	alla	all'	ai	agli	alle
	ahl	AHL-loh	ahll	AHL-lah	ahll	eye	AHL-yee	ahl-leh
di	del	dello	dell'	della	dell'	dei	degli	delle
	dehl	DEHL-loh	dehll	DEHL-lah	dehll	day	DEHL-yee	DEHL-leh
da	dal	dallo	dall'	dalla	dall	dai	dagli	dalle
	dahl	DAHL-loh	dahll	DAH-lah	dahll	deye	DAHL-yee	dahl-leh
su	sul	sullo	sull'	sulla	sull'	sui	sugli	sulle
	sool	SOOL-loh	sooll	SOOL-lah	sooll	SOO-ee	SOOL-yee	SOOL-leh
in	nel	nello	nell'	nella	nell'	nel	negli	nelle
	nehl	NEHL-loh	nehll	NEHL-lah	nehll	nay	NEHL-yee	NEHL-leh

Mastering Pronouns

Pronouns are words that substitute for nouns. There are many different types of pronouns, and mastering them can take time and effort. You've already learned about subject pronouns in Chapter 1; in this chapter we will have a look at direct object, indirect object, reflexive, and relative pronouns, all of which are very useful tools in developing a mastery of the language.

Direct Object Pronouns

A direct object pronoun is used to avoid unnecessary repetition of words in a sentence. Take a look at the following conversation:

Are you reading the newspaper?

No, I am not reading the newspaper.

Do you know if Mary is reading the newspaper?

No, I don't know if Mary is reading the newspaper.

The repetition of the direct object (newspaper) sounds rather strange to a native speaker of English.

In order to avoid this unnecessary repetition, we can use the pronoun "it" in place of the direct object. The following conversation will sound better:

> Are you reading the newspaper?
>
> No, I'm not reading it.
>
> Do you know if Mary is reading it?
>
> No, I don't know if Mary is reading it.

KEYNOTES

In some cases, knowing which pronoun to use is a bit more complicated in Italian than it is in English. The equivalent of "it" can be either lo (used for a masculine singular direct object) or la (used for a feminine singular direct object in Italian); the pronouns li (masculine plural) and le (feminine plural) are used to mean "them."

Direct object pronouns are used the same way in Italian. In Italian the forms of the direct object pronouns (i pronomi diretti) are as follows:

Singular	Plural
Mi me	ci us
mee	chee
ti you (informal)	vi you (informal)
tee	vee
La you	Li you (formal, m.)
(formal, m. and f.)	Le you (formal, f.)
lah	lee / leh
lo him, it	li them (m. and f.)
loh	lee
la her, it	le them (f.)
lah	leh

A direct object pronoun is placed immediately before a conjugated verb.

Leggo il giornale (LEHG-goh eel johr-NAH-lay) becomes Lo leggo (loh LEHG-goh). ("I read the newspaper" becomes "I read it.")

Compro la frutta (KOHM-proh lah FROO-tah) becomes La compro (lah KOHM-proh). ("I buy the fruit" becomes "I buy it.")

In a negative sentence, the word non must come before the object pronoun.

He doesn't eat it.

Non la mangia.

nohn lah MAHN-jah.

Why don't you invite them?

Perché non li inviti?

pehr-KAY nohn lee een VEE-tee

Note that mi, ti, lo- and la change to m', t', and l' in front of a vowel or silent h.

Indirect Object Pronouns

The direct object in a sentence answers the question what? or whom? in relation to the verb. The indirect object nouns and pronouns answer the question to whom? or for whom? in relation to the verb. In English, the word "to" is often omitted: "We gave Paul a watch," instead of "We gave a watch to Paul." In Italian, the preposition a is always used before an indirect object noun. It goes without saying that if an article precedes the noun, then we must use an articulated preposition.

Indirect object pronouns (i pronomi indiretti) replace indirect object

nouns. They are identical in form to direct object pronouns, except for the third person forms gli, le, and loro.

Singular	Plural
mi (to/for) me	ci (to/for) us
mee	chee
ti (to/for) you	vi (to/for) you
tee	vee
Le (to/for) you	Loro (to/for) you
(formal m. and f.)	(formal, m. and f.)
leh	LAW-roh
gli (to/for) him	loro (to/for) them
lyee (like ll sound in the	LAW-roh
English word million)	
le (to/for)	her
leh	

Indirect object pronouns, like direct object pronouns, precede a conjugated verb, except for loro and Loro, which always follow the verb.

370

I'm giving her the keys.

Le do le chiavi.

leh doh leh kee-YAH-vee

They offer us an aperitif.

Ci offrono un aperitivo.

chee OHF-froh-noh oon ah-peh-ree-TEE-voh

We'll talk to them this evening.

Parliamo loro stasera.

pahr-lee-YAH-moh LAW-roh stah-SAY-rah

I'm giving him a watch.

Gli regalo un orologio.

lyee reh-GAH-loh oon oh-roh-LOH-joe

Note that mi and ti change to m' and t' in front of a vowel or silent h.

-QUESTION

Should I use an indirect object pronoun or a direct object pronoun? If the object is preceded by a preposition, that person/thing is an indirect object. If it is not preceded by a preposition, it is a direct object.

Reflexive Pronouns

Reflexive pronouns are used with reflexive verbs, which are verbs whose action falls back on the subject. Take a look at these sentences containing reflexive verbs:

I see myself in the mirror.

They enjoy themselves at the party.

In reflexive sentences, Italian verbs, like English verbs, are conjugated with reflexive pronouns. Reflexive pronouns (i pronomi riflessivi) are identical in form to direct object pronouns, except for the third person form si (the third-person singular and plural form).

Singular		Plural	
mi	myself	ci	ourselves
mee		chee	
ti	yourself	vi	yourselves
lee		vee	

si	himself, herself, itself	si	themselves,
see	yourself(formal)	see	yourselves(formal)

Just like direct object pronouns, reflexive pronouns are placed before a conjugated verb. **Mi** chiamo Michael (mee KYAH-moh Michael).

My name is Michael. (Literally, "I call myself Michael.") Mi, ti, si, and vi may become m', t', s', and v' before a vowel or silent h. Ci may only become c' before an i or e.

She washes **herself** every day.

Maria si lava tutti i giorni.

mah-REE-ah see LAH-vah TOOT-tee ee JOHR-nee.

We enjoy **ourselves** a lot.

Ci divertiamo molto. chee dee-vehr-TYAH-moh MOHL-toh.

Reflexive verbs often have to do with parts of the body or clothing. You can recognize reflexive verbs by the si (oneself) attached to the infinitive. Here are some common reflexive verbs:

addormentarsi   to fall asleep

 ahd-dohr-mehn-TAHR-see

alzarsi   to get up

ahl-ZAHR-see

annoiarsi   to get bored

 ahn-noy-AHR-see

arrabbiarsi   to get angry

ahr-rahb-BYAHR-see

chiamarsi   to be called

kyah-MAHR-see

divertirsi   to enjoy oneself

 dee-vehr-TEER-see

fermarsi   to stop (oneself)

 fehr-MAHR-see

innamorarsi   to fall in love

 een-nah-mohr-AHR-see

lavarsi   to wash (oneself)

lah-VAHR-see

372

prepararsi	to get ready
preh-pahr-AHR-see	
riposarsi	to relax
ree-poh-ZAHR-see	
sposarsi	to get married
spoh-ZAHR-see	
sentirsi	to feel
sehn-TEER-see	
svegliarsi	to wake up
svel-YAHR-see	
vestirsi	to get dressed
vehs-TEER-see	

CHAPTER 3: PRESENTATION AND GREETINGS

When you make contact with people who speak another language, knowing how they say hello and good-bye is especially useful.

This chapter explains how to say the very basics in greetings, as well as how to supplement a greeting with a little small talk.

Looking at Common Greetings and Good-byes

To give you a good start in greeting people in Italian, we want to familiarize you with the most common greetings and good-byes, followed by examples:

✓ **Ciao!** (chah-oh) (Hello and good-bye, informal) Ciao, Claudio! (chah-oh klah-oo-dee-oh) (Hello, Claudio!) **Salve!** (sahl-veh) (Hello and good-bye, neutral/ formal) Salve, ragazzi! (sahl-veh rah-gaht-tsee) (Hi, folks!) Salve is a relic from Latin. In Caesar's time, the Romans used it a lot.

✓ **Buongiorno/Buon giorno** (boo-ohn-johr-noh) [Good morning (literally, Good day), formal]

Buongiorno, signora Bruni! (boo-ohn-johr-noh see-nyoh-rah broo-nee) (Good morning, Mrs. Bruni!) **Buongiorno** is the most formal greeting. When-ever you're in doubt, use this word. It also means "good-bye."

✓ **Buonasera/Buona sera** (boo-oh-nah-seh-rah) (Good afternoon, good evening, formal) **Buonasera, signor Rossi!** (boo-oh-nah-seh-rah see-nyohr rohs-see) (Good afternoon, Mr. Rossi!) You use **buonasera** to say both hello and good-bye after approximately 5 p.m. in the autumn and winter and after 6 p.m. in the spring and summer. Just mind the time of day! When in doubt, say buongiorno if the sun is still out.

✓ **Buonanotte** (boo-oh-nah-noht-teh) (Good-night) **Buonanotte, amici!** (boo- oh-nah-noht-teh ah-mee-chee) (Good-night, friends!)

✓ **Buona giornata!** (boo- oh-nah johr-nah-tah) (Have a nice day!) You often use this phrase when you're leaving somebody or saying good-bye on the phone.

✓ **Buona serata!** (boo-oh-nah seh-rah-tah) (Have a nice evening!) Like **buona giornata,** you use **buona serata** when you're leaving someone or saying good- bye on the phone. The difference is that you use **buona serata** just before or after sunset.

✓ **Addìo** (ahd-dee-oh) (Good-bye, farewell) **Addìo, amore mio!** (ahd-dee-oh ah-moh-reh mee-oh) (Farewell, my love!) **Addìo** is more literary; that is, you see it more frequently in writing than in speech.

✓ **Arrivederci** (ahr-ree-veh-dehr-chee) (Good-bye) **Arrivederci, signora Eva!** (ahr-ree-veh-dehr-chee see-nyoh-rah eh-vah) (Good-bye, Mrs. Eva!)

Deciding whether to address someone formally or informally

✓ You generally use the formal form—Lei (lay) (you, formal singular)—with people you don't know: businesspeople, officials, and persons of higher rank, such as supervisors and teachers. The exceptions are with children and among young people; in those cases, you use the informal.

✓ When you get to know someone better, depending on your relationship, you

may switch to the informal form of address—tu (too) (you, informal singular). You also use the informal with members of your family and with children.

Young people speak informally among themselves, too.

Responding to a greeting

In English, you often say "How are you?" as a way of saying "Hello"—you don't expect an answer. In Italian, however, this is not the case; you must respond with an answer. The following are common ways to reply to greetings.

Formal greeting and reply:

Buongiorno, signora, come sta? boo-ohn-johr-noh see-nyoh-rah koh- meh stah Hello, ma'am, how are you?

Benissimo, grazie, e Lei? beh-nees-see-moh grah-tsee-eh eh lay Great, thank you, and you?

Informal greeting and reply:

Ciao, Roberto, come stai? chah-oh roh-behr-toh koh-meh stah-ee Hi, Roberto, how are you?

Another typical, rather informal, greeting and reply:

Come va? koh-me vah How are things?

Non c'è male. nohn cheh mah-leh Not bad.

Specifying your reuniting

You may want to specify your next meeting when you leave someone. The following common expressions can also be used as good-byes on their own:

✓ **A presto!** (ah prehs-toh) (See you soon!)

✓ **A dopo!** (ah doh-poh) (See you later!)

✓ **A domani!** (ah doh-mah-nee) (See you tomorrow!)

✓ **Ci vediamo!** (chee veh-dee-ah-moh) (See you!)

Although the short form will usually suffice, you can combine Ci vediamo with the other phrases. For example:

✓ **Ci vediamo presto!** (chee veh-dee-ah-moh prehs-toh) (See you soon!)

✓ **Ci vediamo dopo!** (chee veh-dee-ah-moh doh-poh) (See you later!)

✓ **Ci vediamo domani!** (chee veh-dee-ah-moh doh-mah-nee) (See you tomorrow!)

To this basic phrase, you can also add a weekday or a time — for example, **Ci vediamo lunedì alle cinque** (chee veh-dee-ah-moh loo-neh-dee ahl-leh cheen-koo-eh) (See you Monday at 5.) See Chapter 3 for the words for times of day and days of the week.

words to know

buongiorno	boo-ohn-<u>johr</u>-noh	good morning; good-bye
ciao	<u>chah</u>-oh	hello and goodbye
Come sta?	<u>koh</u>-meh stah	How are you?
bene	<u>beh</u>-neh	fine
arrivederci	ahr-ree-veh-<u>dehr</u>-chee	good-bye
Ci vediamo!	chee veh-dee-<u>ah</u>-moh	See you!
grazie	<u>grah</u>-tsee-eh	thank you

Finding Out Whether Someone Speaks English

When you meet someone from another country, your first question is probably "Do you speak English?" To ask whether someone speaks English, you need to be familiar with the verb parlare (pahr-lah-reh) (to speak; to talk). Table 4-1 shows the conjugation of this verb.

Conjugating the Verb Parlare		
Italian Translation	pronunciation	
io parlo speak	<u>ee</u>-oh <u>pahr</u>-loh	I
tu parli singular) speak	too <u>pahr</u>-lee	you(informal,
Lei parla singular) speak	lay <u>pahr</u>-lah	you(formal,
lui/lei parla speaks	<u>loo</u>-ee/lay <u>pahr</u>-lah	he/she
noi parliamo	<u>noh</u>-ee pahr-lee-<u>ah</u>-moh	we speak
Voi/voi parlate you(formal/informal,plural)speak	<u>voh</u>-eee pahr-<u>lah</u>-teh	
loro parlano speak	<u>loh</u>-roh <u>pahr</u>-lah-noh	they

Following are some examples of parlare in action:

✓ **Parlo molto e volentieri!** (pahr-loh mohl-toh eh voh-lehn-tee-eh-ree) (I like to talk!/I am quite talkative!)

✓ **Parli con me?** (pahr-lee kohn meh) (Are you speaking/talking to me?)

✓ **Parli inglese?** (pahr-lee een-gleh-zeh) (Do you speak English?)

✓ **Oggi parliamo di musica americana.** (ohj-jee pahr-lee-ah- moh dee moo-zee-kah ah-meh-ree-kah-nah) (Today we talk about American music.)

✓ **Parlano sempre di viaggi!** (pahr-lah-noh sehm-preh dee vee-ahj-jee) (They always talk about trips!)

Italians have a nice saying: **Parla come mangi!** (pahr-lah koh-meh mahn-jee) (Speak the way you eat!) You may want to say this to someone who speaks in a very sophisticated fashion with a touch of arrogance. This phrase reminds people to speak normally—just the way they eat.

Begging Your Pardon?

When you're getting familiar with a new language, you don't always understand everything that fluent speakers say to you, and you often find yourself asking them to repeat themselves. In those instances, the following sentences are helpful:

✓ **Non ho capito.** (nohn oh kah-pee-toh) (I didn't understand.) Mi dispiace. (mee dee-spee-ah-cheh) (I'm sorry.) Che cosa? (informal) (keh koh-zah) (What?) Come, scusa? (informal) (koh-meh skoo-zah) or Come, scusi? (formal) (koh-meh skoo-zee) (Pardon?) .

If you want to be very polite, you can combine these three expressions: Scusi! Mi dispiace ma non ho capito. (skoo-zee mee dee-spee-ah-cheh mah nohn oh kah-pee-toh) (Excuse me! I'm sorry, I didn't understand).

Scusa (skoo-zah) and **scusi** (skoo-zee) also mean "excuse me," and you use them when you need to beg pardon—for example, when you bump into someone.

Making Introductions

Introducing yourself or introducing acquaintances to one another is an important step in making people feel comfortable. In Italian, what you say and how you say it which form of address you use and whether you use first or last names depends on how well you know the person(s) you're talking to.

Introducing yourself

Chiamarsi (kee-ah-mahr-see) (to be named/to be called) is an important reflexive verb that you use to introduce yourself and to ask others for their names. To get the ring of the verb chiamarsi, practice these easy examples:

✓ **Ciao, mi chiamo Eva.** (chah-oh mee kee-ah-moh eh-vah) (Hello, my name is Eva.)

✓ **E tu come ti chiami?** (eh too koh-meh tee kee-ah-mee) (And what's your name?)

✓ **Lei si chiama?** (lay see kee-ah-mah) (What's your/her name?

You use the same verb form with lui (loo-ee) (he) and **lei** (lay) (she)—for example, **lui si chiama** (loo-ee see kee-ah-mah) (his name is).

As in English, you can also introduce yourself simply by saying your name: Sono Pietro (soh-noh pee-eh-troh) (I'm Pietro).

Young people forgo ceremony and introduce themselves more casually, though still politely—like this:

Ciao! Sono Giulio. chah-oh soh-noh joo-lee-oh Hello! I'm Giulio.

E io sono Giulia, piacere. eh ee-oh soh-noh joo-lee-ah pee-ah-cheh-reh And I'm Giulia, nice to meet you.

The following example offers an informal introduction used only in a very casual situation, such as on the beach or at a disco:

Come ti chiami? koh-meh tee kee-ah-mee What's your name?

Chiara. E tu? kee-ah-rah eh too Chiara, and yours?

Normally, the older person proposes making the switch to the informal form. The older generation tends to be more formal and may not switch to the informal as quickly as younger people do. If you're uncertain, address people formally.

Introducing other people

Sometimes, you have to not only introduce yourself but also introduce someone to other people.

The following vocabulary words may be helpful to you in making introductions check out the section "Talking about yourself

and your family," later in this chapter, for more.

With these terms, you can indicate the relationship between you and the person you're introducing:

✓ **mio marito** (mee-oh mah-ree-toh) (my husband)

✓ **mia moglie** (mee-ah moh-lyee-eh) (my wife)

✓ **il mio amico** (eel mee-oh ah-mee-koh) (my friend [m])

✓ **la mia amica** (lah mee-ah ah-mee-kah) (my friend [f])

✓ **il mio collega** (eel mee-oh kohl-leh-gah) (my colleague [m]) la mia collega (lah mee-ah kohl-leh-gah) (my colleague [f])

Words to Know

conoscere	koh-<u>noh</u>-sheh-reh	to meet
presentare	preh-zehn-<u>tah</u>-reh	to present/to introduce
mi chiamo	mee kee-<u>ah</u>-moh	my name is
piacere	pee-ah-<u>cheh</u>-reh	nice to meet you

Getting Acquainted

378

If you get a good feeling about a person you meet and want to get to know that person better, a conversation usually follows the introduction. This section describes some of the subjects you might talk about.

Talking about where you come from

Meeting people from other countries can be educational. Two common questions, phrased here in the formal, are useful to remember:

✓ **Da dove viene?** (dah doh-veh vee-eh-neh) (Where do you come from?) Di dov'è? (dee doh-veh) (Where are you from?)

The answers are, respectively:

✓ **Vengo da . . .** (vehn-goh dah) (I come from . . .) Sono di . . . (soh-noh dee)

(I'm from . . .)

Into these phrases, you can insert the names of countries, as well as continents or cities

Countries

Country	pronunciation	Translation
America	ah-<u>meh</u>-ree-kah	America
Brasile	brah-<u>see</u>-leh	Brazil
Canada	<u>kah</u>-nah-dah	Canada
Cina	<u>chee</u>-nah	China
Francia	<u>frahn</u>-chah	France
Germania	jehr-<u>mah</u>-nee-ah	Germany
Giappone	jahp-<u>poh</u>-neh	Japan
Inghilterra	een-geel-<u>tehr</u>-rah	England
Irlanda	eer-<u>lahn</u>-dah	Ireland
Italia	ee-<u>tah</u>-lee-ah	Italy
Morocco	mah-<u>rohk</u>-koh	Morocco
Portogallo	pohr-toh-<u>gahl</u>-loh	Portugal
Russia	<u>roos</u>-see-ah	Russia
Spagna	<u>spah</u>-nyah	Spain
Svezia	<u>sveh</u>-tsee-ah	Sweden

Svizzera	sveet-tseh-rah	Switzerland

Some countries (those with a final -a) are feminine, and others (those with the endings -e, -o, and sometimes -a) are masculine.

Canada is an exception; it's masculine but ends in -a.

The United States is masculine and uses a plural article because there are many states.

If you want to talk about nationalities, you have to alter the country names a bit.

As you say in English, "Are you American?" or "I'm Canadian," you say the same in Italian:

✓ **È Americano/a?** (eh ah-meh-ree-kah-noh/-nah) (Are you American?)

✓ **No, sono Canadese.** (noh soh-noh kah-nah-deh-zeh) (No, I'm Canadian.)

Some nationalities are genderless, while others are gender specific.

Genderless Nationalities

Nationality	pronunciation	Translation
Canadese	Kah-nah-deh-zeh	Canadian
Cinese	chee-neh-zeh	Chinese
Francese	frahn-cheh-zeh	French
Giapponese	jahp-poh-neh-zeh	Japanese
Inglese	een-gleh-zeh	English
Irlandese	eer-lahn-deh-zeh	Irish
Portoghese	pohr-toh-geh-zeh	Portuguese
Svedese	sveh-deh-zeh	Swedish

In other cases, nationalities have feminine, masculine, plural feminine, and plural masculine forms.

Gender-Specific Nationalities

Nationality	Pronunciation	Translation
Americana/o/e/i	ah-meh-ree-kah-nah/noh/neh/nee	American
Brasiliana/o/e/i	bra-see-lee-ah-nah/noh/neh/nee	Brazilian
Italiana/o/e/I	ee-tah-lee-ah-nah/noh/neh/nee	Italian
Marocchina/o/e/I	mah-rohk-kee-nah/noh/neh/nee	Moroccan

Russa/o/e/I	<u>roos</u>-sah/soh/seh/see	Russia

Nationlity	Pronunciation	Translation
Spagnola/o/e/i	spah-<u>nyoh</u>-lah/loh/leh/lee	Spanish
Svizzera/o/e/i	<u>sveet</u>-tseh-rah/roh/reh/ree	Swiss
Tadesca/o/he/hi	teh-<u>dehs</u>-kah/koh/keh/kee	German

In English, you put the pronoun in front of the verb. Not so in Italian. Because the verb form is different for each pronoun, you can easily leave out the pronoun you understand who is meant from the verb ending and the context.

You use the pronoun only when the subject isn't clear enough or when you want to emphasize a fact—for example, **Loro sono Americani, ma io sono Italiano** (loh-roh soh-noh ah-meh- ree-kah-nee mah ee-oh soh-noh ee-tah-lee-ah-noh) (They are Americans, but I am Italian).

Table above shows you the conjugation of the verb venire (veh-<u>nee</u>-reh) (to come), which is helpful to know when you want to tell people where you come from or ask other people where their home is.

The right verb/preposition combination in this case is venire da (veh-nee-reh dah) (to come from), as in Vengo dalla Francia (vehn-goh dahl-lah frahn-chah) (I come from France).

The preposition da (dah) takes different forms based on the gender and number of the noun that follows it. You can tell which form of da to use from the article (la, il, or gli) that the noun takes. Here's how it works:

da	+	**la**	= **dalla**
da	+	**il**	= **dal**
da	+	**gli**	= **dagli**

Wondering how you know which article to use? Continue on, dear reader:

- ✓ You use **la** for a feminine, singular noun.

- ✓ Use **il** for a masculine, singular noun.

- ✓ You use **gli** for a masculine, plural noun.

Conjugating the Verb Venire

Italian	Pronunciation	Translation

io vengo	<u>ee</u>-oh <u>vehn</u>-goh	I come
tu vieni	too vee-<u>eh</u>-nee	you(informal,singular)come
Lei viene	lay vee-<u>eh</u>-neh	you(formal,singular) come
lui/lei viene	<u>loo</u>-ee/lay vee-<u>eh</u>-neh	he/she comes
noi veniamo	<u>noh</u>-ee vah-nee-<u>ah</u>-moh	we come
Voi/voi venite	<u>voh</u>-ee veh-<u>nee</u>-t	you(formal/informal,plural)come
loro vengono	<u>loh</u>-roh <u>vehn</u>-goh-nah	they come

The following examples give you some practice with this construction:

- ✓ **Vengo dal Giappone.** (vehn-goh dahl jahp-poh-neh) (I come from Japan.)

- ✓ **Vieni dalla Svizzera.** (vee-eh-nee dahl-lah sveet-tseh-rah) (You come from Switzerland.)

- ✓ **Viene dalla Francia.** (vee-eh-neh dahl-lah frahn-chah) (He/she comes from France.)

- ✓ **Veniamo dall'Italia.** (veh-nee-ah-moh dahl-lee-tah-lee- ah) (We come from Italy.)

- ✓ **Veniamo dagli U.S.A.** (veh-nee-ah-moh dah-lyee oo-zah) (We come from the U.S.A.)

- ✓ **Veniamo dal Canada.** (veh-nee-ah-moh dahl kah-nah-dah) (We come from Canada.)

- ✓ **Venite dalla Russia.** (veh-nee- teh dahl-lah roos-see-ah) [You (plural) come from Russia.]

- ✓ **Vengono dalla Spagna.** (vehn-goh-noh dahl-lah spah-nyah) (They come from Spain.)

You might ask the following questions to initiate an informal conversation:

- ✓ **Sei di qui?** (say dee koo-ee) (Are you from here?)

- ✓ **Dove vivi?** (doh-veh vee-vee) (Where do you live?)

- ✓ **Dove sei nato?** (doh-veh say nah-toh) (Where were you born?)

- ✓ **E' la prima volta che vieni qui?** (eh lah pree-mah vohl-tah keh vee-eh-nee koo-ee) (Is this your first time here?)

- ✓ **Sei qui in vacanza?** (say koo-ee een vah-kahn-dzah) (Are you on vacation?)

- ✓ **Quanto rimani?** (koo- ahn-toh ree-mah-nee) (How long are you staying?)

Being you, being there: Using the verbs "essere" and "stare"

Essere (ehs-seh-reh) (to be) is the most important verb in the Italian language. You use this verb frequently; it's necessary in meeting, greeting, and talking with people. Table 4-7 gives its conjugation.

Conjugating theVerb Essere

Italian	Pronunciation	Translation
io sono	ee-oh soh-noh	i am
tu sei	too say	you(informal, singular) are
Lei è	lay eh	you(formal, singular)are
lui/lei	loo-ee/lay eh	he/she is
noi siamo	noh-ee see-ah-moh	we are
Voi/voi siete	voh-ee see-eh-the	you(formal/informal,plural),are
loro sono	loh-roh soh-noh	they are

The following examples show you how to use the verb essere:

✓ **Sei Americana?** (say ah-meh-ree-kah-nah) (Are you American?) **No, sono Australiana.** (noh soh-noh ah-oo-strah-lee-ah-nah) (No, I'm Australian.)

✓ **Com'è Paola?** (koh-meh pah-oh-lah) (What is Paola like?) **È un po' arrogante.** (eh oon poh ahr-roh-gahn-teh) (She's a little bit arrogant.)

✓ **Siete qui in vacanza?** (see-eh-teh koo-ee een vah-kahn-tsah) (Are you here on vacation?) **No, siamo qui per studiare l'italiano.** (noh see-ah-moh koo-ee pehr stoo-dee- ah-reh lee-tah-lee-ah-noh) (No, we're here to study Italian.)

✓ **Dove sono Elena e Sara?** (doh-veh soh-noh eh-leh-nah eh sah-rah) (Where are Elena and Sara?) **Sono in biblioteca.** (soh-noh een bee-blee-oh-teh-kah) (They are in the library.)   Another verb also means roughly "to be": stare (stah-reh) (to be there, to stay). Stare indicates the current state of affairs rather than an unchanging condition. You also use stare to express the way you feel. Stai bene? (stah-ee beh-neh) means "Are you okay?" and Maria sta male (mah-ree-ah stah mah- leh) means "Maria doesn't feel well."

Conjugate the Verb Stare.

Italian	Pronunciation	Translation

383

io sto	ee-oh stoh	I stay
tu stai	too stah-ee	you(informal,singular)stay
Lei sta	lay stah	you(formal, singualar) stay
lui/lei sta	loo-ee/lay stah	he/she stays
noi stiamo	noh-ee stee-ah-moh	we stay
Voi/voi state	voh-ee stah-teh	you(formal/informalplural)stay
Loro stanno	loh-roh stahn-noh	they stay

The following examples show you how to use the verb stare:

✓ **In che albergo stai?** (een keh ahl-behr-goh stah-ee) (What hotel are you in?)

✓ **State un po' con me?** (stah-teh oon poh kohn meh) (Will you stay with me for a while?

✓ **Non sto bene.** (nohn stoh beh-neh) (I don't feel well.)

✓ **Oggi stiamo a casa!** (ohj-jee stee-ah-moh ah kah-zah) (Let's stay home today!)

✓ **Daniela sta a dieta.** (dah-nee-eh-lah stah ah dee-eh-tah) (Daniela is on a diet.)

Talking about yourself and your family

Small talk often focuses on family: an opportunity to tell a bit about yourself and your home and learn something about the other person's family and home.

Table below gives you the words for family members.

Family Members

Italian	Pronunciation	Translation
madre	mah-dreh	mother
padre	pah-dreh	father
sorella	soh-rehl-lah	sister
fratello	frah-tehl-loh	brother
'figlia	fee-lyah	daughter
figlio	fee-lyon	son
figli	fee-lyee	children
nonna	nohn-nah	grandmother
nipoti	nee-poh-tee	grandchildren

zia	<u>dzee</u>-ah	aunt
zio	<u>dzee</u>-oh	uncle
cugina	koo-<u>jee</u>-nah	female cousin
cugino	koo-<u>jee</u>-noh	male cousin
cognata	koh-<u>nyah</u>-toh	sister-in-law
nuora	noo-<u>oh</u>-rah	daughter-in-law
genero	<u>jeh</u>-neh-roh	son-in-law

The Italian language doesn't have a neutral term for "brothers and sisters," like the word siblings in English.

You have to say sorelle e fratelli (soh-rehl-leh eh frah-tehl-lee) (sisters and brothers). To avoid this long expression, Italians often reduce it to fratelli.

In a casual conversation, you're likely to speak about your own family members.

For this purpose, you need the adjective mio/mia (mee-oh/mee-ah) (my), as in the following examples:

✓ **mio fratello** (mee-oh frah-tehl-loh) (my brother)

✓ **mia madre** (mee-ah mah- dreh) (my mother)

Chatting about the weather

When you're in conversational trouble, you can always talk about **il tempo** (eel tehm-poh) (the weather).

Because the weather is such a common topic, you must be armed with the necessary vocabulary.

Table below gives some common weather-related terms.

Weather Words

Italian	Pronunciation	Translation
il clima[m]	eel <u>klee</u>-mah	the climate
mite	<u>mee</u>-teh	mild
la temperature[f]	lah tehm-peh-rah-<u>too</u>-rah	the temperature
freddo	<u>frehd</u>-doh	cold
caldo	<u>kahl</u>-doh	hot

temperato	tehm-peh-<u>rah</u>-toh	temperature
umido	<u>oo</u>-mee-doh	humid
coperto	koh-<u>pehr</u>-toh	overcast
la nebbia[f]	lah <u>nebb</u>-bee-ah	fog
tempo incerto[m]	<u>tehm</u>-poh een-<u>chehr-toh</u>	uncertain weather
piove	pee-<u>oh</u>-veh	it's raining

When you're talking about the weather, the following idiomatic expressions will make you sound like a native speaker:

- ✓ **Fa un caldo terribile!** (fah oon kahl-doh tehr-ree-bee-leh) (It's terribly hot!)

- ✓ **Oggi il sole spacca le pietre!** (ohj-jee eel soh-leh spahk-kah leh pee-eh-treh)

(Today the sun is breaking the stones!)

- ✓ **Fa un freddo cane!** (fah oon frehd- doh kah-neh) (It's terribly cold!)

- ✓ **Fa un freddo/un caldo da morire!** (fah oon frehd-doh/oon kahl-doh dah moh-ree-reh) (It's deadly cold/warm!)

Da morire (dah moh-ree-reh) (deadly) is a typical expression used for emphasis. You can use it in all kinds of situations: for example, **Sono stanco da morire** (soh-noh stahn-koh dah moh-ree-reh) (I'm deadly tired) or **Ho una sete da morire** (oh oo-nah seh-teh dah moh-ree-reh) (I'm deadly thirsty).

Piove sul bagnato (pee-oh-veh sool bah-nyah-toh) (literally, it rains on the wet) is an idiomatic expression that Italians use when something positive happens to someone who doesn't really need it.

For example, if a millionaire wins the lottery, you could say **Piove sul** bagnato to indicate your feeling that you should've won instead.

CHAPTER 4: DAYS, MONTH AND SEASON

If you're beginning to speak Italian, then it's important to learn the names and the words associated with the days of the week, months of the year and the ever-changing seasons.

Not only will these words help when telling time and planning ahead with newfound friends, but they'll also help you to describe the weather.

The Days of the Week in Italian

> Monday = lunedì
>
> Tuesday = martedì
>
> Wednesday = mercoledì
>
> Thursday = giovedì
>
> Friday = venerdì
>
> Saturday = sabato
>
> Sunday = domenica

Take note that in Italian "dì" makes a "dee" sound. So, for example, lunedì is roughly pronounced as loon-eh-dee.

The above names were all derived from Roman deities and every day is associated to a body in the solar system:

> lunedì = Luna = Moon
>
> martedì = Marte = Mars
>
> mercoledì = Mercurius = Mercury
>
> giovedì = Giove = Jupiter
>
> venerdì = Venere = Venus
>
> sabato = Saturno = Saturn
>
> domenica = Sole = Sun

Also, it's important to note that unlike in English the days of the week in Italian are not capitalized. Here are some examples of the days of the week in sentences:

> Sarò di ritorno a casa lunedì = I'll be back home Monday
>
> Non lavoro fino al prossimo martedì = I don't work until next Tuesday
>
> Mercoledì, quando ci siamo viste, hai dimenticato il tuo portafoglio = Wednesday, when we met, you forgot your wallet.

Andiamo al cinema giovedì = We are going to the movies on Thursday.

Che giorno è oggi? Oggi è venerdì = What day is it today? Today is Friday

Di rado lavoro il sabato = I seldom work on Saturday

Da domenica io sono libero = As of Sunday I'm free

Oggi è venerdì = Today is Friday

Notice that if you add the day of the week at the end of the sentence you can then add the preposition "di".

Io posso vedere Mario solo di sabato = I can only see Mario ON Sunday

Le scuole sono chiuse di domenica = Schools are closed ON Sundays

To indicate habitual days we can use a definite article in a singular form:

Il lunedì vado al cinema = I go to the cinema on Mondays

La domenica incontro i miei amici = I meet my friends on Sundays

Il prossimo sabato vado al ristorante = Next Saturday, I'll go to the restaurant

Tutti i sabati vedo Carlo = On Saturdays I see Carlo

The Months of the Year in Italian

Like days' names, also months in Italian have Roman origins. For example, gennaio (January) comes from Janus, who supported the beginning of all events, febbraio (February) comes from the latin "februare" which means purification, held in honor of the roman goddess Febris, and marzo (March) derives from the Roman god Marte, the god of war, as most wars in the ancient world began in March with the spring thaw.

Aprile is thought to come either from the Greek goddess Aphrodite, to whom April was dedicated, or from Latin "aperire," which means to open (because April is the month when flowers bloom).

Maggio (May) comes from the name of Maia, Roman goddess of the Earth and in Christian culture May is the month of the Madonna (Virgin Mary).

Giugno (June) derives from Giunone, the wife of Jupiter, while luglio (July) was named in honor of Julius Caesar who was a Cancerian, born on the 13th of July.

Agosto (or August) was named after another great Roman, Julius Caesar's heir and the first Roman Emperor, Caesar Augustus.

Settembre (September) and Ottobre (October) come from the Latin words for seven and eight, as they were respectively the seventh and the eighth month in the Roman calendar.

Similarly, novembre and dicembre come from the Latin words for nine and ten. When written, the months in Italian are only capitalized if they're the first word of a sentence.

IN, A prepositions + month = indicates an event taking place within that month

In luglio partiremo per l'Italia = In July, we shall leave for Italy

A dicembre cambierò casa = I'll move in December

388

I corsi iniziano in ottobre = Classes begin in October

Noi andremo a Roma in settembre = We are going to Rome in September

In nord America la primavera inizia in marzo = In North America spring begins in March

The Seasons in Italian

Primavera – Spring is a gorgeous time to visit Italy. Not only you'd skip on the stifling heat of the summer, but you'd get to enjoy nature blooming and visit sites with less of a tourist crush. Festivals, concerts and processions are very common at this time of year. Toward the end of spring temperatures can get quite warm and you can enjoy outdoor dining, strolling, biking or jogging.

Estate – Summer is the hottest time of the year in Italy. Try summers in Sardinia, Sicily and Calabria, which are just some of the many regions in the country with gorgeous beaches. Temperatures at this time can rise above 30 degrees celsius so locals often escape cities to vacation by the sea or near the mountains. August (ferragosto) is the traditional month for Italians to take vacation.

Autunno – Like spring, the fall is a perfect time to visit Italy. Not only will you enjoy cooler temperatures and less crowded cities, but the prices will also be lower. Enjoy traditional tourist destinations, or participate in one of the many festivals held in towns across Italy in the fall. Italian Food festivals (sagre) are very popular and common during this period of the year. Some fall festivals:

Turin Food Festival, October 21-25

Pumpkin Festival (Festival della Zucca)

Festival dell'Aglio (Garlic Festival)

Tortellini Day in Ferrara (October)

Sagra del Tartufo Truffle Festival (October)

A few years back one of these festivals in the area of the Langhe, Piedmont, a white truffle was auctioned off to the tune of 100,000 euros. Altogether 250,000 euros worth of truffles were sold. Autumn in Italy is also celebrated by a flower exhibition in Parma, to celebrate harvest time and the fruits of the fall.

Inverno – Most people think of Italy as a summer vacation spot only and that couldn't be farther from the truth. Italy offers beautiful scenery throughout the winter and boasts great skiing resorts for outdoor enthusiasts. Piedmont offers skiing and mountain sports in the villages that hosted the 2006 Winter Olympics and you can ski anywhere the Olympians did. Cervinia, near the Swiss border, Sappada, Cortina (Dolomites), Val Gardena, Gran Sasso and Roccaraso (Abruzzo) all offer developed ski resort and many other winter sports.

No matter what day you land in what month or what season just remember to enjoy your time in Italy!

CHAPTER 5: WEATHER

Italian weather is pretty much the same as weather anywhere. There are good days, bad (or average, non-newsworthy) days and really bad (or ugly!) days. Like most of us, Italians generally prefer good or ugly—the ho-hum doesn't inspire fabulous conversation.

When the weather is good—Italians actually call it beautiful!—you'll begin your small talk with È bel tempo (It's good weather).

Use these terms to comment on the pleasant moments Mother Nature sends your way:

Sunny

Che giornata di sole! Bel tempo! (What a sunny day! Beautiful weather!)

Even simpler, you might say:

È soleggiato. (It's sunny.)

Clear

È sereno. (It's clear.)

If it's nighttime, try:

Il cielo è chiaro stasera. Guarda tutte quelle stelle! (The sky is clear tonight. Look at all those stars!)

No humidity

Non è umido. I miei capelli sono felici! (It's not humid. My hair is happy!)

Cloudless

Non è nuvoloso. (It's not cloudy.)

Not rainy

Non sta piovendo. (It's not raining.)

Blue sky

Guarda quel bel cielo blu! (Look at that beautiful blue sky!)

Warm breeze

Senti quella brezza calda? È come il bacio di un angelo contro la mia guancia! (Feel that warm breeze? It's like the kiss of an angel against my cheek!)

The Bad: How to Chat About Ho-hum Weather

When something isn't great or terrible, it's ordinario (ordinary). So when the weather is non buono, non molto cattivo, solo ordinario (not good, not bad, just ordinary), there are lots of ways to discuss that!

If you're waiting to be seated in un ristorante a Roma (a restaurant in Rome) and the couple beside you strikes up a small-talk weather conversation, you'll be prepared to respond to "È un tempo normale" ("It's ordinary weather") if you remember these expressions:

Rain

Piove. (It's raining.)

With a shrug, the comment above in its simplest form is useful if you want to discourage further conversation.

Sta piovendo. (It's raining.)

To comment that it's really raining hard say:

Sta piovendo a secchiate! (It's raining buckets!)

Fog

C'è la nebbia. (It's foggy.)

Cloud

È nuvoloso. (It's cloudy.)

Windy

C'è vento! (It's windy!)

If it's very windy, color up your comment by saying:

È così ventoso che gli uccelli non possono volare! (It's so windy the birds can't fly!)

Humid

È un giorno umido! Non mi piace quello che fa ai miei capelli... (It's a humid day! I don't like what it does to my hair...)

Gloomy

È una giornata uggiosa. (It's a gloomy day.)

Cool

Fa fresco. (It's cool out.)

The Ugly: Italian Expressions for Terrible Weather

italian-weather-expressions

Ugly weather? Nessun problema! (No problem!)

I've been in Italy when the snow was falling—hard—and I didn't hear one Italian complain. Not one bit. They all just took it in stride, kept up the small talk about il maltempo (bad weather) and went about their business.

The same happened when I was caught in a downpour in Rome. The rain was being blown sideways but it didn't faze anyone!

So if your small talk begins with "È brutto tempo" ("It's ugly weather"), try these comments to keep the conversational ball rolling:

Cold

Fa freddo. (It's cold.)

È un po' freddo. (It's a little bit cold.)

If it's freezing? Be astoundingly impressive by saying:

È così freddo che i miei occhi sono congelati. (It's so cold my eyes are frozen.)

Stormy

È tempestoso. (It's stormy.)

Mi piacciono i temporali. (I like thunderstorms.)

Troppi tuoni e fulmini! (Too much thunder and lightning!)

Snowing

Sta nevicando! (It's snowing!)

Amo la neve! (I love snow!)

I giorni nevosi sono così romantici... (Snowy days are so romantic...)

Hurricane

Ci aspettiamo un uragano. (We are expecting a hurricane.)

Gli uragani sono rari in Italia ma in un giorno come questo può succedere di tutto! (Hurricanes are rare in Italy but on a day like this anything can happen!)

Hot

È una giornata calda. (It's a hot day.)

Il caldo è insopportabile. (The heat is unbearable.)

Blizzard

Siamo venuti sulle Alpi sperando in una bufera di neve! (We came to the Alps hoping for a blizzard!)

Stiamo avendo una tormenta! (We're having a blizzard!)

Italians are friendly people who love to talk!

So get very comfortable chatting about the weather—and all the snow, rain, wind and sunshine you might experience in Bella Italia (Beautiful Italy).

Make the weather conversation rain down. Throw your inhibitions to the wind and let the sun shine on your small talk talents!

CHAPTER 6: SHOPPING FOR FOOD

C'è un supermercato qui vicino?

(CHEH oon soo-pair-mair- CAH-toh kwee vee-CHEE-no)

Is there a supermarket around here?

Supermarkets (supermercati) have become very popular in Italy only in the past ten to fifteen years, as before Italians preferred to do their grocery shopping in the local generi alimentari (grocery store). Italian supermarkets are no different from those in North America in both the selection of products and the organization of their sections. Very popular supermarket chains are Copp, Sigma, and Sma. More recently, many Italians have started to do their grocery shop- ping also at the ipermercati, superstores that sell just about every- thing, from food items (meat, cheese, deli, bread, frozen food, drinks, wines, beer, etc.) to games for children, home and garden furnishing items, appliances, perfumes, personal items, household cleaning items, over-the-counter medicines, shoes, clothing, etc.

You will find small supermarkets in urban areas. Ipermercati and large supermercati are usually located outside urban areas near high- ways (autostrade) or freeways (superstrade), and they offer ample parking.

In the supermercati and ipermercati, prices are cheaper than in local grocery stores or specialized food stores, though the quality is still excellent. Because of their location, supermarkets are mostly used for weekly grocery shopping, while the daily shopping is done at the generi alimentari or at specialized stores.

When shopping in these stores, check for specials (sconti) in the weekly flyer. If you become a regular shopper in a store, ask for a reward card. Online grocery shopping is also a reality in Italy today. Supermarkets are normally open from 9:00 A.M. to 8:30 P.M. Some ipermercati may stay open until 10:00 P.M., and may also be open on Sunday.

Dove si trova il più vicino ipermercato?

Where is the closest superstore?

DO-veh see TRO-vah eel PEW vee-CHEE-no ee-pair-mair-CAH-toh

Dove sono i carrelli per la spesa/cestini-spesa?

Where are the shopping carts/shopping baskets?

DO-veh SO-no ee cahr-REL-lee pair lah SPEH-sah/cheh-STEE-nee-SPEH-sah

Potrei avere per favore un flyer/volantino pubblicitario?

Could I please have a flyer?

Po-TRAY ah-VEH-reh pair fah-VO-reh oon flyer/vo-lahn-TEE-no poob-blee-chee-TAH-ree-oh

Dov'è il reparto gastronomia?

(Do-VEH eel reh-PAHR-toh gah-stro-no-MEE-ah)

Where is the deli section?

Here are some of the food sections found in a supermarket: panetteria (bakery), ortofrutta (fruit and vegetables), macelleria (meat), and gastro- nomia (literally, "gastronomy section"), which includes dairy products, deli products, and other homemade specialties.

Supermarkets, as well as smaller grocery stores, carry a large selection of gluten-free items, too.

Note that since 2005 Italian supermarkets are allowed to sell "farmaci da banco" (over-the-counter medicines).

Dov'è la sezione frutta e verdura?

Where is the produce section?

Do-VEH lah seh-tsee-OH-neh FROOT-tah eh vehr-DUH-ra

Avete un reparto farmacia?

Do you have a pharmacy (section)?

Ah-VHE-te oon reh-PAHR-toh Fahr-mah-CHEE-ah

Dov'è il bancone pescheria?

Where is the seafood section?

Do-VEH eel bahn-KOH-neh pehs-keh-REE-ah

Dov'è il Servizio Clienti?

Where is Customer Service?

Do-VEH eel sehr-VEE-tsee-oh clee-EHN-tee

Per favore, potrebbe indicarmi il negozio di generi alimentari più vicino?

(Pair fah-VO-reh po-TREB-beh een-dee- CAHR-mee eel neh-GOH-tsee-oh dee JEH-neh-ree ah-lee-mehn-TAH- ree PEW vee-CHEE-no)

Could you please tell me where the closest grocery store is?

Many Italians, particularly those living in small towns, prefer to do their daily grocery shopping at the local generi alimentari (grocery store), where the selection is limited, however.

These stores normally carry dry goods such as pasta and canned food; dairy products; cold cuts; household cleaning items; hygiene products; drinks, wine, beer, liquor; etc.

They normally do not carry meat or fish; some of them might not even carry fruits and vegetables. To buy specialized items Italians go to the macelleria (butcher shop), fruttivendolo or frutta e verdura (fruit and vegetable shop), panetteria (bakery), pescheria (fish market), salumeria (deli store), pasticceria (pastry shop), and gelateria (ice-cream parlor).

Grocery store hours vary; they are normally open Monday through Friday, from 8:00 A.M. to 1:00 P.M. and then from 5:00 P.M. to 8:00 P.M. By law, they must be closed on Sunday and on public holidays as well as one other day during the week, on a rotation basis with other grocery stores throughout the area.

In quale scaffale trovo la pasta?

In which aisle do I find pasta?

Een QUAH-leh scaf-FAH-leh TRO-vo lah PAH-stah

Vendete prodotti surgelati?

Do you sell any frozen food?

Vehn-DEH-teh pro-DOT-tee soor-jeh-LAH-tee

Potrei avere una cassa d'acqua minerale, per favore?

Could I please have a case of mineral water?

Po-TRAY ah-VEH-reh OO-nah CAS-sah DAK-koo-ah mee-neh-RAH-leh pair fah-VO-reh

Avete delle offerte speciali?

Do you offer any specials?

Ah-VEH-teh DEL-leh of-FAIR-teh speh-CHAH-lee

Che giorno è il mercato all'aperto?

(Keh JOR-no eh eel mair-CAH-toh ahl-ah-PAIR-toh)

Which day is the open-air market?

Italians like to shop at the open-air market or farmers' market.

In major cities there is a daily open market, while in many small Italian towns the markets take place once a week, normally in the town square.

In the open-air market you will find all types of vendors, from food to shoes, from clothes to paintings, from household items to hygiene products.

A trip to the market is an experience you should not miss, even if you have no intention of buying.

If you plan to buy something, browse first and check for quality but also for the best prices and occasionissime or sconti (bargains).

Prices, even when indicated by a price tag or told to you by the vendor, are normally inflated; be sure to bargain down the price.

The quality of food is excellent at the open-air markets, especially dairy and deli products as they are often homemade.

 Fruits and vegetables, homemade sweets, preserves and marinated items are also of the highest quality. Meat and poultry are excellent buys.

Il prezzo è un po' troppo alto.

The price is a bit too high.

Eel PRETS-so eh oon po TROP-po AHL-toh

Potrebbe farmi un prezzo migliore, per favore?

Could you please give me a better price?

Po-TREB-beh FAHR-mee oon PRETS-so meel-YOHR-eh pair fah-VO-reh

Lo prendo, se abbassa ancora il prezzo.

I'll buy it, if you lower the price a bit more.

Lo PREHN-doh seh ab-BAS-sah ahn-CO-rah eel PRETS-so

Se ne prendo due, mi fa uno sconto?

If I buy two, can you give a discount?

Seh neh PREHN-doh DOO-eh mee fah OO-no SCON-toh

Mezzo chilo di pane, per favore.

(METS-so KEE-lo dee PAH-neh pair fah-VO-reh)

A loaf (half kilo) of bread, please.

Bread is one of the food staples of Italy, but it is also one of the food items that has the most variation in ingredients, quantity, and shape.

Bread making in Italy is an art.

Often bread is identified as pane regionale (pane toscano, pane calabrese, pane pugliese) or as pane locale (pane ferrarese); other times the bread takes its name from its shape (pane rotondo, filoncino, ciabatta) or by the ingredients (pane di semola, pane integrale, pane di mais, pane di segala , pane di orzo , pane di riso, pane di glutine).

Special and often decorative bread is also prepared for many holidays and festivity days such as St. Anthony, St. Joseph, All Souls', Easter, and Christmas, or for events such as births and weddings.

Some common specialty breads include pane alle olive, pane con uova, pane con alici, etc. Many are called the regional names for bread: la michetta, la biova, la pagnotta, la mafalda.

You may also have the pane insipido (unsalted bread, typical in Tuscany), the pane arabo or pane pita, and the piadina (a variation of the pita bread, typi- cal in Emilia Romagna).

Besides grocery stores and supermarkets, breads can be bought in the local panetteria, panificio, or forno, which normally open very early in the morning and close by midday.

When buying bread, ask for a mezzo chilo di pane or un chilo di pane, or if you prefer, ask for a panino.

Potrei avere quattro panini, per favore?

Could I please have four buns?

Po-TRAY ah-VEH-reh QUAT-tro pah-NEE-nee pair fah-VO-reh

Ha del pane integrale?

Do you have any whole wheat bread?

Ah del PA-neh een-teh-GRAH-leh

Un filoncino, per favore.

A French baguette, please.

Oon fee-lon-CHEE-no pair fah-VO-reh

Quando posso trovare del pane caldo e croccante?

At what time will I be able to find hot and crunchy bread?

QUAHN-doh POS-so tro-VAH-reh del PAH-neh CAHL-doh eh croc-CAHN-the

Un panino con prosciutto e formaggio, per favore.

(Oon pah-NEE-no kohn pro-SHOOT-toh eh for-MAD-jo pair fah-VO-reh)

A bun with prosciutto and cheese, please.

In a salumeria you will find dairy and deli products of all types: prosciutto, mortadella, salame, salciccia,provolone, parmigiano,Romano, crotonese, svizzero, Gorgonzola, pecorino, mozzarella, ricotta, etc.

Many store owners take pride in their homemade and genuine products with no preservatives.

At times you may also find piatti pronti, a hot table, or you may be able to purchase delicious sandwiches with cold cuts. Sandwiches are also available at a paninoteca or piadineria.

Many salumerie will also offer a varied selection of grocery products such as pasta, pasta di casa (homemade pasta), conserve (pre- serves), sottoaceti (pickled vegetables), and sottoli (items in oil), olive (olives), marmellata (jam or jelly), olio (oil), aceto (vinegar), caffè (cof- fee), vini (wines), liquori (liqueurs), acqua minerale (mineral water), insalata (salad), insalata di mare (seafood salad), supplì (fried rice balls), porchetta (roasted piglet), fritti (deep-fried items), etc.

Duecento grammi di mortadella, per favore.

Two hundred grams of mortadella, please.

doo-eh CHEHN-oh GRAM-mee dee mor-tah-DEL-lah pair fah-VO-reh

Potrebbe tagliare il prosciutto a fette più sottili, per favore?

Could you please slice the prosciutto a bit thinner?

Po-TREB-beh tahl-YAH-reh eel pro-SHOOT-toh ah FET-teh PEW sot-TEE-lee pair fah-VO-reh

Potrebbe grattugiarmi un pezzo piccolo di parmigiano, per favore?

Could you please grate me a piece of Parmesan cheese? small

Po-TREB-beh grat-tood-JAHR-mee oon PETS-so PEEK-ko-lo dee pahr-mee-JAH-no pair fah-VO-reh

La ricotta è fresca?

Is the ricotta cheese fresh?

Lah ree-COT-tah eh FREHS-cah

Mezzo chilo di spezzatino di manzo, per favore.

(METS-so KEE-lo dee spets-sah-TEE-no dee MAHN-tso pair fah-VO-reh)

Half a kilo of beef stew, please.

A macelleria specializes in meat and poultry products.

However, simi- lar to a salumeria, you will find many grocery items there.

A macelleria takes pride in offering carni scelte di prima qualità (grade A choice cut), insaccati e affettati di produzione propria (homemade salami products and cold cuts).

You will also be able to find a rotisserie service, which is actually more common in a polleria (poultry shop) or in a rosticceria (rotisserie and hot table).

A polleria is a store similar to the macelleria, but is of course more specialized in poultry and dairy products.

To be more competitive, many store owners combine in their enterprise macelleria, salumeria, polleria, and rosticceria.

Many Italian macellerie offer among their products carne equina (horse meat); you will also find specialized macelleria equina.

Potrebbe darmi dieci cosce/petti di pollo, per favore?

 Could you please give me ten chicken legs/breasts?

Po-TREB-beh DAHR-mee dee-EH-chee CO-sheh/PET-tee dee POHL-lo pair fah-VO-reh

Una dozzina di fettine di vitello,   per favore.

A dozen veal cutlets, please.

OO-nah dots-SEE-nah dee fet-TEE- neh dee vee-TEL-lo pair fah-VO-reh

Ha delle costolette di agnello/ maiale già marinate?

Do you have any seasoned lamb/pork chops?

Ah DEL-leh co-sto-LET-teh dee ahn-YEL-lo/mye-AH-leh jah mah-ree-NAH-teh

Quanto costa un pollo arrosto?

How much does a roasted chicken cost?

QUAHN-toh CO-stah oon POL-lo ar-ROS-toh ?

Questo pesce è di giornata?

(QUEH-sto PEH-sheh eh dee jor-NAH-tah)

Is this fish fresh?

Italians buy fish in a specialized store called a pescheria. Because Italy is surrounded by the sea, the fish is normally di giornata (fresh, literally caught that day).

For obvious reasons, many pescherie open early in the morning.

In towns by the sea, freshly caught fish is sold in open markets near the seashore. Fresh fish is also sold by fishmongers who travel from town to town with their furgoncini or autonegozi.

Note that many fish or seafood restaurants are also called pescheria.

A quanto va il merluzzo?

How much is the cod?

Ah QUAHN-toh vah eel mair-LOOTS-so

Potrebbe darmi una dozzina di spiedini di gamberoni, per favore?

Could you please give me a dozen skewered shrimps?

Po-TREB-beh DAHR-mee OO-nah dohts-SEE-nah dee spee-eh- DEE-nee dee gahm-beh-RO-nee pair fah-VO-reh

Ha delle sardine in scatola?

Do you have canned anchovies?

Ah DEL-leh sahr-DEE-neh een SCAH-toh-lah

Vende pesce surgelato?

Do you sell frozen fish?

VEHN-deh PEH-sheh soor-jeh-LAH-toh

Un chilo di baccalà senza spine, per favore.

A kilo of deboned dried cod, please.

Oon KEE-lo dee bac-cah-LAH SEHN-tsa SPEE-neh pair fah-VO-reh

Mezzo chilo di ciliege, per favore.

(METS-so KEE-lo dee chee-lee-EH-jeh pair fah-VO-reh)

Half a kilo of cherries, please.

To buy frutta di stagione (seasonal fruit) or verdura (vegetables), visit the local fruttivendolo or frutta e verdure or go to the local market.

In many small towns, you will see a fruttivendolo ambulante (traveling fruit seller),who will travel from town to town with his furgoncino (small truck) and a megaphone, inviting people to buy frutta fresca e di stagione (fresh and seasonal fruit).

Becoming more common in the cities now are the mercato degli agricoltori (farmers' markets), where frutta e verdura biologica (organic fruits and vegetables) of the highest quality at very competitive prices are sold.

Un chilo di patate, per favore.

A kilo of potatoes, please.

Oon KEE-lo dee pah-TAH-teh pair fah-VO-reh

Una cassetta di mandarini, per favore.

A case of tangerines, please.

OO-nah cas-SET-tah dee mahn-dah-REE-nee pair fah-VO-reh

Vende prodotti biologici?

Do you sell organic products?

VEHN-deh pro-DOT-tee bee-oh-LO-jee-chee

Un mazzo di rapini, per favore.

A bunch of rapini (turnip greens), please.

Oon MATS-so dee rah-PEE-nee pair fah-VO-reh

Ha delle banane meno mature?

Do you have less-ripe bananas?

Ah DEL-leh bah-NAH-neh MEH-no ma-TOO-reh

Una dozzina di paste, per favore.

(OO-nah dohts-SEE-nah dee PAH-steh pair fah-VO-reh)

A dozen pastries, please.

Italians have an excellent reputation for baked goods. Each region offers a varied and extensive selection of torte, crostate, dolci, paste, etc. Each town takes pride in offering their local and original desserts, which may be purchased at the local pasticceria.

Many pasticcerie take pride in announcing that theirs is a pasticceria artigianale (artisan pastry shop).

The best time to visit a pastry shop is during special holidays such as Christmas and Easter, the St. Joseph feast, or the feast of the patron saint of the town.

During these periods, pastry shops are at their best, even in their displays.

The quality is always excellent, no matter what you buy: a torta di compleanno or torta della nonna, a crostata di mele or a torta al cioccolato, a torta al gelato or a torta alla crema, a dozen of paste or a dozen cannoli alla ricotta,some sfogliatelle or zeppole, half a kilo of biscotti di mandorla or biscotti al pistacchio, a cassata siciliana or some cantucci toscani, torroncini alla mandorla or torroncini al cioccolato, cioccolatini or caramelle or confetti.

Vorrei ordinare una torta alla frutta fresca.

I would like order a fresh-fruit flan.

Vor-RAY or-dee-NAH-reh OO-nah TOR-tah AL-lah FROOT-tah FRES-cah

Potrebbe scrivere "Buon compleanno" sulla torta, per favore?

Could you please write "Happy Birthday" on the cake?

Po-TREB-beh SCREE-veh-reh Boo-ON com-pleh-AN-no SOOL-lah TOR-tah pair fah-VO-reh

Potrebbe darmi mezzo chilo di dolci, per favore? Could you
please give me half a kilo of sweets/cookies?

Po-TREB-beh DAHR-mee METS-so KEE-lo dee DOL-chee pair fah-VO-reh

Quanto costa questa scatola di cioccolatini?

How much does this box of chocolates cost?

QUAHN-toh CO-stah QUEH-stah SCA-toh-lah dee choc-co-lah-TEE-nee

Un cono al cioccolato e nocciola.

(Oon CO-no ahl choc-co- LAH-toh e not-CHO-lah)

A cone with chocolate and hazelnut.

In Italy you will find prepackaged ice cream in supermarkets, local grocery stores, variety stores, etc.

However, for a gelato artigianale, in a cono or a coppetta, go to the local bar, a pasticceria, or to a spe- cialized gelateria to enjoy an ice cream of your favorite gusto (flavor) sitting down at a table.

In the gelateria you will find a wide variety of gelati alla crema or gelati alla frutta, gelati allo yogurt or sorbetti, gelati senza glutine or semifreddi (partly frozen dessert), gelati affogati or gelati drinks, tartufi or spumoni, granite or crepes. If you are served at the table you will also enjoy the elaborate presentation of the ice cream with cookies, fruits, and similar toppings.

Che gusti avete?

What flavors do you have?

Keh GOO-stee ah-VEH-teh

Una granita al limone, per favore.

A lemon granita, please.

OO-nah grah-NEE-tah ahl

lee-MO-neh pair fah-VO-reh

Una coppetta ai frutti di bosco.

An ice-cream cup with field berries.

OO-nah cop-PET-tah aye FROOT-tee dee BOS-co

Un semifreddo al caffè.

A coffee semifreddo.

Oon seh-mee-FRED-doh ahl caf-FE

Chiuso per ferie.

(Kee-OO-zo pair FAIR-ee-eh)

Closed for the holidays/vacation.

Many Italians take their yearly vacations in July and August.

Their preferred vacation period starts on ferragosto (August 15) and lasts two weeks. During this period, many Italian cities are literally deserted and stores are closed. Some stores might have special summer hours (orario estivo).

A sign saying chiuso per turno settimanale or chiusura turno setti- manale: mercoledì indicates that the store is observing by law a day of rest taken in rotation with other stores.

The sign orario unico indicates that the store is not closing for a lunch break, but has continuous hours. Chiusura pomeridiana means that the store will not open in the afternoon. Finally, chiuso per lutto means that the store is closed because of a death in the family.

Chiuso per le feste.

Closed for the holidays.

Kee-OO-zo pair leh FEHS-teh

Orario unico.

Continuous hours.

Oh-RAH-ree-oh OO-nee-co

Chiusura pomeridiana.

Closed in the afternoon.

Kee-OO-zoo-rah po-meh-ree-dee-AH-nah

Chiuso per lutto.

Closed for death in the family.

Kee-OO-zo pair LOOT-toh

CHAPTER 7: MAKING FRIENDS

Ci vediamo in piazza alle dieci.

(Chee veh-dee-AH-mo een pee-ATS-sah AL-leh dee-EH-chee)

Let's meet in the square at ten.

While in Italy, you will likely befriend some Italians. Since many Ital- ians cannot speak English very well, it might be useful to know some phrases which you can use to interact with them or simply have fun trying to speak the language. Italians love to hear when foreigners try to speak their language. This can be a great way of making friends!

In Italy, especially in small towns, it is very common to meet peo- ple outside, either on the main street or in the most important piazza (square) in the city. In winter or summer, young people hang out there for hours and just spend time together doing nothing besides chat- ting. This may be quite different from what North Americans are used to, but it is definitely the most traditional way of meeting people in Italy, especially on a Saturday afternoon.

Nowadays young people are meeting in shopping malls, too, but the old trend of spending time hanging outside together still remains strong. Often, the main street or square is just the place to meet with friends to decide where to go afterward, but such a decision can take some time and you may end up staying in the square for hours! For older people it is more common to make plans in advance and meet directly in restaurants or other places, but in small villages the main— sometimes the only—bar can be a great way to meet locals, young and old alike.

Ti passo a prendere domani pomeriggio alle quattro.

I will come and pick you up tomorrow afternoon at four.

Tee PAS-soh a PREHN-deh-reh doh-MAH-nee po-meh-REED-jo AL-leh QUAT-tro

Mi dispiace, ma domani sera sono occupato. Facciamo sabato?

I am sorry, but I am busy tomorrow night. What about Saturday?

Mee dee-spee-AH-cheh mah doh-MAH-nee SEH-rah SO-no oc-coo-PAH-toh Fat-CHAH-mo SAH-bah-toh

Che cosa facciamo stasera?

(keh co-zah fat-chah-mo stah-seh-rah)

what are we doing tonight?

On Friday and Saturday nights, young people go to the disco or to nightclubs to meet friends or to make new ones. Discos normally ded- icate Friday to young people ages seventeen years and up, while Sat- urday is for younger teenagers (13–16). The local bar, billiard, or video arcade is also an alternative location to meet and make friends.

Facciamo qualcosa tutti insieme domani?

Are we doing something together tomorrow?

Fat-CHAH-mo quahl-CO-zah TOOT- tee een-see-EH-meh doh-MAH-nee

Mi dai il tuo numero?

(Mee DAH-ee eel TOO-oh NOO- meh-roh)

Can I have your number?

Italians are very friendly people and love chatting, so if you approach someone with a smile, you will be greeted similarly. Don't be surprised anywhere in Italy, though, if someone whom you don't know starts talking to you, making small conversation. Similarly, you may want to do the same. However, always remember to respect your interlocutor if he/she does not want to continue your conversation.

Breaking the ice (rompere il ghiaccio), while at a disco or at a night- club, is perhaps a bit more difficult, but the tactics are more or less the same worldwide.

Come va? Tutto a posto?

What's up?

COH-meh vah TOOT-toh ah POH-sto

Ci conosciamo già, vero?

We've already met, correct?

Chee coh-no-shee-AH-moh jee-AH veh-roh

Dove abiti?

Where do you live?

DOH-veh ah-BEE-tee

Mi fa molto piacere conoscerti!

(Mee fah MOHL-toh pee- ah-CHEH-reh co-no-SHEHR-tee)

It's really nice to meet you!

If you are introduced to someone new it is important to stringere le mani (shake hands). Young people do not do it so often today, but if you do shake hands, you'll never go wrong. Really close friends and relatives si baciano sulle guance (kiss each other on the cheeks) upon meeting, especially if they haven't seen each other for a long time. And just like everywhere in the world, a sorriso (smile) is always appreciated.

If you are being introduced to someone new or if you are young and are being introduced to someone older than you, it is always appropriate to dare del Lei (use the Lei form of address) and to use Signore or Signora (Mr. or Mrs.) before their names. However, if you are young and are meeting someone of your age, you can easily dare del tu (use the tu form of address). After being introduced or after getting to know you, Italians will tell you dammi pure del tu, which means you do not have to use the formal Lei address with them any longer.

Ti presento il mio amico Marco.

This is my friend Marco.

Tee preh-SEHN-toh eel MEE-oh ah-MEE-co MAHR-co

I miei amici vogliono conoscerti. Vieni che te li presento.

My friends want to meet you. Come and let me introduce you to them.

Ee mee-AY ah-MEE-chee VOL-yo-no co-no-SHEHR-tee Vee-EH-nee keh teh lee preh-SEHN-toh

Il mio nome è John e sono

My name is John and I am American.

americano. Mi piace molto   l'Italia!

I really love Italy!

Eel MEE-oh NO-meh eh John eh SO-no ah-mair-ee-CAH-no Mee pee-AH-cheh MOHL-toh lee-TAH-lee-ah

Come ti chiami? Non ho capito il tuo nome.

What's your name? I didn't get it.

CO-meh tee kee-AH-mee Nohn oh cah-PEE-toh eel TOO-oh NO-meh

Esci con me stasera?

(EH-shee kohn meh stah-SEH-rah)

Are you going out with me tonight?

Italian males are renowned all over the world as "Latin lovers" and in most cases they want to keep up with that stereotype. So women visiting Italy might be surprised at the forward manner of Italian men. Sometimes they can be very insistent, so women who do not appreci- ate this attention should be very strict and firm in response, which will be enough to make them stop. In any event, to avoid an unpleasant situation, remember that you are in a foreign country and be cautious. Men visiting Italy need only be kind to meet Italian women. If you are a man, these women will most likely expect you to fare la prima mossa (make the first move), which means introducing yourself to them and initiating conversation.

Usciamo a cena insieme?

Shall we go out to dinner?

Oo-SHAH-mo ah CHEH-nah een-see-EH-meh

Verresti al cinema/in discoteca/ a fare una passeggiata con me?

Would you like to go to the movies/ disco/for a walk with me?

Ver-REH-stee ahl CHEE-neh-mah/een dee-skoh-TEH-kah/ah FAH-reh OO-nah pahs-sehj-jee-AH-tah kohn meh

Sei molto simpatica. Mi piacerebbe conoscerti meglio.

You are a really nice girl. I'd like to get to know you better.

Say MOHL-toh seem-PAH-tee-cah Mee peeah-cheh-REB-beh co-no-SHEHR-tee MEHL-yo

Vorrei rivederti, se ti va. Mi dai il tuo numero di telefono?

I'd like to see you again, if you like. Would you give me your phone number?

Vor-RAY ree-veh-DAIR-tee seh tee vah Mee dye eel TOO-oh NOO-meh-ro dee teh-LEH-fo-no

Mi sono pazzamente innamorato di te.

(Mee SO-no pats- sah-MEHN-teh een-nah-mor-AH-toh dee teh)

I've fallen madly in love with you.

If you fall in love with someone in Italy, it might be useful to know a few words to surprise him or her. Keep in mind that in Italian the phrase "I love you" is usually translated as Ti amo, but this expression is used in a different way than the English. Ti amo refers to romantic love; therefore you want to use it only with your partner, only to address people you are passionately in love with. In English, "I love you" is used to address friends, children, or relatives, but you cannot use Ti amo for that: In such cases, use the phrase Ti voglio bene.

If you fall in love with someone, you will exchange baci (kisses), abbracci (hugs), and carezze (caresses); moreover you might call your partner amore mio (my love), cucciolo/a (little puppy), piccolo/a (little one), and other little words which you two can have fun making up. If you end up in a long-distance relationship, you may exchange old-fashioned letters, e-mails, or text messages: When writing to your loved one, use the phrases mi manchi (I miss you), ho voglia di vederti (I want to see you), ho voglia di stare con te (I want to spend time with you), spero di rivederti presto (I hope I'll see you again), penso sempre a te (I am always thinking about you), mi fai felice (you make me happy), and sto male senza di te (I feel bad without you).

Mi piaci molto. Sei una ragazza molto interessante.

I really like you. You are a very interesting girl.

Mee pee-AH-chee MOHL-toh Say OO-nah rah-GATS-sah MOHL-toh een-tair-es SAHN-teh

Mi manchi molto./Mi manchi da morire.

I miss you very much.

Mee MAHN-kee MOHL-toh/Mee MAHN-kee dah mo-REE-reh

Sei molto bella. Ho voglia di baciarti.

You are gorgeous. I want to kiss you.

Say MOHL-toh BEL-lah Oh VOL-yah dee bah-CHAHR-tee

Sei il ragazzo più bello del mondo. Fatti abbracciare.

You are the most handsome man in the world. Let me hug you.

CHAPTER 8: SHOPPING

Dove posso trovare un negozio di vestiti?

(DO-veh POS-so tro-VAH-reh oon neh-GOH-tsee-oh dee veh-STEE-tee)

Where can I fi nd a clothing store?

In Italian the expression fare shopping is widely used and it normally means to go shopping for clothes. Fashion in Italy is a very important business and all over the world Italy is known for fashion brands like Prada, Armani, Gucci, and Versace, which are the most expensive and exclusive ones, but also for other less upscale names like Benetton. Italy is most often associated with style and fashion and many Italians take pride in always being ben vestiti (well dressed) and in keeping with the latest tendenze (trends). Young Italians want to be alla moda (hip with the latest trends) and in most cases would never wear some- thing that is fuori moda (out of style).

The most important city in Italy in terms of fashion is Milan, where you can find the headquarters of all the marche di vestiti (clothing brands). It is a paradise for shoppers; there are stores to satisfy every need.

Fare shopping is something that is normally done on Saturday afternoons, when the main streets of even the smallest towns are full of people who shop for clothes or simply take a peek at the vetrine (store windows). In most cases, the exclusive shops and the boutiques are located in the downtown area of each town, which in Italy is normally the centro storico (historical center). Shops are lined along the streets and usually each town has at least one famous street where shoppers go to look for real Italian-style shopping. In most cases, shops and bou- tiques (elegant shops) are open from Monday through Saturday, from 9 A.M. to 1 P.M. and then again from 4 P.M. to 8 P.M. In large cities or in tourist areas it is more common to find shops which are open all day, mostly from 9 A.M. to 8 P.M. All stores are normally closed on Sunday, except during the Christmas period.

C'è un grande magazzino qui vicino?

Is there a department store nearby?

Cheh oon GRAHN-deh mah-gaht- TSEE-no kwee vee-CHEE-no

Scusi, dov'è il centro commerciale?

Pardon me, where is the shopping mall?

SCOO-zee doh-VEH eel CHEHN-tro cohm-mair-CHAH-leh

Scusi, è questa la strada per l'outlet?

Pardon me, is this the road to the outlet center?

SCOO-zee eh QUEH-stah lah STRAH-dah pair lah outlet

Scusi, sa a che ora chiudono i negozi?

Pardon me, do you know when the shops close?

SCOO-zee sah ah keh OH-rah kee-OO-doh-no ee neh-GOH-tsee

Dove trovo una piantina del centro commerciale?

(DO-veh TRO-vo OO-nah pee-an-TEE-nah del CHEHN-tro cohm- mair-CHAH-leh)

Where can I fi nd a map of the shopping mall?

Centri commerciali (shopping malls) have become very popular in Italy in the last ten to fifteen years, and, even though it is more common to go there to shop for food or for electronics, people love to buy clothes there, too. In most shopping malls, however, there are only grandi catene (chain stores) and less exclusive fashion brands.

Just as in North America, shopping malls in Italy are large places where you can find every kind of shop: negozi di vestiti (clothing stores), scarpe (shoes), elettrodomestici (home appliances), telefoni cellulari (mobile phones), mobili (furniture), giocattoli (toys), and also some cafeterias and fast food. They are usually outside urban areas and sometimes just outside the city center. Normally malls are open from 9 A.M. to 9 P.M. every day of the week, Sunday included. Large shopping malls close only on national holidays in Italy.

Dov'è l'ascensore?

Where is the elevator?

Do-VEH lah-shehn-SO-reh

Come arrivo al parcheggio?

How do I get to the parking lot?

CO-meh ahr-REE-vo ahl pahr-KED-jo

Dov'è il bancomat?

Where is the ATM?

Do-VEH eel BAHN-co-maht

Scusi, dov'è l'uscita più vicina?

Pardon me, where is the nearest exit?

SCOO-zee doh-VEH loo-SHEE-tah

PEW vee-CHEE-nah

Dov'è il reparto donna?

(Doh-VEH eel reh-PAHR-toh DON- nah)

Where is the women's department?

In Italy grandi magazzini (department stores) can be found only in the largest cities like Milan, Rome, Turin, and a few others. The oldest and most upscale department store in Italy is La Rinascente, where you can find all the most well-known fashion brands, including the most expensive ones. Other department stores are Coin and Upim, which are a bit less expensive and exclusive than La Rinascente.

Just like in North America, department stores have different reparti (departments), and they usually sell vestiti da uomo (men's clothing), vestiti da donna (women's clothing), vestiti da bambino (chil- dren's clothing), borse (bags), scarpe (shoes), accessori (accessories), biancheria intima (lingerie), profumi (perfumes), accessori regalo (gifts), and accessori per la casa (home accessories). Some of them also have a reparto gioielleria (jewelry department), where you can find anelli (rings), collane (necklaces), orecchini (earrings), and orologi (watches). In a few trendy department stores, like Coin or La Rinascente, there are also gourmet foods, where the most exquisite products from Italy and other parts of the world are sold.

In most department stores you can also find a nice café or a small restaurant inside, where shoppers can relax and rest from a busy shopping day. These eateries can be very big and divided on different floors and are usually open all day, from 9 A.M. to 8 P.M., sometimes even on Sunday.

Dov'è il reparto uomo?

Where is the men's department?

Do-VEH eel reh-PAHR-toh oo-OH-mo

Dov'è il reparto calzature?

Where is the shoe department?

Doh-VEH eel reh-PAHR-toh

cahl-tsah-TOO-reh

C'è un ristorante in questo grande magazzino?

Is there a restaurant in this department store?

Cheh oon ree-sto-RAHN-teh een QUEH-sto GRAHN-deh mah-gaht-TSEE-no

Scusi, sa dov'è il reparto biancheria intima?

Pardon me, do you know where the lingerie department is?

SCOO-zee sah doh-VEH eel reh-PAHR-toh bee-ahn-keh-REE-ah EEN-tee-mah

411

Quando iniziano i saldi?

(QUAHN-doh ee-NEE-tsee-ah-no ee SAHL-dee):

When do the sales start?

Factory outlet malls (commonly called outlet in Italian) are very popular in Italy nowadays, because in these malls there are outlet shops selling designer and premium brands at a discounted price.

The first and largest outlet mall in Italy is in Serravalle Scrivia, near Alessandria, in northern Italy. It opened only a few years ago and was an immediate success, which led to other outlets being opened around the country.

Today there are at least five or six outlet centers in Italy. Just like shopping malls, they are open all days of the week from 9 A.M. to 9 P.M., and they are usually located far from urban areas but very close to the main autostrade (highways).

Outlet centers are very popular during saldi (sales), when people swarm to them looking for designer brands at an even greater discounted price. Sales do not take place only in outlets but are found in every shop.

Basically there are saldi invernali (winter sales), which normally start around January 10and last until mid-February, and saldi estivi (summer sales), which start around mid-July and last until the beginning of September.

The government of each region decides these dates and each shop must stick to them. Apart from summer and winter sales, there can be other sales called svendita or liquidazione totale, which can take place when a shop is closing or is going to be renovated.

In the larger outlet malls there are good bargains all year round.

Scusi, questo è in saldo?

Pardon me, is this on sale?

SCOO-zee QUEH-sto eh een SAHL-doh

Quant'è lo sconto?

How much is the discount?

QUAHN-teh lo SCON-toh

È in saldo solo la merce estiva/ invernale?

Are only summer/winter clothes on sale?

Eh een SAHL-doh SO-lo lah MAIR-cheh eh-STEE-vah/een-vair-NAH-leh

Ci sono negozi che fanno svendite in questa zona?

Are there shops with sales in this area?

Chee SO-no neh-GOH-tsee keh FAHN-no SVEN-dee-teh een QUEH-stah ZO-nah

412

Vorrei provare questo vestito.

(Vor-RAY pro-VAH-reh QUEH-sto veh-STEE-toh)

I'd like to try this dress/suit.

In large department stores and shopping malls you are free to enter every shop, just browse, and in most cases help yourself with clothes. If you need help, ask the commessa (shop assistant), but usually you are free to choose and try on clothes by yourself. In smaller shops it is more polite to first ask to take a look before browsing in the shop. In most cases, you'll be allowed to look without being disturbed by either the shop assistant or the shop owner. It is, however, important to keep in mind that you cannot mess up clothes in the shop and just leave.

In a clothing store you can usually find vestiti da donna (dresses), vestiti da uomo (suits), pantaloni (trousers), gonne (skirts), maglie di lana (wool sweaters), maglie di cotone (cotton sweaters), felpe (sweat- shirts), camicie (shirts), magliette (T-shirts), giubbotti (jackets), cappotti (coats), sciarpe (scarves), cappelli (hats), guanti (hand gloves), and cravatte (ties). In a lingerie store, however, you can find mutande da uomo (boxer shorts), mutande da donna (ladies underwear), collant (tights), and calze (socks).

In terms of materials or fabrics, either look for clothes di seta (made of silk), di lana (made of wool), di cotone (made of cotton), or acrilici (acrylic).

Dove sono le cabine di prova?

Where are the fitting rooms?

DOH-veh SO-no leh CAH-bee-neh dee PRO-vah

Posso dare un'occhiata?

Can I take a look?

POS-so DAH-reh oon-ok-kee-AH-tah

Ha questa camicia in blu?

(AH QUEH-stah Kah-MEE- chee-ah in blu)

Do you have this shirt in blue?

For many people, color coordination is important for dressing. Which colors go well together? What color combination should be avoided? Which are the accessories (accessori) that need to be coordinated? If color coordination is important for your look (look), get some sound advice or a second opinion by asking the salesperson. White (il bianco) and black (il nero) go well with almost any color. Red (il rosso) goes well (si abbina) with colors of the same tonality (tonalità) like purple (il viola) or pink (il rosa); however, it should not be matched with green (il verde), yellow (il giallo), or blue (il blu).

Come mi sta questa gonna rossa con la camicetta bianca?

How does this red skirt look with the white blouse?

CO-meh mee stah QUEH-stah GOHN-nah RO-sah kohn lah cah-mee-CHEHT-tah bee-AHN-cah

Le scarpe e la borsa rosse sono   molto chic.

The red shoes and purse are very classy.

Leh SKAHR-peh eh lah BOHR-sah ROHS-seh SOH-no MOHL-toh sheek

I jeans chiari e la maglietta gialla sono molto eleganti.

The light-colored jeans and the yellow sweater are very elegant.

Ee jeens kee-AH-ree eh lah mahl-YEHT-tah SO-no MOHL-toh eh-leh-GUN-tee

Potrei provare una tonalità più scura?

Can I try one with a darker shade?

POH-tray proh-VAH-reh OO-na toh-nah-lee-TAH PEW SKUH-rah

Potrei avere una taglia più grande/più piccola?

(Po-TRAY ah-VEH-reh OO-nah TAHL-yah PEW GRAHN-deh/ PEW PEEK-ko-lah)

Can I have a bigger/smaller size?

If you are shopping for clothes in Italy, keep in mind that sizes are different, so make sure you know the right misura (measurement). For sweaters and T-shirts, the system is more or less the same as in North America: there are taglia piccola (small), taglia media (medium), and taglia forte (large).

Usually you can use the English terms "small," "medium," "large," and "extra large," as well, and you will be perfectly understood. Sizes are exactly the same as in North America for jeans also. Measurements are a little different for dresses, skirts, and trou- sers, however.

The following is a size comparison chart, so that you know what to ask the commessa (shop assistant) for. Also keep in mind that there is no difference between taglie da uomo (men's sizes) and taglie da donna (women's sizes).

Italian	American Women	American Men
42	8	32
44	10	34
46	12	36
48	14	38
50	16	40
52	18	42

Vorrei un paio di pantaloni   **taglia 44.**

I'd like a pair of trousers size 34.

Vor-RAY oon PYE-oh dee pahn- tah-LO-nee TAHL-yah quah-RAHN- tah-QUAT-tro

Vorrei cambiare questo vestito perché non mi va bene.

(Vor-RAY cahm-bee-AH-reh QUEH-sto veh-STEE-toh pair-KEH nohn mee vah BEH-neh)

I'd like to exchange this dress/suit because it doesn't fit.

In Italy it is not always easy to return your clothes to the store if you don't like them. Some big chain stores or department stores have a clear return policy which you can easily find on the back of your receipt, but you might want to double-check with small shop own- ers about their return policy.

It may be problematic or they may only allow exchanges within a short period of time. Even if these shop owners will exchange your clothes for other merchandise, it is very unlikely that they will accept your clothes and give you money back (dare indietro i soldi). Most of the time, if clienti (customers) do not want to exchange clothes for other merchandise, they will be given a buono (coupon) for the amount of money they spent, which can be used in the same store within a certain period of time.

Vorrei cambiare questo vestito perché ha un difetto.

I'd like to exchange this dress, because it has a flaw.

Vor-RAY cahm-bee-AH-reh QUEH-sto veh-STEE-toh pair-CHE ah oon dee-FET-toh

Vorrei cambiare questa borsa con un'altra.

I'd like to exchange this purse with another one.

Vor-RAY cahm-bee-AH-reh QUEH-stah BOHR-sah kohn oon-AHL-trah

Potrei avere un buono in cambio?

May I have a store credit in exchange?

Po-TRAY ah-VEH-reh oon boo-OH-no een CAHM-bee-oh

Questa gonna è troppo grande. Posso cambiarla?

This skirt is too big. Can I exchange it?

QUEH-stah GOHN-nah eh TROP-po GRAHN-deh POS-so cahm-bee- AHR-lah

Avete un paio di stivali numero 38?

(Ah-VEH-teh oon PYE-oh dee stee-VAH-lee NOO-meh-ro trehn-TOT-to)

Do you have a pair of boots size 6½?

Certain areas of Italy, like Tuscany, for example, are renowned for their high-quality leather, and there you can find great bargains on shoes and bags. Almost everywhere, there are good quality acces- sories at a fair price.

If you enter a shoe store looking for women's shoes, you might ask for scarpe a tacco alto (high-heeled shoes), scarpe a tacco basso (low-heeled shoes), or scarpe senza tacco (shoes with no heel).

For both men and women you can ask for mocassini (mocassins), scarpe da ginnastica (sneakers), infradito (flip-flops), and stivali (boots).

If you are looking for ciabatte (slippers), you could ask in a shoe store, but it is more common to find them in either a lingerie or clothing store. In terms of shoe brands, there is a big choice: you can either go from the very expensive and stylish brands like Rossetti, Ferragamo, Vicini, or to more affordable but still very trendy brands like Nero Giardini.

Shoe sizes in Italy are different from those in North America. Please see the following chart, so that you know what to ask for. And note that, as with clothing sizes, in Italy there is no difference between men's and women's shoe sizes.

Female (U.S) Female	(Italian)
3½	35
4	35½
4½	36
5	36½
5½	37
6	37½
6½	38
7	38½
7½	39
8	40
8½	41
9	41½
9½	42
10	42½
10½	43

Male (U.S.)	Male (Italian)
5	36½
5½	37
6	37½
6½	38
7	38½
7½	39
8	40
8½	41
9	41½
9½	42
10	42½
10½	43
11	44
11½	44½
12	45
12½	46

Potrei provare quelle scarpe in vetrina?

Can I try those shoes in the window?

Po-TRAY pro-VAH-reh QUEHL-leh SCAR-peh een veh-TREE-nah

Queste scarpe sono piccole. Posso avere una misura più grande?

These shoes are small. Can I have a bigger size?

QUEH-steh SCAR-peh SO-no PEEK-ko-leh POS-so ah-VEH-reh OO-nah mee-ZOO-rah PEW GRAHN-deh

Avete una borsa di pelle e un portafoglio coordinato?

(Ah-VEH-teh OO-nah BOHR-sah dee PEL-leh eh oon por-tah- FOHL-yo co-or-dee-NAH-toh)

Do you have a leather bag and a matching purse?

Regarding borse (bags) and other fashionable accessories, Italy has the largest possible selection to choose from.

Bags are normally sold in either clothing or shoe stores, and all the well-known fashion brands have their own line of bags, so it is really up to your own personal taste to find the perfect one.

The Marche region in Italy is the area where all Italian shoe factories are located, and there you can find the outlets of the most well-known brands—where there are not only shoes and bags but also portafogli da donna (purses), portafogli da uomo (wallets), valige (suitcases), and cinture (belts) of the finest quality at a discounted price. If you are lucky, you might even find places to have shoes made in your design and exact foot size.

Potrebbe incartarmi quella cintura, per favore? È un regalo.

Could you wrap that belt please? It is a gift.

Po-TREB-beh-teh een-cahr-TAHR-mee QUEL-lah cheen-TOO-rah pair fah-VO-reh Eh oon reh-GAH-lo

Dov'è la cassa?

(Doh-VEH lah CAHS-sah)

Where is the cash register?

Today most of the stores accept carte di credito (credit cards) without problems (Visa and MasterCard, at least), but some of the small shops are keen on giving a sconto (discount) if you pay with cash (pagare in contanti). Some small or family-owned stores might also be willing to offer a discount if you buy a large amount of goods. There is no pos- sibility of getting this discount in big department stores, but give it a try with friendly small-shop owners.

In Italy it is very important to always make sure to get your receipt, because you might be asked to show it outside the shop by some ispettori della finanza (sales tax auditors), and if you don't have it you may get a fine

Unlike in North America, in Italy taxes are already included in the price on the tag, so no extra costs will be added at checkout.

The price on the tag, or the price you are told by the shop owner, will be the final price.

Quanto costa?

How much is it?

QUAHN-toh CO-stah

Passo pagare con la carta Di credito?

Can i pay with a credit card?

POS-so pah-GAH-reh kohn lah CAR-tah dee CREH-dee-toh

ECCo lo scontrino.

Here is your receipt.

EC-co lo scon-TREE-no

Potrei avere lo scontrino?

Can i have the receipt

Po-TRAY ah-VEH-reh lo scon-TREE-no

CHAPTER 9: MEANS OF TRANSPORTATION

Getting Around by Plane

If you are flying from the United States or Canada, more than likely you will land in Rome's Leonardo da Vinci–Fiumicino Airport (FCO), or simply known as Fiumicino (fyoo-meh-CHE-noh). You may also fly into Milan's international airport, known as Malpensa (MXP). Each of those cities can serve as a hub to your preferred destination or can be your starting point from where you can begin your journey.

If you are flying from the United Kingdom, you will have more options to fly into other cities, as well as Rome or Milan, directly from either London's Heathrow (LHR) or Gatwick (LGW) airport. Rome and Milan each also have another airport that can serve European passengers, namely Ciampino and Linate, respectively.

Here are a few phrases that can come in handy, even though you'll find a good number of people able to speak English at the airports.

arrival	arrivo
departures	partenze
airport	aeoroporto
flight	volo
flights	voli
direct flight	volo diretto
Is it a direct flight?	È un volo diretto?
What is the flight number?	Qual è il numero del volo?
I have one suitcase.	Ho una valigia.
to change	cambiare
airplane	aeroplano
Do I have to change planes?	Devo cambiare aereo?
I've lost my luggage.	Ho perso la mia valigia
Where is?	Dov'è
Where is terminal two?	Dov'è il terminale due?
When is the next flight to Rome?	A che ora parte il prossimo volo per Roma?

Getting Around by Bus

Getting around by bus can offer some advantages over other forms of transport in Italy. It is typically less expensive than taking a plane or a boat. And they can go into smaller towns where train stations do not exist. First it's important to realize there are basically three types of bus transportation.

Local City Buses

These are your basic buses that you will encounter in just about any Italian town of any size and can take you within a particular city or to a neighboring city. I'm not sure why, but most of the time they are an ugly orange color. You will need to purchase your ticket prior to boarding at a local tabaccaio or tobacco shop. These are indicated with a black "T" outside their storefront. You are supposed to enter from the front or rear of the bus (entrata) and exit in the middle (uscita). There is a validation machine aboard the bus where you are supposed to stamp your bus ticket. Random checks are possible by bus personnel. The driver will not ask you for money or for your ticket as you are boarding the bus.

Regional Buses

These are buses that can take you between major cities such as Florence and Rome. They are run by private companies. Unfortunately, Italy does not have a national bus carrier such as Greyhound in the United States or National Express if you're from the United Kingdom. If you do want to make a long-distance trip from one part of Italy to another, more than likely you will have to change buses a few times. In that case, you would be better off taking a train. Most of the time you will not need to change trains. These buses tend to be colored blue, green, red, or other colors consistent with the company's brand. They typically have air conditioning (aria condizionata). In this case, you will need to show your ticket (biglietto) prior to boarding the bus. Tickets can be purchased at the bus company's ticket window, usually in their bus station or ticket office.

Chartered Buses

These are buses that are also run by private companies, but they are typically done as a group tour to take you from one part of Italy to another. And it is typically a long-distance trip such as Naples to Turin and then back.

arrivo	arrival
departures	partenze
I have two suitcases.	Ho due valigie.
to change	cambiare
bus	autobus
Do I have to change buses?	Devo cambiare autobus?
bus stop	fermata
Where is?	Dov'è?

Where is the bus stop? Dov'e` la fermata dell'autobus?

I've lost my luggage. Ho perso la mia valigia.

Where is the bus for Rome? Dov'è l'autobus per Roma?

Where is the bus station? Dov'è la stazione dell'autobus?

When is the next bus to Naples? A che ora parte il prossimo autobus per Napoli?

Where can I get a bus to the center? Dove posso prendere l'autobus per il centro?

Where can I buy tickets? Dove posso comprare biglietti?

Is this the stop for the museum? È questa la fermata per il museo?

Getting Around by Train

Hands down the best way of getting around Italy between towns is by train. The high-speed trains are getting faster, more convenient, and more comfortable to use.

There are even overnight trains that you can use if you are planning on traversing large distances in Italy.

You do not have to worry about the weight of the luggage, like you do on an airplane.

You do not need to worry about going through security screening, taking off your shoes, etc., like you do at an airport. You do not need to worry about parking and driving through maddening traffic.

Most trains are now air-conditioned and all are smoke-free.

There are even electrical sockets on the high-speed and intercity trains that you can use to plug in your computer, electronic devices, etc. You can just sit back, relax, and enjoy your journey.

Types of Trains in Italy

* Frecce Series (formerly known as Eurostar or ES)

These are the high-speed (185 miles per hour / 300 kilometers per hour) trains that provide service to major Italian cities. They come equipped with air conditioning and offer food, drink, or refreshments. They have different classes of service (first class, second class, business class, etc.) and reservations are required. In theory they can sell out, but that happens on rare occasion. Many times you can purchase tickets at the self-service counter right before departure. There are, however, discounts if you purchase in advance.

The three types for this series include:

Frecciarossa (FR or red arrows) – these trains connect Turin-Milan-Bologna-Rome-Naples-Salerno and can reach speeds up to 225 mph (360 km per hour).

Frecciargento (FA or silver arrows) – these trains connect Rome, Venice, Verona, Bari/Lecce, Lamezia Terme/ReggioCalabria and can reach speeds up to 155 mph (225 km per hour).

Frecciabianca (FB or white arrows) – these trains connect Milan, Venice, Udine, and Trieste. They also connect Genoa and Rome along with Bari and Lecce. These trains can reach speeds up to 125 mph (200 km per hour).

* Inter-City Trains (IC)

The next type of trains is the Inter-City variety (IC). These can also reach speeds up to 125 miles per hour (200 km per hour). These are not as fast as the Freccia trains above and they do not have as many food and refreshment options. A reservation is also required for these trains. Just like the Freccia trains, you can often purchase the same day as departure.

* Espresso, Regionale & Locale Trains

These are the slowest of all Italian trains and will stop in the smallest of towns. A reservation is not required and you can just purchase a ticket and hop on the next train available. If you are traveling from a major city to another major city, like Rome to Naples, you would want to avoid these trains.

train   treno

Alternatively, another word for train, which has an American-Indian type connotation, is ferrovia. Ferro is the word for steel and via means a way or a path.

How much?   Quanto?

train station   stazione ferroviaria

How much does it cost to go...   Quanto costa per andare...

...to Rome?   ...a Roma?

...to Florence?   ...a Firenze?

...to Venice?   ...a Venezia?

I would like one ticket to Rome please.   Vorrei un biglietto per Roma per favore.

one-way   andata

round-trip   andata e ritorno

I would like a one-way ticket to Rome please.   Vorrei un biglietto andata per Roma per favore.

I would like a round-trip ticket to Rome please.

Vorrei un biglietto andata e ritorno per Roma per favore.

When does the train depart to Rome?   Quando parte il treno per Roma?

When does the first train depart to Rome?   Quando parte il primo treno per Roma?

When does the last train depart to Rome?   Quando parte l'ultimo treno per Roma?

What time does the train arrive at Naples?	A che ora arriverà il treno a Napoli?
Does the train stop at Salerno?	Il treno si fermerà a Salerno?
Which track (platform) do I take for Rome?	Quale binario devo prendere per Roma?

What track (platform) does the train from Naples arrive?

A che binario arriva il treno da Napoli?

sleeping car	vagone letto
dining car	carrozza ristorante

Getting Around by Boat

Many people are surprised to learn that many places in Italy can be easily reached via water transportation.

In other words, you can hop on a boat in one part of the country and take a trip to the opposite side of the country.

In fact, you can even enter and leave Italy by boat.

It shouldn't come as a surprise if you think about it...the city of Venice was built on the water and boats are a normal part of their everyday life. And it's been that way for centuries. And cities like Genoa, Amalfi, and Pisa were once powerful maritime republics.

The three main types of boat transport are:

* Ship / Nave (plural – Navi)

These are the largest of the three options and are only capable of going to large port towns such as Naples, Palermo, Genoa, Venice, etc. Some of them are able to carry cars (ferry) and even trains. Some will also have overnight accommodations available. Since these are the largest of the three options, they tend to also be the slowest.

* Boat / Traghetto (plural – Traghetti)

These are smaller boats or ferries and are used for the ports listed above and some of the smaller islands.

* Hydrofoil / Aliscafo (plural – Aliscafi)

This is basically a boat with a couple of foils underneath the hull that lift it off the surface of the water to reduce the friction, thus increasing the speed. These are the fastest way to traverse on water, typically requiring half the time as a ship. Thus, the price is usually twice as expensive as a ship.

where?	dove?
How much?	Quanto?

port	porto

How much does it cost to go...   Quanto costa per andare...

...to Rome?   ...a Roma?

...to Naples?   ...a Napoli?

...to Venice?   ...a Venezia?

I would like one ticket to Rome please.   Vorrei un biglietto per Roma per favore.

one-way	andata
round-trip	andata e ritorno

I would like a one-way ticket to Naples please.

Vorrei un biglietto andata per Napoli per favore.

I would like a round-trip ticket to Naples please.

Vorrei un biglietto andata e ritorno per Napoli per favore.

When is the hydrofoil to Palermo?

Quando parte l'aliscfo per Palermo?

When is the first ship to Genoa?

Quando parte la prima nave per Genova?

When is the last boat to Naples?

Quando parte l'ultimo traghetto per Napoli?

What time does the ship arrive at Naples?

A che ora arriverà la nave a Napoli?

Does the hydrofoil stop at Salerno?

L'aliscafo si fermerà a Salerno?

Driving in Italy

For all practical purposes, driving should be your last-choice method of transport in Italy unless you absolutely can't avoid it.

If you plan on seeing Rome and Florence, which is the itinerary for many first-time travelers, there is no reason to rent a car if you are staying within those cities.

The traffic will drive you bonkers and parking can be a major hassle. And the gasoline prices and auto rental will be more than what you are accustomed to at home.

Most rental companies require that you be 25 years of age to rent a car in Italy. Of course, if you are planning on visiting Venice, you will have to leave your car outside the city limits.

In most cities that have any type of historical center or centro storico, cars are not allowed anyway.

Some cities will have a ZTL zone or a zone of limited traffic (zona di traffic limitato) usually reserved for public officials, public transportation, etc.

They are usually monitored with camera and you must have the appropriate sticker with transponder on your car.

If you don't, you can expect to receive a ticket in the mail from your friendly retentive Italian bureaucrat.

Yes, they will send it to your address back home in the United States if necessary. And of course they will expect payment.

What happens if you don't pay? I can't say with 100% certainty, but you probably won't be able to enter Italy or any country within the European Union without clearing up the fine.

As computers and data sharing becomes more prevalent, I predict one day they may attach some type of lien against your passport that would have to be cleared up before any type of international travel.

If you plan on traveling outside the major cities, through Tuscany or Umbria, for example, then it probably makes sense to rent a car if you are traveling with a group.

Other places that are conducive to a car would include Sardinia, Sicily, Calabria, and the Amalfi Coast. Of course, if you are traveling with kids or a large group of people, it would also be advantageous in those circumstances.

Italian drivers are aggressive but skillful.

They act decisively and quickly. The left lane is only for passing – get in and get out of the lane as soon as you're done with your pass.

If you don't, someone will sure enough come up behind you and flash their high beams to indicate that they want you out of the way.

In addition, most of the gasoline stations are not self-serve, though they are becoming more and more common. The word for self-service is fai da te, or do it yourself.

You must have an International Driver's License (IDL) along with the proper insurance if you want to drive in Italy. You can obtain an IDL at your local Automobile Association of America (AAA) or the equivalent Canadian association.

gasoline	benzina

Note – benzina refers to unleaded gasoline. It is available in 95 or 98 octane. Leaded gasoline is no longer available in Italy.

Diesel	fuel
gas station	benzinaio
Where is the nearest gas station?	Dove si trova il benzinaio più vicino?
Fill her up, please.	Il pieno, per favore.
I would like 10 liters of gas (petrol).	Vorrei 10 litri di benzina.
Give me 20 euros of gasoline.	Mi dia 20 euro di benzina.
road	strada
Can you tell me?	Può dirmi?
Can you tell me the road to Naples?	Può dirmi qual è la strada per Napoli?
Are we on the right road to Florence?	Siamo sulla strada giusta per Firenze?
How do I get to the airport?	Come si va al' aeroporto?
park	posteggiare
Can I park here?	Si può posteggire qui?
left	sinistra
right	destra
straight ahead	sempre diritto
north	nord
south	sud
east	est
west	ovest

CHAPTER 10: HOTELS AND ACCOMODATIONS

L'albergo Aurora, per favore.

(Lahl-BEHR-go Ah-oo-RO-rah pair fah-VO-reh)

To the Hotel Aurora, please.

This phrase could be useful to tell a taxi driver to take you to your hotel. However, as in North America, large hotels have service booths in the major airports and train stations. Obviously the price range varies, depending on the period of travel, the city, and the choice of hotel, but generally prices are quite expensive.

It is common in Italy to find monastery/convent hotels— actual monasteries located in idyllic and historical locations, which are informally rated as the equivalent of three- to four-star hotels.

Their prices vary, but they are generally very affordable: an average of 40 to 50 euros for a single and 80 to 90 euros for a double.

For a three-star hotel the average price is 110 euros; for a modest pensione 80 euros.

Scusi, potrebbe indicarmi un albergo/una pensione qui vicino, per favore?

Pardon me, could you please point me to a hotel/pensione close by?

SCOO-zee po-TREB-beh een-dee- CAHR-mee oon ahl-BEHR-go/ OO-na pehn-see-OH-neh kwee vee-CHEE-no pair fah-VO-reh

Scusi, potrebbe indicarmi come arrivare all'albergo Aurora, per favore?

Pardon me, could you please tell me how to get to the Hotel Aurora?

SCOO-zee po-TREB-beh een-dee- CAHR-mee CO-meh ahr-ree-VAH- reh ahl-lahl-BEHR-go Ah-oo-RO-rah pair fah-VO-reh

C'è un buon bed and breakfast vicino?

(CHEH oon boo-ON bed and breakfast quee vee-CHEE-noh)

Is there a nice bed and breakfast nearby?

Tourism is Italy's largest asset, and therefore there is a great variety of accommodations throughout the country: from luxurious hotels and villas to resort villages, from family-run pensioni to youth hostels, from agriturismo sites to campgrounds. If you are on a tight budget, there are many bed-and-breakfast places and albergo/ostello della gioventù (youth hostels).

C'è un albergo della gioventù in   questa città?

Is there a youth hostel in this city?

CHEH oon al-BEHR-goh dehl-la jo- vehn-TOO een QUE-sta cheet-TAH

Vorrei fare una prenotazione.

(Voh-RAY FAH-reh OO-na preh-no-tah-tsee-OH-neh)

I would like to make a reservation.

Finding accommodations during the tourist season in Italy, especially in tourist areas, can be very problematic; make your hotel reserva- tions well ahead of time.

If it was not possible to reserve ahead, ask someone: Scusi, potrebbe indicarmi un albergo/una pensione qui vicino? (Excuse me, could you please suggest a hotel close by?)

If you get lost after visiting the city or going to an excursion, and you are near the hotel, ask someone: Scusi, potrebbe indicarmi come arrivare all'albergo Aurora? (Excuse me, could you please tell me how to get to the albergo Aurora?) or, simply, L'albergo Aurora, per favore (Albergo Aurora, please).

ùFor reservation purposes, hotels request a proof of identification (normally a passport); small hotels might ask you to leave the key to your room while going out for the day.

Vorrei prenotare una singola/doppia (or matrimoniale) per due notti.

I would like to reserve a single/ double room for two nights.

Vor-RAY preh-no-TAH-reh OO-nah SEEN-go-lah/DOP-pee-ah (or mah-tree-mo-nee-AH-leh) pair DOO-eh NOT-tee

Mi dispiace, ma devo cancellare la mia prenotazione.

I'm sorry, but I need to cancel my reservation.

Me dee-spee-AH-cheh mah DEH-voh can-chehl-LAH-reh la MEE-ah preh-no-tah-tsee-OH-neh

Ha una camera per una notte/per stasera?

(Ah OO-nah CAH-meh-rah pair OO-nah NOT-teh/pair stah-SEH-rah)

Do you have a room available for one night/tonight?

Hotel rooms in Italy are generally comparable to those in North Amer- ica. Even family-run hotels and monastery-hotels are comparable to American standards; generally, they all have a private bathroom (il bagno), bathtub (il bagno) and/or shower (la doccia), television (la televisone), and a comfortably sized room (la camera).

However, to avoid unpleasant surprises, especially with smaller venues, it is always a good idea to ask about what's in a room and to check the room itself.

If you wish, it is also a good idea to point out that you want a nonsmoking room (una camera per non fumatori).

Desidererei avere una camera tranquilla/con veduta panoramica/che dia sul cortile/che non dia sulla strada principale.

I would like a quiet room/a room with a view/a room that overlooks the courtyard/a room that does not face the main street.

Deh-see-deh-REH-ray ah-VEH-reh OO-nah CAH-meh-rah trahn-QUEEL-lah/kohn veh-DOO-tah pah-no-RAH-mee-cah/keh DEE-ah sool cor-TEE-leh/keh nohn DEE-ah SOOL-lah STRAH-dah preen-chee-PAH-leh

La colazione è inclusa?

(Lah co-lah-tsee-OH-neh eh een- CLOO-zah)

Is breakfast included?

Breakfast is often included in the price in many Italian hotels and pensioni, but be sure to ask anyway.

It is usually a rich breakfast buffet for all tastes: uova (eggs), pancetta (bacon), burro (butter), marmellata (jam), croissants, panini (rolls), cioccolata calda (hot chocolate), formag- gio (cheese), Nutella, tè (tea), regular coffee, milk, espresso, cappuc- cino, caffellatte, latte, and many other items. Many hotels also cater to clients with celiac disease and offer a gluten-free breakfast.

Breakfast is normally served between 7:00 A.M. and 10:00 A.M.

A che ora viene servita la colazione?

At what time is breakfast served?

Ah keh OH-rah vee-EH-neh sair-VEE-tah lah co-lah-tsee-OH-neh

Dove posso parcheggiare la macchina?

(DOH-veh POS-so pahr-kehd-JA-reh lah MAHK-kee-nah)

Where can I park my car?

Parking is available in big hotels but you must pay extra. Quite a few smaller hotels and pensioni might offer free parking. Many hotels, including small ones, also include in their price a free in-room Internet connection. However, in some hotels there is an extra cost. Also, many hotels offer free Internet services in the lobby.

C'è il collegamento Internet in camera?

Is an Internet connection available in the room?

CHEH eel col-leh-gah-MEHN-toh EEN-tair-neht een CAH-meh-rah?

Come si fa a regolare il climatizzatore?

(CO-meh see fah ah reh-go-LAH-re eel clee-mah-teets-sah-TO-reh)

Can the air- conditioning/heating be adjusted?

Adjusting the air-conditioning/heating temperature in any hotel room in Europe or in North America can often become a real chal- lenge.

The sentences below will assist you when asking for help. If there is no air-conditioning, or if it is too hot or too cold, ask to be moved to another room. The location of your room might contribute not only to the temperature in it but also to the level of noise you are exposed to.

Be sure to consider that when opting to change rooms.To save energy, some small hotels might use a system which should be manually activated as soon as you open the door to your room. Once you leave the room, the power is deactivated.

Please remember that Italy uses a higher power voltage (220 volts) than North America (110 volts) and differently shaped electrical sockets. Therefore you should pack a plug adaptor for any electric devices.

Fa troppo caldo/freddo nella stanza.

It is too hot/cold in the room.

Fah TROP-po CAHL-doh/FRED-doh NEL-lah STAHN-zah

Manca la corrente.

There is no power.

MAHN-cah lah cor-REHN-teh

Per favore, potrebbe mettermi in un'altra camera?

Could you please move me to another room?

Pair fah-VO-reh po-TREB-beh MET-tair-mee een oon-AHL-trah CAH-meh-rah

Non riesco a capire come funziona la doccia.

(Nohn ree- EHS-co ah cah-PEE-reh CO-meh foon-tsee-OH-nah lah DOHT-chah)

I do not know how the shower operates.

At times, showers or flushing systems in Europe are not very intuitive or are completely different from what you may be accustomed to. The following sentence will help you get some assistance:

Ho problemi con il bagno/ la doccia/il lavandino.

I have problems with the toilet/ shower/sink.

O pro-BLEH-mee kohn eel BAHN-yo/lah DOHT-chah/eel lah-vahn- DEE-no

A che ora è il check-out?

(Ah keh OH-rah eh eel check-out)

At what time is checkout?

Checkout times vary; the most common time to check out is 11:00 A.M. Almost all hotels allow the use of their luggage storage room after checking out. This is a good option if you want to spend the day after checking out visiting the city. You can then pick up your luggage and travel to the airport/train station afterward.

Posso lasciare le valige in deposito dopo il check-out?

Could I leave my luggage in the luggage storage room after checking out?

POS-so lah-SHAH-reh leh vah-LEE-jeh een deh-PO-zee-toh DOH-po eel check-out

A che ora parte la navetta/il pulmino per l'aeroporto?

(Ah keh OH-rah PAHR-teh lah nah-VET-tah/il pool-MEE-no pair eel-POR-toh)

At what time does the shuttle/minibus leave for the airport?

Most hotels also offer transportation to and from the airport, but it is important to reserve a place to avoid unpleasant surprises. If you pre- fer to transfer to the airport by taxi, be sure to call ahead for the cab. Public transportation is also a good alternative to reach the airport as the service is often frequent and rather inexpensive; for example, in Rome there is a train every half hour, to and from the Fiumicino Airport.

Per favore, potrebbe prenotarmi un tassì per le otto domani mattina? Could you please reserve a taxi for me for eight o'clock tomorrow morning?

Pair fah-VO-reh po-TREB-beh preh-no-TAHR-mee oon tahs-SEE pair leh OT-to doh-MAH-ni maht-TEE-nah

Ci sono dei mezzi pubblici per l'aeroporto?

Is there any public transit to the airport?

CHEEH SO-no day METS-tsee POOB-blee-chee pair lah-eh-roh-POR-toh

CHAPTER 11: MEDICAL ISSUES

Hopefully you are like most individuals and will not experience any medical issues during your visit to Italy. The most likely scenario is that you will experience a little bit of jet lag in adjusting to your new time zone. Experts say it takes one day for each hour of time difference for your body to adjust. Therefore if you are traveling from New York to Rome it'll take you six days to adjust to the six-hour time difference. If you are flying from Los Angeles you can expect nine days.

There are ways to shortcut the amount of time necessary so you are not feeling like a zombie during your vacation. If you should succumb to a non-serious illness in Italy your best bet is usually to try to remedy yourself via the pharmacy. Obviously, for major ailments and injuries you should head to the hospital or emergency room, where you are usually seen right away without filling out a ton of paperwork.

Emergency Phone Numbers

112 – Similar to 911 in the United States or 999 in the United Kingdom

118 – Emergency number for the hospital / ambulance

Most of the time, the operator will not speak any English. However, they may be able to transfer you to someone that does. Pharmacies in Italy have been around for hundreds of years. In fact, the Santa Maria Novella pharmacy in Florence is the oldest one in Italy and has been around since 1221.

They are usually on a rotating system of operating hours to ensure that one is always available to the general population. The hours are regulated by Italian law.

In just about every city there is one that is open 24 hours. They are typically located in the center of town near the train station or bus station.

They are indicated with the internationally known symbol of a cross. The cross is usually colored green. Red crosses usually indicate an emergency room (pronto soccorso).

Unlike the pharmacies in the United States or Canada such as CVS or Walgreen's, an Italian pharmacy pretty much is just that – a pharmacy. They will not carry food and beverage items, birthday cards, office supplies, photographic equipment and services, etc.

However, the Italian pharmacist has a lot more leeway than your local pharmacist in the United States. The Italian pharmacist has the ability and authority to prescribe medicine for some of your typical ailments. Or they can recommend an over-the-counter item as well. That's right, if you have the flu or something minor, you should first go to the Italian pharmacist to see if they can help you.

Some useful vocabulary:

I'm not feeling well.

Non mi sento bene.

I have a pain here.

Ho un dolore qui.

headache	mal di testa
backache	mal di schiena
I need a doctor quickly.	Ho bisogno di un medico presto.
Can you call a doctor for me?	Può chiamarmi un medico?
Does the doctor speak English?	Il medico parla inglese?
My ... hurts.	Mi fa male ....
...ankle	...la caviglia.
...arm	...il braccio.
...chest	...il petto.
...eyes	...gli occhi.
...finger	...il ditto.
...foot	...il piede.
...heart	...il cuore.
...kidney	...il rene.

...lung   ...il polmone.

...neck   ...il collo.

...nose   ...il naso.

...skin   ...la pelle.

...stomach   ...lo stomaco.

...throat   ...la gola.

CHAPTER 12: MEETING PEOPLE

Italians are a very warm and fun-loving people. If you make a little bit of an effort with your Italian language, it will go a long way in meeting Italians during your trip. Although, once they find out you speak English, many of them will want to practice their English skills with you as opposed to speaking in their native Italian.

Another thing to keep in mind is that Italy is one of the most visited countries on earth with regards to tourism. That means it is visited by people from Germany, England, France, Spain, Austria, Poland, Sweden, etc. I generally have an easier time meeting tourists from other countries as opposed to Italians. I'm not sure the reason why, but I have my own theory. People from other countries will tend to be in a vacation mode wanting to meet other people. Italians will be busy with their normal routines. The old saying "go with the flow" definitely applies. If you keep your mind open, you're bound to meet interesting people from many different parts of the world.

hello	ciao
What is your name?	Come si chiama?

If you are trying to be more flirtatious with someone of the opposite sex, you would want to use the familiar version for you.

What is your name?	Come ti chiami?
My name is ...	Mi chiamo ...
pleasure (to meet you)	piacere
How are you? (Formal)	Come sta?
How are you? (Familiar)	Come stai?
How is it going?	Come va?
I'm fine, thank you.	Sto bene, grazie.

Where are you from? (Formal)	Da dove viene?
Where are you from? (Familiar)	Da dove vieni?
I'm from the United States.	Sono degli Stati Uniti.
work	lavoro

Note – similar to the word labor

What type of work do you do? (Formal)	Che tipo di lavoro fa?
Can I buy you a drink?	Ti posso offrire una bevanda?
Can I buy you dinner?	Ti posso offrire una cena?
Would you like to dance?	Ti piacerebbe ballare?
You are very pretty.	Sei molto bella.
You are very handsome.	Sei molto bello.
I like your smile.	Mi piace il tuo sorriso.
I like your eyes.	Mi piaciono i tuoi occhi.
I'm with...	Sono con...
...my wife.	...mia moglie.
...my husband.	...mio marito.
...my girlfriend.	...mia ragazza.

...my boyfriend.	...mio ragazzo.
Do you have a boyfriend / girlfriend?	Tieni un ragazzo / una ragazza?
We're here on holiday / vacation.	Siamo qui in vacanza.
We're here for two weeks.	Siamo qui per due settimane.
See you later.	A più tardi.

CHAPTER 13: ANIMALS

In this Rocket Italian lesson we'll be taking a trip to the zoo to talk about all types of animals in Italian – animali! You might have a dog or cat at home, but I bet you don't have a monkey!. After this lesson you'll be able to talk about the animals in your life and also about the more rare animals you don't see every day.

"a cuccia!" (to dog) "down!"

"attenti al cane" "beware of the dog"

"è vietato introdurre cani" "no dogs allowed"

A cavallo On horseback

Andare a caccia To go hunting

Animali domestici Pets

Animali selvatici Wild animals

Bestiame Livestock

I diritti degli animali Animal rights

Il cane abbaia The dog barks

Il cane ringhia The dog growls

Il gatto fa le fusa The cat purrs

Il gatto miagola The cat miaows

In casa abbiamo 12 animali We have 12 pets in our house

Liberare un animale To set an animal free

Mettere un animale in gabbia To put an animal in a cage

Mi piacciono i gatti ma preferisco i cani I like cats but I prefer dogs

Mi piace l'equitazione or andare a cavallo I like horse-riding

Non abbiamo animali in casa We have no pets in our house

CHAPTER 14: ITALIAN AT HOME

Practicing Italian at home can be a good way to prepare for your trip. Use sticky notes to label items in your house, and try to remember some useful terms and phrases. Try teaching some words to your family members so you can quiz each other. It can only help!

Things to Do at Home

You've learned a lot of words and expressions related to travel. Now take a look at some useful verbs that have to do with life at home. Many of them are verbs; see Chapter 2 to review how to conjugate verbs.

to build, to construct

costruire

kohs-troo-EE-ray

to clean

pulire

poo-LEE-ray to

clean/brush one's teeth

lavarsi i denti

lah-VAHR-see eedehn-tee

to close, to shut

chiudere

KYEW-deh-ray

to close/shut thecurtains

chiudere le tende

KYEW-deh-ray leh tehn-deh

to cook

cucinare

koo-chee-NAH-ray

to comb one's hair
pettinarsi
peht-tee-NAHR-see

to do the washing/ laundry
fare il bucato
fah-ray eel boo- KAH-toh

to get up, to rise
alzarsi
ahl-TSAHR-see

to go to bed
andare a letto
ahn-DAH-ray ah leht-toh

to go to sleep / to fall asleep
addormentarsi
ahd-dohr-mehn- TAHR-see

to hang up the washing/laundry
stendere il bucato
STEHN-deh-ray eel boo-KAH-toh

to iron
stirare
stee-RAH-ray

to lie down
sdraiarsi

sdreye-AHR-see

to open
aprire
ahp-REE-ray

to open/draw thecurtains
aprire le tende
ahp-REE-ray leh tehn-deh to paint

to varnish
verniciare
vehr-nee-CHAH-ray

to repair
riparare
ree-pah-RAH-ray

to sit down
sedersi
seh-DEER-see

to sleep
dormire
dòhr-MEE-ray

to take a bath
fare un bagno
fah-ray oon bahn-yoh
to take a shower
fare la doccia

fah-ray lah doh-chah

to turn/switch on

accendere

ah-CHEN-deh-ray

to wash

lavare

lah-VAH-ray

to wash (oneself),to wash up

lavarsi

lah-VAHR-see

KEYNOTE

In Italian there aren't separate words for house (structure) and home (environment).

The distinction is made by using the definite article. Vado a casa means "I'm going home"; Vado alla casa di Paolo means "I'm going to Paul's house."

Inside Your Home

Here are terms you can use to describe the contents of your home:

Appliances and Electronics

air conditioning	l'aria condizionata
	LAH-ree-ah kohn-deets-ee-oh-NAH-tah
alarm clock	la sveglia
	lah svehl-yah
central heating	il riscaldamento centrale
	eel ree-skahl-dah-MEHN-toh chehn- TRAH-lay
computer	il computer
	eel kohm-PYOU-tehr
dishwasher	la lavastoviglie
	lah lah-vah-stoh-VEEL-yeh
DVD player	il lettore DVD

eel leht-TOH-ray dee-voo-dee

electric socket	la presa (di corrente)
	lah pray-zah dee kohr-REHN-tay
electric stove	la cucina elettrica
	lah koo-CHEE-nah eh-LEHT-tree-kah
electrical switch	l'interruttore
	leen-tehr-root-TOH-ray
freezer	il congelatore
	eel kohn-jeh-lah-TOH-ray
gas stove	la cucina a gas lah koo-CHEE-nah ah gahs
iron	il ferro da stiro
	eel fehr-roh dah stee-roh
microwave (oven)	il forno a microonde
	eel fohr-noh ah mee-kroh-OHN-deh
oven	il forno
	eel fohr-noh
printer	la stampante
	lah stahm-PAHN-tay
radio	la radio
	lah RAH-dee-oh
refrigerator, fridge	il frigorifero
	eel free-goh-REE-feh-roh
telephone	il telefono
	eel teh-LEH-foh-noh
television set	il televisore
	eel teh-leh-vee-ZOH-ray
vacuum cleaner	l'aspirapolvere
	lah-spee-rah-POHL-veh-ray
VCR	il videoregistratore
	eel vee-deh-oh-reh-jee-strah-TOH-ray
washing machine	la lavatrice

lah lah-vah-TREE-cheh

KEYNOTE

To practice your Italian, try renting an Italian movie or watching Italian television. Many cable companies in metropolitan areas in the United States offer Italian network television (RAI).

ITALIAN CONVERSATIONS

Learn Italian for Beginners in Your Car Like Crazy.

Lessons for travel & Everyday.

How to speak Italian with Grammar, Vocabulary, Conversations and Common Phrases.

VOL 1

CHAPTER 8: TEST...129

CHAPTER 9: DIALOGUE AND INTRODUCTORY COVERSATION...148

ITALIAN COMMON PHRASES.......................................154

INTRODUCTION...172

INTRODUCTION

This book provides all the key words and phrases you are likely to need in everyday situations. It is grouped into themes, and key phrases are broken down into short sections, to help you build a wide variety of sentences. A lot of the vocabulary is illustrated to make it easy to remember, and "You may hear" boxes feature questions you are likely to hear. At the back of the book there is a menu guide, listing about 500 food terms, and a Numbers and the most useful phrases are listed on the jacket flaps for quick reference.

Nouns

All Italian nouns (words for things, people, and ideas) are masculine or feminine. The gender of singular nouns is usually shown by the word for "the": il or lo (masculine) and la (feminine). They change to l' before vowels. The plural forms are i or gli (masculine) and le (feminine).

Adjectives

Most Italian adjectives change endings according to whether they describe a masculine or feminine, singular or plural word. In this book the singular masculine form is shown, followed by the alternative feminine ending: I'm lost   Mi sono perso/a

"You" There are two ways of saying "you" in Italian: lei (polite) and tu (familiar). In this book we have used lei throughout, as that is what you normally use with people you don't know.

Verbs

Verbs change according to whether they are in the singular or plural. In phrases where this happens, the singular form of the verb is followed by the plural form: Where is/are...? Dov'è/Dove sono...?

CHAPTER 1: COLORS IN ITALIAN

Unfortunately, when it comes to learning the colors in Italian there are some rules you need to memorize. Only a couple of them can be inferred or figured out from what we use in English.

You just have to remember that Italian colors can fall into one of three different categories:

1 – Normal Colors

This will encompass most of the colors of the Italian language. For these colors they must match in gender and number to the object that they are describing.

Gender becomes important = Masculine or Feminine

Number becomes important = Singular or Plural

2 – Neuter Colors

For these cases, gender does not matter. The only thing that matters is the number of items being described.

Gender Does Not Matter

Number Becomes Important = Singular or Plural

3 – Unique or Invariable Colors

For these cases nothing matters! This is a "one color fits all" approach in the Italian language. You don't have to worry about gender or number. This is similar to the approach we use in English.

Gender Does Not Matter

Number Does Not Matter

The above is confusing until you see it in action with some practical examples. However, don't fret about it too much. Italians are very forgiving of errors when it comes to using their language. They will appreciate your eagerness in trying to learn.

1 – Normal Colors

Here are some examples that follow the normal pattern:

azzurro – sky blue

bianco – white

giallo – yellow

grigio – gray

nero – black

rosso – red

a white house	una casa bianca
two white houses	due case bianche

In the example above, the object being described (house) is feminine. To make the plural of house, the last letter "a" changes to an "e." This occurs not only in the noun, but notice how the word for white changes to a plural form (bianca becomes bianche). The letter "a" in bianca is changed to an "e." As we learned earlier in the pronunciation section, the letter "h" is used in between the "c" and the "e" so it keeps the "c" sound, as in cat. Otherwise, without the "h," the "c" sound would revert to the "ch" sound we have in church.

Some more normal examples:

a yellow house

una casa gialla

tre case gialle

three yellow houses

Notice how the word for yellow in Italian ends in an "a" to indicate a feminine noun.

If it were a masculine noun, it would end in an "o" like the example below:

a yellow bridge

un ponte giallo

five yellow bridges

cinque ponti gialli

More examples:

a black cat

un gatto nero

four black cats

quattro gatti neri

ten black cats

dieci gatti neri

2 – Neuter Colors

The main neuter colors in Italian are:

marrone – brown

verde – green

a brown house

una casa marrone

a brown cat

un gatto marrone

In the example above, notice how the word "marrone" stays the same, even though the objects being characterized are feminine and masculine (house and cat, respectively). Thus, that's why it is called a neuter color.

Let's review what would be the scenario with a normal color:

a white house

una casa bianca

a white cat

un gatto bianco

However, with neuter colors, the number (singular or plural) is important in coming up with the correct usage of the color.

Let's review the earlier example in the singular form:

a brown house

una casa marrone

a brown cat

un gatto marrone

Here are the plural variations:

three brown houses

tre case marroni

three brown cats

tre gatti marroni

In this case, the "e" in marrone will change to an "i" to indicate that it is plural.

a green telephone

un telefono verde

five green telephones

cinque telefoni verdi

3 – Unique or Invariable Colors

For these particular colors in Italian, gender does not matter and the number of items being described does not matter.

Here are examples of common unique or invariable colors in Italian:

arancione – orange

blu – blue

rosa – pink

viola – purple

a blue car

una macchina blu

seven blue cars

sette macchine blu

In the above example, macchina changes to macchine to become plural, but blu remains the same.

an orange cat

un gatto arancione

two orange cats

due gatti arancione

In the above example, gatto changes to gatti to become plural, but arancione remains the same.

I've only touched upon the most common colors that you will encounter. Just as in English, Italian has many different variations of colors like teal, aqua, etc. I've chosen to ignore them for this lesson since they tend not to be used in everyday conversation.

CHAPTER 2: CARDINAL AND ORDINAL NUMBERS

You can't get away without knowing numbers, even in small talk. Somebody may ask you how old you are or how many days you're visiting. Numbers are used in restaurants, for dealing with money, and for finding addresses. This chapter helps you navigate your way through these situations by giving you counting related vocabulary to work with.

CARDINAL & DECIMAL NUMBERS

Cardinal numerals (1, 2, 3... etc.) are used for mathematics or for stating quantities. The name of Italian ones works in the following way: 1 to 10 have a specific name, 11 to 16 follow a semi-standard pattern (more or less like English ...-teen), 17 to 19 have a different semi-standard pattern; all the others can be obtained with a fully standard pattern. The following tables show also English sounds.

0 to 10

zero	dzehroh	zero (but also nill, o, etc...)
uno	wnoh	one
due	dweh	two
tre	treh	three
quattro	quah'ttroh	four
cinque	chinqueh	five
sei	sehy	six
sette	seh'tteh	seven
otto	oh'ttoh	eight
nove	nohveh	nine
dieci	dyehchih	ten

Numbers do not change inflection for different genders, except uno, which actually behaves as the same indefinite article and therefore when followed by a matching noun changes as follows: **uno** one (as a digit)

uno scopo, un cane, un occhio one purpose (= a purpose), one dog (= a dog), one eye (= an eye) **una scatola, una chiave, un'oca** one box (= a box), one key (= a key), one goose (= a goose)

But any other number is irrespective of gender (the noun will obviously be plural):

un albero, tre alberi (masculine) one tree, three trees

una casa, tre case (feminine) one house, three houses

un cane, otto cani (masculine) one dog, eight dogs

una chiave, otto chiavi (feminine) eight keys

In written Italian, it is usually more correct to spell small numbers by their names when they state a quantity:

"there were five ships" would be better than "there were 5 ships".

When using articles, the numeral acts like a plural adjective in the "adjective-noun" pattern:

*gli***alberi** - *i* tre alberi (*gli* matches **alberi**, while *i* matches **tre**) the trees - the three trees

*le***case** - *le***tre case** (*le* matches both **case** and **tre**) the houses - the three houses

*i***cani** - *gli* otto cani (*i* matches **cani**, while *gli* matches **otto**) the dogs - the eight dogs

*le***chiavi** - *le***otto chiavi** (*le* matches both **chiavi** and **otto**) the keys - the eight keys

When the numbered noun is single (i.e. "only one"), the adjective **unico** = only can be used:
ilgatto (the cat) - **un gatto** (one cat) - **l'unico gatto** (the only cat) **la strada** (the road) - **una strada** (one road) - **l'unica strada** (the only road) **l'indice** (masc., the index) - **un indice** (one index) - **l'unico indice** (the only index)

Instead, when numbers are treated as nouns, they are always masculine and singular, because Italian assumes that **numero** (= number) comes before them, although in most cases it may be omitted. And, as any other noun, also the word **numero** requires an article:

*il***numero uno** or simply *l'***uno**number one

*il***numero**due or simply *il***due** number two

*il***numero**otto or simply *l'***otto** number eight

il **numero dieci** or simply *il***dieci** number ten

As usual, notice how the article phonetically depends on the following word.

11 to 19

Undici	wndychih	eleven
Dodici	dohdychih	twelve
Tredici	trehdychih	thirteen
Quattordici	quah'ttohrdychih	fourteen
quindici	quihndychih	fifteen
sedici	sehdychih	sixteen
diciassette	dychassehtteh	seventeen
diciotto	dychohttoh	eighteen
diciannove	dychahnnohveh	nineteen

As you see, the first group has a root resembling numbers 1 to 6, followed by the suffix ...dici, a contraction of dieci (ten), with accent falling on the last syllable before the suffix.

The last three numbers, instead, have an opposite pattern: a prefix for ten (dicia...) is followed by the digit, though for fonetic reasons something changes in the overall spelling. The stressed syllable is the same as for the corresponding digits.

The same rules stated above for 0 to 9 are also valid for these numbers (and for the following ones, as well), therefore:

undici   (eleven)

gli **undici cani** (masculine)   (the eleven dogs)

le **undici case** (feminine)   (the eleven houses)

il **numero undici** or simply   *l'***undici** (number eleven)

diciannove   (nineteen)

I **diciannove cani** (masculine)   (the nineteen dogs)

Le **diciannove case** (feminine)   (the nineteen houses

Il **numero diciannove** or simply il diciannove (number nineteen)

FULL MULTIPLES OF 10

venti	**veh**nty	twenty
trenta	**treh**ntah	thirty
quaranta	quah**rahn**tah	forty
cinquanta	chin**quah**ntah	fifty
sessanta	sehs**sahn**tah	sixty
settanta	seh'**ttahn**tah	seventy
ottanta	oh'**ttahn**tah	eighty
novanta	noh**vahn**tah	ninety
cento	**cheh**ntoh	one hundred

So the multiples of ten are not very different from the English ones, as they use a suffix **...anta** (but **...enta** for thirty) in the same way English uses ...ty.

Names of digits slightly change, binding with the suffix. The word cento, instead, actually means hundred (Italian does not require to specify one, as in English). All rules are the same as above:

cinquanta   (fifty)

cento   (one hundred)

i **cinquanta cani**   (masculine) (the fifty dogs)

i **cento cani**   (the one hundred dogs)

le **cinquanta case**   (feminine) (the fifty houses)

le **cento case**   (the one hundred houses)

il **numero cinquanta** or il cinquanta		(number fifty)
il **numero cento** or **il cent**o		(number one hundred)

COMPOUND NUMBERS FROM 21 TO 99

To obtain twenty-one, thirty-two, forty-eight, etc., the pattern is similar to English: bind the multiple of 10 to the digit (with no dash).

ventuno	vehn**t**wnoh	twenty-one
ventidue	vehnty**d**weh	twenty-two
ventitré	vehnty**treh**	twenty-three
ventiquattro	vehnty**quah'**ttroh t	wenty-four
venticinque	vehnty**chin**queh	twenty-five
ventisei	vehnty**seh**ih	twenty-six
ventisette	vehnty**seh'**tteh	twenty-seven
ventotto	vehn**toh'**ttoh	twenty-eight
ventinove	vehnty**noh**veh	twenty-nine

and the same for other numbers:

trentuno	trehn**t**wnoh	thirty-one
trentadue	trehntah**d**weh	thirty-two
trentatré	trehntah**treh**	thirty-three
quarantuno	quahrahn**t**wnoh	forty-one
quarantadue	quahrahntah**d**weh	forty-two
cinquantuno	chinquahn**t**wnoh	fifty-one
cinquantadue	chinquahntah**d**weh	fifty-two

Note that the stress always falls on the digit.

Two observations:

!   when digits start with a vowel (**uno, otto**) the last vowel of the multiple of ten is dropped (**ventuno**, not "ventiuno"; **quarantotto**, not "quarantaotto"); etc.

!   since digit tre is monosyllabic (one syllable), in order to keep the stress on vowel e also in compound numbers, the last vowel is spelled é (with an accent): tre, but ventitré; trentatré; quarantatré; etc.).

476

FULL MULTIPLES OF 100

Very simple!

Just bind each digit to **cento**:

duecento	dwehchentoh	two hundred
trecento	trehchentoh	three hundred
quattrocento	quah'ttrohchentoh	four hundred
cinquecento	chinquehchentoh	five hundred
seicento	sehychentoh	six hundred
settecento	seh'ttehchentoh	seven hundred
ottocento	oh'ttohchentoh	eight hundred
novecento	nohvehchentoh	nine hundred
mille	mylleh	one thousand

COMPOUND NUMBERS FROM 100 TO 999

Also, **cento** behaves in the same way as the previous numbers, although in English you would have to use conjunction and (i.e. one hundred *and* one; three hundred *and* two; etc.):

Centouno   chentohwnoh   one hundred and one **centodue**   chentohdweh
         one hundred and two

centotré   chentoh**treh**   one hundred and three

centoquattro chentoh**quah'**ttroh   one hundred and four **centocinque**   chentoh**chin**que
one hundred and five **centosei**   chentoh**seh**ih   one hundred and six **centosette**
       chentoh**seh'**tteh   one hundred and seven **centootto**   chentoh**oh'**ttoh
one hundred and eight **centonove**   chentoh**nohv**eh   one hundred and nine
centodieci   chentoh**dyeh**chih   one hundred and ten

Note that this time no elisions are made, therefore **cento** always remains the same, also before uno and **otto**.

For greater numbers with a **cento** compound, the pattern is the same:

centoundici (one hundred and eleven)

centoventitré (one hundred and twenty-three)

centocinquantotto (one hundred and fifty-eight)

centonovanta (one hundred and ninety) etc.

Also multiples work out in the same way:

duecentocinque (two hundred and five)

trecentodiciassette (three hundred and seventeen)

quattrocentosessantasette (four hundred and sixty-seven)

cinquecentotrentuno (five hundred and thirty-one)

ottocentocinquantaquattro (eight hundred and fifty-four)

novenentoottantotto (nine hundred and eighty-eight) etc.

FULL MULTIPLES OF 1,000

Mille is slightly different from the **cento** concept: it actually means **one** thousand (not simply thousand): its multiples are therefore made of number + **...mila** (suffix for **mille**), also for numbers greater than 9:

duemila	dweh**myh**lah	two thousand
tremila	treh**myh**lah	three thousand
quattromila	quah'ttroh**myh**lah	four thousand
cinquemila	chinqueh**myh**lah	five thousand
seimila	sehy**myh**lah	six thousand
settemila	seh'tteh**myh**lah	seven thousand
ottomila	oh'ttoh**myh**lah	eight thousand
novemila	nohveh**myh**lah	nine thousand
diecimila	dyehchy**myh**lah	ten thousand
undicimila	wndychih**myh**lah	eleven thousand
dodicimila	dohdychih**myh**lah	twelve thousand
ventimila	vehnty**myh**lah	twenty thousand
ventunomila	ventwnoh**myh**lah	twenty-one thousand
ventiduemila	ventydweh**myh**lah	twenty-two thousand
trentamila	trehntah**myh**lah	thirty thousand
quarantamila	quahrahntah**myh**lah	forty thousand
centomila	chentoh**myh**lah	one hundred thousand
centodiecimila	chentohdyehchy**myh**lah	

one hundred and ten thousand

centocinquantamila	chentohchinquahntah**myh**lah	one hundred and fifty thousand
duecentomila	dwechentoh**myh**lah	

478

two hundred thousand

novecentonovantanovemila

nohvehchentohnohvantahnohveh**myh**lah

nine hundred ninety-nine thousand

Notice how the stress is always carried by the **...mila** suffix.

COMPOUND NUMBERS FROM 1,001 TO 999,999

There is a slight change at this point, as **mille** and **...mila** sometimes need conjunction **e** (= and), where in English it is usually omitted. Follow these examples:

- **mille e uno** (**my**lleh eh **wnoh**) = one thousand one

- **mille e sette** = one thousand seven

- **mille e trentacinque** = one thousand thirty-five

- **mille e cento** = one thousand one hundred

- **mille e trecento** = one thousand three hundred

- **mille e novecento** = one thousand nine hundred

BUT...

- **millecentouno** = one thousand one hundred and one

- **millecentonove** = one thousand one hundred and nine

- **millecentoventotto** = one thousand one hundred and twenty-eight

- **millequattrocentonovantasei** = one thousand four hundred and ninety-six

- **milleottocentotrentatré** = one thousand eight hundred and thirty-three

Therefore, as a general rule, conjunction e breaks the word only when **mille** is followed by numbers smaller than 100, or by full multiples of 100 (**duecento, trecento,** etc.). The unbroken form is used in all other cases.

But in written texts, books, newspapers, etc., such big numbers are uncommon to be spelled with words: "almost two thousand people attended the event" would be more likely than "one thousand nine hundred and eighty-seven people...", or if the right number was required it would often be spelled with numerals: "1987 people". So if you don't become familiar now with these patterns, you can still do well, although you will need to master these numbers for dates (discussed in paragraph 3.4).

NOTE

In English, numbers like 1,100; 1,200; 1,300; etc. may either sound one thousand one hundred, one thousand two hundred, etc., or eleven hundred, twelve hundred, etc.: this never happens in Italian, which only uses the first form (**mille e cento, mille e duecento,** etc.), as the word **cento** does not support digits greater than nine (**novecento**).

479

DECIMAL NUMBERS AND SEPARATORS

While English uses a comma (,) as a separator for thousands, Italian uses a full stop (.).

1,100 (English spelling) becomes **1.000**

344,901 (English spelling) becomes **344.901** and so on.

Obviously, thousand separators do not affect pronounciation: they are simply used as mere graphic elements.

The comma instead, in Italian **virgola**, is used as a separator for decimals, whereas in English a dot is normally used: 1.15 (English spelling) becomes **1,15**

63.05 (English spelling) becomes **63,05**

and so on.

In this case, the word virgola is used exactly as English point, so that in the examples above the pronounciation would be: 1,15 = uno virgola quindici (one point fifteen) 63,05 = sessantatré virgola zero cinque (sixty-three point o five) and so on.

Fractions, instead, will be discussed in paragraph 3.3.

ORDINAL NUMBERS

As suggested by their name, ordinal numbers (1st, 2nd, 3rd... etc.) are used for indicating orders or ranks. In Italian, they have specific forms from 1 to 10, while all the following ones use one same suffix, so they are quite easy to learn. Unlike cardinal numbers, though, ordinals behave like an adjective, therefore they can have both a masculine and a feminine gender, in both singular and plural forms (all of them are regular).

Also in this page English sounds are shown.

ORDINAL NUMBERS FROM 1st TO 9th

primo	**pryh**moh	first
secondo	seh**kohn**doh	second
terzo	**tehr**tzo	third
quarto	**quahr**toh	fourth
quinto	**quihn**toh	fifth
sesto	**sehs**toh	sixth
settimo	**seh'tty**moh	seventh
ottavo	oh'**ttah**voh	eighth
nono	**noh**noh	ninth
decimo	**deh**chimoh	tenth

As found in most Western languages, the expressions first and second are irregular (i.e. they have no phonetic relation with their cardinal numbers one and two), in all the others the name of the digit is still recognizable, though slightly changed:

tre - *ter*zo, **quattro** - *quar*to, **cinque** - *quin*to, and so on, while many suffixes change.

Used as adjectives, they all follow the most common pattern:

primo (masculine singular)

primi (masculine plural)

prima (feminine singular)

prime (feminine plural)

secondo (masculine singular)

secondi (masculine plural)

seconda (feminine singular)

seconde (feminine plural)

And so on with all the others.

Note that there is an adjective derived from uno (one), unico, which means only, in contrast with primo (first). This adjective is regular, although its "...co" ending causes phonetic adjustment:
unico wnyhkoh (masculine singular)

unica wnyhkah (feminine singular)

unici wnyhchyh (masculine plural)

uniche wnyhkeh (feminine plural)

As in English, ordinals require an article, whose gender and phonetics will match the ordinal itself:

Il **prim**o = the first (masculine singular);

la **prim**a = the first (feminine singular);

i **prim**i = the first (masculine singular);

le **prim**e = the first (feminine singular);

*l'***ottav**o = the eighth (masculine singular);

*l'***ottav**a = the eighth (feminine singular);

gli **ottav**i = the eighth (masculine plural);

le **ottav**e = the eighth (feminine plural);

As in English, the article is required both when the ordinal is used as an adjective (i.e. when it is followed by a noun) and when it works as a pronoun (i.e. when it replaces the noun):

la prima casa = the first house

tu sei il terzo = you are the third

il quinto concorrente = the fifth participant

l'ottava a destra = the eighth on the right

In Italian, primo (especially its plural masculine and feminine) in some cases may also have a meaning of the early.... or the earliest..., referred to time, history, etc.: le prime conquiste = the early (earliest) achievements i primi abitanti = the early (earliest) inhabitants le prime tracce dell'uomo = the early (earliest) traces of man i primi esempi di arte bizantina = the early (earliest) samples of Byzantine art

Instead, when quoting the entries of an ordered list, a ranking, etc., the article is dropped (as in English):

primo: XXXXX secondo: YYYYY terzo: ZZZZZ ....

first: XXXXX second: YYYYY third: ZZZZZ ....

ORDINAL NUMBERS FROM 11th ONWARDS

From 11th onwards, you only need to add suffix ...esimo, and to drop the cardinal number's last vowel (except when the last digit is **...tre** = ...three):

undicesimo	wndy**cheh**syhmo	eleventh
dodicesimo	dohdy**cheh**syhmoh	twelfth
tredicesimo	trehdy**cheh**syhmoh	thirteenth
quattordicesimo	quah'ttohrdy**cheh**syhmoh	fourteenth
ventesimo	vehn**teh**syhmoh	twentieth
ventunesimo	vehntuh**neh**syhmoh	twenty-first
ventiduesimo	vehnty**dweh**syhmoh	twenty-second
ventitreesimo	vehnty**treh**ehsyhmoh	twenty-second
trentesimo	trehn**teh**syhmoh	thirtieth
trentunesimo	trehntwhn**eh**syhmoh	twenty-first
trentaduesimo	trehntahd**weh**syhmoh	twenty-second
trentatreesimo	trehntaht**reh**ehsyhmoh	twenty-second
quarantesimo	quahran**teh**syhmoh	fortieth
centesimo	chen**teh**syhmoh	one hundredth
duecentesimo	dwechen**teh**syhmoh	two hundredth
millesimo	myll**eh**syhmoh	one thousandth

The modern way to indicate ordinal numbers is to add their last vowel to the number, in "superscript" style:

1° (primo) or 1ª (prima)

9° (nono) or 9ª (nona)

17° (diciassettesimo) or 17ª (diciassettesima)

etc.

Just like adjectives, they can also have the plural form:

8^i (ottavi) or 8^e (ottave)

22^i (ventiduesimi) or 22^e (ventiduesime)

etc.

Eventually, a circumflex accent (^) may replace any of the superscript vowels:

1^ = 1°, 1ª, 1^i, 1^e

25^ = 25°, 25ª, 25^i, 25^e

130^ = 130°, 130ª, 130^i, 130^e

etc.

The more classic way to indicate an ordinal number in Italian is to use roman numbers: I = 1o (primo) or 1a (prima) IX = 9o (nono) or 9a (nona) XVII = 17o (diciassettesimo) or 17a (diciassettesima) etc. etc... When a roman number occurs in an Italian text, it should always be looked at as an ordinal number, unless it belongs to a date. If you don't feel too confident with these numbers, appendix 1 will show you how they work.

Adding a superscript vowel to roman numbers (i.e. IIIo, Va, etc.) is considered incorrect: since they already

act as ordinal numbers, the vowel would be redundant.

Roman numbers are now still used to indicate volumes, chapters, monarchs, centuries, and very few more categories. However, for some of the aforesaid ones (centuries, rulers) the use of Western numbers would not be considered very elegant. In common speech, ordinal numbers are used according to the "adjective-noun" pattern, i.e. they are always followed by the classified noun, never vice-versa:

il primo giorno (the first day)

le seconde case (the second houses)

la ventesima volta (the twentieth time)

etc.

Instead, when a roman number is used, the ordinal number usually follows the noun:

! when they are used to indicate a monarch, a pope, or other rulers, they are mentioned as in English, but omitting article the:

Leone IV (read as **Leone quarto**) = Leo IV, (in English, Leo the fourth) **Carlo VIII (Carlo ottavo)** = Charles VIII (in English, Charles the eighth).

! When indicating a book's chapter or volume, a play's act, etc.:

volume III (volume terzo), **capitolo XIII (capitolo tredicesimo)** = third volume, thirteenth chapter **atto II (atto secondo)** = second act.

In these cases both forms are accepted, so also **terzo volume, secondo atto**, etc., would be correct if spelled with letters (but not with roman numbers).

! When indicating a century (also in this case both forms are correct):

secolo XVII (secolo diciassettesimo) or **XVII secolo(diciassettesimo secolo)** = seventeenth century.

NOTE

As already said, ordinals greater than 10th do not use the same suffix as the smaller ones, having simplified the inflection to **...esimo** or **...esima.**

In old-style Italian, instead, all ordinals used to follow the pattern **decimo primo** (instead of **undicesimo**), **decimo secondo** (instead of **dodicesimo**), etc., also for larger numbers (**ventesimo quinto** instead of **venticinquesimo**, **settantesimo** nono instead of **settantanovesimo**, etc.), thus keeping the original suffixes of the first nine digits; today this form is very rarely used, and sounds quite archaic.

FRACTIONS

In Italian, fractions work exactly as in English: the first number is expressed as a cardinal number, the second one as an ordinal.

2/3 = due terzi = two thirds

1/7 = un settimo = one seventh

5/8 = cinque ottavi = five eighths

12/45 = dodici quarantacinquesimi = twelve forty-fifths

Number 1 always has the 'short' form un, according to the general phonetic rules of uno, either as a number or as an indefinite article:

1/3 = un terzo = one third

1/10 = un decimo = one tenth

1/90 = un novantesimo = one ninetieth

Fractions whose denominator is 2 read this number as mezzo (half) or mezzi (halves). 1/2 = un mezzo, or simply mezzo = one half, or half

4/2 = quattro mezzi = four halves

5/8 = cinque ottavi = five eighths

12/45 = dodici quarantacinquesimi = twelve forty-fifths

When a fraction is used to state a quantity, the noun to which it refers is introduced by preposition di (of): due quinti di alcool = two fifths of alcohol

cinque ottavi di pollice = five eighths of an inch notice how Italian does not use an indefinite article before inch, nor before any other measure

tre quarti di litro = three fourths of a liter

484

cinquanta centesimi di dollaro = fifty hundredths of a dollar (actually: fifty cents) This last example shows how the word centesimi (hundredths) is also used for cents, to indicate small change of any decimal system currency.

When the object of the fraction is introduced by a definite article (two thirds of the members, etc.), a compound preposition made of di + article will have to be used, instead of di alone. The following samples show the use of both the simple preposition di and of its compound form; although you may disregard the latter now, simply note the difference with the first two. Compound prepositions will be dealt with in paragraph 5.2.

Ordinal numbers always have the masculine form, also when the numbered object is feminine: un quarto di torta = one fourth of cake un quarto di questa torta = one fourth of this cake un quarto della torta = one fourth of the cake

tre quinti di zucchero = three fifths of sugar tre quinti di questo zucchero = three fifths of this sugar tre quinti dello zucchero = three fifths of the sugar

ROUGH QUANTITIES

Besides the common use of una dozzina di... (a dozen...), meaning twelve of something, in Italian the following expressions referring to rough quantities are commonly used:

una decina = about ten

una ventina = about twenty

una trentina = about thirty

una quarantina = about forty

una cinquantina = about fifty

una sessantina = about sixty

una settantina = about seventy

una ottantina = about eighty

una novantina = about ninety

As for the word **dozzina**, these quantities are treated as nouns (i.e. not as pure numbers), therefore they require an article, and are followed by the simple preposition **di** (of), which refers to the counted objects. So, for instance:

una decina di bottoni = about ten buttons

una quarantina di minuti = about forty minutes

un'ottantina di soldati = about eighty soldiers

The noun decina may be combined with exact numbers, to obtain alternative forms:

due decine = una ventina = about twenty

tre decine = una trentina = about thirty

quattro decine = una quarantina = about forty

and so on, up to

nove decine = una novantina = about ninety

485

All the others (ventina, trentina, etc.) are never numbered, i.e. they are always used in the form una ventina, una trentina, etc.

Also una cinquina (about five) and una quindicina (about fifteen) are quite common, although they tend to be rather colloquial.

Other nouns for rough quantities are:

un centinaio (masculine) = about one hundred

plural centinaia (feminine) = hundreds

un migliaio (masculine) = about one thousand

plural migliaia (feminine) = thousands

These two are not really "rough", as their literal meaning is hundred and thousand, but since for counting their equivalent suffixes ...-cento and ...-mila are normally used, centinaio and migliaio often carry a meaning of approximately 100 and approximately 1.000.

cento scatole = one hundred boxes

un centinaio di scatole = some one hundred boxes

trecentocinque mattoni = three hundred and five bricks

tre centinaia di mattoni = some three hundred bricks

novecentocinquanta frammenti = nine hundred and fifty fragments

un migliaio di frammenti = some one thousand fragments

tremilasettantotto spettatori = three thousand and seventy-eight spectators

tre migliaia di spettatori = some three thousand spectators

An exact number may be turned into a rough amount also by using **circa** and **all'incirca**, which mean about, approximately, some.

cento scatole = one hundred boxes

circa cento scatole = about one hundred boxes

trecentocinque mattoni = three hundred and five bricks

circa trecento mattoni = approximately three hundred bricks

novecentocinquanta frammenti = nine hundred and fifty fragments

circa un migliaio di frammenti = some one thousand fragments

tremilasettantotto spettatori = three thousand and seventy-eight spectators

circa tre migliaia di spettatori = about three thousand spectators

The use of circa or all'incirca does not automatically exclude the use of decine, centinaia, migliaia, etc.

circa quaranta minuti = about forty minutes

una quarantina di minuti = (same as above)

circa una quarantina di minuti = (same as above)

all'incirca trecento mattoni = approximately three hundred bricks

tre centinaia di mattoni = (same as above)

all'incirca tre centinaia di mattoni = (same as above)

all'incirca mille frammenti = some one thousand fragments

un migliaio di frammenti = (same as above)

circa un migliaio di frammenti = (same as above)

Also indefinite adjectives such as qualche (some), poche (a few), diverse (several), etc. may combine with decine, centinaia and migliaia: poche decine di minuti = literally: a few tens of minutes (i.e. 40 min.-50 min., or so) qualche centinaio di membri = a few hundred members diverse migliaia di metri = several thousand metres Note that qualche is singular, and can only combine with singular nouns, thus qualche centinaio, qualche migliaio (masculine).

Instead poche is already plural, therefore it has to be poche centinaia, poche migliaia (both feminine).

It is also possible to combine two rough quantities:

due decine di migliaia di abitanti = some twenty thousand inhabitants (literally: two tens of thousands) poche centinaia di migliaia di cellule = a few hundred thousand cells

In the same way also paio (pair), besides its "standard" meaning of two of something, two-piece set, is also commonly used for "slightly more than one" (a couple of, a few, a little, two or three, etc.). entro un paio di giorni = within a couple of days - within a few days un paio di consigli = a couple of tips - a few tips fra un paio d'anni = in a couple of years time - in a few years time Paio (masculine), whose plural is paia (feminine), is never numbered, unless wishing to express the actual meaning of "pair", "a set of two": due paia di scarpe = two pairs of shoes sei paia di guanti = six pairs of gloves circa dieci paia di pantaloni = some ten pairs of trousers una quindicina di paia di occhiali = about fifteen pairs of glasses

CHAPTER 3: THE DAYS AND MONTHS

Before discussing several topics concerning time, it is useful to memorize the adverb quando, which means when, both in positive and interrogative sentences:

quando tornerete ? = when will you (plur.) return ?

quando avremo finito il nostro lavoro = when we will have finished our work To indicate a future action, it is not strictly necessary to use a future tense after quando: present tense still gives the idea of something yet to come, although it may also indicate a habitual action, depending on the context and the meaning of the sentence:

 quando comprerà la nuova automobile = when he/she will buy the new car

quando compra la nuova automobile = when he/she buys the new car (future action)

quando compra qualcosa = when he/she buys something (habitual action)

An idiomatic expression contains this adverb twice: di quando in quando, meaning every now and then, from time to time, occasionally.

 di quando in quando andiamo al cinema = from time to time we go to the movies

THE DAYS OF THE WEEK

The Italian names of the seven days of the week are:

Lunedì	Monday
martedì	Tuesday
mercoledi.	Wednesday
giovedì	Thursday
venerdì	Friday
sabato	Saturday
domenica	Sunday

The Italian week always starts with Monday, while sometimes in English, especially in charts, in tables, etc., it starts with Sunday. Also notice how these names never have a capital (uppercase) letter, as they usually do in English.

These names are all masculine, except domenica which is feminine.

Most names end with ...dì (notice the accent), because the word dì, truncated form of the Latin dies, means day (which has the same Latin origin). In modern Italian, dì alone is not very commonly used, and another word for day, giorno, is often preferred.

Many Italian names of the week have an astronomical-mythological origin, referring to planets (which often bear the name of ancient roman gods and goddesses), but also a few English names have this peculiar origin:

- lunedì means "the day of the Moon" (like English monday);

- martedì means "the day of Mars";

- mercoledì means "the day of Mercurius";

- giovedì means "the day of Jupiter";

- venerdì means "the day of Venus";

- sabato curiously is of Jewish origin (shabbath = Jewish saturday); the English name is linked to Saturn;

- domenica means "the day of the Lord" (Latin dominus); the English name, instead, is linked to the Sun.

When using these names to indicate a precise date, (I will come on Monday, etc.), Italian does not use any preposition to match English on. venerdì comprerò un nuovo televisore = on Friday I will buy a new TV set.

mercoledì, quando sei partito, hai dimenticato le chiavi = on Wednesday, when you left, you forgot the keys

oggi è martedì = today is Tuesday The same form is used when days are not specified: due giovedì di questo mese = two Thursdays in this month (literally "...of this month"), but it can also mean on two Thursdays in this month

The use of a preposition or an article gives the day a habitual meaning: there are several forms for doing so. A definite article is often used:

il lunedì lavoro a casa = on Mondays I work at home

il sabato vado al mare = on Saturdays I go to the seaside

la domenica i negozi sono chiusi = on Sundays the shops are closed

The name of the day can be shifted to the end of the sentence, to give it more emphasis, and in this case the simple preposition di is preferred (though not compulsory):

lavoro a casa di lunedì = I work at home on Mondays

vado al mare di sabato = I go to the seaside on Saturdays

i negozi sono chiusi di domenica = the shops are closed on Sundays

Instead of di, the compound preposition al (= a + il) or alla (= a + la) can be used:

lavoro a casa al lunedì = I work at home on Mondays

vado al mare al sabato = I go to the seaside on Saturdays

i negozi sono chiusi alla domenica = the shops are closed on Sundays But, to make things easier, you can simply memorize either the use of articles, or of preposition di.

A further way to indicate habitual days is to use a definite article in singular form: il lunedì lavoro a casa = on Mondays I work at home

il sabato vado al mare = on Saturdays I go to the seaside

la domenica i negozi sono chiusi = on Sundays the shops are closed The same form is also used to indicate a very specific day (usually, a further specification occurs in the sentence):

il venerdì prima di Natale = Friday before Christmas (but this can also read on Friday before Christmas)

il prossimo martedì = next Tuesday or on next Tuesday

la domenica di Pasqua = Easter Sunday (literally "the Sunday of Easter") or on Easter Sunday But when the specific day is introduced by a demonstrative adjective, the article is always dropped: il sabato prima di Natale = Saturday before Christmas (or on Saturday before Christmas)

...BUT

quel sabato prima di Natale = that Saturday before Christmas (or on that Saturday before....)

NOTE - in the latter case, the specification "before Christmas" is almost redundant, because the use of "that" indicates how this day has already been introduced as a topic, or specified

Some sentences refer to more than one specific day (i.e. the winter Sundays, all Wednesdays in March, etc.), in which case Italian always uses a definite article in plural form: i giovedì di quest'anno = Thursdays of this year

tutti i sabati = all Saturdays

le domeniche estive = the summer Sundays

i primi lunedì del mese = the first Monday of each month, whose literal translation is "the first Mondays of the month", in this case with an actual meaning of "each", but this topic will be discussed at a further stage. In the sentences above, giovedì and lunedì are plural, although the inflection is the same as singular forms because these nouns are truncate.

Instead, sabato and domenica have standard plurals: sabati and domeniche; notice the phonetic h, added to keep the guttural sound of c (i.e. as an English k) before the vowel e.

MONTHS & SEASONS OF THE YEAR

MONTHS

The Italian names of the twelve months of the year are:

Gennaio	January
Febbraio	February
Marzo	March
Aprile	April
Maggio	May

490

Giugno	June
Luglio	July
Agosto	August
Settembre	September
Ottobre	October
Novembre	November
Dicembre	December

They are not very different from the English version, in which the Latin root is even more evident than in Italian.

In most cases, these names have an ancient roman origin: gennaio comes from Janus, the god who patroned the beginning of all events, to whom the first month was dedicated; marzo comes from Mars, god of war; agosto was probably given after the name of the first worshipped emperor, Augustus; settembre through dicembre come from the fact that in ancient times the year had ten months, and these names simply numbered the last ones (Latin septem = 7, octo = 8, novem = 9 and decem = 10).

A main difference with English is that, in Italian, they always have a small (or lowercase) initial letter.

Usually simple preposition in is used to indicate an event taking place within the month: in giugno partiremo per Berlino = in June we shall leave for Berlin

Natale cade in dicembre = Christmas falls in December

Preposition a can be used insted of in, especially in spoken language:

a settembre cambierò lavoro = in September I shall change job

quest'anno Pasqua cade a marzo = this year Easter falls in March Any of the two prepositions can be used: in is more formal, while a is more colloquial.

Unlike day names, months never use a definite article in habitual forms:

febbraio è un mese freddo = february is a cold month

ad (or in) agosto andiamo sempre al mare = in August we always go to the seaside (notice the phonetic use of ad instead of a, because the following word too starts with vowel a)

The article can be used only to indicate a very precise month: il luglio più caldo fu nel 1947 = the hottest July was in (the) 1947 (disregard the comparative form now: it will be discussed further on)

questo è stato un novembre piovoso = this has been a rainy November

dal maggio del 1963 = as of (the) May (of the) 1963

nel giugno del 1970 = in (the) June (of the) 1970

Notice that while English preposition in can be translated either with a or with in when the month does not require an article (as said above), only preposition in is used in forms with an article, as shown again in the followng examples:

in gennaio or a gennaio = in January

...BUT nel gennaio del 1985 (only form) = in January 1985

But when introduced by a demonstrative adjective, the article is always dropped: durante il gennaio del 1985 = during January 1985

...BUT durante quel gennaio del 1985 = during that January 1985 (notice how in this case the specification "1985" is almost redundant, because the use of "that" indicates that this month already was a topic of discussion)

Both in common speech and written language, months are very often introduced by mese di (month of), which affects the need of an article, because mese requires it: in gennaio le fontane ghiacciano = in January, fountains freeze (but using mese)

nel mese di gennaio le fontane ghiacciano = in (the month of) January, fountains freeze

da agosto in poi = from August onwards

(but using mese) dal mese di agosto in poi = from (the month of) August onwards

notice how compound prepositions nel (= in + il) and dal (= da + il) had to be used, instead of simple prepositions in and da because mese cannot stand without a definite article when it introduces a definite month.

SEASONS

The Italian names of the four seasons are:

primavera	spring
estate	summer
autunno	autumn or fall
inverno	winter

Italian also has adjectives referring to each season:

primaverile	(of) spring
estivo (fem. estiva)	(of) summer
autunnale	(of) autumn or fall
invernale	(of) winter

The simple preposition in is commonly used with seasons: in primavera gli uccelli tornano dai paesi caldi = in spring birds come back from (the) hot countries

i contadini fanno il vino in autunno = (the) peasants make (the) wine in autumn

Sometimes, simple preposition di is used, especially with estate and inverno, in which case it is phonetically shortened in d' (with an apostrophe). It is less commonly used with autunno. Obviously, primavera would require a full di, but this preposition is not really used at all with this noun. d'estate il tempo è bello = in summer the weather is fine

quando d'inverno nevica, accendiamo il fuoco = when in winter it snows, we light the fire In some expressions, as the ones above, di is more commonly used, but preposition in could have also been used, and both forms would have been correct, as well.

492

An article is only used to indicate seasons when no event is related to them: detesto l'autunno = I hate (the) autumn

i fiori sono simboli della primavera = (the) flowers are symbols of (the) spring

l'inverno giunse presto = (the) winter came soon

When adjectives are used, no special rule is required:

i lunghi mesi invernali = the long winter months

il clima autunnale è grigio e piovoso = the autumn weather is dull and grey

(notice that clima is a masculine noun, despite the ...a inflection)

le vacanze estive sono sempre troppo corte = (the) summer holidays are always too short

YEARS

In Italian years are pronounced as if they were simple numbers:

1963 nineteen sixty-three

millenovecentosessantatré

(one thousand nine hundred and sixty-three)

1500 fifteen hundred

millecinquecento

(one thousand five hundred)

1701 seventeen hundred and one

(millesettecentouno)

one thousand seven hundred and one

...and so on.

Unlike English, Italian years need a definite article, because they are referred to the word anno (= year).

il 1950 (read il millenovecentocinquanta) = nineteen fifty

nel 1950 = in nineteen fifty

dal 1950 = from (or as of) nineteen fifty

493

fino al 1950 = until or through nineteen fifty f

ra il 1950 e il 1960 = between nineteen fifty and nineteen sixty

When a month is referred to a specific year, the latter needs an article, unlike the English form: il maggio del 1963 = May 1963

nel dicembre del 1995 = in December 1995

dal febbraio del '48 = as of February '48

Sometimes, when the year might be mistaken with a number, the word anno is used:

l'anno 2000 (read l'anno duemila) = year two thousand nell'anno 2 = in year 2

dall'anno 500 = as of (or from) year 500

CENTURIES

The Italian word for century is sècolo (vowel e has been accented for mere tutorial reasons). When writing a specific ordinal number before this word, usually roman numbers are used. Also, western numbers can be used, but a roman numeral is always considered a more elegant choice. If you don't feel confident with roman numbers.

il XIV secolo (read il quattordicesimo secolo) = the 14th century

nel XX secolo (read nel ventesimo secolo) = in the 20th century

The English forms BC (Before Christ) and AD (Anno Domini = Latin for "in the Year of the Lord") correspond to Italian forms aC (avanti Cristo) and dC (dopo Cristo = after Christ).

Only when two or more centuries are mentioned, the numeral part may come after the word secolo:

nel I secolo aC e nel III secolo dC = in the 1st century BC and in the 3rd century AD

may be turned into

nei secoli I aC e III dC = literally in the centuries 1st BC and 3rd AD

DATES

Italian dates are always in the following standard:

!   day, always spelled in western numbers

!   month, spelled either with letters (abbreviated or in full length) or with numbers (western or roman)

!   year, spelled either in full length or by the last two digits.

Separators are more often hyphens (-) or dots (. or ·), but backslashes (/) are also common, or no separator at all.

A few examples: 3 · 5 · 1970 = May 3rd, 1970 (...never March 5th!)

1 gen 1990 = January 1st, 1990

2 - XII - 65 = December 2nd, 1965

494

Unlike English dates, Italian ones need a definite article, referred to the word giorno (= day). As all articles, they require a phonetical match with the number of the day (the first word following the article).

Another important difference is that in Italian date numbers are cardinal, not ordinal as in English:

il 25 aprile (read il venticinque aprile) = April 25th (or on April 25th)

dal 7 giugno (read dal sette giugno) = as of June 7th)

Only number 1 may be read in both ways:

l'1 maggio (read l'uno maggio) = May 1st (or on May 1st)

can also be turned into

il 1º maggio (read il primo maggio) = May 1st (or on May 1st)

Notice how in this case a roman number is never used.

The cardinal number is more common when the month is followed by a year, in a full date:
1.12.1955 would be l'uno dicembre millenovecentocinquantacinque

But

1.12 would more often be il primo dicembre

Anyway, both forms are correct in either case.

Quite often, the simple preposition di (of) is used between number and month: il 24 settembre = September 24th (or on September 24th)

can also be

il 24 di settembre = the 24th of September (or on the 24th of September)

In official or burocratic papers, dates may be read by their numbers: 23.8.97 could sound as ventitré otto novantasette

WHAT TIME IS IT ?

The expression what time is it? in Italian is che ore sono? (literally "which hours are they?"), but also the singular form che ora è? is used.

Italian hours always need a definite article, referring to the noun ora (hour), which is though usually omitted. l'una one o'clock le due two o'clock le tre three o'clock .... le dodici twelve o'clock

It should be noticed how the article is always plural, because the full expressions would be "the two hours", "the three hours", and so on; only one o'clock is singular. All forms are obviously feminine, because the noun ora to which they refer is feminine too.

Italian can use both the 12-hour format and the 24-hour format, the latter being more formal (used in timetables, or in official speech, etc.).

le tredici	one o'clock PM
le quattordici	two o'clock PM
le quindici	three o'clock PM
.....	.....
le ventiquattro	twelve o'clock PM

A practical rule to convert the 24-hour format into the 12-hour format is to subtract 2 from the hour, and then 10:

21:00 21-2 = 19, then 19-10 = 9   9:00 PM

In common speech, though, the 12-hour format is much more commonly used; the "AM" or "PM" specification is usually omitted, since the context of the sentence will provide enough elements to understand which of the two is the right one.

Should the time be possibly mistaken, the hour can be followed by the expressions antemeridiane (= antemeridian, AM) or pomeridiane (= postmeridian, PM). But in common speech and in most texts more common expressions take the place of these "official" ones:

di mattina or del mattino (= in the morning), from 4 or 5 AM to 12 AM

di pomeriggio or del pomeriggio (= in the afternoon), from 1 PM to 5 PM (or 6 PM)

di sera (= in the evening), from 6 or 7 PM to 11 PM

di notte (= at night), , from midnight to 2 or 3 AM

Notice how some forms may use either simple preposition di, or the relevant compound preposition, as an alternative. The form di mattina has del mattino as an alternative (mattina is feminine, mattino is masculine, but both nouns mean morning).

le dieci di mattina (or le dieci del mattino) = ten o'clock AM

le due di pomeriggio or le quattordici = two o'clock PM

le dieci di sera or le ventidue = ten o'clock PM

le due di notte = two o'clock AM

Obviously, time limits are not too strict:

le quattro del mattino (4 o'clock AM) could also be le quattro di notte

le sei di pomeriggio (6 o'clock PM) could also be le sei di sera

etc.

Since hours require a plural article, also verb tenses need to be in plural form:

sono le cinque = it's five o'clock

sono le quindici = it's three o'clock PM

sono le cinque = it's five o'clock

...BUT

è l'una = it's one o'clock

Due to the need of a definite article, only compound preposition are used:

dalle due alle quattro = from two to four

all'una = at one o'clock

sono tornato alle dieci = I came back at ten o'clock

The word ora (literally hour, but whose meaning corresponds to English o'clock) is seldom used, either in case the hour might be mistaken with a different numerical category, or to give emphasis to the expression: il treno parte alle ore quattordici = the train leaves at two o'clock PM la bomba esplose alle ore sedici in punto = the bomb exploded at four o'clock PM sharp But omitting the noun, both sentences would be perfectly correct all the same. The last sentence also shows how the expression in punto corresponds to English sharp (referred to an hour).

FRACTIONS OF THE HOUR

When mentioning fractions of hours, the terms minutes (in Italian: minuti) is usually omitted.

The English form past is translated e (= and):

le cinque e venti = twenty (minutes) past five

le quindici e cinque = five (minutes) past three PM

The English form to is translated meno (= less):

le otto meno dieci = ten to eight

le tre meno cinque = five to three

In Italian, the form "e" can be used all round the hour:

le sette e quaranta = ten to eight

le due e cinquantanove = two fifty-nine (one minute to three)

The form "meno" instead is only used for a time length of twenty minutes or less:

le nove meno cinque = five to nine

le tre meno venti = twenty to three

So 7:50 could be either le sette e cinquanta (more formal) or le otto meno dieci (more colloquial). Instead 4:35 would always be le quattro e trentacinque.

A very colloquial form is also mancano ..... minuti alle ...., which uses the verb mancare = to lack, with the meaning of "a few minutes (are lacking) to reach the given hour":

sono le sette meno dieci = it's ten to seven

mancano dieci minuti alle sette = it's ten minutes to seven

sono le due meno cinque = it's five to two

mancano cinque minuti alle due = it's five minutes to two

sono le dieci meno uno = it's one to ten

manca un minuto alle dieci = it's one minute to ten

Unlike the verb essere in the previous form, here mancare refers to the number of minutes, not to the hour: for this reason the last sentence above needs a singular inflection (manca), since un minuto (= one minute) is singular.

When using this colloquial form, the word minuti (or minuto if singular) must be used.

This form exists also without a verb:

mancano dieci minuti alle sette = it's ten (minutes) to seven

dieci minuti alle sette = ten (minutes) to seven

mancano cinque minuti alle due = it's five (minutes) to two cinque minuti alle due = five (minutes) to two

When the time fraction is ..:15, ..:30 or ..:45 minutes, the expressions un quarto (a quarter), mezza (half) and tre quarti (three quarters) are commonly used:

le cinque e un quarto = a quarter past five

le otto e mezza = half past eight (notice the feminine form mezza, related to ora = hour)

le due e tre quarti (or le tre meno un quarto) = two forty-five (or a quarter to three)

le sei meno un quarto = a quarter to six

Also in this case it is possible to use the form manca un quarto alle ....

5:45 = un quarto alle cinque (literally a quarter to five), though other colloquial alternatives could be le cinque e tre quarti, or le sei meno un quarto, while the "official" form (in timetables, etc.) would be le cinque e quarantacinque.

Since un quarto is singular, notice how the verb inflection too (manca) is singular.

MEZZOGIORNO, LA MEZZA, MEZZANOTTE

The Italian word for mid-day is mezzogiorno, and it can be used in place of le dodici (12 AM); unlike the latter, mezzogiorno does not need an article, and since it is singular, it requires singular verb tenses. Also fractions of the hour can be referred to mezzogiorno:

è mezzogiorno = it's mid-day

sono le dodici = it's twelve o'clock

partiranno a mezzogiorno e venti = they will leave at twenty (minutes) past twelve

partiranno alle dodici e venti = they will leave at twenty (minutes) past twelve

era mezzogiorno e tre quarti = it was twelve forty-five

erano le dodici e tre quarti = it was twelve forty-five

sarà mezzogiorno meno un quarto = it might be a quarter to twelve

saranno le dodici meno un quarto = it might be a quarter to twelve

As you see, mezzogiorno rejects the definite article, thus requiring simple prepositions, and is singular; le dodici instead needs the article, therefore it requires compound prepositions, and is a plural form.

The specific time 12:30 is commonly referred to as la mezza (the half), but it is only used alone. è quasi la mezza = it's almost half past twelve torno da scuola alla mezza = I come back from school at half past twelve

The Italian for midnight is mezzanotte, and it it is often preferred to le dodici (12 PM), since the latter is more often used for 12 AM.

Also either alone or in fractions of the hour.

Also mezzanotte can be used with fractions of the hour; as mezzogiorno, it rejects an article, it needs simple prepositions, and behaves as a singular noun.

è mezzanotte = it's midnight tornò a mezzanotte e cinque = he/she came back at five (minutes) past midnight

fino a mezzanotte meno un quarto = until a quarter to midnight

da mezzanotte alle due = from midnight to two o'clock

TIME ADVERBS & DURATION FORMS

Before introducing duration forms, it is useful to memorize a few adverbs related to time, some of which have already been used in the previous exercises: try to learn them, little by little, as they occur quite often, both in texts and in common speech.

oggi	today
domani	tomorrow
dopodomani	the day after tomorrow
ieri	yesterday
l'altroieri	the day before yesterday (this Italian adverb requires a definite article)
adesso	now
ora	now (remember that, as a noun, ora means hour)
spesso	often
frequentemente	frequently
qualche volta	sometimes (literally: "some time")
talvolta	sometimes

di rado	seldom	
raramente		rarely
prima		before
dopo		after
durante	during	
sempre	always	
mai		never

These adverbs follow the same scheme as adjectives: they may be used either before or after the main subject. Which of the two positions depends on which part of the sentence is more emphasized, since in Italian language the last part of the sentence usually carries more "stress":

uso molto spesso il computer = I use the computer very often (emphasis on the computer)

uso il computer molto spesso = I use the computer very often (emphasis on very often)

di rado lavoro = I seldom work (slight emphasis on work)

lavoro di rado = I seldom work (seldom is more emphasized)

The two adverbs sempre and mai, instead, are used according to a further rule, which will be the subject of a future paragraph. By now, simply memorize their meaning.

DURATION FORMS

The simple preposition da (or its compound, depending on whether the subject requires a definite article or not) is used to express the starting time of a duration, thus translating several English forms:

! the form as of ...:

da giovedì = as of thursday

da oggi = as of today

dal 13 maggio = as of May 13th

! the form since ...:

da giugno del 1958 = since June 1958

dall'altroieri = since the day before yesterday

da mercoledì scorso = since last Wednesday

da quel giorno = since that day

! the form from ..., when followed by to ... (see below for the second part of this expression): dal 1975 al 1980 = from 1975 to 1980 da settembre a ottobre = from September to October

dalle cinque alle nove = from five (o'clock) to nine

da adesso in poi = from now on

The simple preposition a ... indicates the end of a time length.

Remember that when a is followed by a vowel (especially another a), it changes to ad.

This preposition translates English to, when introduced by from (same case as above):

da lunedì a domenica = from monday to Sunday

dal lunedì alla domenica = from (every) monday to (every) Sunday

dalle cinque alle sette = from five (o'clock) to seven

da maggio ad agosto = from May to August (notice ad instead of a, due to agosto)

But, the same preposition a is also used for stating an hour, as English at:

alle sette e mezza = at half past seven

alle nove meno dieci = at ten to nine

all'una e venti = at twenty past one

a mezzanotte = at midnight

When a time length has no definite origin, and only the finishing time is stated, fino a ... is used to express the latter, translating several English forms:

!   the form until (or till):

fino a sabato = until saturday

fino a domani = until tomorrow

fino alle cinque = until five o'clock

!   the form up to ... (also generally used with numbers, measures, etc.):

fino al 1950 = up to 1950

fino ad ora = up to now (notice ad instead of a, because of ora)

fino al quindici = up to number fifteen

fino a sei metri = up to six metres

fino a qui = up to here

!   the form through ...:

catalogo dei prezzi fino al 31 giugno = price catalogue through June 31st

questa tessera è valida fino al 2001 = this card is valid through 2001

501

Sometimes, when the deadline is not a given day but a month, a year, etc. (as in the second sample sentence), the adjective tutto = all is added to the form (fino a tutto ...), to indicate that the month or year mentioned is included within the period. Therefore, the above-mentioned sentence would often be: questa tessera è valida fino a tutto il 2001

The English preposition for ..., expressing duration, is translated by preposition per ...: per cinque settimane = for five weeks

ho lavorato lì per cinque giorni = I have worked there for five days

l'ingresso è gratis per tutto il 1995 = the entrance is free for the whole (year) 1995

In expressing time length, English always uses for + the duration of the action, but Italian also uses another form: da + the duration of the action.

This is the only tricky bit in translating these forms into Italian, so be sure to focus it well. lavoro da due anni = I have been working for two years

non vedo Paolo da cinque mesi = I haven't seen Paul for five months

la radio non funziona da due settimane = the radio has not been working for two weeks

piove da due giorni = it has been raining for two days

In Italian, this form is rather different from the previous one, although it might seem similar in English:

ho lavorato per cinque settimane = I have worked for five weeks

this sentence mainly gives stress to the time length of the action, and little importance is given to when the action started;

lavoro da cinque settimane = I have been working for five weeks the English form gives stress to the fact that the action has taken place habitually for the given time (i.e. "I have worked every day for a time length of five weeks"), while the Italian form carries a meaning of "I have been working every day starting from five weeks ago": this is why preposition da is used, as if to say "from a starting moment, five weeks ago".

So, as a practical rule, preposition per gives a sense of duration in time as any similar English form, while da always has a meaning of "time elapsed from that moment", either referring to the future (translating English from, as of, etc. as explained in an earlier part of this paragraph), or in the past, as in this case, though in English it has to be turned into a different form. Also notice that when preposition da is used for English since, the Italian tense always refers to the latest moment of the action, as if looking at the action back in time, while the English tense refers to the starting moment of the action, or anyway to an earlier time than its end: non vedo Paolo dal 1975 = I have not seen Paul since 1975 vedo (present tense) is referred to "now", while have seen (present perfect tense) refers to "1975" dormo da due ore = I have been sleeping for two hours dormo (present tense) is referred to "now", while have been refers to "two hours ago"

Also when the action happens in the past, there is a difference between the Italian tense and the English one: non vedevo Paolo dal 1975 = I had not seen Paul since 1975 vedevo (imperfect tense) is referred to the time of the sentence, while had seen (present perfect tense) refers to an earlier time ("1975") dormivo da due ore = I had been sleeping for two hours dormivo is referred to the time of the sentence, while had been refers to an earlier time ("two hours before")

ADVERBS prima, dopo, durante

The English adverb before is translated prima. In Italian it is always followed by preposition di when introducing a noun or a date; instead, it is followed by conjunction che (that) when introducing a subordinate clause, requiring subjunctive tenses.

This page only focuses the first case (prima di ...):

prima di giugno = before Jun

e prima del 1970 = before 1970

prima di domani = before tomorrow

lunedì viene prima di martedì = monday comes before Tuesday

The same adverb may also translate before in sequences (almost suggesting a progression in time):

il sette viene prima dell'otto = number seven comes before number eight

la M viene prima della N = (letter) M comes before (letter) N

The adverb after is translated dopo. In Italian it is usually not followed by any preposition (although di is needed in a very limited number of situations, which will be explained in a future paragraph).

dopo giugno = after June

dopo il 1970 = after 1970

dopo i fatti di ieri = after yesterday's events

martedì viene dopo lunedì = tuesday comes after Monday

Also in this case, dopo can be used for sequences, as well:

l'otto viene dopo il sette = number eight comes after number seven

la F viene dopo la E = (letter) F comes after (letter) E

The adverb during ... is translated durante ... (without any preposition), and it is used in the same way as in English:

durante la vacanza = during the holiday

durante l'anno = during the year

abbiamo mangiato il popcorn durante la partita = we eat the popcorn during the match

CHAPTER 4: FAMILY AND RELATIVES

A typical Italian family is composed of father, mother, and oft en just one child, because Italy is one of the countries in the world with the lowest birthrate. Since most Italians live with their parents until they get married, and reside in or near the town where they were born, family relations remain strong. However, the rate of divorce has been growing, especially among people with young children, as have unconventional families.

It is still common for elderly parents who are no longer independent to join their children's household. Whey they cannot, the alternative to a retirement home is to remain at home assisted by a badante (caretaker), usually an immi- grant woman from eastern or central Europe, South America, or the Philippines.

il bambino; il fi glio	child
la famiglia	family
la fi glia	daughter
il fi glio	son
i fratelli [e/o le sorelle] (pl.)	siblings
il fratello	brother
i genitori (pl.)	parents
la madre	mother
la mamma	mom
il padre	father
il papà	dad
la sorella	sister
l(a)'unità famigliare; la famiglia	household
I miei fi gli sono già grandi.	My children are grown up.
Sono in cinque tra fratelli e sorelle	They are five siblings.

Close relatives

la cognata	sister-in-law
il cognato	brother-in-law
il cugino	cousin
il gemello	twin
il genero	son-in-law

il nipote	grandson; nephew
la nipote	granddaughter; niece
i nipotini (pl.)	grandchildren
la nonna	grandmother
il nonno	grandfather
i nonni	grandparents
la nuora	daughter-in-law
il, la parente	relative
la suocera	mother-in-law
il suocero	father-in-law
la zia	aunt
lo zio	uncle
Vedi quella ragazza? È mia nipote.	See that girl? She's my niece.
Vedi quella ragazza? È mia nipote. Carlo frequenta poco i suoi parenti.	See that girl? She's my granddaughter. Carlo doesn't see his relatives much.

Engagements and weddings

la coppia	couple
la fidanzata	fiancée
il fidanzato	fiancé
il marito	husband
la moglie	wife
la sposa	bride
lo sposo	groom
lo sposo; il, la consorte	spouse
il testimone	best man
la testimone	bridesmaid
Sono una bella coppia.	They are a nice couple.
Oggi sposi!	Just married!

Other relationships

l(o, a)'amante	lover

505

il compagno; il, la partner	companion; partner
la fi gliastra (derogatory, rarely used)	stepdaughter
il fi gliastro (derogatory, rarely used)	stepson
il fi glio adottivo	adopted son
la matrigna (derogatory, rarely used)	stepmother
il patrigno (derogatory, rarely used)	stepfather
la mia, tua, sua, etc. ragazza	my, your, his, etc., girlfriend
il mio, tuo, suo, etc. ragazzo	my, your, her, etc., boyfriend
il, la single	single man/woman
la vedova	widow
il vedovo	widower

Sono molto attaccata ai fi gli di mio marito.

I'm very attached to my stepchildren.

Le single sono in aumento.

The number of single women is growing.

Used in the plural, a masculine noun indicates a group of males and a group of males and females: i fi gli, sons or sons and daughters; le fi glie means daughters. Some nouns are gender spe- cifi c in the singular and the plural:

il fratello / la sorella	brother/sister
il genero / la nuora	son-in-law/daughter-in-law
il marito / la moglie	husband/wife
il maschio / la femmina	male/female
il padre; il papà / la madre; la mamma	
father; dad / mother; mom	
l'uomo / la donna	man/woman

Articles

In Italian the defi nite articles are: il, lo, l(o)', i, gli, la, l(a)', le; the indefi nite articles: un, uno, una/ un' (a, an). We can also use indefi nite qualifi ers such as un po' di (a little of; some), molto (very; much; a lot of), poco (too little), tanto (so much), and the preposizione articolata (preposition article) del, dello (dell'), and della (dell', some).

With uncountable nouns, Italian uses the defi nite article and indefi nite quantifi ers, but not the indefi nite article un, uno, etc. We can convey indefi nite quantities of countable nouns in the plural with alcuni (some; any; a few), qualche (some, followed by the singular, but conveying a plural meaning), molte (many; a lot), poche (few), tante (so many), and dei, degli, and delle (some):

l(o)'aff etto (countable and uncountable)	affection; care
l(o)'amore (countable and uncountable)	love; love affair
l(o)'anello di fi danzamento	engagement ring
l(o)'anniversario	anniversary
la bugia	lie
il divorzio	divorce
la fede [nuziale]	wedding ring
la fi ducia (uncountable)	trust; faith
il litigio	argument
la luna di miele	honeymoon
il matrimonio	marriage; wedding
le nozze (pl.)	wedding
la promessa	promise
la relazione [extraconiugale]	(love) aff air
la separazione	separation
il tradimento	betrayal

Provo un grande aff etto per te.

I feel great aff ection for you.

Casanova è famoso per i suoi amori.

Casanova is famous for his love aff airs.

Possessive adjectives carry the article. Th ey do not when they refer to family members in the singular form (note, however, that the possessive adjective loro always carries the article): mia madre (my mother); suo marito (her husband); nostro fi glio (our son), unless a qualifi er, includ- ing a possessive adjective, accompanies the noun: la mia mamma (my mom); il fi glio più grande (the older son). Possessives are coordinated in gender with the person (or thing) to which they re- fer, and in number with the owner and with the "thing" owned.

la zia mia e di mia sorella → nostra zia   our aunt

lo zio di Pietro → suo zio   his uncle

il gatto di Gianna → il suo gatto	her cat
le gatte di Gianna → le sue gatte	her cats

Possessive pronouns always carry the article. And i miei, i suoi, used by themselves, mean: my parents, relatives, etc. We do not use it for the third person plural: i loro.

Possessive adjectives and pronouns

il mio, la mia, i miei, le mie	my; mine
il tuo, la tua, i tuoi, le tue	your; yours
il suo, la sua, i suoi, le sue	his; her; hers; its
il Suo, la Sua, i Suoi, le Sue	your; yours (you formal, sing.)
il nostro, la nostra, i nostri, le nostre	our; ours
il vostro, la vostra, i vostri, le vostre	your; yours
il loro, la loro, i loro, le loro	theirs
il Loro, la Loro, i Loro, le Loro	your; yours (you formal, pl.)

Verbs

abbracciare	to embrace; to hug
abitare (con) (aux. avere); vivere (con)	
to live (with)	
(aux. avere/essere)	
aiutare	to help
amare	to love
andare d'accordo (con)	to get along well (with)
corteggiare	to court
divorziare (da) (aux. avere)	to divorce (from)
fare l'amore (con)	to make love (with)
fi danzarsi (con)	to get engaged (with)
fi darsi (di)	to trust
innamorarsi (di)	to fall in love (with)
lasciare	to leave
litigare (con) (aux. avere)	to argue (with)
odiare; detestare	to hate

508

perdonare	to forgive
piacere (a)	to like; to be pleasing to
promettere (a) (aux. avere)	to promise (to)
rimproverare	to scold
sposare	to marry
tradire	to betray
viziare	to spoil (a person)
voler bene (a) (aux. avere)	to care for; to love
Le piacciono i bambini.	She likes children.
Mio nonno ha vissuto bene e a lungo.	My grandfather had a good and long life.
Bianca è vissuta per molti anni in Brasile	Bianca lived many years in Brazil.

In the infinitive, Italian verbs end in -are, -ere, or -ire: am-are (to love), promett-ere (to promise), pun-ire (to punish). In the refl exive form, they end in -arsi: sposarsi (to get married), -ersi: prendersi cura di (to take care of), and -irsi: sentirsi (to feel) (aux. essere). Th e reflexive form also indicates a reciprocal action, conveyed in English with the phrases one another, each other, mutually, etc.

Si è comportata male.

She misbehaved. / She behaved badly.

Elena e Vincenzo si amano.

Elena and Vincenzo love each other.

Giovanna e Filippo si odiano

Giovanna and Filippo hate each other.

Reflexive pronouns

mi	myself
ti	yourself
si	himself/herself; oneself; itself
Si	yourself (you formal, sing.)
ci	ourselves
vi	yourselves
si	themselves
Si	yourselves (you formal, pl.)

The pronoun si also means one, people, we, you, they, etc. Si is used as an impersonal subject which may or may not include the speaker.

Si va al cinema stasera?

Are we going to the movies tonight?

Si dice in giro che la sua ditta stia fallendo.

People say that his fi rm is going bankrupt.

Used impersonally, si can be followed by the third person singular or plural.

Si apre il negozio alle 9.

The store opens at 9 a.m.

Si aprono le porte del teatro alle 9.

The theater's doors open at 9 p.m.

Describing family relationships

affettuoso	affectionate
affezionato (a)	attached (to)
amato	loved
divorziato	divorced
fidanzato	engaged
innamorato (di)	in love (with)
intimo	intimate
materno	motherly; maternal
paterno	fatherly; paternal
perdonato	forgiven
promesso	promised
sposato (a/con)	married (to/with)
tradito	betrayed
vedovo	widowed

Elsa è una bambina aff ettuosa.

Elsa is an aff ectionate child.

Mio fratello è aff ezionato al suo cane.

My brother is attached to his dog.

10 practice makes perfect Italian Vocabulary

Pronouns When we refer to someone whom we have already mentioned, we can use subject, direct object, or indirect object pronouns.

Subject pronouns

io	I
tu	you
lui/lei	he/she (including pets)
esso/essa	it
noi	we
voi	you
loro; essi/esse	they

Direct object pronouns

ATTACHED TO OR	AFTER THE VERB	BEFORE THE VERB
mi	me	me
ti	te	you
lo/la	—	him/her; it
—	lui/lei	him/her (persons and pets only)
ci	noi	us
vi	voi	you
li/le	—	them (persons and things)
—	loro	them (persons only)

Indirect object pronouns

ATTACHED TO OR		AFTER THE VERB	BEFORE THE VERB	
mi	me	a/per me	to me	
ti	you	a/per te	to you	
gli —	him/her	a/per lui/lei	to him/her (persons and pets) a/per esso/essa to it (things)	
ci	us	a/per noi	to us	
vi	you	a/per voi	to you	
gli	them	a/per loro; loro	to them (persons and pets) a/per essi/esse to them (things)	—

CHAPTER 5: PEOPLE

Italians spend their leisure time with friends as much as with family members. Limited geographical mobility enables people to maintain friendships made even in their childhood or teenage years. People become friends with their peers in col- lege, or through sports, political parties, religious functions, and participation in the countless volunteer organizations existing in Italy, more than through their work environment.

il carattere	character
il cognome	last name
la donna	woman
l(o)'essere umano (m. and f.)	human being
la gente (collective sing.) / le persone; le genti / i popoli	people; peoples
l(o)'individuo (m. and f.)	individual; person
il nome (proprio)	(given) name
la persona (f. and m.)	person
la personalità	personality
la ragazza	girl
il ragazzo	boy
il tipo / la tipa	kind of person; guy; character
l(o)'umore	mood
l(o)'uomo, gli uomini	man
Olga è un bel tipo!	Olga is quite a character!
Sei di cattivo umore?	Are you in a bad mood?

Describing personalities

aggressivo	aggressive
antipatico	off -putting
buono; bravo	good
cattivo	bad
curioso	curious
debole	weak; fickle

dolce	sweet
forte	strong
furbo	cunning
generoso	generous
normale	ordinary; normal
paziente	patient
prepotente	overbearing
profondo	profound
saggio	wise
serio	serious
severo	strict
sicuro di sé	confident
simpatico	nice
superficiale	superficial
timido	shy vivace lively; vivacious

Vittorio è davvero antipatico. Vittorio is really off -putting.

Tuo fi glio è molto prepotente. Your son is very overbearing.

Personality traits

la bontà	goodness
la curiosità	curiosity
la debolezza	weakness
la forza	strength
la furbizia	cunning
la generosità	generosity
la normalità	normality
la saggezza	wisdom
la serietà	seriousness
la stima; il rispetto	respect

Gandhi è un esempio di saggezza.

Gandhi is an example of wisdom.

La bambina prende tutto con serietà.

The little girl takes everything seriously.

We can derive nouns from adjectives that describe personality traits by adding various endings. One of the most common ending is -ità (English -ity, as in curios-ity), which is added to an adjective by dropping the end-vowel, and sometimes modifying it.

curioso	curiosità	curious	curiosity
serio	serietà	serious	seriousness
buono	bontà	good	goodness

In Italian most of these nouns are feminine and uncountable, take the defi nite article, and cannot be used in the plural. We can convey single instances through a periphrasis: un atto di bontà (a good deed), (degli) atti di bontà (good deeds), un atto di generosità (an act of generosity), (degli) atti di generosità (acts of generosity), etc.

Adverbs

Adverbs enable us to add important qualifi cations to situations, actions, and descriptions, by modifying verbs, adjectives, nouns, other adverbs, and entire sentences. With a few exceptions, they change neither gender nor number.

Parla normalmente.	She speaks normally.
La sua gamba è molto debole.	Her leg is very weak.
Sei arrivato troppo tardi.	You arrived too late.
bene	well; good
curiosamente	curiously
debolmente	weakly
dolcemente	sweetly
forte; fortemente	strongly; with great energy
generosamente	generously
male	badly
normalmente	normally
seriamente	seriously

In Italian most adverbs derive from adjectives. Adverbs that emphasize how something is, happens, or is done, are formed usually by adding -mente (-ly, -ily) to the feminine singular of adjectives in -o: aggressiv-o → aggressiv-a → aggressiva-mente (aggressively); or to the singular of adjectives in -e: dolce → dolce-mente (sweetly). When the last syllable of adjectives in -e ends in -le or -re, the fi nal vowel is omitted: umil-e → umilmente (humbly).

Essere

We can add an adjective to the verb essere (to be) to talk about a state of aff airs or a situation. Th e verb does not take any subject and is always in the singular. It can be followed by the present or the past infi nitive, or by a declarative dependent clause introduced by che, when we wish to emphasize who is or should be performing an action. When the main clause conveys possibility, uncertainty, or a subjective opinion or feeling, the verb of the dependent clause will be in the subjunctive.

514

È importante vederla.

It's important to see her.

È certo che Adriana è partita.

It's certain that Adriana left.

È commovente che tu lo abbia perdonato. It's moving that you forgave him.

Here follows a list of common adjectives used with the verb essere.

carino; bello	nice
certo; sicuro	certain
commovente	moving
curioso	curious
difficile	hard; difficult
facile	easy
giusto	right; fair
importante	important
normale	normal
sbagliato	wrong
strano	strange; weird

Social relationships

l(a)'amicizia	friendship
l(o)'amico	friend
la compagnia	company
il complimento	compliment
la conoscenza (f. and m.)	acquaintance
la conversazione	conversation
l(o)'estraneo; lo sconosciuto	stranger
il flirt	flirt;flirtation
il giovanotto	young man

il pettegolezzo	(piece of) gossip
il regalo	gift
la richiesta	request
lo scherzo	joke
(la) signora	lady; Madam; Ms.
(il) signor	gentleman; Sir
(la) signorina	young lady; Ms.; Miss
il silenzio	silence
la solitudine	loneliness; solitude
il vicino [di casa]	neighbor
la visita	visit

«Hai avuto una storia»? «No, solo un flirt». Sono solo pettegolezzi.	"Did you have an aff air?" "No, just a flirtation." It's just gossip.

Keeping company and socializing

accompagnare	to accompany; to go with
annoiare	to bore
aspettare; attendere	to wait (for)
aspettarsi (da)	to expect (from)
chiamare; telefonare (a)	to call
chiamarsi	to be called; to be named
comportarsi	to behave
conoscere (aux. avere); sapere (aux. avere)	to know

Note that conoscere means to be acquainted with; whereas sapere means to know something, to know how infinitive.

Conosci mio fratello?	Do you know my brother?
Sapete la poesia a memoria?	Do you know the poem by heart?
Sapete come fare ad arrivare a casa?	Do you know how to get home?

dare/darsi del Lei	to be on formal terms
dare/darsi del tu	to be on familiar terms
dire (a)	to say (to)
domandare (a); chiedere (a)	to ask fare

una domanda (a)	to ask a question
frequentare	to frequent
importare (a)	to mind; to matter (to)
mettersi in contatto (con)	to get in touch (with)
offendere	to offend
parlare (a/con) (aux. avere)	to speak (to/with); to talk (to/with)
passare (da)	to stop by
ringraziare	to thank
rispondere (a); rispondere al telefono	to answer; to answer the phone
salutare	to greet
scrivere (a)	to write (to)
scusare; chiedere scusa (a); chiedere permesso (a)	to excuse to apologize (with)
spettegolare (aux. avere)	to gossip
stare zitto	to be quiet
toccare a qualcuno (in coda)	to be someone's turn (in line)
uscire (con qualcuno)	to go out (with someone)
vedere; andare a vedere; andare a trovare	to visit
Ti dispiace se abbasso la radio?	Do you mind if I turn down the radio?
Tocca a me, adesso.	It's my turn.

When we wish to convey how something is done we can use an adverb, or a complement introduced by con (with) noun, in maniera feminine adjective (in a   manner), or in modo masculine adjective (in a   way). Experience and context will tell you when it is idiomatically more appropriate to use the adverb, and when to use the complement con noun, or in modo / maniera adjective.

Li ha rimproverati severamente. → Li ha rimproverati con severità. He reproached them severely / with great severity.

Parlava curiosamente. → Parlava in maniera curiosa / modo curioso. She was speaking curiously / in a curious manner/way.

Sharing events with others

accettare	to accept

augurare	to wish
brindare (a)	to toast
celebrare; festeggiare	to celebrate
dare il benvenuto (a)	to welcome
invitare	to invite
offrire (a)	to offer (to)
ospitare	to host
portare	to bring
prendere;portare	to take
presentare (a)	to introduce (to)
regalare	to give
ricevere	to receive; to have someone over
rifiutare	to refuse
Posso presentarla al nostro vescovo?	May I introduce you to our bishop?
Ricevono molto.	They have people over quite often.

Social occasions

l(o)'appuntamento	appointment
la buona educazione (sing.);	
le buone maniere (pl.)	good manners
la cattiva educazione (sing.); la	
maleducazione (sing.); le cattive maniere (pl.)	bad manners
il compleanno	birthday
il comportamento	behavior
la domanda	question
il favore; il piacere	favor
la festa / il party	party
la gentilezza	kindness
l(o)'invito	invitation
il numero di telefono / telefonico	telephone number
l(o, a)'ospite; l(o)'invitato	guest
l(o, a)'ospite; il padrone / la padrona di casa	host; hostess

i ringraziamenti (pl.)	thanks
la risposta	answer
Puoi farmi un favore?	Could you do me a favor?
Mamma mia, che maleducazione!	Good gracious, what bad manners!

Responses

As Donatella and Marianna's conversation shows, adverbs, nouns, adjectives, names, and verbs can be used as interjections, invariable parts of speech which can express emotions on the part of the speaker—Ouch!—or carry specifi c meanings—Hello!

Rosanna non viene. Peccato!	Rosanna's not coming. Pity!
Mamma, ho fame!	Mom, I'm hungry!
arrivederci (informal); arrivederla (formal)	good-bye
buona fortuna	good luck
ciao (informal); pronto (when answering the phone)	hello
cin cin; salute	cheers (when toasting)
congratulazioni; complimenti	congratulations
di niente	not at all
forse	maybe
grazie	thank you
mi scusi; scusi	excuse me; sorry
no	no
per favore	please
prego	you're welcome
sì	yes
Pronto, chi parla?	Hello, who's speaking?
Ciao, Carla, come stai?	Hello, Carla, how are you?

Describing social situations

da solo	(all) alone; by oneself
gentile	kind
(molto) impegnato; occupato	busy
insieme	together
libero	free
malvolentieri	reluctantly

personale	personal
(in) pochi	few (people)
pronto	ready
scortese; sgarbato	impolite
solo	alone
(in) tanti	a lot of (people)
volentieri; con piacere	gladly
Ha pitturato il garage da sola.	She painted the garage herself.
Siamo in tanti!	There are so many of us!

CHAPTER 6: ANIMALS

Gli Animali: Let's Talk Animals in Italian

In this chapter we will focus on Italian vocabulary related to animals, the word for an animal farm in Italian is a false friend. It is is fattoria or fattoria degli animali (the word fabbrica means factory in Italian). If you go to a farm in Italy, you may find some of the following animals:

La capra - goat

L'asino- donkey

Il cavallo- horse

Il maiale - pig

La mucca- cow

La pecora - sheep

La tartaruga- tortoise

Il pavone- peacock

Il gallo- rooster or cockerel

La gallina- hen

Il tacchino- turkey

L'anatra- duck

Il pappagallo- parrot

L'oca- goose

The word for 'zoo' in Italian is also 'zoo' but pronounced 'zoh'. It may also be called giardino zooligico, parco zoo, zoo safarior bioparco. Here you can find other animals, such as:

Il coccodrillo- crocodile

L'elefante- elephant

La giraffa- giraffe

L'ippopotamo- hippopotamus

Il leone- lion

L'orso- bear

Il serpente- snake

La scimmia- monkey

La tigre- tiger

La zebra- zebra

In the wild, these animals would live in the deserto(desert), giungla(jungle), foresta(forest), foresta pluviale(rainforest), savana(savannah), or paludi(wetlands or swamps). To see animals who normally live in the mare(sea), oceano(ocean), fiume(river) or lago(lake), you can go to an acquario(aquarium). In an acquarioyou may be able to see:

Lo squalo - shark

La medusa- jelly fish

Il delfino- dolphin

Il pinguino- penguin

La foca- seal

La lontra - otter

Il cavaluccio marino- sea horse

Il polpo - octopus

La razza- ray

If you're wondering how to talk about your pets in Italian, these are called animali domestici. Here below are some of the most common ones:

Il cane- dog

Il gatto- cat

Il coniglio - rabbit

Il criceto- hamster

Il topo- mouse

La tartaruga- tortoise

Il pesce- fish

La rana - frog

Here you can read a conversation about pets between two people in both Italian and English:

Hai un animale domestico?

No, non mi piacciono molto gli animali.

Davvero? A me piacciono molto!

Tu hai qualche animale domestico allora?

Sì, ne ho cinque.

Quali animali domestici hai?

Ho un canarino, un ratto, un porcellino d'india, una lucertola e una tarantola.

Wow, tanti!

Sì, fanno parte della mia famiglia.

Dove abitano?

Ho delle gabbie. Puoi venire a casa mia a vederli se vuoi?

No grazie!!!

Translation

Have you got a pet?

No, I don't like animals very much.

Really? I like them a lot!

So have you got some pets?

Yes, I have five.

What pets do you have?

I've got a canary, a rat, a guinea pig, a lizard and a tarantula.

Wow, so many!

Yes, they are a part of my family.

Where do they live?

I have some cages. You can come to my house to see them if you'd like?

No thank you!!!

Italian animals make different sounds to English animals, or maybe it is more correct to say that Italians have different ways of describing the sounds animals make, compared to in English. So, what sounds do animals make in Italian? Che versi fanni gli animali in italiano?

I cani abbaiano - dogs bark (bau bau - not woof woof as in English)

i gatti miagolano - cats meow (miao)

I leoni ruggiscono - lions roar (grrrr)

Le mucche muggiscono - cows moo (muuu)

Le api ronzano - bees buzz (zzzz)

I galli cantano - roosters sing (chicchirichí)

I serpenti sibilano - snakes hiss (zsss)

Gli uccelli cinguettano - birds chirp (cip cip)

There are many sayings in Italian related to animals, here is a selection below:

In bocca al lupo - good luck (literally, in the mouth of the wolf). The response is 'crepi!' - let it die!

Non c'è trippa per gatti - there is no hope of getting whatever it is you want (literally, theres no tripe for cats)

Correre dietro alle farfalle - wasting time or chasing after an unachievable goal (literally, chasing butterflies)

Sputare il rospo - spill the beans or spit it out i.e. get something off your chest (literally, spit out the toad)

Fare la civetta - to flirt (literally, to be an owl)

Avere altre gatte da pelare - to have other fish to fry (literally, to have other cats to skin)

Cavallo di battaglia - someone's forte or strong point (literally, battle horse)

Andare a letto con le galline - To go to bed early (literally, to go to bed with the chickens)

Lento come una lumaca - slow as a snail

Ubriaco come una scimmia - drunk as a skunk (literally, drunk as a monkey)

Chi dorme non piglia pesci - the early bird catches the worm (those who sleep don't catch fish)

I hope you have enjoyed this lesson about animals in Italian. In bocca al lupo!!

WORDS TO MEMORISE

l'anatra = the duck

l'asino = the donkey

la balena = the whale

il cammello = the camel

il cagnolino = the puppy

il cane = the dog

il canguro = the kangaroo

il cavallo = the horse

il cervo = the deer

il cigno = the swan

il coccodrillo = the crocodile

il coniglio = the rabbit

l'elefante = the elephant

la farfalla = the butterfly

la formica = the ant

la gallina = the hen

il gatto = the cat

il gattino = the kitten

il ghepardo = the cheetah

la giraffa = the giraffe

il leone = the lion

il lupo = the wolf

il maiale = the pig

la mosca = the fly

la mucca = the cow

l'orso (m) = the bear

la pecora = the sheep

il pesce = the fish

il pollo = the chicken

la rana = the frog

il rinoceronte = the rhino

il rospo = the toad

la scimmia = the monkey

lo scoiattolo = the squirrel

il serpente = the snake

lo squalo = the shark

lo struzzo = the ostrich

la tartaruga = the turtle

la tigre = the tiger

il topo = the mouse

il toro = the bull

il tricheco = the walrus

l'uccello = the bird

la mucca = the cow

la volpe = the fox

la zanzara = the mosquito

la zebra = the zebra

l'animiale domestico = the pet

CHAPTER 7: TRANSPORTATION

If you go to Italy either for work or for vacation, you might find your- self in need of a train or a bus. Unlike many North Americans, Italians are used to using public transportation on a daily basis, even if the service is not always great. And since gasoline is so expensive and public transportation is quite affordable in comparison, in most cases taking the train or the bus is the best solution. The only thing you may need is a little patience. If you must use the train, look for the stazione ferroviaria (train sta- tion). The ferrovia (railway) is well distributed throughout the country, and by train you can reach even secluded locations. Nowadays the system is undergoing some major changes and some train stations are closing. These stations will no longer offer ticketing and infor- mation services, but they will keep their stop. This means that even if a train station is closed, there will still be trains stopping there— however, perhaps on a less frequent basis.

Scusi, c'è un bar in questa stazione?

Pardon me, is there a bar in this train station?

SCOO-zee cheh oon bahr een QUEH-stah stah-tsee-OH-neh

Avrei bisogno di lasciare i miei bagagli in stazione. Come devo fare?

I'd need to leave my luggage in the station. What should I do?

Ah-VRAY bee-ZON-yo dee lah-SHAH-reh ee mee-AY bah-GAHL-yi een stah-tsee-OH-neh CO-meh DEH-vo FAH-reh

È aperta la biglietteria?

Is the ticket office open?

Eh ah-PAIR-tah lah beel-yet-tair-REE-ah

Dove sono gli orari dei treni?

Where are the train schedules?

DOH-veh SO-no lyee oh-RAH-ree day TREH-nee

In order to buy a train ticket, you must go to the biglietteria (ticket office) inside the train station. If you need information before purchas- ing your ticket, you must first go to the ufficio informazioni (informa- tion office).

In small train stations, the ticket office takes care of both tasks, but in larger stations the ticket office and the information office are clearly separated—be sure of where to go first to avoid waiting in a long line for nothing. If the ticket office is closed, buy your ticket at the biglietterie automatiche (automatic ticket machines) which can be found in every train station.

Train tickets can also be bought at some tabaccai (tobacco shops) or giornalai (newsagents) and online on the Trenitalia website (www.trenitalia.com), which has an English link. When purchasing your ticket, you must specify your destinazione (destination), whether you want a biglietto di sola andata (one-way ticket) or a biglietto di andata e ritorno (round-trip ticket), and the type of train you want to travel on.

Trains can be regionali (regional trains), Intercity (long-distance trains), and Eurostar (high-speed long-distance trains). On regional trains there is only one seating class, while on Intercity and Eurostar trains there are prima and sec- onda classe (first and second classes).

Scusi, dov'è la sala d'aspetto?

Pardon me, where is the waiting room?

SCOO-zee doh-VEH lah SAH-lah dah-SPET-toh

A che ora parte il prossimo Intercity per Milano?

What time does the next Intercity train to Milan leave?

Ah keh OH-rah PAHR-teh eel PROS- see-mo Intercity pair Mee-LAH-no

A che ora arriva questo treno a Genova?

What time does this train arrive in Genoa?

Ah keh OH-rah ahr-REE-vah QUEH-sto TREH-no ah JEHN-oh-vah

The most important thing to do before getting on the train is obliterare il biglietto (to validate your ticket), which means looking for small yellow machines which are usually located in the train station main hall and validating your ticket there.

These machines cannot be found on the binari (train platforms), so make sure you find them before looking for your platform.

You must validate your ticket before board- ing, because the controllore (train officer) will surely check your ticket while en route, and if your ticket is not validated, you'll get a fine. Train tickets have a limited validità (validity), which depends on the train type, so make sure to check your ticket for that.

It is also important to know that unused and unstamped tickets can be refunded at the ticket office.

Scusi, dov'è la carrozza 8?
Pardon me, where is the car number 8?
SCOO-zee doh-VEH lah cahr-ROTS-sah OT-toh

Scusi, quello è il mio posto. È prenotato.
Pardon me, that is my seat. It is reserved.
SCOO-zee QUEL-lo eh eel MEE-oh PO-sto Eh preh-no-TAH-toh

Non ha obliterato il biglietto.
You didn't validate your ticket.
Nohn ah oh-blee-tair-AH-toh eel beel-YET-toh

Trains differ greatly in terms of quality and services offered. Regional trains are the least expensive but do not offer any services. For example, on a regional train you will not find a carrozza ristorante (restaurant car), a carrozza letto (sleeping car), or onboard catering. S ometimes you may even have to be prepared for a lack of aria condizionata (air-conditioning) in summer or riscaldamento (heating) in winter. Regional trains are also slower than other trains as they stop in every city, but quite often they are the only way to reach certain destinations.

Intercity and Eurostar trains are more expensive but offer a better service.

They are much faster than regional trains, because they only stop in major cities. In terms of services offered, they have big- ger seats, catering on board, air-conditioning and heating, and posti prenotati (reserved seats). Remember that Trenitalia, Italy's national train company, is under-going some major changes, so be prepared for some ritardi (delays) while traveling.

C'è una carrozza ristorante su questo treno?
Is there a restaurant car on this train?
Cheh OO-nah cahr-ROTS-sah ree-sto-RAHN-teh soo QUEH-sto TREH-no

C'è una carrozza letto su questo treno?
Is there a sleeping car on this train?
Cheh OO-nah cahr-ROTS-sah LET-toh soo QUEH-sto TREH-no

Il treno è in ritardo?

Is the train running late?

Eel TREH-no eh een ree-TAR-doh

Airports and flights in Italy work exactly the same as everywhere else in the world, so if you are acquainted with all standard air travel procedures, you will know what to expect. Nowadays Alitalia, Italy's national airline, is experiencing a difficult period, so it is common to experience ritardi (delays) and scioperi (strikes). Italians previously used air travel to go abroad and relied on the train for internal trans- ports, mostly because internal flight fares were much higher than the cost of a train ticket.

Today, however, because of budget airlines, it is very common for Italians to use air travel for internal transports, too.

Every major city in Italy has one aeroporto (airport), while Rome and Milan have two. The airports are quite far from the city's down- town areas.

They can easily be reached in taxi (by taxi), in autobus (by bus), in treno (by train), or sometimes even in metropolitana (by sub- way). Once at the airport, look either for the arrivi (arrivals) or partenze (departures), depending on your needs.

If you are departing, you must fare il check-in (check in), passare i controlli (go through security controls), and then simply wait at the porta d'imbarco (gate) for your aereo (plane) to leave.

If you are just arriving, after passing though controllo passaporti (immigration and passport control) and dogana (customs), look for the ritiro bagagli (luggage claim) area and then look for the exit. If you are waiting for someone at the airport, go to the arrivals area and check if the flight is in orario (on time), in ritardo (delayed), or cancellato (cancelled).

Scusi, ho perso il volo Alitalia per Milano. Quand'è il prossimo?
Pardon me, I missed the Alitalia flight to Milan. When is the next one?
SCOO-zee oh PAIR-so eel VO-lo Ahl-ee-TAH-lee-ah pair Mee-LAH-no QUAHN-deh eel PROS-see-mo

Ho una coincidenza per Napoli. Dove devo andare?

I have a connecting flight for Naples. Where must I go?
Oh oo-nah coh-in-chee-DEHNT-sahpair NAH-poh-lee DOH-veh DEH-vo ahn-DAH-reh

Si informano i signori passeggeri che il volo è stato cancellato.
We inform passengers that the flight has been canceled.
See een-FOR-mah-no ee seen-YOR-ee pahs-sed-JAIR-ee keh eel VO-lo eh STAH-toh cahn-chel-LAH-toh

When it comes to customs, all countries have more or less the same regulations. For international flights, generally passengers are allowed to check two bags of about 50 pounds each.

Airlines place their own limits on the number, the size, and the weight of what can be carried onto a flight.

Il mio bagaglio è stato smarrito. Mi può aiutare?
My baggage has gotten lost. Can you help me?
Eel MEE-oh bah-GAHL-yo eh STAH-toh smahr-REE-toh Mee poo-OH aye-oo-TAH-reh

Every Italian city has a good public transportation system consisting of autobus (buses), which either run in centro (within the city center) or connect the center with la periferia (the suburbs). There are also buses that run between cities, which are normally called pullman or corriera and are bigger and more comfortable than the city buses.

You can buy tickets for the buses at a tabaccaio (tobacco shop), at a giornalaio (newsagent), at tourist information offices, sometimes in train stations, and surely at the sede centrale (main office) of each bus company. Only in a very few cases can you buy your tickets on board, so make sure you have your ticket before getting on the bus. Finding a cartina or mappa (transit system map) can be a bit difficult; if you need one ask the tourist information office or the bus company's main office.

Once on board, you must validate your ticket. This is important, because you will be fined if your ticket is checked and found not vali- dated. In most cases, you do not need a transfer, as your ticket is valid for unlimited travel for a certain amount of time. If you are transferring from one bus to another, simply carry your ticket with you without validating it another time. Since the system can change slightly from city to city, if unsure, it is always better to ask if a transfer is needed

while buying the ticket. In just a few cities you can find tram (street- cars), too, but they are part of the city bus system, so everything operates the same.

Whatever information you may need while on board, you may ask the autista (driver) or your fellow passengers.

Ferma qui il bus per la stazione?
Does the bus to the station stop here?
FAIR-mah kwee eel boos pair lah stah-tsee-OH-neh

Quante fermate ci sono prima di arrivare al Colosseo?
How many stops are there before getting to the Coliseum?
QUAHN-teh fair-MAH-teh chee SO-no PREE-mah dee ahr-ree-VAH-reh ahl Co-los-SEH-oh

Scusi, qual è la prossima fermata?
Sorry, what is the next stop?
SCOO-zee quahl eh lah PROS-see-mah fair-MAH-tah

Dove devo scendere per andare in centro?
Where must I get off to go downtown?
DOH-veh DEH-vo SHEHN-deh-reh pair ahn-DAH-reh een CHEHN-tro

Today, only a few cities in Italy have a metropolitana (subway system): Milan, Rome, Naples, Turin, Genoa, Palermo, Catania, and Cagliari.

In most cases it is a very small system, consisting of only a few lines. The Perfect Phrases in Italian for Confident Travel biggest system is the one in Milan, where currently there are three lines and another three are under construction.

The metro or subway system works more or less the same as that of buses. Tickets are purchased at a tabaccaio (tobacco shop), at a giornalaio (newsagent), or at the sportelli (ticket counters) in each stazione della metropolitana (metro station), or from biglietterie auto- matiche (automatic ticket machines) if the counters are closed. Usually a ticket is valid only for one trip; therefore it does not have a specific time validity. In most cases, one ticket costs about one euro, and you can buy biglietti giornalieri (daily tickets), biglietti settimanali (weekly tickets), and biglietti mensili (monthly tickets), or buy a carnet, which offers a certain number of tickets at a discounted price.

Sometimes there are also tourist passes, so check with the tourist office or the ticket counter for information. In a few cases, you can use your bus ticket for the subway, too, but since every system is different, make sure it is allowed before relying on that. For subway hours of opera- tion, check with either the tourist office or the subway ticket counter as well.

Vorrei un carnet da dieci biglietti.
I'd like to have a ten-ticket book.
Vor-RAY oon car-NEH da dee-EH- chee beel-YET-tee

Quanto costa il biglietto giornaliero?
How much is the daily ticket?
QUAHN-toh CO-stah eel beel-YET-toh or-nah-lee-EH-ro

Posso usare il biglietto del bus per la metropolitana?
Can I use the bus ticket for the subway?
POS-so oo-ZAH-reh eel beel-YET-toh del boos pair lah meh-tro-po-lee-TAH-nah

Potrebbe darmi una cartina della metropolitana?
Could you give me a subway system map?
Po-TREB-beh DAHR-mee OO-nah cahr-TEE-nah DEL-lah meh-tro-po-lee-TAH-nah

Even if Italian cities have a good public transportation system, a taxi is sometimes needed, perhaps late at night, or when you need to go to the airport and do not want to carry heavy suitcases, or simply to go somewhere quickly.

In a hotel or restaurant, it is easier to have someone call a taxi for you; however, at the airport or train station, you must mettersi in coda (get in line) at the fermata dei taxi (taxi stand) just outside the main exit.

Regardless of how you are traveling, upon arrival in a new city be sure to have the number of a taxi agency handy in case of need.

Once in the taxicab, make sure the tassista (taxi driver) under- stands where you need to go, and, most importantly, make sure you know in advance how much you are expected to pay for the corsa (ride).

If you are unsure about the cifra (amount of money), don't be shy; ask that the driver scriverlo su un pezzo di carta (write it on a piece of paper). Tourists are common prey all over the world and Italy is no exception.

Dovrei andare all'albergo Miramare.
I need to go to the Miramare Hotel.
Do-VRAY ahn-DAH-reh ahl-lahl-BEHR-go Mee-rah-MAH-reh

Quanto costa la corsa per l'aeroporto?
How much is the ride to the airport?
QUAHN-toh CO-stah lah COR-sah pair lah-eh-roh-POR-toh

Quanto ci vuole per arrivare in centro?
How much does it take to get to the city center?
QUAHN-toh chee voo-OH-leh pair ahr-ree-VAH-reh een CHEHN-tro

Potrebbe mandare un taxi al ristorante Margherita?

Can you send a taxi to the Margherita restaurant?
Po-TREB-beh mahn-DAH-reh oon TAH-xee ahl ree-sto-RAHN-teh Mahr-geh-REE-tah

Bikes can be rented only in very few cities in Italy. In some areas of Italy, like the Pianura Padana, where the land is flat, biciclette (bikes) are widely used as a means of transportation, while in the rest of Italy using a bike to go to work or to go to the city center can be difficult, if not dangerous. Most cities have only a few cycle tracks, and cycling in

the city traffic can be a very unpleasant experience. Therefore, finding a bike to rent may not be easy, unless you are in a tourist area.

Bringing your own bike to Italy can be quite challenging as well. However, on certain trains bikes are allowed on board with you, so this could be an interesting and different way of touring Italy. If you are really brave, consider renting a motorino (scooter), but be pre- pared to face the crazy city drivers.

Ci sono piste ciclabili in questa città?
Are there cycle tracks in this city?
Chee SO-no PEE-steh chee-CLAH-bee-lee een QUEH-stah cheet-TAH

Posso salire sul treno con la bicicletta?
Can I get on the train with the bike?
POS-so sah-LEE-reh sool TREH-no kohn lah bee-chee-CLET-tah

Scusi, quanto costa affittare un motorino?
Pardon me, how much is it to rent a scooter?
SCOO-zee QUAHN-toh CO-stah ahf-feet-TAH-reh oon mo-to-REE-no

CHAPTER 8: SHOPPING AND SERVICES

with credit card in hand, you're off to spend, spend, spend! From clothing to jewelry to artisanal products, this chapter will introduce you to the places you can spend money and the questions you should ask about your purchases.

Stores and Businesses

There are many places that will gladly accept your money in exchange for goods and services. Here is a list of the ones you might be most interested in:

Bakery	il fornaio	eel fohr-NEYE-oh
butcher shop	la macelleria	lah mah-chehl-leh-REE-ah
delicatessen	la salumeria	lah sah-loo-meh-REE-ah
department store	un grande magazzino	oon grahn-day mah-gaht-SEE-noh
dry cleaner	la lavanderia a secco	lah lah-vahn-deh-REE-ah ah sehk-koh
fish market	la pescheria	lah pess-keh-REE-ah
fruit stand	il fruttivendolo	lah froo-tee-VEHN-doh-lah
grocery store	alimentari	ah-lee-mehn-TAH-ree
ice cream shop	la gelateria	lah jeh-lah-teh-REE-ah
jewelry shop	la gioielleria	lah joy-ehl-leh-REE-ah
newsstand	l'edicola	leh-DEE-koh-lah
outdoor market	il mercato	eel mehr-KAH-toh
pastry shop	la pasticceria	lah pahs-tee-cheh-REE-ah
pharmacy	la farmacia	lah far-mah-CHEE-ah
store	il negozio	eel neh-GOHT-see-oh
supermarket	il supermercato	eel soo-pehr-mehr-KAH-toh
tobacco shop	il tabaccaio	eel tah-bahk-KEYE-oh

KEYNOTE

You will find that any deli shop, or salumeria in Italian, is likely to offer an extensive variety of local cured meats. Buy a loaf of bread, a jug of wine, and some cured meats for a delicious picnic meal.

Laundromat and Dry Cleaner

Did you spill some Chianti on the only dress shirt you brought with you? Perhaps a smattering of marinara sauce on your blouse? Laundromats and dry cleaners are there to help.

to wash	lavare	lah-VAH-ray
to dry clean	lavare a secco	lah-VAH-ray ah sehk-koh
to dry	asciugare	ah-shoo-GAH-ray
bleach	la candeggina	lah kahn-dehj-JEE-nah
dryer	l'asciugatrice	lah-shoo-gah-TREE-cheh
fabric softener	l'ammorbidente	lahm-mohr-bee-DEHN-teh
to do the laundry	fare il bucato	fah-ray eel boo-KAH-toh
soap	il sapone	eel sah-POH-nay
stain	la macchia	lah mahk-kyah
starch(ed)	inamidato	een-ah-mee-DAH-toh
washing machine	la lavatrice	lah lah-vah-TREE-cheh

Hair Salon and Barbershop

Italian hairstylists and barbers have the reputation of being among the best in the world. You'll find that prices can be reasonable, especially in a barber shop. Hey, you're on vacation—give it a try!

barber	il barbiere	eel bahr-BYEH-ray
beard	la barba	lah bahr-bah
beauty parlor	la parrucheria	lah pahr-rook-eh-REE-ah
brush	la spazzola	lah SPAHT-soh-lah

comb	il pettine	eel peht-tee-neh
curls	i riccioli	ee REE-choh-lee
dandruff	la forfora	lah FOHR-foh-rah
dry hair	i capelli secchi	ee kah-PEHL-lee sehk-kee
hair	i capelli	ee kah-PEHL-lee
haircut	il taglio di capelli	eel tahl-yoh dee kah-PEHL-lee
hairstyle	la pettinatura	lah peh-tee-nah-TOO-rah
hairstylist	il parruchiere	eel pahr-rook-YEH-ray
long	lungo	loon-goh
moustache	i baffi	ee bahf-fee
oily hair	i capelli grassi	ee kah-PEHL-leegrah-see
part	la riga	lah ree-gah
scalp	la frizione	lah freets-YOH-neh
short	corto	kohr-toh
strand	la frangetta	lah frahn-JEHT-tah
trim	una spuntatina	oo-nah spoon-tah-TEE-nah
wig	la parrucca	lah pahr-ROOK-kah
wisp	la ciocca di capelli	lah chohk-kah dee kah-PEHL-lee

Verbs

to blow dry fohn

asciugare con il phon

ah-shoo-GAH-ray kohn eel

to curl

arricciare i capelli

ah-reech-CHAH-ray ee kah-PEHL-lee

to cut

tagliare

tahl-YAH-ray

to perm

fare la permanente

fah-ray lah pehr-mah-NEHN-tay

535

to shave

fare la barba/radere

fah-ray lah bahr-bah/RAH-deh-ray

to wash

lavare

lah-vah-ray

to tease

cotonare

koh-toh-NAH-ray

to do someone's hair

fare i capelli

fah-ray ee kah-PEHL-lee

to dye/to color

tingere

TEEN-jeh-ray

to brush

spazzolare

spahts-soh-LAH-ray

to comb

pettinare

peht-tee-NAH-ray

Clothing and Jewelry

Milan and Rome are at the center of the world's fashion and jewelry industries. Besides the larger department stores and big-name shops, you will find numerous boutique shops that offer stylish (and affordable!) clothing. Shopping can be fun, but it can be overwhelming, too, so be sure to pace yourself.

Clothing

bathing suit   il costume da bagno

eel kohs-TOO-meh dah bahn-yoh

belt   la cintura

lah cheen-TOO-rah

blouse   la camicetta

536

lah kah-mee-CHEHT-tah

boots	gli stivali	lyee stee-VAH-lee
bra	il reggiseno	eel reh-jee-SEH-noh
button	il bottone	eel boht-TOH-neh
cloth, fabric, material	il tessuto	eel tehs-SOO-toh
clothes	i vestiti	ee vehs-TEE-tee
color	il colore	eel koh-LOH-ray
cotton	il cotone	eel koh-TOH-nay
dress	il vestito	eel vehs-TEE-toh
woman	donna	doh-nah
footwear	la calzatura	lah kahl-tsahTOO-rah
glasses	gli occhiali	lyee ohk-KYAH-lee
gloves	i guanti	ee gwahn-tee
handbag	la borsa	lah bohr-sah
hat	il cappello	eel kahp-PEHL-loh
jacket	la giacca	lah jahk-kah
jeans	i jeans	ee jeans
leather	il cuoio	eel kwoy-oh
lining	la fodera	lah FOH-deh-rah
lipstick	il rossetto	eel rohs-SEHT-toh
makeup	il trucco	eel trook-koh
overcoat	il cappotto	eel kahp-POHT-toh
pajamas	il pigiama	eel pee-JAH-mah
panties	le mutandine	leh moo-tahn-DEE-neh
pants	i pantaloni	ee pahn-toh-LOH-nee
perfume	il profumo	eel proh-FOO-moh
pocket	la tasca	lah tahs-kah
raincoat	l'impermeabile	leem-pehr-mee- AH-bee-leh
sandals	i sandali	ee SAHN-dah-lee
scarf	la sciarpa	lah shahr-pah
shirt	la camicia	lah kah-MEE-chah
shoelace	il laccio	eel lahch-choh

shoes	le scarpe	leh skahr-peh
silk	la seta	lah seh-tah
skirt	la gonna	lah gohn-nah
sleeve	la manica	lah MAH-nee-kah
slippers	le pantofole	leh pahn-TOH-foh-leh
sneakers	le scarpe da ginnastica.	leh skahr-peh dah jeen-NAHS-tee-kah

socks	il calzini	eel kahl-TSEE-nee
spike heel	il tacco a spillo	eel tahk-koh ah speel-loh
stocking	la calza	lah kahl-tsah
suit	il completo	eel kohm-PLEH-toh
sunglasses	gli occhiali da sole	lyee ohk-KYAH-lee dah soh-lay
sweater	il maglione	eel mahl-YOH-neh
tie	la cravatta	lah krah-VAHT-tah
T-shirt	la maglietta	lah mahl-YEHT-tah
umbrella	l'ombrello	lohm-BREHL-loh

underwear	la biancheria intima	lah byahn-keh-REE-ah een-tee-mah
velvet	il velluto	eel vehl-LOO-toh
wallet	il portafoglio	eel pohr-tah-FOHL-yoh
wool	la lana	lah lah-nah
zipper	la cerniera	lah chehr-NYEH-rah

Jewelry

amber	l'ambra	lahm-brah
bracelet	il braccialetto	eel brah-chah-LEHT-toh
brooch	la spilla	lah speel-lah
costume jewelry	la bigiotteria	lah bee-joht-teh-REE-ah
cufflinks	i gemelli	da ee jeh-MEHL-lee dah
shirt	camicia	kah-MEECH-ah
diamond	il diamante	eel dee-ah-MAHN-teh
earrings	gli orecchini	lyee ohr-rehk-KEE-nee

538

emerald	lo smeraldo	loh smeh-RAHL-doh
gold	l'oro	loh-roh
gold plated	dorato	doh-RAH-toh
jewelry	i gioielli	ee joy-EHL-lee
necklace	la collana	lah koh-LAH-nah
pearls	le perle	leh pehr-leh
pendant	il ciondolo	eel CHOHN-doh-loh
pin	lo spillo	loh-speel-loh
ring	l'anello	lah-NEHL-loh
ruby	il rubino	eel roo-BEE-noh
sapphire	lo zaffiro	loh zahf-FEE-roh
silver	l'argento	lahr-JEHN-toh
silver plated	argentato	ahr-jehn-TAH-toh
watch	l'orologio	loh-roh-LOH-joh
wedding ring	la fede	lah feh-deh

Useful Verbs

to button up	abbottonare	ahb-boht-toh- NAH-ray
to change, to get changed	cambiarsi	kahm-BYAHR-see
to dress (oneself), to get dressed	vestirsi	vehs-TEER-see
to fit; to suit	stare bene (a)	stah-ray behn-ay ah
to knot, to tie	annodare	ahn-nohd-AH-ray
to measure	misurare	mee-zoo-RAH-ray
to mend, to repair; to darn	rammendare	rahm-mehn-DAH-ray
to sew	cucire	koo-CHEE-ray
to take off, to remove.	togliere	TOHL-yeh-ray
to try	provare	proh-vah-ray
to unbutton, to undo	sbottonare	sboht-toh-NAH-ray
to undress (oneself) to get undressed	spogliarsi	spohl-YAHR-see

Useful Adjectives: Colors

Remember that colors are adjectives and therefore must agree in number and gender with the nouns they modify.

attractive	attraente	aht-trah-EHN-teh
black	nero	neh-roh
(dark) blue	blu	bloo
(pale) blue	azzurro	ahds-ZOO-roh
Brown	marrone	mahr-ROH-neh
comfortable	comodo	KOH-moh-doh
elegant	elegante	eh-leh-GAHN-teh
fashionable,in fashion	alla/di moda	ahl-lah moh-dah
gold (in color), golden	d'orato	doh-RAH-toh
(made) of gold, gold.	d'oro	doh-roh
gray	grigio	gree-joe
green	verde	vehr-day
long	lungo	loon-goh
naked, bare, nude	nudo	noo-doh
orange	arancione	ah-rahn-CHOH-nay
pink	rosa	roh-zah
purple, violet	viola	vyoh-lah
red	rosso	rohs-soh
rough, coarse	rozzo	rohts-soh
short	corto	kohr-toh
silver (in color), silvery	argenteo	ahr-jehn-TAY-oh
(made) of silver, silver	d'argento	dahr-JEHN-toh
soft, smooth	morbido	MOHR-bee-doh
thick	spesso	spehs-soh
tight(-fitting)	stretto	streht-toh
white	bianco	byahn-koh
worn out	consumato	kohn-soo-MAH-toh
yellow	giallo	jahl-loh

Useful Adjectives: Sizes

Shoe and clothing sizes in Europe are different than those used in the United States. Be prepared that the shoe salesman may tell you that you have a size 43 foot.

What size do you wear?
Quale misura desidera?
kwah-lay mee-ZOO-rah deh-zee-deh-rah

I would like . . .
Desidero . . .
deh-zee-deh-roh . . .

I don't know the sizes in Italian.
Non conosco le misure italiane.
nohn koh-NOHS-koh leh mee-zoo-reh ee-tahl-YAHN-eh

It's too big/small.
È troppo grande/piccolo.
eh trohp-poh grahn-day/PEEK-koh-loh

Clothing Size (la taglia/la misura)

Large	grande	grahn-day
larger	più grande	pyou grahn-day
medium	medio	mehd-ee-oh
small	piccolo	PEEK-koh-loh
smaller	più piccolo	pyou peek-koh-loh

CHAPTER 9: PLACES IN TOWN

I would have gone to Italy, but . I should have bought that ticket, but ... Whether by train, plane, boat, or car, get yourself to Italy. There won't be any excuses after you learn these vocabulary words and the conditional tenses (which were used in the first two sentences of this paragraph).

Coming and Going

Whether you're coming or going, you'll have to make sure your passaporto (passport) and visto (visa) are in order. Although most border officials do speak English, it wouldn't hurt for you to start practicing your Italian as soon as you get to the border. Take a look at some of the terms you should know.

At the Border: Common Phrases

Italian	English
Quando arriviamo alia frontiera?	When do we get to the border?
Ecco il passaporto.	Here's my passport.
Mi fermo una senimana.	I'll be staying a week.

Italian	English
Sono qui per affari.	I'm here on business
Sono qui cometurista.	I'm here as a tourist(on vaction).
Sono in visita dai miei nonni.	I'm visiting my grandparents.
Posso telefonare al mio consolato?	Can i phone my consultate?
Devo riempire il modulo?	Do i have to fill in this form?

At the Border: Vocabulary

English	Italian
color of eyes	il colore degli occhi
color of hair	il colore dei capelli
customs	Ia dogana
date of birth	Ia data di nascita

542

departure	Ia partenza
divorced	divorziato (male), divorziata (female)
entry visa	il visto d~ntrata
exit visa	il visto d'uscita
to extend	prolungare
first name	il nome di battesimo
height	Ia statura
identity card	Ia carta d'identita
last name	il cog nome
maiden name	il nome da nubile
marital status	lo stato di famiglia
married	sposato (male), sposata (female)
nationality	Ia nazionalita
occupation	Ia professione
place of birth	illuogo di nascita
place of residence	Ia residenza
to renew	rinnovare
signature	Ia firma
single	celibe (male), nubile (female)

Exchanging money when traveling in Italy doesn't have to be complicated. Often the best rates are through your debit card or credit card using anATM-check you finan- cial institution before leaving home! Be aware that you'll no longer use lire in Italy. As part of the European Union, Italy now uses the common currency called the Euro.

Passport and Itineraries, You're on Your Way!

You've conjugated verbs, learned to roll your rrrs, can pronounce double consonants, and know the difference between passato prossimo and il futuro. Now you want to practice your Italian in Italy! Before you go, here is practical information about traveling, including survival phrases, embassy and consulate information, and tour suggestions. Buon viaggio!

Get Your Papers in Order

Before your first taste of authentic crostini misti and a glass of Chianti, you'll have some paperwork to do. Check to see if you need a passport to enter Italy and return home (returning to the United States with an expired passport is illegal).

Visas are generally required for citizens of the United States only if they stay in Italy for longer than three months. If that's the case, you' 11 need an application form, a detailed itinerary, proof of adequate medical insurance, a valid return airline ticket, and proof of accommoda- tions. Also carry two or more forms of identification on your person, including at least one photo ID. Many banks require several IDs in order to cash traveler's checks.

Getting Through Customs

Going through la dogana (customs) shouldn't be much of a bother as long as you have all the right identifi- cation. In addition, if you've purchased goods and gifts at a duty-free shop, you'll have to pay a duty on the value of those articles that exceeds the allowance established by the Italian customs service.

If you're an EU citizen you can take the EZ-Pass lanes at the airport and breeze right through customs. It's all part of the efforts to ease border-patrol regulations and ease travel between participating countries.

"Duty-free" simply means that you don't have to pay a tax in the country of purchase. Be sure to keep receipts for major purchases while in Italy--non-EU (European Union) citizens can claim a refund for the value added tax (VAT or IVA).

What if You Lose It?

Sometimes it happens no matter what you do to pre- vent it. You thought your wallet was safe in your pocket but you misplaced it Or, your passport fell out of your pocket on that rough ride from Naples to the island of Capri. If you lose your passport, immediately notify the local police and the nearest embassy or consulate. There are consulates in most major Italian cities including Flor- ence, Milan, Naples, Palermo, and Venice. They answer the phone around the clock and also have lists of English- speaking doctors and lawyers.

The U.S. Embassy and Consulate is at Via V. Veneto, 119a, 00187 Rome. They issue new passports the same day but are closed on U.S. and Italian holidays!

Making a Telephone Call

At some point you'll want to speak on the telephone, either to make hotel reservations, purchase tickets to a show, or arrange for a taxi to pick you up. The alfabeti telejonici (phonetic alphabet) is useful when spelling out words over the telephone, for example, or when speaking to officials.

Italians tend to use the names of Italian cities (when there is a corresponding town) rather than proper nouns to spell out words. For example, while you might say "M as in Michael," an Italian is more likely to say M come Milano (M as in Milan). The following table will give you examples for all other letters, including those five foreign letters that sometimes appear in Italian.

The Telephone Alphabet: A Come Ancona

Letter	Representative City	Letter	Representative City
A	Ancona	N	Napoli

B	Bologna	O	Otranto
C	Como	P	Padova
D	Domodossola	Q	Quarto
E	Empoli	R	Roma
F	Firenze	S	Savona
G	Genova	T	Torino
H	Hotel	U	Udine
I	lmola	V	Venezia
J	Jerusalem	W	Washington
K	kilogramrna	X	Xeres
L	Livorno	Y	York
M	Milano	Z	Zara

Telephones aren't the only way to communicate in Italy. Internet cafes, Internet bars, and even Internet laundromats are popping up everywhere, so you can access Web-based e-mail providers and even surf the Web while in Italy.

The Government in Italy

Sometimes it seems as though the Italian government strives to reach new levels of dysfunctionality. After all, there have been over sixty governments since the country formed a democratic republic in 1946 following World War II, and political scandals seem to be the norm rather than the exception. On the other hand, it may be that term limits are simply a theoretical concept, and politicians and their parties mutate as the economy, geopolitics, and social programs demand.

Much like many democratic governments today, the Italian government is divided into three branches. The executive branch has two members: the presidente, who is elected by an electoral college, and the primo minis- tero, who is generally the leader of the party that has the largest representation in the Chamber of Deputies (the prime minister is also sometimes called il Presidente del Consiglio dei Ministn). The legislative branch consists of a bicameral Parlamento, which includes the Senato della Repubblica and the Camera dei Deputati (Chamber of Deputies). The Corte Costituzionale (Constitutional Court) rounds out the government. For a more in-depth look at Italian government, visit the official Italian gov- ernment Web site atwww.govemo.it.

Planes, Trains, and Boats

You can practice your Italian even before arriving in Italy if you fly on Alitalia, the Italian national airline. Its planes have a green, white, and red color scheme and the crew wears uniforms designed by-who else?-Italian designers. Many other airlines have several daily sched- uled flights into the country from worldwide destinations. Ready to get on the airplane? The following table has some useful vocabulary for your airplane trip.

Vocabulary: On the Plane

English	Italian
Aircraft	l'aereo
land	atterrare
airline	Ia compagnia
aerea landing	l'atterraggio
approach	avvicinarsi
pilot	il piIota
arrival	l'arrivo
reservation	Ia prenotazione
crew	l'equipaggio
return ftight	il volo di ritorno
destination	Ia destinazione
seat belt	Ia cintura di sicurezza
emergency	ex~ l'uscita d'ernergenza
stopover	lo scalo
flight	il volo
takeoff	il decollo
flight attendant	l'assistente di volo
ticket	il biglietto
helicopter	l'elicottero
wing	l'ala

Or Take the Train

Rail travel in Italy is relatively easy, and most cities and towns have rail service. There are several different levels of trains on the Ferrovie dello Stato or FS (Italian State Railway). Avoid the locale, which stops at every station along a line-it's only slightly more expensive to ride the diretto or espresso, which stops only at major stations. Then there's the rapido, or InterCity (IC) train, which travels only to the largest cities. The Eurostar trains are the fast trains, which can be pricey but cut down on travel time considerably.

To find out what la biglietteria is and how to inquire about the departure, as well as for other useful vocabu- lary, take a look at the table below.

Vocabulary: By Train

English	Italian
arrival/departure	arrivi/partenze
change trains	cambiar treno
connection	la coincidenza
couchette sleeper	la carrozza cuccette
diningcar	il vagone ristorante
express train	il direttissimo
fast train	il diretto
first-aid station	il pronto soccorso
information office	le informazioni
long distanceexpress	il rapido
money exchange	il cambio
motorail service	la littorina
platform	il binaio
rail car	l'automomotrice
restaurant	il ristorantee
restroom	il gabinetto
sleeper/sleeping car	il vagone letto
suburban train	il treno suburbano
ticket window	la biglieteria
timetable	l'orario
waiting room	la sala d'aspetto

Amenities?

Not all Italian hotels have air conditioning, for exam- ple. So, sorry to break it to you but you'll just have to get used to it! And in the economy pensioni and alberghi, you'll probably have to walk down the hall to use the bathroom. But then, you're here to see the ancient ruins, the Donatello sculptures, and the affreschi (frescoes) by Ghirlandio, not to watch TV in your hotel room. For some help in how to check in and other related vocabulary, see the following table.

Vocabulary: Checking In

English	Italian
bath	il bagno
bill	il conto

blanket	Ia coperta
concierge	il portinaio
corridor	il corridoio
drapery	latenda
elevator	l'ascensore
heating	il riscaldamento
lamp	Ia lampada
lobby	l'atrio
mattress	il materasso
mirror	lo specchio
pillow	il cuscino
plug	Ia spina
refrigerator	iI frigo rifero
room	Ia camera
shower	Ia doccia
sink	illavandino
terrace	ilterrazzo
towel	l'asciugamano

In big tourist towns and at expensive hotels the staff almost always speaks at least enough English to help those who haven't yet mastered Italian. Still, trying to speak Italian will definitely ingratiate you in the eyes of the staff -and it might even get you a better room.

Conditional Use

The present-conditional tense (condili.onale presente) is equivalent to the English constructions of "would" + verb (for example: I would never forget). Forming conditionals is easy: Just take any verb, drop the final-e in its infinitive form, and add an appropriate ending-endings are the same for all three conjugation groups of verbs. The only spelling change occurs with -are verbs, which change the a of the infinitive ending to e. You will need to be familiar with this tense if you want to be polite when traveling in Italy.

Conjugating Verbs in the Present Conditional

Pronoun	-are (Par/are)	-ere (Credere)	-ire (Sentire)
io	parlerei	crederei	sentirei
tu	parleresti	crederesti	sentiresti

lui, lei, Lei	parlerebbe	crederebbe	sentirebbe
noi	parleremmo	crederemmo	sentiremmo
voi	parlereste	credereste	sentireste
loro, Loro	parlerebbero	crederebbero	sentirebbero

Reflexive verbs follow the same scheme, with the addi- tion of the reflexive pronouns mi, ti, si, ci, vi, or si when conjugating them: mi laverei, ti laveresti, si laverebbe, ci laveremmo, vi lavereste, si laverebbero. Here are some examples of conditional-tense sentences:

• Vorrei un caffe. (I would like a coffee.)

• Scriverei a mia madre, rna non ho tempo. (I would write to my mother, but I don't have time.) • Mi daresti il biglietto per la partita? (Would you give me a ticket for the game?)

We Could Hav...

But at the stroke of midnight my coach turns into a zucca! The conditional perfect (condizionale passato), like all compound tenses in Italian, is formed with the condizionale presente of the auxiliary verb avere or essere and the past participle of the acting verb. Conju- gated forms of avere and essere appear here.

Condizionale Prrsente of the VerbsAvere and Essere Person Singular Plum/ I (io) avrei, sarei (noi) avremmo, saremmo II (tu) avresti, saresti (voi) avreste, sareste Ill (lui, lei, Lei) avrebbe, (loro, Loro) avrebbero, sarebbe sarebbero

Here are a few examples of the condizionale passato in action. Remember that verbs conjugated with essere must change their endings to agree in number and gender with the subject:

• Avremmo potuto ballare tutta la notte. (We could have danced all night.)

• Avreste dovuto invitarlo. (You ought to have invited him.)

• Saremmo andati volentieri alla Scala, rna non abbi- amo potuto. (We would gladly have gone to La Scala, but we weren't able to.)

• Mirella sarebbe andata volentieri al cinema. (Mirella would have been happy to go to the cinema.)

Sightseeing Tips and Terms

On your mark, get set, sightsee! It's tempting to try to see everything that's in the guidebooks, checking off churches and museums and historical monuments like a grocery list. Here's a tip: Do as the Italians do and slow down. Enjoy a walk down the street, chat up a store clerk, listen to schoolchildren singing.

The real Italy isn't in a tour or a book or a museum- it's experienced during a delicious lunch in a small, out- of-the-way trattoria, in a park with the smell of cyprus trees everywhere, or in the sound of the church bells every hour. After all, this is the country of la dolce vita. For your own giro turistico (sightseeing tour), check out this vocabulary table.

Vocabulary: Sightseeing

English	Italian

District	il quartiere
embassy	l'ambasciata
excavations	gli scavi
farmhouse	Ia cascina
fountain	Ia fontana
gallery	Ia galleria
gate	il portone
landscape	iI paesaggio
memorial	il monumento commemorativo
mountain	Ia montagna
museum	il museo
oldtown	il centro storico
palace	il palazzo
park	il parco
port	il porto
river	il fiume
subway	Ia metropolitana

English	Italian	
Taxi	taxi.	iltassì
valley	la valle.	Iavaiie
waterfall	Ia cascata.	lacascatah

Travel by Water

taly is a peninsula with beaches that encircle most of the country and has a rich maritime history. There are the islands of Capri and Ischia off of Naples, and the Aeo- lian Islands where volcanoes still spew lava. There are the islands of Sicilia and Sardegna (or Sardinia), homes to two very different cultures, yet still part of Italy. Then there's La Serenissima (the Most Serene One), otherwise known as Venezia, the city on the sea, with lagoons instead of streets and narrow, twisting walkways. (Venezia is acces- sible primarily by vaporetto, water taxi, or gondola. The city itself is comprised of 118 bodies of land in a lagoon, connected to the mainland by a thin causeway.)

For some maritime vocabulary, navigate your way to the next table.

Vocabulary: On Board

English	Italian
Anchor	l'ancora
Barge	la scialuppa
Bay	la baia
Boat	la barca
Bow	la prua
Captain	il capitano
Deck	la coperta
Ferry	il traghetto
fishing trawler	la ba rca da pesca
gangway	la passerella
Lifeboat	la scialuppa di salvataggio
Lighthouse	il faro
Mast	l'albero
Motorboat	il motoscafo
Pier	il pontile
Rudder	il timone
Sailboat	la barca a vela
Steamer	il vaporetto

Museums, Theatre, and Art

The most important source of information for tourists in Italy is the ufficio informazioni turistiche (tourist information office).

The office is normally located in the very center of each city, usually in the piazza principale (main square) or close to the principale attrazione turistica (major tourist attraction) of the area.

Bigger cities and places with a strong tourist vocation might have more than one tourist information office, each located in a different area. In large cities, the ufficio informazioni turistiche is normally open every day, year-round, with longer orari d'apertura (hours of operation) during summer or festivi- ties. In smaller towns, it may be that the office is open only for a few hours a day.

The tourist information office is a great source for tourists and people who are not acquainted with the city. There you can ask for cartine gratuite (free maps) and dépliant della città (city brochures), and you can buy a city pass to visit sites at a prezzo scontato (dis- counted price). In most cases you can book a visita guidata della città Perfect Phrases in Italian for Confident Travel (guided city tour) and even ask for assistance in finding an albergo (hotel) or a ristorante (restaurant).

Vorrei qualche informazione sulla città.
I'd like some information about the city.
Vor-RAY QUAHL-keh een-for-mah-tsee-OH-neh SOOL-lah cheet-TAH

Quali sono le attrazioni principali del posto?
What are the main attractions of the place?
QUAH-lee SO-no leh at-trah-tsee-OH-nee preen-chee-PAH-lee del PO-sto

Saprebbe consigliarmi un buon ristorante?
Could you suggest a good restaurant?
Sa-PREB-beh cohn-seel-YAHR-mee oon boo-ON ree-sto-RAHN-teh

Vorrei prenotare una visita   **guidata per due.**
I'd like to book a guided tour for two.
Vor-RAY preh-no-TAH-reh OO-nah VEE-zee-tah goo-ee-DAH-tah pair DOO-eh

Due biglietti d'ingresso per il museo, per favore.

(DOO-eh beel-YET-tee deen-GRES-so pair eel moo-ZEH-oh pair fah-VO-reh)

Two entrance tickets to the museum, please.

Italy is known all over the world for its beautiful musei (museums) and incomparable opere d'arte (works of art). Almost every town, even the smallest, has at least one important place of interest or historic site.

Main museums and the most significant tourist attractions are normally open year-round with one giorno di chiusura (closure day) dur- ing the week, in most cases on Monday. Most of these are also closed on Christmas Day and a few other national festivity days.

Some of the lesser known sites and attractions may have limited orari d'apertura (hours of operation), and it is a good idea to ask the tourist informa- tion office about that before heading to the site. Museums have different tariffe d'ingresso (admission fares): They usually have a standard fare for adulti (adults), then discounted fares for anziani (seniors), bambini (children), studenti (students), gruppi (groups), and in some cases for people holding a city pass. Sometimes museums and tourist attractions have a giornata a ingresso libero (free entrance day) for special occasions and events, so check with the tour- ist information office.

Most museums and tourist sites offer visite guidate (guided tours) or audioguide (audio guides) at an additional cost. Sometimes mostre temporanee (temporary exhibitions) are not included in the standard admission price, so ask the biglietteria (ticket office) about it if you are interested in visiting a special exhibition as well.

In many museums and tourist sites, you can find a bookstore selling books, gifts, and souvenirs, as well as a bar or a restaurant.

C'è uno sconto per gli anziani?
Is there a discount for seniors?
Cheh OO-no SCON-toh pair lyee ahn-tsee-AH-nee

La mostra di Caravaggio è inclusa nel biglietto?
Is the Caravaggio exhibition included in the admission?
Lah MO-strah dee Cah-rah-VAD-jo eh een-CLOO-zah nel beel-YET-toh

Quando comincia/termina la prossima visita guidata?

When does the next guided tour start/end?

QUAHN-doh co-MEEN-chah/TEHR-mee-nah lah PROS-see-mah VEE-zee-tah goo-ee-DAH-tah

A che ora apre/chiude il museo?

What time does the museum open/ close?

Ah keh OH-rah AH-preh/kee-OO-deh eel moo-ZEH-oh

Scusi, come arrivo alla Cattedrale?

(SCOO-zee CO-meh ar-REE-vo AL-lah cat-teh-DRAH-leh)

Pardon me, how do I get to the cathedral?

Le chiese (churches) in Italy are a very important part of the patrimonio storico e artistico (historical and artistic heritage). Most of them hold precious opere d'arte e di architettura (works of art and architecture) and are worth visiting, no matter your religious beliefs. Most churches are open all day and can be visited freely.

Those with valuable affreschi (frescoes), dipinti (paintings), or sculture (sculptures) may have limited hours, and in a few cases there may be a fee to visit certain areas of the church. Sometimes, the entrance is vietata (not allowed) during the Messa (Mass).

In any case, please remember that these are religious places, and it is important to behave in an appropriate way: be prop- erly dressed, fare silenzio (be silent), and respect the people who are there to pray.

Also, make sure you are allowed to fare fotografie (take pictures) before you start snapping shots.

Quando apre la chiesa?

When does the church open?

QUAHN-doh AH-preh lah kee-EH-zah

Tourism and Sightseeing

Qual è l'orario delle Messe?

What are the Mass times?

QUAHL eh lo-RAH-ree-oh DEL-leh MES-seh

Si possono fare foto in chiesa?

Are photos allowed inside the church?

See POS-so-no FAH-reh FO-toh een kee-EH-zah

Dov'è l'affresco di Giotto?

Where is Giotto's fresco?

Do-VEH laf-FRES-co dee JOT-toh

A che ora parte la gita turistica?

(Ah keh OH-rah PAHR-teh lah JEE-tah too-REE-stee-cah)

What time does the sightseeing tour leave?

Tourist sites offer various sightseeing tours.

They can be a piedi (on foot) within the centro storico (historical center), in pullman (by bus) in large or more diffuse cities, or even in battello (by boat) in a few cases. Most tours are offered in several languages, but it is useful to know a few key phrases in Italian as well.

Sometimes the tours will include some tempo libero (free time) to visit the site independently, but make sure to verify the meeting time and place with the rest of the group. In Italy leaving mance (tips) is not a common practice, but it will be appreciated if you leave a tip for the autista (bus driver) or the guida turistica (tourist guide), especially if it was a long tour and they worked hard to ensure you enjoyed the city or site at its best.

Quanto dura la gita?

How long is the tour?

QUAHN-toh DOO-rah lah JEE-tah

Dov'è il luogo di ritrovo?

Where is the meeting point?

Doh-VEH eel loo-OH-go dee ree-TROH-vo

A che ora è l'appuntamento per il rientro all'albergo?

What time do we meet to return to

the hotel?

Ah keh OH-rah eh lap-poon-tah- MEHN-toh pair eel ree-EHN-tro al-lahl-BAIR-go

Questa è una mancia per Lei. Grazie per il Suo ottimo lavoro.

This is a tip for you. Thank you for the great job.

QUEH-stah eh OO-nah MAHN-chah pair Lay GRAH-tsee-eh pair eel OO-oh OT-tee-mo lah-VO-ro

C'è una spiaggia libera qui vicino?

(Cheh OO-nah spee-AD- jah LEE-beh-rah kwee vee-CHEE-no)

Is there a free beach nearby?

Italy offers not only historical cities and cultural places but also great opportunities to enjoy oneself al mare (at the sea), in montagna (in the mountains), and in campagna (in the countryside). Italy has miles and miles of beautiful sandy beaches, which provide various types of entertainment to the tourists. If you are visiting a place by the sea and want to spend some time at the beach, either go to a stabilimento balneare or bagno (private beach) or to a spiaggia libera (free beach).

To access a private beach, you must pay an ingresso (admission fee) to be allowed in.

Scusi, quanto costa l'ingresso?

Pardon me, how much is the admission price?

SCOO-zee QUAHN-toh CO-stah leen-GRES-so

Vorrei affi ttare un ombrellone e due sdraio.

(Vor-RAY af-feet-TAH-reh oon ohm-brel-LO-neh eh DOO-eh SDRAYE-oh)

I'd like to rent an umbrella and two deck chairs.

To use umbrellas and deck chairs at the beach, you must rent them.

Private beaches normally offer many services, like bagni (toilets), docce calde (hot showers), cabine (small beach huts for changing clothes), giochi per i bambini (games for kids), intrattenimenti (enter- tainment) like tornei di beach volley (beach volleyball tournaments), corsi di ballo (dance courses), and other amusements.

There you can also rent a canoa (canoe) or a pedalò (paddleboat). At a free beach, however, there are no services—in most cases not even toilets or docce fredde (cold showers)—so bring your own umbrellas and deck chairs.

However, in every seaside area there is at least one spiaggia libera attrezzata (free beach with services), where all the basic services are available for a fair price.

Potrei avere la chiave della cabina?

May I have the key for the hut?

Po-TRAY ah-VEH-reh lah kee-AH-veh DEL-lah cah-BEE-nah

Che servizi ci sono in questa spiaggia?

What kinds of services are offered at this beach?

Keh sair-VEE-tsee chee SO-no een QUEH-stah spee-AD-jah

Vorrei uno skipass giornaliero.

(Vor-RAY OO-no skipass jor-nah-lee-EH-ro)

I'd like a daily ski ticket.

In Italy there are beautiful mountains, which can be enjoyed in winter and summer alike.

During winter there are activities like sciare (skiing), pattinare sul ghiaccio (ice-skating), or fare snowboard (snowboarding). Large ski resorts also offer activities for those who do not like to ski.

To hit the big slopes, either bring your own sci (skis), racchette (ski poles), and scarponi (ski boots) or rent them. You can rent pattini da ghiaccio (ice skates) and tavole da snowboard (snowboards) as well. Before ski- ing, however, you must purchase a skipass (ski ticket), which can be giornaliero (daily), mattiniero (for the morning only), or pomeridiano (for the afternoon only).

There are also skipass settimanali (weekly) or mensili (monthly).

Vorrei affittare/noleggiare un paio di sci e degli scarponi.

I'd like to rent a pair of skis and ski boots.

Vor-RAY af-feet-TAH-reh/no-lehj-jee-AH-reh oon PYE-oh dee shee eh DEH-yee scar-PO-nee

Quali sono le piste più difficili?

Which are the most difficult slopes?

QUAH-lee SO-no leh PEE-steh PEW deef-FEE-chee-lee

Dove sono le piste di sci?

Where are the ski slopes?

DO-veh SOH-noh leh PEE-steh dee shee

Dov'è la pista di pattinaggio?

Where is the ice rink?

Do-VEH lah PEE-stah dee pat-tee-NAD-jo

Conosce qualche buon sentiero per fare del trekking?

(Coh-NOH-sheh KWAL-keh boo-ON sehn-tee-EH-ro pair FAH-reh dehl trekking)

Do you know of a good hiking path?

Mountains can be enjoyed during the summer, too. In summer one can walk along the sentieri (pathways), enjoying the breathtaking scenery and resting in the rifugi (mountain huts) that sometimes offer great food and drinks for a good price.

For more sporty types, there are mountain bike rentals and even arrampicata (rock climbing). Your hotel owner or the tourist information office can provide the informa- tion you need to enjoy your stay to the fullest.

Quanto ci vuole per arrivare al rifugio?

How long does it take to get to the mountain cabin?

QUAHN-toh chee voo-OH-leh pair ar-ree-VAH-reh al ree-FOO-jo

Dov'è la funivia?

Where is the cableway?

Do-VEH lah foo-nee-VEE-ah

Vorrei affittare un bungalow.

(Vor-RAY af-feet-TAH-reh oon BOON-gah-lo)

I'd like to rent a chalet.

Whether you are in the mountains, at the sea, or in the countryside, a great way to live in close contact with nature is fare campeggio (to go camping).

There are campeggi (camping sites) almost everywhere in Italy, where you can either rent a bungalow (chalet) or a roulotte (trailer), but you must bring your own tenda da campeggio (tent) if you prefer to camp that way.

In busy tourist areas, campgrounds are quite large and organized, offering various services and entertainment.

Please remember, however, that camping outside proper camping sites in most cases is forbidden, so check with the local tourist infor- mation office about the proper locations for camping.

Scusi, c'è un campeggio qui vicino?

Pardon me, is there a camping site

nearby?

SCOO-zee cheh oon cahm-PED-jo kwee vee-CHEE-no

Scusi, avete una piazzola per una tenda?

Pardon me, do you have a space for a tent?

SCOO-zee ah-VEH-teh OO-nah pee-ahts-SO-lah pair OO-nah TEHN-dah

Devo pagare per parcheggiare all'interno del campeggio?

Do I have to pay to park my car inside the camping site?

DEH-vo pah-GAH-reh pair pahr-ked-JAH-reh al-leen-TAIR-no del cahm-PED-jo

È permesso il campeggio libero in questa zona?

Is free camping allowed in this area?

CHAPTER 10: SPORTS

To experience Italy, you have to be tuned in to the culture. If you'd like to get out to a soccer game or perhaps go to the theater, this chapter introduces you to vocabulary and terms related to sports, pastimes, games, and cultural activities.

Sports and Games

Soccer, by far the most popular sport in Italy (and most other countries in the world!), is by no means the only sport in Italy. You will find numerous sports and games available for your recreational pleasure.

Commonly Heard Words

Some words are common to all sports and games. Whether you're reading the newspaper, watching on television, or observing from the audience, you're bound to hear the following words sooner or later.

ball	il pallone	eel pahl-LOH-neh
championship	il campionato	eel kahm-pee-oh-NAH-toh
competition	la gara	lah gah-rah
defeat	la sconfitta	lah skohn-FEET-tah
to enjoy oneself	divertirsi	dee-vehr-TEER-see
entertaining	divertente	dee-vehr-TEHN-tay
entertainment	il divertimento	eel dee-vehr-tee-MEHN-toh
fan	il tifoso	eel tee-FOH-soh
free time	il tempo libero	eel tehm-poh LEE-beh-roh
game	la partita	lah pahr-TEE-tah
to lose	perdere	PEHR-deh-ray
player	il giocatore	eel joh-kah-TOH-ray
popular	popolare	poh-poh-LAH-ray
to prefer	preferire	preh-feh-REE-ray
race	la gara	lah gah-rah
spectators	gli spettatori	lyee speht-tah-TOH-ree
sport	lo sport	loh sport
team	la squadra	lah skwah-drah
victory	la vittoria	lah veet-TOH-ree-ah

to win	vincere	VEEN-cheh-ray

The Verbs Fare and Giocare

The verb fare (to do, to make) can prove very useful when talking about sports and games. Faccio lo sci nautico can translate as "I am waterskiing (right now)" or "I waterski (in general)." In the present tense the verb fare is irregular.

fare (to do, to make)

io faccio	ee-oh fah-choh
tu fai	tu feye (like the English "eye")
lui, lei, Lei fa	loo-ee, lay fah
noi facciamo	noy fah-CHAH-moh
voi fate	voy fah-tay
loro, Loro fanno	loh-roh fahn-noh

Io faccio . . .

l'alpinismo	mountain climbing
	lahl-pee-NEEZ-moh
la caccia	hunting
	lah kah-chah
il campeggio	camping
	eel kahm-PEHJ-joh
il canotaggio	rowing
	eel kah-noh-TAHJ-joh
il ciclismo	bicycling
	eel chee-KLEEZ-moh
la corsa automobilistica	auto racing
	lah kohr-sah ohw-toh-moh-bee-LEES-tee-kah
la corsa nautica	boat racing
	lah kohr-sah NOHW-tee-kah
l'equitazione	horseback riding
	leh-kwee-tahts-YOH-neh
l'excursionismo	hiking

559

	lehk-skoor-zee-oh-NEEZ-moh
il footing	joggingm
	eel footing
la ginnastica	gymnastics
	lah jeen-NAHS-tee-kah
il gioco dei birilli	bowling
	eel joh-koh day bee-REEL-lee
gli sport	sports
	lyee sport
il nuoto	swimming
	eel noo-OH-toh
la pallamano	handball
	lah pahl-lah-MAH-noh
la pallanuoto	waterpolo
	lah pahl-lah-noo-OH-toh
la pallavolo	volleyball
	lah pahl-lah-VOH-loh
il patinaggio	skating
	eel path-tee-NAHJ-joh
il pugilato	boxing
	eel poo-jee-LAH-toh
lo sci di discesa	downhill skiing
	loh shee dee-SHAY-zah
lo sci di fondo	cross-country skiing
	loh shee dee fohn-doh
lo sci nautico	waterskiing
	loh she NOHW-tee-koh

KEYNOTE

Golf has become increasingly more popular over the past few years in italy. Golf courses are widely available, but greens fees can be expensive. Driving ranges are also available, and they offer an inexpensive way to keep your swing in top form!

The verb giocare i.e to play usually it is used whenever we are referring to the name of the game or particular sport. Gioco a calcio means "I play soccer." It is to ne noted that the verb giocare takes the preposition a when followed by the name of the sport or game.

Giocare(to play)

Io gioco	ee-oh joh-koh
tu giochi	too joh-kee
lui, lei, Lei gioca	loo-ee, Iay joh-kah
noi giochiamo	noy johk-YAH-moh
voi giocate	voy joh-KAH-tay
loro, Loro giocano	loh-roh JOH-kah-noh

Io gioco a....

Baseball	bayz-ball	baseball
Biliardi	beel-YAHR-dee	pool
Bocce	boh-cheh	bocce ball
Calcio	kahl-choh	soccer

LEISURE TIME

I like...	Mi piace/piacciono...	mee pyaceh/pyatchyonoh
...art and painting	...l'arte e la pittura	larteh eh lah peetoorah
...movies and cinema	...i film e il cinema.	ee film eh eel cheenemah
...the theater	...il teatro	eel tehatroh
...opera	...l'opera	loperah

I prefer...	Preferisco...	prefereeskoh...
...reading books	...leggere libri	ledjereh leebree
...listening to music	...ascoltare musica	askoltareh moozeekah
...watching sports	...guardare lo sport	gwardareh loh sport
...playing games	...giocare a qualcosa	jokareh ah kwalkosah
...going to concerts	...andare ai concerti	andareh ahee konchertee
...dancing	...ballare	ballareh
...going to clubs	...andare in discoteca	andareh een deeskotekah

...going out with friends	...uscire con gli amici	oosheereh kon lyee ameechee
I don't like...	Non mi piace...	non mee pyacheh
That bores me	Mi annoia	mee annoyah
That doesn't interest me	Non mi interessa	non mee eenteressah

AT THE BEACH

il telo da mare	eel teloh dah mareh	beach towel
il pallone da spiaggia	eel palloneh dah speeadjah	beach ball
la sedia a sdraio	lah sedya ah sdrayo	deck chair

You may hear...

Divieto di balneazione	deevyetoh dee balneatsyoneh	No swimming
Spiaggia chiusa	speeadja kewsah	Beach closed
il lettino sdraio	eel leteenoh sdrayo	lounge chair

Can I rent...

Posso noleggiare...   possoh noledjareh...

...a jet ski?	...una moto d'acqua?	oonah motoh dakwa
...a beach umbrella?	...un ombrellone da mare?	oon ombrelloneh dah mareh
...a surfboard?	...una tavola da surf?	oonah tavolah dah surf
...a wetsuit?	...una muta subacquea?	oonah mootah soobakweah
sunglasses	gli occhiali da sole	lyee okeealee dah soleh
sun hat	il cappello da sole	eel kappeloh dah soleh
suntan lotion	la lozione solare	lah lotsyoneh solareh
bikini	il bikini	eel beekeenee
mask and snorkel	la maschera e il boccaglio	lah maskerah eh eel bokalyo
How much does it cost?	Quanto costa?	kwantoh kostah?

| Can I go water-skiing? | Posso fare dello sci d'acqua? | possoh fareh delloh shee dakwa? |
| Is there a lifeguard? | C'è il bagnino? | che eel baneenoh? |

Is it safe to... **È sicuro...** **eh seekooroh...**

| ...swim here? | ...nuotare qui? | nwotareh kwee ? |
| ...surf here? | ...fare del surf qui? | fareh del surf kwee ? |

AT THE SWIMMING POOL

i braccioli ee bratchyolee armband

la tavoletta lah tavolettah float

il costume eel kostoomeh swimsuit

gli occhialini lyee okyaleenee swimming goggles

What time... Quando... kwandoh

| ...does the pool open? | ...apre la piscina? | apreh lah peesheenah ? |
| ...does the pool close? | ...chiude la piscina? | kewdeh lah peesheenah ? |

Is it... È... eh...

| ...an indoor pool? | ...una piscina coperta? | oonah peesheenah kopertah ? |
| ...an outdoor pool? | ...una piscina all'aperto? | oonah peesheenah alapertoh ? |

Is there a children's pool? C'è una piscina per bambini?

che oonah peesheenah pehr bambeenee ?

Where are the changing rooms? Dove sono gli spogliatoi? doveh sonoh lyee spolyatoy ?

Is it safe to dive? È sicuro tuffarsi? eh seekooroh toofarsee ?

AT THE GYM

| Is there a gym? | C'è una palestra? | che oonah palestrah |
| Is it free for guests? | È gratuita per i clienti? | eh gratooeetah pehr ee klyentee |

Do I have to wear sneakers?

Devo indossare le scarpe da ginnastica?

devoh eendossareh leh skarpeh dah jeennasteekah

Do I need an introductory session?

Devo fare una sessione introduttiva?

devoh fareh oonah sessyoneh introdootteevah

Do you offer...   Offrite...   offreeteh.....

...aerobics classes?

...lezioni di aerobica?

letsyonee dee aerobeekah

...Pilates classes?

...lezioni di Pilates?

 letsyonee dee pilates

...yoga classes?

...lezioni di yoga?

letsyonee dee yogah

il vogatore

eel vogatoreh

 rowing machine

l'ellittica

lelleeteekah

cross trainer

la step machine

lah step machine

step machine

la bicicletta

lah beecheeklettah

exercise bike

BOATING AND SAILING

Can I rent...	Posso noleggiare...	possoh noledjareh...
...a dinghy?	...un gommone?	oon gommoneh
...a windsurf board?	...una tavola da windsurf?	oonah tavolah dah windsurf
...a canoe?	...una canoa?	oonah kanoah
compass	la bussola	lah boosolah
life jacket	il giubbotto di salvataggio	eel jewbottoh dee salvatadjoh

Do you offer sailing lessons?

Offrite lezioni di vela?

offreeteh letsyonee dee velah

Do you have a mooring?

Avete un ormeggio?

aveteh oon ormedjoh

How much is it for the night?

Quanto costa per notte?

kwantoh kostah pehr notteh

Where can I buy gas?

Dove posso comprare del gas?

doveh possoh komprahray del gaz?

Where is the marina?

Dov'è il porticciolo?

doveh eel porteetchyoloh

My...is broken

Il mio/la mia...non funziona

eel meeoh/lah meeah... non foontsyonah

Can you repair it?

Potete ripararlo/a?

poteteh reepararloh/ah

Are there life jackets?

Ci sono dei giubbotti di salvataggio?

chee sonoh day jewbottee dee salvatadjoh

WINTER SPORTS

You may hear...

È un principiante?

eh oon preencheepeeanteh

Are you a beginner?

Deve lasciare un deposito.

deveh lashyareh oon deposeetoh

I need a deposit.

I would like to rent...	Desidero noleggiare...	deseederoh noledjareh...
...some skis	...un paio di sci	oon payo dee shee
...some ski boots	...un paio di scarponi	oon payo dee skarponee
...some poles	...un paio di racchette	oon payo dee raketteh
...a snowboard	...uno snowboard	oonoh snowboard
...a helmet	...un casco	oon kaskoh

When does...	**Quando...**	**kwandoh...**
...the chair lift open?	...apre la seggiovia?	apreh lah sedjoveeya ?

...the cable car close?   ...chiude la funivia?   kewdeh lah fooneeveeya ?

How much is a lift pass?   Quanto costa un pass?   kwantoh kostah oon pass?

Can I take skiing lessons?

Posso prendere delle lezioni di sci?

possoh prendereh delleh letsyonee dee shee ?

BALL GAMES

il pallone

eel palloneh   soccer ball

il canestro

eel kanestroh   basketball hoop

il guanto da baseball

eel gwantoh dah besball   baseball glove

i polsini

ee polseenee   wristbands

I like playing...	Mi piace giocare a...	mee pyacheh jokareh ah...
...soccer	...pallone	palloneh
...tennis	...tennis	tennis
...golf	...golf	golf
...badminton	...volano	volahnoh
...squash	...squash	skwosh
...baseball	...baseball	besboll

Where is the nearest...	Dov'è il più vicino...	doveh eel pew veecheenoh...
...tennis court?	...campo da tennis?	kampoh dah tennis
...golf course?	...campo da golf?	kampoh dah golf
...sports center?	...centro sportivo?	chentroh sporteevoh

la racchetta	lah rakettah	tennis racket
le palle	leh palleh	tennis balls
la palla e il tee	lah pallah eh eel	tee golf ball and tee

May I book a court...	**Posso prenotare un campo...**	**possoh prenotareh oon kampoh...**
...for two hours?	...per due ore?	pehr dooeh oreh
...at three o'clock?	...per le tre?	pehr leh tray
What shoes are allowed?	Quali scarpe sono permesse?	kwalee skarpeh sonoh permesseh

May I rent...	**Posso noleggiare...**	**possoh noledjareh...**
...a tennis racket?	...una racchetta da tennis?	oonah rakettah dah tennis
...some balls?	...delle palle?	delleh palleh
...a set of clubs?	...un set di mazze?	oon set dee madze
...a golf cart?	...il carrello elettrico?	eel karreloh elettreekoh
la mazza	lah madza	golf club

Hobbies

What to do with all your free time? Here's a short list of some hobbies and pastimes practiced throughout the world:

art	l'arte	lahr-teh
art exhibit	la mostra d'arte	lah mohs-trah dahr-teh
ballet	il balletto	eel bahl-LEHT-toh
book	il libro	eel lee-broh
cinema	il cinema	eel CHI-neh-mah
crossword puzzle	il cruciverba	eel kroo-chee-VEHR-bah
to dance	ballare	bahl-LAH-ray
dancing	il ballo	eel bahl-loh
to draw	disegnare	dee-zen-YAH-ray
drawing	il disegno	eel dee-ZEHN-yoh
horse racing	l'ippica	LEEP-pee-kah
to listen to music	ascoltare la musica	ah-skohl-TAH-ray lah MOO-zee-kah

literature	la letteratura	lah leht-teh-rah-TOO-rah
novel	il romanzo	eel roh-MAHN-zoh
opera	l'opera	LOH-peh-rah
to paint	dipingere	dee-PEEN-jeh-ray
paintbrush	il pennello	eel pehn-NEHL-loh
painting	la pittura	lah peet-TOO-rah
pasttime	il passatempo	eel pahs-sah-TEHM-poh
photography	la fotografia	lah foh-toh-grah-FEE-ah
poetry	la poesia	lah poh-eh-ZEE-ah
to read	leggere	LEHJ-jeh-ray
sculpture	la scultura	lah skool-TOO-rah
theater	il teatro	eel teh-AH-troh

CHAPTER 11: ITALIAN ADJECTIVES

You may remember way back in school, your teacher will have told you that an adjective is a describing word. Well, just like in English, an Italian adjective is added to a noun to give it a quality or to define it in a better way.

You could say that adjectives are all about making the noun better.

Whether it's in English, Italian, or any other language, a world without adjectives would be a very dull and boring world indeed. There would be no fast cars, they'd just be cars. No sunny days, they'd just be days...

So, let's celebrate the power of the descriptive word, and find out all about Italian adjectives.

How to pronounce Italian adjectives

Here are some Italian sentences using adjectives to get you started. Further on in this lesson we will look at the pronunciation of these and more Italian adjectives.

Il cielo azzurro mi diverte -   The blue sky amuses me

Ho bisogno di una sciarpa e una giacca nuove   I need a new scarf and a new jacket

Il gioco nuovo - The new toy

La casa nuova - The new house

L'uomo egoista - The egoist man

Gli uomini gentili - The kind men

Il muro rosa - The pink wall

C'era un grande lago - There was a big lake

Luisa è una bella ragazza -   Luisa is a beautiful girl

Luigi è venuto con la sua bella figlia - Luigi has come with his beautiful daughter

Let's get started...

According to the noun it's linked to, adjectives can have:

An attributive function, when it is linked directly to a noun.

Il cielo azzurro mi diverte.

The blue sky amuses me.

A predicative function, when it is linked to the noun through the verb essere, to be.

Il cielo è azzurro.

The sky is blue.

Adjectives agree always on genre and number with the noun. If they're linked to more than one noun and just one of them is masculine, the adjectives are all defined as masculine.

Ho bisogno di una sciarpa (f) e una giacca (f) nuove.

I need a new scarf and a new jacket.

Ho bisogno di un pullover (m) e una giacca (f) nuovi.

I need a new pullover and a new jacket.

Italian Adjectives: forms and examples

The forms of the adjectives:

1. Adjectives ending on masculine singular with –o

nuov-o (M)

nuov-a (F)

Singular

nuov-i (M)

nuov-e (F)

Plural

Il gioco nuovo

The new toy

I giochi nuovi

The new toys

La casa nuova

The new house

le case nuove

The new houses

2. Adjectives ending on masculine singular with –ista

egoist-a (M)

egoist-a (F)

Singular

egoist-i (M)

egoist-e (F)

Plural

L'uomo egoista
The egoist man

La donna egoista
The egoist woman

Gli uomini egoisti
The egoist men

Le donne egoiste
The egoist women

3. Adjectives ending on masculine singular with –e

gentil-e (M)

gentil-e (F)

Singular

gentil-i (M)

gentil-i (F)

Plural

L'uomo gentile
The kind man

La donna gentile
The kind woman

Gli uomini gentili
The kind men

Le donne gentili
The kind women

4. The following adjectives have an invariable form:

pari (pair) and dispari (odd)

adjectives of colors, which derive from nouns: rosa, ocra, viola, nocciola, marrone

adjectives composed by the prefix anti + noun: antinebbia (fog lights), antifurto (anti-theft)

Il muro rosa
The pink wall

I muri rosa
The pink walls

La casa rosa
The pink house

Le case rosa
The pink houses

The Position of Italian Adjectives
The adjectives can be used before or after the noun.

C'era un grande lago
There was a big lake

C'era un lago grande
There was a big lake

The position gives a different tone to a sentence, according to these rules:

The adjective before the noun has less power than the one after.

Luisa è una bella ragazza
Luisa is a beautiful girl

is less powerful than

Luisa è una ragazza bella
Luisa is a beautiful girl

Sometimes the adjective before the noun has a descriptive function, while after it has a distinctive function

Luigi è venuto con la sua bella figlia
Luigi has come with his beautiful daughter

Luigi è venuto con la figlia bella
Luigi has come with his daughter, the beautiful one

In some cases, the different position can influence the meaning of the sentence.

Il nostro vicino è un uomo povero
Our neighbor is a poor man

Il nostro vicino è un pover'uomo
Our neighbor is a mean man

There are adjectives that are used only after the noun. They indicate:

italiano, tedesco, americano, etc.

nationality

democratico, socialista, comunista, etc.

membership

destro, sinistro, etc.

location or position

cieco, gobbo, etc.

physical characteristics

Adjectives and adverbs

While adjectives are connected with nouns, adverbs complete the verb. Usually adverbs have the same stem of the corresponding adjectives + the suffix -mente.

Adverb

A mio padre piace vivere pericolosamente

My father likes to live dangerously

Adjective

Io amo gli sport pericolosi

I love dangerous sports

Adverb

Sono molto felice

I am really happy

Adjective

Ho molti motivi per essere felice

I have a lot of reasons to be happy

Buono is an adjective, while bene is the corresponding adverb.

buono

good

bene

well

In Italia si mangia bene
In Italy they eat well

La pasta è buona
The pasta is good

Italian adjectives summary

Adjectives in Italian are conjugated as the nouns: masculine ends with -o (plural, -i), feminine with -a (plural -e).

As for the noun, a third type of adjectives ends with -e (plural, -i); these adjectives have the same form for masculine and feminine.

The adjectives can have an attributive or predicative function.

Usually the position of the adjectives in Italian language is after the noun, especially if the adjective indicates color or nationality. Most of the Italian adjectives can be used either before or after the noun.

Adverbs are built using the stem of the corresponding adjective + the suffix -mente

HOW TO USE ITALIAN ADJECTIVE

The big piazza, the clear sky, and the handsome Italian man are all examples with an adjective, or something that gives more information about a noun. Oftentimes this is a description.

In Italian an adjective agrees in gender and number with the noun it modifies, and there are two groups of adjectives: those ending in -o and those ending in -e.

Adjectives ending in -o in the masculine have four forms:

Maschile Femminile

Singolare -o -a

Plurale -i -e

Singolare il libro italiano la signora italiana

Plurale i libri italiani le signore italiane

Singolare il primo giorno la mesa universitaria

Plurale i primi giorni le mense universitarie

COMMON ITALIAN ADJECTIVES ENDING IN -O

allegro

cheerful, happy

buono

good, kind

cattivo

bad, wicked

freddo

cold

grasso

fat

leggero

light

nuovo

new

pieno

full

stretto

narrow

timido

timid, shy

Adjectives ending in -o have four forms: masculine singular, masculine plural, feminine singular, and feminine plural. Observe how the adjectives nero and cattivo change to agree with nouns they modify.

Note that when an adjective modifies two nouns of different gender, it keeps its masculine ending. For example: i padri e le madre italiani (Italian fathers and mothers). If an adjectives ends in -io, like "vecchio - old", the o is dropped to form the plural.

l'abito vecchio - the old suit

gli abiti vecchi - the old suits

il ragazzo serio - the serious boy

i ragazzi seri - the serious boys

Uli è tedesco. - Uli is German.

Adriana è italiana. - Adriana is Italian.

Roberto e Daniele sono americani. - Robert and Daniel are American.

Svetlana e Natalia sono russe. - Svetlana and Natalia are Russian.

Adjectives ending in -e are the same for the masculine and the feminine singular. In the plural, the -e changes to an -i, whether the noun is masculine or feminine.

il ragazzo inglese - the English boy

la ragazza inglese - the English girl

i ragazzi inglesi - the English boys

le ragazze inglesi - the English girls

ENDINGS OF -E ADJECTIVES

SINGULAR

PLURAL

il ragazzo triste - the sad boy

i ragazzi tristi - the sad boys

la ragazza triste - the sad girl

le ragazze tristi - the sad girls

ITALIAN ADJECTIVES ENDING IN -E

abile

able

difficile

difficult

felice

happy

forte

strong

grande

big, large, great

importante

important

intelligente

intelligent

interessante

interesting

triste

sad

veloce

fast, speedy

There are quite a few other exceptions for forming plural adjectives.

For instance, adjectives that end in -io (with the stress falling on that) form the plural with the ending -ii: addio/addii; leggio/leggii; zio/zii. The table below contains a chart of other irregular adjective endings you should know.

FORMING PLURAL ADJECTIVES

SINGULAR ENDING

PLURAL ENDING

-ca

-che

-cia

-ce

-cio

-ci

-co

-chi

-ga

-ghe

-gia

-ge

-gio

-gi

-glia

-glie

-glio

-gli

-go

-ghi

-scia

-sce

-scio

-sci

Where do the adjectives go?

Unlike in English, descriptive adjectives in Italian are usually placed after the noun they modify, and with which they agree in gender and number.

1. Adjectives generally follow the noun.

È una lingua difficile. - It is a difficult language.

Marina è una ragazza generosa. - Marina is a generous girl.

Non trovo il maglione rosa. - I can't find the pink sweater.

TIP: Note that adjectives of colors that derive from nouns, like "rosa", "viola", or "blu" are invariable.

2. Certain common adjectives, however, generally come before the noun.

Here are the most common:

bello - beautiful

bravo - good, able

brutto - ugly

buono - good

caro - dear

cattivo - bad

giovane - young

grande - large; great

TIP: When you place "grande" before a noun, it means "great", like "una grande piazza", but if you place it after, it means "big", like "una piazza grande".

lungo - long

nuovo - new

piccolo - small, little

stesso - same

vecchio - old

vero - true

Here are some examples:

Anna è una cara amica. - Anna is a dear friend.

Gino è un bravissimo dottore. - Gino is a really good doctor.

È un brutto affare. - It's a bad situation.

But even these adjectives must follow the noun to emphasize or contrast something, and when modified by an adverb.

Oggi non porta l'abito vecchio, porta un abito nuovo. - Today he is not wearing the old suit, he is wearing a new suit.

Abitano in una casa molto piccola. - They live in a very small house.

THE FOLLOWING ARE LIST OF ADJECTIVES YOU SHOULD COMMIT TO HEART

Below is a list of the Adjectives, Colors, Shapes, Sizes in Italian placed in a table. Memorizing this table will help you add very useful and important words to your Italian vocabulary.

English Adjectives Italian Adjectives

colors	colori
black	nero
blue	blu
brown	marrone
gray	grigio
green	verde
orange	arancione
purple	viola
red	rosso
white	bianco
yellow	giallo
sizes	dimensioni (or) misure

big	grande
deep	profondo
long	lungo
narrow	stretto
short	breve (or)corto (or)basso
small	piccolo
tall	alto
thick	spesso
thin	sottile
wide	ampio
shapes	forme
circular	circolare
straight	dritto
square	quadrato
triangular	triangolare
tastes	i gusti
bitter	amaro
fresh	fresco
salty	salato
sour	acido
spicy	piccante
sweet	dolce
qualities	qualità
bad	cattivo
clean	pulito
dark	buio
difficult	difficile
dirty	sporco
dry	secco
easy	facile
empty	vuoto
expensive	costoso

fast	veloce
foreign	straniero
full	pieno
good	buono
hard	duro (or)difficile (difficult)
heavy	pesante
inexpensive	economico
light	luce
local	locale
new	nuovo
noisy	rumoroso
old	vecchio
powerful	potente
quiet	tranquillo
correct	corretto
slow	lento
soft	morbido
very	molto
weak	debole
wet	bagnato
wrong	sbagliato
young	giovane / giovani
quantities	quantità
few	pochi
little	poco
many	molti
much	molto
part	parte
some	alcuni
a few	qualche
whole	tutto (or)completo, totale

CHAPTER 12: USING MONEY IN ITALY

The euro became the official currency of Italy, along with most other European countries, back in 2002 after an implementation period that lasted a few years. The United Kingdom still uses the pound, a notable exception.

The symbol to signify the currency is €.

The Euro can be divided into one hundred units called Euro Cents.

100 Euro Cents = 1 Euro Dollar

Although the exchange can vary and fluctuate, the general range of valuation during the last few years has been:

1 Euro = Approximately $1.20 to $1.45 US Dollars

1 Euro = Approximately £0.80 to £0.90 Pounds

There are seven bank notes:

5, 10, 20, 50, 100, 200, and 500 Euro (dollars)

There are eight coins:

1, 2, 5, 10, 20 and 50 Euro cents / 1 Euro (dollar) and 2 Euro (dollars)

Unlike American currency, the bank notes come in different shapes and sizes. The coins also come in different sizes, just like American currency. The different shapes are used to assist

those who are visually impaired, blind, etc.

It's important to note that the comma and period are reversed to express the unit of measurement.

Thus the following would represent two thousand euro dollars and 50 euro cents.

€ 2.000,50

It's also important to note that in Italian the singular and plural for the euro are spelled and pronounced exactly the same.

one euro

un euro

two euros

due euro

one hundred euros

cento euro

There are a few options available for you to have access to money while you are visiting the country of Italy.

ATM / Bancomat

There are now ATM machines (bancomat) on virtually every corner in Italy just like you are probably accustomed to at home. You just insert your card and you will have the option of choosing English as your language of choice, along with Italian, German, and French.

More than likely your bank will charge a fee to access the network. It will still work out better than using a traveler's check, where you often pay a fee to have one issued to you.

Make sure your PIN (personal identification number) is a four-digit number, as anything else will probably not work in Italy. Also be sure to call your bank to let them know you will be using the card overseas so it does not spark a suspicious alert on your account. The last thing you want to happen is to have your card swallowed at an Italian ATM machine.

Other Options

If you have family or friends in the country, if worse comes to worse, you could have someone send them funds via PayPal or Western Union. These options, of course, have some heavy fees associated with them as well, so you should only use in emergency. PayPal allows you to transfer money to family and friends, but if it is against the sender's credit card, the fee is a lot higher than if you use PayPal funds or direct debit from the sender's bank account.

On my most recent trip to Italy, I used an ATM card to withdraw 200 euros and about a week later I sent 200 euros to my relatives via PayPal. The net amount received in euros were almost identical, the only difference is my bank charged me five dollars to use the ATM network. Winner: PayPal.

You should also make sure your credit card has a cash advance feature in case your ATM card is swallowed up by the machine or lost.

Credit Cards

The use of credit cards has also gained acceptance in Italy. VISA and MasterCard are widely accepted. American Express is not as readily available so do not rely on that card as a primary means of credit. Discover Card has not been able to gain any type of acceptance in Italy and I doubt it ever will. You can leave that one at home.

It may be a good idea to carry two credit cards but keep them separate from one another in case one gets lost or stolen.

Some of your mom and pop (smaller) establishments, trattorias, pensioni, etc. may not accept credit cards, so it is best to ask. And if they do, they may assess a surcharge of 3 to 4 percent for the convenience.

bank

banca

You may see this word as masculine (banco) or feminine (banca). There is a distinction that started many years ago but it is not important for tourists. Sometimes a financial institution will use banco for the name and others will use banca. The masculine word technically refers to a bench, or the counter where the bankers used to conduct their business.

Some Useful Phrases:

Where is the nearest bank?

Dov'e' la banca piu' vicina?

Where is the nearest ATM?

Dov'e' il bancomat piu' vicino?

I would like to change some dollars.

Vorrei cambiare dei dollari.

I would like to change some pounds.

129

Vorrei cambiare delle sterline.

letter of credit

lettera di credito

check

assegno

transfer

trasferrimento

credit card

carta di credito

What is the commission rate?

Quanto trattiene di commissione?

Where can I cash a traveler's check?

Dove posso cambiare un traveler's cheque?

What time does the bank open?

A che ora apre la banca?

Do you take credit cards?

Accetate carte di credito?

Can I use a credit card?

Si puo' usare la carta di credito?

What time do you (plural) close?

A che ora chiudete?

Telephones in Italy

Prior to the advent of cellular phones, using a phone in Italy meant using one of the public phone booths that you will still see available throughout the country. Many of the older ones are no longer functioning. They used to accept a token or a gettone, which had a monetary value of approximately twenty cents. They also had phones available for use at the post office for a fee.

The gettone are long gone but you will need to use a prepaid calling card that is inserted into the phone for making a call from a public payphone.

telephone

telefono

cell phone

cellulare

telefonino (which means "little telephone")

Nowadays with cellular service being so popular, many Italians have ditched their landlines in favor of using their cell phone.

You basically have three options if you want to use a cell phone in Italy:

1 – Use your existing phone

If your phone is capable of supporting GSM 900 and GSM 1800 frequencies, it will work in Italy. Call your cell phone provider to find out if you are not sure. And then find out what type of international calling plans they have to offer.

The disadvantage is that your phone calls will be considered international long-distance even if you are calling your cousin in Rome who happens to be on the same block. And when your cousin calls you, they will be charged an international rate. The advantage, of course, is you are using your own phone and your own phone number.

2 – You can purchase a phone

You must make sure you purchase a GSM compatible phone that is unlocked. Or in other words, you are not bound by a contract with a specific service provider. You can find them on Amazon or eBay by doing a search. It must be compatible with the frequencies above or just simply look for a quad band phone. These can be purchased prior to your trip or after you

arrive in Italy.

You then need to purchase a SIM card, which will be your own Italian cell phone number. The advantage is that you will then be charged local rates as opposed to long-distance international rates when calling within Italy.

3 – You can rent a cell phone

There are companies that will allow you to rent a cell phone. Often if you rent an automobile, they will allow you to rent a cell phone for free. I personally like the second option above if you plan on returning to Italy in the future. Or even if you plan on traveling throughout Europe, Africa, or other countries, as you'll have a cell phone at your disposal ready and available.

To Make an International Call from Italy

To Call the United States or Canada

Dialing internationally from Italy means you must use the double zero (00) to indicate that you want to place a call outside the country. Then you will need to dial an international country code.

United States – 1

Canada – 1

Then you will dial the area code and the appropriate phone number. If you are calling a toll-free number within the United States, which usually has a prefix of 800 / 888 / 877 / 866, the call will not be toll-free. You'll be charged normal international rates. Many times, the call will simply not go through using those prefixes.

To Call the United Kingdom

To dial the United Kingdom from Italy you must use the double zero (00) to indicate that you want to place a call outside the country. Then you will need to dial the international country code.

Country Code – 44

You then must dial the appropriate city code (which is 20 for London, etc.) and then the phone number.

To Place Calls Within Italy

If you are making calls within Italy you will not need to dial the 39 country code.

Calling a Landline

These numbers will begin with a zero indicating the city code, which can be two digits, three digits, or four digits. For example, the city code for Rome is 06 and the code for Palermo is 091. You simply dial the city code along with the phone number to place a call. The regular phone number can also be six or seven digits.

Calling a Cell Phone

Depending on your cell phone company, these rates will typically be higher for the recipient than the one placing the call. The country code is not needed and cellular numbers are all 10-digit numbers. They usually begin with the number three (3). There is a three-digit prefix which indicates the cell phone provider. This would be useful, as some providers charge less if you are calling someone on the same network. For example, a TIM subscriber calls another TIM subscriber.

Toll-Free Numbers Within Italy

Toll-free numbers are generally indicated with a green color, sometimes known as a numero verde or a green number. They usually begin with 800, 900, or 199. You typically won't be able to reach those numbers from abroad.

Answering the Phone

For most people all over the world the standard greeting when answering the phone will be the standard "hello" or some variation thereof. However, in Italy the standard greeting is the word "pronto," which means ready. In essence, you are using a protocol telling the other person that you are "ready" to talk. That one word basically means:

"I'm ready to talk, are you ready to talk?"

Useful Vocabulary for the Telephone

telephone number

numero di telefono

area code

prefisso

ringer

la suoneria

phone card

la scheda telefonica

to make a call

chiamare per telefono

dial the number

marcare il numero

The line is open.

La linea sta aperta.

The line is busy.

La linea sta occupata.

Where is the telephone?

Dov'è il telefono?

May I use your phone?

Posso usare il suo telefono?

Hello, who's talking?

Pronto, chi parla?

Where is the nearest phone booth?

Dov'è la cabina telefonica più vicina?

I would like to speak to...

Vorrei parlare con...

When will he / she return?

Quando sarà di ritorno?

Will you tell him / her that I called?

Vuol dirgli / dirle che ho chiamato?

ITALIAN CONVERSATIONS

Learn Italian for Beginners in Your Car Like Crazy.

Lessons for travel & Everyday.

How to speak Italian with Grammar, Vocabulary, Conversations and Common Phrases.

VOL 2

INTRODUCTION

Italian is one of the most spoken languages in Europe. There are around 70 million Italian native speakers in the wold, but only 3 million people know it as a second language which is a very small number compared to for instance French and German. However, knowing the Italian language can enrich your understanding of the Italian history and culture. Italy isn't only known for its art, but it's also got a rich history of literature, music, food, fashion and design.

If you want to truly immerse yourself in the Italian culture, you really need to learn the language. It'll also enhance you career progression and broaden your job oppotunities. Remember that learning a language is a challenge and a long term goal. We're here to help you reach that dream faster and easier.

It doesn't happen overnight, but once you know a language, you know it for life! Essential Vocabulary And Conversation For Beginners is intended to provide the student of Italian with a comprehensive and structured approach to the learning of vocabulary. It can be used right from the outset in beginner, intermediate and advanced undergraduate courses, or as a supplementary manual at all levels including the elementary one to supplement the study of vocabulary.

It is designed to provide the learner with a broad treatment of those vocabulary topics that are not covered as designated areas of study in typical language courses, and thus can be used to "fill in the vocabulary gaps" that such courses invariably leave. Additionally, this book can be easily adapted for profitable use in "Language for Special Purposes" courses.

The guiding principle behind the plan of this book is the idea that students need to acquire a comprehensive control of concrete and abstract vocabulary to carry out essential communicative and interactional tasks an area of learning that is often neglected by other types of textbooks for the simple reason that they are more focused on presenting other aspects of the language.

This book therefore, is designed to: provide a vocabulary training tool that can be used throughout the undergraduate program in Italian as the student progresses through it; provide a practical topic-based textbook that can be inserted into all kinds of course syllabi to impart a sense of how the language can be used in specific ways; promote self-instruction in the language; facilitate the acquisition of vocabulary items to which the student would not ordinarily be exposed; present organized units of vocabulary that can be used in tandem with other manuals and/or course materials; provide exercises and activities for all kinds of classroom and self-study purposes.

Before you dive into the more difficult lessons like grammar and writing, it's best to start with a foundation of basic Italian vocabulary words. Learning these words will give you a running start, and enable you to communicate in a simple, yet clear way in Italian. Below is a list of basic Italian vocabulary words, split into five different categories.

Greetings

Greetings are perhaps the most useful vocabulary words of all, especially when you're traveling. These simple words give you the ability to appropriately greet whomever you encounter or understand those who are greeting you.

Greetings	
Buongiorno	Good morning
Buon pomeriggio	Good afternoon
Buonasera	Good evening
Buonanotte	Good night
Ciao	Hi
Salve	Hello
Arrivederci	Goodbye (informal)
Arrivederla	Goodbye (formal)
A presto	See you soon
A domani	Until tomorrow

Essential verbs

In order to form complete sentences you must have an understanding of the essential verbs. Below are just a few of the most useful verbs to add to your language repertoire.

Verbs

Prendere: (io) prendo, (tu) prendi, (lui/lei) prende, (noi) prendiamo, (voi) prendete, (loro) prendono	To take: I take, you take, he/she takes, we take, you take (plural), they take.
Parlare: (io) parlo, (tu) parli, (lui/lei) parla, (noi) parliamo, (voi) parlate, (loro) parlano	To speak: I speak, you speak, he/she speaks, we speak, you speak (plural), they speak.
Capire: (io) capisco, (tu) capisci, (lui/lei) capisce, (noi) capiamo, (voi) capite, (loro) capiscono	To understand: I understand, you understand, he/she understands, we understand, you understand (plural), they understand.
Bere: (io) bevo, (tu) bevi, (lui/lei) beve, (noi) beviamo, (voi) bevete, (loro) bevono	To drink: I drink, you drink, he/she drinks, we drink, you drink (plural), they drink.

Numbers

To effectively communicate prices in shops, quantities of food, and other items, numbers are extremely useful to know. Below are the numbers one through ten as well as examples of how to use the numbers in sentences.

Numbers

Uno: "C'è solo una mela."

Due: "Sono due sorelle."

Tre: "Costa tre euro."

Quattro: "Ti ho chiamato quattro volte!"

Cinque: "Oggi è il 5 giugno."

Sei:"Lei ha sei anni."

Sette: "Ci sono sette continenti."

Otto: "Ci sono otto fermate."

Nove: "Sono le nove di mattina."

Dieci: "Vai avanti dieci passi."

One: "There is only one apple."

Two: "There are two sisters."

Three: "It costs three euro."

Four: "I called you four times!"

Five: "Today is the 5th of June."

Six: "She is six years old."

Seven: "There are seven continents."

Eight: "There are eight stops."

Nine: "It's nine in the morning."

Ten: "Move forward ten steps."

Introductions

Another basic element of vocabulary are words to introduce yourself. After all, it will be hard to meet a native speaker if you're not sure of how to introduce yourself properly. Below are some vocabulary words for introductions.

Introductions

Sono Lucia	I'm Lucia
Mi chiamo Lucia	My name is Lucia
Piacere!	Nice to meet you!
Come ti chiami?	What's your name? (informal)
Lei come si chiama?	What's your name? (formal)
Abito a Los Angeles	I live in Los Angeles

Politeness

Lastly, there's nothing more important in Italian culture than politeness. When speaking a new language, you can often end up saying things you don't mean out of misunderstanding. The following words will help you fix any situation.

Politeness	
Per favore / Per cortesia	Please
Grazie	Thank you
Di niente	You're welcome
Prego	After you/go ahead
Permesso	May I enter?/ Please let me pass

With these words, you're well on your way to building a strong foundation of basic Italian vocabulary. To help you memorize these words, play some fun grammar games or practice speaking with your family or friends.

FORMAT & SYMBOLOGY

All entries in this book follow the same pattern: extra space separates the English from the Italian or the Italian from the English portions of each word set; the English or Italian call word depending on which word list you're consulting is always shown in boldface roman and its Italian or English counterpart, in lightface roman.

A phonetic representation of the Italian term's pronunciation is appended to each entry, within parentheses and in italics. Throughout, masculine and feminine nouns are signified by an "m." and an "f.," and bigender terms by an "m. & f." Occasionally, you man find an n. (for noun) to distinguish the noun meaning of the word from that of a different part of speech. Adjectives (always shown in masculine form!) are denoted by "(adj.)," positioned after the adjective itself; and verbs (always shown in infinitive form) by "(to)."

Adverbs, conjunctions, pronouns, prepositions, and colloquial expressions are assumed to be self-identifying and / or unimportant to be so distin- guished in the present context, and thus bear no such denotations. In instances where several other noncognate English terms also directly translate to the Italian word, they will conjoin the cognate in immediate succession, separated by commas. Thus, the entry abbreviate, abridge, shorten (to) abbreviare (ahb-breh-vee-AHR-reh) indicates that in addition to the closely spelled term at the far left, the annexed terms are also directly translatable by the Italian word. In more instances than not, a string of English words separated by commas will be closely related and synonymous within itself but not always! For exam- ple, the following pair of entries

desert, wilderness deserto m. (deh-ZEHR-toh) fund, bottom   fondo m. (FOHN-doh)

illustrate that English terms with considerably different meanings can own the same translation in Italian. The learner must be particularly alert to these word strings, and remember to make a separate "flash" device for each elemental pair! Similarly, where more than a single Italian word is a direct translation of the English term(s) at the right, a comma separates them.

Again, the diligent student will provide him- / herself with a "flash" device for every word-pairing listed! Symbolic markings in this book are as follows:

• Where a "bomb" ( ) symbol is appended to an entry, it refers to a subtle spelling or pronunciational differentiation between the English and Italian terms that, without remark, might be missed.

• Where space permits, arrows embracing a word or fragment indi- cate an important similarity (including location of the stressed syllable) between related Italian word forms. Where minor spelling differences are noted, the first character or syllable of a hyphenated -fragment is drawn from the original, and subsequent characters indicate the alteration. Thus the line nfant nfant m. (een-FAHN-teh) f. -ta

indicates that the noun exists in both genders and that the spelling of the feminine form is infanta. Similarly, the entry

negative   negativa f. (neh-gah-TEE-vah) (adj.) -vo

indicates that the noun-related English adjective negative is, in Italian, spelled negativo. And the entry physics fisica f. (FEE-zee-kah) physical (adj.) -co

demonstrates that the two entries need not be identical, but rather only close- ly related to warrant the memory-convenience of single-line placement.

• Arrows embracing an "m.,""f.,""m. & f.," or "(adj.)" denomination signify that the related word they enclose is identical to the listed term.

Thus, the entry

human umano m. (oo-MAH-noh) (adj.)

indicates that the Italian for English adjective human is spelled and pro- nounced exactly as is its related.

• In instances where the learner will gain from additional intelligence about a given term or closely related (but not necessarily cognate) term, it will be provided directly below the entry, flagged by the internation- al "Information" symbol, . Because these notes contain an important wealth of "extra" vocabulary, data, and understanding, the learner is urged to pay careful attention to their content.

CHAPTER 1: HOTEL

I f you're not lucky enough to have friends who can offer you a place to stay when you travel, you have to find a hotel. This chapter shows you how to make yourself understood when you ask for a room or check in. Plus, we give you a crash course on making plurals and using possessive pronouns.

Reserving a Room

When you reserve a room in a hotel, you use many of the same terms as you do when booking a table in a restaurant. Substitute either la camera (lah kah-meh-rah) or la stanza (lah stahn-dzah), both of which mean "the room," for il tavolo (eel tah-voh-loh) (the table).

The little differences between Italian and American hotel terms can cause big trouble if using the wrong ones means that you don't get what you want. So we want to tell you how to ask for what kind of room you want in Italian:

La camera singola (lah kah-meh-rah seen-goh-lah)

is a room with one bed.

La camera doppia (lah kah-meh-rah dohp-pee-ah)

is a room with two twin beds.

La camera matrimoniale (lah kah-meh-rah mah-tree-moh-nee-ah-leh)

has one big bed for two people.

In Italy, you choose not only your room type, but also what meals you want. You can opt for:

La mezza pensione (lah meht-tsah pehn-see-oh-neh), which includes breakfast and one hot meal (dinner in most cases).

La pensione completa (lah pehn-see-oh-neh kohm-pleh-tah), which includes breakfast, lunch, and dinner.

We don't need to tell you that making reservations in advance is important particularly for the alta stagione (ahl-tah stah-joh-neh) (high season).

In Italy, high season is the summer months and the weeks around Easter. If you haven't reserved a room and have to request one when you arrive at the hotel, you may have to compromise.

When making reservations, you may have questions about the available rooms and the hotel's amenities. You'll probably encounter and use some of these common questions and phrases:

Avete stanze libere?

(ah-veh-teh stahn-dzeh lee-beh-reh)

(Do you have any vacant rooms?)

La stanza è con bagno?

(lah stahn-dzah eh kohn bah-nyoh)

(Does the room have a bathroom?)

Posso avere una stanza con doccia?

(pohs-soh ah-veh-reh oo-nah stahn-dzah kohn dohch-chah)

(May I have a room with a shower?)

Non avete stanze con la vasca?

(nohn ah-veh-teh stahn-tseh kohn lah vah-skah)

(Don't you have rooms with bathtubs?)

Avete una doppia al primo piano?

(ah-veh-teh oo-nah dohp-pee-ah ahl pree-moh pee-ah-noh)

(Do you have a double room on the first floor?)

La colazione è compresa?

(lah koh-lah-dzee-oh-neh eh kohm-preh-zah)

(Is breakfast included?)

Può darmi una camera con aria condizionata e televisione?

(poo-oh dahr-mee oo- nah kah-meh-rah kohn ah-ree-ah kohn-dee-dzee-oh-nah-tah eh teh-leh-vee-zee- oh-neh)

(Can you give me a room with air conditioning and a television?)

C'è il telefono nella mia stanza?

(cheh eel teh-leh-foh-noh nehl-lah mee-ah stahn- dzah)

(Is there a telephone in my room?)

The reservations agent might tell you something like this:

614

È una stanza tranquillissima e dà sul giardino.

(eh oo-nah stahn-dzah trahn-koo-eel-lees-see-mah eh dah sool jahr-dee-noh)

(The room is very quiet and looks out onto the garden.)

La doppia viene centotrenta euro a notte.

(lah dohp-pee-ah vee-eh-neh chehn-toh-trehn-tah eh-oo-roh ah noht-teh)

(A double room costs 130.00 euro per night.)

Checking in and Getting Settled

One of the first things you do when checking into a hotel is attend to your luggage. The receptionist might ask

Dove sono i Suoi bagagli?

(doh-veh soh- noh ee soo-oh-ee bah-gah-lyee)

(Where is your baggage?)

In response, you might ask

Può far portare le mie borse in camera, per favore?

(poo-oh fahr pohr-tah-reh leh mee-eh bohr-seh een kah-meh-rah pehr fah- voh-reh)

(Can I have my bags brought to my room, please?)

portare (pohr-tah-reh) (to bring) and dare (dah-reh) (to give).

After you begin unpacking, you may find that you forgot to bring something you need.

Or you may want some special amenity, like una cassaforte (oo- nah kahs-sah-fohr-teh) (a safe) for your valuables or un frigorifero (oon free-goh-ree-feh-roh) (a refrigerator). In these instances, you're likely to ask the front desk or the maid for what you need.

The following phrases can help you:

Non trovo l'asciugacapelli.

(nohn troh-voh lah-shoo-gah-kah-pehl-lee)

(I can't find the hair dryer.)

Gli asciugamani devono essere cambiati e manca la carta igenica.

(lyee ah-shoo-gah-mah-nee deh-voh-noh ehs-seh-reh kahm- bee-ah-tee eh mahn-kah lah kahr-tah ee-jeh-nee-kah)

(The towels must be changed and there is no toilet paper.)

Potrei avere un'altra saponetta?

(poh- tray ah-veh-reh oon-ahl-trah sah-poh-neht-tah)

(May I have a new soap?)

If you want something else, notice that you write the feminine form un'altra (oon-ahl- trah) differently than the masculine un altro (oon ahl-troh). Feminine words that begin with a vowel require an apostrophe after the article; masculine words that begin with a vowel don't.

> Ho finito lo shampo.

> (oh fee-nee-toh loh shahm-poh)

> (I ran out of shampoo.)

> Vorrei un'altra coperta e due cuscini, per favore.

> (vohr-ray oon-ahl-trah koh-pehr-tah eh doo-eh koo-shee-nee pehr fah-voh-reh) (I'd like one more blanket and two pillows, please.)

> Vorrei la sveglia domattina.

> (vohr-ray lah sveh-lyah doh-maht-tee-nah)

> (I'd like to get an early wake-up call tomorrow morning.)

Using Plurals and Pronouns

Digging a little bit deeper into grammar can help you understand Italian better. In this section, we hope to improve your knowledge of Italian plurals and pronouns.

Making more in Italian

You may have noticed that the plural form in Italian isn't as simple as it is in English. In English, you usually add an s to the end of a word to make it plural. In Italian, how you make a noun plural depends on both the gender of the word and, as far as the article is concerned, on the first letters in the word.

Italian nouns are either masculine or feminine. You use a different article with each gender:

The masculine articles il (eel) and lo (loh) accompany masculine nouns, most of which end in o.

The feminine article la (lah) accompanies feminine nouns, most of which end in a.

Masculine nouns that begin with a vowel, such as l'amico (lah-mee-koh) (the friend), or any of the following consonants take the article lo (loh):

z, as in lo zio (loh dzee-oh) (uncle) gn, as in lo gnomo (loh nyoh-moh) (the gnome) y, as in lo yogurt (loh yoh-goort) (the yogurt) s followed by another consonant (sb, sc, sd, and so on), as in lo studente (loh stoo-dehn-teh) (the student)

When the word begins with a vowel, lo is abbreviated as l', as in l'amico. The same is true for feminine nouns that begin with a vowel; la is reduced to l'. There is no feminine equivalent to the masculine lo. In the plural, lo and l' (for masculine nouns) become gli (lyee).

When you understand these rules, forming plurals is easy:

For a feminine noun, such as la cameriera (lah kah-meh-ree-eh-rah) (the chambermaid) or l'entrata (lehn-trah-tah) (the hall), change the final a (in the article as well as the word) to e so that la cameriera becomes le cameriere (leh kah-meh-ree-eh-reh) and l'entrata becomes le entrate (leh ehn-trah-teh).

For a masculine noun, such as il bagno (eel bah-nyoh) (bathroom), the plural article becomes i (ee), and so does the final o of the word. So il bagno becomes i bagni (ee bah-nyee).

With some exceptions, to make nouns ending in e plural for example, la chiave (lah kee-ah-veh) (the key) and il cameriere (eel kah-meh-ree-eh-reh) (the

waiter) — you change the e to i, and the article changes according to the gender — for example, le chiavi (leh kee-ah-vee) (the keys) and i camerieri (ee kah- meh-ree-eh-ree) (the waiters). The masculine articles lo and l' change to gli (lyee), and the feminine l' becomes le (leh).

Personalizing pronouns

As you know, a pronoun is a word that you use in place of a noun, such as I. Sometimes you use a pronoun that not only takes the place of a noun but also indicates to whom it belongs.

For example, when you say "My bag is red and yours is black," the possessive pronoun yours represents the word bag and indicates to whom the bag belongs.

In English, you use the pronouns this and these (called demonstrative pronouns) to indicate what you're talking about.

You can use this or these with any noun as long as you get the number right: this book, these girls, and so on. In Italian, however, which word you use depends on both number and gender because there are masculine and feminine articles. Consider these examples:

Questa è la Sua valigia? (koo-eh-stah eh lah soo-ah vah-lee-jah) (Is this your suitcase?) No, le mie sono queste. (noh leh mee-eh soh-noh koo-eh-steh) (No, these are mine.)

Here you see the feminine version of singular and plural (questa and queste, respectively). The following shows the masculine version of singular and plural (questo and questi):

Signore, questo messaggio è per Lei. (see-nyoh-reh koo-eh-stoh mehs-sahj- joh eh pehr lay) (Sir, this message is for you.) Questi prezzi sono eccessivi! (koo-eh-stee preht-tsee soh-noh ehch-chehs-see-vee) (These prices are excessive!)

Possessive pronouns such as my, your, and his indicate possession of something (the noun). In Italian, the possessive pronoun varies according to the gender of the item it refers to. The possessive pronoun must agree in number and gender with the possessed thing or person. Unlike in English, in Italian you almost always put the article in front of the possessive determiner.

When you want to show that something belongs to you and that something is a feminine noun, the possessive mia ends in a, such as la mia valigia (lah mee-ah vah-lee-jah) (my suitcase). When you refer to a masculine word, the possessive ends in o, as in il mio letto (eel mee-oh leht-toh) (my bed).

So these pronouns get their form from the possessor—il mio (eel mee-oh) (mine), il tuo (eel too-oh) (yours, informal), and so on—and their number and gender from the thing possessed. For example, in è la mia chiave (eh lah mee-ah kee-ah-veh) (it's my key), la chiave is singular and feminine and therefore is replaced by the possessive pronoun mia. Table 10-4 lists the possessive pronouns and their articles.

Following are some practical examples using possessive pronouns:

È grande la vostra stanza? (eh grahn-deh lah voh-strah stahn-dzah) (Is your [informal, plural persons] room large?)

Dov'è il tuo albergo? (doh-veh eel too-oh ahl-behr-goh) (Where is your [informal, singular person] hotel?)

Ecco i Vostri documenti. (ehk-koh ee voh-stree doh-koo-mehn-tee) (Here are your [formal, plural persons] documents.)

Questa è la Sua chiave. (koo-eh-stah eh lah soo-ah kee-ah-veh) (This is your [formal, singular person] key.)

Questa è la sua chiave. (koo-eh-stah eh lah soo-ah kee-ah-veh) (This is his/her key.)

La mia camera è molto tranquilla. (lah mee-ah kah-meh-rah eh mohl-toh trahn-koo-eel-lah) (My room is very quiet.)

Anche la nostra. E la tua? (ahn- keh lah noh-strah eh lah too-ah) (Ours too. And yours [informal, singular person]?)

Vocabularies

La chiave	The key
Il numero della chiave	The key number
Lei è nella camera numero 29.	You are in room number 29.

Directions will be given with reference to floors...

Piano terra	Ground floor
Primo piano	First floor
Secondo piano	Second floor
Terzo	piano
Third floor	Quarto piano
Dov'è l'ascensore?	Where is the elevator?

Dov'è la piscina?	Where is the swimming pool?
Dov'è il ristorante?	Where is the restaurant?
Dove viene servita la colazione?	Where do you serve breakfast?
A che ora è il check-out?	At what time do I need to check out?
Pago adesso o più tardi?	Do I pay now or later?
Quando viene servita la colazione?	When do you serve breakfast?

If your room isn't equipped with all the facilities you'd like, here are some useful phrases...

Ho bisogno di più asciugamani.	I need more towels.
Ho bisogno di più sapone.	I need more soap.
Ho bisogno di più carta igienica.	I need more toilet paper.
Ho bisogno di un'altra coperta.	I need an extra blanket.
Ho bisogno di lenzuola pulite.	I need clean sheets.

Here are some final words and phrases that might come in handy...

un letto matrimonial	A double bed (for two people)
l'aria condizionata	The air conditioning
Il riscaldamento	The heater
Il riscaldamento è rotto	The heater is broken.
Sporco	Dirty
Rumoroso	Noisy
Pulito	Clean
Freddo	Cold
Caldo	Hot
L'acqua	The water
La luce	The light
Rotto/rotta	Broken
Inacettabile!	Unacceptable

CHAPTER 2: VOCABULARY IN TAXI

A taxi can be a viable way to get around some of the major Italian cities for short jaunts or if you are in a small town with limited public transportation and need to get back to the train station or bus station. It can be frustrating for many travelers who are accustomed to hailing a cab right from the curb – this won't work in Italy.

The cabs operate on a radio-dispatch system. Therefore, when you see them, most cabs are either occupied with passengers or en route to picking up a passenger.

You will either have to call the cab company to arrange pickup or you will have to send a text message (SMS) to the messaging center along with the address where you are located. They will text back the approximate pickup time.

** Remember – the fare starts from zero as soon as the cab is dispatched and not when they pick you up.

Only use authorized taxis – they will have a taxi sign on the top of the cab. And they usually have a small placard inside the cab that shows their license along with their identification number. They will also have a meter inside the cab. If they do not have a meter, then they are an unlicensed operator.

In Rome, the taxis are white and have a license number on the side. In most Italian cities they are either white or yellow. In Rome the taxi stands (or ranks) are indicated with an orange sign and are located at all the major tourist attractions.

They are also indicated with the sign that says fermata di taxi. You can find them around both airports, the train station (Termini), Piazza Barberini, Piazza Venezia, Largo Argentina, Piazza della Repubblica, etc.

Beware of private operators that offer to give you a "private" ride. Some of them are legitimate, but some have been known to rip off tourists. It's best if you avoid these operators.

where?	dove?
Where can I find a taxi?	Dove posso trovare un taxi?
Are you free (available)?	È libero (disponibile)?
How much does it cost to go...	Quanto costa per andare...
...to the museum?	...al museo?
...to the airport?	...all'aeroporto?
...to the station?	...alla stazione?
...to the hotel?	...all'albergo?
Turn to the right please.	Giri a destra per favore.
Turn to the left please.	Giri a sinistra per favore.
Go straight ahead please.	Vada sempre diritto per favore.

Stop here, please.	Fermi qui, per favore.
Can you take me...	Mi può portarmi...
...to this address?	...a questo indirizzo?
...to the center (of town)?	...al centro?
...to the airport?	...all'aeroporto?

Conversation

All'hotel Bernini, vicino alla Fontana di Trevi
To the Bernini hotel, near the Trevi Fountain

Va bene, le metto le valigie nel cofano
Ok. I'll put the suitcases in the boot.

Mi scusi, è la strada più veloce? Mi hanno detto che sarebbero stati solo dieci minuti.
Excuse me, are we going the fastest route? I was told it only takes 10 minutes.

In Italia dieci minuti non sono esattamente dieci minuti. C'è molto traffico.
In Italy, 10 minutes does not mean 10 minutes. There is a lot of traffic.

Ma son sicuro di aver già visto questa piazza!
But I'm sure I've seen this square before!

Lo veda come un giro gratuito della città.
Think of it as a free tour of the city.

Calling a cab

dove posso trovare un taxi? where can I find a taxi?

per favore mi chiama un taxi ... please can you order me a taxi ...

... subito

... now

... per le ...

for (time)

Quanto verrà a costare per andare a/al/alla ...

how much will it cost to :

alla stazione	to the station
all'aeroporto	to the airport
all'uffi cio turistico	tourist office
c'è un bancomat qui vicino?	is there a cashpoint nearby?
per favore, mi porti a ...	please take me to ...
mi porti lì, per favore	take me there, please
Questo è l'indirizzo del mio albergo	here's the address of my hotel

le mie valigie sono pesantissime; mi aiuta a prenderle?

my cases are heavy; would you help me with them?

facciamo due fermate   we are going to make two stops

il tassista	taxi driver
il posteggio di taxi	taxi rank
la tariffa	fare
la tariffa notturna	night fare
la tariffa diurna	day fare
la tariffa fissa	fixed fare
il tassametro	taxi meter
il cofano	car boot

le dispiace mettere la cintura di sicurezza?

would you mind putting on your seat belt?

Non riesco ad allacciarmi la cintura

I can't fasten my seat belt

può andare più piano/veloce?

Could you slow down/go faster?

devo prendere il treno

I have to catch a train

sono di fretta/in ritardo

I'm in a hurry/late

il percorso route

il ponte bridge

il tunnel

tunnel

il semaforo

traffic lights

se non rallenta mi sento male

if you don't slow down I'm going to be sick

Getting out

si può accostare qui?	can you stop here?
è più di quanto indicato sul tassametro	it's more than on the meter
come mai è così tanto?	why is it so much?
il supplemento	extra charge
la mancia	tip
si può scordare la mancia!	you can forget about the tip!
la ricevuta	receipt
tenga il resto	keep the change
mi dispiace, non ho moneta	sorry I don't have any change

623

CHAPTER 3: TRAVELING BY BUS AND TRAIN

The previous chapters have provided you with the framework for basic conversation and the building blocks (verbs, adjectives, adverbs, and basic expressions) to expand your communicative ability. This chapter will build on that framework and will provide you with the very practical and useful information you need to travel through train and bus.

The Verb Volere

The Italian verb volere means "to want."

> I want to travel.
>
> Voglio viaggiare.
>
> vohl-yoh vee-ah-JAH-ray

> I would like to travel.
>
> Vorrei viaggiare.
>
> vohr-ray vee-ah-JAH-ray

Volere is an irregular Italian verb. For the purposes of this book, it is presented here in its two most useful forms: the present indicative tense and the present conditional mood. In Italy it is more polite to express your desires and wishes with the present conditional mood.

> I'd like a ticket.
>
> Vorrei un biglietto.
>
> voh-ray oon beel-YEH-toh

The Verbs Andare and Venire These two verbs are also important for travelers to know. Andare means "to go" and venire means "to come." These two verbs are most useful in the present indicative tense and the passato prossimo.

> We are going to Rome.
>
> Andiamo a Roma.
>
> ahn-dee-YAH-moh ah roh-mah

> He's coming with us.
>
> Lui viene con noi.
>
> loo-ee vyeh-neh kohn noy

Present	andare	venire
io	vado	vengo
	vah-doh	vehn-goh
tu	vai	vieni
	veye	vee-EH-nee
lui, lei, Lei	va	viene
	vah	vee-EH-neh
noi	andiamo	veniamo
	ahn-dee-AH-moh	veh-nee-YAH-moh
voi	andate	venite
	ahn-DAH-tay	veh-NEE-teh
loro, Loro	vanno	vengono
	vahn-noh	VEHN-goh-noh

Both andare and venire are conjugated with essere in the past tense (passato prossimo). Though andare has a regular past participle (andato), venire has a slightly irregular past participle (venuto).

KEYNOTES

The verbs andare and venire are both irregular in the present tense. You will notice that several commonly used verbs have irregular conjugations.

Airport and Flight Vocabulary

The hustle and bustle of the airport can be stressful. The following terms and expressions may help to alleviate some of that stress.

People, Places, and Things

airplane	un aereo	oon ah-EH-reh-oh
airport	un aeroporto	oon ah-eh-roh-POR-toh
baggage	i bagagli	ee bah-GAHL-yee

baggage check	la consegna bagagli	lah kohn-SEHN-yah bah-GAHL-yee
boarding pass	la carta d'imbarco	lah KAHR-tah dee eem-BAHR-koh
carry-on luggage	i bagagli a mano	ee bah-GAHL-yee ah MAH-noh
checked luggage	i bagagli da stiva	ee bah-GAHL-yee dah STEE-vah
cart	un carello	oon kah-REHL-loh
check-in desk	il banco di check-in	eel BAHN-koh dee
check-in departures	partenze	pahr-TEHN-zeh
early	in anticipo	een ahn-TEE-chee-poh
late	in ritardo	een ree-TAHR-doh
passenger	il passeggero	eel pahs-sehj-JEHR-oh
passport	il passaporto	eel pahs-sah-POHR-toh
pilot	il pilota	eel pee-LOH-tah
security check	il controllo di sicurezza	

eel kohn-TROHL-loh dee see-koo- REHTS-sah

shuttle	lo shuttle	loh shuttle
steward/stewardess	l'assistente di bordo	lahs-sees-TEHN-teh dee BOHR-doh
visa il	visto	eel VEES-toh

KEYNOTES

You will notice that English is often used for terms related to international travel. La hostess can be used to mean stewardess, il duty free is a duty-free shop, economy and coach are widely used to refer to travel class options, many Italians will check in at il check-in, and un volo con stopover is a flight with a stopover.

Ticket Information

airline	la compagnia aerea	lah kohm-pahn-YEE-ah ah-EH-reh-ah
first class	la prima classe	lah PREE-mah KLAHS-say
flight	il volo	eel VOH-loh
gate	l'uscita	loo-SHEE-tah
one-way ticket	un biglietto solo andata	

oon-beel-YEH-toh soh-loh ahn-DAH-tah

round-trip ticket	un biglietto andata e ritorno	

oon-beel-YEH-toh ahn-DAH-tah eh ree-TOHR-noh

626

terminal	il terminal	eel terminal

Travel Verbs

to board	imbarcare	eem-BAHR-kah-ray
to buy a ticket	fare il biglietto	fah-ray eel beel-YEH-toh
to check bags	consegnare i bagagli	kohn-sehn-YAH-ray ee bah-GAHL-yee
to make reservation	a fare una prenotazione	

fah-ray oo-nah preh-noh-tat-see-YOH-nay

to sit down	sedersi or accomodarsi	

seh-DEHR-see /ahk-koh-moh-DAHR-see

to take off	decollare	deh-kohl-LAH-ray
to land	atterrare	aht-teh-RAHR-ray

Baggage Claim, Immigration, and Customs

Before you can enjoy a nice dish of pasta alla carbonara, you have to get out of the airport. The following list of terms will help you get through customs smoothly.

Arrivals and Baggage

arrivals	arrivi	ahr-REE-vee
baggage claim	il ritiro bagagli	eel ree-TEE-roh bah-GAHL-yee
lost luggage	i bagagli smarriti	ee bah-GAHL-yee smahr-REE-tee

My luggage is lost.   i miei bagagli sono smarriti.

ee myay bah-GAHL-yee soh-noh smahr-REE-tee

Immigration and Customs

immigration	l'immigrazione	lee-mee-grahts-ee-OH-nay
last name	il cognome	eel kohn-YOH-may
first name	il nome	eel noh-may
customs	la dogana	lah doh-GAH-nah
nothing to declare	niente da dichiarare	nee-EHN-tay dah deek-yah-RAH-ray
customs declaration	il modula dogana form	eel MOH-doo-loh doh-GAH-nah

Here's my passport   Ecco il mio passaporto.
ehk-koh eel mee-oh pahs-sah-POHR-toh

I have a visa.	Ho un visto.	oh oon VEES-toh
I don't have a visa.	Non ho un visto.	nohn oh oon VEES-toh
I would like to declare . . .	Vorrei dichiarare . . .	vohr-ray deek-yah-RAH-ray

Train Vocabulary

Traveling by train is often cheaper, faster, and more convenient than traveling by airplane or car within Italy, though there are some exceptions. Italy's bullet train, the Eurostar, offers fast, affordable, comfortable, and somewhat reliable service between major cities.

Train travel from major cities to smaller cities and towns is certainly an affordable option, but it can add time to your trip, especially in southern Italy.

arrival	arrivo	ahr-REE-voh
cabin	scompartimento	skohm-pahr-tee-MEHN-toh
car	carrozza	kahr-ROH-tsah
chief conductor	capotreno	kah-poh-TREH-noh
conductor	controllore	kohn-trohl-LOH-reh

corridor	corridoio	kohr-ree-DOH-yoh
departure	partenza	pahr-TEHN-tzah
family offer	offerta	ohf-FEHR-tah
	famiglia	fah-MEE-lyah
first class	prima classe	PREE-mah KLAHS-seh
luggage rack	portabagagli	reh-TEE-nah/
(overhead)	portabagagli	pohr-tah-bah-GAH-lyee
nonsmokers	non fumatori	nohn foo-mah-TOH-ree
smokers	fumatori	foo-mah-TOH-ree
platform	binario	bee-NAH-ree-oh
railway	ferrovia	fehr-roh-VEE-ah
reservation	prenotazione	preh-noh-tah-TZYO-neh
restaurant car	carrozza ristorante	kahr-ROH- tzah ree-stoh-RAHN-teh
seat	posto	POH-stoh
second class	seconda classe	seh-KOHN-dah KLAHS-seh
sleeper car	vagone	vah-GOH-neh letto LEHT-toh
sleeping	cuccetta	koo-CHEHT-tah
compartment station	stazione	stah-TZYOH-neh
supplement	supplemento	soop-pleh-MEHN-toh
ticket	biglietto	bee-LYEHT-toh
ticket office	biglietteria	bee-lyeht-tehr-REE-ah
toilet	toilette	twah-LEHT
tracks	binari	bee-NAH-ree
train	treno	TREH-noh
validate	timbrare	teem-BRAH-reh
window	finestrino	fee-neh-STREE-noh

The names of some Italian cities are spelled and pronounced differently in English. Here is a list of some of Italy's major cities, with their Italian spellings and pronunciations.

English	Italian	Pronunciation
Florence	Firenze	fee-REHN-tzeh
Leghorn	Livorno	lee-VOHR-noh

Mantua	Mantova	MAHN-toh-vah
Milan	Milano	mee-LAH-noh
Naples	Napoli	NAH-poh-lee
Rome	Roma	ROH-mah
Sienna	Siena	SYEH-nah
Turin	Torino	toh-REE-noh
Venice	Venezia	veh-NEH-tzyah

Some Useful Phrases for Train Travel

Sorry, is this the train   Mi scusi, è questo il treno per . . . ?
to . . . ?

mee SKOO-zee, eh KWEH-stoh eel TREH-noh pehr

Good morning, I have   Buon giorno, ho prenotato il posto . . .
booked a seat . . .

bwohn JOHR-noh, oh preh-noh-TAH-toh eel POH-sto

How long until we get   Fra quanto si arriva a . . . ?
to . . . ?

frah KWAHN-toh see ahr-REE-vah ah

Is the train late?   Il treno è in ritardo?

eel TREH-noh eh een ree-TAHR-doh

Is this seat taken?   È libero questo posto?

eh LEE-beh-roh KWEH-stoh POH-stoh

Yes, have a seat.   Prego, si accomodi.

PREH-goh, see ahk-KOH-moh-dee

No, it's occupied.   No, è occupato.

noh, eh ohk-koo-PAH-toh

CHAPTER 4: USEFUL PHRASES WHEN SHOPPING

Italy is famous for its taste and fashion sense, as well as for the stilisti (stee- lee-stee) (designers) who build on that reputation. Looking at all the well- dressed Italians, you may feel like going shopping so that you can look as good. What better place to shop for gorgeous apparel than in Italy, which leads Europe in fashion and shoe production?

This chapter also covers another Italian favorite: food. From fresh-caught fish to crusty loaves of bread, you can find everything you need at an Italian mercato (mehr-kah-toh) (market).

So how do you say "shopping" in Italian?

You say fare la spesa (fah-reh la speh-zah) (literally, making the shopping) when you buy food and fare spese (fah-reh speh-zeh) for everything else. The good news is that you only have to conjugate the verb fare.

Departmentalizing Your Shopping

North Americans have access to huge centri commerciali (chehn-tree kohm- mehr-chee-ah-lee) (shopping malls), where you can find everything. In Italy, people shop in grandi magazzini (grahn-dee mah-gaht-tsee-nee) (department stores), which are tiny compared to American ones.

In any size of department store, signs help you find your way around:

entrata	(ehn-trah-tah)	(entrance)
uscita	(oo-shee-tah)	(exit)
uscita di sicurezza		
(oo-shee-tah dee see-koo-reht-tsah) (emergency exit)		
spingere	(speen-jeh-reh)	(to push)
tirare	(tee-rah-reh)	(to pull)
orario di apertura		
(oh-rah-ree-oh dee ah-pehr-too-rah) (business hours)		
aperto	(ah-pehr-toh)	(open)
chiuso	(kee-oo-zoh)	(closed)
scala mobile	(skah-lah moh-bee-leh) (escalator)	
ascensore	(ah-shehn-soh-reh)	(elevator)
cassa	(kahs-sah)	(cash register)
camerini	(kah-meh-ree-nee) (fitting rooms)	

Signs pointing to the various reparti (reh-pahr-tee) (departments) may or may not include the word da (dah) (for), as in abbigliamento da donna (ahb-bee-lyah-mehn-toh dah dohn-nah) (women's wear). Other departments you may be interested in include

abbigliamento da uomo

(ahb-bee-lyah-mehn-toh dah oo-oh-moh)   (menswear)

abbigliamento da bambino

(ahb-bee-lyah-mehn-toh dah bahm- bee-noh) (children's wear)

intimo donna (een-tee-moh dohn-nah)   (ladies' intimate apparel)

intimo uomo   (een-tee-moh oo-oh-moh)   (men's intimate apparel)

accessori (ahch-chehs-soh-ree)   (accessories)

profumeria   (proh- foo-meh-ree-ah)   (perfumery)

articoli da toletta   (ahr-tee-koh-lee dah toh-leht- tah) (toiletries)

casalinghi   (kah-zah-leen-gee)   (housewares)

biancheria per la casa

(bee-ahn-keh-ree-ah pehr lah kah-zah) (linens and towels)

articoli sportivi

(ahr-tee-koh-lee spohr-tee-vee)   (sports equipment)

articoli da regalo   (ahr-tee-koh-lee dah reh- gah-loh) (gifts)

Talking with a Sales Clerk

When you have a question or need some advice in a store, you turn to la commessa [f] (lah kohm-mehs-sah) or il commesso [m] (eel kohm-mehs-soh) (the sales clerk) and say

Mi può aiutare, per favore

(mee poo-oh ah-yoo- tah-reh pehr fah-voh-reh)

(Can you help me, please?).

Avere bisogno di   (ah-veh-reh bee-zoh-nyoh dee) (to need)

is a frequent expression in Italian. You use it in any kind of store.

The form that you use goes like this:

Ho bisogno di   (oh bee-zoh-nyoh dee)   (I need)

Simply use the appropriate form of avere (see Chapter 2) and then add bisogno di to the end to say "you need," "he needs," and so on. If you're just looking and a salesperson asks Posso essere d'aiuto? (pohs-soh ehs-seh-reh dah-yoo-toh) or Desidera? (deh-zee-deh-rah) (Can I help you?), you answer Sto solo dando un'occhiata, grazie (stoh soh-loh dahn-doh oon- ohk-kee-ah-tah grah-tsee-eh) (I'm just looking, thank you).

Sizing Up Italian Sizes

Whenever you go to another country, particularly in Europe, the sizes called taglie (tah-lyeh) or misure (mee-zoo-reh) in Italian change, and you never know which one corresponds to yours.

Choosing Colors and Fabrics

Knowing some colori (koh-loh-ree) (colors) is important. Two important words as far as color is concerned are scuro/a/i/e (skoo- roh/rah/ree/reh) (dark) and chiaro/a/i/e (kee-ah-roh/rah/ree/reh) (light). Don't worry over all the vowels at the ends of these words. You use only one of them at a time according to the gender and case of the noun it modifies:

> Use -o with male singular nouns.
>
> Use -a for female singular nouns.
>
> Use -i for male plural nouns.
>
> Use -e with female plural nouns.

You may want to specify a particular type of fabric when shopping for an item. Table 6-4 lists some common fabrics.

Accessorizing

Of course, you want to give your outfit that final touch with beautiful

accessori	(ahch-chehs-soh-ree)	(accessories):
berretto	(behr-reht-toh)	(cap)
borsa	(bohr-sah)	(bag)
calze	(kahl-dzeh)	(stockings)
calzini	(kahl-dzee-nee)	(socks)
cappello	(kahp-pehl-loh)	(hat)
cintura	(cheen-too-rah)	(belt)
collant	(kohl-lahn)	(tights)
cravatta	(krah-vaht-tah)	(tie)
guanti	(goo-ahn-tee)	(gloves)
ombrello	(ohm-brehl- loh)	(umbrella)
sciarpa	(shahr-pah)	(scarf)

Stepping Out in Style

Knowing that Italy is the leader in the shoe industry, you won't find it hard to believe what good taste Italians have in scarpe (skahr-peh) (shoes). If you travel to Italy, have a look into the various shoe shops. You may well find the shoes of your dreams, whether they be a regular paio di scarpe (pah-yoh dee skahr-peh) (pair of shoes), pantofole (pahn-toh-foh-leh) (slippers), sandali (sahn-dah-lee) (sandals), or stivali (stee-vah-lee) (boots).

When you try on shoes, you may need to use these words:

stretta/e	(streht-tah/teh)	(tight)
larga/e	(lahr-gah/geh)	(loose)
corta/e	(kohr-tah/teh)	(short)
lunga/e	(loon-gah/geh)	(long)

Because la scarpa (lah skahr-pah) (the shoe) is female in Italian, we provide you with only the female endings for these adjectives: -a for singular and -e for plural.

Italian uses numero (noo-meh-roh) (number) to talk about shoe sizes, but taglie (tah-lyeh) or misure (mee-zoo-reh) (size) to talk about clothes.

Shopping for Food

People do the bulk of their food shopping in a supermercato (soo-pehr- mehr-kah-toh) (supermarket). But many Italian cities have street markets and little shops, called alimentari (ah-lee-mehn-tah-ree), where you can get everything from latte (laht-teh) (milk) over biscotti (bee-skoht-tee) (cookies) to all sorts of assorted salumi (sah-loo-mee) (cold meats) and formaggi (fohr-mahj-jee) (cheeses).

You may choose to pick out your carne (kahr-neh) (meat) at a macellaio (mah-chehl-lah-yoh) (butcher shop), your fresh prodotti (proh-doht-tee) (produce) at a farmers' market, and your pane (pah-neh) (bread) at a panetteria (pah-neht-teh-ree-ah) (bakery), but you can find everything in a supermarket.

Meats

From the butcher shop, you might select items like these:

agnello	(ah-nyehl-loh)	(lamb)
anatra	(ah-nah-trah)	(duck)
fegato	(feh- gah-toh)	(liver—if not specified, calf liver)
maiale	(mah-yah-leh)	(pork)
manzo	(mahn-dzoh)	(beef)
pollo	(pohl-loh)	(chicken)
vitello	(vee-tehl-loh)	(veal)
bistecca	(bee-stehk-kah)	(steak)
cotoletta	(koh-toh-leht-tah)	(cutlet)
filetto	(fee-leht-toh)	(filet steak)

Seafood

In Italy, you get good fresh pesce (peh-sheh) (fish) when you're close to the sea or a lake. If you happen on a good pescheria (peh-skeh-ree-ah) (fish market), you can order what your palate desires:

acciughe fresche (ahch-choo-geh freh-skeh) (fresh anchovies)

aragosta	(ah-rah-goh-stah)	(lobster)
calamari	(kah-lah-mah-ree)	(squid)
cozze	(koht-tseh)	(mussels)
crostacei	(kroh-stah-cheh-ee)	(shellfish)
frutti di mare	(froot-tee dee mah-reh)	(seafood)
gamberetti	(gahm-beh-reht-tee)	(shrimp)
gamberi	(gahm-beh-ree)	(prawns)
granchi	(grahn-kee)	(crab)
merluzzo	(mehr-loot-tsoh)	(cod)
pesce spada	(peh-sheh spah-dah)	(swordfish)
polpo/polipo	(pohl-poh poh-lee-poh)	(octopus)
sogliola	(soh- lyoh-lah)	(sole)
spigola	(spee-goh-lah)	(bass)
tonno fresco	(tohn-noh freh- skoh)	(fresh tuna)
vongole	(vohn-goh-leh)	(clams)

Produce

When you go al mercato (ahl mehr-kah-toh) (to the market) and here, we're talking about an open-air farmers' market you primarily find

frutta   (froot-tah)   (fruits)

and

verdura   (vehr-doo-rah)   (vegetables).

get tutto l'anno (toot-toh lahn-noh)   (year-round).

We give you the forms in singular and plural. In most cases, you say what you want and the seller picks it out for you. Prices are according to weight, usually by chilo (kee-loh) (kilo). Occasionally, you find little baskets or paper bags, which indicate that you can choose your own frutta (froot-tah) (fruit) or verdura (vehr-doo-rah) (vegetables).

Un etto (oon eht-toh) means 100 grams. Mezz'etto (meht-tseht-toh) is 50 grams, because mezzo (meht-tsoh) means "half." Likewise, a mezzo chilo (meht-tsoh kee-loh) is half a kilo.

636

Baked goods

In a panetteria (pah-neht-teh-ree-ah) (bakery), you can try all sorts of different kinds of pane (pah-neh) (bread), ranging from il pane integrale (eel pah-neh een-teh-grah-leh) (whole wheat bread) to dolci (dohl-chee) (pastries).

In most Italian bakeries, you also find pizza al taglio (peet-tsah ahl tah-lyoh) (slices of pizza), which you buy according to weight. You can choose between pizza bianca (peet-tsah bee-ahn-kah) (white pizza) that is, pizza topped only with mozzarella and olive oil and pizza rossa (peet-tsah rohs-sah) (red pizza), which is topped with mozzarella and tomatoes or tomato sauce. The flavor can vary from bakery to bakery, as it does from region to region.

Paying for Your Purchases

When you want to buy something, you have to pay for it.

In Italian department stores, prices are clearly labeled in euros and include sales tax. Often, during saldi (sahl-dee) (sales), il prezzo (eel preht-tsoh) (the price) on the tag is already reduced, but you may find tags reading saldi alla

cassa (sahl-dee ahl-lah kahs-sah) (reduction at the cash register).

When you want to know the price of an item, you ask

> Quanto vengono?
>
> (koo-ahn-toh vehn-goh-noh)
>
> (How much are they?)
>
> Or
>
> Quanto costano?
>
> (koo-ahn-toh koh-stah-noh)
>
> (How much do they cost?).

In Italy, you can't pay by credit card or check everywhere, so ask before you buy something. Shop doors usually indicate which cards the establishment accepts; some establishments welcome neither checks nor credit cards. Italians generally like to be paid in contanti (een kohn- tahn-tee) (in cash).

The following phrases can help you complete your purchase:

> Posso pagare con la carta di credito?
>
> (pohs-soh pah-gah-reh kohn lah kahr- tah dee kreh-dee-toh)
>
> (Can I pay with a credit card?)

> Mi dispiace, non accettiamo carte di credito. Dovrebbe pagare in contanti.
>
> (mee dee-spee-ah- cheh nohn ahch-cheht-tee-ah-moh kahr-teh dee kreh-dee-toh doh-vrehb-beh pah- gah-reh een kohn-tahn-tee)
>
> (I'm sorry, we don't accept credit cards. You have to pay cash.)

Dov'è il prossimo bancomat?

(doh-veh eel prohs-see-moh bahn- koh-maht)

(Where is the nearest ATM?)

One of the great reasons people like to visit Italy is for the shopping. All of the great fashion brands such as Gucci, Fendi, Dolce e Gabbanna, Ferragamo, etc. are all abundant in the fashion capital of the world. Each of the main shopping meccas in Italy has a famous street where you will pay the best of the fashion industry.

> Florence – Via de' Tornabuoni

> Rome – Via dei Condotti

> Milan – Quadilatero d'Oro

If money is no object, you'll find la crème de la crème of Italian fashion on these streets. However, walking just a few blocks off these streets will enable you to find some better- priced fashion items and perhaps even a sale (saldi) or bargain (sconto).

Can I haggle or bargain with the vendors?

The art of bargaining or haggling over the price of an item is often customary in the street markets and smaller boutiques, especially as you head down south. These outdoor stalls and markets in Sicily and Naples are actually derived from Arab traditions when they ruled southern Italy back in the 800s. If you are in a position of buying multiple items, you will usually have more bargaining power. For example, if you buy two items, the third one will be at half-price.

For items such as food or electronics, haggling is usually not an option.

What are the best things to buy in Italy?

Italy is known for its fashion.

Unfortunately, the days of "Made in Italy" are being replaced by "Made in China" at a cheaper price. They'll use Italian materials but the labor will be Asian. You can thank the capitalist market mechanism for that.

It doesn't mean the Fendi handbag is not a good buy. And it doesn't necessarily mean you'll find a better price in Italy as opposed to Toronto or Los Angeles.

Some Italian exporters will get subsidies from the Italian government so the price you pay may actually be less in New York.

However, it sounds better to say you bought your Fendi handbag in Rome near the Colosseum as opposed to a shop off Broadway.

Other items that Italy is known for producing are leather goods, ceramics, pottery, glass (Murano), gold (18 karat), and jewelry.

Business Hours

Business hours for many shops will of course vary, but they typically will shut down in the middle of the day for lunch. And depending on the business, some will be open later during the summer. Some will close one afternoon or morning during the week, and it'll vary from town to town. Grocery stores may close Wednesday afternoon. Clothing stores may close on Monday morning.

Office hours

Mon – Fri 8:30 AM to 1 PM then 2:30 PM to 5:30 PM

Banks

Mon – Fri 8:30 AM to 1 PM then 2:30 PM to 4:30 PM

Some banks are open during the morning on Saturdays.

cost costa

How much?	Quanto?
How much does it cost?	Quanto costa?
Where?	Dove?
Where is the nearest...?	Dove si trova...

Or

I'm looking for a (an)...

Sto cercando per...

...antique shop	...l'antiquario ...
bakery	...il panificio
...barber	...il barbiere
...bookshop	...la libreria
...delicatessen	...la salumeria
...drug store (pharmacy)	...la farmacia
...dry cleaner	...la tintoria
...fish market	...la pescheria
...jeweler	...la gioelleria
...newsstand	...l'edicola
...post office	...l'ufficio postale
...shoe shop	...il negozio di scarpe
...supermarket	...il supermercato
...wine shop	...il vinaio

Can I use a credit card?

Posso usare una carta di credito?

Do you have this...

Tiene questo...

...in my size?
...nella taglia mia?

...bigger?
...più grande?

...smaller?
...più piccolo?

It's too expensive.
È molto caro.

Yes, I'll take it.
Sì, lo prendo.

No, I don't want it.
No, non lo voglio.

moisturizer
crema idratante

razor
rasoio

shampoo
shampoo

soap
sapone

toothbrush

spazzolino da denti

toothpaste

pasta di dente

CHAPTER 5: IN YOUR COMMUNITY

If you plan on staying in Italy for an extended period of time, you will need to take care of the inevitable day-to-day tasks. This chapter will provide you with common terms and expressions for your everyday interactions with shopkeepers and postal employees. Remember, Italians are very receptive to outsiders who make an effort to speak their language!

At the Market

Food shopping in Italy can be a fun and interesting experience. You will find supermarkets (very similar to their American counterparts) pretty much everywhere. Many Italians, however, prefer to shop at local, privately owned specialty shops or perhaps at the local mercato centrale.

bakery   la panetteria

lah pah-neht-teh-REE-ah

book shop   la libreria

lah lee-breh-REE-ah

butcher shop   la macelleria

lah mah-chehl-leh-REE-ah

central market   mercato centrale

mehr-KAH-toh chehn-TRAH-leh

dairy   la latteria

lah laht-teh-REE-ah

department store il grande magazzino

eel grahn-day mah-gahts-SEE-noh

fishmonger   la pescheria

lah pehs-keh-REE-ah

florist   il fioraio

eel fyoh-REYE-oh

green grocer   il fruttivendolo

eel froot-tee-VEHN-doh-loh

grocery store   un alimentari

oon ah-lee-mehn-TAH-ree

hardware store   la ferramenta

lah fehr-reh-MEHN-tah

jewelry store   la gioielleria

lah joy-ehl-leh-REE-ah

newsstand   il giornalaio

eel johr-nah-LEYE-oh

paper store   la cartoleria

lah kahr-toh-leh-REE-ah

pastry shop   la pasticceria

lah pahs-tee-cheh-REE-ah

perfume store   la profumeria

lah proh-foo-meh-REE-ah

pharmacy   la farmacia

lah fahr-mah-CHEE-ah

supermarket	il supermercato
	eel soo-pehr-mehr-KAH-toh
toy store	il negozio di giocattoli
	eel neh-GOHT-see-oh dee joh-KAHT-toh- lee

In the Shop

cash register la cassa lah kahs-sah closed chiuso kyou-zoh entrance l'entrata lehn-TRAH-tah exit l'uscita loo-SHEE-tah sale i saldi ee sahl-dee special offer offerta speciale ohf-FEHR-tah speh-CHAH-leh open aperto ah-PEHR-toh opening hours orario di apertura oh-RAH-ree-oh dee ah-pehr-TOO-rah

KEYNOTE

Larger Italian supermarkets of the chain store variety will charge you a 1 deposit for a shopping cart, which is returned to you after you've finished your shopping. Also, many supermarkets charge for shopping bags to encourage customers to bring their own bags and reduce waste.

Quantities, Weights, and Measures Knowing the correct terms for quantities, weights, and measures can be very helpful when you are out shopping for food.

How much does it weigh? It weighs . . . kilograms. Quanto pesa? Pesa . . . kili. Kwahn-toh peh-zah Peh-zah keelee

bit, piece un po' di oon poh dee bottle bottiglia boht-TEEL-yah box scattola SKAHT-toh-lah can lattina laht-TEE-nah jar barattola bah-RAHT-toh-lah gram gramma grahm-mah hectogram un etto oon eht-toh kilogram un kilo oon kee-loh liter litro lee-troh

ALERT

When ordering food items by weight, you are more likely to express that weight using hectograms (etti). For example, un etto di prosciutto crudo would be about 3.5 ounces of prosciutto, a little less than a quarter pound.

enough basta bahs-tah more ancora ahn-KOH-rah less, fewer meno may-noh a little un po' di oon poh dee too much, too many troppo trohp-poh

In the Coffee Shop

There seems to be a coffee shop in Italian, il bar on every street corner in Italy. It is the place where people go for a quick breakfast or lunch, a cup of coffee, an aperitif, or a quick snack.

a cup of coffee	un caffè oon	kahf-feh
a cup of tea	un tè	oon-teh
a glass of orange juice un bicchiere di succo d'arancia		
oon bee-KYEH-reh dee soo-koh dee ah-RAHN-chah		

a piece of cake   una fetta di torta

oo-nah feht-tah dee tohr-tah cake la torta lah tohr-tah

chocolate   il cioccolato

eel choh-koh-LAH-toh coffee il caffè eel kahf-feh

cookies   i biscotti

ee beez-KOHT-tee

fruit   tart la torta di frutta lah

tohr-tah dee froot-tah ice

cream   il gelato

eel jeh-LAH-toh

chocolate ice cream il gelato al cioccolato

eel jeh-LAH-toh ahl choh-koh-LAH-toh

strawberry ice cream   il gelato alla fragola

eel jeh-LAH-toh ahl-lah FRAH-goh-lah

vanilla ice cream   il gelato alla vaniglia

eel jeh-LAH-toh ahl-lah vah-NEEL-yah

lemon sherbet   il sorbetto al limone

eel sohr-BEHT-toh ahl lee-MOH-neh

orange sherbet   il sorbetto all'arancia

eel sohr-BEHT-toh ahl-lah-RAHN-chah

raspberry sherbet   il sorbetto ai lamponi

eel sohr-BEHT-toh eye lahm-POH-nee

sugar   lo zucchero

loh ZOO-keh-roh

sweets   i dolci

ee dohl-chee

whipped cream   la panna montata

lah pahn-nah mohn-TAH-tah

At the Post Office

Le Poste Italiane offers numerous services, including banking services, pension services, bill processing, and, last but not least, postal services. The post office is generally open Monday to Friday from 8:30 A.M. to 7:00 P.M. and on Saturdays from 8:30 A.M. to 1:00 P.M. Summer hours will vary, and there may occasionally be a chiuso per sciopero ("closed for strike") sign in the window when there's an important soccer game on television.

address   l'indirizzo

leen-dee-REETS-soh

addressee   il destinatario

 eel dehs-tee-nah-TAH-ree-oh

air mail   la posta aerea

lah pohs-tah ah-EH-reh-ah

coin changer   il distributore monete

eel dees-tree-boo-TOH-reh moh-NEH-teh

commemorative stamp   il francobollo emissione speciale

eel frahn-koh-BOHL-loh eh-mees-YOH-neh speh-CHAH-leh

counter   lo sportello

loh spohr-TEHL-loh

customs declaration   la dichiarazione doganale

lah dee-kyah-rahts-YOH-neh doh-goh- NAH-leh

646

destination	la destinazione
lah dehs-tee-nahts-YOH-neh	
information	l'informazione
leen-fohr-mahts-YOH-neh	
letter	la lettera
lah LEHT-teh-rah	
mailbox	la buca delle lettere
lah boo-kah dehl-leh LEHT-teh-reh	
package	il pacco
eel pahk-koh	
postage	l'affrancatura
lahf-frahn-kah-TOO-rah	
postal clerk	l'impiegato postale
leem-pyeh-GAH-toh pohs-TAH-leh	
postcard	la cartolina postale
lah kahr-toh-LEE-nah pohs-TAH-leh	
post office box	la casella postale
lah kah-ZEHL-lah pohs-TAH-leh	
postman	il postino
eel pohs-TEE-noh	
printed matter	le stampe

leh stahm-peh

receipt   la ricevuta

lah ree-cheh-VOO-tah

to register   ꞁ   fare una raccomandata

fah-ray oo-nah rahk-koh-mahn-DAH-tah

registered letter   la raccomandata

lah rahk-koh-mahn-DAH-tah

sender   il mittente

eel meet-TEHN-teh

small parcel   il pacchetto

eel pahk-KEHT-toh

special delivery   l'espresso

lehs-PRESS-oh

stamp (noun)   il francobollo

eel frahn-koh-BOHL-loh

stamp (verb)   affrancare

ahf-frahn-KAH-reh

stamp machine   il distributore francobolli

eel dees-tree-boo-TOH-reh frahn-koh-BOHL-lee

telegram   il telegramma

eel teh-leh-GRAHM-mah

unstamped non affrancato

nohn ahf-frahn-KAH-toh

value declaration la dichiarazione del valore

lah dee-kyah-rahts-YOH-neh dehl vah-LOH-reh

Weather Words and Expressions

If you're out and about and the weather starts to change, this section will help you come up with the correct words and terms.

How's the weather?	Che tempo fa?	Keh tehm-poh fah
It's sunny.	C'è il sole.	cheh eel soh-leh
It's nice.	Fa bel tempo.	fah behl tehm-poh
It's cold.	Fa freddo.	fah frehd-doh
It's hot.	Fa caldo.	fah kahl-doh
It's snowing.	Nevica.	NEH-vee-kah
It's raining.	Piove.	pyoh-veh
It's windy.	Tira vento.	tee-rah vehn-toh
It's foggy.	C'è la nebbia.	cheh lah nehb-byah
storm	il temporale	eel tehm-poh-RAH-leh
lightning	il lampo	eel lahm-poh
changeable	variabile	vah-ree-AH-bee-leh
air	l'aria	lah-ree-ah
rain	la pioggia	lah pyoh-jah
barometer	il barometro	eel bah-ROH-meh-troh
to rain	piovere	PYOH-veh-reh
blizzard	la tormenta	lah tohr-MEHN-tah
snow	la neve	lah neh-veh
climate	il clima	eel klee-mah
storm	la tempesta	lah tehm-PESS-tah
cloud	la nuvola	lah noo-voh-lah

sun	il sole	eel soh-leh
rainstorm	il temporale	eel tehm-poh-RAH-leh
cloudy	nuvoloso	noo-voh-LOH-soh
dusk	il crepuscolo	eel kreh-POOS-koh-loh
fog	la nebbia	lah nehb-byah
frost	il gelo	eel jeh-loh
hail	la grandine	leh GRAHN-dee-neh
ice	il ghiaccio	eel gyah-choh
mist	la foschia	lah fohs-kyah
weather report	il bollettino meteorologico	

eel bohl-leht-TEE-noh meh-tee-oh-roh-LOH-jee- koh

KEYNOTE

Italy's weather tends to be more moderate than the frigid winters and hot and humid summers in some parts of the United States. Many people consider the spring (April and May) and autumn (September and October) to be the best times to visit Italy. The weather is mild and there are fewer tourists at these times.

CHAPTER 6: AT THE DOCTOR'S OFFICE

Though the hope is that your trip will go off without a hitch, it's possible that you may need to seek a doctor's advice while you're abroad. This chapter contains the words and phrases you might need to know to tell a doctor what's wrong.

Common Ailments and Maladies This section gives a list of common ailments that can help you to get the help you need. You can use the verb avere (to have) with these ailments.

allergy	l'allergia	lahl-lehr-JEE-ah
appendicitis	l'appendicite	lahp-pehn-dee-CHEE-teh
arthritis	l'artrite	lahr-TREE-teh
blood poisoning	la setticemia	lah seht-tee-CHEM-ee-ah
chicken pox	la varicella	lah vah-ree-CHEHL-lah
cold	il raffreddore	eel rahf-frehd-DOH-ray
cough	la tosse	lah tohs-say
diabetes	il diabete	eel dee-ah-BEH-teh
dizziness	il capogiro	eel kah-poh-JEE-roh
fever	la febbre	lah fehb-breh
frostbite	il congelamento	eel kohn-jeh-lah-MEHN-toh
heartburn	il bruciore di stomaco	eel broo-CHOH-ray dee STOH-mah-koh
hypertension	l'ipertensione	lee-pehr-tehns-YOH-nay
insomnia	l'insonnia	leen-SOHN-nee-ah
pain	il dolore	eel doh-LOH-ray
pneumonia	la polmonite	lah pohl-moh-NEE-teh
seasickness	il mal di mare	eel mahl dee mah-ray
sore throat	la faringite	lah fah-rihn-JEE-teh
sprain	lo strappo muscolare	loh strahp-poh moos-koh-LAH-ray
ulcer	l'ulcera	LOOL-cheh-rah
wound	la ferita	lah feh-REE-tah

Another group of illnesses goes with essere (to be); for example, "to be diabetic" is essere diabetico.

asthmatic	asmatico	ahz-MAH-tee-koh
(having) a cold	raffreddato	rahf-frehd-DAH-toh
diabetic	diabetico	dee-ah-BEH-tee-ko

Here are some useful terms for describing your illness:

To need medicine

avere bisogno di medicina

ah-veh-ray bee-ZOHN-yoh dee meh-dee-CHEE-nah to

To have high blood

avere l'ipertensione pressure

ah-veh-ray lee-pehr-tehns-YOH-nay

To have low blood

avere l'ipotensione pressure

ah-veh-ray lee-poh-tehns-YOH-nay

to break one's rompersi

il braccio/la gamba arm/leg

ROHM-pehr-see eel brah-choh/ lah gahm-bah

KEYNOTE

In Italian, possessive adjectives aren't used with body parts, as in "my nose" or "his arm." Instead, reflexive verbs are used: Mi fa male la testa (My head hurts) or Si è rotto il naso (He broke his nose).

Parts of the Body

If you have to talk to a doctor, a working knowledge of the geography of the human body will prove helpful.

ankle	la caviglia	lah kah-VEEL-yah
arm	il braccio	eel brah-choh
armpit	l'ascella	lah-SHEHL-lah
artery	l'arteria	lahr-teh-REE-ah

652

body	il corpo	eel kohr-poh
bone	l'osso	lohs-soh
brain	il cervello	eel chehr-VEHL-loh
calf	il polpaccio	eel pohl-PAHCH-choh
chest	il torace	eel toh-RAH-cheh
collarbone	la clavicola	lah klah-VEE-koh-lah
elbow	il gomito	eel GOH-mee-toh
finger	il dito	eel dee-toh
foot	il piede	eel pyeh-deh
hand	la mano	lah mah-noh
heart	il cuore	eel kwoh-ray
heel	il calcagno	eel kahl-KAHN-yoh
hip	l'anca	lahn-kah
index finger	l'indice	LEEN-dee-cheh
knee	il ginocchio	eel jee-NOHK-yoh
larynx	la laringe	lah lah-REEN-jeh
leg	la gamba	lah gahm-bah
middle finger	il medio	eel mehd-yoh
muscle	il muscolo	eel MOOS-koh-loh
nail	l'unghia	loon-gyah
nerve	il nervo	eel nehr-voh
pinkie	il mignolo	eel MEEN-yoh-loh
rib	la costola	lah KOHS-toh-lah
ring finger	l'anulare	lah-noo-LAH-ray
shoulder	la spalla	lah spahl-lah
skin	la pelle	lah pehl-leh
spine	la spina dorsale	lah spee-nah dohr-SAH-lay
stomach	lo stomaco	loh STOH-mah-koh
thumb	il pollice	eel POHL-lee-cheh
vein	la vena	lah veh-nah
wrist	il polso	eel pohl-soh

When coming up with the plural form of the words for some body parts, you will notice that many of them have irregular plurals: il dito becomes le dita, il ginocchio becomes le ginocchia, and la mano becomes le mani.

The Head Presented here is a list of terms related to the head, face, ears, eyes, nose, and throat:

cheek	la guancia	lah gwahn-chah
chin	il mento	eel mehn-toh
ear	l'orecchio	loh-REHK-kyoh
eyeball	il globo oculare	eel gloh-boh ohk-yoo-LAH-ray
eyebrow	il sopracciglio	eel soh-prah- CHEEL-yoh
eyelid	la palpebra	lah PAHL-peh-brah
face	il viso	eel vee-zoh
forehead	la fronte	lah frohn-teh
gum	la gengiva	lah jehn-JEE-vah
hair	i capelli	ee kah-PEHL-lee
head	la testa	lah tess-tah
iris	l'iride	LEE-ree-deh
jaw	la mascella	lah mah-SHEHL-lah
lip	il labbro	eel lahb-broh
mouth	la bocca	lah bohk-kah
neck	il collo	eel kohl-loh
nose	il naso	eel nah-zoh
palate	il palato	eel pah-LAH-toh
skull	il cranio	eel KRAHN-ee-oh
temple	la tempia	lah tehm-pee-ah
throat	la trachea	lah trah-keh-ah
tongue	la lingua	lah leen-gwah
tonsils	le tonsille	leh tohn-SEEL-leh
tooth	il dente	eel dehn-teh

Going to the Doctor

If you need to see a doctor while traveling, the following vocabulary, in conjunction with the common ailments section, can help you describe your symptoms.

to be cold	avere freddo	freh-doh
to be hot	avere caldo	kahl-doh
to be constipated	avere la stitichezza	lah stee-tee-KEHTSsah
to be pregnant	essere incinta	een-CHEEN-tah
to be sick	essere malato	mah-lah-toh
to be tired	essere assonnato	ahs-soh-NAH-toh

If you have an allergy, use the following phrase:

I am allergic to . . . Sono allergico a . . .soh-noh ahl-LEHR-jee-koh ah

aspirin	l'aspirina	lahs-pee-REE-nah
penicillin	la penicillina	lah peh-nee-chee-LEE-nah

Symptomatic Verbs

to bleed sanguinare sahn-gwee-NAH-reh to cough tossire tohs-SEE-reh

to faint svenire svehn-EE-reh to fall cadere kah-deh-reh to sneeze starnutire stahr-noo-TEE-reh to vomit vomitare voh-mee-TAH-reh

Going to the Hospital Hopefully you won't need to visit a hospital, but the following terms may be helpful if you do:

anesthetic l'anestitico

lah-nes-TEH-tee-koh

blood count il quadro ematologico

eel kwah-droh eh-mah-toh-LOH-jee-koh

blood test l'analisi del sangue

lah-NAH-lee-zee dehl sahn-gway

blood transfusion la trasfusione di sangue

lah trahs-fooz-YOH-neh dee sahn-gway

diagnosis la diagnosi

lah dee-ahg-NOH-zee

to discharge il dimettere dall'ospedale

eel dee-MEHT-teh-reh dahl-ohs-peh-DAH-leh

doctor	il dottore	eel doht-TOH-reh
examination	l'analisi	lah-NAH-lee-zee

to examine	visitare	vee-zee-TAH-reh
hospital	l'ospedale	lohs-peh-DAH-lay
infusion	l'infuso	leen-FOO-zoh
injection	l'iniezione	leen-yehts-YOH-neh

intensive care unit

il reparto di cure intensive

eel ree-PAHR-toh dee koo-reh een-tehn-SEE-veh

medical director	il direttore medico
eel dee-reht-TOH-reh MEH-dee-koh	
night nurse	l'infermiera di notte
leen-fehrm-YEH-rah dee noht-tay	
nurse	l'infermiera
leen-fehrm-YEH-rah	
to operate	operare
oh-peh-RAH-reh	
operation	l'intervento
leen-tehr-VEHN-toh	
patient	il paziente
eel pahts-YEHN-teh	
surgeon	il chirurgo
eel kee-ROOR-goh	

temperature chart

il diagramma della temperatura

eel dee-ah-GRAHM-mah dehl-lah tehm-peh- rah-TOO-rah

visiting hours	l'orario delle visite	loh-RAH-ree-oh dehl-leh VEE-zee-teh to
x-ray fare una radiografia fah-ray		oo-nah rah-dee-oh-grahf-FEE-ah

Going to the Dentist Though you may find it difficult to talk if you've got a terrible toothache, you may want to familiarize yourself with the following vocabulary just in case!

at the dentist's office	dal dentista
dahl dehn-TEES-tah	
tooth	il dente
eel dehn-teh	
abscess	l'ascesso
lah-SHESS-soh	
local anesthesia	l'anestesia locale
lah-nehs-teh-ZEE-ah loh-KAH-lay	
molar	il molare
eel moh-LAH-ray	
braces	l'apparecchio
lahp-pah-REHK-kyoh	
bridge	il ponte
eel pohn-teh	
cavities	le carie
le KAH-ree-eh	
crown	la corona
lah koh-ROH-nah	
cuspid	il canino
eel kah-NEE-noh	
dental clinic	la clinica odontoiatrica
lah KLEE-nee-kah oh-dohn-toy-AH-tree- kah	
denture	la dentiera
lah dehn-TYEH-rah	
to extract	estrarre
ehs-TRAH-ray	
false tooth	la protesi
lah PROH-teh-zee	
fill	otturare
oht-too-RAH-ray	
filling	l'otturazione
loht-too-rahts-YOH-nay	

gums	le gengive
leh jehn-JEE-veh	
incisor	l'incisivo
leen-chee-ZEE-voh	
injection	l'iniezione
leen-yehts-YOH-neh	
jaw	la mascella
lah mah-SHEHL-lah	
nerve	il nervo
eel nehr-voh	
oral surgeon	l'odontoiatra
loh-dohn-toy-AHT-rah	
orthodontist	l'ortodontista
lohr-toh-dohn-TEES-tah	
plaster cast	il modello in gesso
eel moh-DEHL-loh een jehs-soh	
root	la radice
lah rah-DEE-cheh	
root canal work	il trattamento della radice
eel traht-tah-MEHN-toh dehl-lah rah-DEE-cheh	
tartar	il tartaro
eel TAHR-tah-roh	
temporary filling	l'otturazione provvisoria
loht-too-rahts-YOH-neh prohv-veez-OH-ree-ah	
toothache	il mal di denti
eel mahl dee dehn-tee wisdom	
tooth	il dente del giudizio
eel dehn-teh dehl joo-DEET-see-oh	

KEYNOTE

The Italian preposition da does not have an exact translation in English. It is commonly used to mean "at the home/office/place of," as in dal dentista (at the dentist's office) and da Mario (at Mario's house/place).

A Few Dental Verbs

to bleed	sanguinare
	sahn-gwee-NAH-reh
to brush one's teeth	spazzolarsi i denti
	spahts-soh-LAHR-see ee dehn-tee
to lose a tooth	perdere un dente
	PEHR-deh-reh oon DEHN-teh
to pull out, remove	estrarre
	ehs-TRAH-reh
to rinse	sciacquare
	shock-WAH-reh

Going to the Pharmacy

The following words will help you get what you need in a pharmacy. Pharmacies all over Italy can be recognized by the big green cross above the entrance.

pharmacy	la farmacia
	lah fahr-mah-CHEE-ah
pharmacist	il farmacista
	eel fahr-mah-CHEES-tah
ace bandage	la benda elastica

659

lah ben-dah eh-LAHS-tee-kah

adhesive bandage | il cerotto
eel cheh-ROHT-toh

aspirin | l'aspirina
lahs-pee-REE-nah

cough syrup | lo sciroppo per la tosse
loh shee-ROHP-poh pehr lah tohs-seh

digestive tonic | il digestivo
eel dee-jess-TEE-voh

disinfectant | il disinfettante
eel dees-een-feht-TAHN-teh

drops | le gocce
leh goh-cheh

gauze bandage | la garza
lah gahr-zah insect

repellant | l'insetticida
leen-seht-tee-CHEE-dah

laxative | il lassativo
eel lahs-sah-TEE-voh

medicine | la medicina
lah meh-dee-CHEE-nah

pill | la pastiglia
lah pahs-TEEL-yah

prescription	la ricetta
	lah ree-CHEHT-tah
prophylactics	i preservativi
	ee preh-zehr-vah-TEE-vee
remedy	il rimedio
	eel ree-MEH-dyoh
thermometer	il termometro
	eel tehr-MOH-meh-troh
tranquilizer	il tranquillante
	eel trahn-kwee-LAHN-tay
vaseline	la vaselina
	lah vah-zeh-LEE-nah

Emergencies and Disasters

It's more than likely you will never need to know any vocabulary relating to emergencies or disasters, but here are a few key words and phrases:

Help!	Aiuto!
	ah-YOU-toh
Police!	Polizia!
	poh-leets-EE-ah
Thief!	Al ladro!
	ahl lah-droh

661

Watch out!	Attenzione!
	aht-tehnts-YOH-neh
accident	un incidente
	oon een-chee-DEHN-teh
attack	un attentato
	oon aht-tehn-TAH-toh
burglary	un furto
	oon foor-toh
fire	un incendio
	oon een-CHEHN-dyoh
flood	una deluvione
	oo-nah deh-loov-YOH-neh
gunshot	un colpo di pistolla
	oon kohl-poh dee pees-TOH-lah
to rape	violentare
	vee-oh-lehn-TAH-reh
ambulance	un'ambulanza
	oon-ahm-boo-LAHN-zah

CHAPTER 7: HEALTHCARE

Italy has universal health care. Medical personnel will generally treat anyone who present themselves at a hospital.

There are also private hospitals; however, these charge a fee, as do doctors in private clinics and offices. You will find hospitals run by the Catholic Church as well, also at a fee.

URGENT MEDICAL CARE / L'ASSISTENZA SANITARIA URGENTE

There has been an accident.

C'è stato un incidente.

cheh STAH-toh oon een-chee-DEN-teh.

Please help me.

Mi aiuti per favore. (formal)

mee ah>YOO-tee pehr-fah-VOH-reh.

It is urgent.

È urgente.

EH oor-JEHN-teh.

Please get a doctor.

Faccia venire un dottore per favore. (formal)

FAH-cha veh-NEE-reh oon doht-TOH-reh pehr-fah-VOH-reh.

An ambulance.

Un'ambulanza.

oon ahm-boo-LAHN-tsah.

Where is the nearest hospital?

Dov'è l'ospedale più vicino?

dohv-EH los-peh-DAH-leh pee>OO vee-CHEE-noh?

Is the doctor in?

C'è un dottore?

cheh oon doht-TOH-reh?

I would like a doctor who speaks English please.

Vorrei un dottore che parlasse inglese per favore.

voh-RAY oon doht-TOH- reh par-LAHS-seh een-GLEH-zeh pehr fah-VOH-reh.

A specialist.

Uno specialista.

OO-noh speh-chah-LEE-stah.

Please notify my husband.

Informi mio marito per favore.

(formal) een-FOHR-mee MEE-oh mah-REE-toh pehr fah-VOH-reh.

Please notify my wife.

Informi mia moglie per favore.

(formal) een-FOHR-mee MEE-ah MOH-lyee>eh pehr fah-VOH-reh.

Can I call my parents?

Potrebbe chiamare i miei genitori?

(formal) poh-TREHB-beh kee>ah-MAH-reh ee MEE>eh>ee jeh-nee-TOH-ree?

TELEPHONE NUMBERS:

Emergency 911. 113	(centotredici).	* chen-toh-TREH-dee-chee.
Medical Emergency. 118	(centodiciotto).	chen-toh-dee-CHOHT-toh.
Home medical visits.	Guardia medica.†	GWAHR-dee->ah MEH-dee-kah.

EMERGENCY LOCATIONS:

Emergency room.	Pronto soccorso.	PRON-toh sohk-KOR-soh.

Hospital.	Ospedale.	oh-speh-DAH-leh.
Pharmacy.	Farmacia.	fahr-ma-CHEE>ah.

LITTLE EXERCISE

He / She is staying at _____.

È alloggiato / a al _____.

eh ahl-lohj-JAH-toh / tah ahl _____.

Please notify my friends.   Informi i miei amici per favore.

een-FOHR-mee ee mee>EH>ee ah-MEE- chee pehr fah-VOH-reh.

They are staying at _____.

Sono alloggiati al _____.

SOH-noh ahl-lohj-JAH-tee ahl _____.

I would like to rest for a moment.

Vorrei riposarmi un momento.

vohr-RAY ree-POH-zahr-mee oon moh-MEHN-toh.

AILMENTS / LE MALATTIE

Heart Attack and Stroke / L'infarto e l'ictus

I have pain in my chest.

Ho un dolore al petto.

oh oon doh-LOH-reh ahl PET-toh.

I have tingling in my left arm.

Ho un formicolio al braccio sinistro.

oh oon fohr-mee-koh-LEE>oh ahl BRAHCH-choh see-NEE-stroh.

I have shortness of breath.

Ho il respiro affannoso sotto sforzo / sono senza fiato.

665

oh eel rehs-PEE-roh ahf-fahn-NOH-zoh SOHT-toh SFOHR-tsoh / SOH- noh SEHN-sah fee>AH-toh.

Car accident.

Un incidente in macchina / stradale.

on een-chee-DEHN-teh een MAHK-kee-nah / strah-DAH-leh.

He / She is choking.

Sta soffocando.

stah sohf-foh-KAHN-doh.

Contractions.

Le contrazioni.

leh kohn-trah-TSYOH-nee.

Emergency.

Emergenza.

eh-mehr-JEHN-tsah.

Heart attack.

L'infarto.

leen-FAHR-toh.

Miscarriage.

L'aborto spontaneo.

lah-BOHR-toh spohn-TAH-neh>oh.

Stroke.

L'ictus.

LEEK-toos.

I had a heart attack _____ years / months ago.

Ho avuto un infarto _____ anni / mesi fa.

oh ah-VOO-toh oon een-FARH- toh AHN-nee / MEH-zee fah.

I have lost feeling in my right arm.

Ho perso la sensibilità nel braccio destro.

oh PEHR-soh lah sehn-see-bee- lee-TAH nehl BRAHCH-choh DEH-stroh.

I am confused.

Mi sento confuso

mee SEHN-toh kohn-FOO-zoh / zah.

My head hurts.

Mi fa male la testa.

mee fah MAH-leh lah TEHS-tah.

He / She cannot speak.

Non può parlare.

nohn poo>OH pahr-LAH-reh.

He / She cannot walk.

Non può camminare.

nohn poo>OH kahm-mee-NAH-reh.

Other Ailments / Altre malattie

I have arthritis.	Ho l'artrite.	oh lahr-TREE-teh.
Asthma.	L'asma.	LAHZ-mah.
Allergies.	Le allergie.	leh ahl-lehr-JEE>eh.
A blister.	Una vescica.	oo-nah veh-SHEE-kah.
A boil.	Un foruncolo.	oon foh-ROON-koh-loh.
A burn.	Un bruciore.	oon broo-CHOH-reh.
Cancer.	Un cancro.	oon KAHN-kroh.
The chills.	I brividi.	ee BREE-vee-dee.

667

A cold.   Un raffreddore.

oon rahf-frehd-DOH-reh.

Congestion.   Una congestione.

OO-nah kohn-jehs-TYOH-neh.

Constipation.   La stitichezza.

lah stee-tee-KEHTS-tsah.

A cough.   La tosse.   lah TOHS-seh.

Cramps.   I crampi.   ee KRAHM-pee.

Diabetes.   Il diabete.   eel dee>ah-BEH-teh.

Diarrhea.   La diarrea.   lah dee>ahr-REH-ah.

An earache.   Il mal d'orecchi.

eel mahl doh-REHK-kee.

Epilepsy.   L'epilessia.   leh-pee-lehs-SEE>ah.

A fever.   La febbre.   lah FEHB-breh.

Food poisoning.

Un'intossicazione alimentare.

oo-neen-tohs-see-kah- TSYOH-neh ah-lee-mehn-TAH-reh.

The flu.   L'influenza.   leen-floo>EHN-tsah.

Headache.   Il mal di testa.   eel mahl dee TEHS-tah.

Hemorrhoids.   Le emorroidi.   leh eh-mohr-ROH>ee-dee.

High blood pressure.   La pressione alta.

lah prehs-see>OH-neh ahl-tah.

Indigestion.   Un'indigestione.

oo-neen-dee-jehs-TYOH-neh.

Insect bite.   Una puntura d'ínsetto.

OO-nah poon-TOO-rah deen-SEHT-toh.

A migraine.   Un'emicrania.

oo-neh-mee-KRAH-nee>ah.

Nausea.   La nausea.

lah na>oo-ZEE-ah.

Pneumonia.   La polmonite.

lah pohl-moh-NEE-teh.

A sore throat.   Il mal di gola.

eel mahl dee-GOH-lah.

A virus.   Un virus.

oon VEE-roos.

An infection.   Un'infezione.

oo-neen-feh-TSYOH-neh.

An inflammation.   Un'infiammazione.

oo-neen-fee>ahm-mah-TSYOH-neh.

A rash.   Un'eruzione cutanea.

oo-neh-roo-TSYOH-neh koo-TAH-neh>ah.

A sinus infection.   Un'infezione ai seni nasali.

oo-neen-feh-TSYOH-neh AH>ee SEH-nee nah-ZAH-lee.

A sprained ankle.   Una slogatura alla caviglia.

OO-nah sloh-gah-TOO-rah AHL-la kah-VEE-lyee>ah.

A urinary infection.   Un'infezione urinaria.

oo-neen-feh-TSYOH-neh oo-ree-NAH-ree>ah.

A venereal disease.   Una malattia venerea.

OO-nah mah-laht-TEE>ah veh-NEH-reh>ah.

Basic Medical Tests

Blood test.

Le analisi del sangue.

leh ah-NAH-leh-see dehl SAHN-gweh.

Electrocardiogram.

L'elettrocardiogramma.

leh-leh-troh-kahr-dee>oh- GRAHM-mah.

Glucose test.

L'analisi del glucosio.

lah-nah-LEE-zee dehl gloo-KOH- zee>oh.

Hepatitis test.

L'analisi per l'epatite.

lah-nah-LEE-zee pehr leh-pah-TEE-teh.

Pregnancy test.

Il test di gravidanza.

eel tehst dee grah-vee-DAHN-tsah.

Urine test.

L'analisi dell'urina.

lah-nah-LEE-zee dehl-loo-REE-nah.

Medical Tests / Le analisi mediche

Allergy test.

670

Un'esame per le allergie.

oon eh-ZAH-meh pehr leh ahl-lehr-JEE-eh.

Biopsy.

Una biopsia.

OO-nah bee-ohp-SEE>ah.

CAT scan.

Una TAC.

OO-nah tahk.

Colonoscopy.

Una colonscopia.

OO-nah koh-lohn-skoh-PEE>ah.

Cardiogram.

Un cardiogramma.

oon kahr-dee>oh-GRAHM-mah.

Electroencephalogram (EEG).

Un elettroencefalogramma.

Oon eh-leht-troh-ehn-cheh-fah-loh-GRAHM-mah.

Gynecological exam.

Un esame ginecologico.

oon eh-ZAH-meh jee-neh- koh-LOH-jee-koh.

HIV test.

Un test per il virus HIV.

oon tehst pehr eel VEE-roos acca-ee- voo.

Mammography.

Una mammografia.

OO-na mahm-moh-grah-FEE-ah.

MRI.

Una risonanza magnetica.

OO-nah ree-soh-NAHN-tsah mah-nee>EH-tee-kah.

Rectal exam.

Un esame rettale.

oon eh-ZAH-meh reht-TAH-leh.

Thyroid test.

Un'analisi della tiroide.

oo-nah-nah-lee-zee DEHL-lah tee-ROH>ee-deh.

X-rays.

Raggi X.

RAHJ-jee eeks.

Explaining the Pain Away / Dare spiegazioni dei dolori

My stomach hurts.

Mi fa male lo stomaco.

mee fah MAH-leh loh STOH-mah-koh.

My head hurts.

Mi fa male la testa.

mee fah MAH-leh lah TEHS-tah.

My foot hurts.

Mi fa male il piede.

mee fah MAH-leh eel pee>EH-deh.

My arm hurts.

Mi fa male il braccio.

mee fah MAH-leh eel BRAHCH-choh.

He / She has fallen.

È caduto / -a.

eh kah-DOO-toh / tah.

He / She has fainted.

È svenuto / -a.

eh sveh-NOO-toh / -tah.

I feel dizzy.

Ho le vertigini / Mi gira la testa.

oh leh vehr-TEE-jee-nee / mee JEE-rah lah TEHS-tah.

It is bleeding.

Sanguina.

SAHN-gwee-nah.

It is swollen.

È gonfio.

eh GOHN-fee>oh.

I have something in my eye.

Ho qualcosa nell'occhio.

oh kwahl-KOH-zah nehl LOHK-kee>oh.

I do not sleep well.

Non dormo bene.

nohn DOHR-moh BEH-neh.

I am allergic to penicillin / sulpha.

Sono allergico / a alla penicillina / ai sulfamidici.

SOH-noh ahl-LEHR-jee- koh / kah AHL-lah peh-nee-cheel-LEE-nah / aye sool-fah-MEE-dee-chee.

I need a receipt for my medical insurance.

Ho bisogno di una ricevuta per la mia assicurazione medica.

oh bee-ZOH-nee>oh dee OO-nah ree-cheh-VOO-tah pehr lah MEE-ah ahs-see-koo-rah-TSYOH-neh MEH-dee-kah.

Doctor Discussions / Discussioni dal dottore

What is wrong with me?

Che cosa ho?

keh KOH-zah oh?

Quick & to the Point At the Doctor's Office

I don't feel well.

Non sto bene.

nohn stoh BEH-neh.

I have a fever.

Ho la febbre.

oh lah FEHB-breh.

I am vomiting often.

Vomito spesso.

VOH-mee-toh SPEHS-soh.

I have a stuffy nose.

Ho il naso chiuso.

oh eel NAH-zoh kee>OO-zoh.

This hurts (exterior).

Questo qui fa male.

KWEHS-toh kwee fah MAH-leh.

My _____ hurts (organ). Mi fa male _____. mee fah MAH-leh _____.

I have dizzy spells.

Soffro di vertigini.

SOHF-froh dee vehr-TEE-jee-nee.

Specialists Cardiologist.

Il cardiologo.

eel kar-dee>OH-loh-goh.

Dermatologist.

Il dermatologo.

eel dehr-mah-TOH-loh-goh.

Gastroenterologist.

Il gastroenterologo.

eel gahs-troh-ehn-teh-ROH-loh-goh.

Gynecologist.

Il ginecologo.

eel jee-neh-KOH-loh-goh.

Immunologist.

L'immunologo.

leem-moo-NOH-loh-goh.

Neurologist.

Il neurologo.

eel neh>oo-ROH-loh-goh.

Ophthalmologist.

L'oftalmologo.

lohf-tahl-MOH-loh-goh.

675

Podiatrist.

Il podologo.

eel poh-DOH-loh-goh.

Psychiatrist.

Lo psichiatra.

loh psee-kee>AH-trah.

Urologist.

L'urologo.

loo-ROH-loh-goh.

Is it serious?

È grave?

eh GRAH-veh?

What should I do?

Che cosa devo fare?

keh KOH-zah DEH-voh FAH-reh?

Do I have to go to the hospital?

Devo andare all'ospedale?

DEH-voh ahn-DAH-reh ahl-ohs-peh-DAH-leh?

Should I stay in bed?

Devo stare a letto?

DEH-voh STAH-reh ah LEHT-toh?

Is it contagious?

È contagioso?

eh kohn-tah-JOH-zoh?

I feel better / worse.

Mi sento meglio / peggio.

mee SEHN-toh MEH-lyee>oh / PEHJ-joh.

Can I travel on Monday?

Potrò viaggiare lunedì?

poh-TROH vee-ahj-JAHR-reh loo-neh-DEE?

WOMEN'S HEALTHCARE / LA SALUTE FEMMINILE

Useful Words and Phrases / Frasi e parole utili

Abortion.	L'aborto.	lah-BOHR-toh.

Birth control pills.   Le pillole anticoncezionali.

leh PEEL-loh-leh ahn-tee-kohn-cheh-tsyoh-NAH-lee.

Diaphragm.	Il diaframma.	eel dee-ah-FRAHM-mah.
Menstruation.	Le mestruazioni.	Leh mehs-troo>ah-TSYOH-nee.
Menstrual cramps.	I dolori mestruali.	ee doh-LOH-ree meh-stroo>AH-lee.
Miscarriage.	L'aborto spontaneo	lah-BOHR-toh spohn-TAH-neh>oh.

I would like to see a female doctor.

Vorrei una dottoressa.

vohr-RAY OO-nah doht-toh-REHS-sah.

_____ gynecologist. _____ una ginecologa. _____ OO-nah jee-neh-KOH-loh-gah.

I've missed a period. Ho saltato le mestruazioni. oh sahl-TAH-toh leh mehs-troo>ah-TSYOH-nee.

My last period began on _____. Le mie ultime mestruazioni sono iniziate il _____. leh MEE>eh OOL-tee-meh mehs-troo>ah-TSYOH-nee SOH-noh ee-nee- tzee>AH-teh eel _____.

I am / She is _____. Sono / È _____. SOH-noh / eh _____.

You are pregnant.

È incinta. (formal)

eh een-CHEEN-tah.

I am 5 months pregnant.

Sono incinta di cinque mesi.

SOH-noh een-CHEEN-tah dee CHEEN-kweh MEH-see.

MEDICINE / LE MEDICINE

When should I take the medicine?

Quando devo prendere la medicina?

KWAHN-doh DEV-oh PREHN-deh-reh lah meh-dee-CHEE-nah?

Quick & to the Point Over-the-Counter Medications

Antacid medication.

La medicina antiacido.

lah meh-dee-CHEE-nah ahn-tee>AH-chee-doh.

Antidiarrheal medication.

La medicina antidiarroica.

lah meh-dee-CHEE-nah ahn-tee-dee>AHR-roh>ee-kah.

Anti-gas medication.

La medicina anti-gas.

lah meh-dee-CHEE-nah ahn-TEE-gahs.

Asthma inhaler.

L'inalatore per l'asma.

leen-AH-lah-toh-reh pehr LAHS-mah.

Antihistamine.

L'antistaminico.

l'ahn-tee-stah-MEE-nee-koh.

Anti-inflammatory medication.

La medicina antinfiammatoria.

lahn meh- dee-CHEE-nah ahn-teen-fee>ah-mah-TOH-ree>ah.

Anti-itch medicine.

La medicina antiprurito.

lah meh-dee-CHEE-nah ahn- tee-proo-REE-toh.

Aspirin.

L'aspirina.

lahs-peh-REE-nah.

Acetaminophen.

L'acetaminofene.

lah-cheh-toh-mee-noh-FEH-neh.

Cough medication.

Il farmaco per la tosse.

eel FAHR-mah-koh pehr lah TOHS-seh.

Is a prescription required?

Ci vuole una ricetta medica?

chee voo>OH-leh OO-nah ree-CHEHT-tah MEH-dee-kah?

How often should I take the medicine?

Ogni quanto dovrei prendere la medicina?

OH-nyee KWAHN-toh DOH-vray PREHN-deh-reh lah meh-dee-CHEE- nah?

Before / after meals.

Prima dei / dopo i pasti.

PREE-mah day / DOH-poh ee PAHS-tee.

Before going to bed.

Prima di andare a letto.

PREE-mah dee ahn-DAH-reh ah LEHT-toh.

When I wake up.   Appena alzato / a.

                                         ahp-PEH-nah ahl-TSAH-toh / tah.

Items Not Bought at the Pharmacy

Conditioner   Il balsamo.

                                         eel BAHL-sah-moh.

Deodorant.   Il deodorante.

                                         eel deh>oh-doh-RAHN-teh.

Face cream.   La crema per il viso.

                                         lah KREH-mah pehr eel VEE-zoh.

Hair spray.   La lacca per i capelli.

                                         lah LAHK-kah pehr ee kah-PEHL-lee.

Hair mousse.   La mousse per i capelli.

                                         lah moose pehr ee kah-PEHL-lee.

Shampoo.   Lo sciampo.

                                         loh SHAHM-poh.

Toothbrush.   Lo spazzolino da denti.

                                         loh spahts-tsoh-LEE-noh dah DEHN-tee.

Toothpaste.   Il dentifricio.

                                         eel dehn-tee-FREE-choh.

Twice a day.   Due volte al giorno.

                                         DOO>eh VOHL-teh ahl JOHR-noh.

Every 4 to 6 hours   Ogni quattro o sei ore.

                                         OH-nyee KWAHT-troh oh seh>ee OH-reh.

Do I take a teaspoonful?

Dovrei prenderne un cucchiaino?

DOHV-ray prehn-DEHR-neh oon koo-kee>ah-EEN-noh?

THE PHARMACY / LA FARMACIA

Where is the closest pharmacy please?

Dov'è la farmacia più vicina per favore?

DOV-EH lah fahr-mah-CHEE-ah pee>OO vee-CHEE-nah pehr fah-VOH- reh?

I would like to pick up medicine.

Dovrei ritirare una medicina.

doh-VRAY ree-tee-RAH-reh OO-nah meh-dee-CHEE-nah.

I have a prescription.

Ho una ricetta medica.

oh OO-nah ree-CHEHT- tah MEH-dee-kah.

Do you have something for indigestion?

Ha qualche cosa per l'indigestione?

ah KWAHL-keh KOH-zah pehr leen- dee-jehs-TYOH-neh?

THE DENTIST / IL DENTISTA

Dental Terms / Vocabolario dentistico

I have an abscess.	Ho un ascesso.
	oh oon ah-SHEHS-soh.
A broken tooth.	Un dente rotto.
	oon DEHN-teh ROHT-toh.
A cavity.	Una carie.
	OO-nah KAH-ree>eh.
Inside the Mouth	
Abscess.	L'ascesso.
	lah-SHEHS-soh.

681

Canine tooth.	Il dente canino.
	eel DEHN-teh kah-NEE-noh.
Cavity.	La carie.
	lah KAH-ree>eh.
Filling.	L'otturazione.
	loht-too-rah-TSYOH-neh.
Incisor tooth.	Il dente incisivo.
	eel DEHN-teh een-chee-ZEE-voh.
Jaw.	La mascella.
	lah mah-SHEHL-lah.
Molar.	Il molare.
	eel moh-LAH-reh.
Toothache.	Il mal di denti.
	eel mahl dee DEHN-tee.
Wisdom tooth.	Il dente del giudizio.
	eel DEHN-teh dehl joo-DEE-tzee>oh.
Gum disease.	Una gengivite.
	OO-nah jehn-jee-VEE-teh.
Lost a filling.	Perso un'otturazione.
	PEHR-soh oon-oht-too-rah-TSYOH-neh.
A toothache.	Mi fa male un dente.
	mee fah MAH-leh oon DEHN-teh.
Tooth extraction.	L'estrazione del dente.
	lehs-trah-TSYOH-neh dehl DEHN-teh.

Dentist Discussions / Discutere dal dentista

Do you know a good dentist?	Conosce un bravo dentista?
	(formal) koh-NOH-sheh oon BRAH-voh dehn-TEE-stah?
I have a toothache.	Ho mal di denti.
	oh mahl dee DEHN-tee.
My filling has fallen out.	Ho perso l'otturazione.
	oh PEHR-soh loht-too-rah-TSYOH-neh.

682

Do I have a cavity?   Ho una carie?

oh OO-nah KAH-ree>eh?

Do you have to pull the tooth?

Deve estrarre il dente? (formal)

DEH-veh ehs-TRAHR-reh eel DEHN-teh?

Will this require stitches?   Dovrà darmi dei punti?

doh-VRAH DAHR-mee day POON-tee?

Could you give me an anesthetic?   Potrebbe darmi un anestetico? (formal)

poh-TREHB-beh DAHR-mee oon ah-nehs-TEH- tee-koh?

Can you fix my dentures?   Mi può riparare la dentiera?

mee poo>OH ree-pah-RAH-reh lah dehn-tee>EH-rah?

Can you fix my bridge?   Mi può riparare il ponte?

mee poo>OH ree-pah-RAH-reh eel POHN-teh?

Please use a local anesthetic.

Può usare l'anestesia locale per favore? (formal)

poo>OH oo-ZAH-reh lah-neh-steh-ZEE-ah loh-KAH-leh pehr fah-VOH- reh?

Can you give me something for the pain?

Mi può dare qualcosa per il dolore?

mee poo>OH DAH-reh kwahl-KOH-zah pehr eel doh-LOH-reh?

You are hurting me.   Mi sta facendo male.

mee stah fah-CHEN-doh MAH-leh.

THE OPTOMETRIST / L'OCULISTA
Optical Terms / Parole relative all'ottica

Blindness.	La cecità.	lah cheh-chee-TAH.
Cataracts.	La cataratta.	lah kah-tah-RAHT-tah.
Contacts.	Le lenti a contatto.	leh LEHN-tee ah kohn-TAHT-toh.

Vision Emergency

Is there an ophthalmologist nearby?

C'è un oftalmologo qui vicino?

cheh oon ohf-tahl-MOH-loh-goh kwee vee-CHEE-noh?

I can't see.   Non ci vedo.   nohn chee VEH-doh.

I can't see out of my right / left eye.

Non ci vedo dall'occhio destro / sinistro.

nohn chee VEH-doh dahl-LOHK- kee>oh DEHS-troh / see-NEES-troh.

I can only see out peripherally.

Posso solo vedere di lato.

POHS-soh SOH-loh veh-DEH-reh dee LAH-toh.

I can't get my contact lens out.

Non riesco a togliermi la lente di contatto.

nohn ree>EHS-koh ah toh-lyee>EHR-mee lah LEHN-teh dee kohn-TAHT- toh.

I have something in my eye.

Ho qualcosa nell'occhio.

oh kwahl-KOH-zah nehl-LOHK-kee>oh.

It hurts.

Mi fa male.

mee fah MAH-leh.

Soft / Hard.

Morbide / rigide.

MOHR-bee-deh / REE-jee-deh.

Cleaning solution.

Il liquido disinfettante.

eel LEE-kwee-doh dees-een-feht-TAHN-teh.

Glasses.

Gli occhiali.

lyee ohk-kee>AH-lee.

Glaucoma.

Il glaucoma.

eel glah>oo-KOH-mah.

Sty(e).

L'orzaiolo.

lohr-tzah>ee-OH-loh.

Sunglasses.

Gli occhiali da sole.

lyee-ohk-kee>AH-lee dah SOH-leh.

Talking to the Optometrist / Parlare con l'oculista

Do you know a good optometrist?

Conosce un buon oculista?

(formal) koh-NOH-sheh oon boo>OHN ohk-koo-LEES-tah?

My glasses are broken.

I miei occhiali si sono rotti.

ee MEE>eh>ee ohk-kee>AH-lee see SOH- noh ROHT-tee.

Could you repair my glasses?

Mi può riparare gli occhiali? (formal)

mee poo>OH ree-pah-RAH-reh lyee ohk-kee>AH-lee?

When will my glasses be ready?

Quando saranno pronti gli occhiali?

KWAHN-doh sah-RAHN-noh PROHN-tee lyee ohk-kee>AH-lee?

Do you sell contact lenses?

Vende lenti a contatto?

(formal) VEHN-deh LEHN-tee ah kohn-TAHT-toh?

I have lost my glasses (contacts).

Ho perso gli occhiali (le lenti a contatto).

oh PEHR-so lyee ohk-kee>AH-lee (leh LEHN-tee ah kohn-TAH-toh).

Could you examine my eyes please?

Mi può controllare gli occhi, per favore?

(formal) mee poo>OH kohn-trohl-LAH-reh lyee OHK-kee pehr fah-VOH-reh?

CHAPTER 8: ASKING FOR DIRECTION

It's time to master directions in Italian! I wish it were as simple as learning the word for 'where' in Italian and a few Italian road signs, but there's a little more to it than that! In Italy, street names aren't as prominently posted as they are in the U.S. and some other areas, so there's a chance you may make a wrong turn during your travels. Not to worry!

By learning just a few simple questions and vocabulary words, you'll be able to ask for information that'll get you back on track. In this chapter, you'll learn how to ask for directions in Italian and how to understand the directions that you receive.

As you may have already guessed, understanding the directions you are given can be more challenging than asking the questions. But have no fear, just listen to the Italian pronunciation very well and practice saying the Italian words and phrases aloud, as you imagine yourself strolling around Florence or driving through Tuscany!

Asking for Directions in Italian

Asking for directions in Italian is super easy. All you need to remember are some simple question words like "where" and "how." If you need to ask directions from a stranger, always be polite and say "scusi" first. Then you can use any of the following three phrases to ask that person how to get to where you want to go. Any of these are handy if you're looking for a specific place.

Dov'è — Where is...

The simplest way to ask directions to a place in Italian is to start with "dov'è" and add the place you're looking for. For example:

Dov'è il cinema? — Where is the movie theater?

Remember that dove simply means "where," but dov'è means "where is." They're pronounced the same, although when saying "dov'è" you'll want to put more emphasis on the è.

Come vado — How do I go [to]...

Come vado alla piazza [del Duomo]? — How do I go to the piazza [del Duomo]?

You can also use Come si va to make your request more formal and impersonal.

Come si va alla piazza [del Duomo]?

Moving on...

Dove si trova — Where does one find...

Dove si trova la biblioteca? — Where does one find the library?

Common Places to Ask for Directions To

Odds are, you won't always have an exact address of the place you need directions to. Here's a list of common places that you may need directions to.

la biblioteca	the library
l'università	the university
la fermata dell'autobus più vicino	the nearest bus stop

il supermercato più vicino   the nearest grocery store

la stazione dei treni / la stazione ferroviaria — the train station

la piazza — the piazza

It helps to know the name of the specific piazza you need to go to. Otherwise people will just point you towards the main one.

il centro — the center (of the town)

This is where you'll find all the restaurants, bars and fun cultural stuff to do.

la chiesa — the church

It also helps to know the name of the specific church as there are so, so many in Italy. Even for non-religious people, visiting churches in Italy is a treat. In many churches you can see artwork by some of the most famous Italian old masters for free!

la cattedrale — the cathedral

Most large Italian cities have a cathedral, also sometimes called Il Duomo. These are often must-see tourist attractions, but be sure to dress modestly before entering; No shorts, short skirts or sleeveless shirts. (And yes, this rule is enforced by security staff at the entrance.)

Understanding Directions in Italian

Let's say you're driving and have to stop for directions at a roadside café. After trying some delicious Italian coffee, you ask the bartender for directions to a nearby city.

You say, "Come si va a Firenze da qui?" or "How does one go to Florence from here?"

He says, "Firenze si trova al nord del fiume" or "Florence is to the north of the river."

Or he could say something like "Vai al sud per 50 chilometri sull' autostrada, poi si trova l'uscita per Firenze" or "Head south for 50 kilometers on the highway, then you'll find the exit for Florence."

As you can imagine, there are lots of possible responses you might get to the same question, even if they're all "right" answers! You may also encounter lots of different accents and modes of speech. For this reason, in addition to learning important vocabulary, you should also familiarize yourself with authentic Italian speech before attempting to find your way around an Italian-speaking area.

Key words and phrases

so you can not only ask for directions, but understand the directions you're given.

The Cardinal Directions

nord — north

sud — south

est — east

ovest — west

Using Verbs to Find Your Way

When listening to directions, there are a few verbs you should learn that'll come up again and again. Note that many of these verbs are irregular.

andare — to go

girare or svoltare — to turn

andare diritto — go straight ahead

andare indietro — go back

continuare — continue

fermarsi — to stop

partire — to leave

arrivare — to arrive

Using Prepositions to Find Your Way

If you're asking directions for a place that's relatively close by, say within a city as opposed to between cities, you probably won't be given directions using the cardinal directions.

Instead, you'll be given directions that involve knowing your prepositions. This would be a good time to review what preposition are and how to use them, because they're essential for giving and receiving directions.

Below are some prepositional phrases you may encounter when receiving directions. You may especially want to take note of how prepositions combine with articles so that you recognize these phrases in use even when they don't look exactly the way they do below.

a sinistra — left

a destra — right

verso or attraverso — through

accanto a — next to

vicino a — close to

dall'altra parte di / di fronte a / davanti a — across from (opposite)

davanti a / di fronte a — in front of

dietro — behind

fino a — until

Some other words you'll encounter when receiving directions are diritto or dritto (straight ahead), indietro (in the opposite direction) and prossimo/a (next).

Putting It All Together

Now that you know how to ask for directions in Italian, as well as some essential verbs, prepositions and places, you can put all these elements together to find your way no matter how lost you are.

Example #1: Directions to the Store

Tu: Scusi Signore, dove si trova il supermercato più vicino?

Il signore: Va diritto per 200 metri. Poi, gira a sinistra alla prossima strada. Continuare per 50 metri e poi si trova il Carrefour accanto alla pizzeria.

You: Excuse me sir, where does one find the nearest grocery store?

Signore: Go ahead for 200 meters. Then turn to your left at the next street. Continue for 50 meters and then one finds the Carrefour next to the pizzeria.

Note: Short distances are commonly given in meters.

Example #2: Directions to the Bus Stop

Tu: Scusi Signora, come si va alla Piazza del Duomo?

La signora: La Piazza del Duomo è abbastanza lontano da qui. È meglio di prendere l'autobus. La fermata (dell'autobus) più vicino è davanti la biblioteca su Via del Corso. Per arrivare a Via del Corso, va indietro di questa strada e poi, quando si arriva a Via Garibaldi, si gira a destra e si cammina a Via del Corso. La biblioteca, e la fermata dell'autobus, si vede a destra.

You: Excuse me ma'am, where does one find the Piazza del Duomo?

Signora: The Piazza del Duomo is rather far from here. It's better to take the bus. The nearest bus stop is in front of the library on the Via del Corso. To arrive at the Via del Corso, go back on this street and then, when you arrive at the Via Garibaldi, turn right and walk to the Via del Corso. The library, and the bus stop, can be seen to the right.

Example #3: Getting Directions from a Friend

Both of the above examples are using formal language in the third person. When asking complete strangers for directions, especially older people, they'll use formal language, so it's good to practice giving and listening to directions in the third person.

But what about if you ask a friend for directions? Then they'll give you directions in the informal, second person. Here's an example.

Tu: Giovanni, come vado alla facoltà di ingegneria all'università?

Giovanni: Da qui, vai diritto a Via Rossellini, fino alla piazza alla fine della strada. Poi vedi un grande edificio. Quello è la facoltà di ingegneria. L'ingresso è sulla parte ovest.

You: Giovanni, how do I go to the engineering faculty at the university?

Giovanni: From here, go straight ahead to Via Rossellini until you reach the piazza at the end of the street. Then you will see a big building. That's the engineering faculty. The entrance of the faculty is on the western side.

There are a lot of fascinating places to go in Italy. Whether you're just visiting or getting to know your new neighborhood, you'll need to be able to find your way around.

By learning a few simple phrases, you'll be well equipped if you ever get lost or are just looking for a fun new place to visit.

Dove posso trovare la stazione dei treni, per cortesia?

Where can I find the train station, please?

Come posso arrivare alla stazione dei treni?

How do I get to the train station?

Sa (Lei) dove si trova la stazione dei treni?

Do you know where the train station is? (formal)

Sai (tu) dove si trova la stazione dei treni?

Do you know where the train station is? (casual)

Road sign

Another more complete way of asking for directions is by saying...

Mi scusi, potrebbe dirmi dove si trova la stazione dei treni, per favore?

Excuse me, could you please tell me where the train station is? (formal)

Scusa, potresti dirmi dove si trova la stazione dei treni, per favore?

Excuse me, could you please tell me where the train station is? (casual)

Here's a list of some places you might like to go to and places you may pass on the way to getting there.

L'agenzia di viaggio	The travel agency
La strada	The street
Il centro commerciale	The shopping center
Il centro storico	The historic center
La stazione di polizia	The police station

L'ospedale	The hospital
Il parco	The park
Il municipio	The town hall
I bagni pubblici / le toilette pubbliche	The public restrooms
Il centro città	The town center
La periferia	The suburb
Il monumento	The monument
Il bar	The bar

Here are some words and phrases you might get to hear when asking for directions in Italian...

Sinistra	Left
Destra	Right
A sinistra	To the left
A destra	To the right
Dritto / diritto	Straight
Alla fine di	At the end of
All'inizio di	A the beginning of
A ovest	To the west
A nord	To the north
A sud	To the south
A est	To the east

When someone gives you directions in Italian, they'll tell you that you need to take such-and-such street, turn left, and then follow another street...

Prenda... / Prendi...	Take... (formal / informal)
Attraversa... / Attraversi...	Cross (formal / informal)
Segua... /Segui...	Follow (formal / informal)
Vada... / Vai...	Go (formal / informal)
Non attraversare qui.	Do not cross here
Dietro l'angol	Around the corner
La prossima strada a sinistra	The next street to the left.
La prossima strada a destra	The next street to the right.
La prossima strada	The street after the next.
L'angolo	The corner

Il ponte	The bridge
Di fronte a	In front of
Vicino a	Next to

Now, you might want to know whether it is far or not...

È molto lontano?	Is it very far?
È lontano.	It's far.
Non è lontano.	It's not far.
È vicino?	Is it close by?
È vicino.	It's close by.
Non è vicino.	It's not close by

CHAPTER 9: EATING OUT

There is so much about dining and eating in Italy that it could take a lifetime to savor and explain, but I'll try to give you the highlights in this chapter.

To say that food is an integral and important part of the Italian culture would be an understatement. Food is Italy and Italy is all about food. And one of the good things about Italy is that the cuisine is very regionalized and diverse depending on which part of the country you are visiting. That's because a big emphasis is placed on the ingredients that are grown in the local and nearby area.

Despite the differences, which can be many, you should keep the following generalizations in mind:

Northern Italian Cuisine - Characterized by meats, veal, beef, polenta, risotto, butter, cream, stews, soups, prosciutto, and cheese.

Southern Italian Cuisine - Characterized by pasta, fish, pizza, red sauces, olive oil, garlic, salad greens, and peppers.

Some Cultural Differences

Soda Refills

One of the odd things to remember is that there are no soda refills in Italy like you have at some places in the United States and Canada. Partly because whenever you order a Coke they will bring you the can and a glass. It is also commonplace to bring you a lemon to add flavor to the drink.

Many places will not serve ice with your drink unless you specifically ask for it. It used to be considered very odd to serve a drink with ice, especially water with ice. However, Italians are getting more used to the idea and you will see it done more often. You won't get the "you must have three heads" stare if you ask for it.

To-Go Boxes

Another cultural difference is that you won't see any "to-go" boxes if you can't finish your meal. I'm not sure if it's considered an insult to the restaurateur or not, but it would definitely be considered gauche. There are not too many meals that go unfinished anyway in Italy.

They usually have a few courses but the portion sizes tend to be smaller. Although as more and more Americans travel to Italy every year, it is becoming more common to ask for a "to-go" box if you can't finish your meal. It is a trend I'm starting to see that's becoming more evident in the larger cities like Rome and Milan.

Bar

This is the neighborhood staple of Italian establishments. The locals will come here in the morning for their coffee, or at lunch for a sandwich (panino) or a small pizza (pizzetta). It's not what you would typically expect of a "bar" as the term is used in the United States, which is a place that serves alcohol.

Trattoria

Next up on the totem pole of places to dine in Italy is the trattoria. These tend to be more family-run and focus on local cuisine. This is where many of the budget-conscious Italian locals like to dine. The food will be medium-priced and the atmosphere is more casual.

Ristorante (Restaurant)

This is the most upscale of dining experiences in Italy. Consequently, it'll be the most expensive. There is usually a host or a hostess that will seat you. They will often have a sommelier that has extensive knowledge of the wines that are served. This is the place where you would take a client or a potential client to impress them.

Shopping at the Grocery Store (Supermarket)

Another option that is highly worth considering is buying your food at a local supermarket or grocery store. If you are staying someplace that has a stove, you can easily save some money by cooking up your own meals. It doesn't take much to concoct something delicious in Italy. Pasta is very easy to make. You can also buy some bread, along with some olive oil or prosciutto with some olives and you can have yourself a nice picnic. Good local wines can be bought in the Italian supermarkets starting at two euros per bottle.

Water in Italy

For the most part, the water, including the tap water, in Italy is safe to drink. If you visit Rome you will see many fountains spewing water and many of the locals reaching in to grab a drink or refilling their water bottle. It must be safe if they've been doing it for thousands of years. However, you may prefer the taste of bottled water, which is sold all over the place under many different brands. You just need to specify whether you prefer it with bubbles (tonic water) or without.

natural water without bubbles

acqua naturale senza gas

natural water with bubbles

acqua naturale con gas

Coffee in Italy

Italians like their coffee very strong and like to have it at the end of the meal to give you a jolt. They prefer a little cup of espresso coffee as opposed to a cup the size you would be accustomed to using to drink some tea.

Here are some basics on Italian coffee:

Caffè – a shot of strong, black coffee

Caffè macchiato – same as above, with a drop of milk

Caffè lungo – a long coffee, as in watered-down

Caffè americano – typical cup of American joe

Caffè freddo – iced espresso

Caffè corretto – espresso "corrected" with grappa or sambuca

Granita di caffè – coffee-flavored shaved ice

Cappuccino – coffee served with frothy milk, usually warm

Cappuccino senza schiuma – same as above, no foam

Cappuccino freddo – served ice-cold, usually in summer

I would like an espresso please.	Vorrei un espresso per favore.
I would like an American coffee please.	Vorrei un caffè Americano per favore.

Kitchen Utensils / At the Table

Fork	forchetta
Spoon	cucchiaio
Knife	coltello
Plate	piatto
Cup	tazza
Glass	bicchiere
Napkin	servietta
Bottle	bottiglia
Salt	sale
Pepper	pepe
Table	tavolo

At the Restaurant

I'm hungry.	Ho fame.
Waiter	cameriere
Waitress	cameriera
I am vegetarian (male).	Sono vegetariano.
I am vegetarian (female).	Sona vegetariana.

Can you recommend a good restaurant close by?

Può consigliarmi un buon ristorante qui vicino?

Do you know any vegetarian restaurants?   Conosce ristoranti vegetariani?

Do you have a table for four?	Avete un tavolo per quattro?
Do I have to make a reservation?	Devo fare una prenotazione?
I'd like to make a reservation for two at eight o'clock.	
Vorrei prenotare per due persone alle venti. [military time]	
I'm sorry, but we're full.	Mi dispiace, siamo al completo.
Where are the bathrooms?	Dove sono i gabinetti?
The menu, please.	Il menù, per favore.
Can we have a table...	Potremmo avere un tavolo...
...in the corner?	...d'angolo?
...near the window?	...vicino alla finestra?
...outside?	...all' aperto?
The check, please.	Il conto, per favore.

Breakfast Foods

Biscuits	biscotti
Butter	burro
cereal	cereali
omelette	frittata
milk	latte
jelly	marmellata
bread	pane
sausage	salsiccia
tea	tè
egg	uovo
sugar	zucchero
broth	brodo
pasta	pasta
pasta with tomato sauce	pasta al pomodoro
pasta with meat sauce	pasta al ragù
rice	riso
soup	zuppa
Second Courses	Secondi Piatti

Lamb	agnello
Roasz	arrosto
Steak	bistecca
Cutlet	cotoletta
Brains	cervello
Liver	fegato
Tongue	lingua
Hen	gallina
Pork	maiale
snails (escargot)	lumache
chicken	pollo
turkey	tacchino
tripe	trippa

Note – this is a popular Roman specialty. It is the stomach lining of the cow.

Veal	vitello

Various Fish Dishes

Anchovies	acciughe
Eel	anguilla
Lobster	aragosta
Squid	calamari
Mussels	cozze
Shrimp	gamberi
Cod	baccala
Oysters	ostriche
Bluefish	pesce azzurro
Salmon	salmone
Tuna	tonno

Note – Sicily is famous for its tuna, much of which gets exported to Japan for sushi.

Clams	vongole
Trout	trota

sea urchin	ricci

Vegetables / Verdure

Artichokes	carciofi
Carrots	carote
Cabbage	cavolo
Cucumber	cetriolo
Onions	cipolle
Beans	fagioli
Fennel	finocchio

Note – this word is often used in a derogatory manner against male homosexuals.

Mushrooms	funghi
green salad	insalata
lettuce	lattuga
lentils	lenticchie
eggplants	melanzane
peppers	pepperoni

Note – this is easy to get confused with the topping that comes on top of a New York style pizza in the United States.

Celery	sedano
Spinach	spinaci
Pumpkin	zucca
Fruits / Frutta	apricot
albicocca	pineapple
ananas	orange
arancia	banana
banana	cherries
ciliege	fig
fico	cactus fig
fico d'india	raspberries
lamponi	lemon

limone	apple
mela	blueberries
more	peach
pesca	grape
uva	Desserts / Dolci

Italy is known for their desserts, especially their gelato, which is similar to American ice cream. Rome and Florence are cities particularly known for their gelato.

Some of the makers really take it to an artistic level, using only natural ingredients.

Pancakes	fritelle
Cream	crema
ice cream	gelato
cake / pie	torta

torta di...	
...fruit	...frutta
...apple	...mele
...chocolate	...cioccolato
Pudding	budino

Cassata Siciliana

This is a Sicilian specialty – a sponge cake filled with sweet ricotta-like cream cheese usually sprinkled with candied fruits on top.

Meals in Italy

* Breakfast (Colazione)

Most Italians will start off with a breakfast (colazione) around 7:30 AM. It is typically a croissant (cornetto) that can be plain or filled with cream or jelly. And they will typically drink some type of coffee, usually an espresso or a cappuccino. Some Italians will have a different pastry or possibly cereal or yogurt. However, it tends to be a light meal. If you are expecting a nice American- or Canadian-style breakfast with eggs, pancakes, hash browns, and grits, you'll be very much disappointed.

* Lunch (Pranzo)

The biggest meal of the day for most Italians is their lunch (pranzo). It typically starts around 1:30 or 2 PM. The custom of taking a nap afterwards is still very common, similar to the siesta taken in Spain, although the Italians will call is a "pausa." And then the shops will typically open back up again at 4 PM for their second shift of the day. Most restaurants are closed after lunch and then will reopen for dinner, usually around 7 or 8 PM.

* Dinner (Cena)

The final meal of the day (dinner) for most Italians is a light one that typically is one course consisting of pasta, fish, or meat and a salad. It is typically eaten around 8 or 9 PM. In the southern regions where it is hotter and the sun is out longer, it'll tend to be closer to 9 PM.

Italian Meal Courses

When you go to an Italian restaurant the menu will usually be divided into sections depending on the course. Do not feel obligated to order every course. You can mix and match to your choosing – they are usually very accommodating. Here are the basic courses of an Italian meal:

* Antipasto – Appetizers (typically a few Euros each).

* Primo Piatto – First Dish – Is usually pasta, pizza, polenta, risotto – these tend to be lower- cost items.

* Secondo Piatto – Second Dish – Is usually meat and fish, and tends to be more expensive.

* Contorno – Side dishes, hot or cold, vegetables or salad. These typically run a few Euros each.

* Dolce – Desserts.

* Frutta / Formaggio – Fruit and Cheese – the fruit can be of the dried variety. This is when they often serve nuts, almonds, etc.

* Caffè – Coffee – After a meal it is typically an espresso. Cappuccino or other milky coffees are usually not served after a meal. These will typically run about one or two Euros.

CHAPTER 10: DRIVING

Vorrei affittare una macchina sportiva. (Vor-RAY ahf-feet- TAH-reh OO-nah MAHK-kee-nah spor-TEE-vah): I'd like to rent a sports car.

Italy has so many lovely hidden spots to visit that it can be fun to rent a car to drive around freely and make the most of your time. You can find compagnie di autonoleggio (car rental agencies) in every airport or in main train stations. The most common rental agencies are Avis, Hertz, Budget, Europcar, Maggiore, and Sixt. Car rental works exactly as it does in North America; you can prenotare online (reserve online) if you like, and you can ritirare (pick up) your car in one place and riconsegnare (return) it in another. You must pay con carta di credito (with credit card) and have a patente di guida valida (valid driver's licence) and un documento d'identità (a piece of identification) in order to rent a car. When renting a car, there is a large choice of vehicles to choose from: an auto piccola or economica (small car) like a Fiat Panda or a Fiat Punto; an auto di medie dimensioni (medium-size car) like a Volks- wagen Golf; or an auto di grandi dimensioni (large car) like big Audis or Volkswagens. Apart from the rental agency auto classification, in Italy cars are normally divided into utilitarie (economy cars), berline (sedans), station wagons, SUVs, fuoristrada (off-road vehicles), and sportive (sports cars). Most people in Italy buy small cars, because streets are narrow and even parking spots are quite tiny.

Quanto costa affittare una macchina per una settimana?

How much is it to rent a car for one week?

QUAHN-toh CO-stah ahf-feet-TAH-reh OO-nah MAHK-kee-nah pair OO-nah set-tee-MAH-nah

Posso riconsegnare la macchina a Roma?

Can I return the car in Rome?

POS-so ree-kohn-sehn-YAH-reh lah MAHK-kee-nah ah RO-mah

Che tipi di veicoli avete?

What kinds of cars do you have?

Keh TEE-pee dee veh-EE-co-lee ah-VEH-teh

Potrei avere una macchina più grande/più piccola?

Could I have a bigger/smaller car?

Po-TRAY ah-VEH-reh OO-nah MAHK- kee-nah PEW GRAHN-deh/PEW PEEK-ko-lah

Vorrei una macchina con il cambio automatico.

(Vohr- RAY OO-nah MAHK-kee-nah kohn eel CAHM-bee-oh ah-oo-toh- MAH-tee-co)

I'd like a car with automatic transmission.

Normally cars have cambio manuale (standard transmission), but cars with cambio automatico (automatic drive) are available if you ask well in advance. You may want to ask for condizionatore or aria condizio- nata (air conditioner or air-conditioning), chiusura centralizzata (cen- tral locking), and alzacristalli elettrici (electric windows). In terms of fuel, choose between a motore a benzina (gas-powered engine) and a motore diesel (diesel-powered engine). Cars with a diesel-powered engine usually need less fuel and therefore are more economical than those running on gasoline.

La macchina ha il navigatore satellitare?

Does the car have GPS?

Lah MAHK-kee-nah ah eel nah-vee-gah-TOH-reh sah-tehl-lee-TAH-reh

Quanto è il limite di velocità nei centri abitati?

(QUAHN- toh EH eel LEE-mee-teh-dee veh-loh-chee-TAH neh-ee CHEN-tree ah-bee-TAH-tee)

What is the speed limit in the city streets?

When driving in Italy or in any other country, make sure to familiarize yourself with the traffic laws.

For example, in Italy it is against the law to make a right turn on a red light; on a multiple lane highway it is not allowed to overtake another car by passing on the right. Furthermore, you must adapt to the position and height of traffic lights; at times the rotonde (circles or roundabouts) can be a bit confusing; and of course, drivers face traffic jams in many Italian cities.

Si può andare in macchina al centro storico? Are you permitted to drive your car in the historical center of town?

See PWO ahn-DAH-reh in MAHK-kee-nah al CHEN-troh STOH-ree-coh

Corso Italia è un'isola pedonale.

Corso Italia is a pedestrian-only zone.

KOR-soh ee-TAH-lee-ah EH oon EE-soh-la peh-doh-NAH-leh

Scusi, dov'è l'entrata dell'autostrada?

(SCOO-zee doh- VEH lehn-TRAH-tah del-lah-oo-toh-STRAH-dah)

Pardon me, where is the toll road entrance?

After renting a car, start driving and having some fun on the Italian roads. Be cautious, however, as Italian drivers are considered very wild! Roads in Italy are classified as strade statali, provinciali o comunali, which are just standard roads pertaining either to the state, the prov- ince, or the city. Then there are the superstrade (highways), which are faster roads outside the city center, and tangenziali (ring roads or belt- ways), which run around the center of a big city.

The autostrade (toll roads) are fast highways that take you everywhere in Italy, but that request the payment of a ticket. On entering the autostrada, you must stop and take a biglietto (ticket), which you hand in when exiting, at which time you will also pay the necessary fee.

The pedaggio (toll road ticket) can be paid in cash or with credit card; just make sure to choose the corresponding lane upon exiting. Cash lanes have a sign displaying coins; the others a sign displaying cards. Some lanes have employees handling your payment; others have automatic machines.

If your car has a Telepass (a small machine that handles automatic exit and payment), simply look for the Telepass lanes and drive through: the owner of the car will be charged afterward on his or her bank account.

If you ask for directions and distances, remember that distances in Italy are measured by the kilometer, which corresponds to 0.62 miles.

Posso avere la ricevuta del pagamento?

Can I have the receipt?

POS-so ah-VEH-reh lah ree-ceh-VOO-tah del pah-gah-MEHN-toh

Ho perso il mio biglietto. Cosa devo fare?

I have lost my ticket. What should I do?

Oh PAIR-so eel MEE-oh beel-YET-toh CO-sah DEH-vo FAH-reh

Ho sbagliato uscita. Posso rientrare in autostrada?

I have taken the wrong exit. Can I enter the toll road again?

Oh sbahl-YAH-toh oo-SHEE-tah POS-so ree-ehn-TRA-reh een ah-oo-toh-STRAH-da

Quanti chilometri ci sono per arrivare in città?

How many kilometers are there to get to the city?

QUAHN-tee kee-LO-meh-tree chee SO-no pair ahr-ree-VAH-reh een cheet-TAH

Favorisca patente e libretto di circolazione.

(Fah-vo-REE- scah pah-TEHN-teh eh lee-BRET-toh dee cheer-co-lah-tsee-OH-neh)

Driver's licence and logbook, please.

Limiti di velocità (speed limits) on the autostrade vary from 80 kilometers per hour (50 miles per hour) to a maximum of 130 km/h (80 mph); however, on superstrade limits can be between 50 km/h (30 mph) and 110 km/h (70 mph). In cities the speed limit is 50 km/h.

Use caution when driving; multe per limiti di velocità (fines for speeding tickets) can be very high. Remember also that in Italy it is mandatory to wear cinture di sicurezza (seat belts), it is forbidden to use mobile phones when driving, and there are huge fines and criminal charges for guida in stato di ubriachezza (DUI). Controlli stradali (road controls) can be handled by different corps: polizia stradale (highway police), Carabinieri (a different force which is part of the Italian army and deals with security-keeping tasks), polizia provinciale (county police), and vigili urbani (metropolitan police). Officers can pull a car over, even if the driver didn't do anything wrong, just to ask for a controllo (check).

In that case, you'll be asked to show your patente (driver's license) and libretto (vehicle registration certificate), and they may check your bollo d'assicurazione (insurance stamp), which has to be clearly exposed on the windshield.

Ha superato i limiti di velocità e devo farle la multa.

704

You have exceeded the speed limit and I have to give you a ticket.

Ah soo-pair-AH-toh ee LEE-mee-tee dee veh-lo-chee-TAH eh DEH-vo FAHR-leh lah MOOL-tah

Come mai guidava così veloce?

Why were you driving so fast?

CO-meh my gwi-DAH-vah co-ZEE veh-LO-cheh

Potrei vedere il suo certificato di assicurazione?

May I see your insurance documents?

Po-TRAY veh-DEH-reh eel SOO-oh chair-tee-fee-CAH-toh dee ahs-see-coo-rah-tsee-OH-neh

È una macchina in affitto?

Is it a rental car?

Eh OO-nah MAHK-kee-nah een ahf-FEET-oh

Vorrei fare il pieno di benzina verde.

(Vor-RAY FAH-reh eel pee-EH-no dee behn-TSEE-nah VAIR-deh)

I'd like to fi ll up the tank with unleaded gasoline.

Stazioni di servizio or benzinai (gas stations) can be found everywhere in Italy: in the city center or on main highways and of course on the autostrade (toll roads). The most common names are Agip, Esso, Ip, Q8, Api, Erg, Shell, and Tamoil.

The big gas stations on highways usually have a bar and a small shop, while those on the autostrade may even have a snack bar, a restaurant, and a small grocery store. These stations are called autogrill.

In most gas stations, big or small, there will be a car wash, and you can also find oil-change and tire-inflation services. In terms of fuel, you can choose between benzina verde (unleaded gas) and diesel or gasolio (diesel), depending on the engine of your car. Fuel is much more expensive in Italy than in North America.

In the past, diesel was much less expensive than gas, but today the two cost roughly the same. Gas stations usually have benzinai (attendants) who take care of filling up tanks during the day (mostly from 8 A.M. to 8 P.M.), while in the evening or on weekends it is self-service. In large gas stations, however, it is permissible to fill up the tank by yourself, even when attendants are in service, to get a discount. At gas stations you can pay either in cash or with credit cards.

Quanto dista il prossimo autogrill?

How far is the next autogrill?

QUAHN-toh DEE-stah eel PROS-see-mo ah-oo-toh-GREEL

C'è un autolavaggio in questa stazione di servizio?

Is there a car wash in this gas station?

Cheh oon ah-oo-toh-lah-VAHD-jo een QUEH-stah stah-tsee-OH-neh dee sair-VEET-see-oh

Dieci euro di diesel, per favore.

Ten euros of diesel, please.

Dee-EH-chee eh-OO-ro dee DEE-zel pair fah-VO-reh

C'è lo sconto self-service?

Is there a discount for self-service?

Cheh lo SCON-toh self-service

È possibile guidare la macchina in centro?

(Eh poh-SEE- bee-leh gwi-DAH-reh een CHEHN-troh)

Are cars allowed downtown?

In some cities, the historic center of town is off-limits to cars. In these cases, park your car in a public lot and visit the town on foot.

Dove posso parcheggiare la macchina?

Where can I park my car?

DOh-veh POS-soh pahr-keh-JAH-reh lah MAHK-kee-nah

Potrebbe fare un controllo generale alla macchina?

(Po-TREB-beh FAH-reh oon kohn-TROL-lo jeh-neh-RAH-leh AHL-lah MAHK-kee-nah)

Can you do a general check on my car?

If your car has a problem, look for a meccanico (garage). Garages can be found in every city and they are usually open from Monday through Friday from 8 A.M. to 1 P.M. and then again from 3 P.M. to 7 P.M. Some of them may be open on Saturday also, but all of them are surely closed on Sunday and for festivities.

There are small garages on the autostrada, as well; usually each autogrill has one. Garages generally take care of problems related to a car's engine, so if you need some fixing to its body look for a carrozzeria (body shop), and for specific problems with lights and the electrical sys- tem see an elettrauto (electric garage).

In most cases, though, large garages can handle all issues without problems. If there is no specific problem, but you just want a checkup, ask them for a general check or an oil change or some tire inflation, too.

Il faro sinistro posteriore della macchina non funziona. Potrebbe cambiare la lampadina, per favore?

The left rear light of my car is not working. Could you please change the lamp?

Eel FAH-ro see-NEE-stro po-steh- ree-OH-reh DEL-lah MAHK-kee-nah nohn foon-tsee-OH-nah Po-TREB-beh cahm-bee-AH-reh lah lahm-pah-DEE-nah pair fah-VO-reh

Potrebbe dare un'occhiata alle gomme? Mi sembrano un po' sgonfie.

Can you check the tires? It seems as if they are a bit flat.

Po-TREB-beh DAH-reh oon-ok- kee-AH-tah AHL-leh GOM-meh Mee SEHM-brah-no oon po SGON-fee-eh

Avrei bisogno del cambio d'olio.

I need an oil change.

Ah-VRAY bee-ZON-yo del CAHM-bee-oh DO-lee-oh

La macchina fa uno strano rumore. Può controllare?

The car makes a strange noise. Can you check it?

Lah MAHK-kee-nah fah OO-no STRAH-no roo-MO-reh Poo-OH kohn-trol-LAH-reh

Potrebbe suggerire una strada con veduta scenica?

(Poh-TREB-beh su-jeh-REE-reh OO-na STRAH-dah kohn veh-DOO- tah SHAY-nee-kah)

Can you suggest a scenic driving route?

Italy is famous for its beautiful, scenic driving tours. Before going on a driving trip, however, it's best to know the distances involved in order to budget for gas and travel time. Planning ahead is especially impor- tant if you are renting a car.

Quanto dista Pisa da Firenze?

How far is it from Pisa to Florence?

QUAHN-toh DEE-stah PEE-zah dah Fee-rehn-zeh

CHAPTER 11: ENTERTAINMENT

Quale film proiettano questa settimana all'Odeon?

(QUAH-leh feelm proy-ET-tah-no QUEH-stah set-tee-MAH-nah al-LO-deh-on)

What movie are they showing at the Odeon this week?

The Italian film industry has always been considered one of the best in the world. Fellini, De Sica, Bertolucci, Tornatore, Salvatores, and Benigni are Oscar-winning directors. Italian movies such as Ladri di biciclette, 8½, La dolce vita, Umberto D, and many more are regularly listed among the best movies ever made.

Many Italian actors, includ- ing Academy Award winners Sophia Loren and Roberto Benigni and three-time nominee Marcello Mastroianni, are known worldwide.

Italian artists have also won Oscars in original dramatic score, costumes, and other categories. The industry is constantly producing excellent directors, actors, and artists in the international scene. Italian movies do quite well at the box office, even though the market is dominated by American movies dubbed into Italian.

You will not find many Italian theaters that show movies in English. The cost for a movie ticket varies, depending on the day of the showing, from 4 to 5 euros for weekdays to 7 to 8 euros for Saturday and Sunday.

If you need to make a reservation (online or by phone) for very popular movies, the cost is normally 0,50 euro more. Special prices or combo prices (tickets plus snack) might be available in some theaters. The price for a drink and a medium popcorn box is about 7 euros.

Potrebbe suggerirmi una buona sala cinematografica, favore?

Could you please suggest a good per movie theater?

Po-TREB-beh sood-jeh-REER-mee OO-nah boo-OH-nah SAH-lah chee-neh-mah-toh-GRAH-fee-cah pair fah-VO-reh

Potrebbe suggerirmi un buon film comico/romantico, favore?

 Could you please suggest a good per comedy/romantic movie?

Po-TREB-beh sood-jeh-REER-mee oon boo-ON feelm CO-mee-co/ro-MAHN-tee-co pair fah-VO-reh

Quanto costa il biglietto?

How much does a ticket cost?

QUAHN-toh CO-stah eel beel-YET-toh

A che ora inizia/finisce il film/ lo spettacolo?

At what time does the movie/show start/finish?

Ah keh OH-rah ee-NEE-tsee-ah/fee-NEE-sheh eel feelm/lo spet-TAH-co-lo

Cosa rappresentano al teatro greco di Siracusa?

(CO-sah rap-preh-ZEHN-tah-no al teh-AH-tro GREH-co dee See-rah-COO- zah)

What is playing at the Syracuse Greek Theater?

Italy has always produced excellent theatrical authors. Nobel Prize winners such as Luigi Pirandello and Dario Fo, together with Eduardo De Filippo and Carlo Goldoni, are among the best known dramatists in the world. Commedia dell'arte with its masks has influenced world theater for centuries.

Many Italian cities have a teatro stabile; Italian theaters such Teatro alla Scala (Milano), Teatro La Fenice (Venezia), Teatro San Carlo (Napoli), Teatro Massimo (Palermo), Teatro Olimpico (Vicenza), just to name a few, are internationally renowned. Greek theaters such as the ones in Taormina or Syracuse, or the Arena in Verona, are still used for theatrical events.

While in Italy you can enjoy all sorts of theatrical pieces, from Greek tragedies to Latin comedies, from commedia dell'arte to Goldoni, from Molière to Shakespeare, from Ibsen to Shaw. Prices vary, from 15 to 35 euros, according to the theater, the company, city, play, and type of seat. For a premiere show or premiere theaters, prices are much higher. Special prices for students, seniors, schools, and groups are very common. Season tickets are also quite common. During the summer, many towns offer free concerts, theatrical plays, and similar events of good to excellent quality.

Quanto dura lo spettacolo?

How long does the show last?

QUAHN-toh DOO-rah lo spet-TAH-co-lo

Offrite dei prezzi ridotti per studenti/anziani?

Do you offer special prices for students/seniors?

Of-FREE-teh day PRETS-see ree-DOHT-tee PAIR stoo-DEHN-tee/ahn-tsee-AH-nee

Vorrei prenotare due posti in galleria/platea/un palco.

I would like to reserve two gallery/stalls/balcony seats.

Vor-RAY preh-no-TAH-reh DOO-eh PO-stee gal-leh-REE-ah/plah-TEH-ah/oon PAHL-co

A che ora è aperto il botteghino?

At what time does the box office

Ah keh OH-rah eh ah-PAIR-toh open? eel bot-teh-GEE-no

Chi sono i protagonisti del musical?

(Kee SO-no ee pro- tah-go-NEE-stee del MOO-zee-cahl)

Who are the protagonists of the musical?

Even though it has its antecedent in the commedia musicale of the 1950s–70s, the musical, as we know it today, has a very recent history in Italy.

The first long-running show was Grease, staged in 1997 in Rome and Milan; the show was a box-office hit. Since then, musicals have become popular in Italy, especially among the younger generation.

Musicals are also an integral part of the entertainment in many tourist villages and resorts, which has contributed to the success of the genre in Italy. Cabaret shows and shows by Italian leading stand-up comics are also very popular.

An average price for these types of shows is about 40 euros. For prices, show information, and the calendar of events, consult the Spettacoli section in local newspapers, or search the Internet.

Many theaters provide ticket sales online (biglietteria online) with an extra charge of about 2 euros.

È permesso l'uso della macchina fotografica/telecamera durante lo spettacolo?

Is the use of a camera/camcorder allowed during the show?

Eh pair-MES-so LOO-zo DEL-lah MAHK-kee-nah fo-toh- GRAH-fee-cah/teh-leh-CAH-meh-rah doo-RAHN-teh lo spet-TAH-co-lo

Ha un calendario degli eventi per il vostro teatro?

Do you have a calendar of events in your theater?

Ah oon cah-lehn-DAH-ree-oh DEHL-yee eh-VEHN-tee pair eel VO-stro teh-AH-tro

Dove posso trovare informazioni sulla stagione lirica al Teatro alla Scala?

(DO-veh POS-so tro-VAH-reh een-for-mah- tsee-OH-nee SOOL-lah stah-JO-neh LEE-ree-cah ahl Teh-AH-tro AL-lah SCAH-lah)

Where would I be able to fi nd some information about the opera season at the Teatro alla Scala?

Italian is the language of music and opera; Italy has exported this prestigious form of art all over the world. Italian words like aria, concerto, allegro, adagio, andante, piano, soprano, etc. are words rec- ognized by music lovers around the world. Composers, artists, and singers like Verdi, Puccini, Donizetti, Rossini, Scarlatti, Monteverdi, Stradivari, Mascagni, Paganini, Palestrina, Vivaldi, Caruso, Pavarotti, and most recently Bocelli are all household names among music lovers.

Operas such as La traviata, Tosca, Pagliacci, Le nozze di Figaro, Madame Butterfly,and Turandot, and arias such as "Nessun dorma," "La donna è mobile," "Che gelida manina," "Largo al factotum," etc., are all recognizable worldwide.

Prices for opera are quite expensive but not prohibitive, but you need to reserve your seat very much in advance. For example, in the renowned Teatro alla Scala in Milan, you might find tickets as low as 18 euros and as high as 126 euros.

Of course, for premiere perfor- mances, the prices are much higher.

Quando è la prima della Turandot di Puccini?

When is the premiere of Puccini's Turandot?

QUAHN-doh eh lah PREE-mah DEL-lah Too-rahn-DOH dee Poot-CHEE-nee

Quanto costa un abbonamento?

What is the price for a season ticket?

QUAHN-toh CO-stah oon ab-bo-nah-MEHN-toh

Ci sono dei buoni posti disponibili?

Are there any good seats available?

Cheeh SO-no day boo-OH-nee PO-stee dee-spoh-NEE-bee-lee

C'è un festa in paese questo weekend?

(CHEH oon FEH- stah een pah-EH-zeh QUEH-sto weekend)

Is there a festival in town this weekend?

In the typical Italian town, during the summer, there is a different fes- tival almost every weekend. Many are dedicated to the town's patron saint or other religious figures, but Italy also hosts many popular music and cultural festivals.

Mi piacerebbe andare a vedere il Carnevale di Venezia o il Carnevale di Viareggio.

I would like to see the Venice Carnival or the Viareggio Carnival.

Me pee-ah-cheh-REHB-beh ahn-DAH-reh ah veh-DEH-reh eel cahr-neh-VAH-leh dee veh-NEHT- zee-ah oh eel cahr-neh-VAH-leh dee vee-ah-REHJ-jee-oh

A che ora è la processione?

What time is the procession?

Ah keh OH-rah EH la proh-chehs- see-OH-neh

A che ora sono i fuochi d'artificio?

What time are the fireworks?

Ah keh OH-rah SOH-noh ee foo-OH-kee dahr-tee-FEE-chee-oh

Andiamo al concerto di Laura Pausini? (Ahn-dee-AH-mo ahl kohn-CHAIR-toh dee LA-oo-rah Pa-oo-ZEE-nee): Do you want to go to Laura Pausini's concert?

Young Italians, also in view of the high prices of theatrical plays, prefer to go to concerts, to go to the disco, to watch a soccer game at the stadio, or to spend free time with friends at a local bar. The price for a concert normally does not exceed 60 euros; a visit to a disco is about 20 to 25 euros and includes the admission and a drink; for about 50 euros you can get a good seat for a top soccer match.

Chi gioca oggi?

Which (soccer) team is playing today?

Kee JO-cah OD-jee

Dove si comprano i biglietti per il concerto/la partita di domenica?

Where can one buy tickets for Sunday's concert/game?

711

DOH-veh see TROH-vah-no ee beel-yee-EHT-tee pair eel con-CHEHR-toh/lah pahr-TEE-tah dee doh-MEH-nee-cah

Dove posso trovare una buona discoteca?

(DOH-veh POS-so tro-VAH-reh OO-nah boo-OH-nah dee-sco-TEH-cah)

Where can I fi nd a good disco(theque)?

The minimum age to be admitted into a disco in Italy is eighteen; the minimum drinking age in Italy is also eighteen, but unfortunately the laws and controls in Italian discos are very relaxed.

Quanto costa un biglietto per la discoteca?

How much is a ticket for the discotheque?

QUAHN-toh CO-stah oon beel-YET-toh pair lah dee-sco-TEH-cah

Potrebbe suggerirmi un buon night-club, per favore?

Could you please suggest a good nightclub?

Po-TREB-beh sood-jeh-REER-mee oon boo-ON night-club pair fah-VO-reh

Un cocktail, per favore.

(Oon cocktail pair fah-VOH-reh)

A cocktail, please.

The most common drink sold in Italian nightclubs and discos are cocktails and aperitifs, not wine. These locales can serve alcoholic drinks until 2:00 A.M. Italy's production of beer is quite limited; the most popular beers in Italy are Peroni, Moretti, and Messina. Imported beers are also readily available.

Un aperitivo, per favore.

An aperitif, please.

Oon ah-peh-REE-tee-voh pair fah-VOH-reh

Una Peroni, per favore.

A Peroni beer, please.

OO-nah Peh-ROH-nee pair fah-VOH-reh

Una birra alla spina per favore.

A draft beer, please.

OO-nah BEER-ah AHL-lah SPEE-nah pair fah-VOH-reh

Cosa c'è oggi in televisione?

(CO-sah CHEH OD-jee een teh-leh-vee-see-OH-neh)

What's on TV today?

If you prefer to spend time at home, it may be fun to rent an Italian movie or enjoy a television show.

Movie rentals (videonoleggio) are less expensive in Italy than in North America; note, however, that you will be charged by the hour. Remember also that movie rental is not a very popular practice in Italy. Besides sports programs, reality shows and variety shows are very popular in Italy. The most popular shows are aired on weekends.

Avete una guida ai programmi TV?

Do you have a TV guide?

Ah-VEH-teh OO-nah goo-EE-dah aye pro-GRAM-mee tee-voo

Vorrei noleggiare un DVD.

I would like to rent a DVD.

Vor-RAY no-led-JA-reh oon dee-voo-dee

Su quale canale si vede CNN?

What channel is CNN on?

Soo QUAH-leh cah-NAH-leh see VEH-deh chee-EN-neh-EN-neh

CHAPTER 12: MAKING LEISURE A TOP PRIORITY

Hitting the town is always fun, whether you're visiting someplace new or playing il turista (eel too-ree-stah) (the tourist) in your own hometown.

In this chapter, we give you the information you need to talk about having fun and socializing with others. In general, Italians are sociable people who enjoy having a good time.

You see them having espressos together al bar (ahl bahr) (in the bar) or drinks at night in piazza (een pee-aht-tsah) (on the public square). Most Italians love to go out in the evenings, crowding the streets until late at night.

On weekends, Italians like to go out in groups: They meet up with their amici (ah-mee-chee) (friends) for get-togethers.

Acquiring Culture

No matter where you live or travel to, most major cities have a weekly pubblicazione (poob-blee-kah-tsee-oh-neh) (publication) that lists information about upcoming events.

These publications include descriptions and schedules for theaters, exhibitions, festivals, films, and so on.

Of course, advertisements also fill the pages, but the difference between an annuncio (ahn-noon-choh) (announcement) and pubblicità (poob-blee-chee-tah) (advertising) is usually easy to determine.

Newspapers aren't your only source of information about things to see and do.

Asking the following questions can get you the answers you want:

Cosa c'è da fare di sera?

(koh-zah cheh dah fah-reh dee seh-rah)

(Are there any events in the evenings?)

Può suggerirmi qualcosa?

(poo-oh sooj-jeh- reer-mee koo-ahl-koh-zah)

(Can you recommend something to me?)

C'è un concerto stasera?

(cheh oon kohn-chehr-toh stah-seh-rah)

(Is there a concert tonight?)

Dove si comprano i biglietti?

(doh-veh see kohm-prah-noh ee bee- lyeht-tee)

(Where can we get tickets?)

Ci sono ancora posti?

(chee soh-noh ahn-koh-rah poh-stee)

(Are there any seats left?)

Quanto vengono i biglietti?

(koo-ahn-toh vehn-goh-noh ee bee-lyeht-tee)

(How much are the tickets?)

When you're seeing a show, certain verbs are helpful:

cominciare   (koh- meen-chah-reh)   (to start)

and

finire   (fee-nee-reh)   (to end).

Take a few examples:

Il film comincia alle sette.

(eel feelm koh-meen-chah ahl-leh seht-teh)

(The film starts at 7:00.)

Lo spettacolo finisce alle nove e trenta.

(loh speht-tah- koh-loh fee-nee-sheh ahl-leh noh-veh eh trehn-tah)

(The show ends at 9:30.)

Going to the movies

Going al cinema (ahl chee-neh-mah) (to the movies) is a popular activity almost everywhere. You can go

da solo (dah soh-loh) (alone) con un amico (kohn oon ah-mee-koh) (with a friend) in gruppo (een groop-poh) (in a group)

Often, il film (eel feelm) (the film) you want to see is playing at a multisala (mool-tee-sah-lah) (multiplex).

In Italy, American films normally are doppiati (dohp-pee-ah-tee) (dubbed) into Italian, but you can sometimes find the original English version with Italian subtitles.

Following are some common questions about the movies:

Andiamo al cinema?   (ahn-dee-ah-moh ahl chee-neh-mah)

(Shall we go to the movies?)

715

Cosa danno?	(koh-zah dahn-noh)
	(What's playing?)
Chi sono gli attori?	(kee soh-noh lyee aht-toh-ree)
(Who's starring?)	
Dove lo fanno?	(doh-veh loh fahn-noh)
(Where is [the movie] being shown?)	
E' in lingua originale?	(eh een leen-goo-ah [vehr-see-oh-neh] oh-ree-jee- nah-leh)
(Is the film in the original language?)	
Dov'è il cinema?	(doh-veh eel chee-neh-mah)
(Where is the cinema?)	

Note: Dov'è is the contracted form of Dove è.

Movie theaters are often crowded. Therefore, reserving your biglietto (bee- lyeht-toh) (ticket) for a movie in advance is always wise.

Choosing your seat at the theater

The language of the theater and the cinema is very similar.

When you attend a play, opera, or symphony, however, where you sit is more of a cause for discussion. In most cases, seats in the platea (plah-teh-ah) (orchestra) are poltronissime (pohl-troh-nees-see-meh) (seats in the first and second rows) and poltrone (pohl-troh-neh) (seats in the following rows).

Or you can choose posti nei palchi (poh-stee nay pahl-kee) (box seats). Some theaters indicate seats by the number of the row: i primi posti (ee pree- mee poh-stee) (first seats) are in the first five or six rows, i secondi posti (ee seh-kohn-dee poh-stee) (second seats) are in the following ones, and so on.

You may want to avoid certain seats. A doctor who may be called away in the middle of a performance probably doesn't want to sit centrale/i (chehn-trah- leh/lee) (in the middle of the row). Or maybe you don't like feeling hemmed in and want to choose seats laterale/i (lah-teh-rah-leh/lee) (on the sides).

In large theaters and in opera houses, you can sit in il loggione (eel lohj-joh- neh) (the gallery), which is also called la piccionaia (lah peech-choh-nah- yah) (literally, the pigeon house) because it's high up.

Following are a few useful phrases concerning performances:

la replica

(lah reh-plee-kah)

(repeat performance)

la matinée

(lah mah- tee-neh)

(matinee)

lo spettacolo pomeridiano

(loh speht-tah-koh-loh poh- meh-ree-dee-ah-noh)

(afternoon performance)

Going to a concert

Music is the universal language. Some of the most popular forms, such as l'opera (loh-peh-rah) (opera), have a close association with Italian.

Maybe you know a musician who plays an instrument in his or her spare time. You're probably curious and want to ask questions (and will hear answers) such as

Che strumento suoni?

(keh stroo-mehn-toh soo-oh-nee)

(Which instrument do you play?)

Suono il violino.

(soo-oh-noh eel vee-oh-lee-noh)

(I play the violin.)

Dove suonate stasera?

(doh-veh soo-oh-nah-teh stah-seh-rah)

(Where are you playing tonight?)

Suoniamo al Blu Notte.

(soo-oh-nyah-moh ahl bloo noht-teh)

(We play at the Blu Notte.)

Chi suona in famiglia?

(kee soo-oh-nah een fah-mee-lyah)

(Who in the family plays?)

Suonano tutti.

(soo- oh-nah-noh toot-tee)

(All of them play.)

Inviting Fun

Getting or giving un invito (oon een-vee-toh) (an invitation) is always a pleasure, whether you invite a friend to a casual dinner or receive an invitation to what promises to be la festa (lah feh-stah) (the party) of the year. A party is a good opportunity to meet new people. When you feel like entertaining, you can say you want dare una festa (dah-reh oo-nah feh-stah) (to give a party). You can also use the expression fare una festa (fah-reh oo- nah feh-stah) (to make a party). Suggesting an activity in Italian is not so different from the way you do it in English. You can ask Perché non . . . (pehr-keh nohn) (Why don't we . . .) or Che ne pensi . . . (keh neh pehn-see) (What do you think about . . .).

The use of "let's," however, is a little different. In Italian, how you say something and the tone you use differentiates a normal sentence from a suggestion. You say Andiamo! (ahn-dee-ah-moh) (Let's go!) with enthusiasm and punctuate it with an exclamation point, but Andiamo al ristorante (ahn-dee-ah-moh ahl ree-stoh-rahn-teh) (We're going to the restaurant) is a normal sentence. The actual form of the verb doesn't change.

If your invitation is accepted, the person might say Ci sarò (chee sah-roh) (I'll be there).

The word perché is special. We use it here to ask the question "why." However, it can also mean "because." A dialogue can go like this:

Perché non mangi? (pehr-keh nohn mahn-jee) (Why don't you eat?) Perché non ho fame. (pehr-keh nohn oh fah-meh) (Because I'm not hungry.)

Getting Out and About

Everybody likes to get away from the daily grind and check out new environments and activities in their free time. Vacationers flock al mare (ahl mah-reh) (to the beach), head in montagna (een mohn- tah-nyah) (to the mountains) or in campagna (een kahm-pah-nyah) (to the country), or take a trip to a grande città (grahn-deh cheet-tah) (big city) to see the sights.

Maybe you use your fine settimana (fee-neh seht-tee-mah-nah) (weekends) to play sports like calcio (kahl-choh) (soccer) or pallavolo (pahl-lah-voh-loh) (volleyball). Or perhaps you park yourself in front of the TV to watch pallacanestro (pahl-lah-kah-neh-stroh) (basketball). In any case, being able to talk sports and other recreational activities is a plus in any language.

Enjoying the wonders of nature

Maybe you like to go to the mountains to be close to nature. Even when ti godi (tee goh-dee) (you enjoy) Mother Nature on your own, you may want to know some vocabulary to express the wonders you see.

While you're out in the country, you might see some animali (ah-nee-mah- lee) (animals). This book gives you the names of some common ones.

In a couple of the following sentences related to the outdoors, Italian borrows English words—picnic and jog.

Mi piace camminare nel verde.	(mee pee-ah-cheh kahm-mee-nah-reh nehl vehr-deh)
	(I like to walk in nature.)
Facciamo un picnic sul prato?	(fahch- chah-moh oon peek-neek sool prah-toh)
	(Should we have a picnic on the lawn?)
Ti piace il osservare gli uccelli?	(tee pee-ah-cheh eel ohs-sehr-vah-reh lyee ooch-chehl-lee)

	(Do you like bird-watching?)
Faccio jogging nel parco.	(fahch-choh johg-geeng nehl pahr-koh)
	(I go jogging in the park.)
Ho una piccola fattoria.	(oh oo-nah peek-koh-lah faht-toh-ree-ah)
	(I have a small farm.)

Taking a tour

Whether you're in a city or a rural area, you can usually find fun and interesting sights. You can take a car trip, or you can leave the driving to someone else and sign up for a guided tour to visit special places. Use the following questions to help find out more about una gita organizzata (oo-nah jee-tah ohr-gah-neet-tsah-tah) (an organized tour).

Note that Italian has two, basically interchangeable ways to say "go on a tour": fare una gita (fah-reh oo-nah jee-tah) and fare un'escursione (fah-reh oon-eh-skoor-see-oh-neh).

Here are some questions you might ask when booking a tour:

Ci sono gite organizzate?	(chee soh-noh jee-teh ohr-gah-neet-tsah-teh)
	(Are there any organized tours?)
Che cosa c'è da vedere?	(keh koh-zah cheh dah veh-deh-reh)
	(What sights are included?)
Quanto costa la gita?	(koo-ahn-toh koh-stah lah jee-tah)
	(How much does the tour cost?)
C'è una guida inglese?	(cheh oo-nah goo-ee-dah een-gleh-zeh)
	(Is there an English-speaking guide?)

Dove si comprano i biglietti?

(doh-veh see kohm-prah-noh ee bee-lyeht-tee)

(Where do I buy tickets?)

Playing sports

Playing and talking about sports is a favored pastime of people the world over.

Some sports you do in Italian. You pair those words with the verb fare (fah-reh) (to do, to practice). With other sports, you use giocare (joh-kah-reh) (to play).

Finally, a few sports take the verb andare (ahn-dah-reh) (to go), including andare a cavallo (ahn-dah-reh ah kah-vahl-loh) (to ride) and andare in bicicletta (ahn-dah-reh een bee-chee-kleht-tah) (to cycle).

You can follow sports ranging from tennis to pugilato (poo-jee-lah-toh) (boxing) to Formula 1 (fohr-moo-lah oo-noh) (Formula One car racing). Or you can be a bit more active and participate in sports like these:

camminare   (kahm-mee-nah-reh)   (hiking)

fare equitazione   (fah-reh eh- koo-ee-tah-dzee-oh-neh) (horseback riding)

fare snowboarding (fah-reh snoo-bohr-ding) (snowboarding)

fare vela   (fah-reh veh-lah)   (sailing)

pattinare   (paht-tee-nah-reh)   (ice skating)

pescare   (peh-skah-reh)   (fishing)

sciare   (shee-ah-reh)   (skiing)

In Italy, the most popular sports are:

il calcio   (eel kahl-choh)   (soccer)

il ciclismo   (eel chee-klee-smoh)   (cycling)

Just think of the worldwide event known as Giro d'Italia (jee-roh dee-tah-lee-ah), the Italian bicycling tour.

CHAPTER 13: VOCABULARY AT WORK

Business contact with people in other countries continually increases in importance. Because modern technology supports the quick exchange of information over long distances, you may have to talk to foreign business partners or even travel to their countries.

If you happen to have contact with an Italian company or businessperson, knowing some basic Italian business vocabulary is useful.

English is the language of business, though, and Italian has adopted many English computer terms.

Talking Shop

Italian has at least three words for "company," and they're interchangeable:

la compagnia   (lah kohm-pah-nyee-ah)

la ditta   (lah deet-tah)   (which also means "the firm")

la società   (lah soh- cheh-tah)

L'ufficio   (loof-fee-choh)   means "office"

but people often use stanza (stahn-tsah) (room) to refer to their personal office.

Common professions

Il lavoro (eel lah-voh-roh) (job, work) is a popular topic for small talk. When you talk about your profession in Italian, you don't need to use the article a, as in "I'm a doctor." You simply say sono medico (soh- noh meh-dee-koh).

The human element

Even if you're a libero professionista (lee-beh-roh proh-fehs-see-oh-nee- stah) (self-employed person), chances are that your job puts you in contact with other people. All those people have titles, as the following short exchanges show:

Il mio capo è una donna.   (eel mee-oh kah-poh eh oo-nah dohn-nah)

(My boss is a woman.)

Il mio è un tiranno!   (eel mee-oh eh oon tee-rahn-noh)

(Mine is bossy!)

Hai un assistente/un'assistente personale?

(ah-ee oon ahs-see- stehn-teh/oon-ahs-see-stehn-teh pehr-soh-nah-leh)

(Do you have a personal assistant?)

No, il nostro team ha un segretario/una segretaria.

(noh eel noh- stroh teem ah oon seh-greh-tah-ree-oh/oo-nah seh-greh-tah-ree-ah)

(No, our team has a secretary.)

Dov'è il direttore?   (doh-veh eel dee-reht-toh-reh)

                                                       (Where is the manager/boss?)

Nel suo stanza./Nella sua stanza.   (nehl soo-oh stahn-tsah/nehl-lah
                                                       soo-ah stahn-tsah)

                                                       (In his office./In her office.)

Office equipment

Even the smallest offices utilize a variety of equipment. Fortunately, many technology-related words are the same in Italian as they are in English.

For example, computer, fax, and e-mail are used and pronounced as they are in English, and the Italian for "photocopy" and "photocopier" are fairly intuitive fotocopia (foh-toh-koh-pee-ah) and fotocopiatrice (foh-toh-koh-pee-ah- tree-cheh), respectively.

Here's some additional office-equipment vocabulary:

la stampante	(lah stahm-pahn-teh)	(the printer)
il fax	(eel fahks)	(the fax)
la macchina	(lah mahk-kee-nah)	(the machine)
l'e-mail	(lee-mail)	(the e- mail)
un indirizzo e-mail	(oon een-dee-reet-tsoh ee-mail)	(an e-mail address)
il messaggio	(eel mehs-sahj-joh)	(the message)

Non funziona, è rotto.

(nohn foon-dzee-oh-nah eh roht-toh)

(It's not working; It's out of order.)

Chatting on the Phone

Pronto! (prohn-toh) (Hello!) is the first thing you hear when you talk to an Italian on the telephone. This word is special, though: In most languages, you answer the phone with the same word you use for hello in any setting, but in Italian, you use pronto to say hello only on the phone. Pronto means more than just hello. It frequently means "ready," in which case it functions as an adjective and therefore changes according to the noun it modifies. If the noun it modifies is masculine, the adjective ends in -o, as in pronto. If the noun is feminine, it ends in -a, as in pronta (prohn-tah). Consider these examples:

Martino, sei pronto?   (mahr-tee-noh say prohn-toh) (Martino, are you ready?)

cena è pronta.   (lah cheh-nah eh prohn-tah)   (Dinner is ready.)

Another use of pronto that you should know is pronto soccorso (prohn-toh sohk-kohr-soh) (first aid, emergency room). In this context, pronto means "rapid."

Italians are fanatical about cellphones. Finding an Italian who doesn't own a cellphone, which they call il cellulare (eel chehl-loo-lah-reh), is a tough task.

They love these gadgets so much that they've given them an affectionate nickname—il telefonino (eel teh-leh-foh-nee-noh), which literally means "little phone."

If you're the one making the call, you respond to pronto by identifying yourself:

Sono Giorgio.   (soh-noh johr-joh)   (It's Giorgio.)

Sono io!   (soh-noh ee-oh)   (It's me!)

Con chì parlo?   (kohn kee pahr-loh)

(Who am I speaking to?)

The person on the other end of the line, especially in a business situation, might say

Mi dica!   (mee dee-kah)

[Can I help you? (literally, Tell me!)]

Calling from a public phone

We have to tell you something about il telefono pubblico (eel teh-leh-foh- noh poob-blee-koh) (the public phone). If you don't have a cellphone and you need to call someone while you're out and about, you look for una cabina telefonica (oo-nah kah-bee-nah teh-leh-foh-nee-kah) (a phone booth). These phones are either un telefono a monete (oon teh-leh-foh-noh ah moh-neh- teh) (a coin-operated phone) or un telefono a scheda (oon teh-leh-foh-noh ah skeh-dah) (a card phone).

In Italy, a phone card is called either la carta telefonica (lah kahr-tah teh-leh-foh-nee-kah) or la scheda telefonica (lah skeh-dah teh-leh- foh-nee-kah). You can get one at tabaccai (tah-bahk-kah-ee) (kiosks selling tobacco, newspapers, and so on) or at the post office.

Here are some helpful pay-phone phrases:

C'è/Avete un telefono?

(cheh-ah-veh-teh oon teh-leh-foh-noh)

[Is there/Do you have a (public) telephone?]

È a monete?

(eh ah moh-neh-teh)

(Is it coin-operated?)

723

Avete schede telefoniche?

(ah-veh-teh skeh-deh teh-leh-foh-nee-keh)

(Do you sell phone cards?)

Il telefono dà libero.

(eel teh-leh-foh-noh dah lee-beh-roh)

(The line is free.)

Il telefono dà occupato.

(eel teh-leh-foh-noh dah ohk-koo-pah-toh)

(The line is busy.)

Il telefono squilla.

(eel teh-leh-foh-noh skoo-eel-lah)

(The telephone is ringing.)

Rispondi!

(ree-spohn-dee)

(Answer!; Pick up the phone!)

Attacca!

(aht-tahk-kah)

(Hang up!)

If you don't know a numero di telefono

(noo-meh-roh dee teh-leh-foh-noh)

(telephone number), you have three ways to get it:

Look it up in the elenco telefonico

(eh-lehn-koh teh-leh-foh-nee-koh)   (phone book).

If it's a business number, look in the pagine gialle (pah-jee-neh jahl-leh) (yellow pages).

Call the servizio informazioni (sehr-vee- dzee-oh een-fohr-mah-dzee-oh-nee) (directory information).

Calling for business or pleasure

Whether you want to make an appointment, find out what time a show starts, or just chat with a friend, the easiest way is usually to pick up the phone. Text below shows you the conjugations of the verbs parlare (pahr-lah-reh) (to speak) and chiamare (kee-ah-mah-reh) (to call). Sometimes you call just to chat fare due chiacchiere al telefono (fah-reh doo-eh kee-ahk-kee-eh-reh ahl teh-leh-foh-noh). But the person on the other end of the line may not be prepared for it. So you may want to ask (or you may hear that person say):

Sei occupata?   (say ohk-koo-pah-tah)

(Are you busy?)

Ti posso richiamare? (tee pohs-soh ree-kee-ah-mah-reh)

(Can I call you back?)

Asking for People and Leaving a Message

You often use the phone to get in touch with someone for business or pleasure, so it's good to know how to ask for the person you want. In case the person you want isn't available, you need to be comfortable getting a message across.

The following exchange gives you some useful phrases for using the telephone:

Buongiorno, sono Leo. C'è Camilla?

(boo-ohn-johr-noh soh-noh leh-oh cheh kah-meel-lah)

(Good morning, this is Leo. Is Camilla in?)

No, è appena uscita. (noh eh ahp-peh-nah oo-shee-tah)

(No, she's just gone out.)

Quando la trovo?   (koo-ahn-doh lah troh-voh)   (When can I reach her?)

Verso le nove.   (vehr-soh leh noh-veh)   (Around nine.)

Le posso lasciare un messaggio?

(leh pohs-soh lah-shah-reh oon mehs-sahj-joh)

(Can I leave her a message?)

Here's a short dialogue that's more typical of a business situation:

Buongiorno, dica.

(boo-ohn-johr-noh dee-kah)

(Good morning, can I help you?)

Potrei parlare con il signor Trevi?

(poh-tray pahr-lah-reh kohn eel see-nyohr treh-vee)

(May I speak to Mr. Trevi?)

Mi dispiace, è in riunione.

(mee dee-spee-ah-cheh eh een ree-oon-yoh-neh)

(I'm sorry, he's in a meeting.)

Potrei lasciargli un messaggio?

(poh-tray lah-shahr- lyee oon mehs-sahj-joh)

(Can I leave him a message?)

Perhaps you want to check for messages.

You're familiar with the situation: You're waiting for a call, but the phone doesn't ring. Then you have to go out. When you get back, you want to know whether anyone called for you. You can ask that question in several ways:

Ha chiamato qualcuno per me?

(ah kee-ah-mah-toh koo-ahl-koo-noh pehr meh)

(Has anybody called for me?)

Mi ha chiamato qualcuno?

(mee ah kee- ah-mah-toh koo-ahl-koo-noh)

(Did anybody call me?)

Chi ha telefonato?

(kee ah teh-leh-foh-nah-toh)

(Who called?)

Chiamate per me?

(kee-ah-mah- teh pehr meh)

(Are there any calls for me?)

CHAPTER 14: WEATHER PLEASANTRIES

Italy is certainly a land of distinct seasons. Throughout the country, winter can be very bitter with snow, ice and below-freezing temperatures. During this cold time of year, it's common for Italians to take a brief winter vacation. But then spring comes, beautiful and blooming all across the country. Spring is gorgeous in Italy, as everything seems to come back to life. The summer can be extremely hot throughout Italy, so again, this is a common time for Italians to vacation, particularly during August, when people try to escape from the heat to somewhere breezy or to a beach. Autumn, the harvest season, is also a beautiful season in Italy. Knowing how to discuss the weather can also be quite helpful when learning italian language. Italian weather can vary a lot so it helps to be prepared.

Quick Navigation

"What's the weather like?" in Italian

How to talk about good weather in Italian

If the weather's not nice...

How to say "it's raining" in Italian

How to say "it's hot" in Italian

How to say "it's cold" in Italian

How to say "it's snowing" in Italian

How to talk about extreme weather conditions in Italian

Italian Weather Vocabulary

"What's the weather like?" in Italian

A lot of good conversations and ice breakers begin with this question. Here are the different ways to say it in Italian.

Com' è il tempo?	What's the weather?
Che tempo fa oggi?	What's the weather like?
Che tempo fa fuori?	What's it like outside?

If you want to be more specific and detailed about the type of weather you're having, you can ask for the forecast. It will be a great way to help you plan your activities accordingly!

Quali sono le previsioni del tempo per oggi? What's the weather forecast for today?

Quali sono le previsioni del tempo per questa settimana? What's the weather forecast for this week?

Is it sunny out? Is the sky so blue that all your problems seem to disappear when you look up? Does it make you feel like shouting "Guarda quel bel cielo blu!" (look at that beautiful blue sky!")?

During wonderful days like this, here's how to describe the weather in Italian.

C'è bel tempo. It's good/ beautiful weather

Fa bel tempo	It's nice out
È piacevole.	It's nice.
È soleggiato.	It's sunny.
C'e il sole	It's sunny out
È sereno.	It's clear
E' una giornata piacevole	It's a lovely day
E' bello e caldo oggi	It's nice and warm today

To strike up a conversation about the good weather, you can say, " It's sunny day, isn't it?"

If the weather's not nice you can say these instead.

Fa cattivo tempo.	It's bad/ miserable weather.
il maltempo	bad weather
È brutto tempo	It's ugly weather
Fa brutto tempo	Its ugly out
Fa un tempo orribile.	It's terrible weather.

To make things more specific, say:

C'è la nebbia.	It's foggy.
È nuvoloso.	It's cloudy.
C'è vento!	It's windy!
È ventoso.	It's windy.
È un giorno umido!	It's a humid day!
È umido.	It's humid.
È una giornata uggiosa.	It's a gloomy day.
E' afoso, C'e afa	It's muggy

How to say "it's raining" in Italian

When it's pouring out, it can be a great excuse to stay at home, sip on some caffè macchiato (or two), and catch up on your Italian lessons.

Here's how to tell people in Italian that it's raining.

Piove.	It's raining.
Sta piovendo.	It's raining.
Sta piovendo a secchiate!	It's raining buckets!

C'è una pioggia scrosciante	It's pouring
Sta diluviando	It's pouring
Piove tutto il giorno	It's been raining all day

How to say "it's hot" in Italian

Some days are just scorching hot while some are freezing cold!

To express your frustration of these extreme temperatures, here's what to say.

Fa veramente caldo, non è vero?	It's pretty hot, isn't it?
Fa caldo	It's hot out
È una giornata calda	It's a hot day
Fa caldissimo.	It's very hot.
Si muore dal caldo qui dentro!	It's way too hot in here!
Caldo afoso, soffocante	stifling heat
Fa un caldo terribile!	It's terribly hot!

You can also use an idiomatic expression to express just how hot it is. Say: Il sole spacca le pietre! (the sun is splitting the rocks!)

How to say "it's cold" in Italian

Fa fresco.	It's cool out.
Fa freddo	It's cold.
È un po' freddo	It's a little bit cold
È freddissimo.	It's icy.
Fa freddissimo.	It's very icy.
Qui si gela	It's freezing cold here

Quick tip:

If you want to exaggerate a bit how hot or cold it is, you can say "Fa un freddo/un caldo da morire!" (it's deadly cold/ hot!)

How to say "it's snowing" in Italian

Is it snowy outside? As the world outside turns into a snowy wonderland, you can say with glee, "Sta nevicando!" Other examples:

Sta nevicando oggi.	It's snowing today.
Nevicava ieri.	It was snowing yesterday
Nevicava ieri sera.	It was snowing yesterday evening.

How to talk about extreme weather conditions in Italian

Weather it's a storm, a blizzard, or a hurricane, extreme weather can be quite scary for everyone! Quickly, hide inside your house and wait it out! For the meantime, you can practice saying these in Italian:

È tempestoso	It's stormy
C'è il temporale.	There is a storm.
Troppi tuoni e fulmini!	Too much thunder and lightning!
Ci aspettiamo un uragano	We are expecting a hurricane
Stiamo avendo una tormenta!	We're having a blizzard
Abbiamo un'ondata di calore	We are having a heatwave

Italian Weather Vocabulary

Now let's wrap it up by going through this list of Italian words about the weather.

Weather	Tempo
Climate	Clima
Temperature	Temperatura
Wind	Vento
Sun	Sole
Rain	Pioggia
Snow	Neve
Fog	Nebbia
Hail	Grandine
Ice	Ghiaccio / Gelo
Clear sky	Cielo sereno
Sunbeam	Raggio di sole
Clouds	Nuvole
Storm	Temporale
Lightning	Fulmine
Cold	Freddo
Freezing	Gelido
Hot	Caldo
Humid	Umido
Dry	Seco
Cloudy	Nuvoloso

Windy	Ventoso
Rainy	Piovoso
Muggy	Afoso / Soffocante

Quick Note:

The weather is expressed with the verb FARE.

Example: Fa bel tempo.   It's beautiful weather.

When you are referring to climate, use ESSERE.

Example:

Il caldo e' insopportabile.

The heat is unbearable.

CHAPTER 15: TO BE HUNGRY, THIRSTY, HOT, COLD, SLEEPY

These expressions, which describe a condition based on physical sensations, in English require the verb to be followed by the relevant adjective (i.e. I am hungry, you were thirsty, etc.).

Instead, in Italian they require the verb to have (avere), followed by the relevant noun that describes the sensation: i.e. to be hungry turns into to have hunger; to be thirsty into to have thirst, and so on: avere fame = to be hungry (literally: to have hunger) avere sete = to be thirsty (literally: to have thirst) avere caldo = to be hot (literally: to have heat) avere freddo = to be cold (literally: to have cold) avere sonno = to be sleepy (literally: to have sleep) In a similar way, avere ragione = to be right (literally: to have right) avere torto = to be wrong (literally: to have wrong)

Any tense of the verb avere can be used with these expressions, therefore:

egli avrà fame   =   He will be hungry (he will have hunger)

io ho avuto sonno   =   I felt sleepy (I have had sleep)

noi avemmo sete   =   We felt thirsty (we had thirst)

voi avevate ragione = You were right (you had right) and so on.

While to be right and to be wrong are always translated with the verb avere, to be hot and to be cold may also take the verb to feel (i.e. I feel hot, you felt cold, etc.).

In Italian this is obtained by using the verb sentire (to feel), followed by the noun: avere caldo, sentire caldo = to be hot, to feel hot (literally: to feel heat) avere freddo, sentire freddo = to be cold, to feel cold (literally: to feel cold) The verb sentire is never used with hungry, thirsty or sleepy.

The Italian adjectives affamato (hungry), assetato (thirsty), accaldato (hot), raffreddato or infreddolito (cold), and assonnato (sleepy) may also be used, though more sparingly than in English.

In Italian they almost describe a condition, more than a personal feeling. Compare the following examples: essi mangiano un panino perché hanno fame = they eat a sandwich because they are hungry affamati dopo il lungo viaggio, essi si fermarono per un pasto = hungry after the long journey, they stopped for a meal

> io avevo sonno e andai a letto presto = I was sleepy and I went to bed early egli sembrava assonnato perché non aveva dormito = he seemed sleepy because he had not slept

> io avevo caldo (or sentivo caldo) con la giacca, così l'ho tolta

> I was hot / felt hot with the jacket, so I took it off

> io sono accaldato, e sto sudando

I am (feeling) hot, and I'm sweating

In most cases both forms would be correct:

essi mangiano perché hanno fame = they eat a sandwich because they are hungry essi mangiano perché sono affamati = (same as above)

essi dormono perché hanno sonno = they are sleeping because because they are sleepy essi dormono perché sono assonnati = (same as above) However, especially in common speech, the first of the two forms is the one used more often.

There is also a difference in meaning when using raffreddato or infreddolito: raffreddato = cooled, cooled up questo è un motore raffreddato ad acqua = this is a water-cooled engine

raffreddato = running a cold noi eravamo raffreddati e starnutivamo = we were running a cold and we sneezed

infreddolito = feeling cold ella era infreddolita, e indossò un cappotto = she was feeling cold, and she put on a coat Although in the previous examples raffreddato has been used as an adjective, it is the past participle of the verb raffreddare, to cool, cool up. Its reflexive form raffreddarsi, when referred to living creatures has a common meaning of to catch a cold (although the proper way of saying this is prendere un raffreddore).

Since they are very common verbs, it is useful to focus well their different use (and meaning): io raffreddo quest'aqua per ottenere ghiaccio = I cool this water to obtain ice

aprendo la finestra l'aria si raffredda = by opening the window the air cools up

vieni dentro, o ti raffredderai (colloquial) = come inside, or you will catch a cold (= you will turn cold) vieni dentro, o prenderai un raffreddore (proper form) = (same as above)

There is also a similar verb, freddarsi, whose official meaning is to become (too) cold, sometime used in common speech to replace the aforesaid raffreddarsi. Its positive (non-reflexive) form too exists, freddare, always referred to living creatures, with an idiomatic meaning of to shoot someone dead (a rather modern use of this verb):

il caffè si è freddato, non berlo = the coffee has turned cold, don't drink it

quando ho fatto la doccia l'acqua si era freddata = when I took a shower the water had become cold

vieni a mangiare o la minestra si freddera = come to eat, or the soup will grow cold

egli / ella mirò bene, e freddò il nemico al primo colpo = he/she aimed well, and killed the enemy with the first shot As a general rule, freddarsi is preferred to raffreddarsi when a somewhat negative shade of meaning is required, e.g. to become excessively cold, or to become cold (while it shouldn't have), such as speaking of food, hot drinks, water for a shower or a bath, the air in a heated room, etc.

THE POSTPONED SUBJECT

As far as now, in all the sample sentences shown, the subject stood before the verb, and the object followed it (as it always happens in English, as well). il ragazzo apre la porta (transitive verb) subject verb object the boy opens the door

l'ospite era partito (intransitive verb) subject verb the guest had left The early stages of this book, mentioned how in Italian the last part of the sentence often carries the emphasis of the concept expressed: abitavano in una grande casa = they lived in a large house (this tells us where they lived)

abitavano in una casa grande = they lived in a large house (this tells us how was the house they lived in)

When a sentence has no object (a situation that typically occurs with intransitive verbs, but sometimes with transitive ones too), in Italian it is common to shift the subject at the bottom, i.e. after the verb.

A few examples: oggi il tuo amico verrà e pranzerà qui = today your friend will come and will have lunch here could be turned into oggi verrà il tuo amico e pranzerà qui = (same as above)

fai presto, il treno è arrivato! = be quick, the train has arrived! could be turned into fai presto, è arrivato il treno! = (same as above)

una persona era uscita = one person had come out could be turned into era uscita una persona = (same as above) There is no special reason for postponing a subject, except to place a little more emphasis on the last word.

For instance, in the first sentence the usual form puts the emphasis on the fact that your friend will come, while with a postponed subject it means your friend will come. It is not a strong emphasis, i.e. the second form would not mean your friend is coming, not mine, but we are having for lunch your friend, as if the subject (your friend) had not yet been introduced in the conversation.

The usual form, instead, would sound like today your friend (who has likely been mentioned already) will come, and have lunch here. In the same way, the second example puts a little stress on the train, rather than on the fact that it has arrived, while the third example tells us that a person (not two or more, not a dog, but a single individual) had come out, while the usual form would slightly emphasize the coming out of the person, i.e. his action.

Focusing the inflections of the verbs, in the aforesaid samples we see that: verrà matches il tuo amico; è arrivato matches il treno; era uscita matches una persona. Therefore, the postponed subject could rarely be mistaken with an object, because the inflection of the verb always matches the subject, not the object.

This is also clear enough from the meaning of the verb and from the general context of the speech: adesso salirà Paolo = now Paul will go up / climb (i.e. it is Paul's turn to go up) adesso salirà le scale = now he / she will climb the steps

In the first example, the action of climbing is quite evidently carried out by Paul, because Paul cannot "be climbed": despite the noun follows the verb, the person is clearly the subject of the sentence.

In the second example, instead, the stairs are climbed (i.e. they do not climb themselves), so they are the object. Furthermore, salirà, inflection of the 3rd singular person, does not match scale, a plural noun, but either Paul (in the first sentence) or somebody else not mentioned (in the second).

But even if the match had been possible, the meaning of the verb would have been enough to tell the subject from the object. in questo ristorante mangia spesso il mio collega = my colleague often eats in this restaurant in questo ristorante mangia spesso il pesce = in this restaurant he / she often eats fish In this case mangia could match both collega and pesce, but it is obvious that the colleague does the action of eating, i.e. he or she is the subject, while the fish is eaten, thus acts as an object.

However, there are a few cases in which the meaning might be doubted. Compare these two sentences:

> Franco aveva chiamato = Frank had called

> aveva chiamato Franco = Frank had called,

but also he / she had called Frank In the second example both meanings are possible. In these cases the context or the rest of the sentence will provide more clues; for instance:

aveva chiamato Franco, ma tu non eri in casa = Frank had called, but you were not at home aveva chiamato Franco prima di chiamare Elena = he / she had called Frank before calling Helen

The main condition for postponing a subject is that the sentence must NOT have an object.

In fact, this form is used more often with intransitive verbs (which never have a direct object), and less often with transitive ones, as well, if the direct object is missing: lo straniero era arrivato = the stranger had arrived, almost meaning he had finally made it there era arrivato lo straniero = (same as above), almost answering the question: who had arrived?

l'albero è caduto = the tree fell down, almost meaning it did not stand the wind è caduto l'albero = (same as above), almost answering the question: what happened?

presto l'inverno finirà = winter will soon be over, almost meaning it will not last long presto finirà l'inverno = (same as above), almost meaning ...and spring will begin

presto lo studente finirà i suoi compiti = the student will soon finish his homework (only possible form, due to the object)

il campione ha vinto = the champion won, almost meaning he did not lose ha vinto il campione = (same as above), almost answering the question: who won the match?

il campione ha vinto la sfida = the champion won the challenge (only possible form, due to the object)

When the verb used in the sentence is essere (to be), there is no real object, because the verb describes a condition, not an action, therefore the subject may be freely postponed. This occurs very frequently in questions. questa bicicletta è bella = this bycicle is nice è bella questa bicicletta = (same as above)

 il cappotto era vecchio? = was the coat old?

 era vecchio il cappotto? = was the coat old?

 il tempo è buono? = is the weather fine?

 è buono il tempo? = is the weather fine?

non è tutto oro ciò che riluce (proverb) = not all things that shine are gold (the other way is possible, but being a proverb it is only used in this form)

When a subject is postponed, the sentence must end there, i.e. either a full stop must close the period, or a further sentence should be introduced by means of a comma and/or a conjunction (e.g. and, or, so, thus, etc.).

In the following examples the spot where the sentence breaks is shown in yellow, and what breaks it is shown in red. presto finirà l'inverno || e il tempo migliorerà = winter will soon be over and the weather will improve now rejoyces ha vinto il campione , || quindi la folla ora esulta = the champion won, therefore the crowd now rejoyces è caduto l'albero || perché il vento era forte = the tree fell because the wind was strong è arrivato il treno ; || prendi i bagagli = the train has arrived; take the luggage In order to postpone the subject, other parts of the same sentence may sometimes be moved from their original position; compare the following examples: un cane entrò nella stanza = a dog came into the room (the action is slightly emphasized)   !   nella stanza entrò un cane = (same as above, though now the dog is more emphasized) entrò nella stanza un cane = (same, but less common than the previous one)

l'insegnante tornò a scuola = the teacher returned to school (slight emphasis on the action)

a scuola tornò l'insegnante = (same as above, though now the teacher is more emphasized) tornò a scuola l'insegnante = (same, but less common than the previous one)

uno specialista verrà dall'estero = a specialist will come from abroad (emphasis on from abroad) verrà uno specialista dall'estero = (same; both the specialist and from abroad are emphasized) dall'estero verrà uno specialista = (same; now the specialist is more emphasized) Since this particular form does not follow a standard rule, and not all parts of the sentence may be shifted in a similar way, there is no need for the student to memorize every possible disposition, and leave it with its "classic" arrangement (subject + verb + etc. etc.).

In particular, the adverbs are usually left in their original position, i.e. next to the verb, because when an adverb is used it often carries the emphasis: il campione ha vinto = the champion won ha vinto il campione = the champion won il campione ha vinto facilmente = the champion won easily

l'albero era caduto = the tree had fallen down era caduto l'albero = the tree had fallen down l'albero era caduto spesso = the tree had often fallen down

lo straniero arrivò = the stranger arrived era arrivato lo straniero = the stranger arrived lo straniero arrivò tardi = the stranger arrived late

However, also when an adverb is present, the Italian language allows forms similar to the ones discussed so far: ha vinto facilmente il campione... = the champion won easily... era caduto spesso l'albero... = the tree had often fallen... arrivò tardi lo straniero... = the stranger arrived late...

This special form helps to keep the emphasis strong enough on both parts of the sentence, i.e. the adverb and the subject.

It is used when another sentence follows in the same period, to obtain a particular lingering effect: ha vinto facilmente il campione, e la folla lo esalta = the champion won easily era caduto spesso l'albero, ed era diventato storto = the tree had often fallen down, and it had become crooked arrivò tardi lo straniero, e trovò la porta chiusa = the stranger arrived late, and found the door closed

The subject is also postponed so that, after having read the sentence, the reader's attention will somewhat linger on the champion, the tree or the stranger, because the following sentence may likely continue to concern or to describe the same subject. Instead the standard arrangement (subject + verb) does not give the sentence any particular shade nor emphasis, i.e. it simply describes what happens to the subject.

DOUBLE NEGATIVE

In English there are expressions which have a double form according to whether they are used alone or with a negative conjunction.

For instance, the two sentences there was nothing and there wasn't anything have the same meaning, although two different adverbs, nothing and anything, have to be used.

The same pattern occurs for nobody ~ anybody, never ~ ever, nowhere ~ anywhere and so on. Instead in Italian the equivalent adverbs have only one form, which is the negative one (i.e. they match nothing, nobody, nowhere, etc.).

There is only one exception; for the sake of an easier comprehension, this topic will be discussed in the following paragraph.

Provided that in Italian negative sentences always contain the conjunction non (not), the use of the aforesaid pronouns or adverbs turns the sentence two times negative, almost as "I can't see nothing"; "she won't never come"; "we didn't do this neither"; and so on.

In Italian this is the only possible (and correct) way of using negative pronouns and adverbs. nessuno (indefinite pronoun) = nobody, no one, none niente (indefinite pronoun) = nothing nulla (indefinite pronoun) = nothing mai (adverb) = never nemmeno (adverb) = not even, neither neanche (adverb) = not even, neither neppure (adverb) = not even, neither Note how the aforesaid words are compounds (except mai and nulla), and begin with the prefix ne- (from the Latin ne = not), although the final word contains some further alteration: ne + uno (one) >> nessuno (nobody, no one, none) ne + ente (archaic for entity, thing) >> niente (nothing) ne + meno (less) >> nemmeno (not even, neither) ne + anche (also, even) >> neanche (not even, neither) ne + pure (also, even) >> neppure (not even, neither)

Instead nowhere has no Italian equivalent, so the expression da nessuna parte (literally: in no place) is used. In fact, nessuno and its feminine nessuna may be also used with any noun, as an adjective, with the meaning of no....

Note that since nessuno is a compound of uno, before masculine nouns it drops its final o, except when the following noun begins with z or with s + consonant (e.g. sc..., sp..., st..., etc.).

For this phonetic rule refer to the indefinite article uno, paragraph 2.4). nessun amico = no friend nessun timore = no fear nessun rimorso = no regret ...BUT nessuno scambio = no exchange nessuno strumento = no instrument nessuno zio = no uncle

Instead nessuna may undergo an elision and take an apostrophe (nessun') when the following noun begins with the vowel "a".

This change is not compulsory, and with other vowels it is usually avoided: nessuna casa = no house nessuna idea = no idea

nessuna emergenza = no emergency ...

BUT nessun'arma or nessuna arma = no weapon nessun'assenza or nessuna assenza = no absence nessun'attrice or nessuna attrice = no actress

The use of nessun and nessuna will be discussed again, further on, in this same paragraph.

Meanwhile, these are some examples of double negative sentences: in quel cassetto (egli / ella) non trovò niente = in that drawer he / she didn't find anything da lontano (essi) non vedranno nulla = from afar they won't see anything (essi) non hanno letto nessun libro = they haven't read any book quella persona non conosce nessuno = that person doesn't know anybody il lunedì (io) non mangio mai a casa = on Mondays I never eat at home (io) non lo guarderò nemmeno = I won't even look at him / it perché (tu) non vedrai neppure questo film? = why won't you watch this movie either? (egli / ella) non conosceva neppure l'indirizzo = he / she didn't even know the address (noi) non vogliamo nemmeno quello = we don't want that (one) either

Examining these sentences, a first consideration is that the basic structure of double negative expressions is: (subject) + non + (verb) + negative pronoun or negative adverb.

e.g. quella persona (subject) + non + conosce (verb) nessuno (negative pronoun).

Notice how the negative pronouns and adverbs are simply added after the verb; in fact, by dropping them or by replacing them with a definite noun (shown in green in the following samples), the aforesaid sentences turn out "ordinary" negatives: in quel cassetto (egli / ella) non trovò la penna = in that drawer he / she didn't find the pen da lontano (essi) non vedranno i dettagli = from afar they won't see the details (essi) non hanno letto questo libro = they did not read this book quella persona non conosce tuo fratello = that person does not know your brother

When the verb uses a compound tense (passato prossimo, trapassato prossimo, futuro anteriore, etc.), the negative pronouns nessuno, niente and nulla follow the standard pattern shown above: (subject) + non + (verb) + negative adverb or negative pronoun

e.g. essi non hanno letto nessun libro.

Instead the negative adverbs mai, nemmeno, neanche and neppure may either follow the standard sequence, as above, or they may be inserted between the two parts of the compound tense, i.e. the auxiliary verb and the primary verb: (subject) + non + (auxiliary verb) + negative adverb + (past participle of the primary verb)

e.g. essi non hanno letto mai questo libro; alternatively: essi non hanno mai letto questo libro.

A few more examples should make this concept clear enough: il libro non era appartenuto a nessuno (only possible form) = the book had not belonged to anybody

in quel cassetto non ha trovato niente (only possible form) = in that drawer he / she didn't find anything

da lontano non avranno visto niente (only possible form) = from afar they won't have seen anything

non ho mangiato mai a casa = I never ate at home non ho mai mangiato a casa = (same as above)

non avevo guardato nemmeno la TV = I hadn't even watched the TV, but also I hadn't watched the TV either non avevo nemmeno guardato la TV = (same as above)

non aveva visto nemmeno un film = he / she hadn't even seen a movie, but also he / she hadn't seen a movie either non aveva nemmeno visto un film = (same as above)

non avrà letto neppure l'indirizzo = he / she might have not even read the address, but also he / she might have not read the address either non avrà neppure letto neppure l'indirizzo = (same as above)

non abbiamo voluto neppure quello = we didn't even want that (one), but also we didn't want that (one) either non abbiamo neppure voluto quello = (same as above)

When the alternative form is possible, in most cases to use one or the other is a free choice, although the first of the two would give the negative adverb a slightly more emphatic meaning, especially in spoken language (i.e. the voice pitch would slightly raise in pronouncing the adverb), while the second form is less strong, somewhat more stylish, and would be preferred in writing.

A second consideration about the previous examples is that nemmeno, neanche and neppure have the same meaning.

It would sometimes be more stylish to choose a specific one according to the sentence, but in common speech, or for a student's purpose, any of the three may be freely used. non conosceva neppure l'indirizzo = he / she didn't even know the address non conosceva neanche l'indirizzo = (same as above) non conosceva nemmeno l'indirizzo = (same as above) But these adverbs do translate two different English expressions: not even and neither. non conosceva neppure l'indirizzo = he / she didn't even know the address non conosceva neppure l'indirizzo = he / she didn't know the address either In most cases, which of the two is the actual meaning is made clear by the context of the sentence, since neither can only be possible if a first object has already been mentioned (i.e. he didn't know my house - he didn't know my address either).

The form we discussed so far may have both meanings (see once again the previous examples), and is stylistically correct.

However, in Italian it is still possible to distinguish more clearly the two meanings by using different arrangements of the words.

In spoken language, especially in central and southern Italy, to strengthen the meaning of not even it is a common custom to drop the negative conjunction non by replacing it with the negative adverb or pronoun, moved to the front, and to leave the verb at the bottom of the sentence: non conosceva neppure l'indirizzo = he / she didn't even know the address

but this may also be translated as: she didn't know the address either neppure l'indirizzo conosceva (very colloquial) = he / she didn't even know the address

il treno non ferma neanche a Firenze = the train doesn't even stop in Florence   but this may also be translated as: the train doesn't stop in Florence either il treno neanche a Firenze ferma (very colloquial) = the train doesn't even stop in Florence

quella scuola non chiude nemmeno d'estate = that school doesn't even close in summer   but this may also be translated as: that school doesn't close in summer either quella scuola nemmeno d'estate chiude (very colloquial) = that school doesn't even close in summer

This colloquial form is no longer a double negative, having lost non. But remember: although it is commonly heard, according to the official Italian grammar this form is not correct.

When the object of the sentence is a personal pronoun, the two different meanings not even and neither are more clearly understood.

At first, let's see a couple of typical sentences that contain a pronoun as a direct object: non li incontrerò (standard form) = I won't meet them non incontrerò loro (emphatic form) = I won't meet them (i.e. I will meet somebody else)

il giudice non lo ha condannato (standard form) = the judge did not sentence him il giudice non ha condannato lui (emphatic form) = the judge did not sentence him (i.e. the judge sentenced somebody else)

As explained in paragraph 8.1 , forcing the pronoun at the bottom of the sentence gives the latter a stronger emphasis (in the aforesaid example, the pronouns them and him are emphasized).

The same form used with neanche, nemmeno or neppure gives them a clear meaning of neither.

Instead, the standard form used so far (i.e. non + pronoun + verb + negative adverb) would only have the meaning of not even.

Furthermore, in the case of a pronoun used as direct object, the colloquial form explained above is considered correct (i.e. with the adverb moved in front, to replace non), and may be used as an alternative and somewhat stronger expression: non ti guarderò neppure = I will not even look at you neppure ti guarderò = (same as above, but stronger) non guarderò neppure te (emphasized form) = I will not look at you either

purtroppo non lo vidi nemmeno = unfortunately I didn't even see him purtroppo nemmeno lo vidi = (same as above, but stronger) purtroppo non vidi nemmeno lui = unfortunately I didn't see him either

l'anno scorso non le abbiamo neanche invitate = last year we haven't even invited them l'anno scorso neanche le abbiamo invitate = (same as above, but stronger) l'anno scorso non abbiamo invitato neanche loro = last year we haven't invited them either

Among the the indefinite pronouns discussed so far, niente, nulla and nessuno somewhat differ from ordinary ones, such as personal pronouns, relative pronouns, etc.

First of all, they do not have a plural form, due to their respective meaning; this also happens in English. Niente and nulla are both dealt with as masculine singular words.

Also nessuno is a masculine singular pronoun; however, as already mentioned at the beginning of this paragraph, when it is followed by a noun it turns into an adjective, whose English equivalent would be no...(noun): (as a pronoun) nessuno ha detto questo = nobody said this (as an adjective) nessun uomo pesa oltre 300 chili = no man weighs over 300 kilograms (as an adjective) nessuna persona comprerebbe questo libro = no person would buy this book

Used as a pronoun, nessuno does not change; it is considered a masculine word, also when it evidently refers to feminine individuals.

Therefore, if a compound verb's past participle is gender- and number- sensitive (see paragraph 6.4), the pronoun nessuno always requires a masculine inflection. nessuno (pronoun) è entrato nel reparto femminile = nobody entered the women's ward nessuna paziente (adjective) è entrata nel reparto femminile = no (female) patient entered the women's ward

Used as an adjective, instead, nessun and nessuna match the gender of the noun they refer to, as any other ordinary adjective.

While nessun (+ masculine noun) turns again into nessuno when the following noun begins with z or with s + consonant (see previous examples), nessuna (+ feminine noun) may undergo an elision, i.e. the last a dropped and replaced by an apostrophe, when the following noun begins with the vowel a.

This change, though, is facultative, and it rarely occurs when the noun begins with e, i, o, u. nessun vincitore = no winner nessun uomo = no man nessuno sconto = no discount nessuna domanda = no question nessun'amica or nessuna amica = no (female) friend nessuna imposta (seldom nessun'imposta) = no tax

nessun impiegato entrò nell'ufficio = no clerk entered the office nessuno straniero venne in città = no stranger came into town nessun'altra ragazza = no other girl Beware of nouns whose inflection is similar to a typical feminine one, such as atleta (athlete), poeta (poet), artista (artist), omicida (murderer), sosia (lookalike), etc., see paragraph 2.3

Many of them are both masculine and feminine, although a few of them have specific feminine forms (for instance poeta = poet, poetessa = female poet), or are only masculine (for instance programma = program). nessun atleta = no (male) athlete nessun'atleta = no (female) athlete

nessun sosia = no (male) lookalike nessuna sosia = no (female) lookalike

nessun artista = no (male) artist nessun'artista = no (female) artist

nessun poeta = no (male) poet nessuna poetessa = no (female) poet

nessun programma = no program

nessuno schema = no scheme

THE USE OF ALCUNO

The introduction of the previous paragraph mentioned an exception to the use of non + negative adverbs or adjectives.

In fact, the adjective forms nessun and its feminine nessuna are the only expressions among the ones discussed in paragraph 19.4 that have a positive (non-negative) form, which matches the English any. This form is alcuno, more often alcun for phonetic reasons (same as nessun - nessuno), and its feminine alcuna (the latter seldom undergoes an elision, thus turning into alcun').

The phonetic rules by which the aforesaid changes occur are the same ones concerning nessuno and nessuna (see again the previous paragraph 19.4) The use of alcun and alcuna after non avoids a double negative sentence: (io) non ho alcun compito = I do not have any duty (egli / ella) non possiede alcuna casa = he / she does not own any house il soldato non usò alcun'arma = the soldier did not use any weapon quel negozio non vi farà alcuno sconto = that shop will not give you any discount (voi) non avevate commesso alcun reato = you had not committed any offence questa scuola non insegna alcuna lingua straniera = this school does not teach any foreign language

The use of nessun or nessuna after non is still possible, yet rather colloquial. When alcun / alcuna can be used, it is preferrable to avoid a double negative sentence. (io) non ho alcun (colloquially nessun) compito (egli / ella) non possiede alcuna (colloquially nessuna) casa il soldato non usò alcun'arma (nessun'arma) quel negozio non vi farà alcuno (nessuno) sconto (voi) non avevate commesso alcun (nessun) reato questa scuola non insegna alcuna (nessuna) lingua straniera

Instead, when it is used as a pronoun (i.e. not followed by a noun), alcuno does not replace nessuno, therefore the sentence remains twice negative. (essi) non vedono alcuna persona = they don't see any person (essi) non vedono nessuna persona (colloquial) = (same, literally: "they don't see no person") (essi) non vedono nessuno = they don't see anybody

(egli / ella) non conta su alcun amico = he / she does not rely on any friend (egli / ella) non conta su nessun amico (colloquial) = (same as above) (egli / ella) non conta su nessuno = he / she does not rely on anybody questa penna non appartiene ad alcuno studente = this pen does not belong to any student questa penna non appartiene a nessuno studente (colloquial) = (same as above) questa penna non appartiene a nessuno = this pen does not belong to anybody

The form non vedono alcuno, non conta su alcuno, etc. did actually exist in the past, but now it may be found only in old texts, dating back to the 19th century (or older), therefore it can be considered obsolete.

Unlike nessuno, which has a feminine (nessuna) but no plural form, alcuno has the full set of regular inflections for feminine and plural: alcuna, alcuni, alcune.

They may be used either with positive or with negative sentences. The plural forms (alcuni, alcune), though, no longer mean any but some.

Compare the following examples:

(tu) non venderai alcun libro = you will not sell any book (tu) non venderai nessun libro (colloquial) = (same as above) (tu) venderai alcuni libri = you will sell some books (tu) non venderai alcuni libri = you will not sell some books

il poliziotto non sparò alcun colpo = the policeman did not fire any shot il poliziotto non sparò nessun colpo (colloquial) = (same as above) il poliziotto sparò alcuni colpi = the policeman fired some shots il poliziotto non sparò alcuni colpi = the policeman did not fire some shots

(io) non ho visto alcun gatto in giardino = I did not see any cat in the garden (io) non ho visto nessun gatto in giardino (colloquial) = (same as above) (io) ho visto alcuni gatti in giardino = I saw some cats in the garden (io) non ho visto alcuni gatti in giardino = I did not see some cats in the garden

ITALIAN SHORT STORIES

Learn Italian for Beginners in Your Car Like Crazy.
Language Learning Lessons for travel & Everyday.
How to speak Italian with Stories and Conversations.

INTRODUCTION

Reading is the key to improving your comprehension skills and helps you formulate better sentences. But when you're still a beginner or intermediate-level learner, it can be difficult to find proper materials to practice reading. You will also need to consult a dictionary while you're reading, and without audio accompaniment, you will find it difficult to catch new words and how they're pronounced by native speakers. It's easy to get confused. For beginners, reading and listening to short stories can be a fun and painless way of learning Italian. This book will introduce you to new vocabulary and sentence structures, while the accompanying audio material will help you with listening comprehension.

Reading short stories is an effective way to improve your Italian reading and listening comprehension skills. Through learning in this way, you will be able to improve your Italian without the monotonous chore of memorizing grammar rules. This works especially for beginners! Easy, right? In these Italian short stories, you find new vocabulary (words) that you can immediately put to use in everyday life.

Practice your listening skills by listening to a native Italian-speaker narrating the stories.

Enjoyable stories

      Varied vocabulary and sentence structures

      Easy grammar for beginners

      Audio for listening practice

      English translation

      Discover them one by one!

How to Learn Italian with short stories

Since these stories are often pretty straightforward, you don't need to be a professional reader. However, you still need a simple plan for learning effectively with them. To get the most out of your short story, I suggest this three-step approach. Let's called it an Italian experiment! Read the story for the gist, not the details. Focus on trying to understand the main ideas of the story: the characters, the major plot developments, and the setting. Take your time to read it again carefully. Look up unknown words, phrases or grammatical constructions that are unfamiliar to you. Write them down in a notebook or on flashcards to help you memorize them. Look at the translation to read the story one more time. This way, you understand the text fully and have access to the translations and explanations. For further practice, I recommend writing a summary of the story. This way, you'll have a more complete understanding of it and make new vocabulary and grammar topics easier to memorize.

This book contains a selection of 8 finest short stories which have been adapted from originals written by the world's greatest storytellers such as: O. Henry, W.S. Maugham, A. Maltz, W. de Mille; R. Goldberg and others. In addition there are 5 mini-stories presented at the beginning of the book as a "warm-up exercise".

The stories have been thoroughly adapted (to preserve the gist of the original) and translated into Italian language. The stories have been arranged according to their degree of difficulty and each story is accompanied by a "Key Vocabulary".

Although this book can be useful for learners of both English and Italian languages. It was mainly intended as a reading material for learners of Italian language.

LEVEL

The book is intended mainly for Elementary to middle-Intermediate level learners (that is, those who have already studied the basic structures of Italian). It will also be useful for more advanced learners as a way of practicing their reading skills and comprehension of Italian language.

USING THE BOOK EFFECTIVELY

In our opinion it will be most beneficial if you read each story in English first. Then review 'Key Vocabulary' and reread the story once more as a 'parallel text'. Knowledge of the context will enable you to link together English words and phrases to their Italian counterparts, thus expanding your vocabulary and improving your reading comprehension of Italian language. After reading through a story a couple of times you'll notice that you understand an 'Italian version' of the story as if it was written in your native tongue. And remember that your fluency in Italian will grow with each story you read.

Have fun! Divertiti!

ABBREVIATIONS

(used in 'Key Vocabulary')

agg. –   aggetivo (adjective)

avv. –   avverbio (adverb)

cong. – congiunzione (conjunction)

fig. –   figurato (figurative)

intr. –   interiezione (interjection)

prep. – preposizione (preposition)

pron. – pronome (pronoun)

s.f. – sostantivo femminile (feminine noun)

s.m. – sostantivo maschile (masculine noun)

v.aus. – verbo ausiliare (auxiliary verb)

v.intr. – verbo intransitivo (intransitive verb)

v.tr. – verbo transitivo (transitive verb)

v.rf. – verbo riflessivo (reflexive verb)

CHAPTER ONE: THE STORY IN FRENCH WITH ENGLISH TRANSLATION

Classic Fable "Les Trois Petits Cochons"

Section 1

Il était une fois une maman cochon qui avait trois petits cochons. Elle les aimait beaucoup, mais comme il n'y avait pas assez de nourriture pour qu'ils puissent tous manger à leur faim, elle les a envoyé tenter leur chance dans le vaste monde.

Once upon a time there was a mama pig who had three little pigs. She loved them very much, but there was not enough food for all of them to eat, so she sent them out into the big world to seek their fortunes.

Section 2

Le premier petit cochon a décidé d'aller vers le Sud. Alors qu'il marchait le long de la route, il a rencontré un fermier qui portait une botte de paille. Il lui a alors demandé poliment :"Pourriez-vous s'il vous plaît me donner cette paille, que je puisse construire une maison?"

The first little pig decided to go south. As he walked along the road he met a farmer carrying a bundle of straw, so he asked the man politely: "Could you please give me that straw, so that I can build a house?"

Comme le petit cochon avait dit "s'il vous plaît", le fermier lui a donné la paille, et le petit cochon l'a utilisée pour construire une belle maison. La maison avait des murs en paille, un plancher en paille, et à l'intérieur... un confortable lit en paille.

Because the little pig had said "please", the farmer gave him the straw, and the little pig used it to build a beautiful house. The house had straw walls, a straw floor, and inside... a comfortable straw bed.

Section 3

Alors que le petit cochon venait juste de finir de construire sa maison et qu'il s'était allongé pour faire une sieste dans son lit en paille, le grand méchant loup est arrivé près de la maison. Il a senti l'odeur du cochon à l'intérieur de la maison, et cela lui a mis l'eau à la bouche. "Mmm... Des sandwichs au bacon!"

When the little pig had just finished building his house and had laid down for a nap in his straw bed, the big bad wolf arrived at the house. He smelt the scent of the pig inside the house, and his mouth started to "Mmmm ... bacon sandwiches!"

le loup a frappé à la porte de la maison en paille et a dit: "Petit cochon! Petit cochon! Laisse-moi entrer! Laisse-moi entrer!"

So the wolf knocked at the door of the straw house and said: "Little pig! Little pig! Let me in! Let me in!"

Mais comme le petit cochon avait vu les grandes griffes du loup à travers la serrure, il a répondu: "Non, non, non! Par les poils de mon menton!"

But as the little pig had seen the wolf's big paws through the keyhole, he replied: "No! No! No! By the hair of my chin!"

Alors le loup a montré ses dents et a dit: "Alors je vais souffler et souffler et ta maison va s'effondrer!"

Then the wolf showed his teeth and said: "Then I'll blow and I'll blow and your house will fall down!"

Alors il a soufflé et soufflé et la maison s'est effondrée. Le petit cochon est revenu en courant chez lui auprès de sa mère.

So he blew and he blew and the house fell down. The little pig ran back home to his mother.

Section 4

Le deuxième petit cochon a décidé d'aller vers le Nord. Alors qu'il marchait le long de la route, il a rencontré un fermier qui portait un fagot de bois. Il lui a alors demandé poliment:"Excusez-moi, puis-je avoir ce bois pour construire une maison?"

The second little pig decided to go North. As he walked along the road he met a farmer carrying a bundle of wood, so he asked the man politely: "Excuse me, may I have that wood to build a house?"

Comme le petit cochon avait dit "excusez-moi", le fermier lui a donné le bois, et le petit cochon l'a utilisé pour construire une belle maison. La maison avait des murs en bois, un plancher en bois, et à l'intérieur... une solide table en bois.

Because the little pig had said "excuse me", the farmer gave him the wood, and the little pig used it to build a beautiful house. The house had wood walls, a wood floor, and inside... a strong wood table.

Section 5

Alors que le petit cochon venait juste de finir de construire sa maison et qu'il faisait un bouquet pour sa solide table en bois, le grand méchant loup est arrivé près de la maison. Il a senti l'odeur du cochon à l'intérieur de la maison, et son estomac s'est mis à gronder. "Mmm... Du rôti de porc!"

When the little pig had just finished building his house and was arranging flowers on his strong wood table, the big bad wolf came arrived at the house. He smelt the scent of the pig inside the house, and his stomach started to rumble. "Mmmmm ... roast pork!"

Alors le loup a frappé à la porte de la maison en bois et a dit: "Petit cochon! Petit cochon! Laissemoi entrer! Laisse-moi entrer!"

So the wolf knocked at the door of the wood house and said: "Little pig! Little pig! Let me in! Let me in!"

Mais comme le petit cochon avait vu le long nez du loup à travers la serrure, il a répondu:"Non, non, non! Par les poils de mon menton!"

But as the little pig had seen the wolf's long nose through the keyhole, he replied: "No! No! No! By the hair of my chin!"

Alors le loup a montré ses dents et a dit: "Alors je vais souffler et souffler et ta maison va s'effondrer!"

Then the wolf showed his teeth and said: "Then I'll blow and I'll blow and your house will fall down!"

Alors il a soufflé et soufflé et la maison s'est effondrée. Le petit cochon est revenu en courant chez lui auprès de sa mère, qui n'était pas contente!

So he blew and he blew and the house fell down. The little pig ran back home to his mother — who was not happy!

Section 6

Le troisième petit cochon a décidé d'aller vers l'Ouest. Alors qu'il marchait le long de la route, il a rencontré un fermier qui portait un chargement de briques. Il lui a alors demandé poliment : "Bonjour monsieur, puis-je avoir quelques-unes de ces briques pour construire une maison?"

third little pig decided to go West. As he walked along the road he met a farmer carrying a load of bricks. So he asked the man politely: "Hello sir, may I have some of those bricks to build a house?"

Comme le fermier appréciait qu'on l'appelle "monsieur", il a donné au petit cochon quelques briques, et le petit cochon les a utilisées pour construire une belle maison. La maison avait des murs en brique, un plancher en brique, et à l'intérieur... une grande cheminée en brique.

The farmer liked being called "sir" so he gave the little pig some bricks, and the little pig used them to build a beautiful house. The house had brick walls, a brick floor, and inside... a large brick fireplace.

Section 7

Alors que le petit cochon venait juste de finir de construire sa maison et qu'il préparait une grande marmite de soupe dans sa cheminée en brique, le grand méchant loup est arrivé près de la maison. Il a senti l'odeur du cochon à l'intérieur de la maison, et s'est léché les babines."Mmm... Des côtelettes de porc avec de la sauce barbecue et des haricots verts!"

When the little pig had just finished building his house and was cooking a big pot of soup in his brick fireplace, the big bad wolf arrived at the house. He smelt the scent of the pig inside the house, and he licked his lips. "Mmmmm ... pork chops with barbeque sauce and green beans!"

Alors le loup a frappé à la porte de la maison en brique et a dit: "Petit cochon! Petit cochon! Laisse-moi entrer! Laisse-moi entrer!"

So the wolf knocked at the door of the wood house and said: "Little pig! Little pig! Let me in! Let me in!"

Mais le petit cochon a vu les grandes oreilles du loup à travers la serrure, il a donc répondu:"Non, non, non! Par les poils de mon menton!"

But as the little pig had seen the wolf's big ears through the keyhole, he replied: "No! No! No! By the hair of my chin!"

Alors le loup a montré ses dents et a dit: "Alors je vais souffler et souffler et ta maison va s'effondrer!"

Then the wolf showed his teeth and said: "Then I'll blow and I'll blow and your house will fall down!"

Alors il a soufflé et soufflé, encore et encore. Mais il n'a pas réussi à faire s'effondrer la maison. À la fin il était tellement essoufflé qu'il ne pouvait plus du tout souffler.

So he blew and he blew, again and again. But he could not make the house fall down. At last he was so out of breath that he couldn't blow any more.

Le petit cochon se contentait de remuer sa grande marmite de soupe, et de rire.

little pig just stirred his big pot of soup, and laughed.

Section 8

Mais le loup avait tellement envie de manger des côtelettes de porc... il ne voulait pas abandonner! Il s'est faufilé derrière la maison et a grimpé sur le toit. "À présent, j'aurai ce cochon, c'est certain!"

But the wolf had such a craving to eat pork chops... he didn't want to give up! He snuck around the back of the house and climbed onto the roof. "Now I'll get that pig, for certain!"

Le loup s'est laissé glisser dans la grande cheminée en brique et a atterri... PLOUF! Les fesses les premières dans la grande marmite de soupe du petit cochon... qui était alors très chaude! Le loup a hurlé et a bondi hors de la marmite, puis est sorti en courant de la maison et a dévalé la route, serrant très fort ses fesses brûlées.

The wolf let himself slide down the great brick chimney and landed ... PLOP! Bottom-first into the little pig's big pot of soup... which was now very hot! The wolf howled and jumped out of the pot, then ran out of the house and hurtled down the road, clutching his burnt bottom.

Le petit cochon a appelé sa mère et ses deux frères sur son téléphone portable en brique, et les a invité à partager un délicieux dîner de soupe aux fesses de loup.

The little pig called his mother and his two brothers on his brick mobile phone, and invited them to share a delicious dinner of wolf-bottom soup.

La soupe aux fesses de loup était si savoureuse que bientôt tous les gens à cent kilomètres à la ronde ont voulu attraper le loup et le faire s'asseoir dans leur soupe. Le pauvre loup a dû s'enfuir très loin jusqu'à la sombre forêt profonde où il a pu vivre en paix et dans le calme.

The wolf-bottom soup was so tasty that soon everybody within one hundred kilometers wanted to catch the wolf and make him sit in their soup. The poor wolf had to run far away to the deep dark forest where he could live in peace and quiet.

CHAPTER TWO: Aesop and the traveler / Aesop e il viaggiatore

Aesop was a very clever man who lived many hundreds of years ago in Greece. He wrote many fine stories. He was well-known as a man who liked jokes. One day, as he was enjoying a walk, he met a traveler, who greeted him and said:

"Signor, can you tell me how soon I shall get to town?"

Aesop era un uomo molto intelligente vissuto in Grecia molte centinaia di anni fa. Scrisse molte belle storie. Era molto conosciuto come uomo a cui piacevano gli scherzi. Un giorno, mentre si godeva una passeggiata, incontrò un viaggiatore, che lo salutò e disse:

"Signore, può dirmi quanto mi ci vorrà per arrivare in città?" "Go," Aesop answered.

"I know I must go," protested the traveler, "but I want you to tell me how soon I shall get to town?"

"Go," Aesop said again angrily. "Vada," Aesop rispose.

"Lo so che devo andare," protestò il viaggiatore, "ma voglio che lei mi dica quanto tempo mi ci vuole per arrivare in città?"

"Vada," rispose di nuovo Aesop arrabbiato.

"This man must be mad," the traveler thought and went on. After he had walked some distance, Aesop shouted after him: "It will take you two hours to get to town."

"Quest'uomo deve essere pazzo," pensò il viaggiatore e se ne andò. Dopo che ebbe camminato una certa distanza, Aesop gli urlò:

"Ci vorranno due ore per arrivare in città."

The traveler turned around in astonishment. "Why didn't you tell me that before?" he asked.

Il viaggiatore si girò sbalordito. "E perché non me lo ha detto prima?" chiese.

"How could I have told you that before?" answered Aesop. "I did not know how fast you can walk."

"Come avrei potuto dirglielo prima?" rispose Aesop. "Non sapevo quanto veloce lei camminasse."

Key Vocabulary:

o intelligente agg. [in-tel-li-gèn-te] – intelligent, clever.

o vivere v.intr. [vì-ve-re] – to live.

o centinaio s.m. [cen-ti-nà-io] – (about a) hundred,

~a (pl.) – hundreds (meaning 'a great number').

o scrivere v.tr. [scrì-ve-re] – to write.

o conoscere v.tr. [co-nó-sce-re] – to know, to be acquainted with.

conosciuto agg. [co-no-sciù-to] – known, well-known. o piacere v.intr. [pia-cè-re] – to like.

o godere v.tr. [go-dé-re] – to enjoy.

o incontrare v.tr. [in-con-trà-re] – to meet; to run into (s.o.).

o salutare v.tr. [sa-lu-tà-re] – to greet; to say hello (or bye).

o ci vuole = it takes. (pl. form – ci vogliono).

ci vuole un'ora per arrivare qui / it takes one hour to get here. ci vogliono due giorni / it takes two days.

o volere v.tr. [vo-lé-re] – to want.

o arrabbiato agg. [ar-rab-bià-to] – angry.

o pazzo agg. [pàz-zo] – crazy, mad.

o pensare v.tr. [pen-sà-re] – to think.

o certo agg. [cèr-to] – sure.

un ~ | una certa = some, certain.

o girarsi v.rf. [gi-ràr-si] – to turn around, to turn.

o sapere v.tr. [sa-pé-re] – to know (how).

CHAPTER THREE: The doctor's advice / Il consiglio del medico

One time an old gentleman went to see a doctor. The doctor examined him and said: "Medicine won't help you. You must have a complete rest. Go to a quiet country place for a month, walk a lot, drink milk, go to bed early, and smoke just one cigar a day."

"Thank you very much," said the old gentleman, "I shall do everything you say."

Un giorno, un vecchio gentiluomo andò dal medico. Il medico lo visitò e disse: "La medicina non l'aiuterà. Lei ha bisogno di riposo assoluto. Vada in un paese tranquillo per un mese, cammini molto, beva latte, vada a dormire presto e fumi soltanto un sigaro al giorno."

"Grazie mille," disse il vecchio gentiluomo, "Farò tutto quello che mi ha detto."

A month later the gentleman came to the doctor again. "How do you feel?" said the doctor, "I am very glad to see you. You look much younger."

Un mese più tardi, il gentiluomo ritornò dal medico. "Come si sente ora?" chiese il medico, "Mi fa piacere rivederla. Sembra molto più giovane."

"Oh, doctor," said the gentleman, "I feel quite well now. I had a good rest.

I went to bed early, I drank a lot of milk, and I walked a lot. Your advice certainly helped me. But you told me to smoke one cigar a day, and that one cigar a day almost killed me at first. It's no joke to start smoking at my age.

"Oh, dottore," disse il gentiluomo, "Mi sento abbastanza bene ora.

Mi sono riposato. Sono andato a letto presto, ho bevuto molto latte e ho camminato molto. Il suo consiglio mi ha sicuramente aiutato. Ma mi ha detto di fumare un sigaro al giorno, e quell'unico sigaro al giorno mi ha quasi ucciso all'inizio. Non è uno scherzo iniziare a fumare alla mia età.

Key Vocabulary:

o visitare v.tr. [vi-si-tà-re] – to visit; to examine.

o riposo s.m. [ri-pò-so] – rest, repose.

o tranquillo agg. [tran-quìl-lo] – quiet; tranquil.

o soltanto avv. [sol-tàn-to] – only, just.

o ritornare v.intr. [ri-tor-nà-re] – to return; to come back.

CHAPTER FOUR: The clever poor man / Il povero uomo intelligente

One day a poor man was travelling on horseback. In the afternoon, when he was tired and hungry, he stopped tied his horse to a tree and sat down to have his lunch. A rich man came to that place and began to tie his horse to the same tree.

Un giorno, un uomo povero stava viaggiando a cavallo. Nel pomeriggio, quando si sentì stanco e affamato, si fermò, legò il suo cavallo ad un albero e si sedette per pranzare. Un uomo ricco arrivò nello stesso posto e iniziò a legare il suo cavallo allo stesso albero.

"Do not tie your horse to that tree," said the poor man, "my horse is wild, it will kill your horse. Tie it to another tree!"

"Non legate il vostro cavallo a quel albero," disse l'uomo povero, "il mio cavallo è selvaggio e ucciderà il suo cavallo. Lo leghi ad un altro albero!"

But the rich man answered: "I will tie my horse where I like!" So he tied up his horse and also sat down to eat his lunch. A few minutes later they heard a terrible noise and saw that the two horses were fighting. They ran up to them, but it was too late – the rich man's horse was killed.

Ma l'uomo ricco rispose: "Legherò il mio cavallo dove voglio!" Così, legò il suo cavallo e si sedette anche lui per mangiare. Dopo alcuni minuti, sentirono un terribile rumore e videro che i due cavalli si stavano scontrando. Corsero verso di loro, ma era troppo tardi – il cavallo dell'uomo ricco era già stato ucciso.

"See what your horse has done!" cried the rich man. "You will have to pay for it!" and he brought the poor man to the court.

"Hai visto cosa ha fatto il tuo cavallo!" urlò l'uomo ricco. "Ora dovrà pagarmelo!" e portò l'uomo povero in tribunale.

The judge turned to the poor man and asked: "Is it true that your horse killed his horse?" But the poor man answered nothing. Then the judge asked the poor man many other questions, but he did not say anything. At last the judge shouted: "This man is dumb. He cannot speak!"

Il giudice si rivolse verso l'uomo povero e chiese: "È vero che il suo cavallo ha ucciso il cavallo di lui?" Ma l'uomo povero non rispose. Poi il giudice ha chiesto l'uomo povero molte altre domande, ma lui non disse niente. Infine, il giudice urlò: "Questo uomo è muto. Non può parlare!"

"Oh," said the rich man, "he can speak as well as you and I. He spoke to me when I met him." "Are you sure?" asked the judge. What did he say?"

"Oh," disse l'uomo ricco, "lui sa parlare bene quanto lei e me. Mi ha parlato quando l'ho incontrato." "Ma ne è sicuro?" chiese il giudice. E cosa le ha detto?"

"Of course I am sure," answered the rich man. "He told me not to tie my horse to the same tree where his horse was tied. He said his horse was wild and would kill my horse."

"Certo che ne sono sicuro," rispose l'uomo ricco. "Mi ha detto di non legare il mio cavallo allo stesso albero dov'era legato il suo cavallo. Ha detto che il suo cavallo era selvaggio e avrebbe ucciso il mio cavallo."

"Oh," said the judge, "now I see that you are wrong. He warned you before. So he will not pay for your horse."

"Oh," disse il giudice, "ora vedo che lei ha torto. Lui l'aveva avvertito prima. Quindi non pagherà per il tuo cavallo."

Then he turned to the poor man and asked him why he had not answered all questions.

Poi si rivolse verso l'uomo povero e gli chiese perché non avesse risposto a tutte le domande.

The poor man said: "I did not answer you because I knew that you would believe a rich man rather than a poor man. So I wanted him to tell you everything, and now you see who was right and who was wrong."

L'uomo povero rispose: "Non le ho risposto perché sapevo che avrebbe creduto di più ad un uomo ricco invece che ad un uomo povero. Così, volevo che fosse lui a raccontarvi tutto, e ora può vedere chi ha ragione e chi ha torto."

Key Vocabulary:

o sentire v.tr. [sen-tì-re] – to hear; to feel.

o stanco agg. [stàn-co] – tired.

o legare v.tr. [le-gà-re] – to tie (up), to bind.

o iniziare v.tr. [i-ni-zià-re] – to begin; to initiate.

o selvaggio agg. [sel-vàg-gio] – wild, untamed.

o uccidere v.tr. [uc-cì-de-re] – to kill; to murder.

o così avv. [co-sì] – so; like this, this way.

o dopo avv. [dó-po] – after; later.

o vedere v.tr. [ve-dé-re] – to see; to look at.

o scontrarsi v.rf. [scon-tràr-si] – to fight, to scuffle; to clash.

o urlare v.intr. [ur-là-re] – to shout, to cry, to yell.

o dovere v.aus. [do-vé-re] – must; to have to.

o portare v.tr. [por-tà-re] – to carry; to bring; to take.

o rivolgere v.tr. [ri-vòl-ge-re] – to turn; ~ around; to address.

o rispondere v.intr. [ri-spón-de-re] – to answer, to respond.

o muto agg. [mù-to] – mute, dumb.

o torto agg. [tòr-to] – wrong; unfair.

o quindi cong. [quìn-di] – therefore, so.

o avvertire v.tr. [av-ver-tì-re] – to let know; to warn.

o invece avv. [in-vé-ce] – instead of; rather than.

CHAPTER FIVE: Fortune and the man / Fortuna e l'uomo

One day a man was walking along the street. He had only an old bag in his hands. He was wondering why people who had a lot of money were never satisfied and always wanted more. "As far as I'm concerned", he said, "if I only had enough to eat, I would not ask for anything else".

Un giorno, un uomo stava camminando lungo una strada. Aveva solo una vecchia borsa nelle mani. Si chiedeva perché le persone che possedevano tanto denaro non fossero mai soddisfatte e desiderassero sempre di più. "Per quanto mi riguarda", disse, "se solo avessi abbastanza da mangiare, non chiederei niente altro".

Just at this moment Fortune came down the street. She heard the man and stopped.

In quello stesso istante, Fortuna passeggiava lungo la stessa strada. Sentì le parole dell'uomo e si fermò.

"Listen," she said, "I want to help you. Open your bag and I will pour diamonds into it. But every diamond which falls on the ground will become dust. Do you understand?"

"Oh, yes, I understand," replied the man.

"Senti," disse lei, "Voglio aiutarti. Apri la borsa e ci verserò dei diamanti. Ma ogni diamante che cadrà a terra si trasformerà in polvere. Hai capito?"

"Oh, sì, ho capito," rispose l'uomo.

He quickly opened his bag and saw a stream of diamonds was poured into it. The bag began to grow heavy. "Is that enough?" asked Fortune. "Not yet." The man's hands began to tremble.

"You are the richest man in the world now," said Fortune.

Egli aprì velocemente la sua borsa e vide una corrente di diamanti riversarsi in essa. La borsa iniziò a diventare pesante. "È sufficiente?" chiese

Fortuna. "Non ancora." Le mani dell'uomo iniziarono a tremare. "Ora, sei l'uomo più ricco del mondo," disse Fortuna.

"Just a few more, add a few more," said the man. Another diamond was added and the old bag split. All the diamonds fell on the ground and became dust.

"Ancora un po', aggiungine ancora un po'," disse l'uomo. Venne aggiunto un altro diamante e la vecchia borsa si strappò. Tutti i diamanti caddero a terra e si trasformarono in polvere.

Fortune disappeared, leaving the man along on the street.

Fortuna sparì, lasciando l'uomo solo per la strada.

Key Vocabulary:

o camminare v.intr. [cam-mi-nà-re] – to walk.

o chiedere v.tr. [chiè-de-re] – to ask, to request.

o possedere v.tr. [pos-se-dé-re] – to possess, to have, to own.

o soddisfatto agg. [sod-di-sfàt-to] – satisfied, pleased.

o desiderare v.tr. [de-si-de-rà-re] – to desire, to long for.

o riguardare v.tr. [ri-guar-dà-re] – to regard; to concern.

o per quanto mi riguarda – as far as I'm concerned.

o abbastanza avv. [ab-ba-stàn-za] – enough; fairly, quite.

o passeggiare v.intr. [pas-seg-già-re] – to walk, to stroll.

o stesso agg. [stés-so] – same.

o fermare v.tr. [fer-mà-re] – to stop, to halt.

o versare v.tr. [ver-sà-re] – to pour, to spill.

o trasformare v.tr. [trasfor-mà-re] – to transform, to turn (into).

o aggiungere v.tr. [ag-giùn-ge-re] – to add (to).

o ancora avv. [an-có-ra] – still; yet (in negative phrases).

o po' avv. = truncated poco.

o poco agg. [pò-co] – little, not much; few.

o strappare v.tr. [strap-pà-re] – to rip, to split; to tear out.

o sparire v.intr. [spa-rì-re] – to disappear.

CHAPTER SIX: The bellboy / Il fattorino

A tourist was standing in front of the reception desk of a Washington hotel. He was in a hurry. He had only ten minutes to pay his bill and arrive at the station. Suddenly he remembered that he had forgotten something.

Un turista era in piedi davanti alla reception di un hotel a Washington.

Aveva fretta. Aveva solo dieci minuti per pagare il conto e arrivare alla stazione. Improvvisamente si ricordò di aver dimenticato qualcosa.

He called the bellboy and said: "Run up to room 85 and see whether I left a box on the table. Be quick please, I am in a hurry."

Chiamò il fattorino e disse: "Corri su nella stanza 85 e vedi se ho lasciato una scatola sopra al tavolo. Fai veloce per favore, ho fretta."

The boy ran up the stairs. Five minutes passed, while gentleman was walking up and down impatiently.

Il ragazzo corse su per le scale. Passarono cinque minuti, mentre il gentiluomo camminava su e giù impazientemente.

At last the boy came back. "Yes, sir," he said, "you left it there. It's on the table."

Finalmente il ragazzo ritornò. "Sì, signore," disse, "l'ha lasciata lì. È sopra al tavolo."

Key Vocabulary:

o avere fretta – to be in a hurry.

o fattorino s.m. [fat-to-rì-no] – messenger boy; bellboy.

o ricordare v.tr. [ri-cor-dà-re] – to remember.

o dimenticare v.tr. [di-men-ti-cà-re] – to forget.

o correre v.intr. [cór-re-re] – to run.

o lasciare v.tr. [la-scià-re] – to leave; to let.

o fare v.tr. [fà-re] – to make, to do.

o fai veloce – (literally) make it quick.

o mentre cong. [mén-tre] – while.

o finalmente avv. [fi-nal-mén-te] – finally, at last.

CHAPTER SEVEN: Art for heart's sake / Arte per il bene del cuore

Mr. Smith was sitting in his library room reading the newspaper. There was a knock at the door and his servant Koppel came in.

Il Signor Smith era seduto nella sua biblioteca e stava leggendo il giornale.

Qualcuno bussò alla porta e Koppel il suo servitore entrò.

"Will you take your orange juice, sir?" the servant said gently to his master. "No," answered Mr. Smith.

"Desidera un succo d'arancia, signore?" disse gentilmente il servitore al suo padrone. "No," rispose il Signor Smith.

"But it's good for you, sir. It's the doctor's orders." "No."

"Ma le farà bene, signore. Sono gli ordini del medico." "No."

Koppel heard the front door bell and was glad to leave the room. He found

the doctor in the hall downstairs.

Koppel sentì suonare il campanello della porta e fu contento di lasciare la stanza. Nell'atrio al piano di sotto trovò il dottore.

"I can't do anything with the old man," he said to the doctor. "He doesn't want to take his juice. He doesn't want me to read to him. He hates the radio. He doesn't like anything."

"Non posso fare niente con il vecchio," disse al dottore. "Non vuole bere il suo succo. Non vuole che gli legga qualcosa. Odia la radio. Non gli piace niente."

Doctor Jones received the information with his usual professional calm.

He had thought a lot about his patient since his last visit. This was not an ordinary case.

Il Dottor Jones prese l'informazione con la sua solita calma professionale.

Aveva pensato molto al suo paziente dalla sua ultima visita. caso ordinario.

The old gentleman was in rather good shape for a man of seventy six. But something had to be done with him. He needs to be kept from buying things. The fact is that the old man suffered considerably from his purchases.

Il vecchio signore era piuttosto in buona forma per un uomo di settantasei anni. Ma si doveva fare qualcosa con lui. Era necessario trattenerlo dal fare acquisti. Il fatto era che il vecchio soffriva notevolmente per i suoi acquisti.

His latest heart attack happened after his disastrous purchase of a railroad in one of the Western States. Another attack was the result of the bankruptcy of some grocery shops, which he had bought at a very high price.

Il suo ultimo attacco di cuore avvenne dopo il disastroso acquisto di una ferrovia in uno degli Stati Occidentali. Un altro attacco era il risultato della bancarotta di alcuni negozi di generi alimentari, acquistati ad un prezzo molto alto.

All of these purchases had to be liquidated at a great sacrifice both to his health and to his pocketbook.

Tutti questi acquisti dovevano essere liquidati con grande sacrificio sia per la sua salute che per il portafoglio.

The doctor once again reflected on all this before he entered his patient's room. He approached Mr. Smith smiling.

Il dottore ragionò su tutto questo ancora una volta prima di entrare nella stanza del suo paziente. Si avvicinò al Signor Smith sorridente.

"Well, how's the young man today?"

"Umph," came from the figure in the armchair.

"I hear you don't obey orders," went on the doctor. "Who can give me orders at my age?"

"Bene, come sta oggi questo giovane uomo?"

"Umph," udì dalla figura seduta nella poltrona.

"Mi hanno detto che non obbedisce agli ordini," continuò il dottore. "Chi può darmi ordini alla mia età?"

The doctor took a chair and sat down close to the old man. "I have a proposition for you," he said quietly.

Il dottore prese una sedia e si sedette vicino al vecchio. "Ho una proposta da farle," disse con calma.

The old man looked at him suspiciously over his glasses.

"What is it? More medicine, more automobile rides, more nonsense to keep me away from business?"

Il vecchio lo guardò con sospetto sopra gli occhiali.

"Cos'è questo? Altre medicine, altri giri in automobile, altre sciocchezze per tenermi lontano dagli affari?"

"How would you like to study art?" "Nonsense."

"I don't mean seriously, just for fun." "Nonsense."

"Le piacerebbe studiare arte?" "Sciocchezze."

"Non intendo seriamente, solo per divertimento." "Sciocchezze."

"All right," the doctor stood up. "It was just a suggestion, that's all." "Where did you get this crazy idea?"

"Well, it's only a suggestion."

"But, Jones, how can I start, that is, if I am foolish enough to do it?"

"Va bene," il dottore si alzò in piedi. "Era solo un suggerimento, ecco tutto."

"Beh, è solo un suggerimento."

"Ma, Jones, come posso iniziare, cioè, sono abbastanza folle per farlo?" "I've thought of that too. I can get a student from one of the art schools.

He would come here once a week and give you lessons. If you don't like it after a little while, you can send him away."

"Ho pensato anche a questo. Posso trovare uno studente da una delle scuole d'arte. Verrebbe qui una volta alla settimana a darle lezioni. Se dopo un po' di tempo non le piace, potrà mandarlo via."

Doctor Jones went to his friend, the director of an Art Institute, and explained the situation. The director found a suitable person - a young man of eighteen named Frank Swain, who was a gifted student. He needed the money. He was working as a bell-boy at night to pay for his studies at the Institute.

Il Dottor Jones andò dal suo amico, il direttore di un Istituto d'Arte, e gli spiegò la situazione. Il direttore trovò una persona adatta – un giovane di diciotto anni di nome Frank Swain, uno studente dotato. Aveva bisogno di quel denaro.

Lavorava di notte come fattorino per pagarsi gli studi all'Istituto.

The young man was introduced to the doctor. You may imagine how delighted he was when he heard the doctor's offer. Five dollars a lesson! Fine!

Il giovane, venne presentato al dottore. Potete immaginare la sua felicità quando udì l'offerta del dottore. Cinque dollari a lezione! Bene!

The next afternoon Frank came to Mr. Smith's study. The old man looked at him suspiciously.

Il pomeriggio seguente Frank andò allo studio del Signor Smith. Il vecchio lo guardò con sospetto.

"Sir, I am not an artist yet," said the young man. The old man murmured something.

"Signore, non sono ancora un artista," disse il giovane. Il vecchio mormorò qualcosa.

Frank arranged some paper and pencils on the table. "Let's try to draw that vase over there," he suggested. "Umph." The old man took a pencil and made a scrawl.

Frank preparò della carta e delle matite sopra al tavolo. "Proviamo a disegnare quel vaso laggiù," suggerì. "Umph." Il vecchio prese una matita e fece uno scarabocchio.

He made another scrawl and connected them with a couple of lines. Then he looked at the result with satisfaction.

Fece un altro scarabocchio e li unì con un paio di linee. Poi guardò il risultato con soddisfazione.

Frank was patient. He needed the five dollars.

Frank era paziente. Aveva bisogno di quei cinque dollari.

"If you want to draw something you'll have to look at what you are drawing, sir.

Will you look at the vase again?" Frank said gently.

"Se vuole disegnare qualcosa deve guardare a cosa sta disegnando, signore.

Vuole riguardare il vaso un'altra volta?" disse Frank gentilmente.

The old man obeyed. Then he said: "The vase is really quite pretty. I never noticed it before."

Il vecchio obbedì. Poi disse: "Quel vaso è piuttosto carino. Non lo avevo mai notato prima."

At that moment the servant came in bringing a glass of juice for his master.

"Oh, it's orange juice again," said Mr. Smith. Frank left.

In quel momento entrò il servitore portando un bicchiere di succo per il suo padrone.

"Oh, ancora succo d'arancia," disse il Signor Smith. Frank se ne andò.

When he came the following week there was a drawing on the table that had a slight resemblance to the vase.

Quando ritornò la settimana seguente, trovò un disegno sul tavolo che aveva una certa somiglianza con il vaso.

The old man asked him: "Well, what do you think of it?" "Not bad, sir," answered Frank. "But it's a little crooked."

Il vecchio gli chiese: "Beh, che ne pensi di questo?" "Non male, signore," rispose Frank. "Ma è un po' storto."

"I see. The halves do not match," the old man agreed. He added a few lines and colored the open spaces with a blue pencil.

"Capisco. Le due metà non coincidono," il vecchio era d'accordo.

Aggiunse alcune linee e colorò lo spazio aperto con una matita blu.

Then he looked towards the door. "Listen, young man," he whispered, "I want to ask you something before old 'orange juice' comes back."

Poi guardò verso la porta. "Ascolta, ragazzo, "sussurrò, "Voglio chiederti una cosa prima che il vecchio "succo d'arancia" ritorni.

"Yes, sir," replied Frank respectfully."

"Could you come twice a week or perhaps three times?" "Sì, signore," rispose Frank con rispetto."

"Potresti venire due volte alla settimana o magari tre volte?" "Surely, Mr. Smith."

"Good. Let's make it Monday, Wednesday and Friday. Four o'clock." "Certamente, Signor Smith."

"Bene. Facciamo lunedì, mercoledì e venerdì. Alle ore quattro."

The servant entered the room and was surprised to see that this time his master was willing to take his juice.

Il servitore entrò nella stanza e fu sorpreso nel vedere che questa volta il suo padrone era disposto a prendere il succo.

As weeks went by Frank's visits became more frequent. Now when the doctor came to see Mr. Smith, the old man was talking a lot about art. He also proudly demonstrated the stains of paint on his heavy silk dressing gown.

Mentre passavano le settimane, le visite di Frank diventavano sempre più frequenti. Ora, quando il dottore veniva a visitare il Signor Smith, il vecchio parlava molto di arte. Mostrava anche con orgoglio le macchie di pittura sulla sua vestaglia di seta pesante.

He did not allow his servant to send it to the cleaner's. The reason was that he wanted to show the doctor how hard he had been working.

Non permetteva che il suo servitore la portasse in tintoria. Il motivo era che voleva mostrare al dottore quanto si stava impegnando.

The doctor's advice appeared to be working for Mr. Smith. There were no more purchases of companies that cost a lot of money. No more crazy transactions which ruined his health. Art was a complete cure for his financial troubles.

Il consiglio del dottore sembrava funzionare con il Signor Smith. Non ci furono più acquisti di aziende che costavano un sacco di denaro. Niente più transazioni folli che rovinavano la sua salute. L'arte era una cura completa per i suoi guai finanziari.

The doctor allowed his patient to visit art galleries and exhibitions with Frank. An entirely new world opened up its mysteries. The old man seemed to take a great interest in the galleries and the painters displayed in them.

Il dottore permise al suo paziente di visitare gallerie d'arte e mostre con Frank. Un mondo completamente nuovo aprì i suoi misteri. Il vecchio sembrava mostrare un certo interesse nelle gallerie e sui pittori esposti in esse.

How were the galleries managed? Who selected the pictures for the exhibitions? An idea was forming in his brain.

Come erano gestite le gallerie? Chi selezionava i dipinti per le mostre?

Un'idea gli si stava formando nel cervello.

When spring came and the trees were in bloom Mr. Smith made a picture which he called "Trees Dressed in White". The picture was awful but nevertheless the old man announced that he wanted to exhibit it in the summer show at the Lathrop Gallery.

Quando arrivò la primavera e gli alberi erano in fioritura, il Signor Smith fece un quadro che chiamò "Alberi Vestiti di Bianco." Il quadro era orribile ma tuttavia il vecchio annunciò che voleva esibirlo nella mostra estiva alla Lathrop Gallery.

The summer show at this gallery was the biggest art exhibition of the year in quality, if not in size. The lifetime dream of every artist in the United States was a Lathrop prize.

La mostra estiva in questa galleria era la più grande mostra d'arte dell'anno come qualità, se non anche in grandezza. Il sogno di una vita di qualsiasi artista negli Stati Uniti era un premio Lathrop.

And it was in this show that Mr. Smith was going to exhibit his "Trees Dressed in White," which looked like salad dressing which somebody had thrown on the wall of a house.

Ed era a questa mostra che il Signor Smith voleva esibire "Alberi Vestiti di Bianco," che sembrava a del condimento per insalata che qualcuno aveva gettato sul muro di una casa.

"If the papers write about this, Mr. Smith will become a laughing stock.

We must stop him," Frank said in horror.

"Se i giornali scrivono un articolo su questo, il Signor Smith diventerà uno zimbello. Dobbiamo fermarlo," disse Frank con orrore.

"No," protested the doctor. "We can't do that now. We may spoil all the good work we have done."

"No," protestò il dottore. "Non possiamo farlo ora. Rovineremo tutto il buon lavoro fatto."

To the astonishment of all three – and especially Frank – "Trees Dressed in White" was accepted for the Lathrop Show. Not only was Mr. Smith crazy, thought Frank, but the Lathrop Gallery was crazy too.

Con sorpresa di tutti e tre – e soprattutto di Frank – "Alberi Vestiti di Bianco" fu accettato per la Mostra Lathrop. Non era soltanto il Signor Smith pazzo, pensò Frank, ma anche la Lathrop Gallery era pazza.

Fortunately, the painting was displayed in a dark corner where visitors could hardly see it. Frank came to the gallery one afternoon and blushed to the ears when he saw "Trees Dressed in White" an ugly splash on the wall.

Fortunatamente, il dipinto venne esposto in un angolo buio dove i visitatori riuscivano a malapena a vederlo. Un pomeriggio Frank arrivò alla galleria e arrossì fino alle orecchie quando vide "Alberi Vestiti di Bianco" – un orribile spruzzo sul muro.

When two students stopped before the picture, laughing, Frank ran away in terror. He did not want to hear what these young men had to say.

Quando due studenti si fermarono davanti al quadro, ridendo, Frank scappò via terrorizzato. Non voleva sentire cosa questi due giovani avevano da dire.

During the course of the show the old man continued taking his lessons and did not talk about his picture. But every time Frank entered the room he found Mr. Smith chuckling.

Durante il corso della mostra il vecchio continuò a prendere lezioni e non parlò del suo quadro. Ma ogni volta che Frank entrava nella stanza trovava il Signor Frank che ridacchiava.

May be the old man was really crazy. And it was strange that the Lathrop committee encouraged him by accepting his picture.

Forse il vecchio era veramente pazzo. Ed era strano che la commissione di Lathrop lo avesse incoraggiato accettando il suo dipinto.

Two days before the close of the exhibition a long official looking envelope was delivered to Mr. Smith while Frank, Koppel and the doctor were in the room.

Due giorni prima della chiusura della mostra, una lunga busta dall'aspetto ufficiale fu recapitata al Signor Smith mentre Frank, Koppel e il dottore si trovavano nella stanza.

"Read it to me," asked the old man. "My eyes are tired from painting."

"Leggimela," chiese il vecchio. "I miei occhi sono stanchi dal dipingere."

"It gives the Lathrop Gallery pleasure to announce that the First Prize of $1,000 has been awarded to Mr. Collis P. Smith for his painting 'Trees Dressed in White'".

"È con piacere che la Lathrop Gallery annuncia che il Primo Premio di $1,000 è stato assegnato al Signor Collis P. Smith per il suo dipinto "Alberi Vestiti di Bianco."

Frank and Koppel were astonished. The doctor showing his usual professional self-control said: "Congratulations, Mr. Smith! Of course, I did not expect such great news. But, but well, now you'll have to admit that art brings much more satisfaction than business."

Frank e Koppel rimasero stupiti. Il dottore mostrando il suo solito auto controllo professionale disse: "Congratulazioni, Signor Smith! Certo, non mi aspettavo delle notizie così belle. Ma, ma – ora dovrà ammettere che l'arte dà molte più soddisfazioni rispetto agli affari."

"Art is nothing," said the old man. "I bought the Lathrop Gallery last month."

"L'arte non è niente," disse il vecchio. "Ho acquistato la Lathrop Gallery lo scorso mese."

Key Vocabulary:

o bussare v.intr. [bus-sà-re] – to knock.

o atrio s.m. [à-trio] – hall, hallway.

o odiare v.tr. [o-dià-re] – to hate, to detest.

o trattenere v.tr. [trat-te-né-re] – to hold back, to keep; to restrain.

o avvenire v.intr. [av-ve-nì-re] – to take place, to occur, to happen.

o soffrire v.tr. [sof-frì-re] – to suffer.

o notevole agg. [no-té-vo-le] – notable, considerable.

~mente avv. – notably, considerably.

o acquistare agg. [ac-qui-stà-re] – to acquire, to purchase.

o portafoglio s.m. [por-ta-fò-glio] – wallet, pocketbook.

o ragionare v.intr. [ra-gio-nà-re] – to reason; to think, to reflect.

o obbedire v.intr. [ob-be-dì-re] – to obey.

o sospetto agg. [so-spèt-to] – suspicious.

s.m. – suspect; suspicion.

o sciocchezza s.f. [scioc-chéz-za] – foolishness, nonsense.

o folle agg. [fòl-le] – foolish; insane, mad.

o cioè avv. [cio-è] – that is.

o mandare v.tr. [man-dà-re] – to send.

o dotato agg. [do-tà-to] – gifted, talented; endowed.

o presentare v.tr. [pre-sen-tà-re] – to present; to introduce.

o mormorare v.intr. [mor-mo-rà-re] – to murmur; to mutter.

o provare v.tr. [pro-và-re] – to try; to test; to prove.

o disegnare v.tr. [di-se-gnà-re] – to draw; to outline; to design.

o scarabocchio s.m. [sca-ra-bòc-chio] – scribble, scrawl.

o unire v.tr. [u-nì-re] – to unite; to join, to connect.

o piuttosto avv. [piut-tò-sto] – quite, rather, somewhat.

o storto agg. [stòr-to] – twisted, crooked.

o capire v.tr. [ca-pì-re] – to understand.

o coincidere v.intr. [coin-cì-de-re] – to coincide, to match.

o sussurrare v.tr. [sus-sur-rà-re] – to whisper.

o magari inter. [ma-gà-ri] – 1. (as a response) I wish! "Credi di vincere alla lotteria?" – "Magari!" / "Do you think you'll win the lottery?" – "I wish!"

– 2. (in a complete sentence) maybe, perhaps. o disposto agg. [di-spó-sto] – willing, disposed.

782

o vestaglia s.f. [ve-stà-glia] – dressing gown.

o permettere v.tr. [per-mét-te-re] – to permit, to allow.

o motivo s.m. [mo-tì-vo] – motive, reason.

o esposto agg. [e-spó-sto] – exhibited, displayed.

o mostra s.f. [mó-stra] – show, fair, exhibition.

o fioritura s.f. [fio-ri-tù-ra] – blossom, bloom.

o tuttavia cong. [tut-ta-vì-a] – nevertheless, however, but.

o condimento s.m. [con-di-mén-to] – seasoning, dressing.

o rovinare v.tr. [ro-vi-nà-re] – to ruin; to spoil.

o a malapena avv. [ma-la-pé-na] – barely, scarcely, hardly.

o scappare v.intr. [scap-pà-re] – to escape, to run away.

o ridacchiare v.intr. [ri-dac-chià-re] – to chuckle,to giggle.

o incoraggiare v.tr. [in-co-rag-già-re] – to encourage.

o aspetto s.m. [a-spèt-to] – appearance, look; aspect.

o recapitare v.tr. [re-ca-pi-tà-re] – to deliver.

o assegnare v.tr. [as-se-gnà-re] – to assign; to grant.

~ un premio – to award a prize.

o rispetto a – compared with/to; with/in regard to.

o soddisfazione s.f. [sod-di-sfa-zió-ne] – satisfaction.

CHAPTER EIGHT: Jimmy Valentine's retrieved reformation

A guard came to the prison shoe shop where Jimmy Valentine was working and took him to the prison office. There the warden handed Jimmy his pardon, which has been signed that morning by the governor.

Una guardia arrivò al negozio di scarpe della prigione dove Jimmy Valentine stava lavorando e lo portò all'ufficio della prigione. Là, il direttore della prigione consegnò a Jimmy l'indulto, firmato la mattina stessa dal governatore.

Jimmy took it quietly; he was too tired to show excitement. He had been in prison nearly ten months and he had been sentenced to four years.

Jimmy lo prese con calma; era troppo stanco per mostrarsi emozionato. Era in prigione da quasi dieci mesi ed era stato condannato a quattro anni.

True, he had expected to stay only about three months, at the longest. He had a lot of friends and he was sure they would help him.

È vero, pensava di rimanere in prigione solo tre mesi circa, al massimo. Aveva molti amici ed era sicuro che lo avrebbero aiutato.

"Now, Valentine," said the warden, "You'll get out in the morning. You're not a bad fellow really. Stop breaking open safes and be honest."

"Ora, Valentine," disse il direttore della prigione, "Uscirai domani mattina. Non sei un cattivo ragazzo, per niente. Smettila di scassinare casseforti e fai l'onesto."

"Me?" said Jimmy, in surprise. "Why, I've never broken open a safe in my life."

"Io?" disse Jimmy, sorpreso. "Perché, non ho mai scassinato una cassaforte in tutta la mia vita."

"Of course not" laughed the warden. "And what about that Springfield job? Do you mean to say you didn't take part in it?"

"Certo che no" rise il direttore. "E che ne dici del lavoro a Springfield? dirmi che non ne hai preso parte?"

"Me?" said Jimmy even more surprised. "Warden, I've never been to Springfield in my life!"

"Io?" disse Jimmy ancora più sorpreso. "Direttore, non sono mai stato a Springfield in tutta la mia vita!"

"Take him back," the warden said to the guard smiling, "and give him some clothes. Tomorrow unlock him at seven and bring him to the office. You better think over my advice, Valentine."

"Riportalo al suo posto," disse il direttore della prigione alla guardia sorridente, "e dagli dei vestiti. Domani liberalo alle sette e portalo nell'ufficio. Faresti meglio a ripensare al mio consiglio, Valentine."

At a quarter past seven the next morning Jimmy stood in the warden's office. He wore a badly fitting suit and the cheap shoes that the state gives to prisoners, when they are set free.

Alle sette e un quarto del mattino dopo, Jimmy si trovava nell'ufficio del direttore della prigione. Indossava un abito della taglia sbagliata e le scarpe economiche che lo stato dava ai detenuti, quando venivano liberati.

The clerk handed him a railroad ticket and the five-dollar bill with which he was supposed to start a new, honest life.

L'impiegato gli consegnò un biglietto ferroviario e una banconota da cinque dollari con cui avrebbe dovuto iniziare una nuova, onesta vita.

The warden gave him a cigar, and they shook hands. Valentine, 9762, was registered in the books "Pardoned by Governor," and Mr. James Valentine walked out into the sunshine.

Il direttore della prigione gli diede un sigaro, e si strinsero la mano. Valentine, 9762, era registrato nei registri "Graziato dal Governatore", e il Signor James Valentine uscì alla luce del sole.

Paying no attention to the song of the birds, the green trees, and a smell of the flowers, Jimmy went straight to a restaurant.

Senza prestare attenzione al canto degli uccelli, al verde degli alberi, al profumo dei fiori, Jimmy si diresse immediatamente verso un ristorante.

There he ordered a roast chicken and a bottle of white wine and a better cigar than the one the warden gave him before.

Là, ordinò un pollo arrosto e una bottiglia di vino bianco e un sigaro migliore di quello che gli venne dato prima dal direttore della prigione.

After the lunch he walked slowly to the railroad station. He put a quarter into the hat of a blind man who was sitting by the door of the station and then took a train.

Dopo pranzo, si diresse lentamente verso la stazione ferroviaria. Mise un quarto di dollaro nel cappello di un uomo cieco seduto presso la porta della stazione e salì su un treno.

Three hours later he arrived at his native town, went directly to the café of his old friend Mike Dolan and shook hands with Mike, who was alone behind the counter.

Tre ore più tardi, arrivò al suo paese natale, andò subito al bar del suo vecchio amico Mike Dolan che in quel momento si trovava da solo dietro alla cassa e gli strinse la mano.

"Sorry we couldn't make it sooner, Jimmy, my boy," said Mike. "It was not easy this time and we had a lot of trouble. Are you all right?"

"I'm fine," said Jimmy. "Do you have my key?"

"Mi dispiace, non siamo riusciti a farlo prima, Jimmy, ragazzo mio," disse Mike. "Non è stato facile questa volta e abbiamo avuto parecchi problemi. Stai bene?"

"Sì, sto bene," disse Jimmy. "Hai la mia chiave?"

He took the key and went upstairs, unlocking the door of his room. Everything was just as he left it. There on the floor was still the collar-button that had been torn from the shirt of Ben Price – the well-known detective – when Price had come to arrest Jimmy.

Prese la chiave e andò di sopra, aprì la porta della sua camera ed entrò. La stanza era come l'aveva lasciata. Là sul pavimento c'era ancora il bottone del colletto che gli venne strappata dalla camicia da Ben Price – il noto detective – quando Price venne ad arrestare Jimmy.

Jimmy removed a panel in the wall and dragged out a dust-covered suitcase. He opened it and looked fondly at the finest set of burglar's tools in the East. It was a complete set made of special steel.

Jimmy rimosse un pannello dal muro e tirò fuori una valigia coperta di polvere. La aprì e guardò con affetto al set di strumenti da scasso più bello dell'Est. Era un set completo fatto di acciaio speciale.

The set consisted of various tools of the latest design. He had invented two or three of them himself, and was very proud of them. Over nine hundred dollars they have cost him!

Il set comprendeva vari strumenti dal design più recente. Due o tre pezzi li aveva inventati lui da solo, e ne era molto orgoglioso. Gli erano costati oltre novecento dollari!

Half an hour later Jimmy went downstairs. He was now dressed in an elegant new suit, and carried his cleaned suitcase in his hand.

Dopo mezz'ora, Jimmy ritornò giù. Ora indossava un abito nuovo ed elegante, e aveva in mano la sua valigia pulita.

"What are you going to do next? To break another safe?" asked Mike Dolan smiling cheerfully.

"Cosa farai ora? Scassinerai un'altra cassaforte?" chiese Mike Dolan sorridendo allegramente.

"I don't understand. I'm representing the New York Biscuit Company." This statement delighted Mike to such an extent that he burst out laughing.

"Non capisco. Rappresento la Biscuit Company di New York." Questa affermazione deliziò Mike che scoppiò a ridere.

A week after the release of Valentine, 9762, there was a new safe-burglary in Richmond, Indiana. Only eight hundred dollars were stolen. Two weeks after that another safe was opened and fifteen hundred dollars disappeared; securities and silver were untouched.

Una settimana dopo il rilascio di Valentine, 9762, ci fu un'altra cassaforte scassinata a Richmond, Indiana. Furono rubati solo ottocento dollari. Due settimane dopo, venne aperta un'altra cassaforte e sparirono millecinquecento dollari; titoli e argento rimasero intatti.

That began to interest the detectives. A few days later the Jefferson City Bank was robbed and banknotes amounting to five thousand dollars were taken.

I detective iniziarono a interessarsi al caso. Alcuni giorni dopo la Jefferson City Bank venne rapinata e vennero prese banconote che ammontavano a cinque mila dollari.

The amount taken was too high now and it was time for so well-known a detective as Ben Price to begin investigation. Ben Price investigated the scenes of the robberies and noticed a striking similarity in the methods of the burglaries and later he was heard to say:

La somma presa era troppo alta ora ed era il momento che un detective noto come Ben Price iniziasse a investigare. Ben Price investigò le scene delle rapine e notò una somiglianza sorprendente nei metodi dei furti, e più tardi lo sentirono dire:

"That's all Jimmy Valentine's work. He's resumed business. Only he has those fine tools that can open any safe without leaving the slightest trace. Yes, it is Mr. Valentine."

"Questo è tutto lavoro di Jimmy Valentine. Ha ripreso gli affari. Solo lui possiede strumenti così precisi per aprire qualsiasi cassaforte senza lasciare nemmeno la minima traccia. Sì, è il Signor Valentine."

One afternoon Jimmy Valentine and his suitcase climbed out of a train in Elmore, a little town in Arkansas. Jimmy, looking like a student who had just come home from college, walked out of the station and went toward the hotel.

Un pomeriggio, Jimmy Valentine e la sua valigia uscirono da un treno a Elmore, un piccolo paese ad Arkansas. Jimmy, che sembrava come uno studente appena ritornato a casa dal college, uscì dalla stazione e si diresse verso l'hotel.

A young lady crossed the street, passed him at the corner and entered a door over which was the sign "The Elmore Bank." Jimmy Valentine looked into her eyes, forgot what he was, and became another man.

Una giovane donna attraversò la strada, gli passò davanti all'angolo ed entrò in una porta, sopra cui c'era l'insegna "The Elmore Bank." Jimmy Valentine la guardò negli occhi, dimenticò cos'era, e diventò un altro uomo.

She lowered her eyes and blushed slightly. Young man of Jimmy's style and looks were scarce in Elmore.

Lei abbassò gli occhi e arrossì leggermente. Un giovane uomo con lo stile e l'aspetto di Jimmy scarseggiavano ad Elmore.

Jimmy called a boy who was standing on the steps of the bank as if he were one of the stockholders, and began to ask him questions about the town, giving the boy dimes from time to time.

Jimmy chiamò un ragazzo che si trovava sui gradini della banca, come se fosse stato uno degli azionisti, e iniziò a fargli domande sulla città, dandogli ogni tanto qualche centesimo.

After a short while the young lady came out, passed Jimmy again, pretending not to see him, and went on her way.

Dopo un po' di tempo, la giovane donna uscì, passò di nuovo davanti a Jimmy fingendo di non vederlo, e proseguì per la sua strada.

"Isn't that young lady Miss Polly Simpson?" asked Jimmy shrewdly.

"Quella giovane donna non è la Signorina Polly Simpson?" chiese Jimmy astutamente.

"No," said the boy. "She is Annabel Adams. Her father owns this bank. "

"No," disse il ragazzo. "È Annabel Adams. Suo padre possiede questa banca."

Jimmy went to the Planters' Hotel, registered as Ralph D. Spencer, and reserved a room. He leaned on the desk and stated his intentions to the clerk. He said he had come to Elmore to start business.

Jimmy si diresse verso il Planters' Hotel, si registrò come Ralph D. Spencer, e prenotò una stanza. Si appoggiò sul bancone e dichiarò le sue intenzioni all'impiegato. Disse che era venuto a Elmore per iniziare un'attività.

How was the shoe business now in the town? Was it worthwhile opening a shoe store? The clerk was impressed by the clothes and manner of Jimmy and he was ready to give the young man any information he desired.

Com'era il settore delle calzature in paese? Valeva la pena aprire un negozio di scarpe? L'impiegato rimase colpito dall'abbigliamento e dalle maniere di Jimmy ed era pronto a dare al giovane uomo tutte le informazione che desiderava.

Yes, it was worthwhile investing in the shoe business, he thought. There wasn't a shoe store in the town. The business appeared to be a good idea from any point of view.

Sì, valeva la pena investire nel settore delle calzature, pensò. Non c'era un negozio di scarpe in paese. L'attività sembrava una buona idea sotto tutti i punti di vista.

"I hope, Mr. Spencer, you'll decide to stay in Elmore. You'll find it a pleasant town to live in, and the people are very nice," continued the clerk.

"Mi auguro, Signor Spencer, che lei decida di rimanere ad Elmore. Troverà che è una piacevole città in cui vivere, e gli abitanti sono molto cordiali," continuò l'impiegato.

Mr. Spencer said that he would stay for a few days and consider the situation. The clerk wanted to call the boy to carry up the suitcase, but Mr. Spencer said that he would carry his suitcase himself; it was rather heavy.

Il Signor Spencer disse che sarebbe rimasto per qualche giorno per considerare la situazione. L'impiegato voleva chiamare il ragazzo per portare la valigia al piano superiore, ma il Signor Spencer disse che avrebbe portato la valigia da sé; era piuttosto pesante.

Mr. Ralph Spencer, the phoenix that arose from Jimmy Valentine's ashes – ashes left by the flame of a sudden attack of love – remained in Elmore and prospered. He opened a shoe store and was making large profits. In all other respects he was also a success.

Il Signor Ralph Spencer, la fenice sorta dalle ceneri di Jimmy Valentine – ceneri rimaste dalla fiamma di un improvviso attacco d'amore – rimase ad Elmore e prosperò. Aprì un negozio di scarpe e fece grandi profitti. Sotto tutti gli aspetti ebbe successo.

He was popular with many important people and had many friends. And he fulfilled the wish of his heart. He met Miss Annabel Adams, and fell deeply in love with her.

Aveva molto successo tra le persone importanti e aveva molti amici. Riuscì pure a soddisfare un desiderio del suo cuore. Incontrò la Signorina Annabel Adams e se ne innamorò profondamente.

After a year the situation of Mr. Ralph Spencer was this: he had won the respect of most the inhabitants of the place, his shoe store was prospering, and he and Annabel were to be married in two weeks.

Dopo un anno la situazione del Signor Ralph Spencer era questa: si era guadagnato il rispetto di gran parte degli abitanti del luogo, la sua attività di calzature era prospera, e si sarebbe sposato con Annabel tra due settimane.

Mr. Adams, Annabel's father, who was a typical country banker, approved of Spencer. Annabel herself was proud of her fiancé. In fact her pride almost equaled to her affection.

Il Signor Adams, il padre di Annabel, un tipico bancario di paese, accettava Spencer e Annabel era fiera del suo fidanzato. Infatti, il suo orgoglio quasi eguagliava il suo affetto.

One day Jimmy sat down in his room and wrote this letter which he sent to the address of one of his old friends:

Un giorno Jimmy si sedette in camera sua e scrisse questa lettera che spedì all'indirizzo di uno dei suoi vecchi amici:

"Dear Old Chap,

I want you to be at Brown's Café, in Little Rock, next Wednesday at nine o'clock in the evening. I want you to do something for me. And, also, I want to make you a present of my tools. I know you'll be glad to have them you couldn't get such a set for a thousand dollars.

Caro Vecchio Amico,

Voglio che tu venga al Brown's Cafe, a Little Rock, il prossimo mercoledì alle ore nove di sera. Voglio che tu faccia qualcosa per me. E, vorrei anche darti in dono i miei strumenti. Lo so che sarai contento di averli – non riusciresti ad avere un tale set nemmeno per mille dollari.

Billy, I gave up the old business a year ago. I am making an honest living now and in two weeks I'm going to marry the finest girl on earth. I wouldn't touch a dollar of another man's money now for a million.

Billy, ho rinunciato alla mia vecchia attività un anno fa. Mi guadagno da vivere in modo onesto ora e tra due settimane mi sposerò con la ragazza più bella sulla terra. Ora, non toccherei un dollaro di un'altra persona nemmeno per un milione.

After I get married I'm going to sell my shoe store and move west, where there won't be a danger of meeting people who knew me before. I tell you, Billy, she's an angel.

Dopo il mio matrimonio, ho intenzione di vendere il mio negozio di scarpe e di spostarmi verso ovest, dove non correrò il rischio di incontrare persone che mi conoscevano prima. Ti dirò Billy, lei è un angelo.

She believes in me and I would never do another wrong thing for the whole world. Do come to Brown's, because I must see you. I'll bring the tools with me.

Your old friend, Jimmy."

Lei crede in me e non potrei ma fare un'altra cosa sbagliata per niente al mondo. Per favore, viene da Brown's, perché devo vederti. Porterò con me gli strumenti.

Il tuo vecchio amico, Jimmy."

On the Monday night after Jimmy wrote this letter, Ben Price, the detective, arrived in Elmore. He walked around town until he found what he wanted to know.

Il lunedì sera, dopo che Jimmy scrisse questa lettera, Ben Price, il detective arrivò ad Elmore. Camminò per il paese finché scoprì quello che voleva sapere.

From the pharmacy across the street from Spencer's shoe store he took a good look at Ralph D. Spencer.

Dalla farmacia che si trovava sul lato opposto della strada del negozio di scarpe di Spencer, osservò attentamente Ralph D. Spencer.

"Going to marry the banker's daughter, are you, Jimmy?" said Ben to himself, softly. "Well, I don't know!"

"Ti sposerai con la figlia del banchiere, vero Jimmy?" disse Ben tra sé, piano. "Beh, non lo so!"

The next morning Jimmy took breakfast at the Adams' house. He was going to Little Rock that day to order his wedding suit and buy something nice for Annabel. That would be the first time he had left town since he came to Elmore.

Il mattino seguente, Jimmy fece colazione a casa di Adam. Oggi doveva andare a Little Rock a ordinare il suo abito da sposo e acquistare qualcosa di carino per Annabel. Questa sarebbe stata la prima volta che lasciava il paese dopo il suo arrivo ad Elmore.

After breakfast the whole family went for a walk together: Mr. Adams, Annabel, Jimmy, and Annabel's married sister with her two little girls, ages five and nine.

Dopo colazione, l'intera famiglia andò a fare una lunga passeggiata: Il Signor Adams, Annabel, Jimmy e la sorella sposata di Annabel con le sue due piccole figlie, di cinque e nove anni.

They passed by the hotel where Jimmy still stayed, and he ran up to his room and brought his suitcase. Then they went on to the bank.

Passarono per l'hotel dove Jimmy ancora soggiornava, e lui corse su nella sua stanza a prendere la usa valigia. Poi proseguirono verso la banca.

There at the bank stood Jimmy's horse and buggy and the coachman who was going to drive him to a railroad station. All went inside the bank – Jimmy included.

Alla banca si trovava il cavallo di Jimmy, il calesse e il cocchiere che lo avrebbe portato alla stazione ferroviaria. Entrarono tutti in banca – incluso Jimmy.

The clerks were pleased to be greeted by the good-looking, pleasant young man who was going to marry Miss Annabel. Jimmy put his suitcase down.

Gli impiegati erano felici di essere salutati dal quel giovane uomo di bell'aspetto e dai modi piacevoli che stava per sposare la Signorina Annabel. Jimmy appoggiò a terra la valigia.

Annabel whose heart was beating with happiness and youth, put on Jimmy's hat, and picked up the suitcase.

Annabel, che aveva il cuore che batteva di felicità e gioventù, indossò il cappello di Jimmy, e prese la valigia.

"Don't I look nice?" said Annabel. "Oh, my, Ralph, how heavy it is! It weighs as much as if it were full of gold bricks."

"Non sono carina?" disse Annabel. "Oh, mio caro Ralph, ma quanto è pesante. Pesa come se fosse piena di lingotti d'oro."

"There are a lot of nickel shoehorns there," said Jimmy coolly, "that I'm going to return. I decided to take them myself so that to avoid unnecessary expenses. I'm getting awfully economical."

"Ci sono molte calzascarpe in nichel qui," disse Jimmy freddamente, "che devo ritornare. Ho deciso di farmeli da solo per evitare delle spese inutili. Sto diventando terribilmente economico."

The Elmore Bank had just put in a new safe and vault. Mr. Adams was very proud of the vault and insisted that everyone should take a look at it. The vault was a small one, but it had a new modern door.

La Elmore Bank aveva appena installato una nuova cassaforte e una camera blindata. Il Signor Adams era molto fiero della camera blindata e insistette che tutti gli dessero un'occhiata. La camera blindata era piccola, ma aveva una porta nuova e moderna.

It fastened with three steel bolts and had a security system to open it at predetermined hours. Mr. Adams enthusiastically explained how it works to Mr. Spencer, who, however, didn't seem to take a great interest in it.

Era fissata con tre bulloni di acciaio e aveva un sistema di sicurezza per aprirla a ore prestabilite. Il Signor Adams spiegò con entusiasmo al Signor Spencer come funzionava, il quale, tuttavia, non sembrava mostrare grande interesse.

The two children May and Agatha, were delighted to see the shining metal and the funny clock.

Le due bambine May e Agatha, erano entusiaste nel vedere il metallo luccicante e quella divertente sveglia.

While they were thus engaged, Ben Price, the detective, walked into the bank and leaned on his elbow, looking casually inside between the railings. He told the cashier that he didn't want anything; he was just waiting for a man he knew.

Mentre erano così occupati, Ben Price, il detective, entrò in banca e si appoggiò sul gomito, guardando casualmente tra la ringhiera. Disse al cassiere che non voleva niente; stava solo aspettando un uomo che conosceva.

Suddenly there was a terrible scream from the women. Unseen by the elders, May, the nine-year-old girl, while playing with her sister, had shut her in the vault. The old banker grabbed the handle and tugged at it for a moment.

Improvvisamente, si sentì un terribile urlo dalle donne. Non vista dagli adulti, May, la bambina di nove anni, mentre giocava con la sorella, si chiuse nella camera blindata. Il vecchio banchiere afferrò la maniglia e per un momento provò a tirarla.

"The door can't be opened," he cried out. "The clock has not been wound." Agatha's mother screamed again, hysterically.

"La porta non può essere aperta," urlò. "La sveglia non è stata caricata." La madre di Agatha urlò ancora, istericamente.

"Hush!" said Mr. Adams, raising his trembling hand. "All be quiet for a moment. Agatha!" he called as loudly as he could. "Listen to me…" During the following silence they could hear the faint sound of the child crying in the dark vault.

"Silenzio!" disse il Signor Adams, alzando la mano tremante. "Fate silenzio per un momento. Agatha!" chiamò più forte che poté. "Ascoltami… "Nell'attimo di silenzio udirono il debole suono della bambina che piangeva nella buia camera blindata.

"My darling!" cried the mother. "She will die of fright! Open the door! Oh, break it open! Can't you men do something?"

"Tesoro mio!" urlò la madre. "Morirà di spavento! Aprite la porta! Oh, scassatela! Voi uomini non potete fare qualcosa?"

"There isn't a man nearer than Little Rock who can open that door," said Mr. Adams in a trembling voice.

"Non c'è alcun uomo fino a Little Rock che sia in grado di aprire questa porta," disse il Signor Adams con voce tremante.

"My God! Spencer, what shall we do? That child – she can't stand it long in there. There isn't enough air, and, besides she'll go mad from fright."

"Oh, Santo Cielo! Spencer, cosa possiamo fare? Quella bambina – non può rimanere là dentro a lungo. Non c'è abbastanza ossigeno, e inoltre, impazzirà dalla paura."

Agatha's mother beat the door of the vault wildly with her hands. Somebody suggested dynamite.

La madre di Agatha si mise a battere selvaggiamente con le mani sulla porta della camera blindata. Qualcuno suggerì la dinamite.

Annabel turned to Jimmy, her large eyes full of horror, but not yet despairing. To a woman nothing seems impossible to the powers of the man she loves.

Annabel si rivolse a Jimmy, i suoi grandi occhi pieni di orrore, ma non ancora disperati. Per una donna, nulla sembra essere impossibile dall'uomo che ama.

"Can't you do something, Ralph – try, won't you?" He looked at her with a strange, soft smile on his lips and in his eyes.

"Annabel," he said, "give me that rose you are wearing, will you?"

"Non puoi fare qualcosa, Ralph – proverai, vero?" Lui la guardò con uno strano, dolce sorriso sulle labbra e negli occhi.

"Annabel," disse lui, "dammi quella rosa che hai addosso, va bene?"

Hardly believing that she heard him correctly she unpinned the flower from her dress, and gave it to Jimmy.

Incredula di aver capito correttamente cosa gli aveva chiesto, sganciò il fiore dal suo vestito e lo diede a Jimmy.

He put it into his vest-pocket, threw off his coat and pulled his shirt sleeves. With that act Ralph D. Spencer passed away and Jimmy Valentine took his place.

Lo mise nella tasca del suo gilet, si tolse il cappotto e tirò su le maniche della camicia. Con questo atto, Ralph D. Spencer sparì e Jimmy Valentine prese il suo posto.

"Get away from the door, all of you," he commanded, shortly. He put his suitcase on the table and opened it. From that moment on he seemed to be unaware of the presence of anyone else.

"Allontanatevi dalla porta, tutti," ordinò bruscamente. Mise la sua valigia sopra al tavolo e la aprì. Da quel momento in poi, sembrava inconsapevole della presenza degli altri.

He took out strange instruments quickly and orderly, whistling to himself as he always did when he was at work. In the deep silence the others watched him dumbfounded.

Tirò fuori rapidamente e con cura strani strumenti, fischiettando tra sé come faceva sempre quando lavorava. Nel profondo silenzio gli altri lo osservarono a bocca aperta.

In ten minutes – breaking his own burglarious record – he opened the door.

Agatha's mother rushed into the vault and took the child, who was very weak, but safe.

In dieci minuti – battendo il suo stesso record di scassi – aprì la porta. La madre di Agatha si precipitò nella camera blindata e prese la bambina, che era molto debole ma salva.

Jimmy Valentine put on his coat and walked towards the front door. As he went, it seemed to him he heard a voice that he once knew call "Ralph". But he didn't stop for an instant.

Jimmy Valentine si rimise il cappotto e camminò verso la porta principale.

Mentre se ne andava gli sembrò di sentire una voce che una volta conosceva, chiamare "Ralph". Ma non si fermò nemmeno un istante.

At the door a big man stood in his way.

"Hello, Ben!" said Jimmy, still with his strange smile. "At last you're here, are you? Well, let's go. I don't think it matters much now."

Alla porta un grosso uomo gli bloccò la strada.

"Ciao Ben!" disse Jimmy, ancora con il suo strano sorriso. "Finalmente sei qui, vero? Bene, andiamo. Credo non abbia molta importanza ora."

And then Ben Price acted rather strangely.

"I guess, you're mistaken, Mr. Spencer," he said, "I don't believe I recognize you. Your buggy's waiting for you, isn't it?"

Poi, Ben Price si comportò in modo strano.

"Penso che lei si stia sbagliando, Signor Spencer," disse lui, "Non mi sembra di riconoscerla. Il suo calesse la sta aspettando, vero?"

And Ben Price turned and walked down the street.

E Ben Price si girò e camminò giù per la strada.

Key Vocabulary:

o negozio s.m. [ne-gò-zio] – shop, store.

o consegnare v.tr. [con-se-gnà-re] – to hand over; to deliver.

o indulto s.m. [in-dùl-to] – pardon.

o firmare v.tr. [fir-mà-re] – to sign.

o mostrare v.tr. [mo-strà-re] – to show, to display.

~si v.rf. – to show oneself.

o emozionare v.tr. [e-mo-zio-nà-re] – to excite.

~to agg. – excited.

o condannare v.tr. [con-dan-nà-re] – to condemn; to sentence.

~to agg. – condemned, sentenced.

o scassinare v.tr. [scas-si-nà-re] – to break open; to pick (a lock).

o riportare v.tr. [ri-por-tà-re] – to bring again; to take back.

o indossare v.tr. [in-dos-sà-re] – to wear.

o un abito della taglia sbagliata – (lit.) a suit of the wrong size.

o ferrovia s.f. [fer-ro-vì-a] – railroad, railway.

~rio agg. – railroad, railway (attributive).

o stringere v.tr. [strìn-ge-re] – to tighten; to squeeze.

~ la mano a qualcuno – to shake hands with someone. o grazia s.f. [grà-zia] – grace; pardon, mercy.

o prestare v.tr. [pre-stà-re] – to lend, to loan.

~ ascolto a | ~ attenzione a – (lit.) to lend an ear (listen) to | to lend (pay) attention to.

o immediatamente avv. [im-me-dia-ta-mén-te] – immediately.

o presso avv. [près-so] – near; next to, by.

o salire v.intr. [sa-lì-re] – to climb up; to go up; to rise.

~ in treno | autobus – to get on the train | bus. o natale agg. [na-tà-le] – native.

Natale s.m. – Christmas.

o paese s.m. [pa-é-se] – 1. country, state; 2. (small) town; village.

o parecchio agg. [pa-réc-chio] – a lot of; several.

o noto agg. [nò-to] – well-known.

o rimuovere v.tr. [ri-muò-ve-re] – to remove, to move.

o strumento s.m. [stru-mén-to] – instrument, tool.

o comprendere v.tr. [com-prèn-de-re] – 1. to comprise, to include.

2. to understand, to comprehend.

o deliziare v.tr. [de-li-zià-re] – to delight.

o scoppiare v.intr. [scop-pià-re] – to burst, to explode.

o titolo s.m. [tì-to-lo] – title, headline; stock, security.

o ammontare v.tr. [am-mon-tà-re] – to pile up; to amount (to).

o qualsiasi agg. [qual-sì-a-si] – any; whichever, whatever.

o riprendere v.tr. [ri-prèn-de-re] – to take again; to resume.

o sorprendere v.tr. [sor-prèn-de-re] – to surprise, to amaze.

~nte agg. [sorpren-dèn-te] – surprising, amazing, striking. o uscire v.intr. [u-scì-re] – to get out, to come out; to exit.

o appena avv. [ap-pé-na] – just, just now; barely, scarcely.

o abbassare v.tr. [ab-bas-sà-re] – to lower.

o arrossire v.intr. [ar-ros-sì-re] – to blush.

o scarseggiare v.intr. [scarseg-già-re] – to be scarce.

o qualche agg. [quàl-che] – some, a few.

~ centesimo – a few cents.

o fingere v.tr. [fìn-ge-re] – to pretend, to feign.

o proseguire v.tr. [pro-se-guì-re] – to continue; to go on.

o astutamente avv. [a-stu-ta-mén-te] – astutely, shrewdly.

o appoggiare v.tr. [ap-pog-già-re] – to lean (on); to lay/put (down).

o dichiarare v.tr. [di-chia-rà-re] – to declare, to state.

o attività s.f. [at-ti-vi-tà] – activity; business.

o valere la pena – to be worth the effort (to be worth it).

o augurare v.tr. [au-gu-rà-re] – to wish; to hope.

o abitante s.m.|f. [a-bi-tàn-te] – resident; inhabitant.

~i della città – townspeople, inhabitants. o sé – himself, herself, itself; themselves.

lui pensa solo a sé – he only thinks of himself.

da sé – (by) oneself.

o soddisfare v.tr. [sod-di-sfà-re] – to satisfy; to fulfill.

o prosperare v.intr. [pro-spe-rà-re] – to prosper, to thrive.

o uguagliare v.tr. [u-gua-glià-re] – to equal, to match.

o dono s.m. [dó-no] – gift, present.

o tale agg. [tà-le] – such; certain, someone.

o rinunciare v.intr. [ri-nun-cià-re] – to renounce; to give up (sth).

o correre un rischio – to take a chance; to be in danger.

o finché cong. [fin-ché] – until.

o scoprire v.tr. [sco-prì-re] – to uncover; to find out.

o soggiornare v.intr. [soggior-nà-re] – to stay, to sojourn.

o dare un'occhiata – to take a look; to glance.

o bullone s.m. [bul-ló-ne] – bolt.

o prestabilire v.tr. [pre-sta-bi-lì-re] – to prearrange, to predetermine.

o spiegare v.tr. [spie-gà-re] – to explain; to unfold.

o afferrare v.tr. [af-fer-rà-re] – to grab; to grasp.

o caricare v.tr. [ca-ri-cà-re] – to load (up); to charge, to wind.

o morire v.intr. [mo-rì-re] – to die.

o grado s.m. [grà-do] – degree, grade, level.

essere in grado – to be able to.

o impazzire v.intr. [im-paz-zì-re] – to go crazy, to go mad.

CHAPTER NINE: Ruthless / Spietato

Judson Webb was an American business man. He had a comfortable apartment in New York but in the summer he used to leave the dusty city and go to the country.

Judson Webb era un uomo d'affari americano. Aveva un comodo appartamento a New York ma in estate lasciava la polverosa città per andare in campagna.

There he had a cottage which consisted of three rooms, a bathroom and a kitchen. In one of the rooms there was a big closet. Mr. Webb liked his cottage very much, especially his closet where he kept his guns, fishing rods, wine and other things.

Lì aveva un cottage composto da tre stanze, un bagno e una cucina. In una delle camere c'era un grande armadio. Al Signor Webb piaceva molto il suo cottage, soprattutto il suo armadio dove teneva i suoi fucili, le sue canne da pesca, il vino e altre cose.

Judson Webb loved his possessions and even his wife was not allowed to have a key to the closet.

Judson Webb adorava i suoi averi e nemmeno sua moglie aveva il permesso di avere una chiave per quel armadio.

It was autumn now and Judson was packing his things for the winter. In a few minutes he would be going back to New York.

Era autunno, e Judson stava mettendo in valigia le sue cose per l'inverno.

Tra pochi minuti sarebbe ritornato a New York.

As he looked at the shelf where he usually kept the whiskey, his face become serious. All the bottles were unopened except one. It was placed invitingly in front with a whiskey-glass by its side.

Mentre guardava la mensola dove di solito teneva il whiskey, la sua faccia si fece seria. Tutte le bottiglie erano chiuse eccetto una. Era stata disposta in modo invitante davanti con un bicchiere da whiskey a fianco.

The bottle was less than half full. As he took the bottle from the shelf, Helen, his wife, spoke from the next room:

La bottiglia era meno di mezza piena. Mentre prendeva la bottiglia dalla mensola, Helen, sua moglie, gli parlò dalla stanza vicino:

"I've packed everything. Hasn't Alec come to get the keys?" Alec lived in the neighborhood and acted as caretaker.

"Ho messo tutto in valigia. Alec non è venuto a prendere le chiavi? Alec viveva nelle vicinanze e faceva da custode.

"He's at the lake pulling the boat out of the water. He said he would be back in half an hour!"

"È andato al lago a tirare fuori la barca dall'acqua. Ha detto che sarebbe ritornato in mezz'ora!"

Helen came into the room carrying the suitcase. She stopped and looked in surprise as she saw the bottle in her husband's hand.

Helen entrò nella stanza con la valigia. Si fermò e rimase stupita vedendo la bottiglia nelle mani del marito.

"Judson," she exclaimed, "you're not taking a drink at ten in the morning, are you?"

"Judson," esclamò, "non stai bevendo al dieci del mattino, vero?"

"No, dear. I'm not drinking anything out of this bottle. I am just putting something into it." He took two small white pills out of his pocket and put them on the table. Then he opened the bottle.

"No, cara. Non mi sto bevendo niente da questa bottiglia. Ci sto solo mettendo dentro qualcosa." Prese due piccole pillole bianche dalla tasca e le mise sul tavolo. Poi aprì la bottiglia.

"The person who broke into my closet last winter and stole my whiskey will probably try to do it again while we are away," he went on, "only this time he'll be very sorry if he comes.

"La persona che ha forzato il mio armadio lo scorso inverno e ha rubato il mio whiskey, probabilmente ci riproverà mentre siamo via," continuò, "solo che questa volta se ne pentirà se prova a venire."

Then one by one he dropped the pills into the bottle and held it up to watch them dissolve. His wife looked at him in horror.

Poi, una alla volta, lasciò cadere le pillole nella bottiglia e la alzò per vederle sciogliere. Sua moglie lo guardò con orrore.

"What are they?" she asked him at last. "Will they make the man sick?"

"Cosa sono?" finalmente gli chiese. "Faranno male all'uomo?"

"Not only sick. They will kill him," he answered with satisfaction.

"Non solo male. Lo uccideranno," rispose lui con soddisfazione.

He closed the bottle and put it back on the shelf near the little whiskey glass. He was pleased. Then he said:

Chiuse la bottiglia e la rimise sulla mensola vicino al bicchiere da whiskey. Si sentiva soddisfatto. Poi disse:

"Now, Mr. Thief, when you come back, drink as much whiskey as you wish..."

"Ora, Signor Ladro, quando tornerai, bevi quanto whiskey vuoi..." Helen's face was pale.

"Don't do it, Judson," she cried. "It's horrible, it's murder!" Il viso di Helen era pallido.

"Non farlo, Judson," urlò. "È orribile, è un omicidio!"

"The law does not call it murder if I shoot a thief who is entering my house by force."

"La legge non lo chiama omicidio quando sparo a un ladro che sta entrando in casa mia con la forza."

"Don't do it," she begged, "the law does not punish burglary by death, what rights have you?"

"Non farlo," supplicò lei, "la legge non punisce i furti con scasso con la morte, che diritto hai tu di farlo?"

"When it comes to protecting my property, I make my own laws."

"Quando si tratta di proteggere la mia proprietà, le leggi le decido io."

He was now like a big dog which was afraid that somebody would take away his bone.

Ora era come un grosso cane, impaurito che qualcuno gli portasse via il suo osso.

"But all they did was to steal a little whiskey," she said, "probably some boys. They did not do any real damage."

"Ma tutto quello che hanno fatto è rubare un po' di whiskey," disse lei, "probabilmente sono stati dei ragazzi. Non hanno fatto alcun danno reale."

"It does not matter. If a man robs me of five dollars it is the same as if he took a hundred. A thief is a thief." She made one last effort to convince him.

"Non importa. Se un uomo mi ruba cinque dollari è come se ne avesse presi cento. Un ladro è sempre un ladro." Cercò di convincerlo ancora un'ultima volta.

"We won't return here again till next spring. I shall worry all the time knowing that this bottle full of poison is here. Suppose something happens to us and nobody knows..."

"Non ritorneremo qui fino alla prossima primavera. Sarò preoccupata per tutto questo tempo sapendo che qui si trova questa bottiglia piena di veleno. Supponi che qualcosa accada a noi e nessuno sa..."

He laughed at her sincerity. "We'll risk it," he said. "I've made my money by taking risks. If I die, it will all belong to you, and you can do as you please."

Lui si mise a ridere per la sua sincerità. "Rischieremo," disse lui. "I miei soldi li ho guadagnati rischiando. Se muoio, tutto apparterrà a te, e potrai fare come ti pare."

She knew it was useless to argue. He had always been ruthless in business.

She went to the door with a sigh of defeat.

Lei sapeva che era inutile discutere. Era sempre stato spietato negli affari.

Si diresse verso la porta con un sospiro di sconfitta.

"I'll walk down the road and say good-buy at the farmhouse," she said quietly. She had made up her mind to tell everything to caretaker's wife. Somebody had to know.

"Faccio una passeggiata lungo la strada e vado a salutare tutti alla fattoria," disse con calma. Aveva deciso di raccontare tutto alla moglie del custode. Qualcuno lo doveva sapere.

"All right, my dear," he smiled, "and don't worry about your poor little burglar. No one is going to be hurt unless he breaks in."

"Va bene, cara," sorrise lui, "e non preoccuparti del tuo povero piccolo ladruncolo. Nessuno si farà del male a meno che non irrompa in questa casa."

Helen went down the road and Judson started to close the closet door. Then he suddenly remembered that he had not packed his hunting boots that were drying outside on the heavy table in the garden.

Helen camminò lungo la strada e Judson iniziò a chiudere la porta dell'armadio. Poi, improvvisamente si ricordò che non aveva messo in valigia i suoi stivali da caccia che si stavano asciugando fuori sul pesante tavolo in giardino.

So, leaving the door open, he went to get them. But while he was taking his boots he suddenly slipped on a stone and his head struck the massive table as he fell.

Quindi, lasciando la porta aperta, andò a prenderli. Ma mentre stava prendendo i suoi stivali, improvvisamente scivolò su un sasso e la sua testa colpì il massiccio tavolo mentre cadeva.

Several minutes later he felt a strong arm round him and Alec's voice saying" "It's all right, Mr. Webb, it was not a bad fall. Take this – it will make you feel better."

Alcuni minuti più tardi sentì un forte braccio attorno a lui e la voce di Alec che diceva "Va tutto bene, Signor Webb, non è stata una brutta caduta. Prenda questo – la farà sentire meglio."

A small whiskey-glass was pressed to his lips. Half-conscious he drank.

Un piccolo bicchiere di whiskey è stato premuto alle sue labbra. Semicosciente ha bevuto.

Key Vocabulary:

o comodo agg. [cò-mo-do] – comfortable.

o là avv. – over there, there.

o composto agg. [com-pó-sto] – composed, made up of.

o soprattutto avv. [so-prat-tùt-to] – above all; especially.

o fucile s.m. [fu-cì-le] – rifle, gun.

o canna s.f. [càn-na] – cane; fishing rod.

o avere v.aus. [a-vé-re] – to have.

(functions as a noun in plural: ~i = possessions). o nemmeno avv. [nem-mé-no] – neither; not even.

o mettere v.tr. [mét-te-re] – to put, to place.

o cosa s.f. [cò-sa] – thing, matter.

o disporre v.tr. [di-spór-re] – to arrange, to dispose.

o venire v.intr. [ve-nì-re] – to come; to come out.

o vicinanza s.f. [vi-ci-nàn-za] – vicinity, neighborhood.

o tirare v.tr. [ti-rà-re] – to pull; to drag.

o rimanere v.intr. [ri-ma-né-re] – to remain, to stay.

o stupire v.tr. [stu-pì-re] – to surprise, to stun, to amaze.

stupito agg. [stu-pì-to] - surprised, amazed, stunned. o dentro avv. [dén-tro] – in, inside.

o prendere v.tr. [prèn-de-re] – to take; to get.

o forzare v.tr. [for-zà-re] – to force; to break open.

o rubare v.tr. [ru-bà-re] – to steal.

o riprovare v.tr. [ri-pro-và-re] – to retry, to try again.

o pentirsi v.rf. [pen-tìr-si] – to regret, to be penitent.

o alzare v.tr. [al-zà-re] – to lift (up), to raise.

o sciogliere v.tr. [sciò-glie-re] – to melt, to dissolve.

o rimettere v.tr. [ri-mét-te-re] – to put back.

o sparare v.tr. [spa-rà-re] – to shoot, to fire.

o supplicare v.tr. [sup-pli-cà-re] – to implore, to beg.

o furto s.f. [fùr-to] – theft.

o scasso s.m. [scàs-so] – break-in.

il furto con scasso – burglary.

CHAPTER TEN: While the auto waits / Mentre l'automobile attende

The girl in grey came again to that quiet corner of the small park at the beginning of twilight. She sat down upon a bench and began to read a book. Her dress was very simple. Her face was very beautiful.

La ragazza vestita di grigio ritornò a quell'angolo tranquillo del piccolo parco all'inizio del crepuscolo. Si sedette su una panchina e iniziò a leggere un libro. Il suo vestito era molto semplice. Il suo viso era molto bello.

She had come here at the same hour on the previous day, and on the day before that, and there was a young man who knew it.

Era venuta qui alla stessa ora il giorno precedente, e anche il giorno prima di quello, e c'era un giovane uomo che lo sapeva.

The young man saw the girl and came near. At that moment her book slipped from her fingers and fell on the ground.

Il giovane uomo vide la ragazze e si avvicinò. In quel momento, il libro le scivolò dalle dita e cadde a terra.

The young man picked up the book, returned it to the girl politely, saying a few words about the weather, and stood waiting.

Il giovane uomo raccolse il libro, lo ritornò gentilmente alla ragazza, dicendo alcune parole sul tempo, e rimase in piedi in attesa.

The girl looked at his simple coat and his common face. "You may sit down, if you like," she said. "The light is not good for reading. I would prefer to talk."

La ragazza guardò il suo semplice cappotto e il suo viso comune. "Puoi sederti, se vuoi," disse lei. "La luce non è adatta per leggere. Preferirei parlare."

"Do you know," young man said, "that you are the finest girl I have seen. I saw you here yesterday."

"Lo sai," disse il giovane, "che sei la ragazza più bella che io abbia mai visto. Ti ho visto qui ieri."

"Whoever you are," said the girl in an icy tone, "you must remember that I am a lady."

"Chiunque tu sia," disse la ragazza in un tono gelido, "devi ricordare che sono una signora."

I beg your pardon," said the young man. "It was my fault, you know – I mean, there are girls in the parks, you know – of course, you don't know, but..."

"Chiedo scusa," disse il giovane uomo. "È stata colpa mia, sai – volevo dire, ci sono ragazze nel parco, lo sai – naturalmente che non lo sai, ma..."

"Let's change the subject. Of course, I know. Now tell me what you think about these passing people.

"Cambiamo discorso. Certo che lo so. Ora, dimmi cosa pensi di queste persone che passano di qua.

801

Where are they going? Why do they always seem in a hurry? Are they happy?" The young man thought for a moment how to respond, but the girl continued.

Dove stanno andando? Perché sembrano andare sempre di fretta? Sono felici?" Il giovane pensò per un attimo a come rispondere, ma la ragazza continuò.

"I come to this park because it is only here that I can to be near the masses of people. I speak to you because I want to talk to a common man, unspoiled by money.

"Io vengo in questo parco perché è solo qui che riesco a essere vicina alle masse di persone. Parlo con te perché voglio parlare con un uomo comune, non corrotto dal denaro.

Oh! You don't know how tired I am of money – money, money! And of the men who surround me. I am tired of pleasure, of jewels, of travel."

Oh! Tu non sai come sono stanca del denaro – denaro-denaro! E di tutti gli uomini che ho attorno. Sono stanca del divertimento, dei gioielli, di viaggiare."

"I always had an idea," said the young man, "that money must be a very good thing."

"Ho sempre avuto un'idea," disse il giovane uomo, "che il denaro deve essere una cosa molto bella."

"Well, when you have millions! Drivers, dinners, theaters, parties! I am tired of it!" said the young girl.

"Ebbene, quando hai i milioni! Autisti, cene, teatri, feste! Sono stanca di tutto questo!" disse la giovane ragazza.

The young man looked at her with interest. "I have always liked," he said, "to read and to hear about the life of rich people."

Il giovane la guardò con interesse. "Mi è sempre piaciuto," disse lui "leggere e sentir parlare della vita delle persone ricche."

"Sometimes," continued the girl, "if I ever loved a man. I should love a simple man. – What is your profession?"

"A volte," continuò la ragazza, "se mi innamorerò di un uomo, amerò un uomo semplice. – Qual è la tua professione?"

"I am a very simple man. But I hope to rise in the world. Did you really mean it when you said that you could love a simple man?"

"Sono un uomo molto semplice. Ma spero di farmi strada nel mondo.

Dicevi sul serio quando hai detto che potresti innamorarti di un uomo semplice?"

"I really did," she said.

"I work at a restaurant," said he. The girl drew back a little. "Not as a waiter?" she asked.

"Sì, davvero," disse lei.

"Io lavoro in un ristorante," disse lui. La ragazza si ritrasse un po'. "Non come cameriere?" chiese lei.

"I am a cashier in that restaurant you see over there with that brilliant electric sign: 'Restaurant'."

"Sono un cassiere in quel ristorante che vedi laggiù con quella luminosa insegna elettrica: 'Ristorante'."

The girl looked at het watch and rose. "Why you are not at work?" she asked.

La ragazza guardò il suo orologio e si alzò. "Perché non sei al lavoro ora" chiese lei.

"I am on the night shift," replied the young man, "it is still an hour till my work begins. May I hope to see you again?"

"Ho il turno di notte," rispose il giovane uomo, "ho ancora un'ora di tempo prima di iniziare il mio lavoro. Posso sperare di rivederti ancora?"

"I don't know, perhaps. I must go now. There is a dinner and concert tonight. May be you noticed a white automobile at the gate of the park when you came?"

"Non lo so, forse. Ora devo andare. Ho una cena e un concerto stasera. Hai per caso notato un'auto bianca al cancello del parco quando sei arrivato?"

"Yes, I did," said the young man.

"I always come in it. The driver is waiting for me there. Good night."

"Sì, l'ho vista," disse il giovane. "Arrivo sempre con quella. L'autista mi sta aspettando là. Buonasera."

"But it's almost dark now," said the young man, "and the park is full of rude men. May I accompany you to the car?"

"Ma è quasi buio," disse il giovane, "e il parco è pieno di uomini maleducati. Posso accompagnarti all'auto?"

"No, you will remain on this bench for ten minutes after I have left." And she went away.

"No, tu rimarrai qui su questa panchina per altri dieci minuti dopo che me ne sarò andata." E se ne andò.

The young man looked at her elegant figure while she was walking to the entrance of the park. Then he rose and followed here

Il giovane osservò la sua elegante figura mentre camminava verso l'ingresso del parco. Poi si alzò e la seguì.

When she reached the park gate, she turned her head and looked at the car, then walked by it, crossed the street and entered the restaurant with the brilliant electric sign: 'Restaurant'. A red-haired girl left the cashier's desk, and the girl in grey took her place.

Quando lei raggiunse il cancello del parco, girò la testa e guardò l'automobile, la passò e attraversò la strada ed entrò nel ristorante con la luminosa insegna elettrica: 'Ristorante'. Una ragazza dai capelli rossi lasciò la cassa, e la ragazza vestita di grigio prese il suo posto.

The young man put his hands into his pockets and walked slowly down the street. Then he stepped into the white automobile and said to the driver: "To the club, Henry."

Il giovane mise le mani in tasca e camminò lentamente giù per la strada. Poi entrò nell'automobile bianca e disse all'autista: "Al club Henry."

Key Vocabulary:

o crepuscolo s.m. [cre-pù-sco-lo] – twilight, dusk.

o precedente agg. [pre-ce-dèn-te] – previous, preceding.

o avvicinare v.tr. [av-vi-ci-nà-re] – to approach, to come near.

o cadere v.intr. [ca-dé-re] – to fall.

o raccogliere v.tr. [rac-cò-glie-re] – to pick up; to collect.

o adatto agg. [a-dàt-to] – suitable, suited, appropriate.

o preferire v.tr. [pre-fe-rì-re] – to prefer.

o chiunque pron. [chiùn-que] – whoever; anyone.

o gelido agg. [gè-li-do] – icy, freezing.

o discorso s.m. [di-scór-so] – speech, talk; subject.

o riuscire v.intr. [riu-scì-re] – to succeed (in doing); to manage; can, to be able.

o corrotto agg. [cor-rót-to] – corrupt.

o attorno avv. [at-tór-no] – around, round.

o farmi strada nel mondo – (lit.) to make my way in the world.

o davvero avv. [dav-vé-ro] – really, indeed.

o ritrarre v.tr. [ri-tràr-re] – to draw back/in; to retract.

o turno s.m. [tùr-no] – shift (of work); turn.

o sperare v.tr. [spe-rà-re] – to hope.

o maleducato agg. [ma-le-du-cà-to] – impolite, rude.

o osservare v.tr. [os-ser-và-re] – to observe, to watch.

o raggiungere v.tr. [rag-giùn-ge-re] – to reach; to catch up with.

CHAPTER ELEVEN: Three at table / Tre al tavolo

I was a young man. I had just come back from China, but since my family was away, I went to the country to stay with an uncle.

Ero un giovane uomo. Ero appena ritornato dalla Cina, ma siccome la mia famiglia era via, sono andato in campagna a stare da uno zio.

When I got down to the place I found it closed because my uncle was in the South of France; because he was supposed to come back in a few days I decided to stay at the Royal George, a very decent inn, and await his return.

Quando arrivai sul luogo, lo trovai chiuso perché mio zio si trovava nel Sud della Francia; siccome sarebbe dovuto ritornare tra alcuni giorni, decisi di soggiornare al Royal George, una locanda molto dignitosa, e attendere il suo ritorno.

The first day I passed well enough; but in the evening the dullness of the place, in which I was the only visitor, began to bore me, and the next morning after a late breakfast I went out with the intention of having a brisk walk.

Il primo giorno lo trascorsi abbastanza bene; ma nel pomeriggio la monotonia del luogo, in cui ero l'unico visitatore, iniziò ad annoiarmi, e il mattino seguente dopo una tarda colazione, uscii con l'intenzione di fare una camminata a passo spedito.

I started off in excellent spirits, because the day was bright and frosty. The villages through which I passed were old and charming. I lunched luxuriously on bread and cheese and beer in the bar of a small inn, and decided to walk a little further before turning back.

Iniziai di ottimo umore, perché la giornata era luminosa e gelida. I villaggi che attraversai erano vecchi e affascinanti. Pranzai lussuosamente con pane e formaggio e una birra nel bar di una piccola locanda, poi decisi di camminare per ancora un po' prima di ritornare indietro.

When at last I had gone far enough, I turned up a little lane, and decided to find my way back by another route, relying upon the small compass.

Quando finalmente mi sembrava di essere andato abbastanza lontano, svoltai in un piccolo vicolo, e decisi che avrei trovato la via del ritorno seguendo un altro percorso, facendo affidamento sulla piccola bussola.

I had reached the marshes, when a dense fog began gradually to spread. I continued my course until, at four o' clock, while it was getting darker and darker. I had to admit that I was lost.

Raggiunsi le paludi, quando una fitta nebbia iniziò gradualmente ad espandersi. Continuai il mio percorso fino alle quattro, mentre si stava facendo sempre più buio. Dovevo ammettere che mi ero perso.

The compass was no help to me now; I walked about miserably, occasionally shouting in hope of being heard by some passing shepherd or farmer.

La bussola non mi era d'aiuto; girovagai miserabilmente, urlando occasionalmente nella speranza di essere sentito da qualche pastore o contadino che passava di là.

At last by good luck I found my feet on a small road that was going through the marshes, and by walking slowly and tapping with my stick, I managed to stay on it. I had followed it for some distance when I heard footsteps approaching me.

Finalmente, per fortuna, i miei piedi si trovarono su una piccola strada che attraversava le paludi, e camminando lentamente e aiutandomi con il bastone riuscii a rimanere su di essa. L'avevo percorsa per una certa distanza quando sentii dei passi che si avvicinavano.

We stopped as we met, and the stranger, a peasant from the neighboring village, hearing of my situation, walked back with me for nearly a mile. He put me on the main road and gave me instructions how to reach a village that was located three miles away.

Quando ci incontrammo ci fermammo, e lo sconosciuto, un contadino dal villaggio vicino, sentendo la mia situazione, mi accompagnò per quasi un chilometro. Mi portò sulla strada principale e mi diede istruzioni su come raggiungere un villaggio che si trovava a tre chilometri di distanza.

I was so tired that three miles sounded like ten, and besides that, not far from the road I saw a dimly lighted window. I pointed to the window, but my companion shook his head and looked round him uneasily.

Ero così stanco che tre chilometri mi sembravano dieci, e oltre a questo, non lontano dalla strada vidi una finestra illuminata da una fioca luce. Indicai la finestra, ma il mio accompagnatore scosse la testa e si guardò intorno con disagio.

"You won't get any good there," he said. "Why not?" I asked.

"Non troverai niente di buono là," disse lui. "Perché no?" gli chiesi.

"There's something in there, sir," he answered. "What it is I don't know.

Some say that it's a poor mad thing, others say it's a kind of animal; but whatever it is, it isn't good to see."

"C'è qualcosa in quella casa, signore," rispose. "Cosa sia non lo so. Alcuni dicono sia una cosa pazza, altri dicono si tratti di una specie di animale; ma qualunque cosa sia, non è bella da vedere."

"Well. I'll go on then," I said, "good night."

"Beh. Allora ci vado," dissi io, "buonasera."

He went back whistling until the sound of his footsteps faded in the distance, and I followed the road he had indicated. But I was now cold and tired, and decided to go back toward the house.

Lui se ne andò fischiettando finché il rumore dei suoi passi svanì in lontananza, e io seguii la strada che mi aveva indicato. Ma avevo freddo ed ero stanco e ha deciso di tornare verso la casa.

There was no light and no sound from within. I knocked lightly upon the door.

It opened suddenly and a tall old woman, holding a candle, greeted me.

Dal suo interno non traspariva alcuna luce o suono. Bussai leggermente alla porta.

Improvvisamente si aprì e una donna alta e vecchia, con una candela in mano, mi salutò.

"What do you want?" she asked.

"I've lost my way; I want to get to Ashville." "I don't know it," said the old woman.

"Cosa vuoi?" chiese lei.

"Mi sono perso; voglio arrivare ad Ashville." "Non la conosco," disse la vecchia signora.

She wanted to close the door when a man appeared from a room at the side of the hall and came toward us.

Stava per chiudere la porta quando un uomo apparve da una stanza che si trovava a fianco dell'atrio e si avvicinò.

"Ashville is fifteen miles from here," he said calmly.

"If you will direct me to the nearest village, I shall be grateful," I said. He didn't answer, but exchanged a quick glance with the woman.

"Ashville si trova a quindici chilometri da qui," disse lui con calma. "Se mi indica il villaggio più vicino, le sarò grato," dissi io. Lui non

rispose, ma scambiò una rapida occhiata con la donna.

"The nearest village is three miles away," he said turning to me and trying to soften a naturally harsh voice. "If you will give us the pleasure of your company, we'll offer you our hospitality."

"Il villaggio più vicino si trova a tre chilometri," disse l'uomo voltandosi verso di me e provando ad addolcire la sua voce naturalmente aspra. "Se vorrà offrirci la vostra gradita compagnia, vi offriremo la nostra ospitalità."

I hesitated. They were certainly a strange looking couple, and the gloomy hall with the shadows thrown by the candle looked hardly more inviting than the darkness outside.

Io esitai. Erano certamente una coppia molto strana, e l'atrio tetro con l'ombra proiettata dalle candele era poco più invitante dell'oscurità all'esterno.

"You are very kind," I murmured, "but – "

"Come in." he said quickly. "Shut the door, Anna."

"Lei è molto gentile," mormorai, "ma –"

"Entri." Disse lui velocemente. "Chiudi la porta, Anna."

Almost before I knew it I was standing inside and the old woman, muttering to herself, had closed the door behind me.

Senza accorgermene, mi trovai in casa e la vecchia signora, mormorando tra sé, aveva chiuso la porta dietro di me.

With a strange feeling of being trapped I followed my host into the room, and taking a chair warmed my frozen fingers at the fire.

Con la strana sensazione di essere intrappolato, seguii il padrone di casa nella stanza, presi una sedia e riscaldai le mie dita gelate davanti al fuoco.

"Dinner is almost ready," said the old man, "if you will excuse me."

"La cena è quasi pronta," disse il vecchio, "se volete scusarmi."

I nodded and he left the room. A minute later I heard voices: his and the old woman's and, I was sure, a third. Before I had finished my inspection of the room he returned, and looked at me with the same strange look I noticed before.

Annuii e lui uscì dalla stanza. Un minuto più tardi sentii delle voci: la sua e quella della vecchia signora e, ne ero sicuro, una terza. Prima di finire di ispezionare la stanza lui ritornò, e mi guardò con lo stesso strano sguardo che avevo notato prima.

"There will be three of us at dinner," he said. "That is two of us and my son."

I nodded again.

"Noi saremo in tre a cena," disse. "Noi due e mio figlio." Annuii di nuovo.

"I suppose you don't mind dining in the dark," he said.

"Not at all," I answered, hiding my surprise as well as I could, "but really I don't want to intrude. If you will allow me —"

"Suppongo che non le dispiaccia cenare al buio," disse.

"Niente affatto," risposi, nascondendo il mio stupore al meglio che potevo, "ma veramente non vorrei disturbare. Se mi permettete —"

"It's seldom that we have company," he said, "and now that you're here we want you to stay. My son has some eye problems, and he can't stand the light. Ah, here's Anna."

"È raro che noi abbiamo compagnia," disse, "e ora che Lei è qui, vogliamo che Lei rimanga. Mio figlio ha dei problemi agli occhi, e non sopporta la luce. Ah, ecco qui Anna."

As he spoke the old woman entered, glanced at me and began to lay the tablecloth, while my host, taking a chair, sat looking silently into the fire.

Mentre lui parlava, la vecchia signora entrò, mi guardò e iniziò a stendere la tovaglia, mentre il padrone di casa prendendo una sedia si sedette guardando in silenzio il fuoco.

When the table was set, the old woman brought in a pair of chickens ready carved in the dish, and placing three chairs, left the room.

Dopo aver apparecchiato il tavolo, la vecchia signora arrivò con un paio di polli già tagliati nel piatto, e preparando tre sedie, lasciò la stanza.

The old man hesitated a moment, and then, rising from his chair, placed a large screen in front of the fire and slowly extinguished the candles.

Il vecchio esitò un attimo, e poi, alzandosi dalla sedia, sistemò un largo schermo davanti al fuoco e lentamente spense le candele.

"Blind man's holiday," he said, and groping his way to the door opened it.

"Le vacanze di un uomo cieco," disse, e procedendo a tentoni verso la porta, la aprì.

Somebody came back into the room with him, and in a slow, uncertain manner took a seat at the table. And the strangest voice I have ever heard broke the silence.

Qualcuno entrò nella stanza con lui, e in modo lento e incerto si sedette a tavola. E la voce più strana che avessi mai sentito ruppe il silenzio.

"A cold night," it said slowly.

"Una notte fredda," disse piano.

"It sure is," I answered and, light or no light, started eating with appetite. It was somewhat difficult eating in the dark, and it was evident from the behavior of my invisible companions that they also were not used to dining under such circumstances.

"Sì, veramente," risposi e, con luce o senza luce, iniziai a mangiare con appetito. Era piuttosto difficile mangiare al buio, ed era evidente dal comportamento dei miei compagni invisibili che anche loro, non erano abituati a cenare in queste circostanze.

We ate in silence until the old woman came into the room with some sweets and put them upon the table.

Cenammo in silenzio finché la vecchia signora entrò nella stanza con dei dolci e li mise sul tavolo.

"Are you a stranger around here?" asked the strange voice again.

"Lei è uno straniero da questa parti?" chiese ancora una volta la strana voce.

"Yes," I answered and murmured something about my luck in stumbling upon such a good dinner.

"Sì," risposi e mormorai qualcosa riguardo alla mia fortuna di essermi imbattuto casualmente in una cena così deliziosa.

"Stumbling is a very good word for it," said the voice firmly. You have forgotten the wine, father."

"Imbattersi casualmente è la parola giusta," disse la voce con fermezza. Hai dimenticato il vino, padre."

"So I have," said the old man, rising. "It's a bottle of the 'Celebrated' today! I will get it myself." He groped his way to the door, and closing it behind him, left me alone with my invisible neighbor.

"È vero," disse il vecchio, alzandosi. "È una bottiglia per il 'Celebre' di oggi! La prendo io." Si andò a tentoni verso la porta, e chiudendola dietro di sé, mi lasciò solo con il mio vicino invisibile.

There was something so strange about the whole business that I must confess I felt very uneasy. My host seemed to be absent a long time.

C'era qualcosa di molto strano nell'intera faccenda che, devo confessare, mi faceva sentire molto a disagio. Il padrone di casa sembrava essere assente da tanto.

I heard the man opposite lay down his fork and spoon, and it almost seemed to me that I saw a pair of wild eyes shining through the darkness like a cat's.

Sentii l'uomo accanto a me posare la sua forchetta e il suo cucchiaio, e mi era quasi sembrato di vedere un paio di occhi selvaggi brillare nell'oscurità, come quelli di un gatto.

With a growing sense of uneasiness I pushed my chair back, the screen fell over with a bang, and in the light of the fire I saw the face of the creature in front of me.

Con un crescente senso di disagio, spinsi all'indietro la sedia, lo schermo cadde sbattendo, e nella luce del fuoco vidi il viso della creatura davanti a me.

Breathless I got up from the chair and stood with clenched fists beside it. In the red glow of the fire it looked so devilish.

Senza respiro mi alzai dalla sedia e rimasi in piedi accanto ad essa con i pugni stretti. Nel rosso bagliore del fuoco sembrava così diabolico.

For a few moments we looked at each other in silence; then the door opened and the old man returned. He stood shocked as he saw the warm firelight, and then, approaching the table, mechanically put down a couple of bottles.

Per alcuni istanti, ci guardammo a vicenda in silenzio; poi si aprì la porta e il vecchio ritornò. Rimase scioccato quando vide la calda luce del fuoco, e poi, avvicinandosi al tavolo, appoggiò meccanicamente un paio di bottiglie.

"I beg your pardon, said I reassured by his presence, "but I have accidentally overturned the screen. Allow me to replace it."

"Vi chiedo scusa," dissi rassicurato dalla sua presenza, "ma ho accidentalmente rovesciato lo schermo. Mi permetta di sostituirlo."

"No, said the old man, gently, "let it be. We have had enough of the dark." He struck a match and slowly lit the candles.

"No, disse il vecchio gentilmente, "lasciamo stare. Ne abbiamo abbastanza del buio."

Prese un fiammifero e lentamente accese le candele.

Then I saw that the man opposite had the remnant of a face, a horrible face in which one eye, the sole remaining feature, still glittered. I was greatly moved, guessing a part of the truth.

Poi vidi che l'uomo davanti a me aveva solo i resti di un volto, un volto orribile dove un occhio, l'unica caratteristica rimanente, ancora brillava. Ne rimasi molto commosso, intuendo una parte della verità.

My son was injured some years ago in a burning house," said the old man. "Since then we have lived a very private life. When you came to the door we – that is – my son..."

"Mio figlio è rimasto ferito alcuni anni fa in una casa in fiamme," disse il vecchio. "Da allora abbiamo vissuto una vita molto riservata. Quando lei è arrivato alla nostra porta – ossia – mio figlio..."

"I thought," said the son simply," that it would be better for me not to come to the dinner table. But it happened to be my birthday, and my father would not hear of my dining alone, so we come up with this foolish plan of dining in the dark. I'm sorry that I have startled you."

"Pensai," disse semplicemente il figlio, "che sarebbe stato meglio per me non venire a tavola. Ma era anche il mio compleanno, e mio padre non voleva saperne che io cenassi da solo, quindi inventammo questo folle piano di cenare al buio. Mi dispiace di averla spaventata."

"I am sorry," said I, and reached across the table to shake his hand "I am such a fool, but it was only in the dark that you startled me."

"Mi dispiace," dissi, e allungai attraverso il tavolo per stringergli la mano "sono uno sciocco, ma è solo al buio che mi hai spaventato."

"We never see a friend," said the old man, "and the temptation to have company was too much for us. Besides, I don't know what else you could have done."

"Non vediamo mai nessun amico," disse il vecchio, "e la tentazione di avere compagnia era troppa per noi. Inoltre, non so cos'altro avrebbe potuto fare."

"Nothing else just as good, I'm sure," said I.

"Come," said my host, almost gaily, "Now we know each other, draw your chair to the fire and let's celebrate this birthday in a proper fashion."

"Niente altro di altrettanto bello, ne sono certo," dissi.

"Venga," disse il padrone di casa, quasi allegramente, "Ora ci conosciamo, avvicini la sua sedia al fuoco e festeggiamo questo compleanno come si deve."

He drew a small table to the fire for the glasses and brought a box of cigars, and placing a chair for the old servant, asked her to sit down and drink, and we were soon as merry a party as I have ever seen.

Avvicinò un piccolo tavolo al fuoco per i bicchieri e portò una scatola di sigari, e sistemando una sedia per la vecchia serva, le chiese di sedersi e di bere, e presto eravamo tutti così allegri come non avevo mai visto ad una festa.

The night went on so rapidly that we could not believe our ears when in a lull in the conversation a clock in the hall struck twelve.

La notte passò così rapidamente che non credemmo alle nostre orecchie quando in un momento di silenzio durante la conversazione, l'orologio nell'atrio suonò la mezzanotte.

"A last toast before we go to bed," said my host, throwing the end of his cigar into the fire and turning to the small table.

"Un ultimo brindisi prima di andare a letto," disse il padrone di casa, gettando la parte finale del suo sigaro nel fuoco e voltandosi verso il piccolo tavolo.

We had drunk several before this toast, but there was something impressive in the old man's manner as he rose and took up his glass.

Avevamo già bevuto parecchio prima di questo brindisi, ma c'era qualcosa di impressionante nelle maniere del vecchio mentre si alzava e prendeva il suo bicchiere.

His tall figure seemed to get taller, and his voice rang as he looked proudly at his disfigured son.

La sua alta figura sembrava diventare ancora più alta, e la sua voce risuonò mentre guardava con orgoglio il suo figlio sfigurato.

"To the health of the children my boy saved!" he said, and drained his glass in one gulp.

"Alla salute dei bambini che mio figlio ha salvato!" disse, e svuotò il bicchiere in un unico sorso.

Key Vocabulary:

o dignitoso agg. [di-gni-tó-so] – decent, respectable; dignified.

o trascorrere v.tr. [tra-scór-re-re] – to spend, to pass.

o monotonia s.f. [mo-no-to-nì-a] – monotony, routine, dullness.

o annoiare v.tr. [an-no-ià-re] – to bore, to weary.

o spedito agg. [spe-dì-to] – quick, swift, brisk.

o svoltare v.intr. [svol-tà-re] – to turn, to turn a corner.

~ in una stradina | un vicolo – to turn into a side-road | lane. o vicolo s.m. [vì-co-lo] – alleyway, lane.

o percorso s.m. [per-cór-so] – path, course, route.

o affidamento s.m. [af-fi-da-mén-to] – reliance, trust.

fare ~ su – to trust to, to rely on. o bussola s.f. [bùs-so-la] – compass.

o palude s.f. [pa-lù-de] – marsh, marshland, swamp.

o fitto agg. [fìt-to] – thick, dense.

o espandere v.tr. [e-spàn-de-re] – to expand, to spread, to disperse.

o ammettere v.tr. [am-mét-te-re] – to admit, to acknowledge.

o girovagare v.intr. [gi-ro-va-gà-re] – to roam, to wander, to ramble.

o principale agg. [prin-ci-pà-le] – main, principal.

o fioco agg. [fiò-co] – dim, faint, glimmering.

o scuotere v.tr. [scuò-te-re] – to shake.

o disagio s.m. [di-sà-gio] – discomfort, uneasiness, unease.

o intorno avv. [in-tór-no] – around, round, about.

o qualunque agg. [qua-lùn-que] – any; whichever, whatever. (syn. qualsiasi)

o specie s.f. [spè-cie] – kind, sort; species.

o fischiettare v.intr. [fischiet-tà-re] – to whistle.

o svanire v.intr. [sva-nì-re] – to vanish, to disappear, to fade.

o trasparire v.intr. [tra-spa-rì-re] – to shine/to show through; to transpire.

o scambiare v.tr. [scam-bià-re] – to exchange; to swap.

o addolcire v.tr. [ad-dol-cì-re] – to sweeten; (fig) to soften.

o aspro agg. [à-spro] – sour, tart; rough, harsh.

una voce aspra – a rough/harsh voice.

o ospitalità s.f. [o-spi-ta-li-tà] – hospitality.

o tetro agg. [tè-tro] – gloomy.

o oscurità s.f. [o-scu-ri-tà] – darkness, obscurity.

o accorgersi v.rf. [ac-còr-ger-si] – to realize (sth), to notice (sth).

o intrappolare v.tr. [in-trap-po-là-re] – to trap, to catch in a trap.

o riscaldare v.tr. [ri-scal-dà-re] – to warm, to heat.

o disturbare v.tr. [di-stur-bà-re] – to disturb, to bother, to intrude.

o stendere v.tr. [stèn-de-re] – to stretch, to spread (out).

o apparecchiare v.tr. [ap-pa-rec-chià-re] – to make/to get ready.

~ la tavola – to set/to lay the table.

o spegnere v.tr. [spè-gne-re] – to turn off; to extinguish.

o andare a tentoni – to grope (one's way).

o procedere v.intr. [pro-cè-de-re] – to proceed; to go/move (on).

o rompere v.tr. [róm-pe-re] – to break.

o abituato agg. [a-bi-tuà-to] – used, accustomed, habituated.

o imbattersi v.rf. [im-bàt-ter-si] – to stumble on/upon, to run into.

o casualmente avv. [ca-sual-mén-te] – by chance, fortuitously.

o sbattere v.tr. [sbàt-te-re] – to beat; to bang, to slam.

o bagliore s.m. [ba-glió-re] – flare, glint, glow.

o a vicenda – each other, one another.

o rovesciare v.tr. [ro-ve-scià-re] – to knock over; to overturn.

o sostituire v.tr. [so-sti-tuì-re] – to replace; to substitute.

o resto s.m. [rè-sto] – rest, remainder, remnant.

o caratteristica s.f. [ca-rat-te-rì-sti-ca] – character, feature.

CHAPTER TWELVE: The happiest man on Earth / L'uomo più Felice sulla Terra

Jesse felt ready to weep. He had been sitting at the office waiting for Tom.

He was grateful for the chance to rest a little imagining with joy the moment when Tom would say, "Sure, Jesse, you can start working whenever you're ready!"

Jesse era pronto a scoppiare in lacrime. Era rimasto seduto tutto il giorno in ufficio ad attendere Tom. Era grato per l'opportunità di poter riposare un po' immaginando con gioia il momento in cui Tom avrebbe detto, "Certo Jesse, puoi iniziare a lavorare appena sei pronto!"

For two weeks he have been wandering from Kansas City, Missouri, to Oklahoma, through night of rain and a week of burning sun, without sleep or a decent meal, waiting for that one moment.

Per due settimane aveva camminato da Kansas City, Missouri, fino in Oklahoma, tra notti di pioggia ed una settimana di sole cocente, senza riposo o pasti decenti, in attesa di quel momento.

And then Tom had come into the office. He walked in quickly holding some papers in his hands; he had glanced at Jesse and turned away. He had not recognized him... And Tom Brackett was his brother-in-law.

E Tom era arrivato in ufficio. Entrò velocemente con delle carte tra le mani; aveva dato uno sguardo a Jesse e si era girato. Non lo aveva riconosciuto... E Tom Brackett era suo cognato.

Was it because of his clothes? Jesse knew he looked terrible. He had tried to wash at the fountain in the park, but that did not help much.

Era a causa dei vestiti? Jesse sapeva di avere un aspetto orribile. Aveva provato a lavarli alla fontana nel parco, ma non era stato di grosso aiuto.

In his excitement he had cut himself while shaving and now there was a deep scar across his cheek. And he could not shake all dust out of his shabby suit. Or was it just because he had change too much?

Nel suo entusiasmo si era tagliato mentre si faceva la barba e ora c'era una profonda cicatrice sulla sua guancia. E non riusciva a scuotere la polvere dal suo squallido vestito. O era solo perché aveva cambiato troppo?

It's true, they hadn't seen each other for five years, but Tom looked five years older, and that was all. He was still Tom. God! Did he look so different now?

E' vero, non si vedevano da cinque anni, ma Tom sembrava di cinque anni più vecchio, e basta. Era sempre Tom. Dio! Aveva un aspetto così diverso adesso?

Brackett finished his telephone call. He leaned back in his chair and glanced at Jesse with his small, clear blue eyes that were suspicious and unfriendly.

Brackett finì la sua telefonata. Si appoggiò sulla sua sedia e diede uno sguardo a Jesse con i suoi piccoli, chiari occhi azzurri, sospetti e poco amichevoli.

He was a stout man of forty-five, with dark hair and a determined face; his nose was reddish at the tip. He looked like a solid, decent, capable business man, which he really was.

Era un uomo corpulento di quarantacinque anni, dai capelli scuri e il volto determinato; il suo naso era rossastro alla punta. Aveva l'aspetto di un uomo d'affari solido, onesto, capace, e lo era.

He examined Jesse with cold indifference, unwilling to waste time on him. "Yes?" Brackett said suddenly. What do you want?" His voice was decent,

Jesse thought. He had expected that it would be worse.

Esaminò Jesse con fredda indifferenza, non disposto a sprecare del tempo con lui.

"Si?" Brackett disse improvvisamente.

"Cosa vuoi?" La sua voce era buona, Jesse pensò. Si aspettava fosse peggiore.

He moved up to the wooden counter that divided the office into two parts.

He thrust a hand nervously through his hair. "I guess you don't recognize me, Tom," he hesitated for a moment, "I am Jesse Fulton."

Si mosse al bancone in legno che divideva l'ufficio in due parti. Passò nervosamente una mano tra i suoi capelli. "Credo tu non mi abbia riconosciuto, Tom," esitò per un momento, "Sono Jesse Fulton."

"What?" Brackett said. And that was all. "Yes, I am, and Ella sends you her love."

"Cosa?" Brackett disse. Nient'altro. "Si, sono io, ed Ella ti manda il suo affetto."

Brackett rose and walked over the counter until they were face to face. He stared at Fulton again, trying to measure the resemblance to his brother-in-law as he remembered him.

Brackett si alzò e si avvicinò al bancone fino a quando i due si trovarono faccia a faccia. Osservò di nuovo Fulton, cercando di misurarne la somiglianza col cognato che lui ricordava.

This man was tall, about thirty years old. That corresponded! He had straight good features and an erect body. That was right too. But the face was too tired and exhausted, the body was too thin. His brother-in-law had been a solid, strong young man.

Quest'uomo era alto, di circa trent'anni. Questo corrispondeva! Aveva dei bei lineamenti ed un corpo diritto. Anche questo era giusto. Ma il viso era troppo stanco ed esausto, il corpo era troppo magro. Suo cognato era un giovane solido e forte.

Now it seemed to Brackett that he was looking at a faded, badly taken photograph trying to recognize the original; the similarity was there but the difference was tremendous.

Ora a Brackett sembrava di guardare una fotografia sfumata, scattata male, mentre cercava di riconoscere l'originale; la somiglianza era lì ma la differenza era tremenda.

He looked into Jesse's eyes. They certainly seemed familiar, grey with a shy but honest look in them.

Guardò negli occhi di Jesse. Sembravano certamente familiari, grigi e dall'aria timida ma onesta.

Jesse stood quiet. Inside he was burning with rage. Brackett was like a man examining an exhausted horse; there was a look of pure pity in his eyes. It made Jesse furious. He knew he was not as bad as that.

Jesse era immobile. All'interno esplodeva di rabbia. Brackett era come un uomo che ispezionava un cavallo esausto: c'era pura pietà nei suoi occhi. Ciò rendeva Jesse furioso. Sapeva di non essere ridotto così male.

"Yes, I believe you are," Brackett said finally, "but you've certainly changed."

"Si, ti credo, sei tu," Brackett disse finalmente, "ma sei cambiato tanto."

"Sure I have, it's been five years, isn't it?" said Jesse feeling hurt. "And you only saw me a couple of times." Then he said to himself, "What if I have changed? Doesn't everybody change? I am not a corpse."

"Certo, sono passati cinque anni, non è vero?" disse Jesse dispiaciuto. "E mi hai visto solo qualche volta." Quindi disse a sé stesso, "E che fa se sono cambiato? Non cambiano tutti? Non sono mica un cadavere."

"You were strong and healthy," Brackett continued softly, in the same tone of wonder. "You lost weight, I guess?"

"Eri forte e in salute," Brackett continuò dolcemente, nello stesso tono meravigliato. "Avrai perso peso, forse?"

Jesse kept silent. He had to use all his effort not to boil over. But it was only by great effort that he could control himself.

Jesse rimase in silenzio. Doveva mettercela tutta per non esplodere. Ma riuscì a controllarsi con grande sforzo.

The pause extended, became painful. Brackett flushed.

La pausa si allungò, diventando dolorosa. Brackett arrossì.

"Excuse me," he said, lifting the counter. "Come in. Take a seat. Good God, boy" – he grasped Jesse's hand and shook it. "I am glad to see you; don't think anything else! You just looked so exhausted..."

"Scusami," disse, alzando il bancone. "Entra. Siediti. Santo Cielo, ragazzo" – prese la mano di Jesse e la strinse. "Sono così felice di vederti; non pensare a nient'altro! Avevi solo un aspetto così esausto..."

"It's all right," Jesse murmured. He sat down, running his hand through his curly uncombed hair.

"Why are you limping?"

"Va tutto bene," mormorò Jesse. Si sedette, passando la mano tra i suoi ricci e spettinati capelli.

"Perché zoppichi?"

"I stepped on a sharp stone; it made a hole in my shoe." Jesse pulled his feet back under the chair. He was ashamed of his shoes. Two weeks on the road had almost ruined them.

"Ho calpestato una pietra affilata, ha bucato la mia scarpa." Jesse nascose i piedi sotto la sedia. Si vergognava delle sue scarpe. Due settimane per strada le avevano quasi distrutte.

All morning he had been dreaming that before buying anything else, before even a suit, he would buy himself a strong new pair of shoes.

Per tutta la mattina aveva sognato che prima di ogni altra cosa, anche prima di un vestito, si sarebbe comprato un nuovo paio di scarpe forti.

Brackett kept his eyes off Jesse's feet. He knew what was troubling the young man and it filled his heart with pity. The whole thing was terrible.

Brackett evitò di guardare i piedi di Jesse. Sapeva cosa tormentava il giovane e ciò gli riempiva il cuore di pietà. Tutto questo era terribile.

He had never seen anyone who looked more miserable. His sister had been writing to him every week, but she had not told him they were as poor as that.

Non aveva mai visto nessuno dall'aspetto più miserabile. Sua sorella gli scriveva ogni settimana, ma non aveva mai detto che fossero così poveri.

"Well," Brackett began, "tell me everything, how's Ella?"

"Oh, she's quite all right," Jesse replied absently. He had a soft, pleasant, somewhat shy voice and soft grey eyes. He did not know how to start.

"Beh," inizio Brackett, "dimmi tutto, come sta Ella?"

"Oh, sta bene," Jesse rispose distrattamente. Aveva una voce leggera, piacevole, a volte timida e dei delicati occhi grigi. Non sapeva da dove iniziare.

"And the kids?"

"E i bambini?"

"Oh, they're fine... Well, you know," Jesse added becoming more attentive, "the young one has to wear a brace. Unfortunately he can't run around. But he's smart. He draws pictures and he does everything very well, you know."

"Oh, stanno bene... Beh, sai," Jesse aggiunse diventando più attento, "il più giovane deve indossare un sostegno. Non può correre, purtroppo. Ma è intelligente. Disegna le immagini e fa tutto molto bene, devo dire."

"Yes," Brackett said. "That's good."

He hesitated. There was a moment of silence. Jesse turned uneasily in his chair. Now that the time had arrived, he felt awkward.

"Si," disse Brackett. "Molto bene."

Esitò. Ci fu un momento di silenzio. Jesse divenne inquieto sulla sedia. Ora che il momento era arrivato, si sentiva a disagio.

Brackett leaned forward and put his hand on Jesse's knee. "Ella didn't tell me things were so bad for you, Jesse. I might have helped."

Brackett si chinò in avanti e mise la mano sul ginocchio di Jesse. "Ella non mi ha mai detto che le cose erano così difficili per voi, Jesse. Avrei potuto aiutare."

"Well," Jesse said softly, "you've been having your own troubles, haven't you?"

"Beh," Jesse rispose con calma, "hai avuto anche tu i tuoi problemi, non è vero?"

"Yes," Brackett leaned back. His face grew dark. "You know I lost my hardware shop?"

"Si," Brackett si appoggiò all'indietro. Il suo volto si incupì. "Sapevi che ho perso il mio negozio di ferramenta?"

"Well, sure," Jesse answered surprised. "You wrote us. That's what I mean."

"Beh, certo," Jesse rispose sorpreso. "Ce lo hai scritto. E' questo che intendo."

"I forgot," Brackett said. "I still keep on being surprised at it myself. But it wasn't worth much," he added bitterly. "The business was going down for three years. I guess I just wanted it because it was mine." He laughed aimlessly.

"Dimenticavo," disse Brackett. "Continuo ancora a esserne sorpreso. Ma non valeva molto," aggiunse amaramente. "Gli affari stavano crollando da tre anni. Credo lo volessi solamente perché era mio." Rise senza motivo.

"Well, tell me about yourself," he asked. What happened to job you had?" Jesse was silent. "It isn't you and Ella?" Brackett continued anxiously.

"Beh, dimmi di te," chiese. "Cosa è successo al lavoro che avevi?" Jesse era silenzioso. "Non siete tu ed Ella?" Brackett continuò ansiosamente.

"Oh, no," exclaimed Jesse. "What made you think so? Ella and me..."he stopped, laughing, "Tom, dear, I'm just crazy about Ella. She's just so wonderful! She's my whole life, Tom."

"Oh, no," esclamò Jesse. "Cosa te lo faceva pensare? Ella ed io..."si fermò, ridendo, "Tom, caro, io sono pazzo di Ella. E' straordinaria! Lei è tutta la mia vita, Tom."

"Excuse me. Forget it." Brackett said turning away. The young man's love for his wife had upset him. He wished he could do something for them. They were both too good to suffer so much. Ella was like this boy too, shy and soft.

"Scusami. Lascia perdere." Brackett disse girandosi. L'amore del giovane per sua moglie lo aveva sconvolto. Avrebbe voluto poter fare qualcosa per loro. Erano entrambi troppo buoni per soffrire così tanto. Ella era proprio come questo ragazzo, timida e dolce.

me."

"Tom listen," Jesse said, "I've come here on purpose. I want you to help

"Tom ascolta," disse Jesse, "Sono venuto qui di proposito. Vorrei che tu

mi aiutassi."

"Damn it, boy," Brackett said. He has been expecting this. "I can't do much. I only get thirty-five dollars a week and I'm grateful for it."

"Dannazione, ragazzo," rispose Brackett. Se lo aspettava. "Non posso fare molto. Ricevo solo trentacinque dollari a settimana e sono grato per questo."

"Sure, I know," Jesse exclaimed. He was feeling once again the wild anxiety that had possessed him in early hours of the morning.

"Certo, lo so," Jesse esclamò. Sentiva ancora una volta l'ansia selvaggia che lo aveva posseduto nelle prime ore della mattina.

"I know you can't help us with money! But we met a man who works for you! He was in our city! He said you could give me a job!"

"So che non puoi aiutarci coi soldi! Ma abbiamo incontrato un uomo che lavora per te! Era nella nostra città! Ha detto che tu avresti potuto darmi un lavoro!"

"Who said?" asked Tom.

"Oh, why didn't you tell me?" Jesse cried out. "As soon as I heard it I decided to talk to you. For two weeks I've been walking like mad."

"Chi lo ha detto?" chiese Tom.

"Oh, perché non me lo hai detto?" Jesse esclamò. "Ho deciso di parlare con te subito dopo averlo sentito. Per due settimane ho camminato come un pazzo."

Brackett groaned. "You've been walking from Kansas City for two weeks because I could give you a job?"

"Sure, Tom. What else could I do?"

Brackett si lamentò. "Ti sei incamminato da Kansas City per due settimane perché io ti potessi dare un lavoro?"

"Certo, Tom. Cos'altro dovrei fare?"

"My God, there aren't any jobs, Jesse! It's a bad season, there are a lot of unemployed everywhere. And you don't know this oil business. It's special. I've got some friends here but they can't do anything now. Don't you think I would tell you as soon as there was a chance?"

"Mio Dio, non c'è alcun lavoro, Jesse! E' una cattiva stagione, ci sono tantissimi disoccupati ovunque. E non lo conosci questo business dell'olio. E' speciale. Ho alcuni amici qui ma non possono fare nulla ora. Non credi che te l'avrei detto non appena se ne fosse presentata l'opportunità?"

Jesse was struck. That was a blow for him! The hope of the last two weeks seemed to be gone... Then, like a madman, he cried:

Jesse era colpito. Era un brutto colpo! La speranza delle ultime due settimane sembrava persa... Quindi, come un folle, esclamò:

"But listen, this man said you could hire people! He told me! He drives trucks for you! He said you always need men!"

"Ma ascolta, quest'uomo ha detto che potevi assumere delle persone! Me lo ha detto! Guida camion per te! Ha detto che tu hai sempre bisogno di uomini!"

"Oh!.. You mean my department?" Brackett said in a low voice. "Yes, Tom. That's it!"

"Oh! Intendi il mio dipartimento?" Brackett disse con voce bassa.

"Sì, Tom. Questo!"

"Oh, no you can't want to work in my department," Brackett told him in the same low voice. "You don't know what it is."

"Oh, no non puoi voler lavorare nel mio dipartimento," Brackett gli disse con la stessa voce bassa. "Non sai di che si tratta."

"Yes, I do," Jesse insisted. "He told me all about it, Tom. You're a dispatcher, aren't you? You send the dynamite trucks out?"

"Sì, lo so," Jesse insistette. "Mi ha detto tutto, Tom. Sei un distributore, non è vero? Mandi in giro i camion di dinamite?"

"Who was the man, Jesse?"

"Everett, Everett, I think."

"Chi era quell'uomo, Jesse?"

"Everett, Everett, penso."

"Egbert? A man of about my size?" Brackett asked slowly. "Yes, Egbert. He wasn't a liar, was he?"

"Egbert? Un tipo della mia stazza?" chiese Brackett lentamente. "Sì, Egbert. Non avrà mentito, vero?"

Brackett laughed. "No, he wasn't a liar." Then in a changed voice he

added: "Jesse, my boy, you should have asked me before you started off."

Brackett rise. "No, non ha mentito." Quindi, con voce diversa, aggiunse: "Jesse, ragazzo mio, avresti dovuto chiedermelo prima di incamminare."

"Oh, I didn't want to," Jesse explained. "I knew you'd say 'no'! He told me it was risky work, Tom. But I don't care."

"Ma non volevo," Jesse spiegò. "Sapevo che avresti detto 'no'! Mi aveva detto che era un lavoro rischioso, Tom. Ma non mi importa."

Brackett face grew harder. "I'm going to say 'no' anyway, Jesse."

La faccia di Brackett si fece più dura. "Ti dirò comunque di 'no', Jesse."

Jesse was struck. It had not occurred to him that Brackett would not agree. It had seemed to him that reaching Tom's office was the only problem he had to face. "Oh, no," he begged, "you can't refuse me. Aren't there any jobs, Tom?"

Jesse era colpito. Non immaginava che Brackett potesse non essere d'accordo. A lui sembrava che raggiungere l'ufficio di Tom sarebbe stato l'unico problema da affrontare. "Oh, no," pregò, "non puoi rifiutarmi. Non ci sono proprio lavori, Tom?"

"Sure, there are jobs. There's even Egbert's job if you want it." "Has he left?"

"He's dead..." "Oh!"

"Certo, ci sono i lavori. Ci sarebbe anche il lavoro di Egbert se lo vuoi."

"Se ne è andato?" "E' morto..." "Oh!"

"He died on the job, Jesse. Last night if you want to know." "Oh! Then I don't care!"

"E' morto sul posto di lavoro, Jesse. Ieri notte se proprio vuoi saperlo." "Oh! Beh, non mi importa!"

"Now you listen to me," Brackett said. "I'll tell you a few things that you should have asked before you started off. It isn't dynamite you drive. They don't use anything as safe as dynamite for drilling wells. They wish they could, but they can't. It's nitroglycerine!"

"Ora devi ascoltarmi," disse Brackett. "Ti dirò alcune cose di cui avresti dovuto chiedere prima di incamminare. Non è dinamite quella che trasporti. Non usano cose sicure come la dinamite per scavare i pozzi. Vorrebbero, ma non possono. E' nitroglicerina!"

"But I know," Jesse told him quietly. "He warned me, Tom. Don't think that I don't know."

"Ma lo so," gli disse tranquillamente Jesse. "Mi ha avvisato, Tom. Non credere che io non sappia."

"Shut up a minute," Brackett ordered angrily. "Listen! You just have to look at this stuff. Raise your voice and it blows up! You know how they transport it?"

"Stai zitto un attimo," Brackett ordinò arrabbiato. "Ascolta! Dovresti solo darci una occhiata. Alzi la voce e salta tutto in aria! Sai come lo trasportano?"

"Listen, Tom."

"Ascolta, Tom."

"Now, wait a minute, Jesse. For God's sake, just think a little. I know you need a job and need it badly! You have to work, but you must understand. This stuff is transported only in special trucks! At night! They take it along the special route!

"Ora, aspetta un minuto Jesse. Per l'amor di Dio, pensaci su un attimo. So che hai per forza bisogno di un lavoro! Devi lavorare, ma devi anche capire. Questa è roba è trasportata solo in camion speciali! Di notte! E' portata sui percorsi speciali!

They can't go through any city! If they have to stop they must do it in a special garage! Don't you understand what that means? Does not that tell you how dangerous that is?"

Non possono passare da nessuna città! Se devono fermarsi devono farlo in un garage speciale! Non capisci cosa significa? Non ti dice niente tutto questo su quanto sia pericoloso?"

"I'll drive carefully," Jesse said. "I know how to handle a truck. I'll drive slowly." Brackett groaned. "Do you think Egbert didn't drive carefully or know how to handle a truck?"

"Guiderò con prudenza," disse Jesse. "So come si guida un camion. Guiderò lentamente." Brackett si lamentò. "Pensi che Egbert non abbia guidato con prudenza o non sapesse come gestire un camion?"

"Tom," Jesse said passionately, "you can't make me change my mind. Egbert said he was getting a dollar per mile. He was making from five to six hundred dollars a month for half a month's work, he said. Can I get the same?"

"Tom," Jesse disse ardentemente, "non mi farai cambiare idea. Egbert disse che prendeva un dollaro al miglio. Guadagnava dai cinquecento ai seicento dollari al mese per il lavoro di una metà del mese, mi ha detto questo. Potrei avere la stessa somma?"

"Sure you can get the same," Brackett told him angrily. "A dollar per mile. It's easy to say. But why do you think the company has to pay so much?"

"Certo che puoi," Brackett rispose arrabbiato. "Un dollaro al miglio. E' facile da dire. Ma perché pensi che la compagnia debba pagare così tanto?"

It's easy – until you drive over a stone in the dark, like Egbert did, or a tire blows out, or any other thing happens that nobody ever knows! We can't ask Egbert what happened to him. There's no truck, no corpse. There's nothing!

È facile – fino a quando si guida su una pietra nel buio, come ha fatto Egbert, o una gomma esplode, o qualsiasi altra cosa che nessuno saprà mai! Non possiamo chiedere a Egbert cosa gli è accaduto. Non c'è camion, non c'è cadavere. Non c'è niente!

Maybe tomorrow somebody will find a piece of steel left from the destroyed truck. But we never find the driver. Not even a finger nail. All we know that he does not come next day. You know what happened last night?

Forse domani qualcuno troverà un pezzo di ferro del camion distrutto. Ma non troviamo mai il guidatore. Nemmeno un'unghia. Tutto ciò che sappiamo è che non si presenta al lavoro il giorno dopo. Sai cosa è successo ieri notte?

Something went wrong on the bridge. Maybe Egbert was nervous. Maybe his truck ran over a stone. Only, there's no bridge any more. No truck. No Egbert. Do you understand now? That's what you get for your dollar a mile!"

Qualcosa è andato storto sul ponte. Forse Egbert era nervoso. Forse il suo camion aveva guidato su una pietra. Solo che non c'è più alcun ponte. Niente camion. Niente Egbert. Hai capito ora? Questo è quello che si fa per un dollaro al miglio!"

There was a moment of silence. Jesse's face was pale. Then he shut his eyes and spoke in a low voice.

Ci fu un momento di silenzio. Il volto di Jesse era pallido. Poi chiuse gli occhi e disse con voce bassa.

"I don't care about that, Tom. You told me all. Now you must be good to me and give me the job."

Brackett rose from his chair. "No!" he cried.

"Non mi importa, Tom. Mi hai detto tutto. Ora devi essere buono con me e darmi il lavoro."

Brackett si alzò dalla sua sedia. "No!" urlò.

"Listen, Tom," Jesse said calmly, "You just don't understand." He opened his eyes. They were filled with tears.

"Ascolta, Tom," disse Jesse con calma, "Tu non capisci." Aprì gli occhi.

Erano pieni di lacrime.

"Just look at me, Tom. Doesn't that tell you enough? What did you think of me when you first saw me? You thought: 'Why doesn't that beggar go away, what does he want here?'

"Guardami, Tom. Non ti dice nulla nemmeno questo? Che cosa hai pensato di me appena mi hai visto? Avrai pensato: 'Ma perché non se ne va, quel mendicante, che cosa vuole da qui?'

Didn't you think so, Tom? Tom, I just can't live like this anymore. I want to be able to walk down the street with my head up".

Non avrai pensato così, Tom? Tom, io non posso più vivere così. Vorrei poter camminare per la strada con la testa alta".

"You're crazy," Brackett muttered, "Every year one out of five drivers is killed. That's the average. What's worth that?"

"Tu sei pazzo," Brackett mormorò, "Ogni anno un guidatore su cinque rimane ucciso. Questa è la media. Vale qualcosa, questo?"

"Is my life worth anything now? We're just starving at home, Tom. We don't get unemployment relief any longer."

"La mia vita vale qualcosa ora? Stiamo facendo la fame a casa ora, Tom. Non abbiamo più il sussidio di disoccupazione."

"Then you should have told me," Brackett exclaimed.

"Avresti dovuto dirmelo," esclamò Brackett.

"It's your own fault; a man has no right to have false pride when his family has nothing to eat. I'll borrow some money and we'll telegraph it to Ella. Then you go home and try to get the unemployment relief."

"È colpa tua; un uomo non ha il diritto di avere un falso orgoglio quando la sua famiglia non ha nulla da mangiare. Mi farò prestare dei soldi e li telegraferemo a Ella. Dopodiché te ne vai a casa e cerchi di riprenderti il sussidio di disoccupazione."

"And then what?"

"And then wait. You aren't an old man. You've got no right to throw your life away. Eventually you'll get a job."

"E poi?"

"E poi aspetti. Non sei un vecchio. Non hai il diritto di buttare via la tua vita. Troverai un lavoro prima o poi."

"No!" Jesse jumped up. "No, I believed that too. But I don't believe it now," he exclaimed passionately. "I will not get a job just as you won't get back your hardware store. I've been getting the relief for six years. I've lost my skill, Tom. Printing is skilled work.

"No!" saltò in piedi Jesse. "No, lo credevo anche io questo. Ma non ci credo più, ora," esclamò appassionatamente. "Non troverò un lavoro esattamente come tu non riavrai il tuo negozio di ferramenta. Sono sei anni che ricevo il sussidio. Ho perso le mie capacità, Tom. La stampa è un lavoro qualificato.

But the only work I've had during this period was carrying stones. When I got a job this spring I was supposed to be a first-class specialist. But I wasn't. And they have new machines now. In a week I was laid off."

Ma l'unico lavoro che ho fatto in questo periodo era trasportare delle pietre. Quando trovai un lavoro in questa primavera avrei dovuto essere uno specialista di prima classe. Ma non lo ero. E adesso hanno nuove macchine. Mi hanno fatto fuori in una settimana."

"So what?" Brackett said. "Aren't there any other jobs?"

"How do I know?" Jesse replied. "There hasn't been one for six years."

"E allora?" disse Brackett. "Non ci sono altri lavori?"

"Come faccio a saperlo?" rispose Jesse. "Non ce n'è stato uno per sei anni."

"Well, you must have some courage," Brackett shouted. "You have to keep up hope."

"Beh, dovresti avere del coraggio," urlò Brackett. "Devi continuare a sperare."

"I have all the courage you want, but no hope. The hope has melted away during these years. You're the only hope I have."

"Ho tutto il coraggio che vuoi, ma non ho speranze. Le speranze si sono dissolte in questi anni. Sei l'unica speranza che mi è rimasta."

"You're crazy," Brackett muttered. "I won't do it. For God's sake think of Ella for a minute."

"Tu sei pazzo," mormorò Brackett. "Non lo farò. Per l'amor di Dio, pensa a Ella un attimo."

"But, I'm thinking of her!" Jesse exclaimed, looking at Brackett in surprise. "That's why I came."

"Ma sto pensando di lei!" Jesse esclamò, guardando Brackett con sguardo sorpreso. "È per questo che sono venuto."

His voice became very soft and he said in a whisper: "The night Egbert was at our house I looked at Ella as if I had seen her for the first time. She isn't pretty anymore, Tom."

La sua voce divenne molto delicata e disse in un sussurro: "La notte in cui Egbert era a casa nostra io guardai Ella come se l'avessi vista per la prima volta. Non è più carina, Tom."

Bracket waved his hands at Jesse and moved away. Jesse followed him, taking a deep breath.

Brackett agitò le mani a Jesse e se ne andò. Jesse lo seguì, facendo un profondo respiro.

"Doesn't that tell you anything, Tom? Ella was like a little doll, you remember. I could not walk down the street without somebody turning to look at her. She isn't twenty-nine yet but she isn't pretty anymore."

"Non ti dice niente questo, Tom? Ella era una bambolina, te la ricorderai. Non potevo camminare per strada senza che qualcuno si girasse per guardarla. Non ha ancora ventinove anni ma non è più carina."

Brackett leaned forward, staring at the floor. Jesse stood over him, his face pale, his lips were trembling.

Brackett si chinò in avanti, guardando il pavimento. Jesse era in piedi davanti a lui, il volto pallido, le sue labbra tremavano.

"I've been a bad husband for Ella, Tom. Ella deserved a better one. This is the only chance I see in my whole life to do something for her. I've just been a failure."

"Sono stato un pessimo marito per Ella, Tom. Ella ne meritava uno migliore. Questa la vedo come l'unica opportunità in tutta la mia vita di fare qualcosa per lei. Finora sono stato solo un fallito."

"Don't talk nonsense," Brackett protested. "You aren't a failure. No more than me. There are millions of men in the same position. It's just the depression or the 'New policy' or..." He cursed.

"Non dire sciocchezze," Brackett protestò. "Non sei un fallito. Non più di me. Ci sono milioni di uomini nella stessa posizione. È solo la depressione o la 'Nuova Politica' o..." imprecò.

"Oh, no," Jesse said, in a knowing sorrowful tone, "maybe those things will excuse other men, but not me. I should have done something for my family, but I didn't. That is my own fault!"

"Oh, no," disse Jesse, con un tono consapevole e triste, "forse queste possono essere scuse per altri uomini, ma non per me. Avrei dovuto far qualcosa per la mia famiglia, ma non l'ho fatto. Ed è colpa mia!"

Brackett muttered something but Jesse could not make out what he said.

Brackett mormorò qualcosa ma Jesse non riuscì a capire cosa aveva detto.

Suddenly Jesse's face turned red. "Well, I don't care!" he cried wildly. "I don't care! You must give me this job!

All'improvviso il volto di Jesse si fece rosso. "Beh, non mi importa!" esclamò selvaggiamente. "Non mi interessa! Devi darmi questo lavoro!

I've suffered enough. You want me to keep looking at my little boy's legs and tell myself if I had a job he wouldn't be like that?

Ho sofferto abbastanza. Tu vuoi che continui a guardare le gambe del mio bambino per poi dire a me stesso che se avessi un lavoro non sarebbe così?

Every time he walks he seems to say 'I have soft bones because you didn't feed me right!' My God, Tom, do you think I'm going to sit there and watch him like that another six years?"

Ogni volta che cammina sembra dire 'Ho le ossa deboli perché tu non mi hai nutrito come si deve!' Mio Dio, Tom, pensi che io stia lì seduto a guardarlo in quelle condizioni per altri sei anni?"

Brackett sprang to his feet. "You say you're thinking of Ella. How will she like it if you are killed?"

Brackett si alzò in piedi. "Dici di avere Ella in mente. Come le piacerà se tu rimarrai ucciso?"

"Maybe I won't," Jesse shouted back. "Then I am! But meantime I'll get something, will I not? I can buy a pair of shoes.

"Forse non accadrà," Jesse rispose. "O forse si! Ma nel frattempo almeno avrò qualcosa, o no? Potrò comprare un paio di scarpe.

Look at me! I can buy a suit. I can smoke cigarettes. I can buy some candy for the kids. I can eat some myself.

Guardami! Potrò comprarmi un vestito. Potrò fumare le sigarette. Potrò comprare qualche dolciume per i bambini. Potrò mangiarne anche un po' io stesso.

Yes, I want to eat some candy. I want a glass of beer once a day. I want Ella to be dressed decently; I want her to eat meat three time a week, four times maybe. I want to take my family to the movies."

Si, vorrei mangiare qualche dolciume. Vorrei un bicchiere di birra una volta al giorno. Vorrei che Ella fosse vestita decentemente; vorrei che mangiasse carne tre volte a settimana, forse anche quattro. Vorrei portare la mia famiglia al cinema."

Brackett sat down. "Oh, shut up," he said in a tired voice.

Brackett si sedette. "Oh, stai zitto," disse con un tono stanco.

"No," Jesse told him softly, passionately, "you can't get rid of me. Listen, Tom," he said. "I've thought it all out. If I get six hundred a month look how much can I save!

"No," Jesse rispose dolcemente, appassionatamente, "non ti libererai di me. Ascolta, Tom," disse. "Ho pensato a tutto. Se prendessi seicento al mese guarda quanto potrei risparmiare!

If I last only three months, look how much it is – a thousand dollars – even more! And maybe I'll last longer. Maybe a few years. I can provide Ella for all her life."

Se durassi anche solo tre mesi, guarda quanto è – mille dollari – anche di più! E magari durerò più a lungo. Forse qualche anno. Potrei prendermi cura di Ella per tutta la sua vita."

Brackett interrupted him. "I suppose you think she'll enjoy living when you're on a job like that?"

Brackett lo interruppe. "Immagino tu pensi che a lei piacerebbe vivere con te che fai un lavoro così, non è vero?"

"I've thought of that too," Jesse answered excitedly. "She won't know. I'll tell her I get only forty. You'll put the rest on a bank account for her, Tom."

"Ci ho già pensato," Jesse rispose entusiasta. "Non lo saprà. Le dirò che prendo solo quaranta. Metti il resto in un conto bancario per lei, Tom."

"Oh, shut up," Brackett said. "You think you'll be happy? Every minute, walking and sleeping, you'll be wondering whether tomorrow you'll be dead. And the worst days will be your days off, when you're not driving. You'll be free every other day.

"Ma stai zitto," disse Brackett. "Pensi che sarai felice? Ogni minuto, da sveglio o nel sonno, ti chiederai se domani sarai morto. Ed i giorni peggiori saranno quelli festivi, quando non guiderai. Sarai libero in tutti gli altri giorni.

They have to give you these free days, so that you could recover and be fresh for another day's work.

Devono darteli questi giorni liberi, così da poterti recuperare ed essere fresco per lavorare un altro giorno.

And you'll stay at home waiting for that day and wondering if you'll be killed then. That's how happy you'll be."

E starai a casa ad aspettare che quel giorno arrivi e a chiederti se sarà quello il giorno in cui rimarrai ucciso. Questa sarà la tua felicità."

Jesse laughed. "I'll be happy! Don't worry, I'll be so happy, I'll be singing. Tom, I'll feel proud of myself for the first time in six years!"

Jesse rise. "Sarò felice! Non preoccuparti, sarò felice, canterò. Tom, mi sentirò orgoglioso di me stesso per la prima volta in sei anni!"

"Oh, shut up, shut up," Brackett said. The little office where they were sitting became silent. After a moment Jesse whispered:

"Ma stai zitto, stai zitto," disse Brackett. Il piccolo ufficio dove i due erano seduti divenne silenzioso. Dopo un momento Jesse sussurrò:

"You must let me have this job. You must. You must." Again there was silence.

"Devi farmi avere questo lavoro. Devi. Devi."

Ancora silenzio.

"Tom, Tom, - "Jesse begged.

Brackett sighed. "All right," he said finally, "I'll take you on. God help me." His voice was low and very tired. "If you're ready to drive tonight, you can drive tonight."

"Tom, Tom, -" Jesse pregò.

Brackett sospirò. "Va bene," disse finalmente, "ti prenderò. Dio mi aiuti." La sua voce era molto bassa e stanca. "Se sei pronto a guidare stanotte, puoi guidare stanotte."

Jesse didn't answer. He couldn't. Brackett looked up. The tears were running down Jesse's face. He was trying to speak but only uttered strange sounds.

Jesse non rispose. Non poteva. Brackett guardò in alto. Le lacrime scorrevano sul volto di Jesse. Provava a parlare ma emetteva solo strani suoni.

"I'll send a telegram to Ella," Bracket said in the same tired voice. "I'll tell her you've got a job, and you'll send her some money in a couple of days so that she may come here. You'll have a few dollars then – that is, if you last a week, you fool."

"Manderò un telegramma a Ella," Brackett disse con la stessa voce stanca. "Le dirò che hai un lavoro, e tu le manderai dei soldi fra qualche giorno così potrà venire qui. Avrai già qualche dollaro allora – cioè, se duri una settimana, stupido."

Jesse only nodded. His heart was beating wildly. One more minute and it would burst, he thought. He pressed both hands against his breast as if he were afraid his heart would jump out.

Jesse annuì solamente. Il suo cuore batteva fortissimo. Ancora un minuto e sarebbe esploso, pensava. Premette entrambe le mani contro il suo petto come se avesse paura che il suo cuore sarebbe saltato fuori.

"Come back here at six o'clock," Brackett said. "Here's some money. Eat a good meal."

"Thanks," Jesse whispered.

"Wait a minute," Brackett said, "Here's my address."

"Torna qui alle sei," disse Brackett. "Ecco dei soldi. Fai un buon pasto."

"Grazie," sussurrò Jesse.

"Aspetta un minuto," disse Brackett, "Ecco il mio indirizzo."

He wrote it on a piece of paper. "Take any streetcar going that way. Ask the driver where to get off. Take a bath and have a good long sleep."

Lo scrisse su un pezzo di carta. "Prendi una qualsiasi tram che va da quelle parti. Chiedi al guidatore dove scendere. Fai un bagno e fatti una lunga dormita."

"Thanks," Jesse said, "thanks, Tom." "Oh, get out of here," Brackett said.

"Tom!"

"What?"

"Grazie," disse Jesse, "grazie, Tom." "Oh, esci da qui," Brackett disse.

"Tom!"

"Cosa?"

"I just – "Jesse stopped. Brackett saw his face. The eyes were still full of tears, but the thin face was shining now.

"Io – "Jesse si fermò. Brackett vide il suo viso. Gli occhi erano ancora pieni di lacrime, ma il volto sottile brillava ora.

Brackett turned away. "I'm busy," he said. Jesse went out. Tears blinded him but the whole world seemed to have turned golden. He limped slowly, but his heart was full of strange wild joy.

Brackett si girò. "Sono occupato," disse. Jesse uscì. Le lacrime lo accecavano ma il mondo intero ora gli sembrava fatto di oro. Zoppicava lentamente, ma il suo cuore era pieno di una strana e selvaggia gioia.

"I am the happiest man in the world," he whispered to himself, "I'm the happiest man on the whole Earth."

"Sono l'uomo più felice del mondo," sussurrò a sé stesso, "Sono l'uomo più felice sulla Terra intera."

Brackett sat watching till finally Jesse turned the corner of the alley and disappeared. Then he leaned back in his chair. His heart was beating painfully. He listened to it as it beat. He sat still, gripping his head in his hands.

Brackett si sedette a guardare fino a quando Jesse svoltò finalmente l'angolo del vicolo e scomparve. Poi si appoggiò all'indietro nella sua sedia. Il suo cuore pulsava con dolore. Ascoltava ogni battito. Sedeva fermo, con la testa tra le mani.

Key Vocabulary:

o riposare v.intr. [ri-po-sà-re] – to rest, to have a rest; to sleep.

o cocente agg. [co-cèn-te] – roasting, burning, blistering.

o pasto s.m. [pà-sto] – meal.

o cicatrice s.f. [ci-ca-trì-ce] – scar.

o squallido agg. [squàl-li-do] – squalid, shabby, nasty.

o corpulento agg. [cor-pu-lèn-to] – corpulent, obese, stout.

o sprecare v.tr. [spre-cà-re] – to waste, to squander.

o bancone s.m. [ban-có-ne] – counter.

o scattare v.intr. [scat-tà-re] – to go off; to to click, to snap.

~ fotografie – to take (to shoot, to snap) photographs. o ridotto agg. [ri-dót-to] – contracted, shrunken, reduced.

essere ~ male – to be in poor condition/in bad shape.

o mica avv. [mì-ca] – at all, in the least (often used for emphases).

non costa ~ molto – it doesn't cost much at all.

Non sono ~ un cadavere – I am not a corpse, you know! o spettinato agg. [spet-ti-nà-to] – uncombed, ruffled.

o zoppicare v.intr. [zop-pi-cà-re] – to limp.

o calpestare v.tr. [cal-pe-stà-re] – to step on, to trample (on).

o bucare v.tr. [bu-cà-re] – to pierce, to puncture.

o nascondere v.intr. [na-scón-de-re] – to hide, to conceal.

o sostenere v.tr. [so-ste-né-re] – to support, to hold up; to sustain.

sostegno s.m [so-sté-gno] – support, prop, brace, strut. o sentirsi a disagio – to feel awkward.

o incupirsi v.intr. [in-cu-pìr-si] – to darken, to sadden.

o ferramenta s.f. [fer-ra-mén-ta] – hardware, ironware.

o valere v.intr. [va-lé-re] – to be worth;

o amaramente avv. [a-ma-ra-mén-te] – bitterly.

o crollare v.intr. [crol-là-re] – to collapse; to fall down.

o sconvolgere v.tr. [scon-vòl-ge-re] – to disrupt, to disturb, to upset.

o entrambi agg. [en-tràm-bi] – both.

o esclamare v.intr. [e-scla-mà-re] – to exclaim, to cry out.

o lamentarsi v.rf. [la-men-tàr-si] – to groan, to moan; to lament.

o disoccupato agg. [di-soc-cu-pà-to] – unemployed.

o incamminare v.tr. [in-cam-mi-nà-re] – to start off, to get going.

o assumere v.tr. [as-sù-me-re] – to assume; to take on, to hire.

o stazza s.f. [stàz-za] – (of people) bulk, proportions; tonnage (of a ship).

o scavare v.tr. [sca-và-re] – to excavate; to dig, to drill, to bore.

o avvisare v.tr. [av-vi-sà-re] – to warn; to inform.

o roba s.f. [rò-ba] – stuff; things.

o gestire v.tr. [ge-stì-re] – to manage, to operate, to handle.

o ardentemente avv. [ar-den-te-mén-te] – ardently, passionately.

o mendicante agg. [men-di-càn-te] – mendicant, begging.

s.m. – beggar.

o sussidio di disoccupazione – unemployment compensation/relief.

o dopodiché avv. [do-po-di-ché] – after which, then.

o riavere v.tr. [ria-vé-re] – to have again, to have/get back.

o capacità s.f. [ca-pa-ci-tà] – capability, ability, skill; capacity.

o dissolversi v.intr. [dis-sòl-ver-si] – to dissolve, to melt (away), to evaporate; dissolto agg. [dis-sòl-to] – dissolved, melted.

o carino agg. [ca-rì-no] – pretty, cute, nice.

o chinare v.tr. [chi-nà-re] – to bend, to lean, to bow.

o meritare v.tr. [me-ri-tà-re] – to deserve, to merit.

o imprecare v.intr. [im-pre-cà-re] – to swear, to curse.

o risparmiare v.tr. [ri-spar-mià-re] – to save; to spare.

CHAPTER THIRTEEN: Double Dyed Deceiver / Un Imbroglione Matricolato

It happened in Laredo in a gambling house. The players were sitting at a poker game when a quarrel began over some cards.

Il fatto avvenne a Laredo in una casa da gioco. I giocatori erano seduti davanti a una partita di poker quando iniziò un litigio riguardo ad alcune carte.

A young fellow of about Kid's age pulled out his revolver, but just grazed Kid's right ear. When Kid's turn came, he shot the young man and ran away.

Un giovanotto, dell'età di Kid più o meno, prese il suo revolver, e sfiorò appena l'orecchio destro di Kid. Quando arrivò il turno di Kid, sparò al giovane e scappò via.

The young man's friends overtook Kid at the station. Kid turned and aimed his revolver at them. He was a good shot. Seeing his revolver they stopped, turned and disappeared.

Gli amici del giovane superarono Kid alla stazione. Kid si girò e puntò il suo revolver verso di loro. Era un buon tiratore. Vedendo il suo revolver si fermarono, si girarono e sparirono.

The same afternoon Kid took a train, but at the next station he left it because there were telegraph posts along the line and Kid did not trust electricity, he felt safer on horseback. He knew that the man whom he had shot came from a ranch where the people were vengeful.

Lo stesso pomeriggio, Kid prese un treno, ma alla prossima stazione scese perché c'erano dei pali del telegrafo lungo la linea e Kid non si fidava dell'elettricità, si sentiva più sicuro a cavallo. Sapeva che l'uomo a cui aveva sparato proveniva da un ranch dove le persone erano vendicative.

There was a store near the station and Kid saw a saddled horse among the trees. He took it and galloped on. After three days he was on the sea shore. The same day he sailed on a steamer with a cargo of timber and matches.

C'era un negozio vicino alla stazione e Kid vide un cavallo sellato tra gli alberi. Lo prese e partì al galoppo. Dopo tre giorni si trovò in riva al mare. Lo stesso giorno s'imbarcò su una nave a vapore con un carico di legname e cerini.

Thacker, the United States consul at Buenas Tierras, was not yet drunk. It was only eleven o'clock in the morning and he was never drunk until the middle of the afternoon. So, when he saw Kid standing at the door of consulate, he was still in a condition to show the hospitality of a representative of a great nation.

Thacker, il console degli Stati Uniti a Buenas Tierras, non era ancora ubriaco. Erano solo le undici del mattino e non era mai ubriaco fino a metà pomeriggio. Quindi, quando vide Kid in piedi davanti alla porta del consolato, era ancora in condizione di mostrare l'ospitalità di un rappresentante di una grande nazione.

"I am sorry," said Kid. "I was told that people usually called on you before going to see the town. I have just come from Texas.

"Mi scusi," disse Kid. "Mi è stato detto che di solito le persone vengono a voi prima di andare a vedere il paese. Sono appena arrivato dal Texas."

"Nice to meet you Mr.- ?" said the consul.

"Dalton," said Kid. But they simply call me Kid in the Rio Grande country."

"Piacere di conoscerla Signor - ?" disse il console.

"Dalton," disse Kid. "Ma mi chiamano semplicemente Kid nel paese di Rio Grande."

"My name's Thacker," said the consul. "Take a chair. If you intend to buy land, I'll be very glad to help you. Besides, they speak Spanish here and you will need an interpreter."

"Io mi chiamo Thacker," disse il console. "Prenda una sedia. Se ha intenzione di acquistare del terreno, sarò molto lieto di aiutarla. Inoltre, parlano lo spagnolo qui e le servirà un interprete."

"I am not buying anything, "said Kid, "and I speak Spanish much better than English."

"Non ho intenzione di acquistare nulla," disse Kid, "e parlo lo spagnolo molto meglio dell'inglese."

"You speak Spanish?" said Thacker thoughtfully. He looked at Kid in silence.

"Lei parla lo spagnolo?" disse Thacker pensieroso. Guardò Kid in silenzio.

You look like a Spaniard, too," he continued, "and you can't be more than twenty or twenty one. Are you brave?"

"Sembri anche ad uno spagnolo," continuò, "e non puoi avere più di venti o ventuno anni. Sei coraggioso?"

"What do you mean?" asked Kid, suddenly rising and coming up to the consul.

"Are you ready to accept any job?" asked Thacker.

"Cosa intende dire?" chiese Kid, alzandosi improvvisamente e avvicinandosi al console.

"Sei pronto ad accettare qualsiasi lavoro?" chiese Thacker.

"I must tell you, said Kid, "that I took part in a little quarrel in Laredo and killed a man. As I was afraid that his friends would avenge his death, I was compelled to leave the place and come here. So you see that I am ready to take any work."

"Le devo dire," disse Kid, "che ho preso parte in un piccolo litigio a Laredo e ho ucciso un uomo. Siccome avevo paura che i suoi amici volessero vendicare la sua morte, sono stato costretto a lasciare il paese e venire qui. Quindi, come può vedere sono pronto ad accettare qualsiasi lavoro."

Thacker got up and closed the door.

"Show me your hand," he said. He took Kid's left hand and examined the back of the hand very carefully.

Thacker si alzò e chiuse la porta.

"Mostrami la tua mano," disse. Prese la mano sinistra di Kid e esaminò il dorso della mano attentamente.

"I can do it," he said, "your hand will heal in a week." "What do you mean?" asked Kid.

"Lo posso fare," disse, "la tua mano guarirà in una settimana." "Cosa intende dire?" chiese Kid.

Through the window Thacker pointed to a rich white house standing among tropical trees.

Attraverso la finestra, Thacker indicò una casa bianca di ricchi che si trovava in mezzo agli alberi tropicali.

"In that house," said Thacker, "an old gentleman and his wife are waiting for you; they will fill your pockets with money. Old Santos Urique lives there. He owns half the gold mines in the country."

"In quella casa," disse Thacker, "un vecchio signore e sua moglie ti stanno aspettando; riempiranno le tue tasche di soldi. Il vecchio Santos Urique vive là. Possiede metà delle miniere d'oro di questo paese."

"A you drunk?" asked Kid.

"Sit down and I'll tell you everything."

"È ubriaco?" chiese Kid.

"Siediti e ti racconterò tutto."

"Twelve years ago the old gentleman and his wife lost their only son. He was eight years old. Some Americans, who were looking for gold and who often visited the Uriques, told the boy a lot of wonderful things about the States; and a month later the boy disappeared.

"Dodici anni fa il vecchio signore e sua moglie persero il loro unico figlio. Aveva otto anni. Alcuni americani, che cercavano l'oro e che visitavano spesso gli Uriques, raccontarono al bambino un sacco di cose meravigliose sugli Stati Uniti; e un mese più tardi il bambino sparì.

It was said that he was seen once in Texas. The Uriques looked for him everywhere, they spent a lot of money, but in vain.

Venne detto che era stato visto una volta nel Texas. Gli Uriques lo cercarono ovunque, spesero molto denaro, ma invano.

"The mother was quite ill. They say she believes that her son will come back and they never given up hope. On the back of the boy's left hand was tattooed flying eagle."

"La madre era molto ammalata. Dicono che lei creda che suo figlio ritornerà e non hanno mai perso la speranza. Sul dorso della mano sinistra del bambino era tatuata un'aquila in volo."

Kid answers nothing.

Kid non rispose nulla.

"I can do it," continued the consul, "and in a week you will have the eagle tattooed on your hand. I'll call old Urique and when he sees that you have the tattoo mark, that you speak Spanish and can tell him about Texas, the parents will be happy.

"Posso farlo," continuò il console, "e in una settimana avrai l'aquila tatuata sulla mano. Chiamerò il vecchio Urique e quando vedrà che hai il segno del tatuaggio, che parli lo spagnolo e che sai raccontargli del Texas, i genitori saranno felici.

The rest of it is very simple. Old Urique keeps in his house about 100,000 dollars in a safe which a child can open. Get the money, we'll divide it, take a steamer going to Rio Janeiro and let the consulate go to pieces. What do you think of it?"

Il resto è molto semplice. Il vecchio Urique tiene in casa circa 100,000 dollari in una cassaforte che anche un bambino saprebbe aprire. Prendi i soldi, li divideremo, prendi una nave a vapore diretta verso Rio Janeiro e lascia che il consolato vada a pezzi. Che ne pensi?"

"I like your plan," said Kid.

In a few days the tattoo on Kid's left hand was ready and the hand healed.

"Mi piace il suo piano," disse Kid.

Dopo alcuni giorni, il tatuaggio sulla mano sinistra di Kid era pronto e la mano era guarita.

Then the consul wrote the following note to old Urique:

Poi il console scrisse la seguente nota al vecchio Urique:

"Dear Mr Urique,

I have the pleasure to inform you that I have a guest in my house who arrived from the United States a few days ago. I think that he is your son and that he intended to return to you, but at the last moment his courage left him because he doesn't know how you will receive him.

Yours faithfully, Thomson Thacker."

"Egregio Signor Urique,

Ho il piacere di informarla che ho un ospite in casa mia arrivato dagli Stati Uniti alcuni giorni fa. Penso che lui è vostro figlio e che avesse intenzione di ritornare da voi, ma all'ultimo momento il suo coraggio lo ha abbandonato perché non sa come lo riceverete.

Cordiali saluti, Thomson Thacker."

In thirty minutes a carriage drove up to the door of the consulate. A tall man with white hair and a lady dressed in black got out of it.

Thacker met them with the bow.

Dopo trenta minuti una carrozza arrivò fino alla porta del consolato.

Un uomo alto con i capelli bianchi e una signora vestita di nero uscirono dalla carrozza. Thacker li salutò con l'inchino.

They saw a young man with a sunburnt face standing near a desk.

Videro un giovane con il volto bruciato dal sole in piedi vicino alla scrivania.

Donna Urique glanced at his face and his left hand, and crying:"O, my son!" she wrapped Kid in her arms.

Donna Urique guardò il suo volto e la sua mano sinistra, e piangendo disse: "Oh, mio figlio!" avvolse Kid tra le sue braccia.

A month later Kid came to the consulate in answer to a message from Thacker. He was very well dressed and a big diamond shone on his finger.

Un mese più tardi, Kid è venuto al consolato dopo aver ricevuto un messaggio da Thacker. Era molto ben vestito e aveva un grosso diamante che brillava sul suo dito.

"What is the news?" asked Thacker. "Nothing new." answered Kid.

"Quali notizie ci sono?" chiese Thacker. "Niente di nuovo." Rispose Kid.

"It is time to start business. Why don't you get the money? Everybody knows that Urique's safe is full of money."

"È ora di iniziare gli affari. Perché non prendi i soldi? Tutti sanno che la cassaforte di Urique è piena di soldi."

"Oh, there is a lot of money in the house," said Kid, looking at his diamond. "And my adopted father has shown me where the key of the safe is."

"Oh, ci sono molti soldi in casa," disse Kid, guardando il suo diamante. "E il mio padre adottivo mi ha mostrato dove si trova la chiave della cassaforte."

"Well, then, what are you waiting for?" asked Thacker angrily. "Don't forget that I can tell Don Urique and everybody who you really are."

"Bene, allora, cosa stai aspettando?" chiese Thacker con rabbia. "Non dimenticarti che posso dire a Don Urique e a tutti chi sei realmente."

"Listen, said Kid. "When you speak to me, address me as Don Francisco Urique. As to my father's money, let him have it. I don't intend to take it."

"Ascolta," disse Kid. "Quando mi parli, rivolgiti a me come Don Francisco Urique. Per quanto riguarda il denaro di mio padre, lascialo a lui. Non ho intenzione di prenderlo."

"Don't you intend to give me my half then?"

"Non hai intenzione di darmi la metà allora?"

"Of course not," answered Kid, "and I'll tell you why. The first night I was at Don Urique's house, just after I had gone to bed, my new mother came in and tucked in the blanket. 'My dear boy', she said, and tears dropped from her eyes on my face.

"Certo che no," rispose Kid, "e ti dirò il perché. La prima sera che mi trovai a casa di Don Urique, subito dopo essere andato a letto, la mia nuova madre è entrata e mi ha rimboccato le coperte. "Mio caro ragazzo", disse, con le lacrime che le scendevano dagli occhi cadendo sul mio viso."

I have had very little to do with mothers in my life, but I think that this mother must be kept fooled. She stood it once, but she won't stand it twice. That's why things must be just as they are. And don't forget that my name is Don Francisco Urique."

Ho avuto poco a che fare con le madri nella mia vita, ma penso che è meglio continuare ad ingannare questa madre. Lo ha sopportato una volta, ma non lo sopporterebbe la seconda. Ecco perché le cose devono rimanere così come sono. E non dimenticare che il mio nome è Don Francisco Urique."

"I'll tell everybody today who you really are," cried Thacker, red with anger.

"Dirò a tutti chi sei realmente," urlò Thacker, rosso dalla rabbia.

Kid took Thacker by the throat with his strong left hand, drew out his revolver with his right hand and aimed the revolver at the consul's mouth.

Kid prese Thacker per la gola con la sua forte mano sinistra, prese il suo revolver con la mano destra e lo puntò alla bocca del console.

There came a sound of wheels from outside. Kid put his revolver into his pocket, and holding up his left hand with its back toward the trembling consul said:

Si sentì un rumore di ruote giungere dall'esterno. Kid mise il suo revolver in tasca, e alzando la mano sinistra con il dorso rivolto verso il console tremante, disse:

"There is one more reason why things must remain as they are. The fellow whom I killed in Laredo had an eagle on his left hand."

"C'è un altro motivo perché le cose devono rimanere così come sono. La persona che ho ucciso a Laredo aveva un'aquila sulla mano sinistra."

At that moment the carriage of Don Urique stopped at the door of the consulate.

"Where are you, dear son?" called Donna Urique.

In quel momento la carrozza di Don Urique si fermò davanti alla porta del consolato.

"Dove sei, mio caro figlio?" chiamò Donna Urique.

"I am here, dear mother," answered Kid, or, as Thacker has ever since called him, Don Francisco Urique.

"Sono qui, cara mamma," rispose Kid, o, come lo ha sempre chiamato Thacker da allora, Don Francisco Urique.

Key Vocabulary:

o imbroglione s.m. [im-bro-glió-ne] – deceiver, crook, impostor.

o matricolato agg. [ma-tri-co-là-to] – out-and-out, downright, arrant.

un imbroglione ~ – an arrant/an out-and-out deceiver. o fatto s.m. [fàt-to] – fact; event, affair.

o litigare v.intr. [li-ti-gà-re] – to argue, to quarrel (over sth).

litigio s.m. [li-tì-gio] – quarrel, dispute, argument. o più o meno – more or less.

o sfiorare v.tr. [sfio-rà-re] – to graze, to skim (over); to touch lightly.

o superare v.tr. [su-pe-rà-re] – to surpass; to exceed; to overtake.

o un buon tiratore – a good shot.

o provenire v.intr. [pro-ve-nì-re] – to come from; to derive.

o sellare v.tr. [sel-là-re] – to saddle.

~ i cavalli – to ~ the horses; (sella s.f. – saddle; ~to – saddled). o riva s.f. [rì-va] – shore (sea, lake); bank (river).

o imbarcarsi v.rf. [im-bar-càr-si] – to board, to step aboard; to embark.

o nave s.f. [nà-ve] – ship, boat.

nave a vapore – steamer.

o metà s.f. [me-tà] – half; middle.

o ubriaco agg.|s.m. [u-bri-à-co] – drunk (intoxicated); drunk person.

o solito agg. [sò-li-to] – usual; di ~ – usually.

o lieto agg. [liè-to] – glad, pleased.

o pensiero s.m. [pen-siè-ro] – thought.

~so agg. – thoughtful, pensive.

o sembrare v.intr. [pa-ré-re] – to seem, to look (like), to appear.

o intendere v.tr. [in-tèn-de-re] – to intend, to mean.

o siccome cong. [sic-có-me] – as, since.

o guarire v.intr. [gua-rì-re] – to heal; to recover.

o attraverso prep. [at-tra-vèr-so] – across; through.

o trovare v.tr. [tro-và-re] – to find; to locate.

o miniera s.f. [mi-niè-ra] – mine.

miniera di carbone| d'oro / coalmine| goldmine.

o ovunque avv. [o-vùn-que] – everywhere, anywhere. (syn. dovunque).

o spendere v.tr. [spèn-de-re] – to spend.

o dorso s.m. [dòr-so] – back (of body, hand, book etc.).

o aquila s.f. [à-qui-la] – eagle.

o volare v.intr. [vo-là-re] – to fly.

volo s.m. [vó-lo] – flight.

o raccontare v.tr. [rac-con-tà-re] – to tell, to narrate;

o dividere v.tr. [di-vì-de-re] – to divide, to split.

o piano s.m. [pià-no] – 1. floor, story.

abitare al terzo piano / to live on the third floor.

– 2. plan, scheme.

i piani per il futuro / plans for the future.

o abbandonare v.tr. [ab-ban-do-nà-re] – to abandon; to leave.

o bruciare v.tr. [bru-cià-re] – to burn; to set (sth) on fire.

~to – burnt, burned.

o piangere v.intr. [pià-ge-re] – to cry.

o avvolgere v.tr. [av-vòl-ge-re] – to wrap (up); to enfold.

o brillare v.intr. [bril-là-re] – to shine, to sparkle.

o rimboccare v.tr. [rim-boc-cà-re] – to tuck in; to roll up.

o ingannare v.tr. [in-gan-nà-re] – to deceive, to fool.

o giungere v.intr. [giùn-ge-re] – to arrive, to come, to reach.

o esterno agg. [e-stèr-no] – outside, external; outer.

CHAPTER FOURTEEN: The Luncheon / Il pranzo

I saw her at the theater play and during the break I came over and sat down beside her. It was long since we have met but she recognized me at once and addressed me in a friendly voice.

La vidi allo spettacolo teatrale e durante la pausa mi avvicinai e mi sedetti di fianco a lei. Era passato tanto tempo da quando ci incontrammo ma mi riconobbe subito e mi salutò con voce amichevole.

"Do you remember the first time I saw you? You asked me to a luncheon." Did I remember?

"Ti ricordi della prima volta che ti ho visto? Mi volevi portare a pranzo." Mi ricordavo?

It was twenty years ago and I was living in Paris. I had a small apartment in the Latin Quarter and I was earning only just enough to keep my body and soul together.

Accadde venti anni fa ed io vivevo a Parigi. Avevo un piccolo appartamento nel quartiere Latino e guadagnavo quel tanto che bastava per tenere il mio corpo e la mia anima d'un pezzo.

She had read a book of mine and had written to me about it. I answered, thanking her, and then I received from her another letter saying that she was passing through Paris and would like to have a chat with me.

Aveva letto un mio libro e mi aveva scritto a riguardo. Risposi, ringraziandola, e poi ricevetti un'altra sua lettera in cui mi informava che sarebbe passata da Parigi e avrebbe apprezzato fare due chiacchiere con me.

On the following Thursday, she said, she would spend the morning at the Luxembourg and asked me whether I would take her to a little luncheon at Foyet's afterwards.

Il giovedì seguente, disse, avrebbe speso la mattinata in Lussemburgo e mi chiese se l'avrei portata a pranzo da Foyet più tardi.

Foyet's is a restaurant at which the French senators eat and it was so expensive that I had never thought of going there. But I was flattered and I was too young to say "no" to a woman.

Foyet è un ristorante nel quale pranzano i senatori Francesi ed era così costoso che non avevo mai nemmeno pensato di andarci. Ma ero lusingato e troppo giovane per dire "no" a una donna.

I had eighty francs to live on for the rest of the month and a modest luncheon should not cost more than fifteen. If I won't take coffee for the next two weeks, I could manage well enough.

Avevo ottanta franchi con cui vivere per il resto del mese ed un pranzo modesto non sarebbe potuto costarne più di quindici. Se non avessi preso il caffè per le prossime due settimane, avrei potuto farcela abbastanza bene.

I answered that I will meet my friend – by correspondence – at Foyet's on Thursday at half past twelve. She was not as young as I expected and her appearance was imposing rather than attractive.

Risposi che avrei incontrato la mia amica – per corrispondenza – da Foyet il giovedì alle dodici e mezza. Non era così giovane come me l'aspettavo e il suo aspetto era più imponente che attraente.

She was talkative, but since she wanted to talk about me I was prepared to be an attentive listener. I got frightened when the menu was brought, because the prices were much higher than I had expected. But she reassured me.

Lei era loquace, ma visto che voleva parlare di me ero preparato ad essere un attento ascoltatore. Mi spaventai quando ci fu portato il menù, perché i prezzi erano molto più alti di quanto mi aspettassi. Ma lei mi rassicurò.

"I never eat anything for luncheon," she said. "Oh, don't say that!" I answered generously.

"Io non mangio mai niente a pranzo," disse lei. "Dai, non dirlo nemmeno!" Risposi generosamente.

"I never eat more than one thing. I think people eat too much nowadays. A little bit of fish, perhaps. I wonder if they have any salmon."

"Non mangio mai più di una sola cosa. Penso che la gente mangi troppo al giorno d'oggi. Un po' di pesce, forse. Mi domando se abbiano del salmone."

Well, it was early in the year for salmon and it was not on the menu, but I asked the waiter if there was any. Yes, a beautiful salmon had just been delivered, the waiter said, I ordered it for my guest.

Beh, era piuttosto presto durante l'anno per il salmone e non era sul menù, ma chiesi al cameriere se ce ne fosse. Si, un bellissimo salmone era appena stato consegnato, disse il cameriere, lo ordinai per la mia ospite.

The waiter asked her if she would have something while salmon was being cooked.

"No," she answered, "I never eat more than one thing, unless you have a little caviar. I never mind caviar."

Il cameriere le chiese se desiderasse qualcosa nell'attesa che il salmone venisse cucinato.

"No," rispose, "Non mangio mai più di una cosa, a meno che non abbiate un po' di caviale. Apprezzo sempre il caviale."

My heart skipped a beat. I knew I could not afford caviar, but I could not tell her that. I told the waiter to bring caviar. For myself I ordered the cheapest dish on the menu and that was a mutton chop.

Il mio cuore perse un battito. Sapevo di non potermi permettere del caviale, ma non potevo dirglielo. Dissi al cameriere di portare del caviale. Per me ordinai il piatto meno costoso sul menù, cioè una costata di montone.

"I don't advise you to eat meat," she said. "I don't know how you can work after eating heavy things like chops."

"Non ti consiglio di mangiare carne," disse lei. "Non so come tu possa lavorare dopo aver mangiato qualcosa di così pesante come le costate."

Then the waiter came up to us and asked if we'd like to drink. "I never drink anything for luncheon," she said.

Poi il cameriere si avvicinò a noi e chiamò se ci piacerebbe bere.

"Non bevo mai nulla per pranzo," disse lei.

"Neither do I," I answered quickly.

"Except white wine" she continued as if I had not spoken. "These French white wines are so light. They are wonderful for the digestion."

"Nemmeno io," risposi velocemente.

"Tranne il vino bianco" continuò lei come se io non avessi parlato. "Questi vini bianchi Francesi sono così leggeri. Sono fantastici per la digestione."

"What would you like?" I asked her politely.

"My doctor will not let me drink anything but champagne." I ordered half a bottle and said that my doctor had absolutely forbidden me to drink champagne.

"Cosa gradiresti?" chiesi educatamente.

"Il mio dottore non mi fa bere nulla fuorché champagne." Ordinai mezza bottiglia e dissi che il mio dottore mi aveva assolutamente proibito di bere champagne.

"What are you going to drink then?" "Water."

"Cosa berrai allora?" "Acqua."

She ate the caviar and then the salmon. She talked gaily of art and literature and music. But I wondered how much I will have to pay for that luncheon.

Mangiò il caviale e poi il salmone. Parlò allegramente di arte e letteratura e di musica. Ma io mi domandavo quanto dovrò pagare per quel pranzo.

When my mutton chop arrived she began to scold me.

Quando la mia costata di montone arrivò lei iniziò a rimproverarmi.

"I see that you have a habit of eating a heavy luncheon. I am sure it's a mistake. Why don't you follow my example and just eat one thing? I am sure you would feel much better for it."

"Vedo che hai l'abitudine di pranzare pesante. Sono sicura sia un errore. Perché non segui il mio esempio e mangi una sola cosa? Sono sicura che ti sentiresti molto meglio per questo."

"I am eating only one thing," I said as the waiter came again with the menu.

"Io sto mangiando una sola cosa," dissi io mentre il cameriere tornava col menù.

"No, no," she said to him. "I never eat anything else for luncheon. Only one thing! I never want more than that, and even that I eat more as an excuse for conversation than anything else.

"No, no," lei disse. "Non mangio mai nient'altro per pranzo. Solo una cosa! Non voglio mai più di questo, ma anche questo io mangio più come una scusa per la conversazione che ogni altra cosa.

I couldn't possibly eat anything more - unless they have some of those giant asparagus. I should be sorry to leave Paris without eating some of them."

Non riuscirei proprio a mangiare ancora – a meno che non abbiano un po' di quegli asparagi giganti. Mi dispiacerebbe lasciare Parigi senza mangiarne un po'."

My heart skipped a beat. I knew that they were extremely expensive. But I had to order asparagus too.

Il mio cuore perse un battito. Sapevo che erano estremamente costosi. Ma dovevo anche ordinare gli asparagi.

Panic seized me. It was no more a question of how much money would I have left for the rest of the month, but whether I have enough to pay the bill.

Il panico mi assalì. Non era più una questione di quanti soldi avrei avuto per il resto del mese, ma se ne ho abbastanza per pagare il conto.

It would be horrible not to have enough money to pay the bill and be compelled to borrow from my guest.

Sarebbe orribile non avere abbastanza soldi per pagare il conto ed esser costretto a farsi prestare qualcosa dalla mia ospite.

I knew exactly how much I had and if the bill would amount to more, I decided that I would put my hand in my pocket and with a dramatic cry will say that my wallet has been stolen.

Sapevo esattamente quanto avevo e se il conto sarebbe ammontare a più, decisi che avrei messo la mano in tasca e con un pianto drammatico avrei annunciato che il mio portafogli era stato rubato.

Obviously it would be embarrassing if she also did not have enough money to pay the bill. In that case, I could just leave my watch and say I would come back later to pay the bill.

Ovviamente sarebbe imbarazzante se anche lei non abbia avuto abbastanza soldi per pagare il conto. In tal caso avrei potuto solo lasciare il mio orologio e dire che sarei tornato più tardi a pagare il conto.

The asparagus appeared. They were enormous, succulent and appetizing. While my companion ate the asparagus I spoke of the condition in the Balkans. At last she finished.

Gli asparagi comparvero. Erano enormi, succulenti e appetitosi. Mentre la mia compagna mangiava gli asparagi io parlai della condizione nei Balcani. Finalmente lei finì.

"Coffee?" I asked.

"Yes, just an ice cream and coffee," she answered.

So, I ordered coffee for myself and ice cream and coffee for her.

"Caffè?" Chiesi.

"Sì, solo un gelato e un caffè," rispose.

Così, ordinai del caffè per me e del gelato e del caffè per lei.

"You know, there is one thing I believe in," she said as she savored the ice cream. "One should always get up from a meal feeling that he could eat a little more."

"Sai, c'è una cosa in cui credo," disse mentre gustava il gelato. "Bisognerebbe sempre alzarsi da tavola con la sensazione di poter ancora mangiare un po' di più."

"Are you still hungry?" I asked with horror.

"Hai ancora fame?" Chiesi con orrore.

"Oh, no, I am not hungry, you see, usually I don't eat luncheon. I have a cup of coffee in the morning and then dinner, but I never eat more than one thing for luncheon."

"Oh, I see!"

"Oh, no, non ho fame, vedi, di solito a pranzo non mangio. Ho una tazza di caffè al mattino e poi cena, ma non mangio mai più di una cosa a pranzo."

"Ah, capisco!"

Then a terrible thing happened. While we were waiting for the coffee, the head waiter came up to us with a basket full of peaches. But surely peaches were not in season then.

Poi, una cosa terribile accadde. Mentre attendevamo il caffè, il capo cameriere si avvicinò a noi con un cesto pieno di pesche. Di sicuro le pesche non erano di stagione allora.

Lord knew what they cost. I knew too – a little later, because my guest, going on with her conversation, absentmindedly took one.

Dio solo sa quanto costavano. Anche io lo seppi – poco più tardi, perché la mia ospite, mentre continuava la sua conversazione, ne prese distrattamente una.

"You know, you have filled your stomach with a lot of meat – and you can't eat any more. I've just had a snack and I can enjoy a peach."

"Sai, tu ti sei riempito lo stomaco di carne – e non puoi più mangiare. Io ho appena fatto uno spuntino e posso godermi una pesca."

The bill came and when I paid it, I found that I had only enough for a very small tip. She looked at the three francs that I left for the waiter and I knew that she thought I was mean.

Il conto arrivò e quando lo pagai, notai che potevo dare solo una piccola mancia. Lei guardò i tre franchi che lasciai al cameriere e seppi che lei mi considerò cattivo.

But when I walked out of the restaurant I had the whole month before me and not a penny in my pocket.

Ma quando uscii dal ristorante avevo tutto un mese di fronte a me e nemmeno un penny in tasca.

"Follow my example," she said as we shook hands, "and never eat more than one thing for luncheon."

"Segui il mio esempio," disse mentre ci stringevamo la mano, "e non mangi mai più di una sola cosa per pranzo."

"I'll do better than that," I answered. "I'll eat nothing for dinner tonight." "You're a humorist!" she cried gaily, jumping into a cab. "You are quite a humorist!"

"Farò di meglio," risposi. "Non mangerò nulla per cena stasera."

"Sei spiritoso!" esclamo allegramente, saltando in un taxi. "Sei davvero spiritoso!"

I am not a bad man, but looking at her now I thought that I had my revenge at last. Today she weighs over 130 kilograms.

Non sono un uomo cattivo, ma guardarla ora mi faceva pensare di aver finalmente ottenuto la mia vendetta. Oggi, lei pesa più di 130 chili.

Key Vocabulary:

o amichevole agg. [a-mi-ché-vo-le] – friendly, amicable.

o accadere v.intr. [ac-ca-dé-re] – to happen, to take place.

o bastare v.intr. [ba-stà-re] – to be enough, to be sufficient.

o pezzo s.m. [pèz-zo] – piece; part.

o riguardo a – with/in regard to, regarding, about.

o ringraziare v.tr. [rin-gra-zià-re] – to thank.

o ricevere v.tr. [ri-cé-ve-re] – to receive; to get.

o apprezzare v.tr. [ap-prez-zà-re] – to appreciate; to relish.

o chiacchiera s.f. [chiàc-chie-ra] – chat, natter, talk.

fare due chiacchiere – to chat, to natter. o tardi avv. [tàr-di] – late.

più ~ – later; a più ~! – see you later! o lusingare v.tr. [lu-sin-gà-re] – to flatter.

~to agg. – flattered.

o imponente agg. [im-po-nèn-te] – imposing, impressive.

o attraente agg. [at-tra-èn-te] – attractive, cute.

o loquace agg. [lo-quà-ce] – talkative, chatty, loquacious.

o perché avv. [per-ché] – why; because.

o domandare v.tr. [do-man-dà-re] – to ask, to request.

mi domando se – I wonder if/whether. o attesa s.f. [at-té-sa] – waiting, wait.

o a meno che – unless.

o perdere v.tr. [pèr-de-re] – to lose; to miss; to leak.

o battito s.m. [bàt-ti-to] – beat, beating, ticking.

o educatamente avv. [e-du-ca-ta-mén-te] – politely, nicely.

o fuorché cong. [fuorché] – except (for), apart from, but.

o rimproverare v.tr. [rim-pro-ve-rà-re] – to reproach, to scold.

o anche cong. [àn-che] – also, too; even.

o assalire v.tr. [as-sa-lì-re] – to attack, to assault. (fig.) to assail, to seize, to come upon.

o costretto agg. [co-strét-to] – compelled, forced; constrained.

o comparire v.intr. [com-pa-rì-re] – to appear, to come out.

o gustare v.tr. [gu-stà-re] – to taste, to savor; to enjoy.

o attendere v.tr. [at-tèn-de-re] – to wait for, to attend to.

o distrattamente avv. [distrat-ta-mén-te] – absentmindedly.

o riempire v.tr. [riem-pì-re] – to fill up.

o spuntino s.m. [spun-tì-no] – snack.

fare uno ~ – to have a snack.

o mancia s.f. [màn-cia] – tip, gratuity.

dare la ~ – to tip o considerare v.tr. [con-si-de-rà-re] – to consider, to think of.

o spiritoso agg. [spi-ri-tó-so] – witty, humorous, funny.

o ottenere v.tr. [ot-te-né-re] – to obtain, to get, to attain.